The
Why
Who
and
How
of the
EDITORIAL
PAGE

THIRD EDITION

The
Why
Who
and
How
of the
EDITORIAL
PAGE

Kenneth Rystrom

Virginia Polytechnic Institute and State University

STRATA PUBLISHING, INC.
State College, Pennsylvania

Third edition
9 8 7 6 5 4 3 2 1

Published by:
Strata Publishing, Inc.
P.O. 1303
State College, PA 16804

telephone: 1-814-234-8545
fax: 1-814-238-7222

http://www.stratapub.com

Library of Congress Cataloging-in-Publication Data

Rystrom, Kenneth, 1932
        The why, who, and how of the editorial page / Kenneth Rystrom. – 3rd ed.
        p.   cm.
        Includes bibliographical references (p.   ) and index.
        ISBN 1-891136-01-1
        1. Editorials.   I. Title.
        PN4778.R95   1998   070.4'1–dc21   98-26946
                                                 CIP

Text, cover design, and page makeup and composition
by Leon Bolognese & Associates, Inc.

Manufactured in the United States of America by Data Reproductions Corporation.

Credits and acknowledgments appear on pages 349–350 and on this page by reference.

To my children and grandchildren—
May they enjoy, appreciate and love the printed word,
to which I have dedicated myself,
as a reporter, editor and journalism professor,
since receiving a toy printing press at age 8

CONTENTS

Preface

The suggestion that I write this book came from officers of the National Conference of Editorial Writers, who wanted one textbook that could benefit both college students and professional editorial writers. I had three purposes in mind when I wrote the first edition of *The Why, Who and How of the Editorial Page*. First, I wanted to help students and beginning editorial writers learn how to write editorials. Second, I wanted to help them understand what it is like to be an editorial writer today. Third, I wanted to show them both the theoretical and the practical aspects of opinion writing.

Responses to the book encouraged me to keep the book up-to-date. I am grateful to the journalists and journalism professors who have helped make this book the leading textbook on editorial writing, the first editorial writing book in many years to go into a third edition. Several editors have told me they require their new editorial writers to study the book before they start writing editorials. Some editorial writers report that they keep a copy of the book in a handy location in their offices. The book has been widely used in college and university courses with various titles: editorial writing, opinion writing, persuasive writing and feature writing.

In response to the comments and suggestions I have received from many journalists, journalism professors and my own students, this edition retains the basic content and framework of the previous editions. The third edition has been updated to reflect current issues and ideas about editorial writing and the editorial page. Responding to requests, I have expanded discussions of specific skills and types of editorial writing. The new edition also has more examples. Most of the examples in the book are new in this edition.

Description of the Book

As the title suggests, the book consists of three main sections.

Part I, "The Why of the Editorial Page," looks at where editorial writing has come from, where it is today and where it might be headed. Chapter 1 provides what may be the most extensive account of the history of the American editorial page now in print. It points out the changing political and social roles of editorial pages in America. Chapter 2 discusses current issues and possible directions for editorials in the future.

Part II, "The Who of the Editorial Page," describes how people become editorial writers; how they can prepare themselves to become writers, or better writers; and how editorial writers fit into the newspaper organization and the wider community. Included are chapters on relations with publishers, the news staff, the editorial page staff and the community. Over the years, the place of the editorial writer has been changing in all of these relationships. In many ways, editorial writers are better prepared and are being given more responsibility than in the past, but more also is expected of them in terms of knowledge, commitment and integrity.

Part III, "The How of the Editorial Page," is the largest section of the book. It explains how to write editorials and edit opinion pages. Emphasis is placed on how writers and editors can do their jobs better, whether in writing editorials, handling letters to the editor and syndicated features, bringing diverse opinions to the page or attracting readers with innovative design or new features. I have made a particular effort to expand coverage, reflect current issues and provide more examples, while maintaining the fundamental strengths of this section.

Throughout, the book is liberally illustrated with examples of journalists' ideas, thoughts and experiences (some of them contradictory) about how editorials should be written and editorial pages produced. Principles and guidelines are also illustrated with a variety of sample editorials from diverse newspapers and other media.

As I recount some of my own experiences and state my opinions, I hope readers will catch my enthusiasm for editorial page work. I have enjoyed writing my own editorials and editing other people's. I have found pleasure in seeing the results of editing and arranging letters, columns and cartoons on an opinion page. Probably as much as anything I have enjoyed the life of an editorial writer as a recognized member of, and participant in, a community. I hope that, as users of this book read about what writers and editors have said and done, they will conclude that these writers and editors too find their jobs fun, interesting and stimulating.

FEATURES OF THE NEW EDITION

The new edition has been expanded and updated to reflect current issues in the field, as well as suggestions and comments from journalism professors, editorial page writers and my own students. The new edition:

- Provides more instruction on specific types of editorials, including expanded coverage and separate chapters on "Subjects That Are Deceptively Easy" and "Subjects That Are Neglected."
- Provides expanded discussions of several types of opinion writing that are becoming more important to today's editorial and opinion writers: among them, broadcast editorials and cultural reviews.
- Provides more sample editorials, editorial excerpts and other examples. Most of these examples are new to this edition.
- Examines and evaluates new trends in editorial pages, including public journalism, reader participation and new page designs.
- Examines how editorial pages have been affected by, and are likely to be affected by, the electronic media, notably the Internet.
- Explores the trend toward corporate and group ownership and its effects on the policies and practices of editorial pages.
- Examines efforts to provide greater diversity of race and gender in editorial page staffs.

■ Draws on current commentary and scholarship on editorial page issues. The new edition incorporates material from recent *Masthead* articles on the ethics, the art and the practice of putting out an editorial page. It also draws on recent scholarship in persuasion and media effects.

ACKNOWLEDGMENTS

I could not have produced the first edition of this book, let alone the second and third, without drawing on the wisdom and practical experiences of scores of editorial writers and editors. I am indebted to the 90 or so publishers and editors who have given me permission to reprint editorials, reviews, signed articles, editorial pages and op-ed pages. I also want to thank the students who have given me permission to reprint and comment on their work.

As this manuscript nears completion, so do my 40 years in journalism, 20 of them in the newspaper business, 20 in teaching. During 17 of the newspaper years I was associated with an editorial page. During most of my university years I taught an editorial writing course.

I got my start writing editorials on the *Daily Nebraskan* at the University of Nebraska, but I didn't get my first training until, in 1960, I joined the editorial page of the *Des Moines* (Iowa) *Register and Tribune.* The editorial page editor, Lauren K. Soth, had just won the Pulitzer Prize for editorials suggesting an exchange of farm delegations with the then Soviet Union. (Nikita Khrushchev, who came with the Russians, became a hit when he threw corncobs at pestering photographers on the Roswell Garst farm in Iowa.) I suspect that the way I write editorials and teach editorial writing can be traced to what I learned in Des Moines. Much of my understanding of issues grew out of listening to 10 editorial writers sitting around in Soth's office every morning at 9 a.m., talking about the affairs of the world. I came to appreciate the importance of editorial board meetings. I also learned a lot from being called into Soth's office to discuss my latest editorial effort. The basic message of my Des Moines experience was that you should try to convince readers, not harangue them.

After five years, with these lessons not fully learned, I accepted an invitation to return to the newspaper on which I had been a reporter before I went to Des Moines. The *Columbian* in Vancouver, Wash., needed an editorial page editor. Now, instead of 10 people at the editorial conference, I was the only one. I quickly figured out that it was possible to write two editorials a day; handle the letters, columns and cartoons; lay out the page–and still find time to get around the community and have a family and social life. As I look back now, those days seem the most exciting and fulfilling. Much of the reason was that the paper was owned by two brothers, Don and Jack Campbell, who knew what needed to be done to produce a good newspaper and who were willing to provide the resources, guidance and freedom to produce such a newspaper. They were committed to a strong, independent editorial voice.

Several years later, as the paper grew, the *Columbian* added a second, and then a third, person to work on the editorial page. While I was there, the other positions were held by Elisabet Van Nostrand, Dennis Ryerson and Mike Heywood, all of whom have had distinguished editorial writing careers. I must also acknowledge that, during my solo years, I often relied on Erwin O. Rieger, the managing editor, to write the second editorial of the day–and to run the page, in addition to his other duties, when I was out of town. Fellow staff members taught me as much about editorial pages as I ever taught them.

My mother, Zella Rae Borland Rystrom, first inspired and taught me to love the art of writing. My first journalism professor, Nathaniel B. Blumberg, then at the University of Nebraska, introduced me to the wonders and challenges of journalism. During my first stint on the *Columbian*, my managing editor, Erwin O. Rieger, forced me to face the rigors of responsible and accurate reporting. My editorial page editor on the *Des Moines Register*, Lauren K. Soth, fostered such a love of editorial writing in me that, for nearly four decades, I have considered it to be the highest possible calling for a journalist.

I am grateful for the association I have had with countless editorial writers and editors through the National Conference of Editorial Writers. Without the encouragement and contributions of members of NCEW, this book literally would not have been possible. The officers of NCEW have allowed, in fact urged, me to draw as much as I wished upon the rich, varied contents of 50 years of that organization's quarterly, *The Masthead*. Cora Everett, executive secretary of NCEW, has provided friendship, support and assistance in producing all three editions of this book.

My thanks also go to the reviewers whose many substantial contributions helped me refine and improve the book. For the first edition, they were R. Thomas Berner, The Pennsylvania State University; Kenneth Edwards, University of Alabama; Robert C. Kochersberger, Jr., State University of New York, College at Cortland; William McKeen, Western Kentucky University; and Robert M. Ours, West Virginia University. For the second edition, they were Sharon Barrett, University of Montana; David Bennett, Indiana State University; Terry M. Clark, University of Central Oklahoma; Martin L. Gibson, The University of Texas at Austin; and Donald A. Lambert, Ohio University. For this edition, they were Joan Atkins, Morehead State University; Sharon Barrett, University of Montana; Eric Bishop, University of LaVerne; Robert H. Bohler, Georgia Southern University; Max Coursen, Pembroke State University; William A. Fisher, Winthrop University; Kate Hastings, Susquehanna University; Mary S. Haupt, SUNY College at Binghamton; R.V. Hudson, Michigan State University; Saundra Hybels, Lock Haven University; Arnold Mackowiak, Eastern Michigan University; Orayb Najjar, Northern Illinois University; Neil Nemeth, Pittsburg State University; John David Reed, Eastern Illinois University; William J. Roach, University of North Florida; and Jerry Reynolds, Humboldt State University.

In putting out the first edition, as a neophyte to book publishing, I was helped by Mary Shuford, Martha Leff and Kathleen Domenig at Random House. Nearly a decade later, when Kathleen had established Strata Publishing, Inc., she asked me if I would be interested in working with her to publish a second edition. In the preface to that edition I wrote: "The result, from my point of view, has been the smoothest major writing effort with which I had been associated." That is no longer true. Preparation of this edition has superseded it as both the smoothest and the most enjoyable. I've enjoyed working with Kathleen as a demanding, meticulous, creative editor. But she has been more than that. After three editions she knows about as much as editorial writing and editorial pages as I do. I have never doubted that she is as devoted as I am to producing the best possible editorial writing book.

Introduction

Why would anyone want to read an editorial page? It contains no news that the reader has not already come across in the newspaper or on television or on the Internet. It provides no useful information—what movies are showing, how to prepare a low-calorie meal. It provides no entertainment—no crossword puzzle, no bridge column. It offers no personal advice—no Ann Landers or Dear Abby, no horoscope. It offers no financial advice. It offers no sales bargains.

Editors are being told by "outside experts"—and some inside experts– –that the future of newspapers (print and online) depends on providing useful information to their customers, information that they can use in their day-to-day lives.

Editorial page editors are being told that the way to save their editorial pages in this consumer-driven climate is to make a greater effort to turn their pages over to their readers and/or involve their newspapers in organizing and promoting community projects. For the most part, however, the lead in the community-organizing effort is being taken by the newspaper's newsroom, not the editorial staff.

So is the traditional editorial page as out of fashion as lead type?

Of course, I wouldn't be spending all this time and effort putting out a new edition of this textbook if I (and my publisher) thought so.

Actually, surveys show that editorials and letters to the editor are remaining very popular with readers, compared to other parts of the newspaper. A 1993–94 survey ranked editorials sixth (compared to eighth, eight years earlier) and letters seventh (compared to sixth earlier) on a list of 13 reader preferences. As might be expected, both editorials and letters ranked higher with readers who were over 34 years old than with younger readers. Editorials were fourth among older readers, ninth among younger ones.

Letters were fifth among older readers, 11th among younger readers.[3] Strange as it may seem, younger readers apparently are drawn more to editorials than to letters, perhaps an encouraging sign that they are more interested in reading serious comment than erratic, often ill-informed, letters.

Still, there is a lot of truth and common sense in what editors are being told: Readers want a quick read, with pictures and graphics. They don't want to hear about politics and government unless the issues directly affect their lives.

In this climate, editorial page people face two widely differing choices: They can join those who want to make opinion pages more reader-oriented or they can "hang in there," continuing to put out largely traditional pages.

Some editors who have adopted the "join 'em" philosophy are attempting to put out dynamic, stimulating pages that blend editorial comment with more participation from readers. Others have reported success in organizing meetings that help communities reach consensus on troubling issues. Some have joined local television stations in attempts to mobilize their communities in support of causes. Various labels have been applied to a wide variety of activities directed toward greater reader and community involvement: "civic journalism," "public journalism" and "community journalism" (although "community journalism" traditionally has referred to weekly newspapers). One result has been an industry-wide debate over whether newspapers should be engaging in such journalism.

Editors who view "civic journalism" with suspicion, if not downright loathing, contend that a newspaper's credibility is threatened when it promotes community causes. In their view, news people should not be community activists and editorial writers should not be promoters. Such editors also contend that a newspaper's editorial leadership role is weakened when the opinion page is turned over to readers. The result, they say, is likely to be a mish-mash of misinformation, half truths and half-baked opinions. In their view, the role of the editorial page should be the traditional one: commenting on current issues and offering recommendations. (The debate over "civic journalism" is explored further in Chapter 9, "Relations with the Community," and Chapter 19, "Innovations in Design and Content.")

Neither the new "join 'em" option nor the traditional option may be the complete answer for most newspapers. After all, every newspaper faces different circumstances in its community. The sophistication of readers varies. So does the economic status of communities. Some newspapers are located in state capitals or university towns. Others have strong labor unions in their communities. Some are located in racially divided communities, others in fairly homogenous communities. Some communities have a strong tax base. Some are deteriorating economically. Some communities have a strong interest in international affairs. Some are flooded with illegal immigrants. In some communities local leadership is strong; in others, weak.

The point is that editorial writers on most newspapers are not fully free to adopt whatever editorial policy or approach that they please if they expect to appeal to, and retain credibility with, most of their readers. Editorial writers on most newspapers face the challenge of appealing to a wide range of readers. Some editorial page readers are liberal; some are conservative; many are in-between. Some are avid; they read every word on the page. Some are casual, reading whatever catches their attention. Some are occasional, glancing at the page if they have an extra few minutes before they dash off to work. It's been a long time since towns and cities had a variety of newspapers that could appeal to their respective groups of avid, loyal, agreeing readers.

Figuring out a successful formula for an editorial page, for most papers, is likely to depend on devising some combination of options that takes into account the community, the traditions of the newspaper and the personal preferences of the newspaper's policy makers. In most communities, this formula must provide something for everybody. One day the lead editorial might discuss a government issue. The next day it might comment on the first appearance of crocuses, while a second editorial might take a stand on a proposed state law that would require young women to seek their parents' permission before obtaining an abortion.

One day editorials might occupy the traditional space in the left column of the page. The next day an especially incisive letter to the editor might appear in the hallowed position.

From time to time, the newspaper might join other groups in the community in supporting some worthy cause, perhaps even providing leadership in getting it off the ground. But the newspaper would be cautious in the causes that it embraced.

Writers will continue to produce "serious" editorials, but serious editorials don't have to be dull. Editorial writers should, first, write about what readers care about. Second, they should frame issues so they appeal to readers and show how those issues affect them. Third, writers should lure readers with attractive bait: a catchy headline, a startling or intriguing opening, a capsule of the editorial message, graphics, a personal angle.

Not every editorial has to be serious. Editorials can be written, just for the fun of it, with no serious message intended. Editorials also can be written in fun and have a serious message. Art Buchwald has been doing this for decades. Dave Barry, at least on occasion, is doing it today.

If American editorial pages have had one characteristic over the centuries, it has been an ability to adapt—perhaps slowly and reluctantly—to changing times and changing readership. With a few exceptions, editorials no longer are written in the partisan language of the Federalist-era party newspapers, the thundering manner of a Greeley or the sensational style of a Hearst. Today many readers have the choice of only one newspaper. Readers also tend to be better educated and, supposedly, less swayed by emotional, one-sided arguments. The wandering path that American editorial writing has followed, from Colonial days to the present, is described in Chapter 1, "The Editorial Page That Used to Be." A glimpse at where editorial writing today is going—or should be going if it is to survive—is offered in Chapter 2, "The Editorial Page That Should, and Could, Be." The remaining chapters explain and suggest how editorial writers and would-be editorial writers can prepare themselves to meet the challenge of turning out the best possible editorial pages.

SECTION **1** The
Why
of
the
Editorial
Page

CHAPTER 1   The Editorial Page That Used to Be

Editorial writing is not what it used to be. Now, you may assume that I am comparing today's editorial writers with Horace Greeley or James Gordon Bennett or Charles Dana. And I am. No editorial writer today is blessed with the name recognition or devoted readership of these giants of the days of "personal journalism." But I also have a much more recent comparison in mind. Many of today's editorial writers are different from editorial writers of only a few years ago. They are better prepared for their jobs and better known in their communities than those "anonymous wretches" that one participant described as assembling at the first national meeting of editorial writers in 1947.

Editors no longer thunder in the manner of a Greeley, whose editorials could send a screaming mob to New York's city hall or provoke an ill-prepared Union Army into fighting the Battle of Bull Run. Editors of the first half of the 19th century often spoke with the editorial "I," and when they used "we," they meant "I." Editorials didn't have to be signed; readers knew who wrote the editorials in the papers they read.

Readers usually agreed with editorials in the papers they subscribed to. The large number of newspapers in most cities represented a wide variety of political opinions, and people read the papers they found most compatible with their own views. Consequently, editors could be as dogmatic and vitriolic in their editorials as they wished to be and know that their readers would not only agree with what they said but enjoy every nasty word written against mutual opponents. Editors could find comfort in the fact that, even if they did not know any more about an issue than their own political party's line, they were more knowledgeable than the vast majority of their readers. During the days of the "penny press" (when some papers actually did cost only one penny), many readers were immigrants—new to the country and new to the language—and most of them, as well as readers born in America, were only aware of what they read in their papers.

Those were great days for editors who were sure of what they wanted to say and said it boldly. But in addition to spreading their views, they spread a great deal of misinformation and fear among their readers. You have only to recall how the circulation war between Joseph Pulitzer and William Randolph Hearst whipped up a frenzy that helped ignite the Spanish-American War.

No editor of today has that kind of power over the emotions of readers. Today journalists may lament the passing of the great days of personal journalism, but they can't lament the shenanigans, the (sometimes self-) deception and outright lying, those great editors engaged in. The days of the "great editorialist" have been gone for a century.

Compared to Horace Greeley, today's editorial writers are not well known to their readers. They rarely sign their names to what they write. Their editorials are the anonymous opinions of "the newspaper." Since today's readers have virtually no choice of a local daily newspaper, modern editorial writers know that those who read what they write hold as many varieties of opinion as exist in the community. This diverse readership is one reason that editorial writers no longer roar like Greeley. If writers take a strong stand on a controversial issue, they know they will please those who agree with them but displease those who disagree (if these people read the editorials at all). Today's writers suspect that if they come on too strong in their editorials, they will antagonize the readers they think they have the best chance to influence—those in the middle who have not made up their minds. Expression of a strong editorial opinion also may suggest to readers that the paper is using its news columns to advance that same opinion.

Writers know a lot of their readers are as well educated as they. Readers may not see another daily newspaper, but they have many other channels of communication through which they can learn what is happening in their communities and the world. Today's public has a far better chance of finding out whether editorial writers know what they are talking about than did readers of a century ago. If an editorial hands out the party line, those who are unfamiliar with the issue at hand may be swayed for the moment. But if the editorial has told only half the story, and the readers come across the other half at a later time, they are likely to sway right back again—and will thereafter be warier when the newspaper tries to tell them something.

These are some of the ways in which editorial writing is different now from the way it was in the days of Greeley, Bennett and Dana. How, then, does today's editorial writing differ from that of more recent times?

Personal journalism began to die out in the 1870s. Newspapers became corporately, instead of individually, owned. Publishers became more important than editors. Editorial-writing staffs, at least on larger papers, grew in size. If editorials did not specifically represent the handed-down views of the publisher, they were at least the product of a group rather than the thoughts of an independent editorial writer. When the group of "anonymous wretches" assembled for the first meeting of the National Conference of Editorial Writers (NCEW) in Washington, D.C., in 1947, the 26 editorial writers, all men, had not previously met one another. The majority had never heard of most of the others. Only a few of the persons whose work appeared on editorial pages then were very well known. Beginning in the early 1930s, editorial page columnists such as Walter Lippmann, David Lawrence, Raymond Clapper and Arthur Krock had gained many readers through interpreting national and international events. Their bylines were displayed prominently, generally on the right side of the editorial page. But the opinions on the left side of the editorial page, those of "the newspaper," almost invariably were left unsigned. These writers were not well known, and they were not well paid. If they disagreed with what they were told to write, they could try to find another job. Participants at the Washington meeting speculated that they were among the last newspaper groups to form a national organization because their publishers didn't want them to get any ideas about gaining an independent voice.

Since then, editorial writers on many newspapers have carved out for themselves more secure and more prominent positions in relations with their publishers and with their communities. They have adapted to, and helped to change, the conditions in which they work.

Change and adaptation, in fact, have been at work in the evolution of the American editorial page ever since the introduction of the first newspapers on the continent. The changes began long before Greeley, Bennett and Dana appeared on the journalistic scene. The strong editor of personal journalism comes in the third of five general phases through which American newspapers, and editorial pages, have passed since Colonial days. The five phases can be described as follows:

1. During the Colonial era and the period immediately after the Revolutionary War, little effort was made to separate opinion from news. Both appeared intertwined in the columns of the press. Newspapers openly proclaimed that they were partisan voices.
2. With the writing of the new Constitution in 1787 came political parties and the partisan press. Editorials began to appear as distinct forms. Each newspaper was committed to a political party.
3. With the populist ("penny") press that emerged in the 1830s came the strong editor, who initially was concerned with sensationalized news and not with editorials but who, as readers became more literate and sophisticated, began to produce highly personalized editorial pages–and better news products as well. Ties to political parties began to weaken.
4. Following the Civil War, and more so following the turn of the century, anonymous corporate editorial staffs began to replace the famous editors. Writing became more bland. Newspapers, while claiming increasing independence, generally remained committed to conservative editorial policies.
5. In recent years, beginning in the politically active 1960s, a younger, more aggressive and more pragmatic editorial writer has started to emerge. This type of writer tends to be nonpartisan but committed to a general editorial philosophy.

In each of these phases, newspapers and their editorials served different purposes, according to the readers' changing needs. Those papers–and editorials–that succeeded in changing with the times survived; those that did not perished.

The remainder of this chapter will briefly describe the first four phases. The last phase will be discussed in the following chapter and throughout this book.

NEWS MIXED WITH OPINION

During the Colonial period, the first newspapers were heavily influenced by British tradition. The British press was licensed and printers published under the authority of the crown. Licenses could be suspended if the printer published anything that displeased the authorities. The publisher of the first newspaper on American soil, Benjamin Harris, quickly learned what would happen if opinions displeased the Colonial authorities in Boston. In his *Publick Occurrences, Both Foreign and Domestick*, published on Sept. 25, 1690, he said the English had postponed attacking the French because their Indian allies had failed to provide promised canoes. If that were not a clear enough criticism of Colonial policy, Harris proceeded in his news columns to call the Indians "miserable savages, in whom we have too much confided." Harris had not obtained the required license. Members of the Colonial Council did not like what he had written and shut the newspaper down. It died after one issue.

For a large part of the Colonial period, American readers were more interested in what was happening in Europe than what was happening in the Colonies. Events in the Colonies did not seem very important except as they related to events in Europe. Consequently, the Colonialists primarily looked for news from abroad in their early newspapers.

The first generally recognized American newspaper, the *Boston News-Letter*, was started in 1704—14 years after Harris' first attempt—and was a printed version of what had been a written newsletter circulated by Boston postmaster John Campbell. Not much concerned with politics, Campbell avoided Harris' troubles by publishing with the permission of the government. But he did not hesitate to offer opinions, unpolitical though they were. At the conclusion of a news item about a woman's suicide, he said he hoped that the recounting "may not be offensive, but rather a Warning to all others to watch against the Wiles of our Grand Adversary." The reporting of the whipping of a prisoner who had sold tar mixed with dirt was "here inserted to be a caveat to others, of doing the like, least a worse thing befal (sic) them."

With the *News-Letter* already in existence, the father of James and Benjamin Franklin thought James was making a mistake in starting the *New England Courant* in 1721. The continent could not support more than one newspaper, he felt. James Franklin not only dared to publish; he dared to publish without the required license. The *Courant*, carrying little news and few advertisements, contained mostly commentary and essays. One of Franklin's targets was a group that advocated smallpox inoculations. He also attacked civil and religious leaders and questioned some of the religious opinions of the day. Franklin so enraged the Rev. Increase Mather that Mather called the *Courant* the work of the devil. If the government did not do something about the paper, he proclaimed from his pulpit, "I am afraid some *Awful Judgment* will come upon this land, and that the *Wrath of God will arise, and there will be no Remedy*." However, what finally provoked the Colonial Council to charge Franklin with contempt was an allegation that the government had not done enough to protect Boston from pirates. Franklin was thrown into jail and ordered not to publish again. Subsequent issues were listed as being published by his younger brother Benjamin.

Benjamin Franklin began publishing his own *Pennsylvania Gazette* in 1729. He was not averse to inserting opinions into what he wrote, but, being a skilled writer and diplomat, he was able to avoid the trouble that James had encountered. One device that Benjamin Franklin used to help arouse the Colonies was to print a drawing of a snake divided into eight parts representing New England and seven other Colonies, accompanied by the motto "Join or die." It was run with an account of the killing and scalping of frontier Colonists in Virginia and Pennsylvania by the French and Indians.

British tradition also insisted that, in matters of libel, the only task of the jury was to determine whether the alleged words had been published. A comment mixed with news in John Peter Zenger's *New York Weekly Journal* was the first step toward putting an end to that tradition on American soil. Zenger "reported" in a story on election results that voters had been harassed about their qualifications for voting, and in another story that Gov. William Cosby had allowed the French to spy on Colonial naval defenses. In 1734, a year after his first issue had appeared, Zenger was charged with "raising sedition." An elegant appeal by Andrew Hamilton, then an 80-year-old Philadelphia lawyer, convinced the jury that it should ignore English common law, which would have limited the jury to finding Zenger innocent only if the alleged libel had not been published. The favorable decision for Zenger did not immediately change Colonial law, but it encouraged other editors to speak out and finally became accepted practice before the end of the century.

More threatening to most newspapers than the prospect of libel was the Stamp Act of 1765, through which the British attempted to levy a heavy tax on paper to support their military presence in the Colonies. The tax produced vigorous editorial protests. Franklin suspended the *Gazette* for three weeks, during which time he printed as substitutes large handbills headed "Remarkable Occurrences" and "Stamped paper not to be had." The day after the act took effect, William Bradford III's *Pennsylvania Journal and Weekly Advertiser* ran a black border, usually indicating mourning, in the shape of a tombstone.

As the Revolution approached, Colonial papers began to mix more and more editorial comment into the news columns. The papers generally split into three camps: Tory, Whig and Radical. The Tories championed the status quo, continued Colonial relations with Britain. In 1772, one of the most prominent Tories, James Rivington, began publishing *Rivington's New York Gazetteer or the Connecticut, New Jersey, Hudson's River and Quebec Weekly Advertiser*. Rivington tried giving space to all sides of the political issues–an unusual practice at the time. But, to quote Rivington himself, "the moment he ventured to publish sentiments which were opposed to the dangerous views and desires of certain demagogues, he found himself held up as an enemy of his country." In 1775 a party of armed men on horseback broke into his print shop, destroyed his press, carried away his type and melted it into bullets.

The Colonial Whigs represented a rising business class that at first was more interested in protecting itself from economic harassment by the British than in effecting political and social change. One of the most widely published Whigs was John Dickinson, who argued for the preservation of property and for self-taxation in several articles titled "Letters From a Farmer in Pennsylvania." First published in the *Pennsylvania Chronicle* and the *Boston Gazette* in 1767, they were widely reprinted through the Colonies.

One of the most successful publishers of the Revolutionary and post-Revolutionary periods was Isaiah Thomas (who, incidentally, published *The History of Printing in America* in 1810). In 1770 he founded his *Massachusetts Spy*, advertising it as "A Weekly Political and Commercial Paper—Open to All Parties, but *influenced* by None." Thomas tried to open the *Spy* to both Whigs and Tories and to put their respective positions before the public. But he found he could not maintain this stance. The Tories stopped taking his paper, and Thomas concluded that the *Spy* would have to have "a fixed character." Since he was in principle opposed to the British economic measures, he made it a Whig paper. As issues became even sharper, Thomas and other Whigs joined the Radicals.

One of the first avowed Radical publications was the *Boston Gazette and Country Journal.* As early as 1764, publishers Benjamin Eades and John Gill were writing and providing space for anti-British essays. Thomas thought that no other paper or publisher played a greater role in bringing about the independence of the United States.[3]

Samuel Adams, who wrote for the *Gazette,* reasoned that in the cause of liberty events and facts could be twisted and interpreted to help arouse the Colonists against the British. One example, with a slight difference, was the "Journal of Occurrences," in which anonymous authors working for Adams compiled the verbal and physical assaults committed by British soldiers in Boston. In 1768, the "Occurrences" began appearing in John Holt's *New York Journal,* a Radical paper. They were widely reprinted. Although historians have since concluded that some of the "facts" were not quite true, the authors made a point of distinguishing between facts and comments by printing their opinions in italics. This attempt at differentiation between fact and opinion in news columns represented a step toward the use of the editorial as distinct from the news article.

Another Radical opinion writer who helped ignite the Revolution was Tom Paine, more pamphleteer than newspaper writer. His *Common Sense*, which appeared in early 1776, pleaded the cause of independence with an eye to persuading the Whigs who were still on the fence. During the war he published a series called "The Crisis." The papers presented no new facts or arguments but, in the fashion of editorial writers of more than one later era, put ideas into words that could be understood by the less literate.

THE PARTISAN PRESS

The framers of the Constitution in 1787 thought they had achieved sufficient compromises between large and small states, and between the central government and the states, to eliminate the divisiveness that had characterized the late Colonial period. James Madison expressed the hope in "The Federalist," also known as "The Federalist Papers," that under the new government there would be no need for factions. One of the reasons for nominating George Washington, the leader of the Continental Army and symbol of Colonial resistance, as the first president was to rally all Americans around the new government. The "Federalist Papers" themselves, written by Alexander Hamilton, James Madison and John Jay to support ratification of the Constitution, were first published in a newspaper, the *New York Independence Journal.* They were a mixture of fact, argument and opinion.

In spite of the hopes for political unity under Washington, disagreements over how strong the federal government should be began to appear. Hamilton, as secretary of the Treasury, pushed for an active national administration. Since he favored the business community, he wanted firm financial support for the government and, specifically, he wanted a national bank. Thomas Jefferson and others wanted a weaker federal government. The Jeffersonians tended to be favorably disposed toward the French Revolution. Those around Hamilton generally allied themselves with Great Britain. Factions (later called "parties") eventually formed around these two leaders, the Hamiltonians becoming known as Federalists, the Jeffersonians as Democratic-Republicans.

To foster public support for the Washington administration, in which he was a dominant influence, Hamilton provided the inspiration for founding the first partisan newspaper under the new Constitution, the *Gazette of the United States.* It appeared in New York in 1789 under the editorship of John Fenno.

Other Federalist papers followed. *Porcupine's Gazette and Daily Advertiser,* founded by William Cobbett in Philadelphia in 1797, was known for its vitriolic attacks on the opposition. In one instance, calling the French minister to the United States a "blunderbuss," Cobbett lashed out (in part) with these words: "When we see an unprincipled, shameless bully, 'A dog in forehead, and in heart a deer,' who endeavors, by means of a big look, a threatening aspect, and a thundering voice, to terrify peaceable men into a compliance with what he has neither a right to demand, nor power nor courage to enforce, and who, at the same time, acts in such a bungling, stupid manner, as to excite ridicule and contempt in place of fear; when we see such a gasconading, impudent bluff as this (and that we do every day), we call him a *Blunderbuss.*" Cobbett's attacks on the French became such a scandal that President John Adams, a Federalist himself, considered ordering Cobbett to leave the country under provisions of the Alien Act.

A Federal writer of much milder tone was Noah Webster, of dictionary fame. Webster is credited by historian Wm. David Sloan as writing "the first editorial, in the modern sense, ever to appear in an American newspaper."[4] A contribution written by Webster was published under the "Hartford" local news column of the *Connecticut Courant.* Later, while editing a Federalist paper called the *American Minerva* (founded in 1793), Webster placed editorials under the "New York" local news heading, but by 1796 he was placing them under the heading of "The Minerva" (the nickname of the paper). This heading was the forerunner of what we now call the masthead, a box on the editorial page that carries the name of the paper, the names of the main editorial and business persons and other information about the paper. These innovations represented further steps toward differentiating editorials from news.

Once the Federalist press began extolling the virtues of the Washington administration, it was not long before plans were laid to present another point of view. Madison, even though he had contributed to the "Federalist Papers," found himself urging Jefferson, as secretary of state, to provide government subsidies to Philip Freneau to start an anti-Federalist newspaper. The resulting *National Gazette* was published only from 1791 to 1793, but Freneau's virulent attacks on the Federalists inspired other anti-Federalists to speak up. The anti-Federalists opposed increasing the powers of the central government. They opposed increased taxes. They did not want a national bank. Generally they spoke for agricultural interests, the less affluent, the smaller states and Americans who sympathized with the French Revolution.

For most of American history, American citizens have considered George Washington to be beyond reproach. But some of the anti-Federalist writers did not. One of the most outspoken was Benjamin Franklin Bache, grandson of Benjamin Franklin. Bache founded the *Philadelphia General Advertiser*, widely known as the *Aurora*, in 1790. When he wrote that the nation had been "debouched" by Washington, Federalists wrecked his office and beat him. Of Bache, *Porcupine's Gazette* stated: "This atrocious wretch (worthy descendant of old Ben) knows that all men of any understanding put him down as an abandoned liar, as a tool and a hireling. . . . He is an ill-looking devil. His eyes never get above your knees." One day on the street, John Fenno, editor of the *Gazette of the United States*, hit Bache in the face. Bache struck Fenno over the head with his cane. This started a long tradition of street encounters between rival 19th-century editors. The *Aurora* was the first, in 1800, to make its second page specifically an editorial page. It also used the editorial "we." Other editors began to follow both practices.

Several historians have called this the "Dark Age of Journalism" because of the scurrility of the press. But others have seen this emotional outpouring, especially among the anti-Federalists, as a venting of stored-up anger against the British and against anything that resembled the imposition of the strong government that the British attempted to impose on the Colonies. Because of their antipathy toward Britain and sympathy for the French Revolution, the anti-Federalists attacked the administration's inclination to support the British and oppose France. This opposition helped account for the passage of the Alien and Sedition Acts of 1798, which forbade "any false, scandalous and malicious writing . . . against the government of the United States, or either house of the Congress . . . or the . . . President . . . or to excite against them the hatred of the good people of the United States. . . . " The vice president (then Jefferson, an anti-Federalist) was intentionally excluded from the act, which was aimed specifically at the anti-Federalists. The administration of the law was so unfair—so obviously against anti-Federalist editors—that the apparent injustice contributed to the defeat of John Adams and to the election of Jefferson. Jefferson pardoned the imprisoned editors, and the laws were allowed to expire.

With the election of Jefferson, the press became less vicious but remained strictly partisan. Now it was the Federalists' turn to establish a press in opposition to the government. In 1801, the year Jefferson took office, Hamilton founded the *New York Post*, with William Coleman as editor. Hamilton wrote many of the editorials. The *Post* pushed Federalist policies—such as a strong merchant marine and navy and an internal revenue system—and defended the Alien and Sedition Acts. Mostly it saw its purpose as ridiculing the Jefferson administration.

Coleman reluctantly acknowledged that the Louisiana Purchase, one of Jefferson's major accomplishments, was "an important acquisition" but suggested that its principal value might be to trade for the Floridas, "obviously of far greater value to us than all the immense, undefined region west of the river." When Jefferson reported to Congress that up the Missouri River was a mountain of rock salt, the *Post* said:

Methinks such a great, huge mountain of solid, shining salt must make a dreadful glare in a clear sunshiny day, especially just after a rain. . . . We think it would have been no more fair in the traveler who informed Mr. Jefferson of this territory of solid salt, to have added that some leagues to the westward of it there was an immense lake of molasses, and that between this lake and the mountain of salt, there was an extensive vale of hasty pudding, stretching as far as the eye could reach. . . .

Coleman kept up the Federalist fight against Jefferson and later against Madison, but by 1816, when James Monroe was elected president overwhelmingly during the "Era of Good Will," the Federalist Party had dwindled nearly to obscurity. According to the formerly Federalist *Post*, the Republican-Democrats, soon to be known as the Democrats, had taken over the Federalist principles. The *Post* continued as a voice for the commercial community but began espousing Democratic principles.

Beginning with Jefferson, every president through James Buchanan, who was elected in 1856, had an official newspaper in Washington. The principal purpose of the administration paper was to serve as a mouthpiece for the president. The party faithful read the official organ to find out the official line of the party in power. Even though the *National Intelligencer* became the official paper of the Jefferson administration, editors Joseph Gales Jr. and William W. Seaton built a reputation for separating their editorial positions from their news reporting and for providing nonpartisan coverage of Congress.

The most effective use of an official newspaper was made by President Andrew Jackson, who became president in 1829. He first made his influence felt with the party faithful through the *United States Telegraph*, founded in 1825 by Duff Green. When Green switched allegiance to Jackson's rival, John C. Calhoun, Jackson brought Francis P. Blair to Washington to establish a new administration organ, the *Washington Globe*. Blair, who had been on the *Argus of Western America*, the official Democratic Party paper published in Frankfort, Ky., came to have great influence on Jackson and came to be one of Jackson's "kitchen cabinet." Another *Argus* editor, Amos Kendall, became Jackson's principal writer.

The Jackson charm also worked to bring editors under "Old Hickory's" spell, allowing Jackson to gain influence over a substantial number of other newspapers throughout the country. He appointed many editors to government positions. Local postmasterships were among the most popular.

One of the papers that shifted their editorial policies to support Jackson was the *Post*. William Cullen Bryant, who became editor the same year Jackson took office, supported low tariffs and opposed the national bank, positions also held by Jackson. Bryant was one of the first editors to speak out for the right of free speech for abolitionists and the right of labor to organize. Although he loyally supported the Democrats, his editorials—unlike those of the earliest party press—were not marked by excessively partisan, shrill tones. The *Post*, also unlike most other party papers, was seeking to expand its readership beyond a few thousand politically aware readers and merchants. Bryant, who could write to satisfy the best of literary critics with his poetry, used such techniques as beginning an editorial with a humorous saying or an appropriate story to try to win subscribers from among a new and growing working class.

The *Post* succeeded in making the transition from the era of the party press to that of the populist press. Most of the other party papers did not. One reason was that the vast majority of presidents between Jackson and Abraham Lincoln were weak leaders, incapable of inspiring strong journalistic voices. A more important reason was that, unlike the *Post*, the party papers attempted to remain party papers when the new, growing readership in the country was not much interested in politics. Much of the population was barely literate. Partisan politics became extremely confusing during this time: The Whig Party split apart, then died; the new Republican Party came out of almost nowhere; and the Democratic Party divided along North-South lines.

By the time Lincoln became president, designation of an administration paper had become little more than a formality, and Lincoln didn't even bother to seek an official voice. By then most of the readership was concentrated in the populist press. It was this press, not the party press, that became important for politicians.

THE POPULIST PRESS

The first papers that reflected the nation's interest in something besides party politics were the mercantile dailies, which became prominent in the business community in the 1820s. But like the party papers they found only a few thousand readers sufficiently interested to read them regularly. They offered little editorial comment.

Ignored by both party and mercantile press was a rapidly growing potential readership, resulting partly from immigration, partly from increasing literacy. These readers may not have been especially interested in party politics, but they were interested in what was going on in their communities. Out of this development grew an opportunity to publish papers that would sell to the masses.

Day, Bennett, Greeley and Raymond

The first of the populist papers were called the "penny press" because some of them actually cost only a penny. Others cost two or three cents. In the first years much of the content was crime news and gossip. Courts and the police record were favorite sources for stories, many of them full of sex, blood and drunkenness. The readers loved these new papers, and circulation soared into the tens of thousands.

Editorial pages were slow in working their way into these papers. The first of the penny press papers was the *New York Sun*, founded in 1833 by Benjamin H. Day. He allied himself with no political party and employed no regular editorial writer. The few editorials that appeared dealt briefly with the latest sensations, municipal affairs, and morals and manners. One example:

"SUDDEN DEATH–Ann McDonough, of Washington Street, attempted to drink a pint of rum on a wager, on Wednesday afternoon last. Before it was half swallowed Ann was a corpse. Served her right." Another example: "DUEL–We understand that a duel was fought at Hoboken on Friday morning last between a gentleman of Canada and a French gentleman of this city, in which the latter was wounded. The parties should be arrested." The *Sun* had only this to say when the 1843 New York Legislature adjourned: "The Legislature of this State closed its arduous duties yesterday. It has increased the number of our banks and fixed a heavy load of debt upon posterity."

The New York Herald, founded in 1835 by James Gordon Bennett, offered even more sensationalism than the *Sun.* In the early years, Bennett offered little serious editorial comment, but he loved to flaunt his ego and wit before his readers; they loved his swagger and flippancy. He was the first of the editors noted for "personal journalism." Concerning the *Herald,* he wrote: "Nothing can prevent its success but God Almighty, and he happens to be on my side." Although he liked to attack speculators, pickpockets and competing editors for their "crimes and immoralities," his editorials contained more bombast and personal references than solid opinion. Bennett's famous competitor, Horace Greeley, while perhaps not the most objective of critics, accurately characterized Bennett as "cynical, inconsistent, reckless, easily influenced by others' opinions, and by his own prejudices."

Bennett's biting editorial language and sensational news practices earned him occasional physical abuse. Several times he was horsewhipped in the streets. Usually he took advantage of these attacks to parade his fearlessness before his readers. After James Watson, editor of the *Courier and Enquirer,* had pushed Bennett down some stone steps, Bennett reported that he had suffered only a scratch and three torn buttons, but that Watson's "loss is a rent from top to bottom of a very beautiful black coat, which cost the ruffian $40, and a blow in the face, which may have knocked down his throat some of his infernal teeth for anything I know." He concluded self-righteously: "As for intimidating me, or changing my course, the thing cannot be done. . . . I tell the honest truth in my paper, and leave the consequences to God."

Bennett's ego was never more evident than in an editorial announcing his engagement. The heading was: "To The Readers of the Herald–Declaration of Love–Caught at Last–Going to Be Married–New Movement in Civilization." The editorial said in part:

I am going to be married in a few days. The weather is so beautiful; times are getting so good; the prospects of political and moral reform so auspicious, that I cannot resist the divine instinct of honest nature any longer; so I am going to be married to one of the most splendid women in intellect, in heart, in soul, in property, in person, in manner, that I have yet seen in the course of my interesting pilgrimage through human life.

. . . . I cannot stop in my career. I must fulfill that awful destiny which the Almighty Father has written against my name, in the broad letters of life, against the wall of heaven. I must give the world a pattern of happy wedded life, with all the charities that spring from a nuptial love.

In later years, as readers became more sophisticated and Bennett less flippant, the *Herald* developed a serious and thoughtful editorial page. But it is to Horace Greeley that credit traditionally has gone for making the editorial page a significant and respectable portion of the daily newspaper. Greeley might also have been credited with establishing the first penny press. He published his first issue on a snowy day in January 1833, but readers could not get out to buy the paper, and he did not sell enough copies to be able to put out a second issue. His second effort came in 1841 with the founding of the *New York Tribune*.

Tribune editorials, written in a variety of styles but almost always with literary merit, commented on a broad range of topics, generally following a consistent editorial policy. Several writers contributed to the thinking behind the editorials and to the writing of the editorials, but it was customary for readers to think of the *Tribune*'s editorial page, if not the *Tribune* itself, as a one-man show. Subscribers read the paper to see what Greeley thought, and they assumed that every word was his. *The New York Weekly Tribune*, in particular, with circulation across the country, was read with devotion.

With Day's and Bennett's papers appealing mostly to Democratic voters, Greeley's *Tribune* was the first of the populist press with a Whig editorial outlook. But Greeley's philosophy was far more radical than that of most Whigs. He favored high tariffs, as did the Whig party, but not just to protect business; he wanted the creation of an American economy that would benefit merchants, workers and farmers as well. His interest in socialist and utopian ideas reflected the belief that all classes working together in an ideal community could produce wealth and harmony for all. He not only preached this belief in his editorial columns but he traveled the country lecturing to audiences on his ideas.

Greeley strongly believed in Western expansion and supported the march of farmers and merchants westward. But he did not support the methods he saw being used in annexing Texas. The only New York editor to oppose the Mexican-American War, Greeley wrote this editorial after the Senate had voted to annex Texas:

The mischief is done and we are now involved in war! We have adopted a war ready made, and taken upon ourselves its prosecution to the end. We are to furnish the bodies to fill trenches and the cash to defray the enormous expense. Mexico, despoiled of one of her fairest provinces by our rapacity and hypocrisy, has no choice but to resist, however ineffectively, the consummation of our flagitious designs.

Greeley was an early advocate of the abolition of slavery. E.L. Godkin, editor of the *New York Evening Post*, concluded that by the early 1860s Greeley had "done more than any other man to bring slaveholders to bay, and place the Northern fingers on the throat of the institution." Godkin perceived that Greeley had "waged one of the most unequal battles in which any journalist ever engaged with a courage and tenacity worthy of the cause, and by dint of biting sarcasm, vigorous invective, powerful arguments, and a great deal of vituperation and personality."[5]

But, for all that, Godkin accused Greeley of treating his opponents with contempt, of being half-educated "and very imperfectly at that." According to Godkin, Greeley had "no grasp of mind, no great political insight"; his brain was "crammed with half truths and odds and ends of ideas which a man inevitably accumulates who scrapes knowledge together by fits and starts on his way through life." Greeley was saved, Godkin said, by his unflagging enthusiasm, an unshakable faith in principles and a writing style virtually unsurpassed in vigor, terseness, clearness and simplicity. But he was known also for his coarse and abusive language. As Godkin wrote: "He calls names and gives the lie, in his leading articles, with a heartiness and vehemence which in cities seem very shocking, but which out in the country, along the lakes, and in the forests and prairies of the Northwest, where most of his influence lies, are simply proofs of more than ordinary earnestness."

Illustrating both Greeley's penchant for name calling and his devotion to the anti-slavery cause was an editorial titled "Stephen A. Douglas as the Volunteer Executioner," published on Feb. 22, 1854. Greeley depicted a scene in which "a poor, miserable, half-witted and degraded Wretch, who consorted with the negroes," was about to be lynched by a mob. As the execution was about to take place, there was hesitation. He wrote then:

A moment more and there would have gone up in the crowd a cry, "Let him go," "Let him go," but at this moment a person unknown to the crowd was seen to move toward the cart. Springing upon it and rudely seizing the dangling rope, he turned round to the astonished spectators and said: "If none of you will act as hangman, I will. Damn the Abolitionists!" In another instant the fatal cord was adjusted, the cart driven off, and there was suspended between heaven and earth the trembling—the dead—form of an innocent man.

Now who was this hangman? Who was this fierce defender of the peculiar institution? Was he a Southern man? No. Was he a citizen identified with the South? No. It was on the contrary a Northern man, from a free State—in fact, one who had been but two days in the place. It seemed as if, suspecting his own principles, revolting in his heart at slavery and afraid that in the excitement of the hour he might next be arraigned, he took this fearful and terrible office of executioner in order to place himself, as he supposed, on "high Southern ground" . . . . And here is to be seen reflected the true picture of Mr. Douglas's turpitude. Southern men may have in the madness of the hour conceived such iniquity as is embodied in the Nebraska bill. They may have prepared the halter for the neck of the Missouri Compromise—but the last fatal act would never have been undertaken had not the Senator from Illinois volunteered to act as executioner, had been willing to mount the scaffold, and call down the infamy of murdering liberty upon his own head.

Greeley wanted desperately to be elected to high political office. He did win one term in Congress, but his self-righteous attitude toward his colleagues made him unpopular. For a time he was one of the three Whig leaders in New York state, but invariably, just as he thought he was about to be nominated for a position on the Whig ticket, his political allies would outmaneuver him, promising him a chance next time. When the Whigs disintegrated, divided in part over the issue of slavery, he became one of the leaders in the formation of the Republican Party. Finally, when he was old and the nomination was not worth much, some of Greeley's fellow editors and others nominated him for president on a coalition Democratic-liberal Republican ticket in 1872. But he was overwhelmingly defeated by Ulysses S. Grant. Greeley died a few weeks later.

Another editor of the populist press era who was interested in holding public office was Henry J. Raymond, who with George Jones founded the *New York Times.* Raymond, like Greeley, helped form the Republican Party when the Whig Party disintegrated. But he was more successful than Greeley in winning office and in fact was nominated and elected lieutenant governor of New York at a time when Greeley hoped to be nominated.

Raymond's goal in establishing the *Times* was to publish a paper that was more objective in its news columns and less emotional in its editorials than were the *Tribune*, the *Herald* and other populist papers. In this he succeeded. The *Times* was less flamboyant and more respectable than its competitors. It was also less exciting to read. Raymond's inability to make up his mind about whether he was more editor or more politician also affected the vitality of the *Times*. If he had not been lured into politics, he would have been a better editor, in Godkin's view "the most successful journalist that has ever been seen." But, to quote Godkin, Raymond had a tendency to hold doubts about his political convictions and lacked the "temper which was necessary to victory" in the political realm. A "sense of the necessities and limitations of his position as a politician" kept him from being the journalist he could have been.

Other Voices

Historians traditionally have described the journalism of the 18th and 19th centuries, and even the 20th century, as the work of white male editors, most of them in New York City or Washington, D.C. But there were other voices as well, including women and African-Americans, some of whom are only now being rediscovered.

A number of strong newspapers emerged elsewhere in the country in the mid-1800s (but run by white males). In Chicago the *Tribune*, which had been founded in 1847, achieved a formidable reputation after Joseph Medill assumed control in 1855. This paper took a strong anti-slavery stand, promoted the new Republican Party and pushed fellow Illinoisan Lincoln for the presidency. In the Northeast, the *Springfield* (Mass.) *Republican*, founded by Samuel Bowles II in 1824, earned respect for conservative, enlightened, well-written editorials. In 1884, the *Republican* displayed its political independence by switching its support to a Democrat, Grover Cleveland, in the race for president.

As for women editors and publishers, 17 are known to have taken over operations of newspapers following the deaths of their husbands during the Colonial period.[6] The first was Elizabeth Timothy, who became publisher of the *South Carolina Gazette* upon the death of her husband in 1738. The first woman to start a newspaper on her own (in 1762), with the help of daughter Mary Katherine and son William (who didn't stay around very long), was Sarah Goddard, of the solidly Whig *Providence* (R.I.) *Gazette*.

Seventy years later, declaring she had "no party, the welfare and happiness of our country is our politics," Anne Royall launched *Peter Pry*, which Ishbel Ross described as containing an occasional "gleam of common sense sift[ing] through the thick layers of fanatical upbraiding."[7] She fought against corrupt officials, for separation of church and state and against the Bank of the United States. The bank was the subject that she wanted to interview President John Quincy Adams about when she supposedly (quoting Ross) "sat on his clothes while he bathed in the Potomac River and refused to budge until he had answered her questions." In less flamboyant style, Royall published the *Huntress* from 1836 to 1854, advocating Jacksonian principles, free public education, free speech and justice to immigrants and Indians.

Although not strictly an editorial writer, Margaret Fuller wrote essays, reviews and opinion pieces that advanced radical ideas for Greeley's *Tribune*. From 1846 until her death in a shipwreck in 1850, she wrote for the *Tribune* from Europe as the first U.S. woman foreign correspondent.

In 1870 Victoria Woodhull and her sister, Tennessee Claflin, launched *Woodhull and Claflin's Weekly* to promote "Progress! Free Thought. Untrammeled Lives." But, according to Ishbel Ross, they "plunged [so] boldly into the muckraking field . . . all the banned topics of . . . prostitution, free love, social disease, abortion [that] the very words were shocking to the prim readers of the day."[8]

Using a lighter touch, Kate Field, through the columns of *Kate Field's Washington*, published from 1890 to 1896, supported the rights of women and campaigned for Hawaiian annexation, international copyright, temperance, prohibition of Mormon polygamy, and dress reform.[9]

The first African-American newspaper in the United States, *Freedom's Journal*, was begun in 1827 by John B. Russwurm and Samuel E. Cornish to answer attacks on African-Americans coming from the *New York Inquirer*.[10] Most of the readers were white, since few African-Americans were literate. It lasted three years. Forty more African-American newspapers were founded before the Civil War, but most were short-lived. The second paper, the *Weekly Advocate*, another Cornish paper, lasted from 1837 to 1842, an unusually long time. I. Garland Penn, one of the few historians of African-American journalism, edited the *Lynchburg Virginia Laborer*. Most of these publications were much more oriented toward opinion, advancing the anti-slavery cause, than toward news.[11]

A journalist who was both African-American and a woman was Ida B. Wells-Barnett. The daughter of slaves, she spoke out against racial injustice as part owner and editor of the *Memphis Free Speech and Headlight*. When the newspaper office was burned and she was physically threatened, she fled to the North, where she continued to write and lecture in the cause of justice for African-Americans. Each year an Ida B. Wells Award is given to a person who has displayed exemplary leadership in providing employment opportunities in journalism for minorities. Sponsors are the National Association of Black Journalists and the National Conference of Editorial Writers.

Abolition and the Civil War

The Civil War and events leading up to it provided editors with plenty of opportunities to express their strong and diverse viewpoints. We have already noted Greeley's conversion to the cause of abolition. The popularizing of the abolition movement began with the publication of the *Liberator*, founded by William Lloyd Garrison in 1831. At first Garrison was ignored and almost forced into bankruptcy. Even those who sympathized with his views found his blunt, coarse language offensive; in some cases it proved counterproductive. The *Liberator* might have failed in its first year if an African-American preacher named Nat Turner had not led a slave revolt in Virginia that resulted in the deaths of 57 whites. Although Garrison had no subscribers in the South at the time, his writings were perceived to have induced Turner to riot. Southern editors, who wished to place blame on abolitionist interference from the North, began reprinting Garrison's writings as examples of inflammatory material.

Garrison was immediately thrust into the editorial leadership of the abolitionist movement.

Illustrative of Garrison's work was his response when President Millard Fillmore called for new, tougher legislation after abolitionists had defied the Fugitive Slave Act by rescuing a slave from a U.S. deputy marshal in Boston. Garrison wrote:

Nobody injured, nobody wronged, but simply a chattel transformed into a man, and conducted to a spot where he can glorify God in his body and spirit, which are his!

And yet, how all the friends in the pit are writhing and yelling! Not tormented before their time, but just at the right time. Truly, "devils with devils damned firm concord hold!" The President of the United States is out with his Proclamation of Terror, conveying it to us in tones of thunder and on the wings of the lightning; even as though in the old Bay State chaos had come again, and millions of foreign mymidons (sic) were invading our shores! A poor, hunted, entrapped fugitive slave is dexterously removed from the courtroom, and the whole land is shaken! . . . Henry Clay—with one foot in the grave, and just ready to have both body and soul cast into hell—as if eager to make his damnation doubly sure, rises in the United States Senate and proposes an inquiry into the expediency of passing yet another law, by which everyone who shall dare peep or mutter against the execution of the Fugitive Slave Bill shall have his life crushed out!

Abolitionist editors who spoke out strongly risked their property and their lives. Garrison barely escaped an angry mob in Boston in 1835 by jumping out a window and voluntarily spending the night in jail. Threats discouraged abolitionist editor James G. Birney from attempting to organize an abolition movement in Kentucky. When he founded the *Philanthropist* in Cincinnati in the mid-1830s, a mob attacked his office. The abolitionist editor who became the most honored was Elijah Lovejoy. Anti-abolitionists twice destroyed the offices of his *St. Louis Observer*, which had been forced to move from St. Louis to Alton, Ill. When he re-established his paper for a third time, in 1837, a mob destroyed the office and killed him.

One of the editors whom Garrison helped to launch was Frederick Douglass, the best known of the African-American abolitionist editors. Douglass toured the Western states and Europe with Garrison, then went his own way in 1847 to found the *North Star*. The object of the *North Star*, Douglass wrote, "will be to attack slavery in all its forms and aspects; advocate Universal Emancipation; exact the standard of public morality; promote the moral and intellectual improvement of the colored people; and to hasten the day of freedom of our three million enslaved fellow countrymen." Douglass' *North Star*, and his subsequent *Liberty Party Paper*, were not attractive typographically, with mostly solid type, but Douglass' inspired writing and the depth of his convictions made his publications anything but dull. He continued to promote the African-American cause in a series of publications until 1875. By then both he and Garrison were widely honored, at least among African-Americans and Northerners.

The *Post*, under the editorship of William Cullen Bryant, defended the right of the unpopular abolitionists to meet and demonstrate as early as 1833 and spoke sympathetically of John Brown at the time of his raid into Virginia in 1859 to free slaves and incite insurrection. While Southerners were arguing for the extension of slavery, the *Post* foresaw a growing threat of uprising among African-Americans: "But while they speak the tocsin sounds, the blacks are in arms, their houses are in flames, their wives and children driven into exile and killed, and a furious servile war stretches its horror over years. That is the blessed institution you ask us to foster and spread and worship, and for the sake of which you even spout your impotent threats against the grand edifice of the Union!"

Raymond's *Times* characteristically took a more moderate stance, opposing abolition until after the Civil War had begun, even though it had strongly supported the election of Lincoln in 1860. Bennett's *Herald* also remained opposed to abolition until after the war began. It did not favor the election of Lincoln and in fact demonstrated strong sympathy for the South both before and during much of the war. Following the firing on Fort Sumter, the *Herald* contended that "the tempest which now threatens so menacingly" could be entirely dispelled if the Northern states would only call constituent assemblies to ratify constitutional amendments proposed by the South.

At the opposite end of the political and geographical spectrum in the pre–Civil War period were the Southern "fire-eaters." Robert Barnwell Rhett, of the *Charleston* (S.C.) *Mercury,* was ignored in 1832 when he first began writing that the South should secede. In later years, however, he and others not only gained credence but helped convince their fellow Southerners that the North would let the South go.

When the war began, Northern papers supported Union policies, but the *Times* was the only major paper, and only one of three or four of the 17 New York dailies, to consistently support Lincoln throughout the war. On the day after the bombardment of Fort Sumter, the *Times* editorialized:

. . . For the first time in the history of the United States, an organized attempt is made to destroy, by force of arms, the government which the American people have formed for themselves—and to overthrow the glorious Constitution which has made us the envy of the world. The history of the world does not show so causeless an outrage. . . . One thing is certain. Now that the rebels have opened the war, the people will expect the government to defend itself with vigor and determination. There is no room for half-way measures now. . . . *The South has chosen war, and it must have all the war it wants. . . .*

By 1864, however, Raymond feared that Lincoln stood no chance for re-election, barring some bold stroke, but he kept his doubts out of his newspaper columns.

The *Herald,* reflecting its sympathy for the South, chided the Union's misfortune whenever it could find cause and became increasingly bitter against Lincoln. A month after Lincoln took office, the *Herald* referred to the "vicious, imbecile, demoralized Administration." Because the *Herald* was the most widely read American paper in Europe, readers on that continent got many of their impressions of the war from the pro-South *Herald.* After initially promoting Ulysses S. Grant for the Republican nomination for president in 1864, the *Herald* gradually softened its opposition to Lincoln. A rumor indicated that Lincoln had offered Bennett the ambassadorship to Paris. Whether he actually had made such an offer, Bennett wrote a note to Lincoln declining the appointment.

Greeley ran hot and cold on both Lincoln and the war in spite of his alleged strong abolitionist beliefs. Shortly after Fort Sumter, he argued for letting the South secede if that was what the Southern people really wanted. But a few weeks after that, the *Tribune* urged immediate action to bring the seceding states back into the Union. As the summer of 1861 approached, the *Tribune* ran a war slogan atop its editorial page every day for a week:

The Nation's War-Cry

Forward to Richmond! Forward to Richmond!

The Rebel Congress must not be allowed to meet

there on the 20th of July! *BY THAT DATE THE*

PLACE MUST BE HELD BY THE NATIONAL ARMY!

These *Tribune* editorials contributed to the pressures that pushed the Union army to battle prematurely at the First Battle of Bull Run. Casualties were heavy, and the troops retreated in disarray to Washington. The editorials had been written by Fitz-Henry Warren, the *Tribune*'s Washington correspondent, while Greeley was away and Charles A. Dana was in charge of the paper. However, since the slogan ran for a week, Greeley must have known what was being said. In any case, he accepted responsibility for the articles in print and, convinced of the power that he and the *Tribune* had, described himself "as a scapegoat for all the military blunders of the last month." He suffered so much personal remorse that he became physically ill and could not leave his bed.

During the war when things were going well, Greeley was optimistic and tended to speak well of Lincoln. When they were not, he became despondent and blamed Lincoln. In 1864 Greeley suddenly switched to supporting Lincoln after pressing for a substitute presidential nominee. In his case a rumor circulated of a possible postmastership in the second Lincoln administration.

The *Post* strongly supported the war and the administration's measures to wage it, but Bryant became increasingly impatient with Lincoln when the president delayed until 1863 the issuance of the Emancipation Proclamation freeing the slaves. Bryant was also disgusted with newspapers that professed to support the Union but took every possible opportunity to criticize it and taunt it. In fact he published a sarcastic editorial titled "Recipe for a Democratic Paper," which historian Allen Nevins summarized in this fashion:

1. Magnify all rebel successes and minimize all Federal victories; if the South loses 18,000 men say 8,000, and if the North loses 11,000 say 21,000.
2. Calumniate all energetic generals like Sherman, Grant and Rosecrans; call worthless leaders like Halleck and Pope and master generals of the age.
3. Whenever the Union suffers a reverse, declare that the nation is weary of this slow war; and ask how long this fratricidal conflict will be allowed to continue.
4. Expatiate upon the bankruptcies, high prices, stock jobbers, gouging profiteers and "shoddy men."
5. Abuse Lincoln and the Cabinet in two ways: say they are weak, timid, vacillating, and incompetent; and that they are tyrannous, harsh, and despotic.

6. Protest vehemently against "nigger" brigadiers, and the atrocity of arming the slaves against their masters.

7. Don't advise open resistance to the draft. But clamor against it in detail; suggest doubts of its constitutionality; denounce the $300 clause; say that it makes an obvious distinction between rich and poor; and refer learnedly to the military aristocracies of France and Prussia.[12]

Even more anti-Union than the "Democratic Papers" were the Copperhead papers, which spoke for Northern Democrats who openly sympathized with the South. The most prominent of the Copperheads was Clement Laird Vallandigham, who became co-owner of an anti-abolitionist magazine, the *Dayton* (Ohio) *Empire,* in 1847. When the governor of Ohio prepared to answer Lincoln's call for troops after Fort Sumter, the *Empire* declared: "Governor Dennison has pledged the blood and treasure of Ohio to back up a Republican administration in its contemplated attack upon the people of the South. . . . What right has he to make such a pledge? Does he promise to head the troops which he intends to send down South to butcher men, women and children of the section?"

One effect of the Civil War was to put a premium on news. Readers wanted to know how the war was going more than they wanted to know some editor's opinion. Newspapers that could not afford correspondents of their own pooled their resources and formed cooperative news reporting services. Since these services provided news to papers of widely differing editorial viewpoints, they had to be careful to report in as objective a manner as possible to keep from offending the editors. Reliance on the telegraph for transmission provided further incentive to keep stories factual and short. The line between news and editorials became more marked. The press became more impersonal. Shortly after the war, the great populist editors died, Raymond in 1869 at the age of only 49, both Bennett and Greeley in 1872.

"The prestige of the editorial page is done," wrote James Parton, who might not have been the most objective observer, since he had written a highly laudatory biography of Greeley. With the great voices gone, editorials no longer "much influence the public mind, nor change many votes, and . . . the power and success of a newspaper depend wholly and absolutely upon its success in getting, and its skill in exhibiting, the news," Parton wrote.[13]

Woman Suffrage, Native Americans, African-Americans

Among the most common editorial topics immediately following the Civil War were woman suffrage, Native Americans (or Indians), the newly emancipated slaves and economic development. Within a few years it became clear, to say the least, that the Civil War had barely disturbed the white male power balance, at the national level or on editorial pages. Editors were more interested in promoting prosperous communities than in sharing power with another race or sex.

Women such as Susan B. Anthony, Lucy Stone and Elizabeth Cady Stanton, who had been working for abolition, expected that after emancipation and voting rights for African-Americans, woman suffrage would come next. A few editorial voices, among them Greeley's, supported their cause, but others argued that women didn't need the vote, since, according to the

New Orleans Crescent, "they are represented at the ballot box, as well as in the halls of legislation, by their husbands, fathers, and brothers." The *Richmond Whig* saw women's "most effective and irresistible weapon [to be] the artillery of her charms, before which the Columbiad, the Brooke, the Armstrong, and all other guns, 'pale their ineffectual fires.'" Some of the editors expressed the fear that allowing women to enter into the evil world of politics would destroy their traditional superior moral capability, which the St. Louis *Missouri Republican* described as "the aptitude and the habit of the soul to distinguish the finest shades of good and evil, and of what is beautiful and decent."

"It will be a pretty spectacle," wrote an editor for the Memphis *Avalanche*, "to see a strong minded woman haranguing a crowd or squabbling at the ballot box, while her husband is at home darning stockings, making night caps, baking bread and rocking the cradle."

As more and more travelers and settlers headed west after the end of the war, the nation faced difficult choices concerning the Native Americans (Indians) on the Western Plains. A few editors expressed the belief that (in the words of the St. Louis *Missouri Democrat*) "the Indian is endowed with many nobel traits of character, which under proper treatment and training might be rendered highly serviceable to humanity." A few, such as the *Louisville Courier-Journal*, questioned the notion that "civilization must be pushed as far as it will go, that Christianity has to be taught the heathen." But most editors seemed to agree with the *Missouri Republican*, in condemning "the war-path, murdering, scalping and plundering, spreading terror through various settlements and causing mourning in many families." Forget the peace treaties. "Let the Peace Commissioners stand aside for a few months while Gen. Sherman goes in and thrashes these savages till they cry for peace and will be ready to go upon their reservations and stay there." The *Raleigh Standard* was even more blunt: "Let the war of extermination be commenced and followed up until the Indians are either destroyed or driven beyond the limits of the United States."

Most newspapers in the North, but only a few in the South, supported civil and political rights for the newly emancipated African-Americans. Some papers, like the *Memphis Appeal*, lamented that, with the end of slavery, "there . . . never again will be . . . a body of agricultural laborers, so generally contented, so happy, so prolific, with so little disease and deformity among their children, and so little want of common comforts of life among the adults." Some papers, like the Nashville *Republican Banner* (decidedly not a Republican paper), viewed "the Negro [as] indolent by nature, faithless to all their pledges, false to their engagements, deceitful in their contracts, and thriftless and wasteful [and] insolent." The *Charleston Courier* expressed the opinion of many Southern editors concerning the abilities of African-Americans to exercise political rights: "No negro can be so blind as not to know that white men are to be right rulers in this great Republic. Compared with the whites the negros (sic) are as insignificant in numbers as they are deficient in intelligence, and he deceives himself who does not think that intelligence and numbers will not rule."

More sympathy was exhibited toward African-Americans by the relatively few Republican papers in the South and, of course, by the even rarer African-American papers. Responding to concerns similar to those expressed above, the Nashville *Colored Tennessean* said in August 1865: "One set of people declares we won't work, and must be made to. Another is afraid that a war of races will arise. Another thinks we will abandon our Southern homes, and go North. . . . Another thinks we must be made to emigrate. . . . " To all of these, the writer said: "Now, dearly beloved friends, we can solve your problem. A few words will suffice. *Do justly by the Negro, and then let him severely alone.* . . . We are not exceptional beings, we are human. In these dark bodies run the same red running blood. . . . "

The *Missouri Democrat*, in spite of its name, was one of the Republican papers that rather consistently espoused the cause of the African-Americans. It advised the Southern states to accept the terms of Reconstruction and offer "all Constitutional guarantees," including suffrage, to the African-Americans. It warned that "resistance is useless" and that "the attempt to tire out the North will prove suicidal." The suffrage amendment was adopted over the objections of the Southern states. For a time African-Americans and Republicans wielded modest amounts of power and won a few elections in the South. But the Democrat was to be proved wrong. It was not long before the Conservatives and the Conservative editors of the South carried the day and returned to power. During this time several editors were accused of being local and even state leaders of the Ku Klux Klan (which of course they denied).

Dana, Godkin, Watterson

American newspapers were approaching the threshold of corporate journalism, the fourth phase in the development of the editorial page. But, even as most editors were lapsing into corporate anonymity, a few recognizable voices spoke out. Among them were Charles A. Dana of the *New York Sun*, E.L. Godkin of the *Nation* and later of the *New York Evening Post*, Henry Watterson of the *Louisville Courier-Journal* and Henry W. Grady of the *Atlanta Constitution*.

Dana quit the *Tribune* in 1862 after disagreement over Greeley's criticism of the conduct of the Civil War. He felt so strongly about Lincoln's policies that he joined the administration as assistant secretary of war. After the deaths of Raymond and Greeley, Watterson wrote that Dana, then on the *Sun*, was "left alone to tell the tale of old-time journalism in New York." Dana, he said, was as "blithe and nimble" as the young editors in the country, and was "no less a writer and scholar than an editor."

During the early days of his editorship, Dana took editorial swings at the corruption of the Tweed regime in New York and waged campaigns for reforms in government. But as the years went by the *Sun* became more cynical toward reform. Turning a good phrase and enticing readership through humorous, clever writing assumed greater importance. Edward P. Mitchell, later editor of the *Sun* himself, recalled that, before he joined Dana's staff as an editorial writer, he had been told, "Dana's a good teacher for condensation and for saying what you want to say, but as to what he generally wants to say!–"

Dana's sarcasm could be so strong that readers would take him at his literal word. When a public campaign to raise money to erect a statue of Tweed seemed to lag, Dana wrote:

Has Boss Tweed any friends? If so, they are a mean set; it is now more than a year since an appeal was made to them to come forward and put up the ancillary qualities to erect a statue to Mr. Tweed in the centre of Tweed Plaza; but as yet only four citizens have sent in their subscriptions. . . . [T]he hundreds or rather thousands of small-potato politicians whom he has made rich and powerful stand aloof, and do not offer a picayune. . . . [W]e have not decided whether it shall represent the favorite son of New York afoot or a-horseback. In fact, we rather incline to have a nautical statue, exhibiting Boss Tweed as a bold mariner, amid the foretop-gallant buttock shrouds of his steam yacht. But that is a matter for future consideration. The first thing is to get the money; and if those who claim to be Mr. Tweed's friends don't raise it we shall begin the rumor that the Honorable P. Brains Sweeney has turned against him, and has forbidden everyone to give anything toward the erection of the projected statue.

The yacht mentioned in the editorial was one of the luxurious perquisites enjoyed by Tweed but no doubt financed by the public purse. P. Brains Sweeney was Tweed's lieutenant of a slightly different name, Peter B. Sweeney.

Edwin Lawrence (E.L.) Godkin came to the United States to cover the Civil War for English papers. He stayed after the war to found the *Nation* magazine, devoted to discussing political and economic issues. One of his interests was in a more equal distribution of the economic and social benefits of prosperity. Philosopher William James described Godkin as "the towering influence in all thought concerning public affairs" during the 1880s and 1890s. James said Godkin influenced many writers who never bothered to quote him and "determined the whole current of discussion" during that era.

Godkin's style was complex and carefully written, but, when he so desired, lively, humorous and ironic. Concerning the appointment of Elihu B. Washburne as President Grant's secretary of state, Godkin cited the "general, and apparently well-founded belief" that Washburne's "installation in the State Department would be the commencement of his intimate acquaintance with the precedents and principles of international law."

In describing an anarchists' picnic at which there was a riot, Godkin wrote: "The meeting was a great success in the way of promoting practical anarchy, the rioting being protracted to a late hour in the afternoon. Anarchy, like charity, should always begin at home."

Godkin's successor, Edward P. Mitchell, credited Godkin with being the first editor in New York to hold daily conferences with his editorial writers. Mitchell recounted that every writer was encouraged to propose his own topic and to comment freely on topics proposed by other writers. But Godkin had no mercy on unsound and commonplace ideas. "If the junior editor had nothing worth while to say, Godkin would cut across his flounderings with 'O, there's nothing in that,' or 'We said that the other day,' or 'O everybody sees that.'" But, when a writer came up with a new idea, "Mr. Godkin's eye would kindle with interest, he would lean forward alertly, and catching up the theme, he would perhaps begin to enlarge it by ideas of his own, search its depths with penetrating inquiries, and reveal such possibilities in it that the original speaker had the feeling of having stumbled over a concealed diamond." Sometimes, Mitchell recalled, Godkin became so enthusiastic about the idea that he would decide to write on the subject himself.[14]

One of the strong, and extravagant, voices after the Civil War was that of Colonel Henry Watterson of the *Courier-Journal.* Watterson had edited a Southern paper during the Civil War but thought that secession was wrong.

For half a century (from 1868 to 1918) he preached conciliation between North and South—and both sides listened to him, at least to the extent that either listened.

In 1868, when Kentucky was being criticized for having elected anti-Reconstruction Democrats to office, Watterson reminded the North that Kentucky had not seceded during the war: "Kentucky's head was with the Union and her heart was with the South; for it is in the nature of a generous and manly people to sympathize with the weak in its struggle with the strong." Watterson said that the laws were better enforced and there was less crime in Kentucky than in Indiana and Ohio. He concluded:

We are perfectly honest, and think we have a right, as free citizens of a free republic, to decide for ourselves. For so doing and so thinking we are denounced as traitors to our country and a despotism is sought to be placed over us by those who claim that we ought to be forced to vote for Republican candidates and Republican measures, and who declare that if we do not, we are guilty of rebellion and should be punished therefor.

While flamboyant in style, Watterson usually based his editorials on a thorough knowledge of what he was talking about. Most of his editorials were not brief, but one of his most famous was a one-paragraph piece, titled "To Hell with the Hohenzollerns and the Hapsburgs," urging the United States to enter World War I:

Herman Ridder [a German editor] flings Japan at us. Then he adduces Russia. What does he think of Turkey? How can he reconcile the Kaiser's ostentatious appeal to the Children of Christ and his pretentious partnership with God—"meinself und Gott"—with his calling the hordes of Mahomet to his aid? Will not this unite all Christendom against the unholy combine? May Heaven protect the Vaterland from contamination and give the German people a chance! To Hell with Hohenzollerns and the Hapsburgs!

Watterson and Henry W. Grady of the *Atlanta Constitution* have been credited with urging their readers to forget old grievances arising out of the Civil War and to work toward a New South that was more concerned with prosperity than issues.

Promotion and Prosperity

For all his concern for national and international issues, Watterson worked at promoting Louisville, Kentucky and the South, a theme that ran through newspaper editorial pages through the last third of the 19th century and the early part of the 20th century. Editors promoted transcontinental railroads, local and regional railroads, canals, ports, agriculture, paved streets, municipal water, electrical and sewer systems, and schools of higher education. In the eyes of the local editor, his community was the one most deserving of success and prosperity.

Henry W. Grady of the *Atlanta Constitution* may been the pre-eminent promoter. He preached a New South ("sunshine everywhere and all the time") up and down the Atlantic Coast (mostly promoting Atlanta). A promotional trip to Boston, when he was ill, resulted in an early death at age 49, at the height of his prominence.[15]

Community promotion was not limited to the cities. Hal Borland recalled in *Country Editor's Boy* that his father used the *Flager* (Colo.) *News* to editorialize for water, electricity and paved streets.[16] A recent biography of William Allen White of the *Emporia* (Kan.) *Gazette*, generally regarded the ideal small-town editor, reveals that White worked some deals to promote his community that today might be considered conflicts of interest.[17]

Pulitzer and Hearst

For every trend, there is an exception. While most newspapers were headed toward corporate journalism, Joseph Pulitzer and William Randolph Hearst exploded onto the journalistic scene. With the purchase of the *New York World* in 1883, Joseph Pulitzer brought to the East Coast the sensational, aggressive style of news reporting that he had developed with the *St. Louis Post-Dispatch*– and a strong commitment to the editorial page.

In St. Louis, Pulitzer had campaigned editorially for the middle class at the expense of the wealthy. In New York, he took on the cause of the more numerous poor, including workers and the millions of new immigrants. The irresponsible rich, he said, had "the odor of codfish and not the mustiness of age." The *World*'s editorial opinion was that "such an aristocracy ought to have no place in the republic." Pulitzer printed the following list of governmental goals for social justice that the *World* would pursue:

1. Tax Luxuries.
2. Tax Inheritance.
3. Tax Large Incomes.
4. Tax Monopolies.
5. Tax the Privileged Corporations.
6. A Tariff for Revenue.
7. Reform the Civil Service.
8. Punish Corrupt Officers.
9. Punish Vote Buying.
10. Punish Employers who Coerce their Employees in Elections.

At the end of the list, Pulitzer tacked this notice: "This is a popular platform of 10 lines. We recommend it to the politicians in place of long-winded resolutions."

The *World* generally supported Democrats, but it reluctantly backed William McKinley for president in 1896 because Pulitzer thought that the Democratic candidate, William Jennings Bryan, was ignorant on important issues and that the mining and coining of more silver (the "free silver" issue) would not solve the problems of economic depression. But, even though he praised McKinley's election, Pulitzer took the occasion to say that some of the problems that Bryan and the Populists had been talking about were real:

There is no doubt that in this Republic, based as it is upon simplicity and ideas of equality before the law, there are growing inequalities of privilege and increasingly offensive encroachments and vulgarities of the rich.

The trust combinations are fostered by tariffs that protect them from foreign competition. They grow every year more arrogant, more despotic, and more oppressive in their exactions. Yet the laws against them are not only not enforced, but no honest effort is made to enforce them. . . .

In the same way the people have seen bargains made in secret between the Treasury authorities and a Wall Street syndicate for the sale of millions of bonds for 15 cents on the dollar less than their open market value. . . .

They have seen State legislatures of both parties dominated by corporations so that no measure of relief from wrong doing by corporations could become law. . . .

In brief, money is too largely usurping power and influence of manhood.

The New York press was further enlivened when Hearst ventured off his home base in San Francisco in 1895 to out-sensationalize Pulitzer with his newly acquired *New York Journal.* Hearst too undertook the cause of the have-nots, but his editorial approach was a more simplistic, emotional, entertaining appeal to readers. On the first birthday of the new *Journal,* Hearst editorialized:

What is the explanation of the *Journal*'s amazing and wholly unmatched progress? . . . When the paper was purchased by its present proprietor, a year ago today, the work contemplated was at once begun. . . . The *Journal* realized what is frequently forgotten in journalism, that if news is wanted it often has to be sent for. . . .

No other journal in the United States includes in its staff a tenth of the number of writers of reputation and talent. It is the *Journal*'s policy to engage brains as well as to get the news, for the public is even more fond of entertainment than it is of information. . . .

To entice readers, some of whom were not very literate, Hearst used large type for editorials, used large headlines to call attention to the editorials, spread editorials over several columns and sometimes published them on page one. Editorial cartoons added further interest to the page.

Arthur Brisbane, one of the many editors and reporters hired away from Pulitzer, became a master at expressing Hearst's views and promoting his causes in clear, direct language that no reader could misunderstand. The *Journal* addressed such topics as "The Existence of God," "What Will 999 Years Mean to the Human Race?" "Crime Is Dying Out," "Have the Animals Souls?" and "Woman Sustains, Guides and Controls the World." Brisbane editorials often had a simple moralistic tone. An example is "Those Who Laugh at a Drunken Man," written during the prohibition movement following World War I:

How often have you seen a drunken man stagger along the street!

His clothes are soiled from falling. His face is bruised. His eyes are dull. Sometimes he curses the boys that tease him. Sometimes he tries to smile in a drunken effort to placate pitiless, childish cruelty.

His body, worn out, can stand no more, and he mumbles that he is going home.

The children persecute him, throw things at him, laugh at him, running ahead of him.

Grown men and women, too, often laugh with the children, nudge each other, and actually find humor in the sight of a human being sunk below the lowest animal.

The sight of a drunken man going home should make every man sad and sympathetic. . . .

That reeling drunkard is going home.

He is going home to children who are afraid of him, to a wife whose life he has made miserable.

He is going home, taking with him the worst curse in the world—to suffer bitter remorse himself after having inflicted suffering on those whom he should protect . . . .

. . . we cannot call ourselves civilized while our imaginations and sympathies are so dull that the reeling drunkard is thought an amusing spectacle.

The trouble with Spain over Cuba in the late 1890s was ready-made for Hearst in his efforts to overtake Pulitzer. Hearst had a new underdog to champion—the Cuban rebels. Sensationalizing news and editorial comment about Spain and Cuba sold papers, and Hearst's circulation soon caught up with Pulitzer's. Pulitzer responded in kind. The battle between the two to see who could find, or invent, the most grisly revelations about Spanish atrocities helped create the political climate in which President McKinley finally concluded he had little choice but to seek a declaration of war against Spain. Following the sinking of the *U.S.S. Maine* in the Havana harbor in 1898, the *Journal* pretended to withhold judgment concerning the cause of the explosion and to urge caution. But it concluded that, no matter how the investigation turned out, there was no reason not to proceed with freeing Cuba. The editorial stated:

To five hundred thousand Cubans starved or otherwise murdered have been added an American battleship and three hundred American sailors lost as the direct result of the dilatory policy of our government toward Spain. If we had stopped the war in Cuba [between Spain and the rebels] when duty and policy alike urged us to do so the Maine would have been afloat today, and three hundred homes, now desolate, would have been unscathed.

It was no accident, they say. Perhaps it was, but accident or not, it would never have happened if there had been peace in Cuba, as there would have been had we done our duty. . . . The investigation into the injuries of the Maine may take a week, but the independence of Cuba can be recognized today. . . . The American fleet can move on Havana today and plant the flag of the Cuban Republic on Morro and Cabanas. It is still strong enough for that in the absence of further "accidents." And if we take such action as that, it is extremely unlikely that any further accidents will appear.

Both Hearst and Pulitzer had political ambitions. Pulitzer satisfied his ambition with one term in Congress and some service in the Missouri legislature. But it look Hearst a long time to learn that he was not destined for high office. Narrow defeats in races for mayor of New York City and governor of the state did nothing to lessen his efforts to become president. Hearst was a serious contender for the Democratic nomination in 1904, but he deluded himself into thinking he was a possible nominee in the three subsequent presidential elections. Few took him seriously as a candidate in those years.

Hearst's editorial urgings toward war, in the case of the Spanish-American War, were not renewed in the periods leading up to World War I and World War II. The Hearst papers took a pacifist and anti-British position in both news and editorials, in 1914 through 1917. Hearst dismissed critics who charged him with being pro-German. When the United States entered the war in April 1917, the Hearst papers scrambled to support the cause. In World War II, Hearst followed a similar pattern of expressing opposition to entering the war, then switching to a strong support, but in this instance a change of policy on the war did not indicate an end to Hearst's growing bitterness toward President Franklin D. Roosevelt. Part of his resentment resulted from a growing conservatism on social issues; part resulted because Roosevelt was not paying as much attention to Hearst as he had in the early days of his administration.

THE CORPORATE EDITORIAL PAGE

We have already noted the change in emphasis from opinion to news that followed the Civil War. The metamorphosis from prominent editors to anonymous editorial writers came gradually. Dana continued for some years to run the editorial page on the *Sun* as he wished, as did Godkin on the *Post*, Watterson on the *Courier-Journal* and Grady on the *Atlanta Constitution*. Most readers of Hearst's papers knew that Arthur Brisbane wrote the editorials that they read, and many knew that Irvin S. Cobb, Pulitzer's handpicked editorial writer and eventual successor, wrote the editorials on the *World* until Cobb's death in 1923. But few names are remembered today from other papers in the last decades of the 19th century and the first decades of the 20th century.

The *New York Times* epitomized the trend toward editorial anonymity of American newspapers. The *Times* had one brief moment of glory following the Civil War before lapsing into journalistic grayness. One of the underlings of W.M. Tweed, boss of New York's Tammany Hall, had been going from newspaper to newspaper trying to interest editors in publishing records that showed the corruption that existed in city government. Finally, after several editors refused, the *Times*, under the late Henry L. Raymond's partner, George Jones, published the revelations. It listed column after column of fraudulent bills, totaling millions of dollars, that had been paid to Tweed's friends and supporters. The stolen money, the *Times* said editorially, went "to meet the expense of the Ring in the matter of fast horses, conservatories, handsome horses and newspaper editors." After news stories had reported that $360,751.61 had been paid to an obscure carpenter named C.S. Miller for one month's work and $2,870,464.06 had gone to plastering work done by Andrew J. Garvey, a *Times* editorial said: "As C.S. Miller is the luckiest of carpenters, so Andrew J. Garvey is clearly the Prince of Plasterers. His good fortune surpasses anything in the Arabian Nights." (Thomas Nast, with his famous cartoons in *Harper's Weekly*, also helped rouse the public to oust Boss Tweed and send him to jail.)

That was about the last that was heard from the *Times*. "The mistake of the *Times* was in lapsing into the dulness (sic) of respectable conservatism after its Ring fight," Dana wrote in the *Sun* in 1875. "It should have kept on and made a crusade against fraud of all sorts." By the mid-1890s, the *Times* had fallen onto hard financial times. A new owner, Adolph S. Ochs, took over the paper in 1896. Primarily interested in presenting a good news product, Ochs was satisfied with a bland, anonymous editorial page. In recounting the history of the *Times*, Harrison E. Salisbury noted that "there were those who felt he would have been happier had there been no editorial page."[18] The page was plain and dignified: small headlines, regular type sizes, one-column measure, no political cartoons. One of the few *Times* editorial themes in the early 20th century was a defense of industrial entrepreneurs against the encroachment of legislation and the attacks of critics.

Newspapers in general during this period were closely allied with the growing business and industrial community. The papers themselves began to grow more prosperous and to become capitalistic enterprises. They became more dependent on advertising for revenue and on increasing circulation to justify higher advertising rates. The business side of journalism overshadowed the editorial side.

The Social Reformers

By the beginning of the 20th century most of the literary effort directed toward social reform was confined to magazines and books. One reason these publications took on the role that might have been performed by newspaper editorial writers and investigative reporters was that they were able to reach a nation-wide audience for recruiting readers and building a mass circulation. At the local level, readers interested in hearing about the evils of society were a minority in the years before World War I, when the prevalent attitude in America and Western Europe was that the world was making social and economic progress.

The most prominent platforms for the social reform writers, dubbed "muckrakers" by President Theodore Roosevelt, were *McClure's*, Hearst's *Cosmopolitan*, *Collier's* and Edward W. Bok's *Ladies' Home Journal*. The articles that appeared in these magazines, by such writers as Lincoln Steffens, Ida M. Tarbell and Ray Stannard Baker, were part investigative reporting and part editorializing.

One of Steffens's best known efforts was a series of six articles in *McClure's* on corruption in American cities. His findings later appeared in modified form in a book, *The Shame of the Cities*. One of the assumptions of the reformers of an earlier day, including E.L. Godkin on the *New York Evening Post*, was that municipal corruption arose out of the conditions of the poor, the illiterate and the immigrant classes, who in their ignorance were easily manipulated by the bosses. Steffens tried to show that corruption came from the top of the economic and social order, from the business community and the educated: "Don't try to reform politics with the banker, lawyer, and drygood merchant, for these are business men," he wrote in a letter to his father.[19]

Upton Sinclair, another muckraker, wrote in *The Brass Check*, an expose of American journalism, that "American corruption was the buying up of legislatures and assemblies to keep them from doing the people's will and protecting the people's interests."[20] Sinclair set out to show how the press, even the so-called reform press, had sold out to business. He contended that Charles Dana, on the *New York Sun*, while once "something of a radical," had "turned like a fierce wolf upon his young ideals" and now "had one fixed opinion, which was that everything new in the world should be mocked at and denounced."[21] Sinclair recognized Godkin as "a scholar and a lover of righteousness" but wrong in viewing corruption as stemming from the pandering of venal politicians to an ignorant mob. Concerning the typical municipal reformer supported by Godkin, Sinclair wrote: "The candidate was swept into office in a tornado of excitement, and did what all 'Evening Post' candidates did and always do—that is, nothing."[22]

A Few Noted Editors

Several 20th-century editors have stood out. Walter Lippmann, as much a political philosopher as editorial writer and columnist, earned a reputation as a wise analyst in writing, successively, for the *Nation* magazine, the *New York World* and the *New York Herald Tribune*. His column was widely syndicated. Lippmann did, however, have his detractors. He himself acknowledged that he had made a mistake in opposing the League of Nations following World War I. He had criticized it not because of too much internationalism but because of too little, claiming that President Woodrow Wilson had agreed to too many compromises. Later he changed his mind. Lippmann was also criticized for an ambivalent attitude toward the politically powerful. His seeking of their confidence and favor, in some critics' views, posed a conflict of interest. He earned back some of his critics' respect, when he broke, belatedly, with President Lyndon Johnson over the Vietnam War.

William Allen White became the most famous small-town newspaper editor during the first decades of the 20th century. He had written articles exposing social evils for a time for *McClure's,* but he earned his nationwide reputation initially with an editorial titled "What's the Matter With Kansas?" Written in a satirical tone, the editorial argued that the populists, who were complaining that the state was suffering from bankruptcy and an exodus of population, were wrong. White's editorials were widely quoted for their down-to-earth, yet idealistic, approach to national and regional issues. In Emporia, however, a recent biographer reminds us, White was the epitome of the small-town editor, promoting local economic growth and social harmony.[23]

In the days before World War II, White served as chairman of the Committee to Defend America by Aiding the Allies, one of whose purposes was to encourage newspapers to support the Allied cause. Hearst was one publisher who was not convinced by White's efforts. Others included what Henry Luce's *Time* magazine called "the Three Furies of Isolationism,"the three grandchildren of Joseph Medill: Robert McCormick, who had taken over Medill's *Chicago Tribune*; Joseph Medill Patterson, who had founded the *New York Daily News* in the 1920s, and Eleanor Medill "Sissy" Patterson, who became publisher of the *Washington Times-Herald* when the McCormick-Patterson interest purchased that newspaper. In an editorial in the *News,* Joseph Patterson contended that the United States had been pushed into World War I, and that "some of the same forces" were pushing the country into World War II. In two editorials titled "Family Portrait," he said that the Pattersons had descended from a Scotch-Irish ancestor "whose great ambition was to get as far away from England and English aristocratic ideas as they could possible get. . . . It is also natural for us, with our midwestern background, to think first of America in times like these, and to hate to see Americans kidded and cajoled into impossible crusades to remake the world. . . ."

In establishing the paper in New York, Patterson had set out to remake the world of journalism. A tabloid, the *New York Daily News,* championed the cause of the poor and the latest immigrants, and offered them sensational, easy-to-understand news and lots of pictures. But the editorial page, with its casual, simplified, often flippant style, seemed incidental. Soon the *News* had surpassed Hearst's papers in circulation.

At the *New York Post,* a simplification of style was also occurring. Godkin's scholarly editorials had given way to short comments on the news and headlines that summarized the editorials that followed them.

20th-Century Conservatism

During the first decades of the 20th century most of the press was extremely conservative in its politics. The *New York Sun,* which had had a liberal bent under Dana, warned against the perils of American entrance into the League of Nations supergovernment. Hearst expressed anger with France for not using "some of her German indemnity to pay her honest debts to America, especially because if it had not been for America she would now be paying indemnity instead of receiving it." Many newspapers joined in the "witch hunt" for "subversives" in the 1920s.

During the 1920s Americans were routinely electing Republicans as presidents, and most American newspapers were routinely endorsing them. New doubts about the power of the editorial page appeared in the 1930s when readers saw that the press was attacking and opposing the election and re-election of Franklin D. Roosevelt, a candidate whom the voting public continued to support. Editorials may have been the place readers previously had looked for interpretations of current events and general enlightenment. But with Roosevelt's New Deal and the Depression, the United States faced an economic and social, if not political, revolution. The country required greater quantities and kinds of information and insights. Most of the nation's anonymous editorial writers were unwilling or unable to provide what readers wanted. Many of their editorial pens were stuck with automatic reactions to proposals for change. One result was the sudden growth in popularity of bylined columnists, hired by newspapers and syndicated services to explain to readers what was going on, primarily in Washington, D.C. The columns, generally interpretive in nature, were usually published on the editorial page. They were more lively and informative than most of the unsigned editorials that represented the views of the corporate newspaper.

By the 1950s, most newspapers had shed the formal labels that tied them to one party or the other (usually the Republican), but they did continue by wide margins to endorse Republicans for president and, to a lesser degree, Republicans for lower-level offices. In 1952 President Harry Truman leveled the charge of "one-party press" at the newspapers in the race between Dwight D. Eisenhower and Adlai Stevenson. A subsequent study found that the editorial pages of the nation had backed Eisenhower by a margin of almost 5 to 1 but that partiality had been evident in the news columns in only 6 of 35 newspapers studied.[24]

In that same era only a few editorial voices were raised early against "McCarthyism," the emotional and largely unsubstantiated campaign against "communists" and "un-American activities" that took its name from Sen. Joseph McCarthy, a Republican from Wisconsin. Alan Barth of the *Washington Post* was one of those few voices, but the strongest voice was that of Edward R. Murrow. Murrow put together a documented television program on CBS that showed McCarthy for the demagogue that he was. The broadcast helped move public opinion toward eventual support of censure of McCarthy by his Senate colleagues.

One looks in vain for many examples of strong editorial leadership in the 1950s and 1960s. If the Eisenhower administration was content to let social issues lie dormant, so was most of the press. If editorial writers responded to John F. Kennedy's challenge of a "New Frontier" in the early 1960s, it may have been more because of their fascination with the personality and glamour of the new administration than because of concern for civil and social injustices. On the eve of his assassination in 1963, President Kennedy's programs were in deep political trouble, and he himself faced much antagonism among political leaders and voters. The assassination shocked editorial writers, as it did most Americans. One result was that voters and editors rallied around Lyndon Johnson, the new president, and in 1964 overwhelmingly elected him to the presidency. For the first time in the 20th century more newspapers supported a Democrat than a Republican for president. Still feeling the shock of the assassination, editorial writers generally supported a brief flurry of civil rights and social legislation during the Johnson administration.

The euphoria over the Johnson administration did not last long. (Not until 1992, in the Clinton-Bush race, did a plurality of daily newspapers again endorse a Democrat for president.) The high hopes of the "Great Society" proved overly optimistic, partly because funds that might have gone to fight poverty and racial inequality were sent to fight a war in Vietnam. Editorial writers in general, like administration officials, failed to realize that the country was not willing or able to wage full-scale battles on both foreign and domestic fronts, or, in the phrase of the day, to supply both "guns and butter." Only a few editors recognized that the country was unwilling or unable to accomplish what it set out to do in Vietnam. Among the early skeptics over the war were Robert Lasch of the *St. Louis Post-Dispatch* and Lauren Soth of the *Des Moines* (Iowa) *Register and Tribune.* A later skeptic was the *Washington Post,* which continued its support of the war until Russell Wiggins was replaced as editorial page editor by Philip Geyelin.

Editorial endorsements returned to supporting Republicans in the 1968 election when Richard Nixon barely defeated Hubert Humphrey for president. Even though much of the press and the public had grown weary of the Vietnam War and become convinced by that time that it could not be won, the war dragged on, at a somewhat reduced level, for Nixon's entire first term. The press eagerly endorsed Nixon for a second term in 1972, even though many of the revelations later to be known as "Watergate" had been published during the campaign. The documented details of Watergate eventually emerged, and Nixon resigned from the presidency—nearly two years after the break-in at the Watergate complex. A few newspapers, notably the *Washington Post,* deserved credit for the early revelations and for keeping public attention centered on the affair. But the Watergate story was essentially a news story, not an editorial page accomplishment.

Since Watergate, neither editorial pages in particular nor newspapers in general have taken the lead in crusading in national or international matters. Journalists in general were quiescent during the two Reagan terms. In the 1980s the press played no significant role in smoking out the "Irangate" affair, in which Iran bought U.S. military arms with cash that then was sent to support "contra" forces in Nicaragua. In the 1990s editorial writers generally applauded military action in the Iraq war and seemed as overwhelmed and confused by the saving and loan crisis as the rest of the country.

THE NON-IDEOLOGICAL PRESS

During the Bush and Clinton administrations newspapers were as mercurial as the voters. After high popularity (including among the press) during the Iraq war, President Bush's stock suddenly plummeted (for who knows what reason, maybe the economy) to the point that Bill Clinton could win in 1992. Less than a year before the 1996 election, it appeared that almost anyone could beat Clinton. The press certainly was down on him. But by election time (partly because of what the voters saw as excesses by the new Republican congressional majority and partly because of a healthy economy), Clinton became a shoo-in. The press generally supported him, in spite of a pending legal suit charging him with sexual improprieties and suspicions of an improper role in Whitewater investments while he was governor of Arkansas. No sooner was he re-elected than he was embroiled in accounts of how he and the Democratic Party had been raising money during the fall campaign, offering the Lincoln Bedroom in the White House to celebrities and big donors and accepting big bucks from people from a "China connection."

Historical summary

In the nearly three centuries in which editors on the North American continent have been commenting on public issues, opinion has taken different roles. For the first century or so, editorial comment was sparse and generally intermixed with (often highly personalized) accounts of news. Then, as tension mounted between the Colonies and Great Britain, editors began to feel called to a cause. As the Revolutionary War approached, journals tended increasingly to be filled with opinion.

In the first decades following the ratification of the Constitution in 1787, any newspaper, including its editorial page, served as a mouthpiece for political parties. The function of editorials, which began appearing during this era on a designated page, was to argue the party line as forcefully as possible for the party faithful. The stronger and more emotional the tone of the editorial, the more likely it was to please the reader.

Beginning in the 1830s, the new populist press began appealing to a much broader and less political group of readers. At first these penny papers offered mostly crime, sex and gossip. Unsophisticated readers were not interested in editorial comment. But as readers became more literate and editors more concerned about issues, the populist press became more serious. In the two decades before the Civil War the major issues facing the nation got a thorough, if highly emotional and personalized, airing in the editorial columns. Editors did not hesitate to put into print their concerns about the conduct of the Civil War.

The Civil War brought new interest in news, and the day of the great personalized editorialist began to wane. A few voices still spoke out; writers such as Charles Dana, E.L. Godkin, William Randolph Hearst and Joseph Pulitzer raised a ruckus in the late 19th and early 20th centuries. But the trend was clear. Editorial writers were retreating into anonymity on conservative newspapers owned by corporations. One looks in vain for more than a few examples of strong, enlightened editorial leadership on national and international issues during the period dominated by the corporate press.

Only in a few instances have readers had reason to look to editorial pages for insightful examinations of the national and international issues of the day—and to expect to find anything except predictable responses to issues. The picture is brighter at local, regional and state levels. Here at least some editorial writers are speaking out with knowledge and conviction. In the next chapter we will look at what several of these writers and their newspapers have been doing and at what editorial writing could, and should, be in the future.

Questions and Exercises

1. Why did writers for the Colonial press see little reason to make a distinction between news and opinion in the accounts that they wrote?

2. What brought about the decline and eventual demise of the partisan press of the first years of the Republic under the Constitution?

3. Why were Benjamin Day and James Gordon Bennett not interested in editorial comment during the early days of the populist press?

4. What accounts for Horace Greeley becoming the most famous editor of the mid-19th century? Do you think the esteem in which he was held was fully merited?

5. From examples in the chapter (plus other samples if available) contrast the writing styles of Horace Greeley and William Cullen Bryant. What does the difference suggest concerning readers of their papers?

6. Why has Charles Dana remained better known than E.L. Godkin?

7. Based on material in this chapter and information from other sources, does it seem reasonable to hold the *New York Journal* and the *New York World* primarily responsible for the political atmosphere that allowed the Spanish-American War to occur?

8. Why did most of the writing exposing social problems in the early 20th century appear in magazines rather than in the daily press?

9. What factors contributed to the trend toward anonymity of editors in the corporate newspaper era?

10. Why have recent decades produced no modern-day Horace Greeleys, Henry J. Raymonds, William Randolph Hearsts, Joseph Pulitzers or William Allen Whites?

CHAPTER 2 The Editorial Page That Should, and Could, Be

Nothing but a newspaper can drop the same thought into a thousand minds at the same moment. A newspaper is an adviser that does not require to be sought, but that comes of its own accord and talks to you briefly every day of the common weal, without distracting you from your private affairs.

—ALEXIS DE TOCQUEVILLE[1]

The first step toward understanding the role that the American editorial page can play today is to understand the nature of the readership of the page. In general, readers today are better educated than readers of the past. They are probably also more sophisticated, although many may not be as interested in public issues as were the faithful followers of editorials in the more partisan papers of the past. Most of today's readers do not read editorials as consistently as readers did when they could subscribe to, and relish reading, a newspaper with which they agreed politically. In most communities today's readers have little or no choice of a daily paper; they take the one that is available or none at all. In fact, a growing percentage of families today does not subscribe to a daily paper. Those who do subscribe represent not the narrow range of the faithful, as in the past, but a diverse political, philosophic, economic and social range. Unlike newspaper readers of the past, most of today's subscribers are exposed to many other sources of information and opinion from media–television, radio, cable, Internet, magazines, satellite, fax–and from social, civic, labor and business organizations.

All of these related characteristics of the modern editorial page audience suggest major implications for editorial page editors and writers who want to do the most effective jobs of informing and persuading their readers. The purpose of this chapter is to examine those implications and to see how editors deal with them in an age of a more diversified, more disinterested audience. My major point will be that there is still room for strong editorial leadership–for editorial crusades–but the best chances for editorial writers to achieve credibility and to be persuasive lie in being informed, reasonable, articulate and sensitive to the feelings and opinions of others.

A FEW BUGLE CALLS

"Today's editorial trumpet, when it sounds at all, too often sounds not so much like a trumpet as like a kazoo." That's the judgment of Robert Reid, former editorial writer, now associate professor at the University of Illinois. He sees a need especially for editorials "of an outrageous or even irresponsible" type. "We need loud, clamorous, jarring, persistent voices in our newspapers, hitting people hard enough in their prejudices to make them think and act in the public arena rather than in effect encouraging readers to slouch around feeling as if what they think doesn't matter or won't do any good," Reid wrote in an article titled "More Hell-Raising Editorials."[2]

Over a period of more than a year, the *Lexington* (Ky.) *Herald-Leader* raised hell in a series of editorials titled "To Have and to Harm: Kentucky's Failure to Protect Women from the Men Who Beat Them." In several of the editorials, writer Maria Henson told in graphically horrifying terms what had happened to victims of beatings. A first editorial labeled "A Death Foretold" began in this manner:

Betty Jean Ashby's life was in danger. She knew it. Her family knew it. Her neighbors in Louisville's Shepherd Square knew it.

Louisville police knew it.

The Jefferson County Courts knew it, too.

Had the threat come from a mugger, rapist, or holdup man, the authorities might have seen their duty more clearly. But this was what the law calls a "domestic" case. The man who was stalking Betty Ashby was Carl Branch, her common-law husband and the father of her four children. . . .

In fear, Betty Ashby turned to the law. She went through all the steps. She appeared in court, signed sworn statements, told her story to police. But nothing, it seemed, could keep Carl away. . . .

The neighbor . . . could only hug her 4-year-old daughter and cry "Lord Jesus! Lord Jesus!" as Carl hit Betty in the head again and again until she sank to the floor, dead at 22.[3]

Another editorial began: "Lynn Milam has five metal plates in her head to remind her of the night her former boyfriend nearly beat her to death." Some of the editorials commented on what courts, law enforcement agencies and social agencies could or should be doing. Editors of the *Herald-Leader* reported that the editorials "have led to dramatic improvements in Kentucky's efforts to shield women from violent men." The editorial series also earned Henson and the newspaper the 1992 Pulitzer Prize and the Sigma Delta Chi Award in Journalism.

In 1972 Congress passed a law establishing the Golden Gate National Recreation Area. A provision stated that the military post known as the Presidio, established by the Spanish in 1776, would be transferred to the National Park Service if the U.S. Army moved out. In 1988 Congress passed a law authorizing the closing of the Presidio. The National Park Service began devising plans to use the park as a "working laboratory to create models of environmental sustainability that can be transferred to communities world-wide." In 1993, however, legislation was introduced in Congress creating a "public benefits corporation" that would bring "cost-effective management" to make the park self-sustaining. In 1994 the *Bay Guardian* reported that powerful business interests were quietly moving to take control of the Presidio and to

The Presidio Precedent

Well, there they were, the big shots from Washington—Reps. Nancy Pelosi (D-S.F.) and George Miller (D-Martinez), Interior Secretary Bruce Babbitt, and National Park Service director Roger Kennedy—all in San Francisco last week, confirming the bad news we've been reporting for five months now. The Democratic troops were saying that money is tight back in Congress, and that Reaganomics had to be imposed on the national park system.

The message is alarming: For the first time in history, we're supposed to let our national parks be controlled by private, for-profit uses, demolishing a century-old taxpayer tradition of publicly funding these public treasures as a resource and a legacy for future generations.

Pelosi, Miller, Babbitt, and Kennedy have each announced that the quasi-government corporation being proposed by Pelosi for the conversion of the 218-year-old Presidio military post would be duplicated in other urban park settings. Thus, the privatization of the park system could start here in San Francisco, where environmental fights stopped the building of a nuclear power plant at Bodega Bay, stopped freeways going through Golden Gate Park, and stopped the downtown high-rise boom.

How can such a monstrous precedent even be considered in San Francisco in 1994? Pelosi's plan for the Presidio treats San Francisco's environmental past and future with contempt. If the same sort of proposal were being carried by the previous Reagan/Bush administrations, environmentalists here and in Washington would be up in arms. Instead, most of them are going along for the ride.

Supporters of the Pelosi plan insist that the Park Service will remain in control of the Presidio and that the corporation will operate openly. But already Pelosi has acknowledged that leasing deals will probably be done behind closed doors. Furthermore, "openness" at the Presidio has been illustrated by a secret deal between the Park Service and Pacific Gas and Electric Co., which planned to take over the Presidio's multimillion-dollar electrical system. Pelosi is unwilling to speak to the public in an open forum, where the merits of her plan can be debated by the growing number of people opposed to allowing Reaganomics into the Presidio. She won't even come to the phone or respond to five months' worth of *Bay Guardian* phoned and faxed inquiries.

Now the Park Service wants to set up corporate management structures at other national parks without at least waiting to see what havoc will be caused by the one at the Presidio, in violation of every norm of common sense and public policy.

The Park Service's Kennedy even had the gall to stand before the Commonwealth Club of California and declare that the age of entitlements was over, when the public well knows that entitlements are alive and well for the rich, for oil companies, for private utilities, and for other private companies with fleets of Washington lobbyists. The Clintons, the Gores, our Bay Area representatives Tom Lantos and George Miller, Sens. Barbara Boxer and Dianne Feinstein, our Sacramento delegation, and the S.F. supervisors are all going along with the Pelosi plan without a whimper, ready to hand over the Presidio and possibly other national parks to private control. We didn't see that in their campaign literature.

This is an impending national scandal of historic proportions. It is once again the story of the West as a plundered province, of whether public or private interests control public resources. This was the key issue in some of the historic battles in conservation history—battles like Hetch Hetchy, Teapot Dome, and Dinosaur National Park. Now the latest battleground is the Presidio and the issue is whether Clinton and local Democrats are going to continue to fight the wrong war in the wrong place at the wrong time and help kill our national park system, with the quiet consent of environmentalists. On guard!

Bay Guardian

---

market it as a commercial shopping mall.[4] Among a series of editorials condemning the Presidio legislation was one titled "The Presidio precedent." What more appropriate example of a bugle call! The editorial even ends with: "On Guard!"

Unfortunately, from the *Bay Guardian*'s point of view, the legislation that eventually emerged was a sellout to commercial interests. Two years later, an editorial titled "Who lost the Presidio?" accused local politicians, local members of Congress and environmental organizations with compromising without a fight.[5] Bugle-call editorials, after all, don't always lead successful charges.

Between 1955 and 1965 six Southern newspaper editorial writers won Pulitzer Prizes for daring to speak out about civil rights. One of these was Buford Boone, publisher of the *Tuscaloosa* (Ala.) *News*. When the board of trustees refused to allow Autherine Lucy to be admitted to the University of Alabama in 1956, Boone, in a front-page editorial, criticized the board for having "knuckled under to the pressures and desires of a mob" and for making "an abject surrender to what is expedient rather than what is right." He concluded: "Yes, there's peace on the University campus this morning. But what a price has been paid for it!"[6]

Hazel Brannon Smith, editor-owner of the *Lexington* (Miss.) *Advertiser*, knew speaking out on civil rights was risky. She had written: "There was a time, almost a decade ago, when we Mississippians were free . . . we did have the habit of liberty. Newspaper editors were free to write editorially about anything in the world, giving our honest opinions, and there was no fear of economic reprisals or boycott. Today a newspaper editor thinks a long time before he writes anything that might be construed as controversial." That fear did not keep her from speaking out, among other occasions, about the bombing of the home of an African-American man who had tried to register to vote. "This kind of situation would never have come about in Holmes County if we had honestly discharged our duties and obligations as citizens in the past; if we had demanded that all citizens be accorded equal treatment and protection under the law. This we have not done."[7] She received the Pulitzer Prize in 1964.

Some publishers allowed their newspapers to take a stand on the controversial issues surrounding the Vietnam War and Watergate. A number of editors risked public (and their publishers') wrath by speaking out against the Vietnam War in the middle and late 1960s. One of these editors was Robert Lasch of the *St. Louis Post-Dispatch*. The paper I was working for at the beginning of the war, the *Des Moines* (Iowa) *Register and Tribune*, also spoke out early. The *New York Times* and the *Washington Post*, in spite the federal government's opposition, fought to print the Pentagon Papers, which revealed how the United States had been drawn into the Vietnam War. The *Chicago Tribune*, traditionally a very conservative paper, created a stir when it became one of the first major newspapers to call for the resignation of President Nixon during the Watergate affair.

In most instances in which a newspaper achieves an editorial goal, it is difficult, if not impossible, to determine precisely to what extent an editorial campaign contributed to the outcome. This was true for the hardest fought campaign waged by the *Columbian* of Vancouver, Wash., while I was on the paper. The Port of Portland, a local government agency, wanted to expand the runways and parking areas of the Portland International Airport by dumping a square mile of fill into the Columbia River. The river separates Portland from Vancouver as well as Oregon from Washington. The Portland newspapers and, at the beginning, the major public figures in Portland firmly supported the expansion. In Washington some citizens were concerned that altering the course of the river would have detrimental effects, especially on the Washington bank. But others feared that, if the airport were not expanded at that location, convenient to Vancouver, the port would relocate it on the other side of Portland.

Two people whose homes sat on the Washington bank came to the newspaper with research they had done on the hydrological and legal aspects of changing the channel. They were trying to raise money to retain a prominent environmentalist as an attorney to press a court suit. They convinced me that they had a worthy cause. We supported them and questioned the wisdom of expanding into the river. During the next two to three years opponents of the expansion won not a single court decision. Fortunately for them, the port had agreed to wait until the last legal hurdle had been cleared.

Our paper was able to make no discernible impact on opinion in Oregon, but in a succession of editorials over those years we made a strenuous effort to shore up support on our side of the river, while the opponents carried their battles through the courts and later to Congress. Delay proved the undoing of the project. A new projection of future usage of the airport scaled down the original estimates. The environmental movement began to gain strength about this time. Finally, a new mayor, Neil Goldschmidt, was elected in Portland. He began questioning the expansion. Soon the port abandoned its plan and came up with one that would fit on existing land. In this instance several factors came together to scuttle this project, but I am convinced that without the bugle-call editorials of the *Columbian*, calling on Washingtonians to stand their ground, the airport would have been built.

A number of picturesque images have been used to warn editorial writers against expecting too much from editorial campaigns. Bernard Kilgore, when he was publisher of the *Wall Street Journal*, said he thought it was all right for newspapers to regard themselves as thunderers and for editorial writers to picture themselves "with a bolt of lightning in each hand about to smash down on something." But he urged writers to be "very careful about demolishing a subject with one swoop, because good subjects for the editorial pages are very hard to come by."[8] He was warning editorial writers that most topics require analysis and comment over a period of time, not a single definitive pronouncement. Donald Tyerman, at the time editor of the *Economist* of London, reminded editorial writers at a meeting of the National Conference for Editorial Writers (NCEW) that they are neither Moses nor God. He warned against the Tablets of Stone theory—"that you can hand down the truth or, indeed, that you have it to hand down." Nor did he believe that editorial writers can effect a conversion such as occurred to Saul of Tarsus on the road to Damascus.[9]

At another NCEW meeting Philip Geyelin of the *Washington Post* recalled that James Cain, who served with Walter Lippmann on the *New York World* and wrote *The Postman Always Rings Twice*, had argued that a newspaper ought to fight for its beliefs as hard as it could. He turned to music for an illustration, noting that a piano has eight octaves, a violin three, a cornet two, but a bugle has only four notes. "Now if what you've got to blow is a bugle there isn't much sense in camping yourself down in front of piano music," Cain said. To which Lippmann replied, "You may be right, but goddamit, I'm not going to spend my life writing bugle calls."[10] A bugle call may be appreciated by readers once in a while, and it may mobilize them in a worthy cause, but readers can quickly tire of answering bugle calls. Editorial writers may not have an eight-octave persuasive tool at their disposal, but they ought to be able to play more complex tunes than Reveille and Charge!

A MORE COMPLEX MELODY

Readers look to the editorial page for more than bugle calls. One newspaper survey found that the highest percentage of regular readers followed the page either to feel they were participating in current events or to strengthen their arguments on issues. Others read the editorial page to help make decisions on issues, to use in discussion with friends, to determine what is important, to keep up with the latest events, to agree with editorial stands or to help form opinions. These results suggest that readers use the editorial page more to gain information than to seek guidance in forming opinions.[11]

I am not one to urge editors slavishly to fashion their journalistic products to reflect readership surveys. The decisions that editors face—whether to give readers what they want or what the editors think they should have—must still be made. A wise choice may be a compromise between the two, but if a choice must be made, editorial writers generally ought to come down on the side of facts and logic. The aim of the writer should be toward the mind, editorial writers were advised by Lenoir Chambers, who, while on the *Virginian-Pilot* of Norfolk, Va., was one of the six Southern Pulitzer Prize winners mentioned earlier. Editorial writers had better aim for the mind, he said, "for everybody is better educated now, and the editorial writer has a harder job to stay out in front." If writers don't know what they are talking about, readers soon spot them for phonies.[12]

Columnist James J. Kilpatrick, formerly of the *Richmond News Leader*, has warned editorial writers: "Unless an editorial can add something to what appears in the news columns—something besides mere opinion—it has no business in the paper." He urged writers to use historical background, comparisons of parallel situations, fresh facts from other publications and research sources, interpretive analysis and the setting straight of misinformation.[13]

It is easy to dash off an editorial that merely expresses opinion or rewrites the news. It is harder to write an editorial that adds something substantive to public dialogue on an issue. W.C. O'Donovan, editor and publisher of the *Virginia Gazette*, was recognized for doing exactly that when he was awarded the "Mims Award" in 1996 for outstanding editorial leadership displayed in a Virginia newspaper of under 40,000 circulation. O'Donovan told the judges that the *Gazette*'s goals for editorial leadership were:

- to explain issues simply but in context to the community
- to support ambitious policies and projects for the community
- to criticize shortcomings, but offer realistic solutions
- to stay ahead of the curve with fresh ideas on a variety of issues

Several of the editorials that he submitted dealt with problems in the public schools, notably involving discipline and rezoning between two high schools. O'Donovan said two editorials, run several months apart, "were instrumental in keeping teacher and parental pressure on the School Board to tighten discipline." "Discipline dissed" is an example of an editorial that not only states a position but also offers specific suggestions for carrying out a tougher disciplinary policy.

The second editorial, titled "Toughen up, now," got even more specific. Calling on the school board to "sharpen the edges" of the tools it had available "to punish and to heal," the editorial offered 20 suggestions for "things to do right now." Among them:

- "Implore" the police to cruise the streets around the school "to spot suspects such as those who invaded the campus twice last week."

- "Demand an explanation" why the principal had cut back on security guards.

- "Re-authorize teachers to exercise absolute control over their classrooms."

- "Condense the rules and regs to a wallet-size card and mail them to all parents. Require parents and teens to sign the cards and require the kids to have the cards on them at all times."[14]

These two editorials are examples of the results that can come from digging for information and applying imagination, by a less-than-full-time editorial writer (whose other hats are, in this case, editor and publisher).

A community at war with itself was the challenge that the *Southwest Virginia Enterprise* in Wytheville faced over a two-year period. The newspaper's efforts to bring the community back together after a fight over a proposed prison won it a first-place award for editorial writing from the Virginia Press Association in 1996.

A private company's proposal to build a prison in the community had turned longtime friends into enemies. Threats were made against county supervisors who favored the prison as a partial solution to the county's economic problems. Eighteen percent of the residents were living in poverty, according to federal standards. Between 25 and 30 percent of the county's adults were functionally illiterate. Unemployment rates were among the highest in the state, by several points. The employment that a prison would provide could bring money, jobs and new hope for revitalizing a depressed area.

An organization known as CAP (Citizens Against the Prison) mobilized opposition. Materials the newspaper submitted to the press association said "the group let nothing stand in its way in opposing the prison." Eventually the company decided to look elsewhere, but "a bitter taste remained in people's mouths." By that time, residents of the community "had forgotten how to disagree [civilly]."

The *Enterprise* saw its role as trying to heal the wounds, "reminding people of the problems" the community faced and "guiding them toward community-built solutions." The newspaper did not take a specific stand on the prison. An

EDITORIAL

Discipline Dissed
W.C. O'Donovan

Kicking unruly kids out of school is serious business, but so is school.

Just when you thought it was safe to go back to Lafayette High because the discipline code was shaped up, things are worse than ever.

Instead of a crisper, tighter code, Lafayette's is mushy. Superintendent Jim Kent has been quietly modifying suspensions, interpreting liberally instead of to the letter. Nothing radical, but tweaking here and there. He's intent on retaining in-school suspensions over out-of-school. That may sound like a narrow distinction, but the teachers insist it undermines the entire fabric of discipline.

Here's why. Last year the code came under scrutiny because the same Superintendent Kent cut a break for the son of a School Board member. That led to a probe of the entire document, which turned out to be full of ambiguities.

Despite adding clarity and brevity to the code, nothing else has apparently changed. Kent has absolute authority to overrule anyone and has shown a penchant for in-school suspensions. Although they carry the same weight, out-of-school is preferred by teachers to get the miscreants away from the campus.

Teacher Oliver Jones said it best in a protest letter to Kent: "Students need to understand that their actions have consequences, sometimes serious ones. A three-day suspension for a serious infraction does not send the message. Moreover, the majority of students are penalized when we bend over backward to keep disruptive students in class. Lowering the number of suspensions may seem desirable, but not if it means overlooking behavior problems."

Kent and the School Board have labored long to dismantle the alternative school where unruly kids used to be sent so they could start one of their own. That failed once before, but a smaller and more focused version in the old CDR house holds promise. Part of their motivation was to mainstream these kids, but another motive was that the private contractor was doing a poor job of rehabilitating them. Face it, some kids can't cut it in school.

Egregious behavior can get a student sent to the new regional Enterprise Academy, but teachers feel the need for a more hard-core approach, such as a juvenile school that stops short of juvenile jail. They correctly feel that a pecking order of severity needs to be clearly established.

Kent has the right idea of mainstreaming, but Jones teaches in the real world, where that's not working. His colleagues have ventilated in the *Last Word* with specific examples that make outsiders cringe. Kent said these teachers need more understanding.

He also said, "Maybe some teachers need more advice and support than others." Support for a strict code would be advice enough. Shipping a few kids over to the old CDR would get the word out.

The problem is not just the bad kids, but the cumulative effect. From another teacher: "Let me assure you that your student's education is suffering as a result of these policies. Isn't it time for our community to respond to this misguided attempt at discipline?"

Try this instead.

Change in-school *suspension* to in-school *probation*, but with a twist. Develop an exchange with York Schools to swap unruly kids. By getting them out of their own home high school and into another environment, they'll be isolated from other troublemakers but allowed to make a fresh start.

Don't choose Bruton High. Pick York High, which is farther away.

As a condition for probation, require parents to pull the driver licenses of their kids. Since the buses don't run between York High and Lafayette, this will force the parents to drive them to and from school. That will give them plenty of quality time to chat up the day's events.

In an effort to play down his influence, Kent said he's "just one part of the discipline process," but as the superintendent he's the biggest part. He needs to send a new message that he's determined to be tough and consistent.

Virginia Gazette

CAP's New Direction

Almost as soon as Wythe CAP's first newsletter hit the streets, talk about its contents erupted. In some corners of the county, especially local government offices, it fueled controversy.

For those who haven't seen the newsletter, which was only sent to CAP members, it is primarily an opinion publication reflecting the views of CAP on issues such as the development of a jail and County Administrator Bill Branson's threat to sue the Board of Supervisors. There's reflection on CAP's past success and talk of plans for the future.

Looking to the future, including choosing a new organizational name, is the newsletter's strength. As a single-issue grassroots organization, there's no denying CAP's success, but its potential for long-term influence on Wythe County is yet to be decided.

The keys to developing a positive group are present. The people are in place. Momentum exists. There's certainly no dearth of important issues.

However, CAP's challenge is to move from a group established during a passionate controversy over a single issue into a more broad-spectrum organization. Sustaining the passion and support, including finances, can be tricky once the founding issue is resolved.

The idea of a newsletter is a good one—so is a new name (hopefully, one with positive connotations).

A passage in the newsletter reads, "Wythe-CAP has demonstrated what a genuine grass-roots effort can accomplish. We must now see that the abilities and energies of this organization are directed most effectively to the future best interests of this community, this county, this country that we all love."

If that noble goal is kept in sight, this county may reap benefits from a "new" grassroots organization.

However, to achieve that goal, CAP must address its weaknesses.

First, CAP's leadership must be willing to do what it so frequently demands of others—be accountable.

Nowhere in the eight-page newsletter does someone take responsibility for the publication. There's no list of CAP officers. No editor or writer is named. That's a particularly serious exclusion since much of the newsletter is opinion-based rather than purely fact. To judge credibility, readers deserve to know who wrote the opinions.

Without a claim of ownership, the newsletter simply lacks legitimacy.

The newsletter also contains a glaring omission. In a recap of the past year, an article talks about looking forward to the first meeting of the newly elected board of supervisors in January since two prison supporters had been removed in the fall election. However, the article mentions no meeting before the Feb. 6 board meeting when Branson's resignation was accepted—something CAP had long sought.

The newsletter article completely ignores an unannounced Jan. 15 meeting of the board held in private business offices during which no minutes were kept. During this meeting, both state law and the public trust were violated. Yet, CAP, an organization which clamored for accountability among government officials and open government, chose to ignore this blatant violation of open meeting rules.

In another article, it is only mentioned that Branson planned to take board members to court because "of the failure to record minutes for that meeting." In essence, by remaining silent, CAP condones the board's actions.

While CAP has long wanted to see Branson out of office, it should not overlook abuses that occurred during that process because the outcome was to its liking. CAP's legitimacy will suffer if its course appears to be anything other than fair.

CAP earned the respect of many citizens during its battle against the prison. To keep that respect and to progress, CAP must maintain the same level of accountability that it demands from others.

Southwest Virginia Enterprise

editorial titled "Don't miss the bigger issue" acknowledged that there were two sides to the issue and suggested that there might be "a middle road between building a local jail vs. the regional jail effort." The editorial also warned that it was "short-sighted to believe that Wythe County will always be able to go it alone," that in the future it "will need alliances with other Southwest Virginia localities more than ever."[15]

After the CAP forces won, and the company decided to go elsewhere, the *Enterprise* expressed concern in an editorial titled "CAP's new direction." It acknowledged CAP's success but said that "its potential for long-term influence on Wythe County is yet to be decided." The challenge was to move from a one-issue to a broad-spectrum organization.

In its submission to the press association, the paper said its efforts to bring the community together were meeting with some success. Officials were discussing a regional jail. A free medical clinic, which the paper had supported, "has treated hundreds of people in its first year of operation." And "[w]ork is under way, with the newspaper's leadership, to reorganize a homeless shelter."

These two relatively small newspapers exhibited the type of the editorial leadership we must expect from today's media. They are examples of "editorial pages that could, and should, be."

A VARIETY OF TUNES

The diverse composition of today's editorial page audience presents another challenge to editorial page editors. Not only must they recognize, when they write their own editorials, that readers hold a variety of opinions, but they also need to create opportunities for those viewpoints to be presented. Because of time limits and the fleeting nature of messages of film and tape, most of the broadcast media do not find it possible to carry varied viewpoints in depth. That responsibility must fall to the print media. When you are the only newspaper in town, that responsibility falls on you.

Providing opportunities for and encouraging readers to write letters to the editor represents a start in this direction. But providing this forum is not enough. Some readers are less inclined to write than others, or are less likely to write on one side of an issue than another, or are less likely to write on some subjects than on others. So the editor must seek to diversify opinion on the editorial page in other ways. Syndicated columns for 60 years or so have been a traditional source of some diversity. The columnists have their limitations, since most write on national and international news and have their favorite topics. Trying to find provocative non-regular writers requires time and effort, but these offer an opportunity to bring varied and fresh views to the editorial page. The addition of an op-ed (opposite-editorial) page on an increasing number of papers has expanded opportunities for publishing material that can not be squeezed into a single page. (Some of the ideas that editors have come up with to provide a variety of tunes are discussed at greater length in Chapter 19, "Innovations in Design and Content.")

Opinion pieces in one newspaper can't be expected to replicate faithfully all viewpoints of a community's readers. But with a little help from friends, and adversaries, newspapers should be able to create opinion pages that make readers feel their views are being taken into account.

TODAY'S SONG WRITERS

So how do today's editorial writers see their role? A 1994 survey conducted by Ernest Hynds and Erika Archibald found that 62 percent of editorial writers saw "expressing a viewpoint or opinion" as the primary function of editorials, compared to 38 percent in 1977. Almost half (47 percent) cited "quality of argument" as an important factor in writing editorials, compared to 29 percent in 1977. Only 23 percent saw "taking a strong stand" as important, but that exceeded the 5 percent who cited it in the earlier survey. Editorial writers in both surveys expressed strong support (79 percent in 1994, 73 percent in 1977) for presenting views opposed to those supported by the newspaper.[16]

The editorial writers generally expressed confidence that their editorials have influence, but the influence varied in terms of its effect on officials, elections, and social and moral issues:

	Much influence	*Moderate influence*	*Sum of the Two*
Officials	38	49	87
Elections	23	53	76
Social issues	24	51	75
Moral issues	15	45	60

These figures ring true with me. It makes sense that editorial writers think they have their greatest impact on local officials, who follow the news more and are more interested in public affairs than most readers. Editorial writers tend to write about the same public affairs with which these officials are involved. Editorials may have more actual effect on the outcome of elections than might be apparent, because in many elections a 5 percent swing in the vote can make the difference. A study I made of California elections made clear that endorsements had more apparent effect on social ballot measures (schools, taxes, etc.) than moral issues (abortion, homosexual teachers, etc.).[17]

Citing examples of perceived influence, Hynds and Archibald reported that an Eastern metropolitan newspaper said its editorials helped elect the city's first African-American mayor. Another said it had influenced negotiations on a state budget. A large Southern paper said it had helped change the form of city government. A Midwestern paper helped change child-welfare laws. A middle-sized Southern paper pushed local government to look for additional water sources. A small paper in the West provided support for a school board to adopt a sex-education curriculum that emphasized abstinence but included information on birth control.[18]

Some newspaper editors are not content these days simply to have editorials speak out on public issues. They want to play a more active role, involving the newspaper in the community and involving their readers (the community) in public affairs. The "movement" has been described in various terms: "civic journalism" and "public journalism" being the most popular. Whatever it's called, it has set off a coast-to-coast debate over the proper role of a newspaper (or a broadcast station) in a community. The person generally recognized as the intellectual fountainhead of what he calls "public journalism," Jay Rosen of New York University, believes that part of the purpose of journalism is "to encourage civic participation, improve public debate and enhance public life, without, of course, sacrificing the independence that a free press demands and deserves."[19]

Several newspapers have embraced some form of "public" journalism, among them the *Charlotte Observer*, the Spokane *Spokesman-Review* and the *St. Paul Pioneer-Press*. (See Chapter 19 for more about what these newspapers have done.) Editors who are not sold on public journalism say they fear that, in organizing and promoting civic activities, "involved" newspapers risk abandoning the traditional role of newspapers–providing the news and commenting on it. (See Chapter 9, "Relations with the Community," for more of this debate.)

THE TUNE PLAYER

Finally we come to editorial writers themselves, the player of the tunes.

Because of the unique role that an editorial page plays in a community, it has become fashionable in editorial-writing circles to describe the page as the conscience of the community, the soul (or heart or personality) of the newspaper, the moral substructure of the paper. Editorial writers should hope their pages are all of these and more. But writers who set out to be the conscience/soul/heart of the community/paper risk committing one of the follies of editorial writing. At a time when philosopher-kings and prophets are rare and the credibility of institutions is low, the role of truth-seeker should be a humble one. Modern readers don't want truth through revelation; they want to feel they are discovering it for themselves. Writers who would lead must become servants of those readers.

The editorial writer is "uniquely equipped to stand at the corner of life and represent us all," somewhat like the person who hangs around in the piazza in the little towns in Italy, Pacific Northwest editorial writers once were told by R.S. Baker, assistant professor of humanities at what was then Oregon College of Education at Monmouth. Baker said he had often wondered how Italians, who read very few newspapers, could be so well informed. The mystery was solved when he observed the buzzing chatter, the exchange of information and gossip and the constant movement of people in the piazza, the public square. Over a period of days, you could spot the person who was the equivalent of the editorial writer. Baker described the person in this manner:

> He is usually middle-aged with a face made grave by experience yet softened by flickers of humor. Most of the time his head is inclined in attentive listening while his eyes scan the square, alert and skeptical. But when he speaks he is listened to. He does not orate. He does not preach. He does not even adopt a tone of outraged innocence. Softly but clearly, he suggests how the matter appears to him. In his words there is a ring of wisdom based on his balancing of claims of past, present and future, the claims of the ideal and the actual, the desirable and the probable. If he lived here he would have your job–would, from his station in the piazza, keep one eye on the new-book shelf in the library and the other on City Hall, on the till.

Baker urged the writers to drop the pose of divine authority and accept simple humanity. "Do not aim to be Zeus the Thunderer (your 19th- and early 20th-century crusading editor) nor even Jove the All-Seeing (your cool, shrewd commentator on legislative/administrative matters). Rather, you should settle for being wily Odysseus, content to be—in all its terror and glory—a man among men, *primus inter pares.*"[20]

CONCLUSION

How does the editorial writer become the woman or the man in the piazza instead of a publisher's mouthpiece, an ivory-tower dweller, an impersonal penman or a judgment imposer? No secret magic will cause such a transformation. The chapters that follow are intended to offer suggestions for writers who may not have all the answers but, like the wise one in the piazza, want to be listened to when they speak.

Questions and Exercises

1. Examine newspapers in your area for a period of several days. Do you get the impression from reading the editorial pages that the editors are trying to find a wide variety of opinions to present to their readers? In what forms do these opinions appear?
2. Examine the editorial pages of these papers for evidence of the personalities and individual opinions of editorial writers. Are the writers faceless persons, or do their names appear on the masthead or on bylined articles?
3. What seems to be the general tone of the editorials on these papers? Are the writers issuing bugle calls or something more subtle and complex? If a mixture, is the tone chosen for individual editorials appropriate?
4. Put in your own words what you think R.S. Baker meant by likening the editorial writer to the person in the piazza.

SECTION **2**

The
Who
of
the
**Editorial
Page**

Chapter 3 Anybody for Editorial Writing?

Here we are, the practitioners and champions of a profession which, we modestly like to think, assists the sun to rise and set—and we are doing very little, seemingly, either to seek out the young people with brains and judgment who we hope will be our successors or to interest them in the virtues and satisfactions of editorial writing.

—Robert H. Estabrook,
Washington Post[1]

Why would anyone want to become an editorial writer? What kinds of people make the best editorial writers, and where do they come from? These are some of the questions raised in this chapter, which is intended to give prospective editorial writers some idea of what it is like to be an editorial writer.

In the 1950s and early 1960s, when I was beginning my newspaper career, few young journalists gave much thought to becoming editorial writers, at least not until they had had their fill of walking a news beat. So I was surprised when, at age 28, I was asked by a friend and former professor if I would be interested in an editorial writing job he knew about in Des Moines, Iowa, on the *Register and Tribune*. Having left my native Nebraska and taken a job in the Pacific Northwest only three years before, I was not keen on returning to the Midwest. But the editor of the editorial page in Des Moines, Lauren Soth, had recently won the Pulitzer Prize for editorial writing, and I had enjoyed writing editorials on my college newspaper. So I applied for the job, got it and never looked back. Editorial writing became my new life.

My professor-friend said something else when he was trying to interest me in that editorial writing job. "Someday," he said, "you ought to have an editorial page of your own." I could not possibly have dreamed that five years later the publishers I had been working for in Washington state would hire me back as editorial page editor of their newspaper. I had my own editorial page at age 33.

THE ATTRACTIONS OF EDITORIAL WRITING

What have I and other editorial writers found so attractive about working on an editorial page?

Editorial writing offers the chance to step back a pace, to take a broad view of the stream of news that rushes through the pages of a newspaper. Reporters, from time to time, have opportunities to write interpretive articles that attempt to put news into perspective, but only editorial writers spend their entire working day trying to understand what's happening in the world. To interpret the news, editorial writers must have enough time to do a quality job of researching and writing. Editorial writers, at least on some papers, can take half a day, if need be, to dig out information for an editorial that, when set in type, might be only five or six inches long. Editorial writing tends to appeal to people who take pleasure in careful writing. Of all the duties editorial page people may be pressed to perform, the one they are likely to enjoy the most is turning out the one or two editorials that must be written each day.

Another attraction of editorial writing is having a ready-made "soap box" from which you can explain and persuade. Readers, of course, don't always fall in line with the editorials they read in their local newspapers, but over a period of time an editorial page with credibility will influence the thinking and direction of the community. It is exciting and rewarding to be a part of the decision-making process of a community.

The job of editorial writer may carry more importance at the newspaper and in the community than it did not so many years ago. Editorial writers may not get their names in print as often as star reporters, but the position tends to be one of the most prestigious on the paper. An increasing number of papers are providing opportunities for writers to become known to the public, partly through signed articles on the editorial page. While most editorial writers don't spend as much time out in public as reporters, they do, in fact must, get out and become acquainted in the community.

From a financial standpoint, editorial writing also has its advantages. Editorial writers generally are better paid than reporters and newsroom editors, and their job tenure is usually longer. A survey in 1988 found that 72 percent of editorial writers thought they were paid "very well" or "well" compared to other staff members of their newspapers. Sixty-eight percent said their jobs were "very satisfying," and an additional 29 percent said "satisfying."[2]

Despite these attractions, a survey of newsroom staffs showed that only about 30 percent of news reporters and editors were interested in editorial writing.[3] Interest was expressed primarily by those under age 30 who had pursued more formal education. The most frequently mentioned reason for not going into editorial writing–mentioned by about 20 percent–was personal disinterest. Almost as many saw too many restrictions and a lack of freedom of expression. Smaller numbers saw the job as too removed from reality (too much ivory tower). Some saw themselves as lacking the necessary scholarship or experience.

The survey caused William W. Baker of the *Kansas City* (Mo.) *Star* to conclude that "our little niche in the profession does not command the respect that it might among our fellow workers across the room." He wondered whether news staffs had the impression that editorial writing was "dull, uninteresting and downright boring." To overcome that impression, he suggested that editorial writers come out of their ivory towers and into the newsroom more often, work at creating more stimulating writing and frown "a bit less frighteningly when we tackle our typewriters."[4]

THE QUALIFICATIONS FOR EDITORIAL WRITING

Surveys suggest that it is not just discomfort with the editorial ivory tower, but also the demanding qualifications, that leads newsroom people to shy away from editorial writing. A significant 58 percent of the respondents to one survey thought that the qualifications for a competent editorial writer were different from those for a competent news staff writer, pointing in particular to the need for more education and knowledge. Also mentioned were the need for more analytical skills, more experience, sharper insights, better grasp of issues and trends, and better writing.[5]

What qualities are required for editorial writers?

First, they need a wide variety of interests. Editorial writers on large staffs may have opportunities to specialize in subject matter, but those on most papers need to be able to write on almost any subject on almost any day. Even those who specialize need to understand how their topics fit into the broader world. Writers need to know about economics, politics, history, sociology, the arts and the sciences. In stressing the catholic interests of editorial writers, Warren H. Pierce of the *St. Petersburg* (Fla.) *Times* said that writers "should know more about all these subjects than any except a specialist in one of the fields, and enough of each so that even the specialist will not scoff" at their opinions.[6]

Second, editorial writers need to be good reporters. They must be able to dig out information and to recount accurately what they find. No editorial is stronger than the facts behind it. Previous experience as reporters can help editorial writers know where to go and with whom to talk when they need information.

One might think that, because editorial writers deal with opinion, they require less ability to be objective than do reporters. But the capacity to understand an issue or situation fully may be even more important for editorial writers than for reporters. In arguing for the need for objectivity, David Manning White, then a professor at Boston University, said. "To the editorial writer is given the power to exercise the most unrestrained use of language in the name of rhetoric and persuasion," and for this reason editorial writers must check and double-check that what they write "conforms as closely as possible to objective, examinable truth."[7]

A third qualification is good writing. Editorial writers must write succinctly, since the editorial page is usually tighter for space than the news pages. Writers also need to be able to write in an interesting and convincing manner. Newspaper readers may have to read the news columns if they want to know about news, but they don't have to read the editorials, and they won't if editorials are dull or don't say anything.

Fourth, editorial writers need a quality that is sometimes called a sense of fairness or justice, sometimes called a spirit of the reformer, a commitment to principles, or integrity. The subjects they write about should be approached with a sense of purpose.

A fifth qualification is the desire to express an opinion. Hoke Norris of the *Chicago Sun-Times* saw reporters who became editorial writers as moving "from the sidewalk to the parade, from the press table to the speaker's table." As participants, Norris, said, editorial writers "must study, weigh, deliberate, contemplate, meditate, judge, discuss, talk over, think through and generally know all there is to know about any given subject, and . . . must be capable, at times, of completing the entire process in five minutes."[8]

Another desirable quality is the ability to reason cogently. Warren Pierce, a professor at the University of Oregon, had this ability in mind when he quoted the philosopher Arthur Schopenhauer as saying that geniuses share one characteristic: an ability to proceed from the particular to the general. Pierce thought that editorial writers need that ability, as well as the ability to do the reverse. Editorial writers must be able to go from one specific case of juvenile delinquency to the general causes of such delinquency, and "from one deep-freeze or white convertible Oldsmobile to a proposition of ethical conduct in public office." They should be equally able to give meaning to reciprocal trade agreements in terms of a clothes-pin factory in their community or of cotton or corn growers in their state.[9]

One view of an editorial writer's qualities was expressed by Irving Dilliard, editorial page editor of the *St. Louis Post-Dispatch*, who compiled an impressive list in an article titled "The Editor I Wish I Were." His principal points: Editorial writers should know their community, state, nation and world and read a great deal. They should be courteous, treating readers as individual human beings. They should be cooperative, working with associates to produce the best possible newspaper. They should be curious; perhaps they are not the first to learn everything in the community, but they at least should know more new things than anyone else. They should have imagination, seeing opportunities for improving the press in content, service and leadership. They should be persons of conscience and courage, with the ability to stand up to interest groups or a superior editor or publisher. They should have judgment, avoiding "the heavy artillery . . . if a spatter of birdshot will suffice." They should be able to criticize others, but also able to accept criticism. They must take care to avoid activities that might prove embarrassing or detrimental to editorial independence. Writers should be "sparing" in friendships because friendships outside their newspapers "may at any time force the hard choice between personal kindness to a friend and devotion to duty as an editor."[10]

Frederic S. Marquardt of the Phoenix *Arizona Republic* was so overwhelmed by Dilliard's description of the ideal editor that he asked: "Doesn't the guy ever have any fun?" The need to find out about so many places in the world "would give most newspaper auditors acute melancholia," Marquardt said. "I would need at least 72 hours [a day] to keep up with Dilliard, even if I didn't stop for a short beer now and then." Marquardt was especially critical of the admonition to be sparing in friendships. "Show me an editor who bends an elbow in a neighborhood tavern once in a while, or who occasionally sees if he can fill an inside straight, or who goes to a football game without the slightest intention of improving his mind, and I'll show you an editor who knows more about life than all the Ivory Tower boys," Marquardt said.[11]

Who are these journalists who become editorial writers? Surveys show that they tend to be male, white, college-educated, middle-aged and leaning politically toward the Democratic Party. The picture is changing, but more slowly than most editors who are doing the hiring would like.[12]

A 1995 survey of editorial page *editors* found their average age to be 48.8 years, with an average salary of $55,191. Seventy-one percent of editors were male. Politically, 26 percent were Democrats, 15 percent Republicans, 32 percent independent and 16 percent "none" (whatever that is). Eighty-three percent were married and, on average, had 1.7 children. Forty-nine percent were Protestant, 17 percent Catholic, 8 percent Jewish, 3 percent Universalist and 22 percent "none." Forty-six percent had graduate degrees. On average, they had worked on editorial pages for almost 13 years.[13]

A survey of editorial *writers*, at about the same time, found that 80 percent were male and about two-thirds were in the 35–50 age group. Only 10 percent were 34 and under, 22 percent were 51 to 65 and 3 percent were over 65.[14]

More significant than these snapshot pictures are the trends in the makeup of editorial page staffs.

The number of women on editorial pages has been increasing. Compared to the 20 percent in the 1995 survey cited above, women accounted for 16 percent in 1988 and 5 percent in 1977.[15] A survey in the early 1990s found that 34 percent of newspapers had at least one woman on the editorial page staff, compared to 24 percent in 1983 and 12 percent in 1978.[16] But a study in 1988 concluded that women would not "attain levels in newspaper editorships on a par with their level of the population (53 percent) until the year 2055."[17]

More women are becoming editorial page editors. The surveys cited found a greater percentage of women working as editorial page editors (29 percent) than as editorial writers (20 percent). By the year 2000, six of the most recent 10 presidents of the National Conference of Editorial Writers (NCEW) will have been women.

A survey aimed at comparing women and men on the editorial page concluded that "the hiring of women on editorial page staffs does bring about a more diversified staff. Women tend to offer different expertise, somewhat different motivation, a possibly different generational outlook, and a different political orientation than do their male colleagues."[18] The survey found that women who were editorial page editors tended to be on smaller papers, and that women who were writers tended to be on larger papers. Women tended to be younger, to have less journalistic experience but more post-graduate education. They had lower salaries. They were more likely to be Democratic than male editors were, although "independent" was the largest designation for both women and men. Women were more likely to regard themselves as specialists or experts in specific subject areas, notably science and health, "women's issues" (defined in the survey), education and minority issues.

Apparently little if any progress has been made in bringing racial minorities onto the editorial staff or the news staff. The 1995 survey found 97 percent of editorial page *editors* were white, 1 percent Asian and 1 percent Hispanic. The 1988 survey of editorial *writers* found 97 percent were white and 3 percent of racial minorities.[19] In a *Masthead* symposium on "In Search of Diversity,"

Chuck Stokes recounted that at his first NCEW convention he wondered "how could it be" that he could count "the African-American, the Hispanic-American and the Asian-American editorialists on one hand."[20] Rekha Basu of the *Des Moines Register* recognized that the solution "isn't entirely within the power of NCEW to fix, although the organization has been making a concerted effort to recruit minority members and include diversity sessions at many of its get-togethers." She said that the deficiency at the conventions, and by extension in editorial boards, "is reflected in the missing perspectives on a whole gamut of issues—from rap music to the death penalty, from the presidential campaign to the L.A. riots, to international affairs."[21]

Annual reports prepared at Ohio State University suggest that the cause may lie with academic institutions. No significant changes were found over a 30-year period in numbers of B.A. degrees granted to minority students. In fact a "soft decline" was observed.[22]

"Now, some might argue that mainstream media is for mainstream ideas," Caroline Brewer of the *Dayton Daily News* wrote in noting a lack of diversity of both faces and opinions. "And that if people with alternative views want to express them, then they ought to find alternative media." Still, she wrote, "there was a time when what's called mainstream media used to be a place for the exchange of varying ideas. Remember when Martin Luther King Jr.'s advocacy for civil rights 'right now' was considered out of the mainstream?"[23]

WHERE EDITORIAL WRITERS COME FROM

Because editorial writing requires so many skills and qualities, it is not surprising that editors and publishers despair when they face the task of finding an editorial writer. Any publisher or editor who has found the right person will say without a doubt that such success is one of the most satisfying experiences in the field of newspapering. I know; I have experienced both despair and success.

It is infinitely more difficult to predict the potential ability of a would-be editorial writer than it is to decide whether a candidate will make a good reporter. Few guidelines exist for judging whether a former reporter, a college professor, a recent liberal arts graduate or an editorial writer from another newspaper will do the job a publisher or an editor has in mind. For one thing, most people who hire editorial writers, no doubt thinking of some of those qualities mentioned above, are not certain whether editorial writers are born or made. Some editorial writers seem to have what it takes, and some seem not to. James H. Howard, a professor at the University of California, Los Angeles, thought that editorial writers probably had innate talent but that "those not blessed with the talent at birth" could be taught to improve their research, sharpen their writing and "present readable results of logical thinking."[24] Donald L. Breed of the *Freeport* (Ill.) *Journal Standard* said his experience on small newspapers showed that adequate editorial writers were usually found "only by accident."[25]

One dilemma faced by an editor looking for a new writer is whether to look in the newsroom for a person with no editorial page experience or to search outside for a person who has had editorial experience in another community. Most of the editors in a *Masthead* symposium said they looked first in their newsrooms but were not especially optimistic about finding exactly the right person.[26] An employer identified only as "an editor in the West" said he was discouraged by what happens to good reporters "who can pound out several thousand words of news copy a day" when they sit down in front of the editorial typewriter. "That clear, decent prose becomes stilted, 'literary' or arch. Why can't they relax?" One reporter who started on Monday ran out of things to say by Thursday. Another didn't work out because of lack of background. "I don't think he's read a book since he left college," the editor said.[27]

William D. Snider of the *Greensboro* (N.C.) *Daily News* said he found that good editorial writers often come from non-journalistic backgrounds. He cited Ed Yoder, who had come to the *Daily News* after majoring in English and then studying philosophy, politics and economics as a Rhodes Scholar at Oxford. He had been editor of his college paper. Between stints at the *News* he taught college history. From Greensboro, Yoder went to Washington, where he became the last editorial page editor of the *Star* (then a syndicated columnist, and a college professor again). Snider himself had been secretary to two governors before returning to the newspaper world.[28]

I must acknowledge that, in seeking new editorial writers on the *Columbian,* we did no more planning than most papers. My first search represented a classic case of frustration. An ad in *Editor & Publisher* elicited more than 100 applications. Few came close to the person we thought we wanted. Some were "hacks," old-timers looking for an easy chair. Many were acquainted with neither editorial writing nor the territory. Almost in desperation, we allowed a *Columbian* reporter, who eagerly wanted the job, to try out for it. Here was the exact opposite of the reporter who has trouble moving from fact to opinion. After a few weeks of overexuberantly expressing her opinion, she settled down to become a fine, if still flamboyant, editorial writer. In the next search for a writer, we hired a person who had been an editorial writer, in fact the editor, on a small daily newspaper in California. He knew how to write editorials, and it didn't take him long to learn the territory.

My first editorial writing employer hired me when I knew very little about editorial writing and even less about Iowa, where the newspaper was located. But my return to the Vancouver paper represented an almost ideal set of circumstances. I had become acquainted with that community during three years of news reporting. I had had five years of editorial writing experience under a respected editorial page editor and excellent teacher. To make my situation even sweeter, I was brought back to Vancouver six months before the retiring editorial page editor was to leave the paper, enough time to get re-acquainted again in the community and break in slowly. I recommend this combination of experiences but recognize that these opportunities do not arise often.

CONCLUSION AND A WARNING

My comments and the surveys of editorial writers may suggest that editorial writers think highly of themselves. They think that they practice the best of professions. The jobs they hold require all those "fantastic" qualities discussed above. Thus if they hold those jobs, editorial writers reason, they must be fantastic themselves.

Some of this self-esteem is merited. Some of the best informed, most talented, incisive, conscientious people I know are editorial writers. In my experience, nothing can be more stimulating than bringing editorial writers together at an editorial staff meeting or a meeting of writers from several papers. But as praiseworthy as these wordsmiths generally are, perhaps a warning about too much self-congratulation is in order.

Editorial writers may be well-educated, draw good salaries and have their own offices, but they are still newspaper people. Newspaper people tend to be held in high esteem these days—higher than half a century ago certainly. But much of this esteem comes from the jobs they hold, not from their own individual qualities. Press critic Ben Bagdikian has warned that, with newspapers becoming "a respectable institution and editorial writers the most respected of all," newspaper people shouldn't forget where their journalistic predecessors came from. "Newspapers were born and raised in the bloody arena, kicking and gouging their newspaper competitors in the ring while the crowd screeched. . . . " Now most of the competitors have been "carried out on stretchers" and the few that are left are not scrapping but giving their audiences pompous "lecture[s] on the Manly Art."[29]

Among middle-aged and older members of NCEW, perhaps the best-remembered call for humility came from Jonathan W. Daniels, editor of the Raleigh, N.C., *News and Observer*, who delivered an address titled "The Docility of the Dignified Press" to a 1965 NCEW convention. Speaking at an evening banquet at an exclusive country club on the outskirts of Milwaukee, Daniels told the writers that the editors and publishers who gathered for meetings of the Associated Press and the American Newspaper Publishers Association at the Waldorf-Astoria Hotel each spring were "indistinguishable from bankers." He quickly added: "You look pretty impressive yourselves." He reminded them that they were courted by senators, cabinet members and generals. "You really cannot blame the press for wanting a little dignity," he said. "Its members, as their social positions improved, naturally did not want to seem to be like Horace Greeley, who before he founded the famous *Tribune* was fired from one paper because its owner wanted 'only decent looking men in the office.'" Why shouldn't members of the press like their "pants pressed—sometimes striped?" He acknowledged that, "if [the press] didn't appear full-armored from the brow of Jove, it doesn't twist genealogy more than some other people do in suggesting that it is descended from the Bill of Rights." But he reminded his listeners that there were other ancestors. "There was the guitar player on the back of the patent medicine salesman's wagon. Also there was the ink-stained impertinent fellow who began long ago to put embarrassing reports on paper."

Now it had become more fashionable, he said, to look like Walter Lippmann, the distinguished columnist, than Heywood Broun, the disheveled-looking columnist of the 1920s and 1930s who had rankled publishers by trying to organize labor unions in their newsrooms. Perhaps it was at this point in Daniels' speech that one of the editorial writers suddenly rose from his table, lurched drunkenly toward the right side of the room, uttered a profane epithet at Daniels and staggered out, never to be seen at an NCEW meeting again.

Daniels bade him farewell and continued with his speech: "There is, of course, something disreputable about any business devoted to prying into matters," he said. "It is a nosey business. And it should remain so. Anybody who would never wish to hurt anybody's feelings, who never wishes to make anybody mad, should stay out of the newspaper business. The editor who deserves the respect of his community can be no respecter of persons in his community. He must be nosey and often a public scold."[30]

So when editors and publishers want to hire a new editorial writer, all they have to do is find a man or a woman who is a writer, a thinker, a scholar, an objective viewer, a critic, a scold and a person with humility. Is it any wonder that good editorial writers are hard to find–or any wonder that, once found, they think pretty highly of themselves?

Questions and Exercises

1. What are the reasons for trying to find a new editorial writer in an editor's own newsroom?
2. What are the reasons for looking elsewhere?
3. How do you account for the slowness in opening editorial page positions to women and racial minorities?
4. Are there women editorial writers or members of racial minorities on editorial pages in your area? How long have they been editorial writers? What education and experience did they have when they became editorial writers?
5. What do you regard as the most important qualities of an editorial writer?
6. What aspect of editorial writing would appeal to you most? What would appeal to you least? Why?
7. If you wanted to land an editorial writing position on a major newspaper within 10 years, what route would you attempt to follow?
8. On what newspapers with which you are acquainted could you feel philosophically comfortable writing editorials?

CHAPTER 4 Preparation of an Editorial Writer

It is hard to imagine any discipline that would not benefit a journalist.

—A RESPONSE TO A QUESTIONNAIRE CONCERNING COLLEGE CURRICULA[1]

Everybody has a sort of reading anxiety neurosis.

—ROBERT B. FRAZIER, *EUGENE* (ORE.) *REGISTER-GUARD*[2]

Preparing oneself to be an editorial writer is like preparing oneself for life. Everything that the potential editorial writer thinks, learns or experiences is likely to become pertinent someday in the writing of some editorial. The same is true of journalists who are already editorial writers. Every word they read can provide an idea or information for an editorial. Compulsive readers who find themselves reading the sides of the breakfast cereal box may write an editorial that day, or another day, about the dangers of the sugar content in children's breakfast foods or the lack of meaningful nutritional information. A casual conversation may provide an insight into Social Security or the minimum wage.

In this chapter a discussion of the unending education necessary for editorial writing is limited to five areas: undergraduate education, continuing education, firsthand experiences, reading and culture. A sixth area, professional experience, was discussed in the previous chapter.

UNDERGRADUATE EDUCATION

Bring an editor and an educator–or even two editors or two educators–together and you will have a debate on how best to prepare students for careers in journalism.

Journalism schools are a rather recent invention. Many editors before World War II saw little need for them. They hadn't gone to journalism school–perhaps not even to college. Reporting and editing, they knew from experience, could be learned on the job. But the world was becoming more complex, and readers were becoming more knowledgeable and sophisticated. To the GI Bill, which provided educational and other benefits for World War II veterans, must go much of the credit for sending more Americans than ever before to college. Students poured into journalism and every other field of study. Before many postwar classes had graduated, the competition for jobs made a college degree a necessary ticket for many positions.

Skills vs. Liberal Arts

With the legitimacy of journalism programs gradually becoming accepted, the debate turned to skills courses versus liberal arts. How many courses in journalism were necessary to prepare students to write a news story? How many courses in "academic" subjects were necessary to prepare students to know what they were writing about? Out of that debate came general acceptance of the 75:25 ratio set by the American Council on Education for Journalism, the national accrediting agency in journalism. In other words, 75 percent of graduation credits should be in liberal arts and related areas and not more than 25 percent in journalism. More recently this arbitrary rule has been relaxed, but it still remains a reasonable guideline for educators who want to ensure that prospective journalists get a broad liberal arts background.

Green Eyeshades vs. Chi-Squares

Next came arguments over which journalism courses should be offered and required. The protagonists in these arguments were sometimes referred to as the "green eyeshades" and the "chi-squares." Now you hear these disagreements discussed more in terms of "professional" versus "history and theory" courses.

"Green eyeshades" was a reference to the transparent green bills that copy editors used to wear to cut the glare of overhead lights. "Chi-square" is a mathematical procedure used in statistics to measure differences in sets of numbers. The green eyeshades feared that journalism schools were shifting from old-fashioned skills to theory and research. They wanted the schools to concentrate on reporting, news writing, feature writing, copy editing and editorial writing, plus courses in media law and history. They wanted attention paid to spelling, grammar, punctuation and style.

The chi-squares were interested in creating courses in communications theory, communications research, surveys of mass communications, media effects, and mass media and society. One of their goals was to make journalism and communications academically respectable among their research- and theory-oriented colleagues in other university departments. Coupled with this emphasis has been a sharp trend toward valuing advanced degrees over professional experience in hiring new faculty members.

Members of the newspaper business and some educators have expressed concern. Hugh S. Fullerton, associate professor at the University of North Florida, in a letter to the newspaper division of the Association for Education in Journalism and Mass Communication (AEJMC), complained: "The 'academic' side has raised barriers against the professionals. I know many professionals who would be happy to teach if they received the respect that they have earned by many years' experience. But instead, we professionals are told again and again that we are unqualified because we don't have Ph.D.'s."[3]

Anticipating what concerned Fullerton, when I switched from newspapering to teaching I immediately enrolled in a Ph.D. program within commuting distance of the school at which I was teaching. Six years and an editorial writing textbook later, I was able to obtain a position at a university that regarded degrees, research and publications as important. Since then, these qualifications have become even more important at most four-year schools. The trend is not likely to be reversed.

Non-Professional Courses

Some critics argue that journalism programs have no place in higher education. "Indeed, a good case can be made for abolishing J-schools," Jake Highton, associate professor at the University of Nevada–Reno, has written. "What journalism students need is an education–not a journalism education . . . . [Time] would be better spent having students take courses in literature, history, political science, fine arts and economics," with some "critical analysis of media performance."[4]

Most editors probably would not go so far as to advocate abolishing journalism programs but would agree with Otis Chandler, then publisher of the *Los Angeles Times*, when he complained that among job applicants "we're getting too many hopefuls who lack a background in economics, literature, philosophy, sociology and the natural sciences" and who "know little of government." He also deplored journalism students' inadequate exposure to ecology, energy, land-use planning and economics, as well as the physical sciences, birth control and bureaucracies.[5] When NCEW (National Conference of Editorial Writers) members were asked to recommend areas of study, they suggested, in this order, U.S. history, composition, state and local government, introduction to sociology, principles of economics, critical writing, constitutional law, comparative economic systems, geography, history of political thought, political parties, history of modern Europe, economic history of the United States, public financing, urban and regional planning, and philosophy.[6]

Some educators have concluded that, because of the need to know about so many things, the journalism program should be a five-year one. Such a program might lead to a master's degree.[7] Other educators think that four years is enough to produce a working newspaper person, that he or she can grow on the job and later pick up additional education on the side or return for a master's degree, perhaps in another discipline.[8]

Because reporting and commenting on the news are becoming more specialized as the world becomes more complex, the student who comes to a newspaper with training in a particular field–economics, the arts, the health sciences or the criminal justice system, for example–can prove to be a valuable asset to a news or editorial staff, especially when a newspaper seeks to fill a beat or an editorial writing position that requires knowledge in that field.

Practical Experience

One method of impressing students with the need to learn basics–and to teach them at the same time–is through an internship on a newspaper or with another news operation. If interns have at least a couple of news writing and reporting courses, within a three-month internship they can acquire the ability to substitute on several of the regular beats, handle most stories that come into the newsroom and write a simple feature story. The internship experience helps when applying for a job after graduation. The prospective employer knows that the applicant has had some practical experience, and that the internship supervisor can provide an evaluation of the applicant's work. Often a successful internship can lead to a job on the paper on which the student worked as an intern.

Another valuable experience is reporting and editing on a campus newspaper, especially if the work is supervised and criticized by faculty advisers or knowledgeable senior staff members.

In an NCEW online discussion of the best preparation for a would-be editorial writer, participants most recently mentioned news reporting. "The more one knows about each beat on the paper, the better," wrote Kurt Rogahn of the *Cedar Rapids Gazette.* "Knowing the school beat, city hall, county government, politics, even the police beat, keeps an editorialist from asserting impractical ideas, drawing faulty conclusions, misleading the reader and generally messing up." Several editorial writers cited the value of copy-desk experience as well as general knowledge and experience in other areas.[9]

CONTINUING EDUCATION

Editorial writers and would-be editorial writers should never stop trying to expand their educations. Science, mathematics, agriculture, medicine, politics, geography, education—all have vastly changed from the days in which many of today's editorial writers were in college.

Educational Fellowships

The most formal way for writers to recharge themselves intellectually and psychologically is through educational programs. An editorial writer for the *Boston Globe* was given a year's leave of absence to study law at Harvard Law School. "I cannot urge too strongly the desirability, for editorial writers particularly and working journalists generally, a good dose of formal legal education," Anson H. Smith Jr. said. "It sharpens the mind, provides valuable sources of information and advice on legal issues in the news, and generally enhances one's understanding of the legal process."[10] After completing a fellowship at Stanford University, Sig Gissler of the *Milwaukee Journal* said the experience gave him the chance to think about "the big, tough questions that editorial writers seldom have time to dig into deeply." He added: "Think how rewarding it would be to spend nine months at a great university contemplating these concerns—without deadlines, spats with the boss, phone calls from ired readers; without mandatory term papers or exams; without significant restraints on your freedom to explore and reflect."[11]

Probably the most prestigious fellowship is the Nieman Fellowship for Journalists at Harvard University. Information about this and other fellowships can be obtained through most journalism schools. From time to time *The Masthead* publishes a listing of fellowships and other educational offerings.[12]

Seminars

Among programs of a briefer nature, the best known is at the American Press Institute (API) in Reston, Va. For four decades API has provided one- and two-week seminars in almost all phases of newspapering, including sessions on editorial writing and editorial pages. The seminars are financed through tuition fees. Participants meet in small groups to criticize and praise each other's editorials and editorial pages, in larger groups to discuss current issues with experts in journalism and other fields.

From time to time various universities and colleges offer short courses in specific areas of newspapering or in state government or business. (NCEW and the University of Maryland periodically co-sponsor seminars on public issues.) Editorial writers who feel the need for more education can enroll in one or more courses in a nearby college. Evening courses in such areas as economics or public administration can give editorial writers knowledge that might improve their editorials.

Visiting Professorships

One way to learn is to teach. Possibilities exist at several universities for editors and writers to return to the campus as visiting editors or visiting professors. The William Allen White School of Journalism at the University of Kansas, for example, has brought a series of editors to campus. The University of Montana, which from time to time has money for a professional visitor, invited me to teach during the fall quarter of 1976 while I was an editor. The experience was so satisfying that, when a few months later I had a chance to teach an entire year at Washington State University, I accepted the offer.[13] Teaching forces you to think about what you have been doing as a matter of unreflective habit.

FIRSTHAND EXPERIENCES

The editorial writer who hopes to address a changing world must get out of the office. "There is no real substitute in journalism for the face-to-face confrontation," Terrence W. Honey of the *London* (Ontario) *Free Press* wrote in an article titled "Our Ivory Tower Syndrome Is Dead."[14] Unfortunately for some editorial writers it is not dead.

Local Level

Busy editorial writers are often tempted to write editorials on local topics on the basis of what has appeared in the news columns, interpreted in the light of past editorial policy, rather than attend meetings of city councils and local citizen bodies that can become an every-evening job. Most of the time spent at these gatherings may seem boring and unproductive, so writers tend to put off going to local meetings until a hot issue comes along. Attending only at crucial times is better than not attending at all. But most of the work of local government bodies is done in regular, humdrum meetings in the absence of the eyes of the public. Editorial writers who want to know how a council or council member functions under normal circumstances should attend at least some of these dull assemblages. Editorial writers also can boost their credibility with members of local organizations and with anyone else who happens to be at these meetings.

More informative than public meetings are private ones, perhaps over lunch, with key persons. Editorial writers, or the editorial board, may find it advantageous to meet separately with members of opposing sides of issues. On other occasions inviting representatives from all sides to meet together to discuss an issue may prove an effective way to gain information. To make certain that such conferences are not limited to times of crisis–and that lethargy does not win over good intentions–some editorial boards schedule a weekly meeting to which they invite one or more sources. Writers should meet, from time to time, with labor officials (as well as rank-and-file members), Chamber of Commerce leaders, other business groups and individuals, environmental groups, utility officials, energy-interest groups, consumer groups, education groups (professional and citizen), religious leaders, social activists, sports people, transportation people and even people from rival media.

It also is important for journalism students to become acquainted with people who are making, or trying to make, public policy. An editorial writing course offers an opportunity to bring speakers to class or to take students out into the community to learn first-hand what they are writing about.

State Level

Face-to-face confrontation can be more difficult at the state level. Unless a newspaper is located in a state capital, legislative sessions and committee hearings are difficult and time-consuming to attend. Most provide little immediate information for editorials, since the legislative process is spread over an extended period of time. But much of what was said about local meetings applies here too. Writers need to get a feeling for the process at its usual slow pace to see how it works and how its practitioners function. Editorial writers need to show their faces and make their presence known, at least among their local legislators. Credibility with the legislators, as well as knowledge, is the goal.

It was easier to follow legislatures when they met for short sessions every two years. Now critical moments in the process are spread out, and opportunities for strategically directed editorials become more difficult to spot. Some of the difficulty can be alleviated if a newspaper assigns skilled reporters to the legislature to keep editorial writers informed about the timing of bills as well as to track down information for editorials.

Maintaining contact with the executive branch of state government is even more difficult from a distance. Decisions can come at any time and often without public notice. Probably the best approach to establishing contact is through people at the assistant level–governors' aides, assistant attorneys general, the elections supervisor in the secretary of state's office, a key assistant in the state planning office, a high-level career employee of the tax commission. These second-level people are more likely to be expertly informed than their bosses and, even more important, are usually easier to get on the telephone.

Another way to keep abreast of state affairs is to watch for statewide conferences of such groups as county commissioners and city officials, as well as meetings on specific issues, such as taxation, education and legislative or judicial reform.

Students who attend a university in a state capital should find it easy to become acquainted with officials and issues by following the media and dropping in on legislative- and executive-branch meetings. I have found that taking students to the capital (200 miles away) for even a few days helps awaken their interest in state government, particularly when the legislature is in session. It is easier to arrange these visits if the news and editorial people from the capital city newspaper help with the arrangements.

National Level

For national issues, most editorial writers must rely heavily on the news services and newspapers such as the *New York Times,* the *Washington Post,* the *Wall Street Journal,* the *Christian Science Monitor* or the *Congressional Quarterly.* Editorial writers with Washington bureaus have access to information at the national level. Close contacts with the offices of the state's two senators and the local representative can be useful. Most of these officials will have offices in the district or the state, but sources there are likely to prove beneficial primarily on matters of local interest or on subjects relating to the committees on which the senator or representative serves.

Short visits to Washington, D.C., may seem even less productive for an editorial writer than trips to the state capital. But through periodic visits to the capital, a writer can begin to cultivate sources in the federal government, especially in departments that deal with issues pertinent to the writer's own region.

From time to time the Department of State invites editors and editorial writers to Washington for briefings on world affairs. I found the first one I attended fascinating because of the opportunity to see famous personages. But by the second briefing I began to realize that the presentations offered little more than I could have obtained by reading readily available publications.

I have taken some of my students on three-day travel seminars to Washington, D.C., to meet with people of differing opinions, usually on international topics. These have been arranged with the assistance of the local YMCA and some of the campus ministries.

Attendance at national political conventions can benefit an editorial writer, although not as much as it did in the days before television. The principal benefit is probably in getting some of the flavor of the proceedings and watching the home-state delegation.

International Level

The American Association for the United Nations sometimes invites editorial people to meetings and briefings at the United Nations headquarters in New York City. Again, the principal value is in getting a feel for the personalities and the atmosphere. Probably more productive are visits to foreign countries— that is, if the writer has made substantial advance preparation. A quick tourist- or host-conducted visit may distort rather than provide insight into affairs abroad. In recent years NCEW has sponsored a series of overseas tours for members that provide participants with background information about and interpretation of what they are seeing. I found an NCEW trip to Eastern

Europe in 1990 and a trip to Mexico and Cuba in 1993 to be exciting and eye-opening. Of course, these trips are expensive; the cost may be prohibitive for small papers. Projected trips usually are announced in *The Masthead.*

Of course personal travel abroad, especially if you are conversant in a foreign language, can be educational and useful to the editorial writer. I benefited from three trips to Central America, arranged by a local campus ministry, that were led by residents of the countries that we visited. They knew the places to visit and the people to see, and could help us with the language and local customs.

Professional Level

Associating with journalists with similar interests can help rejuvenate editorial writers' enthusiasm for their work and challenge them with ideas for doing a better job. One of the main purposes of NCEW is to improve the quality of editorial pages by bringing editorial writers together for sessions of mutual enlightenment and criticism. A valuable and consistent feature of NCEW's annual meeting has been the day- or half-day-long critique session in which participants study the editorial pages before arriving and analyze, praise and criticize one another's pages. Held at some time in nearly every section of the country, the NCEW meetings have given members a firsthand (though brief) look at other communities. The speakers are almost consistently good. From time to time regional or state versions of these meetings take place.

The Masthead has carried accounts of two regional meetings, one in Virginia, the other in New England. In both instances the organizers enlisted the help of a state or regional newspaper, an "organization with deeper pockets and more clerical help than any one or two editorial writers could muster alone."[15] Both invited out-of-state editorial page editors to critique their pages. One organizer suggested that part of the educational process was leaving "enough free time that participants can get acquainted" and learn from each other.[16]

THE EDITORIAL SHELF

Robert B. Frazier of the *Eugene* (Ore.) *Register-Guard* once surveyed 100 editorial writers to determine their reading habits.[17] Later he wrote an article for *The Masthead* titled "The Editorial Elbow," in which he offered a "more-or-less compleat (sic) listing of reference works useful, day by day, to the editor, reporter and copyreader."[18] From the two efforts Frazier concluded that writers consistently thought they read too little, that probably no other group in the country "read more or more catholically" and that writers on smaller papers, with smaller editorial page staffs, followed a more varied reading diet than writers on larger staffs.

Nonfiction was more popular than fiction. Only about 40 percent said that fiction accounted for a quarter or more of their reading. Half said they read essays, poetry or plays. About 10 percent read often in a foreign language. Some bought only two or three books a year, but one bought 200. Forty percent were regular patrons of libraries. A quarter of them said they read in bed. Two got up to read in the middle of the night. Three read early in the morning. Four admitted to being bathroom readers. One had read Gibbon and one Spinoza. Shakespeare appeared on several lists.

Columnist James J. Kilpatrick thinks that editorial writers do not read enough, and "it shows up with painful transparency in the superficiality, the shallowness, the gracelessness, of our editorial writer."[19] He advised writers to read the Bible and Shakespeare and to read heavily "in the older classics"— Thucydides, Plutarch, Homer, Aeschylus, Disraeli, Gibbon, De Quincey, Spinoza, Voltaire—and then the more recent works of Thorstein Veblen, William James, John Dewey, Alfred North Whitehead and Peter Finley Dunne. To this assignment, Kilpatrick added a list of poets, from Alexander Pope to Edna St. Vincent Millay, and fiction writers, from Charles Dickens to O. Henry. Irving Dilliard of the *St. Louis Post-Dispatch* said an editorial writer should be "familiar with the monumental publishing projects of his time in biography, in history, in the social sciences, regional life, in the messages and papers of the great Americans—Franklin, Adams, Jefferson, Lincoln."[20]

Magazines and Newspapers

In moments when they are not reading the classics, where do, and should, editorial writers turn for help in writing their daily assignments? An insight was provided by editorial writers' answers to a survey question about how they became familiar with their newspapers' ideologies. The smaller-newspaper editors tended to say they read their own newspapers. Editors on larger news-papers tended to read other newspapers.[21] Editorial writers should be reading other newspapers, either on paper or on the Internet. They should read their state and regional papers and such major newspapers as the *New York Times, USA Today,* the *Washington Post,* the *Wall Street Journal,* the *Christian Science Monitor* and the *Los Angeles Times.* A 1994 survey found that 14 percent of edito-rial writers read the *New York Times,* 10 percent the *Wall Street Journal* and 3 percent *USA Today* (the only papers mentioned).[22]

One might expect that most editorial writers would subscribe to a weekly newsmagazine. But the 1994 survey found that only 37 percent did. Of the writers surveyed, 18 percent subscribed to *Newsweek,* 11 percent to *Time* and 8 percent to *U.S. News & World Report.* These magazines give a more compre-hensive account of some news than daily news stories do and, maybe more important, provide essays and reports on such areas as religion, science and the arts. Back sections of *Newsweek* and *Time* can provide ideas for nonpolitical editorials.

Writers should seek out varying points of view on public issues, if only to know what the opposition is saying. One way is to subscribe to an opinion magazine such as the *New Republic,* the *Nation,* the *Standard* or the *National Review.* The 1994 survey indicated that 3 percent of the editorial writers subscribed to the *New Republic;* no measurable number to any other U.S. opin-ion magazine.[23] *Harper's* and *Atlantic* traditionally have been popular with editorial writers. *Business Week* publishes easy-to-understand articles on busi-ness and economics, as well as well-written editorials that discuss issues beyond a narrow business orientation. *Foreign Affairs* offers writing by recog-nized international experts. The *Economist* offers a British point of view, but includes a strong section on the United States. (Three percent of editorial writers took the *Economist*.) *Columbia Journalism Review* and *American Journalism Review* are helpful in keeping up on media issues.

Periodical Research Materials

Available generally on a weekly basis are the following sources of information:

> *Facts on File*, a weekly service that boils down the essential elements of the news into a ready-reference form. It is a good source of elusive facts. Facts on File, 460 Park Ave. South, New York, NY 10019.
>
> *The CQ Researcher* (formerly *Editorial Research Reports*) provides background material on a variety of current issues 48 times a year. Congressional Quarterly, 1414 22nd St., N.W., Washington, DC 20037.
>
> The *National Journal*, published 50 times a year, provides weekly reports on current national issues and more in-depth reports on major topics. National Journal, 1730 M St. N.W., Washington, DC 20036.

Published on a daily basis while Congress is in session is the *Congressional Record*, which can be obtained through your senator or representative in Congress. This publication provides a day-to-day account of what happens in Congress (and some things that don't happen but that legislators wish had happened). The *Record* also contains a large amount of reprinted material, including editorials. The daily volumes present a storage problem and far too much material for most editorial writers. One way to use the *Record* is to glance through the index that arrives every 10 days or so. It does not take long to look up your state and district legislators to see what they have said or inserted into the *Record*. Current, and especially regional, topics also can be checked quickly, as can the names of editorial writers' newspapers and the cities in which the editorials are published. It is nice to know when you have been reprinted in the Record. (The *Congressional Record* is also available online. One access page is at http://rs9.loc.gov/home/search_cr.html/.)

Internet and Data Bases

The 1994 survey cited above found that 58 percent of editorial writers said lack of time for research was a "major" problem. Optimists think that instant access to unlimited amounts of information through the Internet will solve that problem: Once editorial writers find out where they want to go on the World Wide Web, they will be able to do all the research they can possibly desire. The realists say it won't be that simple. First, you have to know where you want to go. Second, you may have to pay to get the information. Third, you may be inundated by so much information that you are no more prepared to write a comprehendible editorial *with* the information than you were *without* it. Finally, you may have no idea of the reliability of the information that you obtain.

A survey published in 1997 found that editorial writers on larger papers were more likely to use the Internet and their newspapers' own databases than writers on middle-sized papers were and even more than writers on small papers did. But the differences were relatively small. The largest papers averaged 5.50 on a scale of 1 to 7, the medium-sized papers 5.28 and the smallest 4.86.[24]

One source available to newspaper people that carries as much credibility as you can find is Facsnet, sponsored by the Foundation for American Communications (3800 Barham Boulevard, Suite 409, Los Angeles, CA 90067-1042; telephone: 213-851-7372, fax: 213-851-9186; http://www.facsnet.org). Sources available through Facsnet have been pre-screened. Other Internet services you can rely on include Lexis, which offers full-text access to many newspapers, magazines and newsletters. Nearly every major (and not so major) newspaper, magazine, and broadcast network has its own website that you can access directly. (From time to time I call up the website of the *Wallowa County Chieftain* in eastern Oregon, where I sometimes vacation. It is exciting to catch up on the news and to see colored pictures of the rodeo at "St. Joseph Days" and snow-covered mountains 3,000 miles away.)

The NCEW has established a website (http://www.ncew.org). The site includes information about NCEW, editorial writing and journalism in general. NCEW also offers an online "mailing list," in which messages are shared among whoever chooses to speak up.[25] (Instructions for joining this mailing list can be obtained at NCEW's website.) One exchange among participants concerned how to set up procedures to obtain permission to reprint magazine articles. (See section on open pages in Chapter 19, "Innovations in Design and Content.") In another exchange an editorial writer, who had been invited to participate in a panel on editorial advisory boards, requested information from other writers who had had experience with such boards. Someone else asked if anyone knew of a good book on opinion writing. (One response was: "Well, of course, there is NCEW member Keith Runyan's text book on opinion writing." In recounting this exchange in *The Masthead*, webmaster Phineas Fiske wrote: "Here's an example of the pitfalls of online conversations . . . Ken Rystrom . . . is the textbook's author.")[26]

You don't need a computer to use the old-fashioned *Reader's Guide to Periodical Literature* (which indexes about 200 magazines) or the *New York Times* Index. The Gale Research Company produces an annual, *The Directory of Directories*, which provides a guide to nearly 10,000 directories. The *American Journalism Review* annually publishes a "Directory of Selected News Sources." Lois Horowitz has published a book titled *Knowing Where to Look*. Most public libraries have these references.

Permanent Reference Materials

Every editorial office, and certainly every good-sized library, should have a supply of reference materials that include an encyclopedia of fairly recent date, *Webster's Third International Dictionary* (or the *Second* if the writers are purists), foreign language dictionaries, a thesaurus, a quality atlas, a music dictionary or encyclopedia, a biographical dictionary (or *Current Biography*), a geographical dictionary, a medical dictionary, a legal dictionary (or at least a media law dictionary), one or more annual almanacs, a book of quotations, *Who's Who in*

America, probably *Who Was Who,* a regional *Who's Who,* the *Congressional Dictionary,* the *United States Government Manual,* the annual *Statistical Abstracts of the United States,* the *Official Postal Guide* (plus a book of ZIP codes), a state directory usually referred to as the "Blue Book," city directories going back as many years as possible, telephone books from assorted cities, the Bible, perhaps the works of Shakespeare.

Books on Language Usage

Here are a few books on language usage that may be helpful to editorial writers:

The Elements of Style. William L. Strunk Jr. and E.B. White (Boston: Allyn and Bacon, 1979, paperbound).

Working with Words: A Concise Handbook for Media Writers and Editors. 2nd ed. Brian S. Brooks and James L. Pinson (New York: St. Martin's, 1993, paperbound).

The New Fowler's Modern English Usage. 3rd ed. Edited by R.W. Burchfield (Oxford: Clarendon, 1996).

The American Heritage Book of English Usage. (Boston: Houghton Mifflin, 1996).

REA's Handbook of English Grammar, Style and Writing. (Piscataway, N.J.: Research and Education Association, 1996).

The Chicago Manual of Style. 14th ed. (Chicago: University of Chicago Press, 1993).

The Careful Writer: A Modern Guide to English Usage. Theodore M. Bernstein (New York: Atheneum, 1977).

Watch Your Language. Theodore M. Bernstein (New York: Atheneum, 1976, paperbound). Out of print; look for it in used-book stores.

The Associated Press Stylebook and Libel Manual. (paperbound).

Tools of the Trade

Members of the NCEW were asked to list three indispensable reference tools.[27] Here is the compilation of responses:

Congressional Quarterly	*Washington Post*
Wall Street Journal	*Webster's Dictionary*
Editorial Research Reports	The morning mail
Encyclopedia Britannica	WordPerfect Thesaurus
My own files	*World Almanac*
Almanac of American Politics	*Statistical Abstract*
My Rolodex, my dictionary and my wife	The Internet
	Rystrom's *The Why, Who and How of the Editorial Page*
Newspaper library	
Nexis	Macdougall's *Editorial Writing*
New York Times	The wire
Bartlett's Familiar Quotations	The telephone
Richard Morris' *Encyclopedia of American History*	The community
	The metro staff
Roget's Thesaurus	Local TV news

Stylebook
Rodale's synonym finder
Webster's synonyms
Legislative guide
The phone book
Oxford English Dictionary
The budget
Aristotle's *Rhetoric*
Foreign Affairs
One-volume *Columbia
    Encyclopedia*
A good atlas
Access to a college library
Local interviews
The criminal code
Facts on File
Grolier Yearbooks
The Bible
My own clipping files

Files of campaign literature and
    government budget papers
America Online
magazines and dictionaries
Infinet to search the
    World WideWeb
My squirrel-pile of
    possibly-useful-someday stuff
Encyclopedia of American History
    in one volume
The U.S. Constitution
State statutes
City charter
Congressional and federal staff
    directories
John Bremner's *Words on Words*
William Safire's
    Safire's Political Dictionary
Longest-serving reporter

CULTURE (POP AND OTHERWISE)

Editorial writers should know something about and be comfortable at a symphony concert, whether the orchestra is playing Beethoven or some composer whose work features only drums, cymbals and whistles. Writers should be somewhat knowledgeable about art and be comfortable at an exhibit of Monet or a local artist. They should know something about various religions and the divisions among religions even though they may not be comfortable at services that are much different from their own, if they attend them.

Editorial writers may scoff at television as trivial and entertainment-oriented. But nearly every family has at least one television set, and one show may be watched by as many as 60 million Americans. If editorial writers want to know what their fellow citizens do and think about in their leisure hours, they had best watch the tube enough to know what's on. They should watch the three network news broadcasts, the talk shows, CNN, a sampling of the cable channels and enough local broadcasts to know the types of news their readers are getting. They will never know when television is presenting quality programs unless they read *TV Guide* or the daily TV listings. Columns by television critics are worth following.

Much of radio is an intellectual wasteland. News is sketchy, except for all-news stations. But writers should know the types of songs the younger generation and not-so-young generations are listening to. They may never write an editorial about any of the top-40 tunes or country music, but they almost certainly will write about the people who listen to this music. Writers ought to tune in from time to time to the call-in programs. Public radio and public television offer more intellectual stimulation, with more extensive news coverage and programs on topics worthy of editorial comment. I would guess that many editorial writers listen to "All Things Considered," an hour and a half or more of news, comment and reports on a variety of topics aired on public radio; and that they watch the MacNeil NewsHour on public television.

Writers also need to keep abreast of the movies—not necessarily seeing every major show but making certain they are aware of what is being seen by their readers. And they should follow the newspaper comics. Most comics may be intended for entertainment, but they often provide insights into what is going on in the younger, or older, or middle generation. Some are works of art. Some carry political messages that are as forthright and controversial as any editorial on an editorial page. Editorial writers should look in on MTV.

CONCLUSION

Perhaps more than anything else, editorial writers must come to editorial writing equipped with curiosity and a good memory. They must want to find out about everything that comes within touch or sight or hearing. Editorial writers who hope to address the human condition must know about that condition in all its aspects. The specific list of books or newspapers or television programs that writers tackle is not as important as the open, searching attitude good writers bring to whatever they approach. If they are restless, energetic and curious, enough material worth examining will come to their attention to keep them on a productive search for information, insight and truth that will last a lifetime.

If what writers find in their quest goes "in one ear and out the other," the time they have spent will have been wasted. Writers must assimilate and remember—or at least remember where they can find what they want. Shakespeare and the Bible may be worth reading and rereading, and so may a few other books. But demands on the time of editorial writers are too great, and life is too short, to have to spend time searching for information and ideas that they should have tucked away in their heads or for materials that they should have at their editorial elbows.

Questions and Exercises

1. What do you regard as the ideal undergraduate preparation for a potential editorial writer? For a journalist?
2. The American Council on Education for Journalism, the national accrediting agency for journalism schools, is reluctant to allow a school to give more than a minimum number of credit hours for internships because the council considers that most of the journalism credit hours should be earned under close supervision of faculty members. Do you think that this limitation is reasonable? Why or why not?
3. Among the periodicals you are acquainted with, which do you think would prove most beneficial to an editorial writer? Why?
4. What reference books and books on writing do you consider most appropriate for your own personal library?
5. What computerized data bases are available at your school?

CHAPTER 5 Who Is This Victorian "We"?

Who would not be an editor? To write
The magic we of such enormous might:
To be so great beyond the common span
It takes the plural to express the man.
—J.G. SAXE IN *THE PRESS* (1855)[1]

A good deal of confusion exists among readers, and even among newspaper people, over the identity or identities behind the editorial "we." That confusion is reflected in a humorous piece that *The Masthead* reprinted in *Quill* magazine. It was written by Fred C. Hobson Jr., professor at the University of North Carolina. Here is a portion of it:

> It was not intended this way, but when I started to write we got so pronounly—er, profoundly—confused we changed my mind.
>
> Besides, when we sat down at my typewriter, I first-personally felt singular.
>
> Hopefully now, what I say, you see—in an editorial, why am I we? Enough poetics. Now for how I—er, we—got confused.
>
> We had an interview the other day. It went fine until we wondered if the person I was interviewing were plural too. If so, then I was we and he was they. But if I am we and he is they, then how the hell is *he*?
>
> And should was be were, if I be we? Or is be are, if she be they? . . .
>
> After all this, I've decided to stick to the editorial I. You should too. After all, there is an old adage . . . we Southerners especially like. . . . You can't legislate plurality.[2]

This confusion did not exist in the days of the Popular and Populist press in the 19th Century. When the *New York Tribune* published an editorial in the mid-1800s, readers knew who wrote it, or thought they did. Subscribers read the *Tribune* to find out what Horace Greeley had to say, and, if someone else on his staff wrote it, everyone assumed that it expressed Greeley's point of view.

When the days of the great editors began to pass, following the Civil War, it became less clear who was writing the editorials and for whom the editorials spoke. As the era of corporate newspapers emerged, editorial writers retreated anonymously into their ivory towers and took to writing what a publisher or an editorial board asked them to write. When Greeley said "we," he meant "I." When these writers used "we," they may have meant the views of "the publisher, the editor, an editorial board, or even a member of the staff or a newspaper reader who has persuaded the board of the rightness of a certain position."[3] The purpose of this chapter is to discuss who the speakers of editorials are on American newspapers today and to examine competing arguments over whom editorials ought to speak for.

The Case for the Unsigned Editorial

Surveys that show that a large majority of editorials are published anonymously suggest that the owners and publishers of most newspapers want their editorials to speak for someone or something other than an individual writer. One survey found that more than 70 percent of 178 editors and editorial writers said they never signed editorials. Sixteen percent said they signed them occasionally; 14 percent signed regularly. More signatures appeared in smaller than in larger papers.[4]

One reason advanced for unsigned editorials is that, even when written by a specific editorial writer, they reflect policy set by the paper's owner or the publisher. Robert U. Brown, editor and publisher of *Editor & Publisher*, asked: " . . . whose name should be put on the editorial when the owner-publisher—whose prerogative cannot be questioned—says 'tomorrow we will endorse such-and-such candidate and I want a strong editorial endorsing him'?"[5] An editorial writer may write all of the words of an editorial, but the editorial speaks for the publisher. No editorial writer, on the basis of his or her own convictions, "has a right to demand a share of ownership's private forum," Floyd A. Bernard of the *Port Huron* (Mich.) *Times Herald* has written.[6]

But with the trend toward group ownership, publisher domination of editorial pages may be waning, if results of a poll conducted in 1988 are an indication. Twenty-seven percent of editorial writers on family or independently owned newspapers reported that their owners or publishers exerted little or no influence in determining priority given to editorial topics. In contrast, little or no influence was reported by 72 percent of writers on private group-owned papers and by 77 percent on public group-owned papers. The poll also revealed what appeared to be a widening gap between the political views of publishers and editorial writers. In a 1979 survey 62 percent of editorial writers had said that their views and their publishers' were similar on most issues. In 1989 that percentage dropped to 47. The percentage of those who agreed with their publishers only about half the time increased from 24 to 33.[7]

These figures seemed in line with the results of a survey in 1980 that showed that 85 percent of group editors did not ever consult with group headquarters before taking a controversial editorial stand; 11 percent said they did consult. In contrast, 71 percent of editors on independently owned papers said they consulted with owners, compared to 27 percent who did not.[8] (Of course, the local owner or publisher was likely to be in an adjoining office.) A symposium conducted by *The Masthead* found that 11 out of 12 groups surveyed reported that editorial policies were set at the local level. A representative of the Gannett Co., owners of more daily newspapers than any other group, reported that local editors and publishers were free to determine their own editorial policies. He said that Gannett asked local executives a lot of questions about business and technology, "but how the newspapers stand on this or that editorial policy is *not* one of the queries because that would violate the local autonomy that has been a keystone of the Group policy ever since the late Frank E. Gannett began accumulating newspapers. . . . "[9]

Another of the large groups, then known as Knight and later to become Knight-Ridder, "chooses its editors carefully and gives them their heads," an editor reported. He said the group had no "corporate line" or "group line" on editorial policy, "but neither does the top management of the organization have a 'don't-give-a-damn' view of the individual paper's editorial policies." For months editorial writers would not hear from headquarters. When they did, comment was informal, and editors who disagreed with the comment were free to state their views and go on about their business.[10]

The only decidedly different report came from Merrill Lindsay, president of Lindsay-Schaub Newspapers, who said that local papers had full responsibility for policy on local issues, but that on state, national and international issues, a group of editorial writers at a central office researched and wrote the editorials.[11]

An article in *Journalism Quarterly* questioned whether local papers were as autonomous as the respondents to the survey had insisted. After studying presidential endorsements from 1960 through 1972, the authors found that the vast majority of groups had generally homogeneous endorsement patterns in those elections—data that "would appear to contradict clearly" the proposition that group-owned newspapers were independent in their political endorsement policies.[12] The study did not attempt to look at endorsements at state or local levels or at editorial stands on other issues, where group influence might be expected to be less.

If an increasing number of editorials do not reflect policies of the owners, and perhaps not even those of the publishers, for whom do they speak?

The most often heard explanation for unsigned institutional editorials is that they express more than one person's opinion. *Editor & Publisher*'s Brown pointed out that many times an editorial is not the product of one writer's opinion "but the amalgam of thought pounded out in an editorial conference of several people." He wondered what purpose it would serve to attach to the editorial "the name of the technician (a skilled editorial writer, albeit) who was assigned to express in words the agreed-upon thought or policy?"[13] The opinion might be a general one worked out over time among writers on a paper, or it might be worked out on a single issue during a morning editorial conference. In any case the writer would be expressing a combination of ideas. It might then make as much sense to put every staff member's name on the editorial as that of the actual writer. Sometimes the actual writing of an editorial will end up being the work of more than one person. Most editorials must pass through an editor or a publisher before they go into print. Since the editor or the publisher has the final say, the end product may be slightly, or greatly, different from the original version. Whose name, or names, should go on in this case? The original writer might not want to be identified with the editorial after the editor or the publisher has made substantial changes.

Sometimes institutional editorials are explained as something more than the sum of the opinions of the members of the editorial page staff. "Editorials express the opinion of an institution, sometimes older than the writer," a Florida editor argued in response to a bill in the Florida Legislature that would have required editorial writers to sign their names.[14] "Editorial writers come and go. . . . But The Paper stays in the community for decades, through depression and prosperity," another editor wrote.[15]

Some defenders contend that unsigned editorials carry more weight with readers because they are not just the personal opinion of an individual. "A signed editorial carries about as much punch as a letter to the editor," Ann Merriman of the *Richmond* (Va.) *News Leader* wrote in arguing that signed editorials have no place under the masthead of a newspaper's editorial page, "even though it would be a good thing if every editorial were written as if it were to be signed."[16]

What about the one-person editorial page staff where it is fairly obvious who is writing the editorials? When Michael J. Birkner took over as editorial writer for the *Concord* (N.H.) *Monitor*, he wrote a bylined column introducing himself. He explained that he would become the "anonymous voice" that henceforth would appear every day in the upper-left-hand corner of the opinion page. "The anonymous voice representing the opinion of this newspaper is, of course, not truly anonymous," he wrote. "A fallible, flesh and blood person can be found behind the 600 or so words that fill the editorial space every day. . . . The editorial 'we,' in this case, is me."[17]

Editorial Boards

On a number of newspapers, probably a growing number, the editorial "we" is an editorial board. In some cases it remains anonymous to readers, but in other cases the masthead on the editorial page identifies the names and positions of board members. The makeup of boards varies widely. In some instances the board is limited to members of the editorial page staff. In addition some boards include an editor with responsibility for both news and editorial departments, the publisher (or general manager) or representatives of other departments of the newspaper. In some instances not all staff members who write editorials are included on the board. Some newspapers have experimented with asking people outside the newspaper to serve on editorial boards. The *Hartford Courant* has invited readers to spend two to three months as visiting members of its board, and to participate in all deliberations. (The part-time job paid an honorarium of approximately $200 a week.)[18]

The main purpose of an editorial board is to set general editorial policy. In addition, a board might determine editorial stands on major issues and decide on editorial endorsements. The power that boards exert over the day-to-day editorials varies greatly from paper to paper. Meetings may be formal or informal, regular or irregular.

Richard T. Cole, a professor of public relations, has suggested that the editorial board is a "great charade" or at least a "polite fiction" on most newspapers. Citing the two major dailies in Detroit, he wrote in *The Masthead*: "Neither has a formal editorial board, although I would venture to say I could introduce you to dozens of politicians, business, labor, association and public relations leaders who would say they have appeared before them. There are no voting members, no quorums, no amendments, no regular meetings, no public notice. Editorial chiefs assemble colleagues and staff to hear a case. My guess is that if an important person insists on meeting the editorial board, the meeting gets called an 'editorial board meeting,' and the innocent fiction lives on. Long live the editorial board."[19]

Cole's experience may reflect the practices, or lack of practices, of some newspapers, but it certainly does not coincide with my perception, based on examining editorial pages from across the country. It seems evident to me that more and more newspapers are establishing formal editorial boards to make clear to policy-setters and readers just who speaks for the editorial "we."

Sometimes the first-person plural in an editorial can be confusing or amusing. Examples of both occurred in an editorial in the Eugene, Ore., *Register-Guard* about a local young woman who was among the first women admitted to Virginia Military Institute. The editorial began this way: "At 17, many of us would have told Beth Hogan: 'You can have it.'" Readers might wonder whether the newspaper has so many editorial writers that it can refer to "many of us." Of course, on second thought, most people will recognize that "us" means readers as well as editorial writers (or even people in general). Later, however, the editorial uses "we" to refer to the newspaper: "We hope she's also physically, mentally and emotionally tough." Then comes, to my mind at least, a humorous image: "We would no more attend VMI than we would bungee-jump off the U.S. Bank building in downtown Eugene." Who is this "we" that declines to bungee-jump? It's hard to imagine a *newspaper* jumping. It's also hard to imagine an entire editorial page staff jumping (maybe holding hands together as they go down?). More seriously, the reference suggests that more than one person wrote the editorial. Of course, an editorial may have been edited or modified by one or more persons before it reaches print, but most editorials are *written* by one person.

A few newspapers have opened their editorial board meetings to the public. George Neavoll recalled that editorial colleagues around the country were "aghast" when they heard of his open-door policy at the *Wichita Eagle-Beacon*. "It's good for the editorial writers, myself included, to have real, live readers in our midst as we make our editorial decisions," he said. "Their presence reminds us that our editorials are written for people, after all, not for some bloodless amalgam without form and void."[20]

THE CASE FOR THE SIGNED EDITORIAL

The most persistently heard objection to unsigned editorials, and the most frequently heard argument for signed editorials, is that editorials are generally the work of individuals and that, while they may reflect some broad newspaper policies, the thinking and the words that go into them are more important than any general philosophy. A flamboyant argument along these lines, in the form of an attack on "editorial transubstantiation," was made by Sam Reynolds of the *Missoulian* in Missoula, Mont. In Roman Catholic and Eastern

Orthodox rites, bread and wine are transubstantiated (or converted) into the body and blood of Christ although their appearance is unchanged. "I view editorial transubstantiation with less awe," he wrote. "Editorial transubstantiation is the basis for editorial anonymity. It is not a miracle; it is nonsense." He argued that "flesh-and-blood human beings" write editorials, and usually it is only one of them who does so. How does the work of a human being become the product of an institution? "The answer must lie in faith, not fact," Reynolds said. Editorial transubstantiation "is merely a lie; a lie eloquently defended by its many priests, but in the end a complete lie."

When Reynolds switched from unsigned to signed editorials he found that he was no longer blamed for editorials that someone else had written and that the advertising staff no longer had to "fend off attacks from persons aroused by my editorials." He also found his editorials had more influence, and he felt that signing editorials was more honest than pretending that editorials represented an institution.[21]

A similarly rewarding experience was reported by George J. Hebert of the *Norfolk* (Va.) *Ledger-Star*, which began attaching writers' names to opinion pieces in 1976. The switch attracted wide attention in editorial writing circles. In announcing the change, the editors said readers had told them that they wanted to know who was writing the editorials. "There will be real people with real names on our end of what we hope will be a continuing exchange of views between us and our readers," the editors said. They hoped to give their writers freer rein and an opportunity to "have more time to probe issues and sharpen their comments." The change elicited almost unanimous approval by readers. The paper additionally emphasized its writers by inserting sketches of their faces alongside the editorials.[22]

The most elaborate case for signed editorials was a two-part series in *The Masthead* written by Professor Warren G. Bovee of Marquette University.[23] Bovee set out to debunk what he saw as seven myths about editorial anonymity.

The first myth was that newspapers traditionally have run unsigned editorials. Our look into the history of the editorial page in Chapter 1 has shown that anonymity is only about a century old.

The second myth was that editorials represent the views of the paper, not an individual. Bovee argued that, "until the time arrives when editorial positions are decided by the total personnel of a newspaper. . . . it is misleading to attribute those positions to 'The Paper' . . . ." While publishers might set broad guidelines, he likened them to "the ball field within which the editorial writers must still decide how to play the game." He said that "editorial writers say more than most publishers would ever think of saying."

The third myth, that editorials represent an editorial conference point of view, could be resolved by all members signing the editorial, he argued.

A fourth myth, that "anonymity is necessary to protect the writer from verbal and physical abuses," Bovee saw as the "real, secret reason" why readers think editors do not sign editorials. His comment was that writers ought to be as subject to "phone calls, crank letters, crosses burned on the lawn and stones thrown through picture windows" as readers whose signed letters also appear on editorial pages. My own experience is that this fear of personal abuse figures minimally in editorial anonymity. Most editorial writers I know would appreciate more public recognition.

A fifth myth is that, if an editorial is signed, it becomes only a personal article or column. But Bovee contended that signed pieces by William Randolph Hearst and Jenkin Lloyd Jones were regarded as editorials.

As to a sixth myth, that unsigned editorials carry more weight, Bovee argued that the impact depends more on what the editorial says than on who signs it.

To the seventh myth, that there are no good reasons for signing editorials, Bovee replied that signing might help overcome reader mistrust of newspapers, giving writers greater freedom to write. "If the occasion demands it," he said, "the signed piece can be as personal and informal as a love letter, or it can be as formal and impersonal as a doctoral dissertation."

Finally, Bovee argued, when a paper has a number of editorial writers, there are bound to be occasions on which the writers disagree with one another. By allowing each to offer his or her view with a byline, the paper would have a more interesting editorial page.

When editors of *The Masthead* asked 11 editorial writers to describe the "we" for whom they spoke, nine remained firmly committed to speaking anonymously for the newspaper, two expressed some interest in departing from anonymity, but only one took a strong stand for signed editorials. That one, Everett Ray Call of the *Emporia* (Kan.) *Gazette*, argued that writers who sign their names are likely to take more pride in their work and make more effort to check their facts than writers who know they will not directly be associated with what they write. He also thought that, in a time when people feel overwhelmed by institutions and readers see newspapers as corporate units, signing editorials helps readers relate more closely to their newspapers. While the *Gazette* had gained a name for personal journalism in the early 20th century when William Allen White had become editor and publisher, the practice of signing editorials came much later, following publication of an anthology that was supposed to include only editorials of William Allen White. After the book was published, White noticed that about two-thirds of the editorials in the last section had not been written by him but by his son, William L. White. "Since then," Call wrote, "initials have been used at the end of editorials that appear in the *Gazette*."[24]

A case for using initials, at least sometimes, was offered by Robert Schmuhl, associate professor of American studies at the University of Notre Dame.[25] His interest in identifying writers grew out of his students' reports that they found editorials "bland and boring." One answer to "Why?" was: "It's as though there's no one behind what's being said."

"Initialing editorials provides an authorial recognition in an understated yet useful way," Schmuhl wrote. "The writer receives credit for composing the editorial, while the finished product appears in a manner quite distinct from a bylined column or even a signed editorial." He hoped that "this modest attribution" would encourage previously anonymous writers to write in a "more engaging, spirited and possibly more persuasive way." The newspaper would appear to have a human voice. "We" would continue to be used. Editorial writers' names would be listed in the masthead.

A COMPROMISE—BYLINED ARTICLES AND COLUMNS

Some of the fire may have been taken out of the debate over signed editorials by an increasing use of articles and columns bearing the names of editorial writers. Publishers have been able to give their writers public recognition and increased opportunities to express their individual views without giving up the principle of the institutionalized editorial. One survey of editorial writers found that almost all of them wrote signed articles, as contrasted with signed editorials, at least on occasion.[26] In a 1994 survey 30 percent of editorial writers said they were using a more personal writing style.[27]

The advantages most cited in the survey were that signed articles help make the editorial page more human, allow for more casual and informal writing and provide more space than editorials for background or firsthand accounts, especially about local matters. Less often mentioned was the function of the signed article as an expression of a writer's views that might be at variance with the paper's editorial policy. This function can provide an outlet for frustrated editorial writers, but it also can cause problems. Some publishers may be willing to allow writers to express contrary opinions; some publishers may not. Some publishers may be willing to allow writers to disagree on some issues but not on others.

Most publishers probably would have no objection to the balance between signed and unsigned pieces that we maintained on the *Columbian*, in Vancouver, Wash. In my later years there, when three of us were writing for the editorial page, I urged other writers to write bylined articles and on occasion to write pro-con articles, with each person signing one of the articles. We did not use those articles to express opinions directly opposed to the official editorial policy, but through the use of the byline we gained a greater feeling of editorial freedom for ourselves.

If most newspapers have been reluctant to give up the anonymous editorial "we," they have at least largely abandoned the "we" in personal columns and in obvious references to individuals. The change in philosophy on this point can be illustrated by the case of David V. Felts, who wrote a personal column for half a century for the Lindsay-Schaub newspapers. After his retirement Felts wrote an article for *The Masthead* in which he said: "I chose to use first-person plural 'we' in order to avoid the capital I, which seemed at the time . . . to suggest a vanity I did not care to confess, or an arrogance I would deny. So I rejected Teddy Roosevelt's 'I' and instead went along with Queen Victoria's 'We.'" However, Felts acknowledged, logical extension of the "editorial we" can be embarrassing and even ridiculous. He recalled that on one occasion a radio disc jockey, who was a friend of his, quoted from his column. Felts wrote: "I had written, so he read, 'When we stepped on the bathroom scales this morning. . . .' Then my friend observed: 'Oh, well, couples who weigh together, stay together.'" Felts then wrote: "Should I someday be assigned to one of those golden typewriters in the great city room in the sky to write celestial chit-chat, I will use the first person singular pronoun, even if only a modest, chastened lower-case i. Queen Victoria probably will not be amused, but Teddy Roosevelt surely will be 'dee-lighted.'"[28]

There is no historical evidence, or even a suggestion, that Horace Greeley could have done what Dave Felts did—look back years later and laugh at a ridiculous use of "we." Greeley's editorials abounded with "we's." In 1846, for example, Greeley was recalling the first election in which he had taken an interest, the presidential race of 1824: "We were but thirteen when this took place."[29]

PERSONAL EXPERIENCES

In my 12 years on the *Columbian*, we ran editorials that were not signed, presumably to indicate to readers that they represented the opinions of the newspaper, not just one person. But I would have counted myself as among those who did not consult with the owners in most cases. My co-publishers and I had spent considerable time, before they hired me, sounding out each others' views. When they decided we were compatible, they, in effect, handed me the editorial "we" to use as I wished (subject of course to cancellation at any time they thought we should go our separate ways). On occasion the publishers were not wholly pleased with what I had written, but for the most part they kept silent. At one point one of the publishers thought the paper should be taking a stronger stand in favor of legalizing marijuana, but he made no attempt to change the policy. On another occasion I found out (several months later) that this publisher had not been in sympathy with the paper's strident opposition to plans to expand Portland International Airport onto a square mile of fill in the Columbia River. But he had made no effort to soften or change our editorial stand.

You learn who the real "we" is during elections, especially presidential ones. In the 1972 election my publishers had their minds set on endorsing Richard Nixon for re-election, and neither the other editorial writer on the paper nor I could budge them from that decision. We argued no endorsement, since we saw neither Nixon nor George McGovern as meriting our support. I wrote an editorial pointing out the weaknesses of both candidates, but the publishers wouldn't consider it. I suggested that it be published as a signed article elsewhere on the editorial page. The publishers said no; readers might be confused by conflicting viewpoints on the page. Neither the other writer nor I was required to write the Nixon editorial. A semi-retired former managing editor, who had written editorials over the years, accepted the assignment.

The only other disagreement over who "we" was in those 12 years also involved an election, this one for a local judgeship. The publishers had their candidate. Two other editorial writers and I preferred another candidate, although we would have settled for kind words for both. In this instance the publishers agreed to look at an editorial that said either candidate would be a good judge. What emerged in print, however, was an editorial, using many of the words I had written, that added praise for the publishers' choice and a firm conclusion backing their candidate. That was one occasion when it would have been impossible to have put one person's name on an editorial.

CONCLUSION

The pendulum that had swung so far from the personal journalism of Horace Greeley to the anonymity of the corporate newspaper has begun to swing back. A small, but seemingly growing, number of newspapers publish signed or initialed editorials. Many more promote the identities of editorial writers through encouraging signed articles and columns and by listing names on mastheads. Some writers are allowed to express opinions contrary to their newspapers' official policies.

Editorial writers are getting out of their offices and becoming better known in their communities. Editorial writers are also strengthening their positions on editorial boards. Editors on group newspapers think they have more independence from management in setting editorial policy than do editors on independent papers. On all papers, personal expertise provides the best opportunity for editorial writers to achieve stronger and more public voices. In an era of complex issues, writers who know what they are talking about stand a good chance of convincing not only their readers but also their editors and publishers. They stand a good chance of getting a piece of the editorial "we."

Whether editorials are signed or unsigned, newspapers perform a service to their readers—and bolster their own credibility—when they spell out exactly who determines editorial policy. Readers should have the right to know who is telling them what to think and what to do.

In even the most compatible relationships between editorial writers and publishers, writers are almost certain to find out from time to time that, as smart and knowledgeable as they think they are, they are not the final bosses. If they have too many disagreements, they need to find other jobs or try some other lines of work.

I asked students in one of my editorial writing classes about the types of disagreement they thought they could tolerate with a publisher. Almost to a person, they said they would quit if asked to write an editorial contrary to their opinions on apartheid or abortion, but they generally would not quit because of disagreement over a president, a local judge or a school bond measure. "I don't think that editorials endorsing presidential candidates really make that much impact on the voters," one student said, but on abortion she would tell her publisher that, because of her "religious belief and moral attitudes, I could not write an editorial that supported taking away legalized abortion." She said she would ask "very nicely" to have someone else write it, and "take the consequences of my actions."[30]

Questions and Exercises

1. Try to find a newspaper with signed or initialed editorials and read them for three or four days. Compare them in terms of tone and style with unsigned editorials on the same subjects published in other newspapers. Do you think that readers would respond differently to these editorials?

2. Look through a number of editorial and op-ed pages of papers in your area. Try to find bylined opinion articles by editorial staff members. Do these articles express opinions that differ from the papers' editorials? Analyze how a reader is likely to respond to specific editorials and opinion articles that express different views.

3. Select an editorial with which you disagree and write a signed opinion piece expressing your view that would be suitable to publish alongside the editorial.

4. Select several editorials that use the editorial "we" in referring to the newspaper's opinion. Does the "we" clearly convey the impression of a corporate opinion behind the editorial? Rewrite the sentences to make the same point without the use of "we."

5. Can you find a column in which the writer refers to himself or herself with the Victorian "we"? Could "I" have been used just as well?
6. Write a letter to an editorial writer on one of the papers in your area to ask about specific instances in which he or she and the editor or publisher might have disagreed on issues. How were the disagreements resolved? Did the writer end up producing an editorial he or she disagreed with? Was he or she allowed or encouraged to write a dissenting opinion? How often and on what kinds of issues has disagreement occurred?
7. Can you uncover, perhaps by reading *Editor & Publisher*, instances in which editorial writers have resigned or moved to non-editorial positions because of disagreement over editorial policy?

CHAPTER 6 Relations with Publishers

When they drew up the Bill of Rights in the late 1780s, the Founding Fathers did not have to worry about whether they intended freedom of the press to apply to publishers or to editors because most of the printers who produced periodicals, books, pamphlets and handbills were owner editors. The authors of the First Amendment anticipated, in the words of Hugh B. Patterson Jr. of the *Arkansas Gazette,* "that the editor would most likely be the owner whose resources as well as reputation would be at stake; that newspapers would be vigorous critics and advocates on public questions; that newspapers would generally be locally owned and controlled; and that readers would have available from different publications a variety of views, sometimes directly competitive, from which to choose, whether the question was local, regional or national in scope."[2]

Today the editor and the owner (or publisher) most often are not the same person. With the demise of the owner-editor, the relationship between editor and publisher became what Bernard Kilgore called "a new kind of problem." Kilgore experienced the problem from both sides, as editor and then later publisher of the *Wall Street Journal.* "The question which somebody is likely to ask," Kilgore said, is "whether publishers are necessary."[3] In any other industry, he said, the job parallel to that of publisher would be clear: He or she would hire and fire. But in the newspaper business, "that's where we get into all the trouble. . . . A publisher just does not hire and fire editors because our business is not that kind of business." The difference is that the product a newspaper sells is "a completely intangible thing." Newspaper people should remind themselves that all the physical plant and machinery around the newspaper business provide only the package or container of the product, "just something to wrap up the ideas that editors have" and carry these ideas to the public. But the newspaper business has become "a great big manufacturing operation and great big selling operation," Kilgore said. Consequently, "the general management of a newspaper has more and more come to be regarded as a job for a manufacturer or a salesman, and the editorial function . . . has tended to become a secondary consideration."[4]

LOCAL VS. GROUP OWNERSHIP

The era of the local family-owned newspaper may look rosier in retrospect than it actually was. Many papers did not make enough profit to produce a good product. Some of the owner-publishers did not know what a good journalistic product was, and some didn't care. But the publishers were products of their communities and those who wished could do what they wanted with their papers without worrying about satisfying a bigger boss somewhere else. The publisher-editor who runs the whole show "in theory . . . is the happiest of mortals, if he can keep his separate selves from warring with one another," wrote Donald L. Breed, editor-publisher of the Freeport, Ill., *Journal-Standard.*[5] Even those owner-publishers who did not write editorials tended to dominate their papers. Editorial writers tended to be "anonymous wretches," as Ralph Coghlan of the *St. Louis Post-Dispatch* referred to writers who attended the first meeting of the National Conference of Editorial Writers (NCEW) in 1947. Indeed, a survey of editorial writers in 1951 found that fewer than 50 percent thought they could stand up for what they believed without risking financial disaster and 63 percent said they wrote opinions that were not always their own.[6]

Since then, group ownership has come to most cities with daily newspapers. Most publishers are no longer home-grown. Often they are sent in for a few years, then transferred elsewhere. Another publisher from another community is brought in. Many of these group publishers are strictly business people.

A survey of newspaper editors sponsored by the American Society of Newspaper Editors found that editors who worked for a group thought they had better career opportunities and greater access to shared ideas, financial resources and outside experts, while editors on independent papers had larger newsroom budgets, a closer involvement with their communities, less bureaucracy and "a tendency to be peculiar."[7]

This survey and an earlier one under the same sponsor suggest group ownership may offer some advantages for editors and editorial writers. The first survey found that, before taking a stand on a controversial issue, 85 percent of group editors said they did not consult with group headquarters, while only 27 percent of independent editors said they did not consult with their owners.[8] In the more recent survey, 39 percent of group editors said they had consulted the publishers (or group headquarters) six or more times during the preceding 12 months before taking a controversial stand, compared to 50 percent of independent editors.[9] These figures suggest that out-of-town ownership and non-newspaper-oriented publishers may provide opportunities for editorial writers on group newspapers to emerge less cautiously and more outspokenly from publisher's offices and editorial conference rooms.

A survey conducted by David Demers, however, suggested that it was not group ownership but the corporate form of the organization that accounted for the relative freedom to set editorial policy. In corporate newspapers, he concluded, the owners and top managers were "more insulated" because they generally came from out of town and stayed for relatively brief periods; their orientation was more to the corporation than to the community. He also suggested the decisions made by corporate editors tended to be "more heavily influenced by professional norms and values, which place a higher premium on truth and criticism than on local parochial interests."[10] Demers also found that corporate papers run more editorials and letters, carry more staff-written pieces and publish more editorials critical of mainstream groups.[11]

Somewhat similar results were found in a survey of editors of independent and group-owned newspapers, who were asked to identify what they saw as the principal editorial roles of their newspapers. Those who conducted the survey were surprised to find that differences were less between independent and group newspapers than among large, medium and small groups. Editors with the larger groups more often identified their newspaper's editorial role as "adversary," "global interpreter" and "critical watchdog." The surveyors interpreted the findings as suggesting that, as the news organizations increase in size and prominence, their "editorial orientations" tend increasingly toward activism. They concluded that this tendency could be good or bad depending on whether the larger organizations "choose to harness their structurally determined editorial activism to promote their own ends or to serve the public interest."[12]

A study of editorials in cities with two newspapers found that, unless the newspapers had different ownerships, chances were slim for substantial differences in editorial policies. If the newspapers operated under a Joint Operating Agreement, they were as similar in their editorial policies as joint monopoly newspapers were.[13]

Of course each year more independent newspapers are taken over by groups, and the groups are getting larger and larger. If these studies are to be believed, there is some good news: Perhaps editorial pages will become aggressive, more critical of mainstream groups and ideas. But it seems ironic that this supposed benefit has been made possible because the new newspaper managers are more concerned about corporate issues than local affairs.

A dying breed as they are, locally-owned family newspapers should not be sold short. Some of the best newspapers that I am personally acquainted with are still (at least basically) family-owned: the *Free Lance–Star* in Fredericksburg, Va., the *Riverside Press-Enterprise* in California, the Eugene *Register-Guard* in Oregon, the *Columbian* in Vancouver, Wash., and the *Daily News* in Longview, Wash.

An editorial page, however, can be restricted as much by financial as by editorial restraints. When a newspaper is locally owned, the publisher can determine the profit levels that seem proper and desirable. But, with group newspapers, budgets and required profit margins tend to be set at group headquarters. In addition, with groups and major newspapers going public and selling stock on the market, owners are becoming even more concerned about profits. If profits lag, the stock is likely to fall in value. If the newspaper ventures into an area of controversy in its news or editorial columns—and perhaps stakes its reputation in tackling a sensitive public issue—the paper's stock may skid in value. Robert T. Pittman of the *St. Petersburg* (Fla.) *Times* perceived "a basic conflict" between an editor's responsibility to readers and the responsibility of an investor-owned newspaper to its stockholders: "What's good for Media General stock isn't necessarily what's good for the country."[14]

Defenders of groups contend that ownership of several papers allows the groups to use their combined resources to enable an individual paper to stand up to the pressures of advertisers or other special interests. That may be true, if the owners are sufficiently dedicated to the newspaper business to be willing to forgo some of the profits while the paper fights its battle. But, if the publishers and groups must answer to stockholders who are interested in profit, not journalism, it may not be possible to remain so idealistic.

David Halberstam, in *The Powers That Be*, noted that the Washington Post Company had gone public only two days before publisher Katharine Graham had to decide whether to defy the government and publish the Pentagon Papers. "The shadow of the stock hung very much over the editorial deliberations," Halberstam wrote. "The timing for everyone concerned could not have been worse. In addition to everything else, there was one little clause in the legal agreement for the sale of the stock that said that the sale could be canceled if a catastrophic event struck the paper." If the government halted distribution of the *Post*, that might be such an event; so might an indictment for contempt of court. The effect on the stock was one of the matters considered by the *Post* in deciding to follow the lead of the *New York Times* in publishing the papers.[15] Court injunctions obtained by the federal government temporarily halted publication, but a 6-3 decision by the U.S. Supreme Court removed the injunctions and allowed the newspapers to resume publication.

In a growing number of instances newspapers and other media have become only minor parts of corporations with investments in a variety of industries. At best, the media owned by these conglomerates are viewed as business operations that must produce their share of the corporation's revenue. At worst, the conglomerate may view profitable media as sources of funds to shore up its weaker operations. Corporations that were once primarily newspaper-oriented have become involved in telephone-book publishing, timber, cable television, billboards, Bibles, television, radio and magazines. Diversity may help ensure profitability and stability, but it also tends to produce a corporative hierarchy that is primarily business- rather than newspaper-oriented. Basic decision-making is removed farther from the editor and editorial writer. When these large corporations are committed to doing a good job in news and editorial operations they have the resources to do so. But when they are not committed to doing a good job, chances are slim for influencing their editorial priorities.

THE PUBLISHER'S ROLE

Weighing on the publisher's mind almost as heavily as making a profit is maintaining "harmonious relations" among employees. Publishers like to run smooth operations and generally do not like to employ personalities that clash. Publishers dislike friction between news and advertising or between news and editorial operations. Publishers tend to subscribe to the philosophy expressed in *The Economics of the American Newspaper*, by Jon G. Udell, which suggests to news and editorial people that the entire newspaper staff is in this together and that no one can benefit without everyone helping. So why doesn't everyone cooperate and forget differences of opinion and interest?"[16]

One of the threats to the why-can't-everyone-be-friends atmosphere is posed by the publisher's responsibility to negotiate with labor unions. Most editorial writers do not have to worry about coming into conflict with the publisher in contract negotiations, since most are excluded from newsroom organized labor groups. But a publisher who is worried about a threatening strike, or angered by what he or she sees as an unfair tilt of federal or state labor relations laws, may hold a strong opinion about what editorial writers ought to be saying concerning organized labor. More than one newspaper has departed from its generally moderate-to-liberal social philosophy when the subject of labor has arisen.

Since publishers' first concerns are usually to function successfully in the economy, they are also likely to have firm views on business topics. "There is one special interest always present, and that is the pro-capitalist bias of a newspaper," publisher-editor Donald L. Breed wrote. "Privately owned and operated newspapers are expressions of newspaper enterprise, and they must make a profit to survive. . . . Therefore, it must be taken for granted that American newspapers will support the free enterprise system."[17] But the free enterprise system has been made substantially less free by government support and protection of business, direct and indirect government intervention in the economy and increasing control by huge corporations. Commenting intelligently on the economy these days requires a lot more information and sophistication than it used to. Publishers may be up-to-date on economic matters affecting their own businesses and fellow local merchants. They may also be familiar with property and income taxes, state and federal health and safety requirements, unemployment and workmen's compensation, and perhaps local zoning and building regulations. While experiences in these areas may provide publishers with some insights for editorial comment, they need to recognize that they are parties with special interests in these matters.

If publishers have contributions to make in evaluating economic issues, they probably have fewer to make in other areas. It is not that publishers, given time and resources, are not smart enough to hold their own with editorial writers. But most publishers are likely to have neither the time nor the frame of mind for knowledgeable editorial writing. Publishers are often hard-pressed to find time to read their own newspapers thoroughly. (One of my publishers, acknowledging this difficulty, asked that his staff forewarn him about any news or editorial items that were likely to bring him a phone call or personal comment.) Publishers simply do not have the time to be editorial writers. Therein lie the makings of both conflict and a good working relationship between publisher and writer.

If publishers try to act as editorial writers, they are likely to drive the editorial staff out the door, up the wall or into the closet. The result will be a weak, submissive staff that stands no chance of putting out a vigorous editorial page. On the other hand, if publishers allow themselves to be too busy to think about the editorial page or to discuss ideas and issues with the writers, conflict is likely to occur at some point. The publisher should exercise leadership continuously and cooperatively, rather than intermittently and imperiously. Almost as annoying as having publishers constantly breathing down the necks of editorial writers is having them descend suddenly and unpredictably into the editorial department.

Surveys of publishers and opinion-page editors found substantial participation—but not necessarily control—by publishers in editorial policy-making. Sixty-two percent of the publishers said they attended editorial page conferences at least once or twice a week. Sixty-six percent said they express their views at these conferences most of the time. Forty-five percent said they discuss social, economic and political issues with executives once a day; another 33 percent once a week. Fifty-nine percent said they had the final decision on editorials. At the same time, the same percentage of publishers said they were "not concerned" or "only a little concerned" that the writing of editorial page staff members may not be consistent with the newspaper's editorial stands.[18] As noted in Chapter 5, "Who Is This Victorian 'We'?" about three-quarters of editorial writers on group-owned newspapers reported that owners and publishers exerted little or no influence in determining the priority given to editorial topics.[19]

One of my publishers used to say that he expected disagreements to arise between us, although he expected me to convince him of my point of view most of the time, since I (presumably) knew more about the subject than he did. That usually proved to be the case, or at least he let me think so. The degree of freedom that individual editors achieve thus lies partly within their own control. As author Robinson Scott has said, editors owe whatever freedom they enjoy to "force of character, . . . knowledge and the strength of [their] convictions."[20]

GETTING ALONG WITH PUBLISHERS

Relationships between editors and publishers probably vary as widely as do the personalities of editors and publishers. The relationship depends partly on the rules that are set when a publisher hires an editor. Some publishers and editors are easy to get along with; some are not. Some personalities work better together in an editor-publisher relationship than others. Publishers and editors are almost certain to encounter some differences of opinion. (The survey of publishers and editors mentioned above found that the two groups gave measurably different opinions when asked a series of questions about liberal, conservative and pragmatic issues, but neither group was consistently more liberal or more conservative than the other.)[21]

Disagreeing with the Publisher

The first thing that editors need to recognize is that, even in the most congenial relations, an editor and a publisher are bound to disagree from time to time. "Editorial-page editors and their publishers should fight," in the opinion of Meg Downey, editorial page editor of the *Poughkeepsie* (N.Y.) *Journal*. "How else can a paper consistently come up with good editorials? 'Good' in the sense of researched, definitive, you-can-tell-where-we-stand editorials. Arguing helps clarify positions and quickly knocks down ones that are poorly defended."[22] David Holwerk of the *Lexington* (Ky.) *Herald-Leader* made the point more picturesquely: Conflicts are not inevitable, he said, "if either you or your publisher is a brain-dead cretin who doesn't give a fresh-frozen's rat's rump what your paper stands for."[23]

Of course no editorial writer wants to be constantly battling with the publisher over policy, if for no other reason than that when fights go all the way to the mat, the publisher almost always has the authority to win and usually does.

A survey of editorial page writers concluded, however, that communication channels with publishers are "fairly" open. "Not only do editors in all circulation categories indicate a high frequency of opinion exchange at [editorial] conferences with publishers, but they also stress that editors' opinions prevailed in these conferences very frequently." The writers reported that publishers very infrequently pressured them to write editorials from a certain viewpoint. The survey found that opinions of editorial writers expressed in editorial conferences were (slightly) more likely to prevail on the larger newspapers. Writers on middle-sized papers were (slightly) more likely to meet with their publishers during editorial conferences. The middle-sized-paper editors also were (slightly) more likely to be asked to write editorials from certain viewpoints, but the frequency was very low on all three sizes of newspapers.[24]

Choosing a Publisher

The first advice for editorial writers is to choose their papers and publishers carefully. Writers need to know enough about the personality of a prospective publisher to have a pretty good idea that they can get along despite disagreements. They need to know enough about the prospective newspaper's editorial policy so that they can, in most cases, feel comfortable writing editorials expressing that policy.

Throughout the country editorial writers looking for jobs may find some middle-of-the-road (apple pie and motherhood) newspapers on which writers of moderate convictions might be able to muddle through a lifetime of editorial writing. Kenneth McArdle of the *Chicago Daily News* may have had these papers in mind when he said, referring to publishers, "Generally speaking, it would be hard to be utterly out of synch with them unless you, yourself, were on the kooky side, because they tend to be rational people."[25] But at least some newspapers, to their credit, have stronger editorial convictions, and, fortunately, so do some editorial writers and would-be writers. Nevertheless, unless a writer's views fall within the middle 50 to 60 percent of the political spectrum, opportunities for signing on with a congenial editorial page are limited.

The task of finding a congenial editorial page may also be more difficult today than in earlier times because journalists don't seem to hop around the country from newspaper to newspaper as much as they once did. They get married, raise families, buy houses and try to find decent school systems in attractive communities. They put their roots into their communities and may develop as deep a concern for them as any publisher. Their concern for and knowledge of their communities, in fact, may go deeper than publishers' because of the newspaper groups' practice of moving their publishers around.

Writers may feel they have bigger stakes in their communities than the representatives of ownership do. Such feelings are not likely to ease working relationships with publishers who have different ideas on editorial policy.

Speaking the Publisher's Language

Dialogue helps to keep editors and publishers from suddenly being surprised to learn that they hold differing opinions on important issues. If publishers and editors can talk about issues before it is necessary to make decisions, chances of compromise improve greatly. Bernard Kilgore warned that misunderstandings between publishers and editors are sometimes caused by editors. He suggested that editors should "get into the business side of a newspaper and try to see what the thing is all about."[26] Editors who want a bigger slice of the corporate budget might stand a better chance of succeeding if they could convince the business side that they understood the problems of producing income and holding down costs. On occasion my publishers took several department heads out to solicit new subscriptions. My principal memory of those occasions was of all the reasons that people had for not taking the paper. For a greater understanding of the community as well as for purely pragmatic business reasons, editorial writers should keep abreast of circulation and advertising lineage figures. If they have a head for figures, so much the better. (In my experience, journalists and journalism students tend to shy away from anything that sounds like math.) If editorial writers can talk the publisher's and the circulation manager's languages they are more likely to project an image of having their feet on the ground—and stand a better chance of selling their editorial ideas.

Educating Publishers

One of the principal functions of editorial writers may be to educate their publishers. "If the editor is willing to educate everybody, including the world, and foreign countries, then it is also necessary for the publishers and the owners to be educated," Kilgore said.[27] But the writer must educate the publishers with what Hoke Norris of the *Chicago Sun-Times* called "a certain tact—even a tenderness." Norris described an editor friend who saw his function in "the care and feeding" of the publisher: "His publisher always believes that he originates the ideas and holds his own opinions. This is perhaps a harmless deception and it might even save a publisher, on occasion, from making a damn fool of himself."[28] A writer who is more educated and informed than the publisher must handle the boss with special care. Otherwise, the writer may run the risk of making the publisher feel resentful or intimidated rather than favorably impressed. As Frank Taylor of the *St. Louis Star-Times* put it, "More than one inferiority complex parades the precincts of publishers."[29]

Publishers might feel less intimidated if they availed themselves of opportunities to keep abreast of current events, took time to dig deeply into local issues or enrolled in a course at a local college. Houstoun Waring, publisher of the *Littleton* (Colo.) *Independent*, warned that it is "only partially effective to educate the reporter and the feature writer if the arteries of the man who calls the tune continue to harden. . . . Publishers may feel they are omniscient, but adult education programs are good for them, too."[30] He had in mind such formal programs as the Nieman Fellowship and other sabbatical opportunities, local press councils and discussions over breakfast with local sources. Nathaniel B. Blumberg, professor of journalism at the University of Montana, recalled press critic "A.J. Liebling's essentially accurate aphorism that without a school for publishers no school of journalism can have meaning."[31] The American Press Institute offers sessions for publishers, but establishing a service-oriented editorial policy for a community, if it is done at all, is likely to rank far down the line on the agenda after more business-related subjects.

Methods generally available to editors for educating publishers, however, are likely to be much less formal. Editors can send memos and background articles (although probably not books) across publisher's desks to help them understand issues before decisions are made, although busy publishers may not find time to read the material. Editors can invite publishers to public meetings, speeches, panel discussions and workshops where a variety of points of views are likely to be aired. Editors can invite publishers to lunch to exchange, in a less formal atmosphere than the editorial conference, ideas about what their newspapers should be doing and saying.

Publishers who want a hand in editorial policy should accept as much responsibility as editorial writers to sit and plow through all the material necessary for making intelligent decisions. Publishers also need to understand that editorial writers do not appreciate being descended upon at the last minute, after all the hard work is done, to give an opinion, even if the opinion is a modest one.

To avoid unexpected, last-minute opinions or decision changes, editorial conference members should try to establish the habit of delaying decisions on important matters until all members have aired their opinions and the issue at hand has been fully discussed. Once a person—especially a publisher, who could lose face before employees—declares even a tentative position on an issue, moving off that position becomes difficult. An editorial page staff that anticipates disagreement with the publisher might find it advantageous to meet before the editorial conference to plan a strategy. If the writers anticipate that they will not be able to convince other conference members of their opinion, they might try to agree beforehand on a compromise that they would find acceptable.

Coping with the Publisher's Special Interests

Editorial writers need to be especially sensitive to editorial topics that touch on activities or causes with which the publisher is personally involved. In a survey of editorial page editors, 94 out of 101 reported that their publishers were active in community affairs. Only about a fourth of them (25), however, reported that the publishers' activities had "affected how editorials were written." Several editors said their publishers voluntarily excused themselves from participating in decisions concerning their activities. One editor said the publisher checked with the editorial board before joining boards of local organizations. Another editor said that the publisher would sometimes suggest editorials "but will ask us not to comment on activities he is involved in."[32] A number of editors thought that publisher involvement was good for the newspaper and for the community. "Those who advocate volunteer involvement and shirk it are guilty of the worst hypocrisy," said one editor. Still, the potential conflict of "boosterism" remained a major concern of the editors.

Phil Duff, executive editor of the Red Wing, Minn., *Republican Eagle*, argued in *The Masthead* that publisher involvement benefits the newspaper and the community, especially in a small community. "There's an inverse proportion at work," he wrote. "The smaller the newspaper and the smaller the town, the more extensively the publisher may legitimately involve himself in civic-political affairs."[33]

How should a writer respond to a special-interest request from a publisher? If the editorial idea is a good one and seems in the interest of the community, the writer should produce it—posthaste. If the request is obviously self-serving or out of character with the paper's policy or contrary to reason and common sense, the editorial writer has a problem. The best course is to dig into the subject, document arguments against writing the editorial and present them to the publisher boldly and positively. Confidence and facts are the best weapons. By no means should a writer ignore or delay action on such a request—even if he or she thinks that an idea is so far out of line that the publisher couldn't be serious about it. Chances are, just as a writer is congratulating himself or herself on successfully having avoided doing anything about the request, the publisher will issue a sharp reminder. At that point the publisher has the upper hand. The writer is embarrassed, apologetic, off balance and in a poor position to convince the publisher of the idea's lack of merits. (I found myself in this spot when a publisher asked me to write an editorial on certain practices of labor unions that offended him. In addition to convincing him that the idea was not a good one, I faced the task of convincing him that I had not intentionally ignored him.) A writer stands a better chance of fending off undesirable requests by confronting the publisher and risking an argument than by ignoring the request. Publishers don't like to be ignored.

To the publisher who has a yen to write, editors might be tempted to suggest a personal column. But editor-publisher Donald L. Breed of the *Freeport* (Ill.) *Journal-Standard* warned that publishers who write "should have exceptional capacity for self-criticism" and for evaluating the criticisms of others. "It is perfectly obvious that many publishers who write editorials or 'columns' have no power or will to step aside and look at themselves and their work," Breed said. "Publishers who write columns about their personal friends, their daily lives, their travels can sometimes be interesting, but the balance of experience is against them."[34]

Writers who have a disagreement with their publishers or editorial boards might seek to express their dissident opinions in a signed article or column on the editorial or op-ed page. But many publishers and some editors are reluctant to open this avenue for contrary opinions from staff members.

Taking on the Publishers

Several articles in *The Masthead* have suggested that editorial writers as a group "take on" their publishers. One of the first rallying cries came in 1970, from Curtis D. MacDougall, professor of journalism at Northwestern University. He quoted with approval a statement that had been made by one of the (unidentified) founders of NCEW a couple of years earlier: "During our first two decades we have educated ourselves. Now let us devote our energies toward doing the same for our publishers."[35]

Over the years editorial writers have carried a lot of ideas back to publishers from conferences of NCEW. At the following year's meeting writers often report that suggestions that emerged from critique groups were accepted back home and that the editorial pages were better for them. That is one way of bringing the collective enlightenment of editorial writers to bear on publishers. But ideas are not always accepted. Editorial writers on some papers receive criticism for the same deficiencies year after year. When asked why they don't change, the answer is usually that the publisher (or editor) "wants it that way."

An editorial writer once issued a battle cry for a full-fledged offensive against the publishers. In 1977 Sam Reynolds, editorial page editor of the Missoula, Mont., *Missoulian*, wrote: "We must lay down standards of what is good in a publisher, and what is bad. We must, as an organization, sharply criticize shabby publisher performance. . . . It must be done because nothing so retards healthy editorial comment in America as lame-brained, narrow-minded, unimaginative, cowardly, sluggish, dogmatic, and imperial publishers . . . . Until the vital step of ripping up publishers who sit like slugs upon editorial spirit and quality is taken, this organization is simply bird-doggin' it, a representative group of aggressive slaves, or hired guns." Reynolds suggested using *The Masthead.* He called on NCEW to encourage good publisher practices and to attack the bad. "Growl! Snap!" he wrote; "it's time we blew the whistle."[36]

Reynolds' call for NCEW to "blow the whistle" seemed to go unheeded. *The Masthead* carried no further references to his proposal. Perhaps editorial writers did not know what they wanted to put into a code of ethics for publishers. One survey, of the 101 editorial page editors, found that 56 of their newspapers had ethics codes. In 34 instances the codes applied to the publisher, but only 17 applied to the publisher's involvement in community activities.[37]

What should a code of ethics for publishers contain? For starters, NCEW members might look to their own statement of principles, especially sections dealing with personal favors and conflicts of interest. A code might include a provision emphasizing the integrity of the editorial decision-making process— the need for previously agreed-upon procedures to be followed in setting editorial policy. It might contain some variation of the NCEW statement that says that an editorial writer "should never write anything that goes against his or her conscience." The statement of principles also emphasizes that "sound collective judgment can be achieved only through sound individual judgments" and implies that editorial policy should evolve through discussion, not be imposed from the top. A code might state that publishers should participate in editorial decision-making only when they have participated in the information-gathering and discussion phases of the process. It might state that publishers (and editors too) should refrain from participating in editorial decisions that involve conflicts of interest.

Perhaps members of NCEW were reluctant to take on publishers because they faced a tough enough task back home dealing with publishers who didn't pay a lot of attention to them. They might have feared that, if they stirred up trouble, they would end up with a bigger battle on their hands. The way most

American newspapers are run today, publishers may lose a skirmish now and then, but they rarely allow themselves to lose the big battles they are determined to win.

THE CASE FOR THE EDITOR

A survey of editorial page editors on 82 of the largest daily newspapers found that more than half (45) reported to a news-side editor, compared to 37 who reported directly to a publisher. Those who reported to the publisher tended to argue that their chain of command was better suited to maintaining a wall of separation between news and editorial departments. "If the editorial page is put in charge of an editor who is also in charge of news, that indicates a lack of concern for the opinion function," said one editorial page editor. "It makes it just another so-called function of the newspaper." But those who reported to an editor contended that their structure kept editorials from being tainted by the business side of the newspaper. "The drawback in reporting to the publisher is that in the final analysis the publisher is a businessman," said one of the respondents.[38]

Whether the editorial page editor reports to a publisher or an editor, a strong case can be made for the argument that, once the editorial page editor gets the job, he or she should be entrusted to set a newspaper's editorial policy. Hugh B. Patterson Jr., publisher of the *Arkansas Gazette*, contended that editorial page editors ought to be given room to set policy, and owner-publishers should support them completely. He thought that, just as career politicians are generally best suited to hold high public office, so "career newspaper editors are best qualified to run newspaper editorial pages."[39] Frank Taylor of the *St. Louis Star-Times* saw publishers as "God-fearing, decent men who would much rather push a cash register button than pull a tiger's tail." He thought that "a majority of editorial writers would measure up well on the God-fearing test but would come through 100 percent plus on pulling a tiger by the tail."[40]

Sevellon Brown III, editor of the *Providence* (R.I.) *Journal-Bulletin*, saw three reasons why "the editor *ought* to be the one—and only one—to make final decisions on editorial policy." First, the editor "is relatively uncluttered by other professional duties and responsibilities." The publishers, with all the other duties they must perform, can give only limited time and energy to the editorial page. Editing an editorial page is a full-time job. Second, the editor is the person "in closest, broadest touch with the news," one of the primary ingredients in editorial policy-making. Third, the editor is best qualified because he or she is, or ought to be, "*relatively* disinterested, *relatively* uncommitted to any particular cause or faith or point of view." The publisher, properly so, comes from the business side and represents only a business point of view. With brains, "moxey" and endurance, the editor can become a lightning rod for all points of view—for business, labor, politicians of all parties, enthusiasts for public education or world trade "or what-have-you, do-gooders of all kinds." The editor, in dealing with a specific issue, can sort out and synthesize the varied pressures and interests "into something like a reasoned, intelligent conclusion"—and there is the paper's editorial policy.[41]

An editor who has fortitude and convictions can attain a strong, unique position in relations with a publisher. As Kilgore pointed out, much to the chagrin of some editorial writers, " . . . you cannot make a five-year-old eat. No amount of force or physical violence will work. . . . Authority, you see, does not accomplish things. With editors it is somewhat the same thing." You can't force an editorial writer to write, and even more fundamentally you can't force an editorial writer to think. The relationship between editor and publisher, Kilgore said, is "a case where you have a boss who is not really a boss, and a case where you have a workman who is not really a workman."[42]

Yet, when it is necessary to make basic policy and settle disagreements, someone must assume the final authority, and it is a rare newspaper where that final authority does not rest with the publisher, general manager or representative of ownership. "Ownerships generally last longer than editorships," William H. Heath, editor-emeritus of the *Haverhill* (Mass.) *Gazette*, wrote. "Therefore, policy made by ownership is more stable. There is a rock-of-ages quality about a newspaper that is distinguished by editorial policy. This quality strengthens public confidence in the paper."[43]

CONCLUSION

Publishers do have the final say on most newspapers. But on many papers editors and editorial writers have more say than they did several years ago. Editorial writing is increasingly regarded as a career, not just a job that a newsperson from some other part of the paper has wandered into at a late stage in his or her working life. The job on many papers is beginning to lose its image as a mouthpiece for the bosses. Publishers are hiring editors and giving them increased editorial freedom. One reason for this new confidence is that editorial writers and editors are better prepared for their jobs. In recent years they have become better educated, more interested in their communities and more willing to speak up for what they know and believe. Knowledgeable, confident writers these days can expect to win a considerable amount of freedom from publishers, at least from those publishers who recognize the value of strong, enlightened editorial pages.

Questions and Exercises

1. If you were a publisher, what role would you choose to play in regard to the editorial page? If you were an editorial page editor, what would you want the role of the publisher to be?
2. Should the role of publisher vary with the size of the newspaper? Should whether a paper is owned locally, by a distant owner or by a group make a difference in the role of the publisher?
3. Judging from the newspapers with which you are acquainted, what chances do you think you would have to sign on with a publisher with wholly compatible views on issues?
4. Among the group-owned newspapers with which you are familiar, have you detected any evidence of control of editorial policy by the group headquarters? Have you seen any evidence of similar editorial policies among newspapers of the same group?
5. What do you think are the most effective ways for an editorial writer to keep a publisher happy and to achieve a maximum sphere of freedom?
6. If editorial writers were "to take on the publishers," as suggested in *The Masthead* articles mentioned in this chapter, what steps might they take?

CHAPTER 7　Relations with the Newsroom

Historically the relationship between the newsroom and the editorial page has been a one-way street. The newsroom produces the news. The editorial writers sit back in Olympian reflection, rearrange their dandruff into new patterns, and then write comments on or interpretations of that news.

—CLIFFORD E. CARPENTER, ROCHESTER (N.Y.) *DEMOCRAT AND CHRONICLE*[1]

American newspapers have grown out of an early tradition that made no effort to keep editorial views or comment out of the news sections. For the last hundred or more years, most newspaper owners have subscribed to a policy, more or less successfully, to keep editorials and news separate. Most provide separate editorial pages and tell readers that is where newspapers' opinions should go.

Sometimes, intentionally or unintentionally, editorial policies will influence how a news story is written or played in the paper. Sometimes, intentionally or unintentionally, the news side will influence the editorial side. Ideally, news will be written and played in as objective a manner as writers and editors are capable of achieving. Ideally, people on the news side will keep their opinions to themselves, not sharing them with editorial writers, sources or readers. To encourage this separation, most newspapers—certainly large and middle-sized ones—have erected a journalistic barrier, if not a physical wall, between their news and editorial departments. In some extreme cases, an editorial writer in a newsroom is viewed as suspiciously as an advertising sales representative.

But times change. One change, as noted in the previous chapter, is that newspaper bosses have begun to subscribe to the philosophy that, because everyone on the paper is in the same business, everyone should understand and help everyone else. Another change is a growing realization, among news and editorial staff members, that they can help each other without threatening the integrity of either of their departments.

A survey of editorial page editors of 82 of the largest newspapers found that 69 (84 percent) saw the need for a wall between news and editorial, but nearly half of those (32) added that such a wall should not rule out communication between the two departments.[2] Reporters can be especially helpful to editorial writers, providing tips, insights, fact and contacts. Unfortunately, because of the tradition mentioned above, jealousy, antipathy or misunderstanding, much of that potential help never gets past the partition that separates the offices.

"In the eyes of some editorial writers," wrote Edward M. Miller of the *Oregonian* of Portland, "the news department is manned by fugitives from the world of intellect. The news department is notable for misjudging the news. It is concerned with trivialities at the expense of Things That Really Matter." To news people, the editorial page is staffed by "fugitives from the world of reality." Editorial writers "commune with God, and do that with considerable reluctance."[3]

Another source of news-editorial trouble is the resentment sometimes felt by news personnel who disagree with a paper's editorial policy, especially policy involving endorsement of candidates. Readers, they contend, assume that editorials speak for the entire journalistic side of the paper (or the entire paper), when in fact editorials represent the views of only a few policy makers. On occasion newsroom people have been known to purchase advertisements in their own paper to support policies or candidates different from those endorsed by the editorial page.

Sometimes relations between news and editorial people can be soured by an excessive amount of competition. Editorial writers may take delight in scooping the news department—finding a story and writing an editorial before the story appears in the news columns. Once in a while reporters may find sardonic pleasure in reporting a story that makes the editorial staff look as though it didn't know what it had been writing about. Repeated efforts on one side of the news-editorial partition to embarrass the other can be destructive to the morale of a newspaper staff and can harm the credibility of the paper. But a little friendly competition between news and editorial can help keep both departments on their toes. It may provide the only such competition in one-newspaper communities.

Problems of a different sort arise when a firm partition is not maintained between news and editorial content, when a publisher does not insist that editorial writers hold complete responsibility for policies expressed in the editorial columns and that news personnel have complete responsibility for the news columns. The editorial staff must not expect the news department to produce articles aimed at bolstering an editorial viewpoint, and the news staff must not allow its opinions to filter into news articles.

REPORTERS AS SOURCES

Whatever the reason, reporters and editorial writers have tended to go their own ways. In many cases in which editorial comment is called for, editorial writers have no need to talk with reporters. They have their own sources, or the subject of the editorial may already have been fully explained in the news columns. But ignoring help available on the news side is a "recipe for disaster," in the words of one of the editorial page editors included in the survey cited above. "Your perspective can get limited without talking with the beat reporter[s]. . . . You can go off half-cocked if you don't talk to them."[4] Since a newspaper invariably has more reporters than editorial writers, the news people are likely to have more sources of information and spend more time in the community than editorial writers. They may have information, not yet ready for print, that might make a big difference in how editorial writers evaluate an issue.

Ellen Belcher, who spent time as a reporter after being an editorial writer, said she could personally attest to the value of checking with the newsroom. "In part because I saw how much information reporters knew that they couldn't fit into their stories, I . . . promised that . . . I'd redouble my effort to make sure that I talk to reporters before I write my editorials, asking them even more questions than I had previously."[5] Reporters, William J. Woods of the *Utica* (N.Y.) *Observer-Dispatch* pointed out, "are invaluable in keeping the egg of silly mistakes off the editor's chin."[6]

Editorial writers who want to tackle a subject in which they are not experts can ask a knowledgeable reporter to brief them on the subject. If a proposed zone change is coming before the city council, a reporter may be able to recount the history of the case, from the developer through the planning staff and zoning commission. The reporter may also be able to provide technical information on zoning procedures. The editorial writer might ask the reporter to clarify the issues involved—to recap the arguments of the developer, the protesting neighbors and the zoning commissioners.

REPORTERS IN THE OPINION PROCESS

"There's nothing wrong with editorial writers sitting down with news types to get their observations," one editorial page editor said. "You have to be careful, though, because if you carry it too far the reporters begin to articulate your policy, and that's not good."[7] In the zoning case, the editorial writer might ask the reporter for a personal opinion on the issue. The reporter might reply that, in comparison with other similar changes, this one does not seem out of line— or perhaps that the change does seem out of line. In seeking an opinion, the editorial writer should be wary. Reporters are responsible for maintaining the appearance of fairness in reporting the news as well as fairness in their writing. A city editor who is concerned about the credibility of reporters may not appreciate having reporters offer opinions to an editorial writer on subjects that they write about. A reporter's relations with a news source can be adversely affected if it becomes known that the reporter has voiced an opinion. To think public matters through to editorial conclusions is the job of the editorial writer, not the reporter.

Some editors—on both news and editorial sides—are receptive to encouraging reporters to express opinions, in print and personally. Desmond Stone of the *Rochester Democrat and Chronicle* reported that inviting reporters to participate in editorial board meetings for a period of two weeks was one way that his paper and its sister paper, the *Times-Union*, tried to make news personnel feel more a part of the editorial decision-making.[8] Rufus Terral of the *St. Louis Post-Dispatch* suggested picking two promising writers in the newsroom to contribute editorials from time to time, so that they could fill in when members of the editorial staff were on vacation or ill and possibly become regular editorial page staff members when a replacement was needed.[9] Some papers ask reporters to write editorials or bylined opinions on a regular basis on particular subjects on which they are experts, but this practice runs the risk of the dangers cited above in weakening the wall between news and editorial sides.

In the survey of editorial page editors cited above, a few said they would be willing to undertake joint projects with the news department. "I'd like to be able to send out a reporter and an editorial writer for six weeks to cover a controversial issue and have the reporter write the news story and the editorial writer write the editorials," one said. "Now, when the news side does a big investigation, the editorial page gets left out until the stuff appears in the paper, and then we have to play catch-up."[10]

David H. Beetle of the *Albany* (N.Y.) *Knickerbocker News* once asked several reporters based in Washington to write a 500-word appraisal of the current administration. The reporter from the Albany paper responded that writing a signed opinion article on the editorial page would brand him as biased forever. As a reporter, he dealt only in facts; he was proud that, in public, he had no opinions. Beetle asked other editors what they thought. They were divided. "Ridiculous," said one editor. "Our city hall reporter writes straight news daily and once a week tells what he thinks of it all. No one believes he is biased." But another editor argued, "If a city hall reporter writes opinion, he'll instantly become 'suspect' when he gathers news."[11]

When I was an editor with supervision over both news and editorial sides, I did not encourage reporters to write articles that expressed opinion about the subjects they were reporting. I did, however, encourage them to write in-depth, analytical articles for use in either the daily news columns or the Sunday opinion section. My experience as both a reporter and an editorial writer convinced me that something happens inside writers when they write pieces that express opinions. As an editorial writer, I often ended up having much stronger opinions on a subject after I had written an editorial. Once a writer has thought through the arguments and embraced one of them, his or her attitude on an issue is likely never to be the same again.

EDITORIALS IN THE NEWS COLUMNS

Two ideas for introducing editorials into the news pages were considered in early issues of *The Masthead*. Neither idea has been given much credence by editors.

The first is the front-page editorial. Such editorials have become rare in recent years, but occasionally an editor or publisher will run an editorial on page one to call attention to a statement considered to be especially important. Fred A. Stickel, president and publisher of the *Oregonian*, wrote a signed page-one editorial urging Oregonians to vote against a ballot measure that would have restricted the rights of homosexuals.[12] Nathaniel B. Blumberg, while a professor at Michigan State University, found enough page-one editorials during the 1952 election that he wrote an article for *The Masthead* titled "The Case Against Front-Page Editorials." Blumberg argued that page-one editorials may confuse readers about what is news and what is opinion and may increase their "suspicions that the news coverage might not be impartial."[13]

Some papers summarize election endorsements in a front-page box, and some editorial page editors use front-page teasers to call attention to editorials on the editorial page. At least some criticisms of front-page editorials might apply to these practices as well.

Another suggestion for bringing opinion into the news columns apparently originated in 1935 with historian Douglas Southall Freeman, then editor of the *Richmond* (Va.) *News Leader*. While going through old *News Leader* files in the early 1950s, James J. Kilpatrick found that Freeman had suggested to his publisher that the news needed interpreting when and where it was printed. The reader should not have to wait until the next day, "when his interest in it has been diminished or has been distracted by some new event." Freeman suggested that the editorial page be abolished and that interpretation and comment be appended at the end of news stories that merited opinion.[14] Kilpatrick's resurrection of the proposal prompted the laboratory newspaper at the University of Michigan, the *Michigan Journalist*, to try Freeman's proposal. Students found that one advantage of tacking an editorial on the end of a news story was that the editorial did not require so much space; there was no need to rehash factual information. But the professor who worked with the students said he feared that readers would think that news sources had not been "given a square shake if the newspaper proceeds to bludgeon those views editorially in the same news column." He also feared that the instant editorial would encourage off-the-cuff reactions and discourage double-checking, digging for more information and calm reflecting required for first-rate editorial comment.[15]

EDITORIALIZING ABOUT NEWS POLICIES

One approach to lowering the bar between news and editorial that seems justified is the use of editorial columns to explain news policies and practices—and editorial practices, for that matter. An editorial or a signed article on the editorial page can be a proper forum for telling readers why certain types of news and not others are covered in the news columns or why new features have been added and others dropped.

In the last couple of years in which I was on a newspaper, I regularly wrote a Sunday op-ed column, which I usually devoted to a journalistic issue. Some of the columns dealt with my own paper's policies and practices. Others concerned matters of more general interest, such as protecting the confidentiality of news sources, libel, invasion of privacy and the signing of editorials. Reader response seemed good. Subscribers wanted to know more about their newspaper, and the press in general.

Some newspapers assign a full- or part-time person to respond to complaints of readers and to write about media matters. Their work usually is published on the editorial or op-ed page. When the remarks of these media critics have pertained to the newspaper industry in general, they have been given considerable freedom to draw conclusions. On some newspapers, however, when criticism comes too close to home, critics find that they don't have as much freedom as they may have thought.[16]

CONCLUSION

The newspaper that wants to maintain the credibility of its news and editorial columns must draw a line between the two and take every opportunity to remind readers of this line. But news and editorial are two parts of a package. It may be possible to produce an outstanding news product without a good editorial page. It is virtually impossible to produce an outstanding editorial page without the support of a good news product. Editorial writers need reporters more than reporters need editorial writers: They simply don't have enough arms and legs and eyes and noses to do their jobs all by themselves.

Questions and Exercises

1. Why do you think that editorial writers have tended to ignore reporters and newsroom editors?
2. Do reporters, in your opinion, have a legitimate complaint when the editorial page expresses views with which they strongly disagree? What steps should be open to them?
3. Should news persons be allowed to purchase advertising space in the newspaper for which they work to express views contrary to those of management?
4. Should reporters be invited to write editorials on subjects with which they are familiar? Or to write signed opinion pieces for the editorial and op-ed pages?
5. Do reporters on papers in your area write editorials and/or signed articles for the editorial or op-ed pages? How far do they go in expressing their opinions?
6. Do you think that editorial writers should ask reporters for their opinions on issues that the reporters are covering?
7. Are there occasions when a page-one editorial can be justified? What about page-one election endorsements?
8. What do you think of the idea of tacking editorial comments to the ends of news stories?

CHAPTER 8 The Editorial Page Staff

An editorial page staff, no matter how large or small, never seems quite the right size for all members. Ask editorial writers if they need more help in putting out the editorial page, and chances are they will answer "Yes." But ask a writer who puts out a page all by himself or herself—or better yet one who used to put one out alone–and chances are you will get a lecture on the freedom and rewards, and misery, of doing the whole job by yourself.

Writers on one-person staffs know they are overworked and don't get enough time to write editorials. Writers on some two-person and three-person staffs, especially on larger papers, think they need more help. On some days, on papers with large staffs, a writer may wish that not so many colleagues were competing for space, promotion and community recognition. Some members of large staffs think back fondly to the days when they wrote all the editorials, handled the letters and still found time for a Chamber of Commerce luncheon. I did when the editorial staff on the *Columbian* grew from one to two, and then from two to three members.

Just as editorial-page people hold a variety of views about staff size, so do they have differences of opinion concerning how much freedom each member of the staff should have and how much members should collaborate through editorial conferences.

THE ONE-PERSON STAFF

A survey of editorial writers in 1979 found that the one-person staff was the most prevalent on U.S. daily newspapers (27 percent of all papers) and that 17 percent had no full-time person at all. Another 17 percent had two persons; 14 percent had three; 10 percent had four;

8 percent had five; 6 percent had more than five.[3] I think there is little reason to think that these percentages have changed much.

Putting out a page by yourself has its advantages. You can write what you wish if you have a good relationship with your publisher. You don't have to worry about disagreements among staff members. You get full credit, or discredit, for whatever you do. Your readers know whom to praise or blame. You can go home at night and point to what you have accomplished.

"I should confess that I still recall with pleasure some of the aspects of those years when I wrote editorials for a semi-weekly and later a small daily newspaper without conferring with anybody in advance," recalled Wilbur Elston, then of the *Detroit News.* "I won't say those editorials could not have been improved. Obviously they could have been. But they were all mine. Whatever praise or criticism I heard from readers was especially pleasant to my ears." Unfortunately, Elston also recalled, most of the editorials "were, I fear, written off the top of my head."[4]

The one-person show is a tough one, and it's not for everyone. In the words of Don Shoemaker of the *Asheville* (N.C.) *Citizen,* it's like being "the keeper of the zoo." Shoemaker, who was the inspiration for the leading character in Jeff MacNelly's cartoon strip, "Shoe," saw the single editorial writer as "more put upon" than any other person in the field of newspapering. The writer had to please "crotchety and sour-bellied" printers, select and edit editorial page features that would complement the locally written editorials and satisfy the publisher—and know all about proofreading, page layout and makeup. The writer had to worry about "any novice journeyman who happens to be around the shop" fouling up the page. At the same time the one-person staff had to "keep a weather eye cocked for the passions and prejudices" of the community, the state and the region. "As any fool kin plainly see, the curator has an impossible, a thankless, a miserable job," Shoemaker wrote. But mostly the "fool" loves it. "I (ugh!) do," he concluded. "But there are moments."[5]

One of the big pluses is satisfaction of the ego. Shoemaker spoke of the "complete identity with a whole product . . . come gripe or praise." When you are a one-person staff, you don't have to worry about bylines. Readers who are familiar with your page will know who wrote the words they agree or disagree with. The letters to the editor that comment on editorials are written to you. Members of the community who want support from the editorial page know whose door they should knock on.

Michael Loftin was reminded of a scene from the movie *Raiders of the Lost Ark:* "Archeologist Indiana Jones, having captured an ancient artifact, is trying to escape from a giant rolling boulder chasing him through the tunnel. Think of the boulder as the looming daily deadline and the production of 800 to 900 words of (reasonably intelligent) commentary as the goal and you can understand why those of us in this situation were cheering for Mr. Jones."[6]

Turning out the letters, the columns, the cartoons and the page layout, while handling telephone calls and office visitors, can account for a good share of the working day. But, once you get into the swing of it, composing one thoughtful, researched editorial and another quick one every day turns out not to be impossible. Topics always abound. Karli Jo Hunt, of the *Home News* of New Brunswick, N.J., said that she has learned "to get through a five-day week writing seven days' editorials, . . . to read, read, read, clip, clip, clip, and pace my 'production' so that Thursdays and Fridays are only nine- or 10-hour sessions at the tube."[7]

When she finds herself under the pressure of time, Linda Egan, of the *Santa Barbara* (Calif.) *News-Press,* said she "fudges," explaining: " . . . we may publish two live editorials, instead of our customary three a day. We say then that our readers deserve more detailed background on this tricky subject. We mean that we don't have time to write short. Sometimes we don't even have time to write long, so we flesh out the column with a space-eating illustration that dresses up one of the editorials. We call that a treat for our readers."[8]

Some editors—in fact, some editors who also double as publishers or managing editors—are able to produce two, three or four editorials a day and say something significant in each of them. They seem able to cover an unlimited range of topics. But my experience has been that single writers make the best use of talent and time if they concentrate on one major topic a day, a topic they know about.

IF NOT ONE, HOW MANY?

The 1979 survey of editorial writers cited earlier in this chapter did not attempt to compare staff sizes with circulations of the newspapers. But an earlier survey had found that 54 percent of dailies with less than 100,000 circulation had only one full-time or part-time editorial writer. "Is it any wonder that performance occasionally falters?" asked Laurence J. Paul of the *Buffalo* (N.Y.) *Evening News* after reviewing the findings. "Apparently all this ink-stained Solomon is expected to do, in addition to whatever other sideline duties he may have, is to comment stylishly, thoughtfully and consistently on a broadening array of complex subjects in 15 to 25 lucid editorials a week. And after the value judgments are made, Solomon, don't forget the waste baskets before you leave." Paul found it scarcely more reassuring that 16 percent of writers on papers that had more than 100,000 circulation worked on staffs of no more than two full-time members. The deficiencies he saw included superficial analysis, clumsy style, convenient subject matter, padded editorials and "even the canned editorials (God save us)."[9] (Canned editorials are opinion pieces supplied by editorial writing services or representatives of interest groups that a newspaper passes off as its own editorials.)

One tendency of an overworked editorial staff is to write about national and international issues that have been researched and reported by the national wire services, news magazines, the *New York Times* or other publications. It is no trick to turn out several of these editorials in a few hours. Information is not likely to be so easily available on local, regional and state topics. Fewer editorial voices are easily available to listen to and imitate. Consequently these topics tend to be ignored when deadlines approach.

Paul thought it ought to be possible to set guidelines for the size of the editorial page staff based on a newspaper's circulation. He suggested that the National Conference of Editorial Writers recommend that papers with circulations between 50,000 and 100,000 have a minimum of two writers, that papers with 100,000 to 150,000 have at least three and that those with 150,000 to 200,000 at least four.

In one sense, the circulation of a newspaper has little to do with the size of the staff needed to turn out a high-quality editorial page. A column of editorials must be written, columns and letters must be handled and callers and visitors must be dealt with. An editorial page in a paper with a small circulation is the same size as the page in a larger paper. One difference, of course, is that a larger paper may produce seven editions a week instead of five or six, have two opinion pages a day instead of one and publish an opinion section on the weekend. The main reason that larger papers should maintain larger editorial page staffs is that they have greater resources with which to do so. Because they have more circulation, more advertising and more money to spend, they should be expected to put more resources into the editorial page.

Another reason: Larger papers tend to serve not just a local community but a region or an entire state. These papers thus have the opportunity to provide leadership in public affairs in the areas they serve. They will not make full use of that opportunity unless they provide their writers with the time and the incentive to do their own research and their own thinking on the issues.

DIVISION OF DUTIES

A one-person staff doesn't have to worry much about how to split up the duties of producing an editorial page. He or she does whatever needs to be done. But help, primarily with letters to the editor, might be available from a newsroom secretary, copy clerk or someone with clerical skills. That helper could check addresses of letters, enforce the newspaper's rules concerning letters to the editor and retype letters on video display terminals. The person might be encouraged to try writing headlines for letters. Assistance with letters is probably the greatest help that a one-person staff can get. Next best is with messages and phone calls.

As staffs increase in size, one person may be assigned the letters to the editors as a full- or part-time job, another the syndicated columns and the layout. Both may write editorials as they find time. One person may have responsibility for the weekend opinion section. The editorial page editor will probably edit the editorials of other staff members and meet with the public and newspaper management.

As staffs increase in size, writers may have their own special subject areas. Specialization can produce a more knowledgeable editorial writer and thus more knowledgeable editorials. If an editorial is directed primarily toward experts in the subject, it may fully serve its purpose. But specialization has limitations. First, writers may become so engrossed in their specialties that the editorials they turn out are incomprehensible to the average reader. Second, when a paper's specialist on a subject is sick or on vacation, or has left the staff, an editor may find that no one else on the staff is capable of writing on that topic. Ideally, editorial writers should be able to write about many subjects in addition to their specialties.

EDITORIAL CONFERENCES

Editorial writers and editors divide sharply over the value—or lack of value—of regular editorial conferences. Proponents argue that they provide an opportunity to bring the thinking of several people to bear on topics, that give-and-take discussion can produce ideas that might otherwise not emerge. Discussion can also reveal that a topic needs more research or possibly ought to be dropped entirely as unworthy of comment. John G. McCullough of the *Philadelphia Evening Bulletin* said that when his staff skipped the morning editorial conference he and the other writers missed it. "When the free give-and-take of these conferences is missing, I feel it shows in [the resulting editorials]," he said. "They seem to have a structural narrowness reflecting the absence of other, counter, views. Such editorials come through as a whoosh of heated opinion." He said the editorials lacked the persuasive logic that is provided by "the extra ingredients fed into the mix during the editorial conference."[10]

Some of the critics of conferences contend that this mixing contributes to bland editorials. Hugh B. Patterson Jr., of the *Arkansas Gazette* of Little Rock, acknowledged that discussions could help clarify and sharpen arguments but could also result in "the lowest common denominator of mutual agreement."[11] Pat Murphy, of the Phoenix *Arizona Republic*, contended that his staff members did not need editorial conferences. "Our staff is made up of self-starters who spin out ideas and suggestions and hit the ground running every morning," he said. Instead of holding a conference, he made the rounds of staff members first thing in the morning to suggest ideas and listen to their proposals. "Fie on daily conferences," he said. "They're a waste of time."[12]

Various combinations of people involved in setting editorial policy might be tried. Editorial writers might meet each morning with the editorial page editor to discuss that day's topics. At less frequent intervals the editorial page editor might meet with the newspaper editor or the publisher. Daily staff meetings, coupled with the editorial page editor conferring with the editor, were our policy when I was on the *Des Moines* (Iowa) *Register and Tribune*. On the *Columbian*, in Vancouver, Wash., we had a daily meeting of editorial writers and a biweekly meeting of the editorial board, which consisted of the editorial staff members, the co-publishers and two or three representatives of other departments. Another possibility is for the publisher to sit in on all daily conferences. This arrangement helps assure that the publisher is informed on editorial issues, but it may have an inhibiting effect on discussion of sensitive issues.

Sitting in on an Editorial Conference

In preparing for this edition, I asked whether students in my editorial-writing class and I could sit in on a conference at the *Roanoke Times*. We went on two consecutive days and observed two quite different meetings. They were a reminder that, even for a specific editorial board, no meeting is quite like any other.

On both days, after acting editorial page editor Geoff Seamans explained to the students how the editorial board works at the *Times*, staff members set about deciding what they were going to write about that day. One news item the first morning (Wednesday) was another in a rash of domestic-violence killings. One editorial writer, Betty Strother, pointed out that, while radio reports were urging women to look for warning signs, they did not say what those signs were. She recalled that she had a contact in Williamsburg who had done some work in domestic violence cases. She would try to reach her. Betty also wanted to comment on plans for allowing more development on Mill Mountain, which overlooks the city.

That morning the newspaper had also carried a colored picture of prisoners painting buildings in a county park. Margie Fisher thought the sheriff deserved a plug for his efforts to make good use of prisoners for the benefit of the public—at a time when public sentiment was to keep prisoners locked up.

The banner headline that morning had announced that CSX and Norfolk Southern railroads had reached an agreement on dividing up Conrail. Geoff expressed interest in that topic. Roanoke has long been a railroad town, once the headquarters of the Norfolk and Western. It took a blow when the merged Norfolk Southern put its headquarters in Richmond. Employment cutbacks over the years have depleted local railroad employment, but many citizens retain stock in NS. The story said the new tracks NS would get could open up new opportunities to ship to New York and beyond.

Several other issues were discussed: requiring tuition for public school students to attend in other local districts, the threat of the Grant family to remove Ulysses S.'s body and the governor's closing of some hearings.

The discussion of the issues was limited and mild.

The second day started with a mention that public school tuition and Mill Mountain development were still on the table. Then came a rather heated exchange between Margie and Geoff that illustrated the problem editorial writers face when they have a pretty good idea of what should be done but the political climate is not right.

Virginia is one of the most conservative states in the country in terms of willingness to pay taxes. Its income, sales and property taxes are all low compared to most states. As a consequence, when the economy has not been booming, social services and education, especially higher education (but not prisons), have suffered. The *Roanoke Times* had carried several editorials suggesting more revenue was needed, but limited its suggestions to a higher tax on cigarettes and alcohol. It also had called for removing the sales tax on food.

A couple of weeks earlier, when the lieutenant governor, Don Beyer, had announced he would run for governor in the fall, he had suggested the possibility of a tax increase. As a result of public outcry, he soon backtracked. What prompted the exchange between Margie and Geoff was Beyer's announcement the day before that he wanted to remove the sales tax on non-prescription medicine. Margie pointed out that the loss to the state would be a lot less than would result from removing the tax on food. She saw Beyer's proposal as a cheap way for Beyer to put himself on the tax-cut side, and thought that should be pointed out. Geoff's concern seemed to be that, by coming down on Beyer's proposed tax cut, the newspaper risked reinforcing the boost-the-tax image that some letter writers seemed fond of attributing to the paper. The conclusion was that Margie, a long-time reporter in the state capital before she became an editorial writer, would take all these matters into consideration when she wrote the editorial. (Unspoken during this exchange was my assumption that the *Times* would endorse Beyer, a conservative Democrat. The paper had been much more critical of his opponent, Attorney General James Gilmore, a Republican. See Chapter 15, "Editorials on Elections," for editorials Virginia newspapers carried during the Beyer-Gilmore race.)

Both days the editorial staff members did something I had not heard of before. They rated that day's editorials (from 1 to 4) in terms of five attributes: "focused," "topical," "engaging writing," "effective headline" and "fresh perspective." On both days the students and I participated in the critiques. The students also were urged to comment on their own ratings. In many cases the ratings patterns were similar, item by item, but the students tended to give higher ratings than the staff members. I was somewhere in between.

Both days the editorial conferences lasted about an hour and a half. My guess is they would have run about an hour if the students had not been there.

On Thursday, the domestic-violence piece appeared at the top of the page, followed by the prisoners editorial and a short piece that had not been discussed during the conference. On Friday, the Beyer editorial (titled "Don Beyer's cop-out on the food tax") appeared at the top with the railroad piece beneath it. Saturday's page carried the Mill Mountain and Grant's Tomb editorials. The latter noted that the condition of Grant's tomb had become so bad that his descendants were threatening to move his remains. Legislators in Illinois had joined in the protest. The last sentence said: "Should the tomb fall again into disrepair, we'll know times have changed if Virginia joins Illinois in demanding more respectful treatment for the grave of the man who defeated Robert E. Lee." (*Times* readers are well aware that Lee is also buried in Virginia, in fact within the circulation area of the newspaper.)

Long-range planning

Editorial writers, even those who hold regular meetings, need to step back a pace or two from time to time. Gilbert Cranberg of the *Des Moines Register and Tribune* found that putting out two editorial pages a day kept his staff members so occupied that they had no chance to examine how they really operated or how the pages could be improved. Cranberg tried a 90-minute luncheon for the writers and found that the session produced ideas for improving use of syndicated features, increasing locally written material for the pages and instituting a sabbatical leave program.[13]

When I was on the *Columbian,* the three of us left the office early on a couple of afternoons, with a six-pack of beer, to talk about the broader issues, some details and the interaction among our personalities. The result was to clear the air in a way that could not have happened in a hurried morning meeting and to allow us to develop some ideas for improving the page that did not spring full-blown from the mind of any one participant.

A more elaborate get-together, a one-day retreat, was tried by the editorial page staff of the *News Journal* in Wilmington, Del. Two weeks' worth of newspapers had been sent to an outside editorial page editor. The first two hours were devoted to his critique, with staff members asking questions. Then, Editorial Page Editor John H. Taylor Jr. reported, "[W]e started on our principal concerns": page content, letters, editorial board agenda, community advisory board and page design. "What the retreat offered," he said, "was a chance to talk and argue without interruption, to come to an agreement all could live with." He counted it a success.[14]

THE TYPICAL DAY

A "typical day" for editorial writers on most papers is a contradiction in terms. Writers who have contact with the outside world or with other members of the staff are not likely to have a *typical* day. It is hard, if not impossible, to plan a day and stick to a schedule. Nevertheless, editors of *The Masthead* asked several writers to describe how they spent their days.[15] If you could average the various schedules of the 25 or so respondents, the result might look something like this:

6 a.m. to 8 a.m.: at home, read the morning newspaper(s) while drinking coffee and eating breakfast

8:30 a.m. to 9 a.m.: peruse other newspapers and the news wires

9 a.m. to 9:30 a.m.: attend editorial board meeting to discuss and pick topics for editorials

9:30 a.m. to noon: conduct research and begin writing assigned editorial

noon to 1 p.m.: lunch, perhaps with fellow staff members, perhaps with sources

1 p.m. to 2 p.m.: complete editorial

2 p.m. to 4 p.m.: work on another editorial, a long-range project, get out of the office for first-hand research, etc.

4 p.m. to 5 p.m.: check page proofs, tend to correspondence, perhaps some time to read

Now all this assumes that someone else is handling the letters, the syndicated columns and the cartoons (local and syndicated), as well as taking telephone calls and dealing with walk-ins. It also assumes that someone else is managing the budget, meeting with the editor or publisher and attending all the meetings and training sessions that modern managers want their employees to participate in. The schedule doesn't include time for long-range planning, election interviews or special projects outside the daily run of editorials. It does not include 7:30 to 10 p.m. a night or two a week, during which the conscientious editorial writer is likely to be attending a civic, political, cultural or social event. Nor does it include family or personal time for Little League or high school basketball games, school concerts, ballet lessons or choir practice.

"Managing time wisely is the single most difficult job that editorial page editors [and writers] face," Morgan McGinley of the *Day* in New London, Conn., wrote in a *Masthead* symposium on "Managing Time and Money." "You must periodically review and reinvent the good ideas you have, and throw out bad ones that have not worked." Acknowledging all the tasks that tend to keep writers in the office, McGinley's advice was: "Free up writers to work on special assignments. Get them out of the building and let them feel there is more to life on the editorial page than long, boring meetings in which the same people give familiar, predictable views on a subject."[16]

CONCLUSION

The staff size that editorial writers are likely to regard as ideal may depend on their own prior experience. To writers who have run a one-person show, a two-person staff may look like a luxury. To writers who have worked on a larger staff, two persons are likely to seem wholly inadequate. Although some attempts have been made to prescribe staff sizes for papers of varying circulation sizes, the circulation of a newspaper has little correlation with the work that needs to be done on an editorial page. The page must come out every day, whatever the circulation; columns and letters must be edited; a certain number of editorials must be written; visitors and callers must be dealt with; meetings, editorial conferences and research must be attended to.

All things being equal, a larger editorial page staff should be able to turn out a better product. If writers have an opportunity to spend time thinking about one or two areas of editorial writing, instead of having to render the judgments of Solomon on all issues, they should be better editorial writers. If they write only one editorial a day, they should be able to do a better job than if they have to write three. However, if they overspecialize, they may work themselves out of their jobs. Editorial writers must never stop being generalists.

Questions and Exercises

1. Editorial page staffs on the average apparently have not been growing in size. What does this seem to say about the attitudes of publishers and other holders of the newspaper budget purse strings?
2. What are the advantages of a one-person editorial page staff? The disadvantages? Do you think the disadvantages outweigh the advantages?
3. Determine the number of editorial page persons on papers in your area. How do these staffs compare in size with the staff sizes mentioned in this chapter?
4. How are the editorial duties distributed among the staff members of these papers?
5. How do the editorial conferences—if any—work on these papers? Who attends? How often do they meet? How are assignments made? Does the editor, the publisher or the editorial board make the final decisions?

CHAPTER 9 Relations with the Community

In general, I think it is acceptable to contribute money to organizations whose purposes are endorsed by one's paper.
—SUSAN HEGGER, ST. LOUIS POST-DISPATCH[1]

I choose to remain virginal.
—NORMAN A. CHERNISS, RIVERSIDE (CALIF.) PRESS ENTERPRISE[2]

Some of the toughest decisions that editors and editorial writers face involve the degree to which they allow themselves to participate in or contribute to civic, business and political causes. Implicit in these decisions is the question: How can editorial writers be a part of a community without becoming biased, or appearing to be biased, through associations with groups with special interests? Closely related to this aspect of maintaining integrity and the appearance of integrity is the problem all journalists face: To what extent, if any, can you accept drinks, meals and trips from people with whom you deal without compromising yourself? These questions have provoked a lot of conscience-searching among editorial writers and have led several organizations in the newspaper business to conclude that consciences need help through codes and guidelines.

TO PARTICIPATE OR NOT TO PARTICIPATE

Those who defend participation in community affairs contend that editorial writers should recognize that they are part of their communities and should feel a responsibility to help make them better places in which to live. But others contend just as strongly that, if writers become involved, they compromise their credibility in commenting on community affairs.

If editorial writers were to subscribe wholeheartedly to either philosophy, decision-making would be easy. If they thought that working through organizations was as appropriate for them as molding opinions through their writing, they would say yes when asked to participate in a worthy cause. If they thought they should undertake no obligations, they would say no. Most editorial writers, however, seem to think that there are some occasions when they can or should become involved and some occasions when they cannot or should not. Places for drawing the line are almost as numerous as editors and writers themselves. When 13 editorial writers participated in a 1966 *Masthead* symposium on the question of proper community involvement, they gave 13 different answers.[3]

Political and Civic Activities

Editorial writers generally agree they ought to avoid public partisan politics. A poll in 1988 found that 89 percent of editorial writers said they agreed or strongly agreed that they should avoid partisan political organizations. Only 9 percent (down from 19 percent in 1979) reported that they had given money or bought tickets to help a party or a candidate. A similar percentage had urged individuals to vote for a party or candidate. Only 7 percent had attended meetings, rallies or dinners not required by their jobs. The poll revealed that 46 percent of the newspapers prohibited political participation by employees and that an additional 37 percent discouraged or strongly discouraged participation. These percentages marked a sharp increase over polls taken in 1971 and 1979, when 0 (!) percent and 29 percent of newspapers, respectively, prohibited participation.[4]

When asked about professional and civic organizations, however, editorial writers were not so clearly in agreement. According to the same poll, 66 percent participated in professional journalism societies; 46 percent in civic, religious, fraternal and veterans groups; 31 percent in non-profit, non-governmental organizations. Of the respondents, 13 percent had participated in public issue groups (foreign policy, civil liberties) and 6 percent in governmental boards or agencies. Only 12 percent said they had not participated in any civic or professional groups.

The principal argument against joining and participating in political and civic activities is that association with organizations and causes may cause "conflicts of interest, real or apparent," in the wording of the Basic Statement of Principles of the National Conference of Editorial Writers (NCEW). Conflicts, or at least the appearance of conflicts, can sneak up on you when you least expect them. Paul Greenberg, editorial page editor of the *Pine Bluff* (Ark.) *Commercial,* agreed at one time to serve as president of his local temple. He thought that certainly that position would present no risk of conflict with his editorial duties. But within two months the temple became involved in a zoning controversy. Since then, he said, he has been more cautious about volunteering for causes. "I would say that serving spaghetti at a fundraising dinner is the highest role to which the editorial writer ought to aspire," he told a panel on ethics at an NCEW convention.[5]

For David Boeyink, one-time editorial page editor of the *Owensboro* (Ky.) *Messenger-Inquirer,* a personal friendship led to a potential conflict of interest. As a newcomer to Owensboro, Boeyink renewed what had been a casual acquaintance with a fellow student at Harvard Divinity School. The families of the two became friends. They attended the same church. As staff member of the Owensboro Chamber of Commerce, the friend "was a great source of insights into local political figures," Boeyink recalled. Then the staff member moved up to become chief administrative officer. "His new prominence . . . provided a few moments of concern, particularly on rare editorials involving the chamber," Boeyink wrote in an article in *The Masthead.* "But with our principal focus on government and education, the problem of possible favoritism never became acute." Then the friend decided to run for mayor and at the same time became executive director of a citizens committee on education, of which Boeyink was a member. Boeyink immediately resigned from the committee. The two stopped talking politics in any informal setting. The families saw each other less and less frequently. To have cut off all ties, he said, "would have meant leaving the congregation we loved and virtually all the best friends we had in Owensboro," a price that was "too high." Boeyink said he was certain he could have written editorials critical of the new mayor's policies, although the newspaper generally supported the programs he was proposing. Boeyink, however, was never put to the test, since, in a decision that had nothing to do with the situation, he changed careers and left Owensboro.[6]

While he was on the *Richmond* (Va.) *News Leader*, James J. Kilpatrick accepted an appointment to a state commission that at first seemed innocuous but eventually came to embarrass him. For eight years he served on the state Commission on Constitutional Government, an agency organized to encourage states to defend their reserved powers under the federal government. He also was chairman of publications for the commission. But when the commission came under attack in the Virginia General Assembly, Kilpatrick said he found himself in a trap. "I could not defend the Commission's publications without appearing to be saying what a great guy am I." In the end, he said, he wrote a "lame piece" to the effect that the incident ought to have taught him a lesson about becoming involved with boards and commissions.[7]

Kilpatrick said that he recognized that, while a newspaper's policy may admonish editors and editorial writers to avoid positions with groups that might be the subject of editorial comment, "in actual practice it tends to get bent around the edges." What is an editor to do when asked to serve on the board of the local library, the symphony orchestra, the community college or the art museum? Or perhaps a committee on public parks or race relations? Sometimes, he said, editors can get away with saying no, but inevitably requests catch up with them. Accepting some of these requests may leave the editor's "editorial purity something less than that of Ivory soap," he said, but they also are likely to make the editor "a better informed and more useful citizen of the community on which the paper depends."[8]

In the same vein, Laird B. Anderson, professor at American University, has expressed concern that, in overreacting to disconnect themselves from public people and events, editorial writers and other journalists have become second-class citizens. "In following this road to second-class status so that we can be viewed as more ethical and credible, we have righteously denied ourselves equality with the citizens whose consciousness we want to reach," Anderson said. "Our offices have all too often become havens, a refuge to scurry back to after dipping a toe in the vast sea of public affairs and then writing about what we've seen or learned. Many of us, I suspect, like this protective buffer. It uncomplicates our lives."[9]

Some of those who try to draw a line between the acceptable and unacceptable differentiate between reporters and opinion writers. Don Lowery, editorial director of WHDH-TV in Boston, told an NCEW convention panel that he had chaired a portion of the local United Way campaign, served on the board of a Special Olympics organization and participated in a public policy group. "As a reporter, I would have declined all such activities," he said. "But my role as an editorialist is different. As an advocate for editorial positions, I see nothing wrong with promoting activities we support."[10]

When editorial writers were asked in a *Masthead* symposium about the ethics of contributing to charities, several drew the line between what Lewis A. Leader of the *Monterey County* (Calif.) *Herald* called "joining a non-profit group and contributing to one."[11] Susan Hegger of the *St. Louis Post-Dispatch* said she thought it was generally "acceptable to contribute money to organizations whose purposes are endorsed by one's paper" but not to organizations "whose platforms or principles run counter to one's editorial page."[12] Van Cavett of the Allentown, Pa., *Morning Call* reported that, because his paper "supported policies advocated by Planned Parenthood," he and his wife Caroline saw no conflict when she was asked to serve on the local board of the organization. "We realized going in that financial contributions and participation of fundraisers would be necessary," he said.[13]

Other writers took a harder line. Charles J. Dunsire of the *Seattle Post-Intelligencer* said he limited his contributions to the local United Way (payroll deduction), his church and a non-profit hospital foundation. He admitted, however, that he contributed annually to his alma mater, the University of Washington, "because such contributions have become necessary to retain the privilege of buying season tickets to the games of one of the nation's most successful and popular football programs."[14]

Civic or Public Journalism

The issue of what is appropriate community involvement at the level of the newspaper itself also has been raised by what is sometimes called "civic journalism" or "public journalism." For several years journalists have been discussing, debating, praising or denouncing "civic journalism." (Sometimes it is called "community journalism," but traditionally this term has referred to weekly newspapers.) As the variety and confusion of names suggests, editors have different ideas about what constitutes such journalism, but all agree that it poses two questions: To what extent should a newspaper seek input from readers in setting its news and editorial agendas? To what extent should a newspaper become involved in community issues?

The person generally recognized as the guru of "public journalism," Jay Rosen of New York University, has said that, while traditional journalism seeks to "inform the public" and acts as a "watchdog" over government, public journalism "tries to strengthen the community's capacity to recognize itself, converse well and make choices."[15] Its purpose, according to Rosen, is "to encourage civic participation, improve public debates and enhance public life, without, of course, sacrificing the independence that a free press demands and deserves."[16]

To William F. Woo of the *St. Louis Post-Dispatch*, however, talk about organizing communities sounds as though newspapers have declared "that they have become the electorate." Woo asks, "What if IBM or the Yellow Pages or Bill Gates were to [designate] themselves as the convener of the community?" Woo expresses concerns about where news and editorial decisions are made:

"Are they made in the newsrooms or at the town hall meeting, within the deliberations of the editorial board or in the place where the editor sups with the civic coalition?"[17]

The extent of disagreement among editors was illustrated during an exchange on the electronic mailing list of the NCEW. The discussion was provoked by an Associated Press news story citing the views of Michael Gartner, editor of the *Ames* (Iowa) *Tribune,* who had just won the Pulitzer Prize for his editorial writing. Gartner had given a speech in which he described "civic journalism" as the "worst thing to come along in our business in my lifetime." The news pages, he said, are "supposed to explain the community, not convene it," and reporters are "supposed to explore the issues, not solve them." Furthermore, he said, "civic journalism" encourages reporters and newspapers to "abandon their detachment from events they cover."[18]

Gartner was "right on the money," according to an unidentified respondent on the Cleveland *Plain Dealer.* "Having worked with my share of 'attached' reporters in my previous incarnation on the city desk, I couldn't agree more with him," the person said. "It's hard enough to keep reporters from grabbing the pulpit on issues about which they feel strongly. Encouraging them, as a matter of policy, to prime the pump for 'solutions' is ludicrous." Furthermore, "editorial writers don't speak with the voice of God" either.[19]

In reply, Jerry C. Ausband of the *Sun News* in Myrtle Beach, S.C., accused Gartner of "fail[ing] to understand" public journalism, which Ausband described as "all about letting the readers help you, the newspaper, shape what is news" and "getting their opinion in a formal way and responding to what they think and what they want to read." In his view, such journalism "does not replace traditional journalistic values."[20]

But, to another defender of "civic journalism," Jason Alt of Penn State's *Daily Collegian,* Ausband's description sounded "much like a marketing department conducting reader surveys instead of editors conducting nightly news meetings." Alt said he saw surveys as providing "information to redirect newsroom priorities, so that journalists can bring together the many voices of a community to help them be empowered to figure out the best solutions."[21]

After these and other opinions had been expressed, the NCEW list moderator, Phineas Fiske of *Newsday,* said he thought a principal problem was that "civic journalism" has not been clearly defined. "It seems to range from finding out what's on your community's mind, at one end, to directing your community to solutions for its problems, in the middle, to leading your community by the hand to those solutions, at the other end." He saw the first alternative as "unexceptionable" and the second as "problematic for news-side but well within the ambit of the editorial page." He saw the third as "asking for trouble when pursued news-side (although that's where it tends to be pursued, I gather), and a little worrisome for an editorial page."[22]

Descriptions and examples of what several newspapers have done with "civic journalism" appear in Chapter 19, "Innovations in Design and Content."

Business Interests

The business, as well as civic, interests of publishers and other non-news, noneditorial executives on a newspaper also can make credible editorial writing more difficult for staff members and hurt the overall credibility of the newspaper. Nor can editorial writers themselves expect exemption from the effects of economics. For one thing, the newspaper is a business; one of the first concerns of the owners is to make a profit. One of the editorial writer's concerns is to make enough money and have a steady enough job to live securely and comfortably.

To a larger extent than many businesses, the profitability of a newspaper is tied to the growth and prosperity of its community. When a community expands, a local supermarket may find its monopoly challenged; another supermarket (which incidentally becomes a potential new advertiser) moves in. The same can be said about service stations and real estate offices, even radio stations. But for the newspaper the result is likely to be more circulation and more advertising, not a new competitor. The temptation to ally a newspaper with whatever brings growth and income to a community has been a fairly consistent one in most communities. This temptation may have proved easier to resist in recent years, with growing evidence of the financial and environmental costs of unplanned growth. Still, it remains difficult not to get excited editorially when a major industry, especially a "clean" one, is considering your town for a new plant.

The *Greensboro* (N.C.) *News & Record* faced that situation when local business leaders seemed about to convince the Carolina-Virginia Fashion Exhibitors to move from another North Carolina city to Greensboro. The local leaders hoped the new headquarters would provide a catalyst for lagging downtown renewal. The newspaper gave the story major front-page coverage. Initial editorials praised the community's efforts and urged the organization to move. But, "when the price tag for city tax contributions in support of the effort fluctuated, the newspaper editorialized that campaign leaders should keep the citizenry better informed and 'lay out the facts as quickly as possible,'" John Alexander, editorial page editor of the *News & Record*, said. Meanwhile, the other community leaders, including the newspaper, waged an all-out, eventually successful, effort to keep the organization. "The contrast in approaches has been a sore point with many business and government leaders ever since," Alexander said. "Asked to give examples of the newspaper's purported 'negativism' and lack of enthusiasm for community projects, these leaders still point to the *News & Record*'s restrained coverage, to that editorial questioning aspects of the proposal's financing, and to the [publisher's] lack of personal involvement in the recruiting effort." Alexander saw no perfect solution for situations such as this, but he concluded: "Whatever the newspaper's involvement as a corporate citizen, the editorial page must be free to state its opinions freely, consistent with its own philosophy—even if it means not backing a favored project, or raising questions about it."[23]

Closely related to the temptation to look favorably on growth is a tendency among editorial writers toward what might be called local or regional provincialism. Writers should take pride in their cities, their states and their regions. They should want to see their areas prosper and become attractive places in which to live. But it is hard sometimes for them to see beyond their own circulation areas—and such provincialism can become a vested interest. For example, a writer may condemn a proposed federal dam halfway across the country as a congressional boondoggle but praise a proposed local dam as an economic necessity. An editor in Southern California may look with longing toward what appears to be an excess of water flowing into San Francisco Bay, but an editor in Northern California is likely to argue that water in the north should stay there. One challenge for editorial writers is to lift their sights and those of their readers beyond the city limits and the near bank of the next river.

Another concern for editorial writers in the economic arena involves the ever-present threat of a clash between business interests and news or editorial policy. What does a newspaper do when a major advertiser threatens to withdraw advertising because of something that has appeared or might appear in the paper? Does the publisher stand firm and let the advertiser pull out? What does a newspaper do when it learns that an advertiser has been caught in an unfair trade practice or a sex discrimination practice? Does it publish its findings and condemn them on the editorial page? What happens when a local supermarket wants to build a new store or local business leaders want to build a football stadium in an area that the community had previously designated as non-commercial? Do the editorial writers feel free to come out against the promoter if they think the proposal is wrong?

Taking a strong stand against business interests can be tough, especially if the financial well-being of the newspaper itself is at stake. In the long run, newspapers probably serve themselves best if they take a firm stand at the beginning of a confrontation. A publisher who refuses to back down to an advertiser's threats will let it be known to other potential threateners that the paper will stand firm against them as well. A paper that can take an editorial stand against its own immediate financial interests can gain public respect that may eventually help not only its credibility but its economic condition as well.

Personal Experiences

In the nearly two decades in which I worked on editorial pages, I tried to limit my civic activities to those that required little time and seemed to pose little risk of conflict with editorial policy. Looking back, I think I should have limited myself even more. I inherited a Rotary Club membership from my predecessor on the *Columbian*, faithfully attended luncheon meetings for nearly 12 years and never encountered any conflict of interest that I recognized. I was never asked to serve on the publicity committee. I never had an occasion to write an editorial either praising or criticizing the club or its activities. Membership benefited me, I thought, because it brought me into contact with leaders of the business community whom otherwise I might have found difficult to get to know. I allowed myself to think my membership benefited the newspaper too. Instead of being an unknown person in an ivory tower, expressing opinions more liberal than most of those of the club's members, I was a fellow member whom they could poke fun at over typographical or other errors that appeared in the paper. I tried to avoid such activities as clerking at the club's rummage sale and selling tickets for its travel series.

An organization in which I was not so successful in avoiding conflict was Design for Clark County. It consisted of civic-minded citizens who wanted to ensure good government and a good environment for the community. The conflict began when I agreed to head one of four goals committees, the one on government. The committee proved to be the most active of the four, perhaps because goals can be expressed more specifically in government than in other areas of the community. Because of the attention the committee received and because the goals generally coincided with the *Columbian*'s editorial policies, some members of the community began to think that the newspaper and I were running Design. I later backed off sharply in my participation, but the association between the paper and the organization had been established so strongly in people's minds that it was several years before the effect of my initial involvement was forgotten. Design might have been more effective if it had been perceived as a voice more independent of the newspaper.

I also served for a short time on the board of the Washington Environmental Council, a private non-profit organization. No problems resulted as long as the council focused on general environmental policies, but when it began to talk about supporting and opposing candidates for the legislature, I got out fast. I found myself in Kilpatrick's shoes, however, when I agreed to serve on the Washington State Planning Commission. It was not a real planning commission. I would not have served on an official state policy agency. It was a two-year ad hoc committee of citizens and officials charged with proposing a new state planning act. Mostly it held hearings on what other people thought the state should do. Eventually the staff, with some help from commission members, drew up a model act to submit to the legislature. The act didn't get very far—or I probably would have encountered greater conflict than I did. I thought I should not comment editorially on the proposal, although I did write an article for the op-ed page trying to explain the model act (with an editor's note pointing out my connection with the commission). Participation on the commission made for two interesting and informative years. If the act had been seriously considered for adoption, though, a conflict of interest would have prevented me from commenting editorially on it and probably would have hurt the credibility of anything the *Columbian* said, even if someone else had done the writing.

I felt less concern about the four years that I served on the Washington Commission for the Humanities, a private, non-profit organization that awarded money mostly to local groups to bring the ideas of humanities scholars to bear on public issues. Some of the awards were controversial among the commission members, but I don't remember any award that would have called for editorial comment in my newspaper. (This was before the National Endowment for the Arts and, to a lesser degree, the National Endowment for the Humanities, became matters of public controversy.) One reason I enjoyed the commission was that it gave me the chance to know and associate with the other members. It was a stimulating group, concerned with projects that generally were far enough away from my circulation area to present few chances for conflict. Besides, I told myself, an editorial writer needs to have some stimulating, continuing associations beyond those of family, religion and the Rotary Club. Editorial writers aren't supposed to be hermits.

To Accept or Not to Accept

Another potential conflict of interest concerns what to do about "freebies," the gifts, large and small, that people with views to push are only too willing to share with newspaper people. In recent years government and business, including the newspaper industry, have tended to become more sensitive to possible conflicts because of such gifts. Tighter codes have been written for public officials, and in many instances editorial writers have written in support of the tougher restrictions. If newspapers expect public officials to observe a higher standard, should not newspapers themselves observe an equally high standard?

In the mid-1970s, following the lead of other journalism organizations, NCEW tightened its Basic Statement of Principles. The conflict-of-interest portion of the original statement, adopted in 1949, had merely said: "The editorial writer should never be motivated by personal interest, nor use his influence to seek special favors for himself or others. He should hold himself above any possible taint of corruption, whatever its source." The revised statement now reads:

The editorial writer should never use his or her influence to seek personal favors of any kind. Gifts of value, free travel and other favors that can compromise integrity, or appear to do so, should not be accepted.

The writer should be constantly alert to conflicts of interest, real or apparent, including those that may arise from financial holdings, secondary employment, holding public office or involvement in political, civic or other organizations. Timely disclosure can minimize suspicion. Editors should seek to hold syndicates to these standards.

The writer, further to enhance editorial page credibility, also should encourage the institution he or she represents to avoid conflicts of interest, real or apparent.

The Professional Standards Committee and the Executive Committee of NCEW had wanted more specific language on freebies: "Gifts, free travel and other things of value can compromise integrity. Nothing of more than token value should be accepted." A majority of NCEW members, however, preferred to rely on their own consciences, rather than on a strict rule, to tell them what was acceptable and what was not.

Free Trips

The wording in the statement regarding travel was softened partly because NCEW officers at that time were hoping to arrange a trip for members to the People's Republic of China, and a trip partly paid for by the Chinese was seen as the only way to get there. Similar concerns were expressed by all six editorial writers who responded to invitations to participate in a *Masthead* symposium on junkets. Basically they argued that the benefits of subsidized trips abroad outweighed any dangers that might arise from possible conflicts of interest. H. Brandt Ayers of the *Anniston* (Ala.) *Star* said he never would have been able to travel to the then Soviet Union and meet leaders firsthand if the trip had not been subsidized. "What we wrote is a better standard for judging independence, intelligence and integrity than who paid for the trip," he said.[24] John Causten Currey of the *Daily Oklahoman* and *Oklahoma City Times* said that familiarization trips offered by the armed services provided the only way that editorial writers could see what the defense budgets bought. He said a paid trip to Israel as an official guest provided him a picture of the Middle East he could not have obtained as a private citizen.[25] Smith Hempstone, then a syndicated columnist, contended that any problems involved in accepting a subsidized trip could be overcome by letting readers know who paid for the trip.[26] Richard B. Laney of the *Deseret News,* Salt Lake City, wondered how free travel could be compromising to those who accepted it, since he suspected that invitations are extended only to those known, or thought to be, friendly. "The persuasion of those already persuaded may not be gutsy PR," he wrote, "but it's hardly an attack on editorial morality either."[27]

One of the earliest, and strongest statements concerning the dangers of accepting free trips was made more than 20 years before NCEW tightened its code. In 1952 Robert Estabrook of the *Washington Post* wrote:

At least a respectable argument can be made that the public interest is served in making available to newspaper readers more information about governmental programs, particularly programs abroad. The plain fact is that many newspapers, if left to their own resources, would neglect these areas and their readers would be the poorer for it. . . .

If we expect to persuade our followers there is something wrong with unreported political funds or junkets by Congressmen at the taxpayers' expense, then we have an obligation, it seems to me, to pay our own way. We properly criticize "influence" with public officials, but I wonder if our readers, if they knew of the all-expense tours, would see much difference.[28]

Stricter codes, unless one stays home and makes no junkets, cost more money. In general, however, newspapers and the other media are more prosperous than they were when Estabrook wrote. If editors and publishers think their staff members should be sent off somewhere for a story, they should pay as much of their way as they possibly can. What they pay out in money they will regain in credibility with readers.

Gifts

When newspaper salaries were notoriously low, some reporters reasoned that free liquor and tickets to shows and games helped make up for the bucks they didn't get. Today salaries are up and gifts are down. Some newspapers have attempted to stop the flow of gifts, however inconsequential. "We no longer see cases of scotch arriving for the sports staff at Christmas," Catherine Ford, associate editor of the *Calgary* (Alberta) *Herald,* wrote in a *Masthead* symposium on ethics. "The shopping columnist does not furnish his house with presents from retailers; the fashion editor buys her own clothes. No newspaper with any sense of ethics at all accepts free trips, considerations from advertisers or free gifts to staff members. Only rarely will an editor approve of staff participation in media events offering prizes, or accept complimentary tickets for staff."[29]

Some editors contend that if writers can be bought for a bottle of whiskey or a lunch they have no integrity worth buying. Mark Clutter of the *Wichita* (Kan.) *Beacon* has asked why newspaper people should "be offended by gifts of whiskey, ham or similar items." Sometimes the gifts are a matter of "public relations routine"; sometimes they are "expressions of genuine friendship or admiration," he said. "Whatever the motive, it would be churlish to refuse. . . . No one can give payola to a man of integrity. To a man who has no integrity, practically everything is payola."[30] Jack Craemer of the *San Rafael* (Calif.) *Independent Journal,* however, said everyone on that paper sent everything back to donors, even though they "look upon us as goof-balls."[31]

CONCLUSION

Probably few editorial writers, and newspaper people in general for that matter, are directly influenced by the gifts, travel and other favors they receive. The publicity over tougher codes has made many of them sensitive to the most blatant forms of handouts. They know that they are not being influenced by the ticket or the drink. Editorial writers may know that they have made every effort possible to report objectively on a free trip they have taken. But do their readers know? If they were told, would they believe it?

When conflict of interest is involved, appearance can be as important as reality in maintaining credibility.

Questions and Exercises

1. As an editorial writer, where would you draw the line on participation in political and civic affairs? Would the size of the community make a difference?
2. Does an editorial writer or editor have a responsibility to participate in the life of the community in addition to contributing through work on the paper? Again, might the answer depend on the size of the community?
3. Should an editorial writer feel freer to accept a civic task that is less likely than other tasks to affect the community in which the paper circulates? Does distance, in other words, make a difference?
4. Should an editorial writer feel freer to contribute to causes supported by the editorial policy of the newspaper than to other causes?
5. Should newspaper management people feel freer to participate in community affairs than news and editorial people do?
6. Should a newspaper establish a code that spells out what freebies, trips and other perquisites news and editorial people can accept? If so, where should the paper draw the line?
7. If a newspaper does not establish a code, how should it avoid conflict of interest or the appearance of conflict of interest?
8. How do you respond to the argument that, if journalists are not honest and trustworthy, no code will make them so?
9. If you were an editorial writer, what trips would you regard as acceptable?
10. Have you seen evidence in the columns of newspapers in your area that indicates the writers do or do not accept free trips? If they do, do they explain the circumstances to their readers?
11. Do the papers in your area have official codes concerning professional conduct? If so what do they prescribe?

SECTION **3**

The
How
of
the
Editorial
Page

CHAPTER 10 Nine Steps to Editorial Writing

No magic formulas exist for writing editorials. No two editorials are ever exactly alike. Editorial writers have their own styles. Newspapers have different editorial policies. Each day brings new topics for comment. Yet, in spite of all the many possible ways to approach writing editorials, the process is basically the same.

An experienced writer may be able to turn out a prize-winning editorial in an hour or so. A beginner may struggle all day. But each, consciously or subconsciously, proceeds through a succession of steps to produce the journalistic writing form that we call an editorial. The purpose of this chapter is to walk the editorial writer or would-be editorial writer through these steps, one by one. The steps can be defined in different ways, but for our purposes let us identify these nine:

1. Selecting a topic
2. Determining the purpose of the editorial
3. Determining the audience
4. Deciding on the tone of the editorial
5. Researching the topic
6. Determining the general format
7. Writing the beginning of the editorial
8. Writing the body of the editorial
9. Writing the conclusion

To provide an illustration, we will select a topic for an editorial and follow the writing of the editorial through the nine steps.

SELECTING A TOPIC

Selecting a topic usually involves deciding among a variety of subjects that might seem appropriate on any one day.

Editorial writers typically scan the morning newspaper, which usually carries international, national, regional, state and local stories that might be worthy of comment, plus off-beat stories that can provide topics for change-of-pace editorials.

On a several-person staff, where writers have their own specialties, some of these topics may automatically fall to certain writers. Selecting a topic may be more difficult on a small, especially a one-person, staff. Writers with limited time for editorial writing are likely to select subjects that they know about or that they can research easily. When time runs short, it is often easier to write about a national or international issue than about a regional or local one, on which you are likely to have to do your own digging for information. Even where writers are few, they should try to select topics from day to day that will provide readers with a variety of subjects at different levels, from local to international.

Questions a writer might ask in deciding on a topic: Can I make a significant contribution to public understanding on this topic? Do I have information or insights that are not generally held among my readers? Is discussion of the topic timely: does it come at an appropriate time for public discussion? Some of these questions may overlap with our next steps, determining the purpose and the audience of the editorial, but they are part of the process of picking a topic.

For the example in this chapter, let us decide that, from among the topics available to write about on this day, we will select a story about a North Carolina jury that awarded $5.5 million in punitive damages to Food Lion supermarket in a civil suit filed against ABC News. ABC had aired a segment on "PrimeTime Live" that used undercover employees and undercover cameras to show out-of-date meat handled and sold in unsanitary conditions. The verdict and the award were based on the deceptive actions of two ABC producers. The topic should be of interest to all journalists, because it raises legal and ethical questions about some practices of investigative reporters.

Picking editorial topics is by itself an important part of the process of trying to persuade readers. Communication research shows that the mass media exert their strongest influence when they help set the agenda for public discussion. What the media choose to write and talk about is seen as having a more significant effect on the public than what the media say about the chosen topics.[2] Selecting also is the first step toward getting readers to read what you write. You should not pick topics solely to attract the most readers, but if you write about obscure, technical or dull topics, potential readers are certain to move on to other parts of the paper.

DETERMINING PURPOSE AND AUDIENCE

Determining the purpose and determining the audience of an editorial are related. The purpose of an editorial is to convince a certain audience to think or do something. The purpose may not be to persuade all of our readers. We may want to urge all readers to vote for a certain candidate for office, or we may want to direct our editorial primarily toward convincing readers who are not inclined to be favorable to this candidate. We may want to urge readers in general to turn out for a public hearing on a proposed freeway through the city, or we may want to convince members of the highway commission that the freeway is not a good idea.

We may have more than one audience in mind for an editorial. We may want both to convince the highway commission and to get people to turn out for a hearing. On occasion an editorial, addressed to readers in general, will contain sufficient technical information to speak to the experts as well. On other occasions an editorial will be directed specifically to the narrower group. In two-level editorials, writers should be careful not to become so involved in the fine points that they lose their general readers.

"Don't kill toxics law" is an editorial, published in the Eugene, Ore., *Register-Guard*, that is specifically aimed at Oregon House members and the governor. The editorial opposes a measure, already passed by the Senate, that would invalidate a tough toxics-disclosure requirement for industries in Eugene. But the editorial also is directed at disclosure supporters, pointing out to them that they have a responsibility to see that the requirement, if it remains, works economically and does not become a "job destroyer."

Most editorials are less specific in terms of intended audience or intended action. In many cases editorials, at least on state, national or international issues, will never be read by the people likely to make the decisions on those issues. In such instances, an editorial may urge some action, but the purpose is primarily to enlighten and convince local readers.

Such was the case involving another Oregon issue that appeared in the *St. Petersburg* (Fla.) *Times*. In an incident that got national attention, a prisoner's private confession to his priest was surreptitiously taped by local law enforcement authorities, who planned to use the confession in court. Since most readers probably would not be aware of a case from that far away, and because the circumstances were complex, the writer provided an extended explanation. The editorial ("The sanctity of the confessional") cited the position of the Catholic Archdiocese of Portland and civil rights groups in support of the claim that the tape should not be used and should be destroyed. (Eventually the courts ruled that the tape should not be admitted into evidence.)

The purpose of an editorial and the audience for it will depend partly on our understanding of how persuasion through editorials takes place. Half a century ago mass communications were thought to exert a strong, direct influence on audiences. The Bullet Theory (or Hypodermic Needle Theory) that was popular then suggested that information and opinion from the media flowed directly into the heads of recipients. Editorials, presumably, would be read and acted upon by readers. Then in the 1940s researchers began to find that audiences were not paying as much attention as had been thought and were not being persuaded to the degree anticipated.[3] To explain this apparent inattention, researchers came up with the Two-Step Flow Theory. It maintained that ideas tended to flow from the media to a select group of opinion leaders, who in turn passed ideas on to the general population. Thus, if only 20 percent of readers read editorials every day, this theory suggested, that was all right, since presumably these few were the opinion leaders. But that theory didn't last long either. Further research showed that information flow is much more complex. The population is not neatly divided into leaders and followers. Much information goes directly to users of the media, not through a

Don't Kill Toxics Law
Fears of its effects are premature

The Oregon Senate has approved a bill invalidating the "toxic right to know" charter amendment approved by Eugene voters last year. In addition to intruding on local communities' prerogative to govern their own affairs, the bill responds to fears that stand a good chance of never being realized. The House should reject the repeal attempt, and failing that, Gov. John Kitzhaber should veto it.

During the next several months the board will be accepting suggestions for clarifications and improvements in the guidelines, giving Hyundai or any other company an opportunity to point out any provisions it can't live with.

The toxic right to know law calls upon private companies to track and report their purchase, use and disposal of toxic chemicals in greater detail than is required under state and federal regulations. Some businesses fear they won't be able to comply, exposing them to fines of up to $25,000 a day. Hyundai Semiconductor of America, in particular, has told legislators that it will close the computer chip manufacturing plant it is building in west Eugene and cancel planned expansions unless the Legislature overrides Eugene's law.

Hyundai should have issued that warning last fall, when Eugene voters were deciding whether to support the charter amendment. Though concerns about chemical exposure and environmental contamination are not limited to a single company, Hyundai's arrival in Eugene was clearly the catalyst for the right-to-know campaign. The election result might have been different if Hyundai had said the law would force the company to pack its bags. In the absence of such a stark choice, voters decided the benefits of tighter reporting processes outweighed any potential inconvenience.

If Hyundai did not know in November that the toxic right to know law was a plant killer, it's hard to understand how it can reach that conclusion in June. The city's Toxics Board is only now completing its handbook of guidelines for compliance. During the next several months the board will be accepting suggestions for clarifications and improvements in the guidelines, giving Hyundai or any other company an opportunity to point out any provisions it can't live with. Companies won't actually begin implementing the guidelines until Jan. 1, 1998, and their first reports won't be due until April 1999.

This timetable should drain the urgency from companies' concerns about the toxics law. It also undermines the case for a compromise being discussed in the House, which would allow Eugene's law to stand but would block enforcement actions for two years. By the time companies have gained a year's experience with the chemical tracking system and are required to submit their first reports, the Legislature will be back in session. If the law proves to be impossibly cumbersome, discriminatory in its effects or unbearably expensive, the Legislature can provide whatever remedy is warranted by actual experience. Better yet, Eugene voters could correct whatever defects are discovered in the law they've adopted.

Senate supporters of the preemption proposal—Senate Bill 1226—say they want to preserve uniformity in statewide regulations governing toxic chemicals. It has yet to be shown, however, how an absence of uniformity will create any problems for Eugene or the rest of the state. And if uniformity is desirable, it has yet to be shown whether local standards should be relaxed to conform with statewide regulations or whether it would be better to bring statewide rules into line with Eugene's more stringent processes.

Indeed, the unspoken concern in Salem may not be that Eugene's charter amendment won't work but that it will work too well, leading other communities to adopt toxic right to know laws. The charter amendment's supporters have a strong interest in making the process work economically and without punitive enforcement—if it proves to be a job destroyer, the entire concept will be discredited in Eugene and beyond. It will be necessary to monitor the toxics law's effects closely, but that is Eugene's responsibility, not the state's. Certainly the state need not intervene before the experiment even gets under way.

Register-Guard

▬▬▬ The Sanctity of the Confessional

Of the recognized privileged communications, the confession of a penitent to a priest would seem the most sacred. The act of confession, ridding one's soul of the missteps in a life, is by its nature incriminating to the penitent. That is especially true when the confession is heard in a jail and, unbeknownst to priest and prisoner, is taped by officials.

That is what happened in Eugene, Ore., last month. A 20-year-old prisoner implicated in the deaths of three teens asked for a Catholic priest. But before the Rev. Tim Mockaitis met with Conan Wayne Hale, prison authorities arranged for the confession to be taped without the knowledge of either of the participants. A confession is sacred, and its confidentiality is protected by law. The tape should be destroyed. Prison officials should be disciplined in such a way that this will not happen again.

The district attorney in Lane County where this occurred, Doug Harcleroad, cites a portion of Oregon law that he says allowed the taping.

He acquired the tape through a court order and may decide to use it in the prosecution of Hale. His primary concern is to solve the triple homicide, an admirable sense of purpose if he were not trampling rights, laws and long-held customs in the process. Hale faces burglary and theft charges in the triple deaths.

The Catholic Archdiocese of Portland called for the tape to be destroyed, quoting to Harcleroad the portion of Oregon law that protects the confidentiality of what is said between priests and followers.

The American Civil Liberties Union also protested. The Catholic League for Religious and Civil Rights, an association of lay Catholics, called for a federal investigation of the incident.

All of this is an appropriate uproar over an egregious invasion of privacy and an assault on freedom of religion. No question, the tape should be destroyed.

St. Petersburg Times

---

middle level.[4] Reader surveys show that relatively large percentages of readers read editorials at least once in a while.[5]

Current theory suggests that it is upon this general audience that a newspaper's editorials have the most effect over a long period. The effect is produced not so much by the persuasion of specific editorials as by the day-to-day dripping of the editorial writer's ink on the stone of the public consciousness. It is the members of a community who decide elections, decide whether to stay or move to another city, or feel good or bad about their community. All these people are the editorial writer's principal audience, even when an editorial calls on a school board to fire a superintendent or criticizes a city manager for a mistake. Public officials are as likely to be motivated by an aroused public as by an editorial's eloquent logic.

One purpose in developing the Food Lion story in this chapter is to explore the implications for covering investigative stories in the future. Journalists will be interested in this aspect. But the general public should also be concerned about whether it will be less well served in the future by constraints on "watchdog" media. We will try to evaluate the expected effects of the verdict from the viewpoints of both supporters and critics.

DECIDING THE TONE

At least as far back as Aristotle, writers have been concerned with how they can best persuade their audiences. Aristotle identified three avenues available to the persuader: the character of the persuader, the attitude of the hearer and the arguments themselves.[6] The more credible the persuader, the more likely it is that an audience will be persuaded. If an editorial page has attained credibility with its readers over the years, editorials on that page are likely to be viewed favorably. Aristotle thought the communicator needed good sense, good will and a good moral character—appropriate prescriptions for an editorial writer.[7] Concerning the attitude of the audience, Aristotle saw that "persuasion is effected through the audience when they are brought . . . into a state of emotion." For example, "pain or joy, or liking or hatred" can have an effect in changing attitudes. Concerning the third avenue, he saw that "persuasion is effected by the argument themselves."[8] Thus, at least from the time of Aristotle, persuaders have recognized that they have a choice: They can appeal to the emotions or to the rationality of their audiences.

When editorial writers select a tone for an editorial, they have many choices, ranging from deeply serious to satirical and humorous. As for the choice between an appeal primarily to emotion or one primarily to reason, some recent research suggests that emotion and reason may not necessarily be in opposition to each other and that simultaneous appeals to both may serve to reinforce persuasion.[9] For the purposes of most editorials, however, writers choose between an appeal based mainly on feelings, values and symbols and one based mainly on information, evidence and logic. Their decisions will depend on the subject matter and the occasion as well as their own preferences. On the day following the assassination of a prominent political figure, for example, a writer might use an emotional tone to express outrage and grief over the tragedy. The next day the writer might take a more rational approach to talk about what contributed to the killing and how to prevent such incidents in the future. An emotional approach might be appropriate to provide entertainment, to arouse readers to action, to chastise or to praise. A rational approach might be more appropriate to explain to readers something they don't know or to convince them of the correctness of the editorial writer's conclusions.

Emotion undoubtedly plays a smaller role in editorial writing today than several decades ago, when daily newspapers were numerous and subscribers could take the paper that came closest to expressing their own opinions. Readers relished reading emotional, partisan appeals, and, if opinions were not changed, they were at least reinforced. Today's editorial writers must appeal to readers with a much broader spectrum of opinions. A rousing editorial based mostly on bombast may please a small group of partisans but leave other readers unconvinced or repulsed. Today's readers are better educated than readers of a hundred years ago and people as a whole are better informed; they should be more able to recognize incorrect or incomplete information. It may be more fun to dash off an editorial that attacks a person or policy without mercy, and perhaps without much thought; such an editorial may draw the strongest, most immediate response from readers. But what value does the editorial have beyond giving a momentary emotional high to some readers and long-term pain to others? Henry M. Keezing of the *New Britain* (Conn.) *Herald* said that one of his prized possessions was a letter to the editor lauding a flamboyant editorial he had whipped up in a matter of minutes. The letter was highly complimentary but it "was written in pencil, in a scrawling longhand, on a piece of paper which a beer distributor gives to cafes and taverns for use for menus." Keezing had made a hit with someone in a tavern. But he said he would have much preferred to hear from a community leader, a legislator or a person of influence.[10]

Columnist James J. Kilpatrick, who writes with about as much indignation as any American newspaper writer, has described how the complexities of today's world have inhibited him from just sounding off. He noted that writing about something you know nothing about is easy; "when research fails, prejudice is there to prop you." But "what raises the sweat and paralyzes the fingers on the keys is to grapple with an issue in which the equities are divided," he said. "It is a maddening thing, but damned little in the editor's world is all white or all black; the editor's world is full of mugwump grays."[11]

The time has come now for us to decide on the tone that we will take in our editorial about "PrimeTime Live." That should be an easy decision after the discussion above. Subjects relating to First Amendment rights might, on occasion, be written in an emotional manner. It might be necessary to raise a public outcry against the trampling of journalistic or religious freedoms. If a newspaper reporter has been held in contempt of court and jailed for trying to report a trial, we might sound off in loud protest against the actions of the judge. The subject we have picked probably will require considerable explanation. While we will hope to convince readers of our point of view, we will not be asking them to take up pickets and march around the courthouse. A rational approach seems to be needed here.

RESEARCHING THE TOPIC

When we decide whether our editorial will be primarily emotional or rational in tone, we also determine the type of research we will have to do to write the editorial. If we can write the piece off the tops of our heads, we can skip research. If we are going to present only one point of view (about which we will say more when we discuss the next step) we can limit our research to the arguments on one side. The amount of research conducted by writers depends to some extent on how much time they have and the availability of resource materials. Very few writers have the luxury of going to the public library or a law library or the city hall or the courthouse to dig out information for that day's editorial. A telephone call—to an office across town or to the state capital—may provide a writer with the only opportunity to obtain information that is not immediately available in the newspaper office. So the kinds of reference materials mentioned in Chapter 4 should be nearby.

The first news story that I read concerning the outcome of the Food Lion trial appeared in the *Roanoke Times* on Jan. 23, 1997. As it turned out, the story in my second morning newspaper, the *Washington Post*, was the same except for a couple of paragraphs omitted from the Roanoke paper. The *Roanoke Times* editors had decided to use the *Post*'s account rather than the Associated Press story (which probably was shorter).

Even though editorial writers face daily deadlines, the Internet has opened up all kinds of possibilities for instant research on current topics. In the Food Lion case, editorial writers could be fairly certain that on the morning of Jan. 23 every newspaper's website would have an article on this case. Using the Internet, I called up the *New York Times* story.

The *Washington Post* had quotes from Roone Arledge, ABC News president; Richard Wyatt, Food Lion attorney; Tom Smith, Food Lion chief executive; the jury foreman; Bruce Sanford, First Amendment lawyer; Jane Kirtley, the executive director of the Reporters' Committee for Freedom of the Press; and William Serrin, chairman of the journalism department at New York University. (Serrin said the "PrimeTime Live" production was "typical television fare, not particularly good journalism.")[12]

The *New York Times* quoted Arledge of ABC; Smith of Food Lion; Neville L. Johnson, a lawyer who had filed numerous hidden-camera cases; Tom Rosenthiel, the director of the Project for Excellence in Journalism; two jurors; and Neal Shapiro, the executive director of rival NBC's "Dateline." (Rosenthiel said that "those pursuing a noble journalistic goal are being punished for the excessive and trivial use of hidden cameras.")[13]

Both stories made clear that the truth of the broadcast was not an issue, but, as the *Times* reported, CBS "used techniques like having producers submit fake resumes to get jobs in the meat department of company stores, and then used hidden cameras to film there."

So it appears that the case is not a simple one. The accuracy of the report is not at issue. Both newspapers quoted media sources who were not pleased with the tactics ABC employed. According to the *Times*, "several jurors said . . . that, although they supported investigative reporting, they took issue with ABC's methods."

From reading these accounts we get the idea that, while investigative reporters may have some cause for concern, the reason ABC got in trouble was that its producers may have exceeded acceptable limits in their undercover operation.

DETERMINING THE GENERAL FORMAT

Deciding whether to be basically emotional or rational in our editorial does not determine how the editorial will be written, especially if we decide on a rational tone. Communication researchers have devoted a lot of effort to trying to discover how arguments can be presented in the most persuasive manner. Among their concerns have been (1) one-sided versus two-sided arguments, (2) the ordering of arguments and (3) the degree to which opinions can be changed.

Research going back to World War II suggests that the one-sided versus two-sided decision partly depends on the audience being addressed. One-sided arguments were found to be more persuasive when the receivers of messages were in agreement with the arguments or when receivers were of lower intelligence or less educated. This approach was also found to be more effective when the receivers were not familiar with the issue being discussed and were not likely to be exposed to opposition arguments in the future, and when the topic was not controversial.[14] Presentation of opposing arguments was more effective when the receivers were initially hostile to the persuader's view, were highly educated, were accustomed to hearing both sides of an argument or were likely to hear the other side eventually.[15]

Researchers have come up with contradictory findings about the order of arguments. Both primacy (the favored argument first) and recency (the favored argument last) have been found to be persuasive. The primacy approach has the advantage of drawing an early favorable opinion from the audience, an opinion that may remain unchanged during the remainder of the presentation. The recency approach has the advantage of giving the last impression a better chance of being remembered. One line of reasoning suggests that, if you have arguments that are likely to be received favorably by your audience, you should present them first to establish a favorable setting for less favorable arguments later. If you have a solution for a problem or a need, it may be better to present the problem or the need first, then suggest your solution.[16] Researchers agree that the weakest spot for an argument is in the middle of the message, so you might put arguments unfavorable to your position there.[17]

The third aspect of communication research involves the extent to which readers can be persuaded to change their opinions. It seems clear that readers' first inclinations are to seek and perceive information that reinforces their present viewpoints. Some studies suggest that reinforcing opinions is about all that can be expected of editorials. Readers, they point out, tend to ignore, disbelieve or reinterpret information that does not conform to their own beliefs. Still, some research shows that readers sometimes seek out information that is contrary to their beliefs and, within limits, are willing to modify their beliefs. A person presumably is able to feel comfortable with a different opinion if it is perceived to fall within a certain comfort zone. The closer the offered opinion is to the outer edge of that zone, the greater the change that will have to occur in the person's opinion. If the offered opinion is even barely outside the zone, however, it is likely to be perceived as more divergent than it actually is, and therefore unacceptable. The trick for the editorial writer is to know enough about the newspaper's readers to be able to push for a maximum amount of opinion change without going so far as to antagonize readers with demands for too much change.[18]

In deciding whether to present one or two sides in our editorial on "PrimeTime Live," we might keep in mind that the initial reactions of journalists (and perhaps much of the public) were shock and dismay that a newsmagazine could be punished so severely for exposing bad meat-handling practices. If we want to defend that point of view, a one-sided, indignant argument might be appropriate. But, if we want to persuade readers that the case is not that simple, a two-sided argument seems called for. The editorial would acknowledge the danger of a "chilling effect" on investigative reporting but a take a closer look at aspects of the case that kept it from being a run-of-the-mill undercover story. If we do a good job of balancing our arguments, readers may not know until the end what we will conclude about the judgment.

In teaching editorial writing classes, I have found it helpful in explaining these, and other, formats, to designate types of editorials using formulas that look like something that might come out of a chemistry course. SA_1A_2DC describes a two-sided editorial. S stands for the statement of the *situation* that prompted the editorial. A_1A_2 indicates the presentation of the *argument* on one side of the issue (A_1) followed by *argument* on the other side (A_2). D is *discussion*, following by the *conclusion* (C). SAC indicates a one-sided editorial with the conclusion at the end; CSAC, a one-sided editorial with the conclusion stated at the beginning. Not many editorials are written strictly according to these formulas, but they give the beginning editorial writer an idea of the options that are available.

WRITING THE BEGINNING

The beginning of an editorial may be the most important part. The first few words must prove sufficiently interesting to attract readers to the editorial. Although we have noted types of editorials that start by stating the conclusion, the most common beginning is a brief statement of the proposal, incident or situation that has prompted the editorial. It may be a simple restatement of information that has been reported in the news columns. This approach is especially appropriate for readers who have no previous knowledge of what the editorial writer is talking about. It also provides a way into the editorial without antagonizing readers who may hold views different from the editorial writer's.

Sometimes a writer needs to present an even broader approach than a statement of the facts of the situation. Starting with some background (designated B in our editorial-writing formula) might help readers understand how the immediate topic relates to more general information with which they may be familiar. Sometimes an effective way to get readers to modify their opinions is to begin with the statement of a generally accepted point of view. After readers have become comfortable with what the editorial writer is saying, the editorial can take what I call a "Yes, but" switch to try to convince readers that another point of view makes even more sense. This approach might be particularly effective in an editorial that seeks to debunk commonly held views or takes a stand that may surprise readers. This approach is not the same as building up an artificial argument to be knocked down. The opening argument needs to be credible. "Yes, but" might be useful when a newspaper wants to change or modify an earlier editorial stance on an issue. This type of editorial can be readable and persuasive, especially if the writer sneaks up on the reader and presents the counterargument unexpectedly.

An editorial sometimes can be started with a question (Q). This question can serve to focus the point of an editorial immediately and tell readers that they can expect to find the answer by reading the editorial. A question that arouses curiosity can be effective in attracting readers. But, if a question simply asks, "What should be done about such-and-such?" and the reader answers, "I don't care" or "I don't know," the editorial writer has lost a reader. A meatier question might suggest alternatives: "Should River City continue with the city manager form of government or return to a system with elected commissions?"

If we wanted to write an editorial taking a firm stand and presenting only one side, our first sentence quite likely would make our stand clear to readers. Two opinion articles on the Food Lion case that appeared on the op-ed pages of the *New York Times* did just that. One writer wrote that, after the jury's verdict become known, "the press mostly circled the wagons and declared it a travesty. But what the Fourth Estate is defending is shoddy journalism, unworthy of the best tradition of investigative reporting."[19] The other writer started this way: "The multimillion-dollar legal and public relations battle Food Lion has waged against ABC News is really a war against investigative reporting."[20] The author of the first article was Paul Starobin, a *National Journal* staff writer and contributing editor of *Columbia Journalism Review*. The author of the second article was Roone Arledge, president of ABC News. Obviously, they had different points of view about the verdict.

In our case, since we want to consider both sides, an editorial could begin with a statement of the situation (S) such as this: "A North Carolina jury has awarded Food Lion $5.5 million in punitive damages for a PrimeTime Live program that showed supermarket employees selling old meat under unsanitary conditions." But how dull! First, it's not much, if any, different from a news lead. Second, even more important, it doesn't frame the issue we want to talk about: the implications of the verdict and award. A more interesting opener: "Some of our fellow journalists are worried that a recent $5.5 million punitive judgment against ABC News in the Food Lion case will put them out of the investigative journalism business."

WRITING THE BODY OF THE EDITORIAL

The steps we have discussed thus far, starting with picking a topic, have covered a number of pages and involved quite a lot of explanations. Except possibly for research, most of the steps could have been taken quickly. Not more than a few seconds may be required for an experienced editorial writer to select a topic, decide on the purpose and the proper audience, determine the tone and select the general approach. Much of the process takes place without conscious reflection. After writing editorials for a few years, editorial writers get a feeling for the right way, for them, to write an editorial. With the beginning determined, at least tentatively, and all the other steps behind them, they are ready to write the body of the editorial–the explanations, the arguments and the analysis. Here is where they either will or will not convince their readers. Here is where they win or lose in the battle to persuade.

If we decide to use the opening sentence that appears at the end of the last section, we will need to compose an editorial based on the SBA_1A_2DC model. That opening must be followed by an explanation of what the case was about (fraud)–and what it was not about (tainted meat). We will use two short paragraphs to provide this background (B). Since we decided our editorial would start by expressing concerns about the verdict, it seems natural to present our first set of arguments on this side (A_1): Some media people expect the case to have the effect of severely curtailing the ability of journalists to do their job of looking out for the public's interests. Undercover journalism has proved beneficial in the past, they point out, citing Upton Sinclair and the meat-packing industry early in this century. In the *Post* article, ABC President Arledge said that undercover reporting is a tradition "going back to Nellie Bly." (Writing about the same time as Sinclair, Nellie Bly exposed injustices by posing as an insane person in a mental institution and as an inmate in a women's prison.)

As a transition to the second argument (A_2), words such as "however," "on the other hand" or "at the same time" sometimes prove handy. They tell the reader that the other argument is about to begin. In our editorial, we will use a somewhat less obvious transition that uses "other" in a different manner, referring to "purists on the other side of the argument." That phrasing flags the other argument, but also implies that some on that side are *not* purists, do not take a black-and- white stand. As it will turn out, the editorial will try to take a middle ground. The main arguments here are that journalists should never engage in deception and that there are other, more reputable ways to get even the toughest story.

The move to the discussion (D) is signaled in this manner: "Between these two camps are some journalists . . . . " Then come sentences that try to differentiate between acceptable and unacceptable undercover methods.

In the conclusion (C) we reiterate the point that deceptive practices generally should be avoided, but might be used as a last resort on some occasions

The Case of the Dirty Hands

*Must journalists always need clean hands
to go after people with dirty hands?*

S — Some of our fellow journalists have expressed the fear that a recent $5.5 million punitive damage award in the Food Lion v. ABC News case will have a "chilling effect" on legitimate news reporting.

B — The verdict by a North Carolina jury did not turn on whether supermarket employees actually handled and sold old meat under unsanitary conditions. Food Lion did not attempt to dispute the allegations of the "PrimeTime Live" program.

What the verdict did turn on was the fraudulent manner in which two ABC producers got, and carried out, their jobs as undercover employees. Food Lion claimed that it had been misled to believe that the two were experienced meat handlers and that, once hired, the crew members displayed disloyalty to their new employer. The jury bought these arguments.

A₁ — Some people in the media industry think this verdict, if allowed to stand, will severely curtail the ability of newspaper, television and radio reporters to expose crime, fraud and corruption. The losers, they say, will be the American people. A First Amendment lawyer has said he expects the award to have the effect of giving "us more stories about Dennis Rodman and Madonna instead of more stories that are important to us." Those who view the verdict in this manner say that some stories that the public needs to know about require a certain amount of deception. The "bad guys" are not going to openly acknowledge they have been doing bad things. Defenders of deceptive practices like to point to Upton Sinclair, who early in this century went undercover to expose horrible conditions in the nation's slaughterhouses, and Nelly Bly, who went undercover in a mental institution and a women's prison.

A₂ — Purists on the other side of the argument contend that reporters should never pretend to be anything but reporters, and in fact should forthrightly present themselves as such. They say there are other ways to dig out most stories. In the Food Lion case, they suggest, ABC might have bought meat and had it tested. The producers could have settled for interviewing employees (which they did). Even Lou Hodges, an ethics professor at Washington and Lee University, who testified on behalf of ABC, acknowledged under cross-examination that there were other ways to get the story.

D — Standing somewhere between these absolutist stances are journalists who point out that there are degrees of deception, from passive to active. Surreptitiously observing, even filming, a person suspected of wrongdoing is one thing. Actually lying about one's qualifications on an application and submitting fake recommendations, as was done in the Food Lion case, is something else. Apparently the reason the "PrimeTime Live" crew thought it had to employ these practices was that it needed dramatic pictures for a "news magazine" that has become more entertainment than news. The supervisor of the crew acknowledged as much when he pointed out that newspapers, some of which had criticized the show, aren't primarily about pictures.

C — The lesson for journalists in this case is that deception should be resorted to as the last tactic, not the first, in covering a hard-to-crack story. Reporters and editors need to remember that, when they set out to expose people with dirty hands, they need to keep their own hands clean.

after careful consideration by editors. We conclude that it is important for journalists to keep their hands clean when they go after people with dirty hands.

WRITING THE CONCLUSION

Well-written beginnings help attract readers. Well-written endings help convince readers. Possible conclusions for an editorial are as infinite in number and variety as the manner in which the editorial is written. Conclusions vary according to the purposes of the editorial, but a conclusion should express what the writer intends the editorial to accomplish.

In the case of our Food Lion editorial, we conclude that there may be rare occasions when deception might be justified, but that generally journalists should avoid deception. The last sentence adds a nice touch: keep your hands clean when going after people with dirty hands. When readers reach this point, they will understand the title of the editorial: "The Case of the Dirty Hands," a reference to the dirty hands of both the meat-handlers and the ABC producers.

Editorial conclusions vary according to the degree of firmness intended by the writer. I have found it helpful, in acquainting would-be editorial writers with possible varieties of conclusions, to think of them as coming in six general forms. Within each form are variations that primarily reflect degree of firmness. In order of descending firmness, the six categories are urge, approve, disapprove, conclude righteously, take consolation and come down softly. The categories, ranked in that order, are explained below. The examples within each category are also ranked in descending order of firmness. (I go on at some length about these conclusions, partly to call attention to the wide variety of subject matter covered in editorials.)

Urging

The most specific and direct conclusion is one that urges readers, a government official or a private party to do something. An editorial may urge voters to support or oppose a candidate or ballot proposition. It may urge the president or Congress to compromise on tax cut proposals or welfare reform. It may urge a city council to lower the speed limit on a street or fire the city manager. It may urge readers in general to support something, such as a chemical weapons freeze.

1. *Do*—write or vote or give (to the United Way, for example). This conclusion urges readers to perform a specific action. When the *Reston* (Va.) *Times* wanted readers to attend a public meeting on plans for a massive redevelopment project, the editorial writer concluded the editorial with a two-word sentence: "Do come."
2. *Must*—intended to leave no doubt in the reader's mind about what the editorial writer wants to have done. When Wal-Mart ran into public opposition to plans to build a super-store near George Washington's boyhood home at Ferry Farm, the *Free Lance-Star*, of Fredericksburg, Va., concluded: "Wal-Mart executives—with all their good business sense and marketing innovations—must recognize that a new approach

is needed." When the United States and Western European countries were dillydallying about sending troops to Bosnia, the *San Francisco Chronicle* said: "The U.N. must act quickly–to save both Bosnia and itself."

3. *Ought*–less forceful than "must" but still a firm stand. The *Press-Enterprise* of Riverside, Calif., said the decision to build a low-level nuclear dump site in a nearby area "ought to hinge on its safe suitability, not Sacramento's anxiety to get a dump."

4. *Should*–slightly less emphatic than "must" and "ought." The *Oregonian*, concerned that the state might provide inadequate or unsafe care for Medicare recipients, stated: "This Legislature should find a way to pass the Adult Foster Care Protection Act." The *Miami Herald*, noting that the U.S. Sentencing Commission was "appalled at the number of black men in prison," said: "After the heat of the election, Congress should look at these sentences with fresh eyes and a sense of costs and benefits."

"Should" can have two meanings, and editorial writers need to make certain their readers know which they intend. The manner in which "should" was used in the two preceding examples implies obligation, necessity or duty. The other usage implies expectation or anticipation of an occurrence. The *Miami Herald* provided an example of this second usage when an automobile agency's proposal to lease air rights over a canal apparently produced more public debate than anticipated. Such a debate, said the *Herald*, "is the least . . . that the public should expect from its stewards of public lands and water." To avoid confusion, some writers prefer to stick with "ought" to express obligation and reserve "should" for expectation.

5. *We urge*–appropriate, if not overused, when urging voters or public officials to take specific actions. "We urge community support of the Heart Association's annual fund campaign in February so that all of us may benefit," said the *Page* (Va.) *News and Courier*.

6. *Needs to*–similar to "ought" and "should." The *Oregonian* said that, because the collective bargaining system established to decide pay raises for state employees was not intended to give either side "everything it wants," the Legislature "needs to recognize that as it passes judgment on this deal."

7. *Hope*–"We hope" is a much overused phrase that tempers a recommendation by suggesting it is only the newspaper's opinion. Some newspapers try to avoid, or even forbid, the use of "we." Usually the point can be made without "we." The *Rocky Mountain News* used a variation of "we hope" in commenting on public hearings about the assault on the Branch Davidian compound at Waco, Texas: "let us hope they will generate sound policies on how to bloodlessly contain armed fanatics." (Note: Although you will find "hopefully" in the conclusions of editorials, it is not an acceptable substitute for "we hope." "Hopefully" is an adverb and, as such, modifies a verb or an adjective.)

Approving

Sometimes no specific action is expected on a public or private matter. Perhaps some action already has been taken that deserves praise, such as a contribution an individual has made to the community or a decision made by a governmental body. Sometimes an editorial writer may want to commend a proposal without going immediately to the next step to urge its approval; additional study or changes may be needed. The following, in descending order of enthusiasm, are variations of positive editorial endings.

1. *Badly needed*–The *Daily News* of Newport News, Va., said, concerning plans of a local special affairs network to televise coverage of the Virginia General Assembly, "Such coverage is badly needed."

2. *Critical*–The *Daily News-Record* of Harrisonburg, Va., said that "scrutiny and oversight of all government functions, of which higher education is one, is critical to achieving the kind of accountability taxpayers expect, and deserve."

3. *Best*–"Continued firmness in the area of weapons inspection and control is the best way to deal with Saddam [Hussein]," the *Houston Chronicle* concluded.

4. *Giant step*–The *Denver Post* said the "courage and perseverance against all odds" of Lane Kirkland and the AFL-CIO, which he headed, to advance the free labor movement "have taken humankind a giant step closer to the day when the term 'the free world' will mean the *whole* world."

5. *Wise*–The *Arizona Republic* said that a proposal that a legislative subcommittee keep tabs on an Arizona Department of Transportation search for a new contractor "is a wise and prudent suggestion, one that ADOT should embrace with enthusiasm." The *Miami Herald* said it was "wise" for a U.S. attorney "to bow out–for the political stakes of his boss, Bill Clinton, yes, but equally to maintain the integrity of an office whose effectiveness is crucial to South Florida."

6. *Encouraging*–The *Florida Times-Union* found it "encouraging to see a new breed of populists emerge and start correcting course" in Florida politics.

7. *Worth hailing*–Despite the effects of welfare reform, the *San Antonio News-Express* expressed confidence that "the state's needy still are getting help." It concluded: "That's an accomplishment worth hailing."

8. *About time*–When the school system's financial service was consolidated with the city's, the *Norfolk Virginia-Pilot* said: "It's about time."

9. *Good*–The same newspaper concluded "Good for them" after stating: "Speaking through its Business–Higher Education Council, corporate Virginia has called upon the legislature to spend tens of millions more for colleges and universities than Mr. [Gov. George] Allen would. Ex-Govs. Godwin, Holton and Baliles have amplified the call."

Disapproving

The types of editorials that end in disapproval are similar to those that end in approval, except that the editorial writer decides to come down on the negative side rather than on the positive side. My search through a large number of editorials suggests that disapproving editorials are not nearly so abundant as approving editorials (so much for the supposed reputation of editorial pages as being negative) and that they come in only a few identifiable forms. Here, in descending order of disapproval, are examples of negative endings.

1. *Quick death*–Referring to "blatant payoffs to corporations," *USA Today* said that "[t]hey deserve a quick death, before they kill trust in the nation's security markets."

2. *Should not*–No matter how the U.S. Supreme Court might rule about admission of women to Virginia Military Institute, the *Pittsburgh Post-Gazette* concluded the court "should not foreclose such options" for other single-sex schools. The *St. Louis Post-Dispatch* said that "[t]o avoid trouble with the EPA–more important, clean up the air that is hurting children and old people–Missouri shouldn't permit another summer to pass with ozone above safe levels."

3. *Unfortunate*–The *Rappahannock* (Va.) *News* lamented that "it is unfortunate" that a proposed highway bypass had become "clouded with unrelated issues."

4. *Trouble*–When the *Shreveport* (La.) *Journal* found that legislators were meeting in secret to decide on settling lawsuits against the state, it stated: "We don't let legislators meet in secret when they decide on dispensing our money for other reasons; we see only trouble in letting them do it for lawsuits."

5. *Mistake*–Noting the federal government's failure to allow for flexibility in welfare reforms, the *Baltimore Sun* concluded: "The states, soon to take over the job of disbursing welfare money, cannot afford to repeat that mistake."

6. *Last thing*–The *Denver Post* warned that "[t]he last thing Denver needs is to virtually invite the violation of federal clean-air standards, the penalties for which, not so incidentally, are visited not just upon the downtown area, but upon the entire metropolitan area."

7. *Fool's bargain*–The *Post* also came up with a disapproving phrase I had not previously seen in an editorial. It said that a proposal to eliminate Selective Service "to save an unnoticeable $20 million in the federal budget is a fool's bargain."

8. *Better way*–Much more blandly, the *Post* suggested that the ways problems were being handled at a local hospital "are little more than a stark reminder to everyone of the old truism, 'There's gotta be a better way.'"

Concluding Righteously

One of the ministers in Vancouver, Wash., used to call me "the village preacher." Being a preacher himself, he must have intended this epithet as a compliment. I accepted it as such, since I thought I was upholding the moral standards of the community. The adjectival form of "preacher," when applied to an editorial, is not particularly complimentary; readers may resent "preachy" editorials. Still, one purpose of an editorial page is to serve as a community conscience, and one duty of editorial writers is to protect and promote the public good, as they perceive it. So, if editorials take on a high moral tone from time to time, perhaps no one should complain about a little preaching. Here are a few examples of concluding righteously.

1. *The public's rights*–a favorite touchstone for editorial writers making a case against government secrets or private interests. Writers find particularly gratifying the invocation of rights involving the First Amendment and freedom of information. Newspapers can perform a worthwhile

function speaking up for these rights, though it is easy for such editorial statements to become clichés. The public gets tired of being preached to about rights, especially when they seem to benefit editors and reporters more than readers. In Montana, the Bureau of Land Management released the names of persons and companies that had "nominated" (proposed) various federal lands for coal leasing but refused to reveal who had nominated what lands. Concluded the *Missoulian*: "The public has a right to know who wants to glom onto what public coal. It has a right to have coal development carefully controlled." In this instance, the paper was contending that the public should know the names, but some who opposed publication might have argued that the *Missoulian* wanted the names for the purpose of publishing an interesting news story.

2. *Preservation of liberties*–another strongly righteous conclusion. In an editorial titled "Freedom's Protector," the now-defunct *Los Angeles Herald Examiner* noted "the never-ending assault on liberty itself by powers that protect themselves–or seek to–by forbidding public criticism of their actions." The editorial saw "the best protector of existing human liberty as a free press, whose importance cannot be overstated," then concluded: "Preservation of these liberties is critical to the health and even the survival of any true democracy. Keep that in mind the next time another judge tries to interfere with full press coverage of a public trial."

Taking Consolation

When events don't go exactly the way an editorial writer wishes, an alternative to disapproving is taking some consolation that the outcome isn't all bad. Here are three of these endings:

1. *Yes, but . . .* –a conclusion that may acknowledge that something untoward has occurred but insist that things aren't so bad as they may seem. When Montana voters turned down an initiative that would have restricted nuclear power plant development in the state, the *Missoulian* concluded: "Industry beat Initiative 71. That means people do not want a ban. But that does not mean the people want nuclear power development."
2. *But at least . . .* –a conclusion that suggests some, but not enough, progress has been made. The *Florida Times-Union* noted that a plan for removing land mines in Bosnia was "painfully slow . . . , but at least it is progress."
3. *Not without faults, but . . .* –a way for editorial writers to indicate that something is less than desirable. The *Danville* (Va.) *Register and Bee* described a health care plan as "not without its faults, but at least it opens the debate on [the] issue."

Coming Down Softly

As any reader of the editorial page knows, not every editorial reaches a firm or clear conclusion. In fact, many editorials purposely remain inconclusive. (Others, unfortunately, arrive at no conclusion in spite of the writer's efforts to

A Word About Libel

W. Wat Hopkins VIRGINIA POLYTECHNIC INSTITUTE AND STATE UNIVERSITY

The notion that a person could be punished for expressing an opinion is obnoxious to most Americans. Deeply rooted in the heritage of a free press is the concept that newspapers have a duty to comment upon matters of public concern. That concept has been endorsed by the U.S. Supreme Court, but in a roundabout way.

The court's grant of protection for expressions of opinion is one of the murkiest areas of libel law. Indeed, in the case in which the court made it clear that opinion is constitutionally protected, the court specifically said that opinion is *not* constitutionally protected.

The oddly worded opinion was written by Chief Justice William Rehnquist in a case called *Milkovich v. Lorain Journal* (1990). The case began when a sports columnist criticized a finding of a state high school athletics panel that cleared a wrestling coach from wrongdoing in a brawl that occurred during a match. The columnist opined that the coach beat the charge with "the big lie." The columnist claimed he was expressing an opinion, but the court found that calling someone a liar was not an opinion, but a statement of fact. Indeed, Justice Rehnquist wrote that opinions, as a category of speech, are not protected by the First Amendment. He added, however, that the court, in a previous case, had held that for a libel case to be maintained, the plaintiff in the case must be able to prove that the objectionable statement is false (*Philadelphia Newspapers v. Hepps*, 1986). Without proof of falsity, therefore, there is no liability.

In effect, then, because a statement of pure opinion cannot be proved to be true or false, it cannot be the basis of a libel suit. "The mayor is incompetent," therefore, cannot be the basis of a libel action, because one cannot prove that the mayor is or is not competent. "The mayor is a crook," however, is not a statement of opinion; it is a statement of fact, and, even if the statement appears in an editorial, it may be the basis of a libel action. Nor is the statement protected if it is prefaced by the words "we believe" or "in our opinion." The heart of the statement is still that the mayor is a crook—a statement that can be proved to be true or false.

---

do so.) Writers might use inconclusive endings when they want to interpret what is happening or bring their readers information and insights that have not appeared in the news columns. Writers also may resort to this form if they can envision no solution to a problem. Editorial writers, after all, don't have to know all the answers. Here are some examples in decreasing order of firmness.

1. *Could*–used to indicate uncertainty or a suggestion. Uncertainty: The *Free Lance–Star* of Fredericksburg, Va., noted that a new Wal-Mart store in the area would undoubtedly produce notable increases in sales tax revenues, "[b]ut the long-range costs to the community could be much greater." Suggestion: The *San Francisco Chronicle* said President Clinton "could demonstrate that his loyalty to the welfare of America's economy is as important to him as his political future by firing [Commerce Secretary Ron] Brown before his administration is stained even more by suspicion, or worse."

2. *Might*–used to indicate an uncertain conclusion. Concerning a proposal that the Canadian prime minister visit South Africa, the *Calgary Herald* concluded: "A formal visit . . . might be in order, but only if he can be sure it would help, not hinder."

3. *But . . .* —suggests that the writer is not fully convinced one side is wholly right. A writer on the Cleveland *Plain Dealer* was not convinced by a study that showed redlining (a bank loan process that makes it harder for African-Americans to obtain financing to purchase homes) was not a problem in Ohio. "Continued scrutiny is warranted," the editorial said. "But this study is worth noting."

4. *No easy solution*—when no answer seems to be a good one. For example, when sheriff's deputies were searching students attending concerts at the University of Montana, the *Montana Kaimin*, the student newspaper, said "people should be safe from injury [from thrown bottles and cans], but they also have the right to be safe from a random search without a warrant." The editorial concluded: "There is no easy resolution to the problem. UM students and officials should attempt to devise an equitable way to ensure safe concerts."

5. *No solution*—when an editorial writer has no solution at all to offer. Lamenting previous studies aimed at eliminating duplication in the Montana college system, the *Helena* (Mont.) *Independent Record* concluded: "We thus hesitate to advocate another study. Nor do we offer any solutions. Meanwhile—uneasy rests the head wearing the crown."

6. *No issue*—the final step toward softness. These are for editorials that don't even attempt to present an issue. Noting changes in fashions in slang, for example, the *Montana Standard* of Butte said that things used to be "cool" and "neat" but now were "weird," and that "type" was being attached to a word to create an adjective: "Many newspapers today use a photo-printing process that yields something called 'cold type,' to distinguish it from the actual 'hot metal type' of days gone by. So far, we haven't heard anybody refer to cold-type type, but it's bound to happen. We've got no particular reason for discussing these things. We just did it to be weird."

CONCLUSION

Experienced editorial writers do not consciously follow the nine steps to editorial writing that we have taken in this chapter. (In fact, it is arbitrary even to suggest that editorial writing involves nine steps.) But, consciously or subconsciously, writers need to give thought, before they begin writing, to the purpose of an editorial, the audience for which it is intended and the approach that is likely to be most effective with that audience. Sometimes writers can dash off a high-quality editorial without looking for additional information, but trying to find all you can about a subject (given your time constraints) usually pays off. Experienced editorial writers may not give much conscious thought to the organization of their editorials or to the formulas suggested in this chapter. But I have found that beginning writers find the models of one-sided and two-sided editorials helpful in presenting their arguments. I also have found that they appreciate being introduced to various ways to start an editorial and the myriad ways to conclude it. After a few weeks, they no longer need to be reminded of the nine steps, the formulas for editorials or the classifications for endings. They have internalized the process of editorial writing.

1. Find editorials on the same subject that are written in at least three different formats. How are the facts (background information, etc.) handled differently by the writers? What seem to be the writers' assumptions concerning the pre-existing attitudes and prior knowledge of their readers? In what ways are these assumptions different? The same?

2. Find editorials on the same subject that are different in tone. How would you describe the tone of each? Would the approach of any tend to antagonize readers? Cause readers to identify with the writer? Put readers to sleep?

3. Pick a topic and write two editorials using distinctly different formats, for example, SA_1A_2DC and CSAC. Which do you think would be more convincing to most readers in this instance?

4. Select an editorial on a topic that interests you. Then rewrite it in an entirely different tone. Use any of the formats YOU like. Which editorial is likely to convince more readers?

5. Find several examples of each of the six major types of editorial conclusions. Can you find endings that would fall into categories other than these six?

6. Without substantially changing the editorial, rewrite a coming-down-softly ending to create a conclusion expressing firm approval or disapproval. Do the reverse with an editorial that has a firm conclusion.

7. Select an editorial that is directed toward a single audience and rewrite it as a two-level editorial (addressing a dual audience). For example, pick an editorial that seems directed primarily toward a city council and rewrite it so that general readers will understand how the issue being discussed will affect them and what they ought to do about it.

CHAPTER 11 Nine Steps to Better Writing

By "good writing," I mean writing that is first, clear; and second, clear; and third, clear. I would have sentences that go snap, crackle and pop. . . . [Unless] they convey meaning, and add something affirmatively to the development of an idea, I would strike them out.

—JAMES KILPATRICK[1]

Now that we have taken a look at the basic steps in writing an editorial, let us turn our attention to some of the finer points of turning out an editorial that is convincing, terse and well written, concentrating on the following nine areas:

1. The right amount of fact
2. Logical conclusions
3. Consistent point of view
4. Clear referents and antecedents
5. Sentences of appropriate length
6. Economy of words
7. Correct grammar
8. Absence of clichés and jargon
9. Proper use of individual words

To provide examples of how editorials can be improved in these nine areas, I will use two editorials written by students in my editorial-writing classes. "The Playboy Option" and "Sex Objects" were written in response to the announcement that *Playboy* would send a photographer to the Virginia Tech campus to take pictures of women students for a future issue. "The Playboy Option" appears on page 159 with a critique based on principles discussed in this chapter. "Sex Objects" appears on page 160. On page 161 is an edited and partly rewritten version of this editorial ("Sex Objects II"), which also reflects the point made in this chapter. I will also cite portions of other editorials to help illustrate these nine points.

THE RIGHT AMOUNT OF FACT

Editorials should contain only those facts that are necessary for the purposes for which the editorials were written. "Facts are precious things, and to be thoroughly enjoyed must be tasted sparingly and drooled over leisurely," Vermont Royster of the *Wall Street Journal* advised editorial writers.[2] Usually the detail required in an editorial is less than that needed in a news story on the same topic. In many cases editorial readers will have read the news reports and will not need a repetition of all the facts before finding out what the editorial writer has to add. Still, editorial writers cannot assume that all readers have seen or remember the original story. So a compromise between a brief reference and a full factual account must be worked out. Editorial writers must rely on their judgment, but should try for brevity. Space in editorial columns is far more limited than in news columns.

The *Playboy* editorials are fairly brief (340 and 388 words). They do not seem overburdened with unnecessary information. The announcement that prompted the editorials, of the *Playboy* photographer coming to town, requires little explanation. "The Playboy Option" goes into a little more detail about the tryout procedure, but the detail will tie in with the conclusion the editorial writer draws.

LOGICAL CONCLUSIONS

It is not always easy to judge whether an editorial presents logical arguments that lead to an appropriate conclusion. To a large extent, whether the arguments work depends on the point of view of the person who is judging.

For the class assignment on the *Playboy* incident, students were instructed to write an SA_1A_2DC editorial (see Chapter 10 for a discussion of this formula), presenting opposing arguments before reaching a conclusion. In "The Playboy Option" the writer first argues that women students could benefit from a paycheck and from something vaguely referred to as "beneficial experience." Then the writer, using "however" as a standard transition to the opposing argument, notes that opponents were concerned about women students degrading themselves and harming their reputations. At that point the writer drops the A_1A_2 arguments and abruptly takes a new tack, pursuing neither the "beneficial" nor "degrading" lines of reasoning. The issue now is a woman's right to decide what she wants to do with her body. Since *Playboy* has given her some options (fully clothed, semi-nude or nude), she is free to make a choice. The editorial then jumps to a conclusion, which I don't follow, that this choice suggests the *Playboy* layout will be tasteful. In other words, the writer seems to start out with one set of arguments, switch to another line of argument, then arrive at an unsubstantiated conclusion.

In "Sex Objects" the writer draws on letters to the editor to provide the arguments. Those opposed to posing contend that *Playboy* is a magazine that exploits women and that women who participate will be degraded. Women are asked to boycott the tryouts. The letters on the other side, mostly from men, say that women should take advantage of the opportunity to appear in a quality magazine, that women are free to choose whether to participate and that Tech could use the exposure. The writer then uses an effective transition to move into the discussion section. "These men" refers back to the male letter

The Playboy Option

Women have a choice in how they would be photographed

(ORIGINAL)	(CRITIQUE)

(ORIGINAL)

Playboy magazine visited the Virginia Tech campus last week in search of young women to pose in their October 1992 "Women of the Big East" issue.

Female students were invited to the Blacksburg Marriott Hotel to be interviewed and to complete a questionnaire. They were also asked whether they would like to be photographed fully clothed, semi-nude or nude.

Students and faculty members believe that such exposure to a well-known magazine would be a beneficial experience for the young women who choose to appear. Many students also view the paycheck as a practical way to pay for the rising cost of tuition.

However, many feminists on campus expressed their displeasure at the thought of *Playboy* visiting Virginia Tech. They solely believe that students attend college in order to receive the best education possible, not to take off their clothes for a national magazine. Many believe the magazine will feature the women in a degrading light, thus harming their reputations.

We as students of Virginia Tech have the right to decide whether we would like to participate in this experience. As with the issue of abortion, a woman has the sole right to do as she pleases with her body. The same principle is applied to this case. If a struggling young student needs help with tuition costs and decides to pose only for the money, don't look down upon her. Yes, there may be other ways in which to earn extra money, but it is up to her to decide how she will go about it.

The young women are also given the option as to how they would like to be photographed. This is to assure them that they do indeed have a voice in the matter. This further implies that the layout will be presented in a tasteful manner. If Playboy wished to degrade these women, then they wouldn't be given so many opportunities in which to voice their opinion.

(CRITIQUE)

Playboy magazine is singular; use "it"

"Students and faculty" implies "all students and faculty"; use "Some"

Use "benefit from" instead of "would be a beneficial experience for"

"Many" is vague; also what may seem many to one person may not to another

"Solely" is misplaced; it should modify "receive"

"In order to" is wordy; "to" is sufficient

"Believe" implies faith in something; use "think" here

With "we," a sudden switch from third person to first; keep the same person

You should say "Women **should** have the sole right" and "the principle **should** be applied"

With " don't . . . ," you switch to second person

"There may be" is weak construction; try "The student has other ways to . . . "

They "were" given the choice; that was last week

Use "option of," not "option as to how"

"This" doesn't refer to anything specific; try "Offering them a choice assured them . . . "

You need "had wished"

You need "wouldn't have been"

"Opinion" not right word; try "options for posing"

Sex Objects

Playboy photographs feed on exploitation of women

(ORIGINAL)

A photographer from *Playboy* magazine was in town last week to recruit women for their upcoming Big East college issue.

Women were asked to go to the Blacksburg Marriott prepared to have pictures taken of them, preferably in a bathing suit. The incentives given for trying out for this issue were exposure in a best-selling magazine and a large sum of money.

Just a few days after the announcement of the photographer being in town, letters to the editor started appearing in papers of the region every day. The first group of letters to appear in the *Collegiate Times*, the Virginia Tech newspaper, consisted of angry women, condoning such activity going on in a college atmosphere. The degradation of women was an argument, with women being viewed only as sex objects. Some people consider *Playboy* a pornographic magazine that exploits women. In the letters, women were asked not to degrade themselves and to boycott the tryouts.

The responses to the letters from women were mostly from men, who thought it was a great advantage to Tech to be featured in such a famous magazine. They felt that Tech needed the exposure, as well as deserved it. They felt that women have the freedom to choose to do this so it is perfectly justified. Many felt that *Playboy* is a quality magazine and the women of Tech should take advantage of the opportunity.

What these men, as well as the women who went to the tryouts, did not think about is how much their way of thinking contributes to sexist beliefs. When women are treated as sex objects, as they are in *Playboy*, the men reading the magazine believe that what they see is what they get. The women are in the magazine only for the sexual pleasure of men. The women in the pictures are usually the perfect exceptions of nature, or the object of plastic surgeons that fool men into believing what the perfect woman's body is. They are also fooled into believing what the perfect woman wants, judging from her provocative pose and her lack of adequate clothing.

Women should be lucky that they have the freedom of choice. They should explore this freedom of choice, and choose not to contribute to sexist beliefs created and fed by the exploitation of women in the pages of *Playboy*.

---

writers of the previous paragraph. The "as well as women who went to the tryouts" quickly enlarges the group to whom the discussion is addressed. "What these men . . . did not think" also allows the writer to move from the letter writers' arguments to the points the writer wants to make. The writer then launches into a full-scale attack on the sexual stereotypes that *Playboy* is perceived to encourage. The final paragraph, citing "freedom of choice," also harks back to the language of the A_2 argument: Women should feel fortunate that they have a choice and should explore it. But it turns out in the writer's view that there really is no choice at all for anyone who does not want to contribute to the exploitation of women. Some may question whether this wording has misled the reader concerning the matter of choice, but it seems clear to me that the writer's basic point is clear and that the conclusion follows from the points made in the arguments and in the discussion.

CONSISTENT POINT OF VIEW

The editorial writer should use a consistent point of view in an editorial: the first-person ("we"), second-person ("you") or third-person ("he," "she," "they").

Some papers discourage or forbid the use of "we" in editorials. Other papers regard it as appropriate. In any case, care should be taken to use "we" infrequently. If you use "we" to refer to the paper, do so consistently; don't switch back and forth between "we" and the name of the paper.

On occasion writers find it appropriate, especially when writing on informal topics, to address editorial readers in the second-person "you." Once adopted, this form of address should be maintained throughout the editorial. Use of "you," of course, can be overdone. Writers must be careful not to switch suddenly to a "you" point of view in the middle or at the end of an editorial.

I detect no switching of persons in "Sex Objects." But, as noted in the critique, the writer of "The Playboy Option" briefly slips into the third person. Another example of what I am talking about occurred in another student editorial. The editorial asked why people are so offended by *Playboy*: "Why don't they just accept the fact that some people think of the human body as an art form and are going to pose for *Playboy* no matter what they say? And in response to the statement that women are in it just for money, we ask you what is wrong with making some extra money doing something you see nothing wrong with and possibly even enjoy?" The writer, after using the third-person "they," suddenly and for no apparent reason switches to "we" and "you." The remainder of the editorial is third-person again. The wording can be changed

Sex Objects II

Playboy photographs feed on exploitation of women

(REVISED)

A photographer from *Playboy* magazine provoked a debate over sexual exploitation when he came to town to recruit women for the fall Big East college issue.

Women were invited to the Blacksburg Marriott to have their pictures taken, preferably in bathing suits. They were offered the incentives of exposure in a best-selling magazine and possibly large sums of money.

Protesting letters to the editor immediately began appearing. The first group of letters, in the *Collegiate Times*, the Virginia Tech newspaper, came from angry women, condemning such activities in a college atmosphere. Some of the letters described *Playboy* as a pornographic magazine that exploits women. They asked students not to degrade themselves by posing. They called for a boycott of the tryouts.

In response came letters, mostly from men, who argued that Tech could benefit from being featured in such a famous magazine. They contended that *Playboy* is a quality magazine and that Tech needs, and deserves, the exposure.

They urged women to take advantage of the opportunity but pointed out that they had the freedom to choose whether to pose.

What these men, as well as those who went to the tryouts, did not think about was how much their way of thinking contributes to sexist attitudes. When women are treated as sex objects, as they are in *Playboy*, men reading the magazine believe that what they see is what they get. The women are in the magazine only for the sexual pleasure of men. The women in the pictures are usually the perfect exceptions of nature, or the products of plastic surgeons who fool men into thinking that these are the perfect woman's bodies. They are also fooled, by the provocative poses and lack of clothing, that they represent what the perfect woman wants.

Women should feel lucky that they have the freedom of choice to pose for *Playboy*. They should exercise this freedom, but they then should choose not to contribute to the sexist atmosphere created and fed by the exploitation of women in the pages of *Playboy*.

easily, and trimmed: "What is wrong with women making some extra money doing something they see nothing wrong with. . . . "

Another inconsistency to avoid is a shift in the intended audience. Unless there is a clear reason, a writer should not start an editorial talking to one audience, then switch to another. For example, a writer should not begin an editorial addressing the general readership about the city's potholed streets and then at the end switch to talking directly to the mayor: "Mr. Mayor, we think you should do something about this."

CLEAR REFERENTS AND ANTECEDENTS

To avoid repeating words in a boring fashion, writers sometimes use pronouns to take the place of nouns. To avoid repeating phrases and sentences, even whole paragraphs, they use "that" or "that idea" or "that concept" or "that development." Sometimes readers become confused by this shorthand. Professor R. Thomas Berner of Penn State referred to pronouns as "those unemotional, ambiguous, spineless parasites we use to refer to other parts of speech somewhere else in the same sentence, or, on occasion, in another sentence in the same paragraph, or, the worst of all possible contortions, in another paragraph." Berner cited the following sentence as an example of what he was talking about: "The city collects only swill from the university, and because of it, it has determined that the rate was higher than it should have been."[3] The only unambiguous "it" in the sentence is the last one, referring to the rate. But to what do the first two refer? According to the rules of grammar—a pronoun should refer to the nearest preceding logical referent—both of them should refer to university. But the first "it" apparently stands for the whole idea that only swill comes from the university, and who knows whether the second "it" means the university or the city?

The two reprinted *Playboy* editorials provide no examples of this problem, but another student wrote: "Whatever the reason for accepting the fact that someone will be chosen and indirectly represent Tech in *Playboy*'s 'Women of the East,' it will not stop the exploitation of women that will occur in that and every issue of the magazine." "It" seems to refer all the way back to "whatever the reason," but can a reason for accepting participation be expected to stop exploitation? The same editorial uses the sentence "This may sound harsh" to start a new paragraph with "this" apparently meant to refer to rambling thoughts in the previous sentence. Another student wrote: "If a student appears in the issue, it would mean publicity for Tech." No referent exists for "it."

SENTENCES OF APPROPRIATE LENGTH

You might expect to find that sentences in editorials would tend to be longer and harder to understand than those in news stories. Yet at least two studies made 20 years apart have shown that readers have found editorials easier to understand than news stories. Professor Galen R. Rarick, who did one of the studies, speculated that the apparent anomaly occurred partly because most editorial writers have been in the writing business longer than most reporters.

Another reason, he suggested, was that news writers may be better at reporting and investigating than at writing. Editorial writers also have a longer time to rewrite and polish their work than most reporters do, and so should produce better writing.[4]

The earlier study was based on a book called *The Art of Readable Writing,* by Rudolph Flesch. This book and a subsequent one by the same author, *How to Test Readability,* attracted considerable attention in the late 1940s and 1950s.[5] Since longer sentences were considered harder to understand than short ones and longer words were considered more abstract than short ones, Flesch came up with a scale based on two factors—average sentence length (number of words) and average word length (number of syllables per 100 words). Using the scale, a "standard" rating of 65 (seventh- or eighth-grade level) could be obtained by various combinations. If sentences were short, words could be longer; if words were short, sentences could be longer. A "standard" rating could be obtained by sentences that averaged 15 words in length if 100 words had no more than 149 syllables, but by sentences that averaged only 10 words if 100 words had 157 syllables.

Although Flesch himself warned against taking the scale too seriously, the response to his books was such that Francis P. Locke of the *Dayton* (Ohio) *Daily News* felt moved to write an article for *The Masthead* titled "Too Much Flesch on the Bones?" "We have created a cult of leanness," he wrote. "The adjective is packed off to a semantic Siberia. The mood piece, if tolerated at all, must be astringent and aseptic." He feared "the growing pressure to water everything down to the thinnest possible pablum for the laziest possible minds."[6] So simplification can be overdone.

Writers should realize that readers, even of editorial pages, are usually in a hurry. Today's readers are not likely to labor over the type of heavy prose that an E.L. Godkin or a Charles Dana gave readers a century ago. Yet simplistic writing can be boring, and if a writer has a fairly complex thought to express, a complex sentence may be necessary. The complexity of the writing should depend on the editorial and the concepts discussed. A good rule is to try to keep the writing simpler than you are at first inclined, since it is still likely to be perceived by most readers as more difficult than you expect.

So how do the "Playboy" and "Sex Objects" editorials rate on the Flesch scale? In spite of some differences in sentence length and number of syllables, the editorials rated similarly, either at "standard" or between "standard" and "fairly difficult." Rewriting "Sex Objects" shifted that editorial from "standard–fairly difficult" to "standard."

	Number of words	*Words/sentence*	*Syllables/100 words*	*Score*	*Rating*
Playboy Option	324	19	147	65	standard
Sex Objects	388	20	151	60	standard–fairly difficult
Sex Objects II	340	19	147	65	standard

The Flesch scale should be regarded as only one indication, and a rather arbitrary one, of writing quality. Using easily understood words and sentences can provide a start toward comprehendible writing, but good writing requires more than keeping words and sentences short.

Neither original editorial has a problem with long sentences, but examples can be found in other students' work. A long, complex sentence (40 words): "It seems as though *Playboy* is playing on the fact that (1) college students are willing to try just about anything, (2) college students always need money and (3) careers in modeling are seen as big opportunities for a lot of college women." A shorter, clearer rewrite (28 words): "*Playboy* seems to be taking advantage of college students, willing to try anything once, who are lured by promises of always-needed money or of careers in modeling."

Another confusing example: "While proponents for *Playboy* agree [with opponents] that one's body is sacred, their view diverges in that posing nude for millions to view is a matter of free expression." The writer could have said: "Proponents agree that one's body is sacred, but they believe that exposing one's body for millions to view is a matter of free expression."

Economy of Words

Long or confused sentences are a tip-off to wordiness. But wordiness also can show up in words and phrases that may be part of short sentences. Following are examples from other (unprinted) *Playboy* editorials.

A phrase that often signals wordiness and the use of the passive voice is "there is" and its various forms (there are, there will be, etc.). Usually you can strike "there is" and insert a stronger verb elsewhere in the sentence. An example from one of the unprinted editorials:

There were a number of sorority women who were interested in auditioning:

Improved:

A number of sorority women were interested in auditioning.

Usually "the fact that" can be chopped out:

Why don't they accept the fact that some people think of the human body as an art form . . . ?

Improved:

Why don't they accept that some people think of the human body as an art form . . . ?"

"Whether" sometimes can be similarly chopped out:

[They] were given the option on whether they wanted to pose nude, semi-nude or clothed.

Improved:

[They] were given the option of posing nude, semi-nude or clothed.

(Also notice the awkward use of the preposition "on" with "option." You should say "option of posing." "Option on" would be appropriate if you had an option on a piece of property.)

Here a repetition of words can be avoided:

> Many argued that posing nude is degrading. Those arguing this feel that . . . .

Improved:

> Many argued that posing nude is degrading. They feel that . . . .

An extreme case of wordiness:

> She should also consider the ramifications of what this decision will mean to those around her.

Improved:

> She should consider what this decision will mean to those around her.

Here are examples of wordiness (and suggested improvements) in the opening sentences of other student editorials:

ORIGINAL

Computers unlock opportunities to learn and explore different topics, and judging from the Internet's popularity, guidelines for viewing certain material must be established before the medium grows any larger. For instance, the Freedom of Information Act (FOIA) requires federal agencies to provide any person access to records that do not fit any of the exceptions defined by Congress. Computers now hold much of this information, which must be available to the public. Every U.S. citizen should have direct access to any computerized information concerning federal agencies.

REVISED

With easy access to computers and the Internet, U.S. citizens should be able to obtain a vast amount of information about their government. But, unless out-of-date pre-Internet rules are redefined, we may be cut off from much of the information we deserve.

ORIGINAL

Now that the Information Age is upon us, the Internet has bombarded our lives and taken control of our computers. And just as with every new product that comes into the home, a controversy has arisen around this new one. What it entails is the idea of censorship and the deleting of certain material on the Internet.

Recently complaints have been made about some specific graphic pictures and disturbing contents that can be accessed on the Internet. Almost everyone could agree that some of this material can be very vulgar and some might possibly state that it should not be allowed.

REVISED

Complaints have been mounting concerning some of the graphic pictures and other disturbing contents accessible on the Internet.

ORIGINAL

The Freedom of Information Act allows reporters and anyone else to have access to public documents.

Although reporters find out the names of those involved in crimes, it is up to the managing editor of a newspaper to decide whether or not to print them.

REVISED

Editors of student newspapers have the right to print the names of fellow students who are charged with crimes. But should they?

ORIGINAL

Expressing one's opinion is a sure way to get attention. Working for the *Collegiate Times* is a sure way to gain enemies. Since the existence of the op-ed page, the *CT* has received an increasing amount of complaints. Apparently people do not understand the definition of the word opinion.

On Sept. 10, 1996, a man wrote a letter to the editor claiming that he did not believe the Holocaust existed (and objecting to an article that talked about the Holocaust).

REVISED

Responses that the *Collegiate Times* received to op-ed articles suggest that some readers do not understand the meaning of the word "opinion."

On Sept. 10, 1996, a man wrote a letter to the editor claiming that he did not believe the Holocaust existed (and objecting to an article that talked about the Holocaust).

Correct Grammar

A person who attains the august position of editorial writer should automatically use correct grammar. Agreement of subject and predicate can be tricky, however, when the two are separated by a prepositional phrase such as one from "Sex Objects": "The response to the letters from women were mostly from men. . . . " "Response," of course, is the subject and requires a singular verb.

Agreement of nouns and pronouns is another problem. One writer wrote: "As Virginia Tech changes their conference. . . . " The writer properly provided Tech with a singular verb–but a plural pronoun. Another writer referred to *Playboy* and "their" October 1992 issue.

Everyone and anyone (both singular) can be troublesome. One person wrote, " . . . everyone is the master [hardly the right word when referring to women] of their own body." In this case, since only women were involved, "her" would have been appropriate. Sometimes the plural form solves the problem: "People have control over their own bodies."

I am chagrined by how often comma splices occur in student editorials. The previous example was part of a sentence with a comma splice: "Whether someone wants to pose is not really the issue, after all everyone is the master of [her] own body." Two sentences are needed.

Absence of Clichés and Jargon

Clichés and jargon, in a sense, are at opposite ends of the spectrum in terms of comprehensibility by the general reader. Clichés tend to be used in everyday conversation by the sophisticated and the unsophisticated, the educated and the not-so-educated. Jargon is a special set of words used by a specific group of people. Everyone understands clichés; only the ingroup fully understands jargon. The editorial writer must resist the easy temptation to use both–jargon, because many readers will not easily understand what the words mean, and clichés, because good writers need to make clear that they are thinking their own thoughts, not echoing someone else's. Clichés may be appropriate on occasion if they truly are appropriate and no better way can be found to make a point. Some of these expressions have been around for a long time, and they do "ring bells" with readers, but in most cases a little more thought can produce a more exact phrase than the cliché. Instead of "ring bells," I could have said "are easily understood by readers."

Problems with jargon tend to increase with the specialization of editorial writers. When writers associate with educators, lawyers, doctors, sociologists, government bureaucrats, politicians or farmers, they pick up their language and tend to forget that many words full of meaning to these people are either incomprehensible or lacking in meaning to many readers. Writers must constantly be on guard against such words sneaking into their writing.

The two editorials reproduced here seem to be clear of clichés and jargon. Another editorial, however, said the *Playboy* incident was one of the "hot topics" on campus. Another said we should think of "the big picture." Other student editorials contained the following:

. . . left a bad taste in students' mouths.

We do not throw away a whole bushel because of a few bad apples.

One bad apple spoils opportunities for others . . .

People are still smoking up a storm.

. . . a step in the right direction.

. . . protect what all Americans hold dear.

. . . pawns on a global chess board.

. . . time that the administration . . . got off their collective backs. [Note also the disagreement between noun and pronoun.]

From a short stack of editorials written by professional editorial writers, I came across these clichés:

It'll soon be time to fish or cut bait.

Montanans can breathe a sigh of relief . . . .

Inflation has reared its ugly head.

Time marches on.

The country went absolutely bananas . . . .

That's a real can of worms.

. . . time to stir the pot again.

. . . the computer . . . coughed up the latest . . . report.

A natural tendency to "let George do it."

Into the breach leapt the Jaycees.

In 1955, long before the widespread use of computerized machines, the *Wall Street Journal* suggested that editorial writers might find a use for an IBM gadget called a Wordwriter. It could store up to 42 words or phrases and all the writer would have to do was punch a letter on the machine and out would come the word or phrase. The *Journal* cited the following list as possible entries:[7]

"A": will be for "As we have reminded our readers time and time
    again . . . . "
"B": "Both sides of this question have merit . . . . "
"C": "Considering all the factors involved . . . . "
"D": "Doubtless some will disagree with this view . . . . "
"E": "Except for the particular circumstances surrounding the case in
    question . . . . "
"F": "Fortunately, things are not always as they seem . . . . "
"G": "Generally speaking . . . . "
"H": "However, the public believes the facts are . . . . "
"I": "Indeed, there is no gainsaying . . . . "

And so on.

Some of the overworked words and phrases that I have come across over the years include:

alarming trend	on closer examination
amazing	only time will tell
basic	problem
broadly speaking	program
factor	remains to be seen
gratifying	responsible observers
incredible	the economy
in fact	thoughtful people
in order ("A new examination	to be deplored
is in order.")	underlying ("underlying causes"
in terms of	unquestionable
major ("major event")	would seem
obvious	

PROPER USE OF INDIVIDUAL WORDS

After all of these potential writing traps have been checked, we also need to check for weak or inappropriate words.

Beginning editorial writers (and some non-beginners) often misuse "hopefully" to mean "we hope." "Hopefully" is an adverb meaning "full of hope." It must modify a verb. To suggest how "hopefully" might be used, I tell my students: "I am looking at you hopefully to see that you have understood my explanation of 'hopefully.'" One of my student writers, referring to family, friends and professors of a student who decided to pose for *Playboy*, began the conclusion of an editorial: "Hopefully they will support her, because it is her decision." Why not: "They should support her" or "They ought to support her."

"Think," "feel" and "believe" create problems for writers of news stories as well as editorials. In most instances writers should use "think," when they are recounting the thoughts and ideas of their sources. "Feel" should be reserved for statements concerning feelings and emotions. "Believe" implies a faith or conviction about something.

In "Sex Objects" the writer uses "felt" three times: "They felt that Tech needed exposure. . . . " "They felt that women have the freedom to choose. . . . " "Many felt that *Playboy* is a quality magazine. . . . " "Feel" did not seem the proper word in any of these cases. Several possibilities exist for changes: "They thought that Tech needed exposure. . . . " "They said that women have the freedom to choose. . . . " "Many saw *Playboy* as a quality magazine. . . . "

The same writer had this sentence: "They ['many feminists'] solely believe that students attend college in order to receive the best education possible, not to take off their clothes for a national magazine." "Believe" seems fine here, since that is their conviction. (With "solely" where it is the sentence implies that this is their only belief. "Solely" belongs before "to receive," and "in order" can be dropped.) Another writer offered this: "Students and faculty members believe that such exposure to a well-known magazine would be a beneficial experience." This seems borderline to me, but I prefer "think."

A possible use of "feel" is: "The administration felt embarrassed [or didn't feel embarrassed] by the *Playboy* dispute."

Earlier I mentioned not-quite-right prepositions. Here is another example: "What will her family, friends or professors think about her when they find out she has been in a 'skin' magazine." To think "about" is to remember her. To think "of" her is what the writer meant to say.

In "Sex Objects" we have this sentence: "The first group of letters . . . consisted of angry women, condoning such activity going on in a college atmosphere." Obviously the writer meant to use "condemn" instead of "condone." Letters do not "consist of" women but "come from" women. In the same editorial: "The degradation of women was an argument. . . . " Degradation of women is "a concern" not an argument; degradation of women might be used as an argument. The writer referred to the "perfect" woman as being "the object of plastic surgeons. . . . " Such a woman might have been the "object" of those who regarded her as a sex symbol, but she was the "product" of the plastic surgeon.

"Many" is a word much abused by editorial writers. With their license to state opinions, perhaps they think they can get away with using the word when they would not think of using it in news columns. Too often editorial writers use this ambiguous word to support a point when they have no idea how many "many" is. What may seem "many" to supporters of a proposal may not seem "many" to opponents. In one editorial the writer said: "Many feminists on campus expressed their displeasure at the thought of *Playboy* visiting Virginia Tech." "Many feminists" sounds like a lot more feminists than I have been aware of at Tech. "Many" is certainly more than the number of voices that had been heard in public. As well, the writer implies that only "feminists" had expressed displeasure and that those who had expressed displeasure were "feminists." Neither assumption seemed justified under the circumstances.

Somewhat similarly, the same writer stated: "Students and faculty members believe that such exposure to a well-known magazine would be a beneficial experience for the young women who chose to appear." This statement suggests all students and faculty members believe this. "Some" may be an appropriate word in cases like this. "Some students and faculty members" puts more emphasis on what the group thinks than on the specific or relative size of the group.

Here are some examples from other student editorials of not quite using the right word:

Student Wording	*Improved Wording*
The university could start to *aid* in this problem.	The university could start to *solve* this problem.
The university is poorly *represented* when its athletes commit crimes.	The university has a poor *reputation* for handling crimes committed by athletes.
The coaches should suspend players *whom* they feel have an ill effect on	The coaches should suspend players *who* they feel have an ill effect on . . . .
The football team thinks *they* are above the rules that the *remainder* of the *campus* must follow.	The football team thinks *it* is above the rules that the *rest* of the *student body* must follow.
It would not be *fair* to say that all students at Tech study livestock on a farm.	It would not be *accurate* to say that all students at Tech study livestock on a farm.
In fact, the animal science department *represents* a small portion	In fact, the animal science department *accounts for* (*makes up*) a small portion . . . .
If the situation were turned on them	If the tables were turned on them . . . [but this is a cliché], or: If they found themselves in a similar situation . . . .
Some people *forget* to realize	Some people *fail* to realize . . . .
The problem has become more *evident then* just getting different types of people onto the same campus.	The problem has become more *complicated than* just getting different types of people on the same campus.
Why are *their* no resources	Why are *there* no resources . . . .
The university should go out of *there* way to accommodate them.	The university should go out of *its* way [but, if the plural were proper, it would be *their*].

The last three examples contain what might be called a "spell check" error (then-than and there-their). No doubt most writing instructors will agree that students' spelling improved remarkably with the introduction of the "spell check" function, but most spelling checkers cannot tell students whether they should use *then* or *than; there* or *their; accept* or *except; it's* or *its; rein, reign* or *rain*–or, for that matter, *for* or *four*. Nor can they save students from errors in spelling possessives, such as *the students papers*. The check cannot recognize this last error, let alone tell the writer whether the apostrophe should go before or after the *s.* All the writer can do is try to memorize these examples and double-check during proofreading. In addition, only careful proofreading can catch some errors, such as the occasional missing word.

In attempting to get away from dull, plain words, students sometimes get carried away. Slick footpaths, one student wrote, "could easily spawn broken bones and twisted ankles, not to mention plenty of embarrassing moments and soiled clothes." As a Pacific Northwest person, I got a lot of enjoyment imagining all the things that salmon could spawn as they worked their way up the Columbia River. Another student, although technically correct, also provoked a mistaken vision in my mind on first reading: "Asphalt is much easier to plow over than gravel," she wrote. Missing the "over," I could see snowplows plowing asphalt into huge piles (which, unlike snow, would never melt).

Avoiding Biased Words and Phrases

Editorial writers—all writers in fact—need to be especially sensitive to words and phrases that reflect or imply bias toward one sex or the other; toward members of a race, religion or nationality; or toward persons of a certain age, physical condition or lifestyle.

Nouns and pronouns that refer only to males, and thereby suggest that females are not included, should be avoided. Frequently a sentence can be recast to change "he" or "his" to the plural "they" or "them." Sometimes that change can create problems too. For example, in one of the editorials about *Playboy,* a student wrote:

. . . everyone is the master of their own body.

In this instance, since the "everyone" being talked about was a woman, "his own body" would make no sense. The writer turned to the plural "their," but of course "everyone" is singular. In addition, if the writer had thought about it, no doubt some word other than the male "master" would have been used. One way to solve both problems:

People [or women] should have control of their own bodies

Generally recasting the sentence in plural form is the simplest solution. "Himself or herself" sounds awkward and should be avoided.

Words containing "man" often introduce gender bias. Here are several possibilities for alternatives:

Biased	*Alternative*
man-made	manufactured
man-hours	hours
layman's terms	lay terms
man-on-the-street interviews	on-the-street interviews
manhole cover	utility cover
policemen	police officer
fireman	firefighter
founding fathers of journalism	pioneers of journalism
Founding Fathers of the nation	Founders of the nation
foreman	supervisor
workman's compensation	worker's compensation

Sensitivity is needed in referring to race, especially because references that were acceptable to members of a race in one decade may be unacceptable in another decade, or may be acceptable to some members and not others. During the last century "colored," "Negro," "black" and "African-American" have each, in succession, become the name that seemed most generally–but not universally–preferred by people of that race. "Native American" has become a preferred name, supplanting the generally accepted "Indian" of earlier years. Several high schools and colleges have been asked to change the names of their athletic teams from Indians, Chiefs and Braves. These names, along with Bears, Lions, Huskies, Ducks and Cougars, suggested that Native Americans were akin to wild animals or team mascots. Some teams changed their names. Some didn't. Some defenders of the original names said those names should be considered compliments.

A few years ago, some people raised objections to the Washington professional football team's name, "Redskins." Assigned to write an editorial on that topic, one student wrote that those who objected "perceive 'Redskins' to be a relic of white frontiersmen who judged the various tribes they encountered to be wild, uncivilized and violent–none of which is the type of self-image anyone would like to possess, especially a traditionally oppressed race in American society." But another student wrote that "proponents of the nickname say that they, indeed, are honoring Native Americans, and, if they didn't have the utmost respect for the group, they wouldn't waste their beloved team's moniker on the Indian."

The American Society of Newspaper Editors has distributed a card that contains a guide to "acceptable" and "unacceptable" terms to use in writing about the disabled. A person who is "handicapped" ("acceptable") is not necessarily "crippled" or "deformed" ("unacceptable"). A person "uses" a wheelchair, not "is confined to a wheelchair."[8] Also a person "resides in," and is not "confined to," a nursing home.

These are only a few suggestions that might improve your writing. Additional suggestions on how to avoid bias in writing can be found in *Without Bias: A Guidebook for Nondiscriminatory Communication.*[9] Several books on writing in general were suggested in Chapter 4, "Preparation of an Editorial Writer."

Conclusion

Simply following all of these steps, and those described in the preceding chapter, will not guarantee a good editorial. Thought, imagination and lively writing, none of which can be reduced to a simple how-to formula, are even more essential than the format of the editorial or the correctness of the words. No matter how technically correct or skillfully organized, an editorial is not likely to be effective unless it also carries hard-to-define qualities that attract and persuade readers.

James J. Kilpatrick has described the goal of the editorial writer "to be, in 300 words or less, temperate, calm, dignified, forceful, direct, catchy, provocative, stimulating, reasoned, logical, literate, factual, opinionated, conclusive, informative, interesting and persuasive. And put a live head on it."[10]

That's all it takes to write an editorial.

Questions and Exercises

1. Find an editorial with what you regard as an overabundance of factual informtion. Rewrite the piece using only those facts that are necessary to make the subject understandable.

2. Apply a heavy editing pencil to an editorial to remove unnecessary words and phrases.

3. Try to find an editorial in which the arguments and evidence presented do not support the conclusion. With the information that is contained in the editorial, can it be rewritten to bring the conclusion into line with the supporting material?

4. Count and average the number of syllables for every hundred words and the number of words per sentence in the editorials of several newspapers. How do the editorials compare in terms of word and sentence length? Are the editorials with longer words and sentences more difficult to understand? If not, why not?

5. In examining these same newspapers, do you find a general trend in individual papers toward long sentences and long words or short sentences and short words, or do editorials vary within the papers?

6. Find an editorial in which the simplified style of the writing seems condescending to readers. Can you rewrite the editorial to overcome this problem?

7. Scan a handful of editorials for clichés. Which–if any–can you justify? How could you eliminate the remainder?

8. Rewrite an editorial that relies excessively on government or other types of jargon. Translate the offending language into understandable English.

9. Examine several editorials for euphemisms and for more difficult words and phrases than are necessary to convey meaning.

10. Find improper and ambiguous uses of "it" and "that" as referents. Rewrite to clarify the meaning.

11. Find several sentences that begin with a form of "there is" and rewrite them in a clearer and more direct manner.

CHAPTER 12 Subjects That Are Hard to Write About

Is it necessary or desirable to fill the editorial columns with pieces on government and politics to the virtual exclusion of all else . . . ?

—CREED BLACK, *NASHVILLE TENNESSEAN*[1]

Any survey of American editorial writers would reveal that government is the favorite topic of editorial writers. This shouldn't be surprising, since the news business seems concerned primarily with public affairs, and much of public affairs involves government. Writers also may follow this tendency as a matter of least resistance, since their own interests are likely to lie in this direction. The nonpolitical subjects may not get written about, or taken seriously, for at least three other reasons. First, writers may regard some subject areas as too difficult to write about—at least in the time available to them. Second, they may regard a subject as so easy to write about that they dash off an editorial devoting little time or thought. Third, they may regard a nongovernment topic as not sufficiently serious to warrant taking time from the "great issues of the day." This chapter will look at the first of these editorials: subjects that are tough to write about. The next chapter will look at subjects that are deceptively easy and subjects that editorial writers often ignore.

Any subject can be hard to write about if you don't know what you are writing about. Over the years, I have found that, because of the fear of not knowing enough about the topic, writers have tended to shy away from seven subject areas: economics, legal issues, international affairs, culture, medicine and health, religion and sports.

ECONOMICS

For the writer who wants to write more than clichés, the editorial on economics is one of the hardest to write. Of all the topics I assign my students, economics is the one they resist most. Those who have taken introductory economics courses seem bewildered by theories, laws and graphs.

Those who have not taken these courses are filled with horror at the thought of writing about what has been called "the dismal science." Part of the reluctance of both groups stems from their impressions that editorials on economics are boring and filled with numbers. If they have read editorials on the subject, they probably think of them as dealing with taxes (too high), government spending (too much), unemployment (too high) or inflation (too rapid). Or they think that editorials on economics deal with the theories of John Maynard Keynes, Milton Friedman or Arthur Laffer. None of this seems to have much to do with daily life.

But economics does relate to how readers live. The supply and price of gasoline affect nearly every American, so editorials about decisions made by the OPEC nations stand a good chance of being read if they talk about how these decisions will be reflected at the gas pump. Editorials about the easing of the capital gains tax, extending the sales tax to food and drugs or boosting the gasoline tax can be written about in a manner that will make readers understand how and why they are affected. So how does a writer produce an editorial on economics that does not end up simply saying the government shouldn't be spending so much money or employees should, or shouldn't, pay a larger share of medical insurance premiums?

Several suggestions have been offered by Lauren K. Soth, veteran at writing editorials on economics as editorial page editor of the *Des Moines Register* and as a syndicated columnist. Economics editorials, according to Soth, should explain and interpret, not merely spout official newspaper policy. They should discuss "what is happening here and now" and concentrate on how current economic phenomena actually affect people's well-being. This means avoiding the temptation to "pontificate on every little economic event in terms of . . . grand ideologies." Soth emphasized that organization of the subject matter is extremely important, that the writer needs to proceed in a manner that seems logical to readers—from the known to the unknown, spelling out each major step of reasoning from the beginning to the conclusion. Each editorial should concentrate on one central idea and drive it home, avoiding getting involved in side issues.

While Soth did not contend that economics can be made simple and entertaining, he believed that the writer can, and should, arouse interest by talking in terms of what people are interested in—people. "Instead of saying, 'Wheat acreage increased to 10 percent,' why not say, 'Farmers planted 10 percent more acres of wheat'?" Without oversimplifying complex issues, the writer can make them understandable. For instance, instead of stringing facts and figures together in prose comparisons, data can be organized in tables and rounded off for easier comprehension.[2]

Instead of citing impersonal facts and figures, why not frame an economic issue in terms of real people? When an independent taxi company succeeded in getting a toehold in Denver, a *Rocky Mountain News* editorial ("The birth of Freedom Cabs") referred by name to three "minority entrepreneurs [who had] celebrated the opening of Freedom Cabs." The editorial was a tribute to their efforts, which ultimately led to a state law to allow more competition among taxi companies. After recounting these efforts, the editorial considered the question of whether opening the door to more cabs would hurt existing companies, but agreed with one of the entrepreneurs that talent and energy should be allowed to compete in a free market.

The Birth of Freedom Cabs

Mayor Wellington Webb says he wants additional input on affirmative action. He should consider the very affirmative action just taken by Leroy Jones, Ani Ebong and Girma Molalegne.

THE ISSUE:
A new Denver taxi company for the first time in decades

OUR VIEW:
Minority business people need free and open markets

On Tuesday, these minority entrepreneurs celebrated the grand opening of Freedom Cabs. (Originally, the name was Quick Pick Cabs. You'll understand the reason for the change shortly.)

Not since 1947 has a new cab company gone into operation in Denver and this opening came about only after four long, hard years of fighting by Jones et al. What did they have to overcome? The government's refusal to allow them to start their own business.

Consider: One government agency establishes minority set-aside programs and battles— as in the Adarand Constructors vs. Peña case— right up to the Supreme Court to preserve its power to award contracts based on race. Meanwhile, another government agency refuses to permit minority businessmen to start their own enterprises using no government favors and no taxpayer money.

As comedian Yakov Smirnoff would say: "What a country!"

To win their battle, Jones, Ebong and Molalegne first enlisted attorneys from the Washington-based Institute for Justice who filed a lawsuit challenging Denver's taxicab monopoly. The institute took the case as part of its effort to restore "economic liberty," the right of all Americans "to pursue a business or profession free from arbitrary or excessive government regulation."

In the end, however, the three aspiring businessmen had to persuade the Colorado legislature to pass a new taxi law instructing the Public Utilities Commission to change its mission from preserving a "regulated monopoly" to enforcing "regulated competition."

In June, the PUC finally authorized Freedom Cabs to go into business with 50 taxis. In the fall, another new firm, American Cabs, also plans to start operating.

Soon, Denver will have 800 cabs instead of 700. PUC commissioners fear that if they allow more taxis than that on the streets, the result might be a "destructive competition" that could knock one of the cab companies out of business.

We tend to agree with Jones, who told the *Rocky Mountain News'* Ann Imse that he didn't see why it should be the government's concern if the market weeds out companies that don't compete effectively.

Indeed, getting government out of the way so that minority entrepreneurs may enter the market and compete freely—using all the talent and energy they can muster—might be the most affirmative action of all.

Rocky Mountain News

The *St. Paul Pioneer-Press* took an informal approach in trying to entice readers into an editorial about a business establishment. When Dayton's department store announced it would have fewer sales and instead emphasize service, the *Pioneer-Press* published a conversational editorial titled "Fewer Sales? Shirley, you're kidding!" Not many years ago news and editorial departments never would have gratuitously mentioned or promoted the name of a commercial firm; that was considered free advertising. If a store wanted its name in print (except for engaging in some nefarious practice), it could take out an advertisement. But these days, when newspapers pride themselves on being consumer-oriented, an editorial about the demise of special sales no doubt will attract more readers than the other editorial the *Pioneer-Press* ran that

FEWER SALES | Shirley, You're Kidding!

"O K, Mr. Shirley, now where do you think you're going?"

"Um, there's an emergency, sir."

"What kind of emergency, Shirley?"

"Well, um, you see, sir, there's yet another hurricane approaching America's shores."

"We're in Minnesota, Shirley."

"One can never too careful, sir. Besides, there's, um, something else."

"I'm waiting."

Dayton's says it's changing its marketing strategy.

"Trial of the Century, sir. I've been called as a surprise witness."

"Trial's over, Shirley."

"UN women's conference in Beijing?"

"Over."

"Million Man March?"

"Not till next week. Look, Shirley, admit it, you're going to a sale at Dayton's."

"Oh, sir, it's worse than that! Dayton's says its changing its strategy—fewer sales! They're going to hire more sales staff instead, and reemphasize customer service and leading fashion."

"Get off it, Shirley."

"Would I lie to you, sir? The worst part is, retail analysts will probably like the idea of more differentiation among Dayton Hudson's different stores—Dayton's, Mervyn's and Target. Plus they'll see the prospect for more focus and better cost control in the department store division. But, sir, don't you see? I've got to go tell them they're ruining my life, sir. I don't know how to cope without Dayton's sales!"

"You've told some whoppers before, Shirley, but this is ridiculous. Out of my way."

"Where are you going, sir?"

"Um, I've got to catch my bus."

"But sir . . ."

St. Paul Pioneer-Press

---

day. It was titled "Bring computer access to every classroom," and even it was a commentary on the changing interests of potential newspaper customers.

Not every editorial on an economic issue can be personalized or jazzed up to attract the casual reader. Some of the toughest editorials to write are those that contradict generally held views about how best to promote your community economically. The *Register-Guard* of Eugene, Ore., undertook that task in an editorial titled "Who needs tax breaks?" In an effort to diffuse an immediate negative response from readers, the writer began the editorial with: "What would happen if all the states agreed to stop all economic incentive programs as of Jan. 1?" If the states would stop trying to out-promise each other, "state and local governments would start saving millions of dollars they now give away in the form of tax breaks for new industry," the editorial said. The editorial cited specific examples of how various industries had taken advantage of state and local incentives.

LEGAL ISSUES

Discussion of a legal issue can become so involved that readers may stop trying to understand what an editorial writer is talking about. Writers need to keep in mind that most readers know little about legal matters, so legal terms should never be used when plain English will do. If a legal term is used, it should be defined in the simplest language possible. Writers should keep a pocket law dictionary handy. Simplifying complex and technical legal matters, however, may distort information or mislead readers. So care must be taken to include enough of the complexities to persuade those knowledgeable of the subject.

■■■■ Who Needs Tax Breaks?

What would happen if all the states agreed to stop all economic development tax incentive programs as of Jan. 1?

The only certainty is that state and local governments would start saving millions of dollars they now give away in the form of tax breaks for new industry. But no one knows whether the locations chosen for new plants would be far different from those chosen now.

The business of using tax incentives to attract business is a competitive trap. It resembles the pre–oil embargo price wars that used to erupt among gasoline stations. As soon as one state offers concessions, neighbors feel compelled to follow suit.

It's easy to see why almost all states now use tax incentives to lure business and stimulate job creation. All feel strong pressure to keep up with the others.

Register-Guard reporter Sherri Buri provided a good run-down Wednesday on Oregon's two biggest programs, the Strategic Investment Program that caps the taxable property value of big manufacturing plants at $100 million and the enterprise zones that give businesses settling herein a full property tax exemption for three to five years. Hyundai will take advantage of an enterprise zone exemption when it builds a $1.3 billion computer chip plant in west Eugene.

Criticism of these programs has increased now that one big company, Sumitomo Sitix, says it still wants to build a $912 million wafer plant in Newberg even though Yamhill County commissioners denied the company's request for an $8 million tax break.

Gov. John Kitzhaber is reported to be planning to review all of the state's economic development incentive programs. He could begin by reading a new review of national studies of tax incentives commissioned by the Department of Economic Development. Completed in April, the 19-page review was done by Anthony Rufolo, a Portland State University urban studies professor, and graduate student J. O'Shea Gumusoglu.

It's a good summary of the arguments for and against these programs, but the conclusion is predictably ambivalent. "In general," the authors say, "the literature does not find tax incentives to be an effective way to promote economic development, but it does not allow a blanket statement that they can never be effective."

One relatively new aspect of tax incentives not covered by past studies deserves special attention. It was mentioned to Buri by Bill Conerly, senior vice president and economist for First Interstate Bank in Portland. He noted that property tax breaks help correct a disproportionate property tax impact on capital intensive plants.

High tech plants such as the one Hyundai plans for Eugene and the laser disc factory Sony is building in Springfield use extremely expensive equipment that is subject to property taxation. Giving them an initial tax exemption cuts this potential cost.

For a start-up exemption (of three to five years) to be fair to the community, of course, the benefiting companies need to be around long enough to pay some taxes later on. Yet in the rapidly changing world of computers and telecommunications, companies themselves have no way of knowing how long a given plant may operate.

This is only one of the difficulties the governor and appropriate legislative committees might examine. They should also consider the possibility that economic development tax incentives should be used mainly during recessionary times and tempered or turned off when the economy heats up. A little Keynesian response to the business cycle would seem appropriate here.

Register-Guard

The 40th anniversary of *Brown vs. Topeka Board of Education*, the Supreme Court case that ordered the desegregation of public schools, prompted an editorial in the *Plain Dealer* of Cleveland ("40 years after Brown vs. Board"). The editorial makes two basic points, neither of them stated in legalese. The first is that equal education for all children still has not been achieved. The editorial quotes the easily understandable opinion written by Chief Justice Earl

40 Years after Brown vs. Board

Forty years ago this week, the halls of education trembled and the walls of education tumbled down when the U.S. Supreme Court ruled that separate but equal public school facilities for black and white children were unconstitutional.

It was a mighty decision—one that shocked the South and forced the country's white leadership to loosen its grip on the racist notion that blacks were inferior human beings. It signaled the beginning of a humane revolution, though not a bloodless one, for civil rights activists were to lose their lives in coming years in the fight to desegregate the rest of American society.

Where has that historic ruling gotten us four decades later? You might determine little progress has been made if you looked to some of America's inner-city school districts, including Cleveland's, for the answer. If you read, not knowing where they came from, the words Chief Justice Earl Warren wrote in the unanimous decision, you might not realize they speak to the state of public education in 1954. This is how the morning-after edition of *The Plain Dealer* described the decision Warren penned:

" . . . he (Warren) said education today is 'perhaps the most important function' of state and local governments, and it is 'doubtful that any child may reasonably be expected to succeed in life if he is denied the opportunity to an education.

"'Such an opportunity, where the state has undertaken to provide it, is a right which must be made available to all on equal terms.'"

Do those observations not pertain to the state of public education in 1994? The controversies flaring nationwide about equitable school funding necessitates a "yes" answer to that question.

The Brown decision, in its intent and in the way that intent was executed, has shaped public education in those intervening years. Busing became the favored means of integrating schools, ordered by federal judges against school systems that balked at the high court's verdict.

Cleveland was one such city: Years after the Supreme Court issued the Brown opinion, Cleveland school officials still were purposefully segregating black pupils in specially built buildings. On their way to these buildings, they would pass schools near their homes that were reserved for white children.

Certainly, the ideal of classrooms full of children from all backgrounds, races and ethnicities is worth pursuing. But, in retrospect, busing was not the vehicle on which that ideal would ride to fruition. Many whites, upset that their children could not go to the school down the street, either moved out of the city or put their children in private or parochial schools. Blacks packed up, too, and moved out to the suburbs, leaving the city with a decimated middle class and a weak tax base with which to finance public education.

Now it is not a question of how to integrate the schools. The dilemma is how to integrate the city, a far more intractable problem.

Meanwhile, education for those who remained in Cleveland public schools, and in similar circumstances in cities around the country, has not improved. Equal educational opportunities, as Chief Justice Earl Warren described them in Brown, still have not been achieved. Moreover, it is hard to imagine how even the highest court in the land could bring quality, let alone equality—each a desirable goal—to every school in the land. Providing a good public education to all children has rightly become the country's top educational priority.

But the worth of Brown vs. Board of Education should not be measured only by what occurred inside the classroom. It was meant to strike at what happened inside the corridors of legislative power, where state and local governments created and perpetuated discriminatory public policy. The decision sent the message throughout the country that the American version of apartheid was unacceptable and doomed.

Indeed, that message was sent beyond our national borders. Immediately after the Warren court made its pronouncement, the Voice of America began airing radio broadcasts of the opinion around the world and particularly to Eastern Europe, where Communist leaders had loudly decried U.S. segregation.

It is far more productive, and appropriate, to look back on the Brown decision for the accomplishment of tearing down those officially built walls of separation. It may not have brought the level of educational quality Americans rightly demand, but it did away with one of the most odious of injustices.

Plain Dealer

Warren, suggesting that what Warren said about education could apply to Cleveland at the time the editorial was written. But then the editorial finds encouragement in that the worth of the decision surpasses its effect on education, claiming that the message to state and local governments and to the American people was that "the American version of apartheid was unacceptable and doomed."

Another *Plain Dealer* editorial ("Free speech OK'd, not a free-for-all") attempted to simplify a complex First Amendment issue by saying the two opposing sides had "won a joint victory." Readers who wondered how that could be were enticed into reading the editorial. The Ohio State Supreme Court had issued a ruling concerning the right to picket the home of a suspected Nazi death camp guard. Both supporters and opponents were assured the right to demonstrate outside John Demjanjuk's house. The main point of the editorial was to urge the two sides to use restraint in their protests.

Newspaper writers are especially likely to be attracted to issues concerning the press and "the people's right to know" about government, but most readers

Free Speech OK'd, Not a Free-for-all

Permission for opposing groups to picket Demjanjuk home assumes that demonstratiors will remain peaceful

Groups that support suspected former Nazi death camp guard John Demjanjuk and others that advocate his deportation have won a joint victory in the Ohio Supreme Court. By a 7-0 margin, the court said both sides could picket simultaneously outside Demjanjuk's home in Seven Hills, reversing a Common Pleas Court decision that was upheld in the 8th District Ohio Court of Appeals.

The high court's ruling was a stout affirmation of free speech in its purest form. Protesters who believe Demjanjuk helped carry out Adolf Hitler's Final Solution and those who contend conventional accounts of the Holocaust are exaggerated or, even more incredibly, that it never took place, may now brandish placards at each other on a usually tranquil suburban street.

Justices made it plain that in the absence of a clear and present danger of violence, there were no grounds to prohibit picketing. Their expectation, of course—and we hope it is realized—is that the opposing demonstrators will stay peaceful.

Seven Hills originally attempted to ban residential picketing. That was clearly unconstitutional, however great a burden permitting the simple exercise of First Amendment rights might place upon a community.

But when Common Pleas Judge Daniel Gaul, in a 1993 ruling, said that it was all right to gather outside Demjanjuk's home but not for opposing groups to do so at the same time, *The Plain Dealer* praised what appeared to be a compromise that would protect free speech and also minimize the risk of violence.

An appeals court adopted the same position. But the American Civil Liberties Union, acting in part for a Jewish activist, took the case to the Supreme Court. Rabbi Avi Weiss, who says he has picketed Demjanjuk 10 times since the latter was released by an Israeli court on war crimes charges in 1993, said it was important to face members of groups that say the Holocaust never happened.

Now, if they file in Seven Hills for permission to picket, Weiss and opposing white-supremacist groups such as the Ku Klux Klan will have the right to confront each other within view of Demjanjuk's residence. Seven Hills officials cannot be blamed if they hope such encounters are rare. And the entire community will join in urging whatever groups show up in the suburb to confine their exchanges to verbal ones.

Plain Dealer

Report Shows Public Records Not Always Public

Public records and other matters in the office of any officer at all times during office hours shall be open to inspection by any person.

It's really not difficult to understand. Arizona's Public Records Law has been on the books since before Arizona was state—adopted by the territorial Legislature in 1901. It's a simple, straightforward law—the way laws used to be before the professional law-writers took over and lawyerized everything.

But in the 94 years since those 25 words were written and OK'd, legislators and bureaucrats have found enough loopholes and crafted about 200 exceptions to turn the law into a tattered remnant of what was intended.

In this week's special report by Arizona members of The Associated Press, including the *Citizen*, it is glaringly clear that it is increasingly difficult for you to know what your government is up to.

Lawmakers frequently justify punching holes in the Public Records Law by saying it is the only way to rein in overly nosey reporters out to soil the reputations of honest, hard-working public servants.

Reporters do make frequent use of the law—but we are far from the only ones affected when public records are sealed. This is not a journalists' right to know—it is *your* right to know what your government is doing.

The AP series found gross inconsistencies in the way public employees interpret the law. Police records that are a cinch to obtain in Tucson are sealed in Tempe. Some county records are available, others are sealed, depending on the whims of the county attorney handling the request.

In the meantime, the Legislature last session considered a myriad of requests that would have closed more public records. The results were mixed: Some records previously open now are sealed, but the actions weren't as Draconian as some lawmakers had hoped.

It's pointless to expect the Legislature to be receptive to laws that open government to inspection when lawmakers exempt themselves from many open records and open meeting laws, routinely meeting in secret to hatch their nefarious plans.

It is unlikely government will make its actions more open—unless you make it abundantly clear to the legislators who represent you that that is what you want and what you expect.

Tucson Citizen

---

are not likely to get very excited about an editorial on public records. The *Tucson Citizen* ("Report shows public records not always public") tried to get around that hurdle with a second sentence that read: "It's really not difficult to understand." The sentence referred to the state's Public Records Law, but also encouraged readers to continue on into the editorial. The point of the editorial was that, since the 25-word law had been adopted in 1901, it had been limited by 200 exceptions. Among the worst offenders were the legislators themselves, "exempt[ing] themselves from many open records and open meeting laws, routinely meeting in secret to hatch their nefarious plans." Readers were urged to put pressure on the legislators.

On a more optimistic open-government note, the *Dickenson Star*, published in the coalfields of Virginia, carried an editorial titled "A Rare, Startling Moment–County Needs More Like It." The county board of supervisors, in "a rare, almost startling moment," had declined to resort to "its infamous executive sessions." The result was an open exchange over an exploration company's proposed changes in an agreement involving underground injection wells. More than half the editorial, however, discussed past instances in which the supervisors had resorted to closed sessions. The supervisors were told that opening more of their meetings would foster more participation by citizens of the community.

INTERNATIONAL AFFAIRS

International subjects may be both the hardest and the easiest topics to write about. They are easy in the sense that, when you write about a faraway country, you will not have your mayor, governor or next-door neighbor calling to say you don't have your facts straight, as they might on a local topic. Writers used to say the safest editorial was a hard-hitting one about Afghanistan. That led to the term "Afghanistanism" to describe editorials on topics that no one knows or cares about. Then came the Soviet invasion of Afghanistan in 1979, and writers were likely to find themselves commenting on affairs in Kazakhstan, Kirgizstan and Uzbekistan as well.

Whether they are about Afghanistan or Mexico, editorials on international topics probably are the least read editorials in the United States. When I ask students in my editorial writing class to tally the editorials in the newspapers they are assigned to read, international editorials always come in last. The little international news people get mostly comes from the 6 o'clock or 11 o'clock news, where a news item might get 15 seconds and a fleeting news clip. The next morning the headline and the first paragraph of the news story seem pretty much to replicate what was on television, even if the story is eight or 10 inches long, so the reader is likely to skip the story.

That's the bad news. The good news is that editorial writers have an opportunity to provide more than a 15-second take, a headline and a lead. Readers are in a hurry when they scan the news pages. They slow down when they come to the editorial page. For a few minutes they are receptive to reading longer articles, considering differing opinions and thinking about issues outside their own little worlds.

"But," say some editorial writers, "I don't know any more about international matters than my readers. If I write on an international subject, the best I can do is repeat what someone more knowledgeable has written." Several editorial writers were asked, in a symposium in *The Masthead*, for their advice on writing knowledgeable, pertinent, international editorials.

The most frequent suggestion: Make what you write relevant to your readers. "Make them look local," said Stein B. Haughlid of *Dagens Naeringsliv* in Oslo, Norway. "When it is a theme like ex-Yugoslavia or Somalia, where American troops are sent in, personification or localizing should not be too difficult. The same goes for the embargo of Iraqi oil that might affect the price of oil all over the world, including the local gas station, the owner's profits and hence the contribution to the church and local tax revenue."[3]

Joe Geshwiler of the *Atlanta Constitution* noted that a place like Peoria, Ill., the headquarters for Caterpillar Tractor, "which does business all around the globe," is "home to a multitude of international business specialists with high standards about the quality of their informational sources." He suggested, as sources for international editorials, "a local university with overseas connections, or a service or religious organization with projects overseas, or

A Rare, Startling Moment— County Needs More Like It

The Dickenson County Board of Supervisors had a legal excuse to retire into the comfort of one of its infamous executive sessions but instead declined to use it.

It was a rare, almost startling moment. Dickenson County needs to see more just like it.

It happened the night supervisors held a special meeting and planned to meet privately with Equitable Resources Exploration Inc. to talk about clarifications and substantial changes the company wanted in its so-called six-point agreement with the county over underground injection wells.

Then-chairman Damon Rasnick broke from the formal agenda that listed, as it routinely does, an executive session to consult legal counsel on a legal matter. Rasnick informed a meager audience that County Attorney Don Askins had advised the board that it didn't really need to meet with EREX behind closed doors.

EREX seemed surprised, too. Company attorney George Mason asked for time to consult with his colleagues before agreeing to proceed. They retired to a private back room and emerged ready to present publicly the deal they wanted from Dickenson County.

What unfolded before the public was open discussion and genuine exchange between two groups with a vested interest in the final outcome.

EREX's presentation—although understandably somewhat promotional and a little heavy on sometimes-confusing legal and engineering jargon—addressed many pertinent issues. Supervisors asked some solid questions and offered some to-the-point observations, mostly grounded in concerns about the safety of injection wells and protection of Dickenson County.

In the end, the two reached agreeable compromise.

Dickenson County citizens need to see more of this kind of exchange. In this instance, not only was the public privy to the initial polite discussion, but also to the meeting that followed to hash out finer details.

Citizens were not left guessing about what happened. They heard with their own ears what supervisors were thinking—what issues troubled them, what positive arguments they had to make. They heard EREX respond. Their information was not filtered through a closed session.

Unfortunately, this example of open decision-making is the exception to the rule for the current board and those before it. Standard procedure for Dickenson County supervisors is to regularly convene behind closed doors,

---

far-sighted businessmen, or an ethnic community in your midst." The "trick," said, "is to identify the connection" to the local community.[4]

Edward Alden of the *Vancouver* (B.C.) *Sun* pointed out that "[e]very city in North America is being reshaped by international events, most significantly by the largest influx of immigrants since the turn of the century, and by the growing importance of international trade and investment."[5]

Philip Taubman of the *New York Times*, which has full-time writers on international issues, said he looks for "ways to make foreign issues accessible and relevant to our readers." He said he liked to "feel we're talking to a reader across the kitchen table, not lecturing someone in an auditorium."[6]

Editorial writers on small staffs should not be expected to provide new insights on tribal wars in a Central African country, but, if they follow the news, read a few national newspapers and magazines, peruse the Internet and check out local sources, they should be able to provide intelligent comment on issues relevant to their readers.

frequently for hours on end. They insist the private sessions are legal and necessary. They say they are acting in the best [interests] of the county. They say we just don't understand.

We say they are wrong. Board members who endorse frequent and prolonged closed sessions are operating under some misguided notions about why they need to conduct so much of the public's business where the public can't hear them.

Citizens understand that some closed meetings are appropriate. It is important to protect the privacy of an individual whose job performance, for example, is at issue. The interest of the county at large is best served by not discussing openly such matters as sensitive negotiations for a property purchase when disclosure could result in the artificial inflation of the price the county and its taxpayers might have pay. No one expects supervisors and the county attorney to publicly plot legal strategy when a lawsuit has been filed or seriously threatened.

Are supervisors breaking the state's open meeting law with such frequent closed sessions? Honestly, the Virginia Freedom of Information Act is a hard law to break, written vaguely as it is and providing plenty of latitude for public bodies to convene out of public earshot.

We have confidence that Dickenson County supervisors do not intentionally break the letter of the law and that their legal council would advise them against it if they tried to.

But the test of good government, as supervisors so aptly demonstrated with EREX, goes beyond the ability to adhere to the letter of the law.

It is the spirit of the law that Dickenson County supervisors seem routinely to break. Like too many officials who held these offices before them, they leave the impression that they look for ways to slip behind closed doors. In fact, lawmakers specifically state the opposite intent.

But the board and its advisors have fallen into the sloppy habit of trying to keep much about government decision-making a secret. The assumption is that they are the owners of the information, that only they, the executives, know best. Supervisors and their advisors certainly have the advantage over the public when they hold all the information cards and won't even let the public peek.

Are supervisors really protecting citizens? From what—knowledge? Once shared, information can enlighten anyone. Informed, the public might help play a better hand.

With all the issues facing Dickenson County, supervisors should welcome the help of an informed citizenry. Instead of putting off the public by keeping secrets, the board should open up the process and flow of information. By doing so, they would foster citizen participation as an important function of government.

Dickenson Star

No Cause for Fear of United Nations

We hear it said across coffee shop tables in North Louisiana and on the conservative airwaves. The United States faces the very real possibility of takeover by the United Nations.

This was all the right-wing rage in the 1950s and 1960s in Louisiana. The slogan was "get U.S. out of the U.N."

And this whole perception of the U.N. was then and is now ridiculous. Bunk. Hokum. Forget it, and the Trilateral Commission.

Most Americans, thankfully, don't believe such nonsense. Those who read a newspaper or hear the news realize the U.N. is stretched thin in Bosnia, Rwanda and Somalia.

Yet, the far-fetched criticism of the U.N. has caused the Clinton administration to withdraw funding from some U.N. peacekeeping operations.

We even hear that the U.N. is planning to invade the U.S. With what? And, remember, the U.N. can do only what its members—including the superpower U.S.—want it to do.

The issue of the U.N. is not whether it will become a "world government."

The issue is will the U.N. have the means of undertaking humanitarian missions with declining support and wild-eyed, ridiculous criticism.

Shreveport Times

In an editorial in support of the United Nations, the Shreveport, La., *Times* sought a local angle and found it in Northern Louisiana coffeeshop tables and talk radio ("No cause for fear of United Nations").

A local angle isn't always necessary. Some major international events call for comment in their own right. When South Africa adopted a new constitution, the *Sun-Sentinel* of Fort Lauderdale ("Grace, intelligence in evidence as South African nation matures") noted the personal strains between Nelson Mandela and F.W. de Klerk, but remained optimistic concerning prospects for "the transformation from a repressive apartheid society to one in which blacks control."

Grace, Intelligence in Evidence as South African Nation Matures

South Africa impressed the world with its transformation from a repressive apartheid society to one in which blacks control a democratic government. Now, in two days of high political drama, the nation adopted a constitution and watched with anxiety as the National Party withdrew from the coalition government.

The most rational way to interpret the party's action is to take F.W. de Klerk's explanation at face value—and factor in other aspects. De Klerk pulled his mainly white party out of the coalition, he said, as part of the renewed nation's growing maturity and normalization. As he explained, South Africa needs a strong, confident opposition, which the National Party intends to supply. Also, the new constitution doesn't provide for a continued coalition government anyway, after the next election in 1999, so he inevitably would have taken his party into opposition within three years.

All of that is convincing and reasonable, and there's no justification for concluding South Africa is in a political crisis. President Nelson Mandela, with whom de Klerk shared the Nobel Peace Prize in 1993, has a comfortable majority and easily can govern alone. Besides, de Klerk and his party won't give up their seven Cabinet seats until June 30, allowing ample time for Mandela to fill them with his own choices.

Those positive points are doubtless important, but it's also necessary to note the increasing personal strain between Mandela and de Klerk. At best they were uneasy partners in the government, with de Klerk noticeably uncomfortable as deputy president, in a subordinate role to Mandela. Although in public appearances they managed to be mostly civil, the two argued vehemently in private. At one point, they were observed shouting at one another in a parking lot.

De Klerk, after all, had been president during apartheid's endgame, and although he ordered Mandela's release from prison after 27 years, a degree of bitterness remained. When an angry Mandela called de Klerk a "joke," for suggesting some members of Mandela's party should be prosecuted for their role in the armed struggle against apartheid, outsiders could see the frayed partnership tearing apart.

At times in the evolution of nations with parliamentary systems, coalition governments become necessary. In South Africa, the coalition's end came a little quicker than expected, but it's being handled intelligently and with as much grace as both sides can scrape up.

Considered in full context, the new South Africa remains an astonishing accomplishment. Mandela and de Klerk deserved their Nobel Prize, as they have earned the world's plaudits for overcoming deeply rooted antagonism on behalf of all the country's citizens, whatever their color.

Events of the past few days are a little unsettling, but hardly cataclysmic. Investors in the new South Africa should realize the country's future remains promising.

A national maturity is emerging, and although the process may well be shaky, it's necessary. Growing pains, yes. But a national crisis? No.

Sun-Sentinel

Arts and Culture

Surveys show that newspaper readership of news about the arts ranks low compared to most other features. Few daily newspapers have good arts and music coverage, even though the surveys have encouraged papers to expand and beef up their "life style" sections. As for opinion pages, according to a former editorial writer turned art-center director, Aubrey Bowie, "[e]ditorial writers seem to turn their attention to the arts only when something very good or very bad grabs the headline and catches their eye, [and] in either case, they are forced to shoot from the hip without the day-to-day research that they do routinely on other community issues."[7]

Arts In Education: A Basic, Not a Frill

KATHLEEN NEFF is a Vinton mom who thinks her kid's first place in a state poetry contest should get a share of the attention heaped on student athletes. She's right. And a small but insistent number of successful businessmen from around the country would agree.

Neff wrote a letter to the editor ("Kids who excel in arts are ignored," Feb. 4) bemoaning how, at a recent awards ceremony in Roanoke County, television cameras focused exclusively on three young athletes, overlooking her 16-year-old daughter and eight other students who had won art and writing honors.

"This incident really bothered me because it illustrates again how important athletes and athletic organizations are in this state, and how irrelevant are the arts."

It bothers us too—not because the arts are irrelevant in Virginia, but because they too often are treated as though they were.

The arts enrich our lives. They're valuable for their own sake, as an expression of humanity, of our aspirations to beauty. Every kid should do art and music and poetry for the fun of it. So should every adult.

But a sound arts education is also economically valuable. Indeed, it becomes imperative as repetitive, standardized tasks in the workplace give way to jobs requiring more creativity.

Interestingly, a cadre of businessmen is convinced of this, having found it out the hard way: by coping with business reversals and worker shortages. The arts, they say, comprise the fourth R of the basic education that students need to compete in the job market. And American schools aren't providing it.

James Houghton, chairman of the National Skills Standards Board and retired chairman and CEO of Corning Inc., is among those once-burned who now believe. Corning's Montgomery County plant has become a model of the high-performance workplace likely to prosper into the next century. A decade ago, the company was ailing. The difference? Ongoing, company-wide training that includes computers, graphics and design.

In an era in which technology changes rapidly, the work world needs people who can learn constantly and see problems in new ways. Yet most school systems aren't changing accordingly—certainly not fast enough.

Schools that marginalize arts education—here a part-time teacher doing it on the side, there an elective course first to be cut when the budget ax falls—are failing not just their students, but the nation's future.

So, please, school officials across the region and Virginia: Get with the program. Well-integrated into basic subjects such as math, English and science, an effective arts education not only civilizes; it helps students prepare to think and solve problems creatively. It's no frill.

On top of which, Houghton told *The Christian Science Monitor* recently, "Art classes are the only ones where students do their personal best, not just enough for a passing grade."

Very much as sports nurture personal excellence.

Roanoke Times

According to Bowie, funding of the arts should get as much careful attention as the funding of more traditional public programs. Bowie noted, however, that changes in federal tax laws have reduced the tax advantages for contributions to non-profit organizations, that federal government support for the arts has been decreasing and that direct government involvement in the arts is a growing issue. Policy makers and editorial writers have been asking: Should the government be supporting the arts? And, if so, under what circumstances?

The *Roanoke* (Va.) *Times* used the occasion of a letter to the editor, complaining about a neglected poetry award, to make a case for supporting arts education in local schools. In "Arts in education: a basic, not a frill," the editorial writer endorsed not only the arts "for their own sake" and art "for the fun of it," but also for its benefit in the work place. It cited a "model" experience at a nearby manufacturing plant.

Part of the task of editorial writers concerned about the arts is to encourage their readers to support and participate in the arts in their own communities. In an editorial titled "So much to do today," the *Santa Barbara News-Press* urged readers to join the third annual Surfrider Foundation Beach Cleanup, to visit an annual Chinese Festival, to "swing by the Medieval Mayfaire Festival

So Much to Do Today

For those of you at a loss for things to do today, we offer an eclectic itinerary that's sure to leave you feeling good about yourself and your community.

The costs will be minimal and the rewards great.

We suggest you start, as so many things do in Santa Barbara, at the beach. Any of several beaches actually.

A year's worth of trash and debris, swelled by the violent winter storms, has accumulated on our beaches. So today, scores of volunteers will be hitting the sands along the South Coast as part of the 3rd annual Surfrider Foundation Beach Cleanup. It will run from 11 a.m. until 2 p.m.

Participants can meet at West Beach near Stearns Wharf; Leadbetter Beach; Goleta Beach County Park on the north side of the pier; or Campus Point Beach and Coal Oil Point Beach on the UCSB West Campus.

You don't need any special skills. Just your enthusiasm and a desire to help. You also may win one of several prizes donated by local merchants.

After you've added some sparkle to the coastline, you can head over to Oak Park for the annual Chinese Festival. Although this is the Year of the Boar, your time spent here should be quite interesting.

There will be Chinese music, traditional folk dances, martial arts demonstrations and, of course, lots of great ethnic food. The festival runs from 10 a.m. to 7 p.m.

For a total change of gears, you could also swing by the Medieval Mayfaire Festival, from 11 a.m. to 7 p.m. in Mission Fields at St Anthony's Seminary, 2300 Garden St. The day will feature plays, parades, storytelling, food, drink and music. There is a cost for this, but admission is discounted a dollar if you come in costume.

To cap off the day, you might consider one of two student productions. At 8:15 p.m. at Our Lady of Sorrows Catholic Church in Santa Barbara, the Santa Barbara High School Madrigal Singers and A Cappella Choir will perform. And at 3 and 7 p.m. in Santa Maria, films and videos produced by current and former Hancock College students will be featured in Film Fest '95. There is a charge for both events.

Finally, if you make it through all that, plan to sleep in on Sunday.

Santa Barbara News-Press

The Art Experience
There's more to I Madonnari than chalk on the sidewalk

If you are inspired by great art, the Santa Barbara Mission is the place to be this weekend. Preparation for the famous Italian street painting festival known as I Madonnari is in progress as you read these words.

In fact, dozens of local artists have been gathering supplies and plotting strategy for weeks and are, at this moment, executing those plans on the plaza at the foot of the Mission's front steps, beginning the works of art that will result in a colorful array of pastel patches for everyone's enjoyment.

Although this weekend marks the 10th annual rendition of I Madonnari in Santa Barbara, it is an event that has been going on in Italy since the 16th century. It is called "Madonnari" because Italian artists were fond of reproducing one of their favorite images—the Madonna.

Over the centuries, the festival of traveling artists has settled generally into one village, Grazie di Curatone, where the International Street Painting Festival is held each August in front of the local Catholic church.

Now, you can save up your allowance and travel to Italy in August if you wish, but you will get the same kind of excitement and the same soul-thrilling artwork right here in front of the mission, beginning at noon today and open to the public through late Monday afternoon.

Individual and groups of artists, including many children, "buy" squares on the Mission plaza, and use their chalks to bring those dull pavers to colorful, vibrant life. Visitors can wander the grounds, mingling with the artists and enjoying their labors, while at the same time buying an Italian ice to ward off the rigors of a warm day, or the wares of other on-site vendors. There also will be live music throughout the three-day festival.

Not only will you have the opportunity to view some truly breath-taking art creations, you also will be part of fund-raising for the Children's Creative Project, a local non-profit organization administered by the County Education Office that sponsors various art projects throughout the county school system.

For example, by the end of the school term this year, the Children's Creative Project will have given more than 22,000 local school children the opportunity to learn from 40 artists-in-residence in the visual and performing arts. Also by school year's end, more than 36,000 young students at 150 school sites will have seen more than 550 performances by 50 touring companies, among them the Kahurangi Maori Dance Theatre of New Zealand.

So, you see, I Madonnari is more than a gaggle of local artists getting down on their hands and knees to entertain thousands of curious visitors at the Mission. It is a fund-raising event that is key to the enhanced art education of literally tens of thousands of local school children.

Who needs Italy?

Santa Barbara News-Press

---

and to "cap off the day" listening to student vocal groups singing at Our Lady of Sorrows Catholic Church. On another occasion ("The art experience") the newspaper urged readers to turn out for "the famous Italian street painting festival known as I Madonnari," a fund raiser that was modeled after an event that has been taking place in Italy since the 16th century.

MEDICINE AND HEALTH

The health sciences represent another area in which editorial writers may feel ignorant. "Few issues more readily trip the typical editorialist into silence, drivel or pompous balderdash," D. Michael Heywood of the *Columbian* of Vancouver, Wash., wrote in a *Masthead* symposium on health care. "Anything deeper than a turf battle between ambulance companies involves chopping through layers of increasing complexity. Burrowing through a vein of valuable explanation or suggestion for public action can seem as daunting as attempting heart surgery with kitchen cutlery."[8] Writers need to display knowledge of the topic as well as an understanding of and sympathy for those who hold different opinions, on abortion, AIDS, euthanasia, artificial insemination, life-preserving treatment, organ transplants and holistic medicine. Heywood's admonition to the opposing sides on abortion: "Our pro-choice position gains strength and validity if we've troubled to keep on talking after we've been branded babykillers. Our antipathy for *Roe vs. Wade* ought to have its corners rounded by sympathy for survivors of the back alley."

In another symposium, editors of *The Masthead* asked writers in 21 communities with relatively low incidences of AIDS to describe how they were writing about the disease.[9] Several writers said commentary was difficult because of conflicting medical evidence. Some suggested the emotion and confusion aroused by AIDS issues could be minimized by treating AIDS as a public health epidemic that demanded governmental attention and public education. The writers indicated that they detected less hysteria among members of the public than previously, but a substantial amount of ignorance resulting more from self-deception than from misinformation in the news media.

One long-running medical issue that is related to AIDS, as well as other ailments, is the medicinal use of marijuana. In California, for example, in 1994, both houses of the legislature approved a medicinal marijuana bill, but Gov. Pete Wilson vetoed it. In 1995, in a "non-election year," the *San Francisco Chronicle* expressed the hope that "compassion and good sense" would result in passage of a similar bill ("Marijuana as Medicine"). Efforts to pass the bill were no more successful. Then in the fall of 1996 voters in California (and Arizona as well) approved an initiative allowing for the use of marijuana. The legislative actions provoked a rash of court challenges as well as efforts by the Clinton administration to keep all uses of marijuana illegal. The actions also provoked legislators and editorial writers in other states.

RELIGION

Religion has been a subject that newspapers traditionally have not covered or commented on, except for the most mundane stories about church activities and the public controversies that spring up within and between religious groups. Reporters and editors don't want to get bogged down in what Susan Willey describes as "the complexity and diversity within religion" or to try to determine appropriate sources. A journalist who is not very knowledgeable about religious matters finds it "much easier to fall back on traditional journalistic news criteria and cover religion on the basis of conflict and aberration," she wrote in *Quill.* They are much more comfortable dealing with facts than with opinions and beliefs, she said. "They lean toward the concrete rather than the abstract."[10] Within journalism, and in fact within American society, there

Marijuana as Medicine

WHAT A SENSE of justice and relief many AIDS, cancer, glaucoma and multiple sclerosis patients felt last year when both houses of the state Legislature passed a bill allowing them to use marijuana to ease their pain and nausea.

Some otherwise law-abiding citizens already had been using the illegal weed to combat the ravages of their diseases. Others were aware of the helpful effects of pot and wanted to try it but could not bring themselves to defy laws against marijuana use and possession. When both the state Senate and Assembly approved the medicinal marijuana measure by Senator Milton Marks, D-S.F., both groups expressed gratitude.

Patients should not have to break the law to get relief

But their victory was short-lived. Despite its legislative approval after substantive hearings, Governor Wilson vetoed the bill.

Let us hope that in this non-election year, compassion and good sense rule and that an identical measure, by Assemblyman John Vasconcellos, D–San Jose, passes and, this time, is signed by Wilson.

The Assembly did the right thing last week by approving the measure. Now it is up to the Senate and the governor to provide the opportunity for relief from suffering for many patients for whom marijuana controls nausea caused by anti-cancer and anti-AIDS drugs, lowers eye pressure caused by glaucoma and reduces muscle spasms and pain related to multiple sclerosis.

The measure is narrowly drawn and would not change laws against marijuana possession and use for the general public. It simply would allow suffering patients—with doctor approval—to possess or cultivate marijuana for personal use.

Several medical studies have shown marijuana does ease pain and nausea for many patients. Recognizing this, a number of communities have chosen to look the other way when known cancer—and other—patients grow pot. But neither the patients nor law enforcement should be forced to disobey the law to provide medical relief.

The patients' hopes were raised, then dashed, last year. A repeat of that cruel outcome is not acceptable.

San Francisco Chronicle

---

also long has been a belief that one's religion is a private matter and therefore is not a proper topic for public discussion. Most Americans, for example, are embarrassed by public preaching in the streets.

Despite inclinations toward reticence, journalists have been increasingly forced in recent years, in spite of themselves, to report and comment on moral and religious issues: prayer in the schools, aid to parochial schools, abortion, gays as church leaders and church members, birth control, religious symbols on public property, creationism vs. evolution. Religious and religion-related groups that traditionally have not been politically active have become not only active but also politically astute at wielding influence. (A few years ago that last sentence would have referred to "church groups." Now writers talk about the activities of churches, mosques, temples, synagogues and religious cults, and not every group is connected with a specific denomination–the Christian Coalition, for example.)

These issues come before the Supreme Court. They come before state legislatures and state boards of education. They come before town councils and local school boards. They spring up on the Internet. Editorial writers can not ignore these issues. In fact they should relish the opportunity to wrestle with subjects that at least some of their readers really care about, and care about deeply. They need look only to their own letters columns to see that readers are writing about abortion, creationism, school prayer, subsidized private-school tuition and a host of other religion-related topics. By writing on these topics, they may encourage other readers to recognize that religious issues are important and merit public discussion.

Quite likely, on many of these issues, readers who really feel strongly on an issue are in the minority. On abortion, for example, some say abortion should never (or almost never) be an option for a woman, while some say any woman should have the right to obtain an abortion under almost any circumstances. You can count on both groups to react and respond when you write an editorial on this issue (those disagreeing with you, of course, responding more vociferously). Most of your readers, however, fall between these two extremes. They have mixed feelings about abortion. They certainly don't want to encourage it, or face the need for it in their families, but they don't want to deny the right to women for whom abortion may be better than other alternatives.

So what is the role of the editorial writer when addressing abortion? Abortion issues have a lot of nuances (parental notification, trimester abortions, federal funding, etc.), so it is not possible to prescribe the best way to address a readership consisting of two extreme groups and a larger, less committed group in the middle. But the writer should try to do at least three things: (1) defuse the highly emotional atmosphere that surrounds these issues

The Folly of Militant Creationism

Maybe it takes more mental agility than we possess, but it just doesn't compute that teaching the scientific fact of evolution affronts the religious convictions of someone who chooses to believe that the world was created by God from nothing in six days.

It doesn't compute and yet, increasingly, so-called creationists are using that argument to challenge the teaching of evolution in public schools. What's worse, in a disturbing number of cases they're winning and, in the process, crippling science curriculums and doing violence both to science and religion.

As reported Thursday by *Tribune* reporter Jeremy Manier, a school district in Colorado dropped a video that had been used to teach human reproduction because it contained a brief explanation of evolution, a fundamental concept in biology.

The son of a church pastor complained that by teaching evolution as scientific fact, not merely theory, the film offended his religious beliefs.

All over the country, creationists have tried to bully school boards and other public educa-

tion authorities into disallowing the teaching of evolution or at least diminishing its importance, often by presenting it as merely an unproven "theory" or "belief."

Too often, these attempts at intimidation have been successful. And often the creationists have won even when they lost. Teachers say they have trimmed their treatments of evolution to avoid hassles.

The tragedies here are manifold. First of all, children who don't learn properly about evolution can't fully understand modern biology. They are being shortchanged educationally.

Secondly, popular understanding of science is damaged. Instead of a patient and humble search for understanding through observation, hypothesis and testing, science comes to be viewed as simply a matter of opinion and belief.

And finally, religion, which really is about belief and things supernatural, is contorted into absurdities like "creation science," a set of propositions that are neither religious nor scientific.

In the name of God, such foolishness ought to stop.

Chicago Tribune

▬▬ Veto School Prayer

Some of the Legislature's worst moments have involved efforts to resurrect group prayer in Florida's public schools. Remember? A rabbi was berated during a Senate hearing. Relationships were strained. Debates turned acrimonious.

AVOID NEEDLESS RANCOR Governor Chiles should not subject the state to this divisive issue.

The last thing Florida needs is for this divisive issue to be argued again by each of Florida's 67 school boards and, quite possibly, by various high schools' student councils and parent-teacher groups.

Could it happen? That's up to Gov. Lawton Chiles. The bill that's likely to reignite this debate around the state—and trigger costly lawsuits—was due on the governor's desk this week. He'll have 15 days to sign it, veto it, or let it become law without his signature.

Vetoing this bill would be an act of courage because public support is strong in much of the state. Moreover, the prayer proviso seems innocuous. It would let students organize prayers that are nonsectarian and nonproselytizing at events where students' attendance is "voluntary." Yet that doesn't reckon with the reality of peer-group pressure and how readily teenagers stigmatize the slightest deviation from the norm.

Mr. Chiles is a religious man. He speaks freely of his faith. He's also sensitive to minorities and respectful of First Amendment rulings on church and state. What complicates the situation for him is the rest of HB 1041, a bill raising academic standards for high school graduation. Were it not for its prayer amendment, this bill would be welcome.

Yet condemning the whole state to relive the Legislature's ugly debate again and again is too high a price to pay. So there's no compelling reason why Mr. Chiles, perhaps after prayerful deliberation, shouldn't veto this flawed bill.

Miami Herald

---

by discussing as calmly and rationally as possible the issues and the differences of the various parties, (2) demonstrate an understanding of the feelings and beliefs of people on the extremes (especially those least in sympathy with your editorial position) and (3) inform and arouse people in the middle so they will assert themselves and make their views known. In other words, the writer should try to expand the dialogue to include the whole range of opinion.

I use abortion only as an example. Editorial writers should not expect to change many views on these emotional issues, but if they can bring some civility into the public discussion they will have made a contribution.

A *Chicago Tribune* editorial ("The folly of militant creationism") displayed a degree of charity, or at least forbearance, in responding to people who said they were religiously offended by teaching evolution as a scientific fact. The editorial did not attack the beliefs of those who chose to "believe that the world was created by God from nothing in six days." But it did take a firm stand against creationists' efforts to cripple science curricula in the public schools. In a surprising ending, the writer invoked the name of God.

In contrast to the *Tribune*'s forbearance, the *Miami Herald* gave no quarter to supporters of prayer in the public schools, in an editorial urging Gov. Lawton Chiles to veto a recently passed bill. While recognizing strong public support for school prayer, the editorial, a relatively short one ("Veto school prayer"), urged the governor to spare the state from having to "relive the Legislature's ugly debate . . . too high a price to pay."

Sometimes an editorial writer cannot resist taking a poke at some pompous, self-righteous religious leader. *The Roanoke Times & World-News* offered this comment as part of an editorial titled "Another Televangelist Falls":

The televangelist is more than an ordinary preacher. He is at once a show-business personality and a business tycoon. He is the custodian of tens of millions of dollars. His contributors send him dough in complete trust. That kind of money conveys power. And power can be an aphrodisiac. The celebrity feasting on the adulation of his followers finds the forbidden fruit is readily available. And it takes fortitude to resist.

But "Thou shalt not commit adultery" is only one of the rules of conduct laid down in the book the televangelist waves before his audience. There are other passages that deal with greed and deception and the worship of material goods.[11]

SPORTS

The sports world seems more and more regarded as an appropriate subject for editorial comment. One reason is that sports pages have broadened their coverage far beyond the mere reporting of the outcome and description of events. At the high school level, local citizens argue whether athletes need to maintain passing grades in all subjects. College issues involve minimal scholastic standards, illegal payments to athletes, the professionalization of college athletics and imbalance in women's and men's sports. At the professional level are arguments over "instant replay," players' salaries, foreign ownership of golf courses and baseball teams, and exclusion of countries from the Olympic

CSU Football Team Dropped Unfairly

It's hard not to root for the Central State University football team as it takes to the road (mostly) on a courageous 1996 campaign.

The Marauders are practicing in spartan conditions while the university sorts out its financial mess. The defending NAIA Division I national champions have just two home games this year. The rest are on the road, including a possible trip to South Africa. The team will face five NCAA Division I teams and play some of the best predominantly black schools in the country.

With the university's problems, this could possibly be the football program's last season. But CSU, which has won three of the last six NAIA Division I championships and has sent many players to the National Football League, is pressing on to forge a team on half of last season's budget.

It is the kind of story of fortitude and determination Americans love.

So it is hard to understand the decision by the New York Urban League to drop CSU from the Whitney Young Classic Sept. 28 at the New

The players have the qualities the team sponsors should be championing.

Jersey Meadowlands. The school stood to make 125,000 to 150,000 badly needed dollars from the game.

The Urban League officials' explanation was weak, that news reports in New York of CSU's problems caused concern over the viability of the game. They replaced CSU with Virginia State.

What is ironic here is that in CSU the game's organizers had a team from a traditionally black state school that is struggling to survive, a team that is moving ahead despite its disadvantages, and is the defending national champion.

Are not those the very things the Urban League, founded in 1910 to fight discrimination in education, employment and housing, should be championing?

Dayton Daily News

Games. Many times, of course, sports editorials praise teams and individuals for outstanding performances or offer condolences over losses. Expressing pride in the hometown team is an appropriate editorial function, but sports editorials, like other editorials on the page, serve readers best when they seek to enlighten or evaluate.

Sports topics are not always good news. "CSU football team dropped unfairly" was the title of a *Dayton Daily News* editorial that concluded that the Central State University football team had been dropped by the New York Urban League from the Whitney Young Classic. "[B]adly needed dollars" thus

Let 'em Strike, Already
And then retire all the old records of a game that's changed too much.

Quick, now—how many major-league baseball teams are there? How many playoff games would a team have to win to become the world champ?

If you missed them, it figures. The rulers of today's big-time sports, who view baseball not as an American institution to be cherished but simply another entertainment phenomenon to be milked, have so butchered up America's game that few bother to keep track anymore. Where once there were two distinct groups of teams whose champions fought it out in the World Series, today there are six divisions, meaning six champs. In one of those divisions today, not one contender is winning even half of its games. A few lucky breaks in the playoffs and the World Series could be a duel between a couple of losers.

To a greater degree than any other sport, baseball is an amalgam of skill, speed, strength, strategy and science. The distance from plate to pitching mound is perfectly calculated to test the eye of the batter against the arm of the pitcher; the bases are spaced precisely to test the speed of the runner against the reflexes of defenders. As yet, the spoilers haven't dared to tamper with these dimensions.

But on the theory that high scoring sells tickets, the strike zone has been reduced to the size of a postage stamp, the ball enlivened, and in three of the six divisions, a "designated hitter" who couldn't catch a pop fly in a basket hits for the pitcher. Never mind how the changes denigrate the hard-earned achievements of baseball's earlier heroes. Outfielders of marginal ability (and less enthusiasm) who couldn't carry Babe Ruth's jock find themselves chasing his home-run record.

And now the players, who average $1.2 million per year plus perks, are preparing to go on strike.

So strike, already. And forget settling in time for playoffs, with their big-money TV contracts. It's time for true fans to turn their backs on what baseball has become; to demand an end to the mockery being made of what was once the greatest of team sports.

Call it quits. Write off the '94 season and close the books for good on the game America grew up with. It should have happened earlier, but now is as good a time as any to call it an era, accept as final and forever all the records that stood at the end of the '93 season, and write the history of a great American tradition. Let 1996 mark the beginning of a new era, chronicled on the fresh, empty pages of new record books.

But let us never again allow the moguls of modern baseball to get richer off the glory of the past. Let them never compare some phony strike-out record racked up against a too-thin line of hitting talent with the records of a Bob Feller or a Walter Johnson or a Sandy Koufax. Let them never add up pop-fly home runs and breathlessly announce the eclipse of the unmatchable feat of Hank Aaron. Let their broadcasters continue to label every catch of every routine fly ball "unbelievable," but do not allow them to invoke the name of Willie Mays or Joe DiMaggio or Carl Furillo in the same breath.

The heroes of the past belong to the legends of a great game. Let the perpetrators of this spectacle played out on a field of mediocrity develop one of their own.

Des Moines Register

had been denied to a traditionally black state school and a team struggling with financial problems. The editorial suggested that the school and the team were exactly what the Urban League should support in its efforts to fight discrimination.

Nor are sports editorials always written in awe of the grandiose nature of sports. When the baseball players were threatening a strike, the *Des Moines Register* titled an editorial "Let 'em strike, already." With the proliferation of teams and the spreading around of mediocre talent, the editorial argued, the game was no longer the same. Current players were not equal to the heroes of the past.

Sports editorials are not limited to activities that involve teams or individual performers. Hunting, fishing, bicycling, backpacking and mountain climbing can also be worthy of comment. The *Idaho Statesman* pointed out that both hunters and non-hunters had an interest in helping keep sandhill cranes away from farmers' fields ("Broad plan can control cranes") and proposed alternatives to hunting.

TOUCHY TOPICS

Sometimes editorials are hard to write when writers know that what they say will offend a few or many of their readers. Three examples are from Idaho and Utah, generally considered conservative states with strong Church of the Latter-Day Saints (Mormon) influence.

Broad Plan Can Control Cranes

Both hunters and non-hunters can help keep sandhill cranes away from farmer's fields in southeastern Idaho, where the big birds are causing thousands of dollars in crop damage.

Thanks to a good decision by the Pacific Flyway Council, sportsmen may be assigned the task of thinning troublesome flocks. That's preferable to the Idaho Fish and Game Commission's original plan—nixed by the Flyway Council—which called for birds to be killed by government shooters.

A small, tightly controlled crane hunting season this fall can appease Southeast Idaho farmers and allow hunters to maintain their traditional role in controlling numbers of wild game. When hunters are involved, the birds are more likely to end up as nourishment on the table, instead of wasted in a government laboratory.

But before the state sets crane policies beyond this fall, non-lethal methods need to be more fully explored.

Non-hunting alternatives can ensure that the state does not overly rely on killing as a management tool. "Lure crops," for example, can be planted to draw the birds away from fields where they are not welcome.

Clearly, a sizeable group of Idahoans favors something other than hunting. During a month-long comment period last year, Fish and Game received 221 comments on the possibility of crane hunting. Of the total, 44 percent supported hunting, but 56 percent did not.

All sides deserve to have their views reflected in state policy.

The Audubon Council hopes to raise $40,000 to plant a lure crop next spring. Those who prefer this alternative can help by donating to the Sandhill Crane Fund at any First Security Bank.

Idaho Statesman

Repeal State Fornication Law

Take your pick: Lose your job or change your personal life to make it "moral." If you don't meet the arbitrary standards of the local prosecutor, you might wind up in jail. This is wrong.

Until Idaho's fornication law is repealed, government will continue to stick its nose into our bedrooms. Lawmakers can remedy the situation by acknowledging the fornication law is a bad law and repealing it.

Mountain Home Police Chief Tom Berry forbids his officers to engage in premarital sex. Maybe he has a point. It is, after all, against the law. Police officers should uphold the law.

In one case, Berry threatened to dismiss Cpl. Jeff Rhodes unless he married the woman whose child he fathered. Rhodes complied last August. Now, a year later, the couple has filed for divorce.

Details about the warning issued to a second officer are not available.

This case comes on the heels of Gem County Prosecutor Doug Varie's prosecution of a 17-year-old Emmett girl under the fornication statute.

It's hard to see how dragging a young mother through the courts or threatening a veteran police officer's job is enhancing society. It's easy, though, to see how someone could abuse the law if he or she wanted to.

Since we're not going to toss the vast majority of Idahoans into jail, prosecution and enforcement must be selective. That can lead to abuse of the law. As was alleged in the Emmett case, should young mothers who seek public assistance be the ones who are punished? Should every police department follow Mountain Home's lead and set policy for officers' personal lives—even when their actions in no way impact on their job performance?

Most officials seem to recognize how unreasonable the law is. But, just like fire hoses in hotels, it's behind the glass. Break in case of emergency. What some may call an emergency can be a chance to punish a person or group of people.

Times change. So must the law.

The fornication law has outlived its usefulness. It can be used unfairly. Erase it from the books.

Idaho Statesman

"Repeal state fornication law" proclaimed the headline (in large bold type) on an editorial in the *Idaho Statesman.* It was prompted by a police chief's order that his officials not engage in premarital sex. The editorial said that, since "the vast majority of Idahoans" were not going to be tossed into jail, prosecution under the law would be selective. The editorial called for removing the law, but warned: "Until Idaho's fornication law is repealed, government will continue to stick its nose into our bedrooms."

The *Salt Lake Tribune*, on the same day, carried editorials supporting liquor advertising and a homosexual club in a public school. One editorial ("No Popularity Contest") accused the state liquor control commission of "fishing for good excuses for Utah's strict prohibition on alcohol advertising, which faces a tough legal battle now that Rhode Island's more modest law, a ban on price ads, has been declared unconstitutional." In another editorial, "Needless school upset," the *Tribune* said the Salt Lake City school had "created a state and national scandal by assuming that [homosexual students, in asking to form a club] were up to no good and overreacting with a punitive policy against all extracurricular activities."

No Popularity Contest

Weird is the proper word for the Utah Alcoholic Beverage Control Commission's call for public advice on liquor advertising.

The commission apparently is fishing for good excuses for Utah's strict prohibition on alcohol advertising, which faces a tough legal battle now that Rhode Island's more modest law, a ban on price ads, has been declared unconstitutional.

Last month, the commission invited residents to answer these, among other questions, by Aug. 15 for consideration at an Aug. 23 hearing:

Should Utah regulate alcoholic beverage advertising? If so, what interests are served by such regulations and whose interests are advanced by it? What types of ads should be regulated, and which should be allowed? Which, if any, Utah restrictions on alcoholic beverage advertising would need to be changed as a result of the Supreme Court decision?

Perhaps the input will be used to steer legislators toward specific revisions of the law or to help state attorneys defend Utah's laws in court. The Rhode Island ruling, after all, left room for advertising limits that serve a higher purpose than commercial speech. Given recent reports about

Needless School Upset

There comes a time when people must grow up. That time has come for Salt Lake City School District, where some school board members still are trying to figure out a way to keep homosexual students from meeting in the schools.

In a study session late last month board members were advised that homosexual students, like other community groups, can rent space in the schools after academic hours. This didn't set well with those who, for the sole purpose of ejecting homosexual clubs from district campuses, decided earlier this year to do away with all student clubs not affiliated with the school curriculum.

Superintendent Darline Robles did her best to defuse the situation, suggesting development of regulations to help principals cope with current building-use policy another year. No matter how much she welcomes fairness and diversity, after all, the school board is her employer.

Hasn't the school board created enough heartburn over this issue by now? Yes, the school board. Although homosexual students pressed for recognition as an extracurricular club, the school board created a state and national scandal by assuming they were up to no good and overreacting with a punitive policy against all extracurricular clubs.

Board member D. Kent Michie now fears the rental policy would permit "through the back door what we wouldn't allow through the front door." Is he willing to expose the district to more claims of discrimination or to shut the schools to all community groups? If students are not doing anything illegal in their gatherings, those are his options.

Public schools can become invaluable centers of activity for communities trying to build cohesion to strengthen support systems for children, families and adults in need. They can divert residents from crime, abuse and hopelessness. Another regressive rule from sophomoric school board members would undermine the utility of public schools at the expense of whole communities.

Salt Lake Tribune

the inaccuracy of the liquor commission data on local drinking habits, outside information may be needed to prove that Utah's law actually serves the community by controlling alcohol consumption.

But what does it say about the political and legal acumen of the commission and its attorneys if they must turn to the public for legal analysis and strategy? Ordinarily, public reactions are solicited for specific policy proposals. And do commissioners seriously wonder which Utah interests are best served by advertising limits?

The fact that the liquor commission is not ultimately responsible for Utah's strict liquor laws makes the request for public comment stranger still. Except for implementing regulations, the commission neither makes nor interprets the law. It cannot act on the responses it receives.

And even if it could act on its own, it would be out of line to solicit public opinion on this issue. This is not a popularity contest. Nor is it a political decision about, say, the size of wilderness. Liquor advertising is a matter of free speech—an individual American right shielded by the U.S. Constitution from majority rule.

The courts aren't going to consult Utah residents about their attitudes toward liquor advertising. They are going to refer to the nation's most fundamental laws. The first of those laws tells judges to be especially skeptical of regulations that try to keep people in the dark for what government—or the majority—perceives to be their own good.

Salt Lake Tribune

Conclusion

Editorials on the subjects discussed in this chapter are not hard to write if you do enough homework to know what you are writing about and if you write in a manner that enables readers to understand what you are writing about.

Questions and Exercises

1. Find an editorial on an economic topic. Compare the writing and approach to the suggestions offered in this chapter. Does the editorial follow these suggestions, especially concerning the use of figures and the personalizing of the writer's points? If not, how could it be improved?

2. Analyze an editorial that talks about taxes, property taxes if possible. Is it easy to understand? Could it be simplified? Should more points be spelled out?

3. Find an editorial that relies excessively on legal terms. Rewrite it using more common language.

4. Can you find an editorial that formerly would have been labeled an "Afghanistanism"? Does the editorial seem to have absolutely nothing to do with the interests of the readers most likely to read the editorial? Could the subject have been made more pertinent to readers?

5. Find an editorial on an international topic that stands a good chance of catching the reader's attention—one that is not on a current hot topic. What is it about the editorial that makes it readable?

6. Compare several editorials on cultural subjects. Which seem to have been written simply to get promoters of causes off the backs of the editorial writers? Which are most likely to attract readers? Could the run-of-the-mill editorials have been made more interesting or pertinent?

CHAPTER 13 Subjects That Are Deceptively Easy

If you don't like people, you're called a misanthrope. And if you detest holidays, you're called an editorial writer. [If you decide not to run an editorial on Columbus Day], stand by for irate calls and letters from what seems like every Italian-American for miles around.

—JAMES E. CASTO, *HERALD-DISPATCH*, HUNTINGTON, W.VA.[1]

Several standard types of editorials have acquired the reputation among editorial writers as being easy to write. They usually can be dashed off, without much thought. Of course they usually are worth no more than the effort that went into producing them. A score or so of editorial writers had fun on the Internet exchanging tongue-in-cheek messages identifying some of these clichéd editorials. Here are some of them with their short-hand designations:

DBI—a "dull but important" editorial
C&D—condemn and deplore
DFS—deserves further study
Q&E—quick and easy
EI—evil incarnate (somebody we hate does something stupid)
LJ—lapse of judgment (somebody we like does something stupid)
US2—an issue so big that everyone is writing about it, so we'll weigh in, too

In this chapter I look at four categories of deceptively easy-to-write editorials: obituaries, the local pride piece, the favorite subject (or "easy shot") and the "duty" piece. In each of these categories, the writer often is tempted to dash off, perhaps cynically, a standard piece that just gets by.

OBITUARIES

De mortuis nil nisi bonum is not a good rule for writing editorials about persons who have died. Speaking nothing but good of the dead may be fine for funeral orations, but telling readers only some of the facts has no more place in an obituary editorial than it has in any other kind of editorial. Relating the full story is relatively easy when you write about a national, or even state, figure. Information is often readily available and indisputable. The family of the deceased is not likely to see the editorial, at least not immediately after publication, so the writer can feel free to tell the good and the not-so-good. But when the person is a local figure, inhibitions take hold. The temptation is to stick with the favorable facts and throw in a dash of "she'll be missed." This is no time to add to the family's bereavement, the reasoning goes. Yet undeserved praise is no praise at all, since those likely to care the most about what is written will know that the words are hollow.

In my experience, families often respond favorably to obituary editorials that mention the human, less than perfect side of the deceased. When I wrote that a civic activist had a booming voice and had been something of a glad-hander (not quite in those words), his widow told me, "That was Bob, all right." Another time I wrote that a woman who had been involved in many activities was something of a character and that she sometimes said things

Jacqueline Kennedy Onassis, 1929–1994

She was the epitome of eloquence, grace

It's hard to fathom the death of Jacqueline Kennedy Onassis.

The former first lady's glamour epitomized the administration of John F. Kennedy. Her dignity carried the nation through the shock of his assassination. And her charm captivated the nation for so many decades that she seemed as durable as the White House itself.

Her friends remember her with a series of vivid images: highborn and sophisticated. Bright, beautiful and charming. Caring and warm. Unshakable. The perfect wife, mother, friend.

But the nation remembers her more as a modern American fairy tale.

Born July 28, 1929, Jacqueline Lee Bouvier was a debutante and a socialite who married Kennedy, a young senator, in 1953 and was 31 when he became the nation's 35th president.

Then she was in the limousine in Dallas on Nov. 22, 1963, cradling her husband's shattered head, holding the hands of her young children at his funeral, and walking behind his casket to the cemetery.

President Clinton called Mrs. Onassis "a model of courage and dignity for all Americans and all the world. More than any other woman of her time, she captivated our nation and the world with her intelligence, elegance and grace.

"Even in the face of impossible tragedy, she carried the grief of her family and our entire nation with a calm power that somehow reassured all of us who mourned," he said.

Afterward, Kennedy's widow fiercely shielded her children from publicity until they were grown, then rejected her role as the keeper of Camelot to marry Greek shipping tycoon Aristotle Onassis in 1968. After the 1975 death of her second husband, she began a career in publishing and was an editor at Doubleday at the time of her death.

With her wealth, she didn't need to work. But she had a mind that needed challenges and the compulsion to help those around her. And she developed into a good editor, one who was insightful and literate.

She lived a life somehow larger than life.

And she lived it as she wanted to live it, disregarding the public dismay that came with her marriage to Onassis.

She lived her life as far from the prying public eye as she could, although she never escaped the crowds and the cameras totally. They were just outside her apartment door as she died Thursday in New York City.

America will miss her. In fact, we never thought she would leave us.

Great Falls Tribune

other people didn't understand. Shaking his head, her son told me, "That's the way Mother was, and we loved her for it." Of course, in small and medium-sized communities, if not in larger ones, there are limits to telling the full truth. You would not want to dig up something especially embarrassing from a person's past, particularly something the person had lived down.

The trick to writing an obituary editorial is to catch some detail—words, behavior, description—that makes the person seem unique and human, something that distinguishes him or her from everyone else, something for which the person can be remembered. You don't always have to write about a widely known person. Fitting subjects might be a person who had taught a long time in the local schools, someone who had been quietly helpful to neighbors and friends, a mail deliverer, someone who had clerked in the same store for many years, a person who had sold newspapers on the same corner ever since anyone could remember.

Many newspapers wrote editorials when Jacqueline Kennedy Onassis died. She had been in the national limelight—one of the most respected Americans—for much of five decades. Readers of all ages felt their own special relationship with her. No editorial could express all the emotions of these readers. The *Great Falls Tribune* ("She was the epitome of eloquence, grace"),

Mortimer Charles Lebowitz

H E WAS in business, but broke so many of its unwritten rules in Washington. He spoke softly about tolerance, but enforced his beliefs with unbending will. And he put money where his principles stood—and where it easily could have ruined him. But to Mortimer C. Lebowitz, who died last week at the age of 84, racial justice—integration—was so absolutely right that he and his chain of Morton's department stores would abide nothing less. He didn't have to trumpet his cause, because his deeds alone spread the word of equal opportunity with a force that rocked the old-line southern business climate here.

When Mr. Lebowitz opened the first Morton's in 1933 at 7th and D streets NW, he broke ground on two fronts: He introduced the concept of discount department stores, and he opened them to all people in ways that white businessmen just didn't do then. Other retailers had separate fitting rooms and toilets for black people, who "were treated very cruelly and clearly were not made to feel welcome," as Mr. Lebowitz recalled in a 1993 interview. "Everyone at the time felt they would lose white customers if they catered to black customers."

There were stores that did not even allow black customers to try on clothes; but from opening day ever after, Morton's stores had dressing rooms and restroom facilities to be shared by all customers. Daring? Foolhardy? For Mr. Lebowitz, there was no question. "Many thought what I did was stupid from the business viewpoint, but I could not see myself discriminating against black customers." Neither could Mr. Lebowitz see himself retaining white members of his staff who were angered by his policies of openness. He replaced them with black employees, and it wasn't long before most of his staff—managers included—were black.

Black Washington came in great numbers to shop, and the businesses grew. Mr. Lebowitz practiced his principles, not only in the marketplace but also in any circles he found himself. He sent his children to the leading integrated school of the day, Georgetown Day School, was a longtime board member and eventually president of the Washington Urban League and gave generously of time and money to local projects.

He was a gentle man with a brave past, who looked back on that past and said, "I feel as though I have been very lucky in life." The luck was Washington's.

Washington Post

Kirsten

In her graduation speech at South Eugene High School six years ago this month, Kirsten Frohnmayer said: "My family jokes that by having this serious health problem, we provide an important community service. We remind people that things in their own lives may not be as bad as they seem."

That was no joke. Following the joys and sorrows of the Frohnmayer family has been a community activity here for more than two decades. Their lives are at least more instructive than soap operas. Kirsten's own story, her cheerfully determined battle against a mysterious disease with a strange name and a lethal record, has been particularly gripping.

But not all stories have happy endings. This one is particularly sad because all of us were rooting so hard, hoping against hope. The community genuinely grieves with the Frohnmayers, as in some degree does the whole state.

At 24, mentally and spiritually Kirsten had done more living than many people twice her age. She had an immense capacity for life. Partly because of her disease, she had a keen appreciation for each day's possibilities.

Her positive outlook calls to mind the obituary editorial famed Kansas editor William Allen White wrote 76 years ago after his own 16-year-old daughter was killed in a freak riding accident: "Her humor was a continual bubble of joy. . . . No angel was Mary White, but an easy girl to live with, for she never nursed a grouch five minutes in her life."

On the list of personal tragedies to which humankind is vulnerable, the death of a child must rank at the top. It does not matter whether the child is struck by a limb while riding her horse or is worn down over many years and finally defeated by a vicious disease; the loss is tremendously hard to bear.

Hearts go out to David and Lynn Frohnmayer and to Kirsten's three remaining siblings. But we know, too, that they will manage, because they are blessed with intelligence and strength of spirit—and because they understand the wisdom of what Kirsten told her classmates at the close of her remarks in 1991:

> "A final thought I'd like to share with you tonight is my belief that sometimes we should live for the day. Too often life consists of anticipation of the future or regrets about the past. But we can't change the past, and we don't know what the future will hold. So, at least some of the time, we should concentrate on the present. Whatever path you've chosen, whether you're talking about college, a job, volunteer work, or family, you're talking about life and life must be fun. Find the fun in life, for as Ferris Bueller said on his day off, 'life moves pretty fast, and if you don't stop and look around once in a while, you are going to miss it.'

> "So . . . I hope that you will remember to appreciate and protect what you have, be optimistic and constructive in the face of adversity, and stop to smell the roses. Good night and good luck."

Register-Guard

> **At 24, mentally and spiritually Kirsten had done more living than many people twice her age. She had an immense capacity for life.**

eschewing sentiment and pathos, suggested that people had become so accustomed to the presence of Jacqueline Kennedy Onassis that they were likely to have a hard time realizing that she would no longer be around. The editorial matter-of-factly sketched the key events in her life. When a much publicized and much admired person dies, readers have their own private thoughts and feelings. Nonetheless, an editorial can help them decide how they feel about the loss.

In contrast, the *Washington Post* faced the task of explaining to readers who Mortimer Charles Lebowitz was and why he merited an obituary editorial. Lebowitz had started a chain of discount department stores in 1933 that had long since faded from the Washington scene. The *Post* not only credited him with introducing the concept of the discount store but also with opening his stores to all people "in ways that white businessmen just didn't do then." The *Post* called him "a gentle man with a brave past" who "spoke softly about tolerance, but enforced his beliefs with unbending will."

Perhaps the toughest job is writing an obituary about a young person who has died. A writer on the Eugene, Ore., *Register-Guard* faced that task in commenting on the death of a second child of a prominent family who died from a mysterious ailment. The life and death of Kirsten Frohnmayer had been widely reported in the local media. Her father, David Frohnmayer, the president of the University of Oregon, had been state attorney general. Her uncle, John Frohnmayer, attained national attention in the 1980s as the controversial head of the National Endowment for the Arts. The editorial writer chose to focus primarily on the bright spots, pointing out that, in her 24 years, Kirsten had exhibited an "immense capacity for life." The writer was reminded of one of the best-known obituary editorials ever to appear in American newspapers: William Allen White's tribute to his 16-year-old daughter Mary. The editorial ends with the concluding remarks Kirsten had given her high school graduating class six years previously: "Good night and good luck."

LOCAL PRIDE

Second cousin to the obituary editorial is the local pride editorial, which comments on the activities of local people, local teams or local organizations. As with obituaries, there are ways to make these editorials more than sheer puffery. Sometimes, for example, an editorial may boost the spirits of some person or organization after a disappointment. Sometimes residents of a community need to take a realistic look at how they appear to others. Is the community as friendly as its promoters say it is? Does it have residential areas that those concerned with its image do not talk about much? Are residents going elsewhere to shop because they can't find what they want in local stores? Are building and development restrictions keeping out all but a select, privileged class of citizens?

Editorial writers cannot be expected to be able to view their communities completely objectively. After all, if these writers didn't think their communities were pretty decent places, why would they be living there? Writers should take pride in their communities and should work hard to make them better places. But without true understanding of the limitations as well as the advantages of their areas, writers cannot help their communities deal with problems and successes.

The *Idaho Statesman* found only good news to hail about a rejuvenated downtown Boise ("Here's to dynamic downtown"). An editorial praised new investments, public facilities and cultural activities, but it noted that, when major retailers left the downtown would have little more than offices for lawyers and government workers.

A variation on the local pride editorial is one that warns that the community's assets may be adversely affected by some action or lack of action. When Wal-Mart proposing building next door to George Washington's childhood home, the *Free Lance–Star* of Fredericksburg, Va., while acknowledging that not much had been made of the home up to then, pointed out that "George

Here's to Dynamic Downtown

Downtown Boise is a success story—and growing bigger and better every day. It's a credit to those who can envision such prosperity and to those who invest in the downtown district.

New shops and businesses are opening. The downtown district is becoming the place to go for entertainment, dining and simply to window shop. As the weeks and months go by, downtown is getting the reputation of the "place to be."

Credit for downtown's rejuvenation belongs to a number of sources. The Capital City Development Corp. has a plan of action. Currently, a streetscape plan is in full swing to add trees, brick sidewalks, benches, bike racks and historic lighting in an eight-block area.

Then there are the investors; the people who see hope in an abandoned building and renovate it or open up a small business. Dozens of businesses, restaurants, shops and services have opened. Visitors now can eat lunch, shop for unique items, even get a quick massage and still have lots of things left to do.

Let's not forget about the events. Alive After Five and First Thursday are mainstays, but more and more organizations are discovering the Grove is a great place to hold a celebration.

And the future is even brighter. The West-Coast Hotel and Bank of America Centre promise to bring more activity to the downtown district.

Boise could have turned out to be like so many other cities. As major retailers left the downtown district, it could have fallen into disrepair and decay. It could have become an embarrassment to the city and state. It could have become an area inhabited by a few lawyers' offices and assorted government bureaucracies.

Instead, downtown Boise is vibrant. Hats off to all of those who have helped turn downtown into a showplace and who continue to lead the way for even better things in the future.

Idaho Statesman

Ferry Farm and Its Gravel Pit

George Washington's boyhood home at Ferry Farm probably has never had as many visitors as it has in recent days, thanks to the controversy over Wal-Mart's plans to build a store next door.

NBC's "Today" show crew was among those who stopped by the property yesterday, on the anniversary of George Washington's birthday.

Much of the "Today" show discussion centered on Ferry Farm's inglorious 20th-century history.

Russell Harper, a Richmond real estate developer, pointed out that there's already a Food Lion, a 7-Eleven and a McDonald's nearby.

He also noted, correctly, that the Ferry Farm property was once used as a gravel pit.

Therefore, Mr. Harper and others imply, it's OK to slap up a Wal-Mart, too. The more, the merrier, right?

It's hard to believe that back in Wal-Mart headquarters in Arkansas that executives analyze things that way.

When presented with evidence of four mistakes, do they commit themselves to a fifth just to be consistent? Or do they step back a bit and try to figure out how to keep the problem from snowballing?

Building a Wal-Mart within coin-throwing distance of Ferry Farm won't erase previous planning mistakes. Nor will it enhance those mistakes.

George Washington's boyhood home has tremendous potential as a tourist attraction. It doesn't take much imagination or knowledge of history to figure out why.

But that potential has never been mined quite as efficiently as gravel.

Although well-meaning, Stafford officials have not managed the project wisely through the years. Fund-raising efforts at Ferry Farm have been grossly mishandled, and community leaders and residents of the Fredericksburg area have not given it sufficient attention.

Wal-Mart executives—with all of their good business sense and marketing innovations—must recognize that a new approach is needed.

Free Lance–Star

Ferry Farm: Nationally, Locally

The long-neglected boyhood home of George Washington at Ferry Farm is drawing more and more national attention. It is likely to increase in the days ahead as Wal-Mart moves forward with plans to build a store next door.

Among those now participating in the debate over Ferry Farm is Richard Moe, the president of the National Trust for Historic Preserva-tion. He was among the leaders in the successful battle against Disney's America.

Mr. Moe, who says he visits Fredericksburg two or three times a year, was here a few days ago to tour Ferry Farm for the first time and talk to local leaders about Wal-Mart's plans.

> 'If anyone wants to see the future, it's sitting right there on west Route 3.'
>
> —Richard Moe
> National Trust for Historic Preservation

His observations ought to be weighed carefully by local residents and public officials. His organization has led many preservation efforts nationwide and has accumulated a wealth of data on the damage that uncontrolled development can wreak on a local economy and, in particular, a community's tourism efforts. We'll talk more about that data in future editorials.

The national trust opposes Wal-Mart's plans primarily because Ferry Farm "is a place of national significance" that should be preserved and opened up for all Americans, according to Mr. Moe.

He said the proposed Wal-Mart and adjacent shopping center are only part of the threat to Ferry Farm. The construction of a Wal-Mart there would likely lead to sprawl that would forever alter State Route 3 east of the city.

"If anyone wants to see the future, it's sitting right there on west Route 3," Mr. Moe says.

He says the proposed Wal-Mart would threaten the viability of existing small businesses and the long-running effort to revive the downtown area.

Stafford County may gain money from taxes on Wal-Mart's sales, but—Mr. Moe points out—local economies don't stop at political boundaries.

If downtown Fredericksburg declines, it will have a ripple effect in surrounding counties.

The threat to tourism is significant, too. The competition for tourism dollars is intense, and visitors who see sprawling development obliterating historic sites in Stafford and the rest of the region will go elsewhere, Mr. Moe says.

Richard Moe urges community leaders and Wal-Mart executives to go slower with this project and examine the potential long-term results.

That's sound advice.

The estimated $565,000 a year that would be generated from sales taxes and property taxes at the new Wal-Mart is appealing.

But the long-range costs to the community could be much greater.

Free Lance–Star

Washington's boyhood home has tremendous potential as a tourist attraction" ("Ferry Farm and its gravel pit"). A day later another editorial speculated that the long-run costs of the big store would overwhelm any prospective new revenue from sales or property taxes and threaten existing small businesses and efforts to revive the downtown area ("Ferry Farm: Nationally, locally"). Ultimately Wal-Mart decided not to build there.

Another local pride approach is pointing out that strong leadership or public support will be needed to carry out a worthy project. In one such case, the *Oregonian* warned that, if the Portland regional government's 50-year plan for concentrating development along light-rail corridors was to succeed, the state legislature would need to provide its share of funding of the rail system. "Light rail isn't just an expensive toy train for Portland," the editorial said. "It's an engine driving growth management for the state's most populated metropolitan area." Returning to the same metaphor, the editorial ("Push light rail")

Push Light Rail

*Legislative leaders must step forward if this
region is to maintain prosperity, livability*

Some legislators have it wrong: Light rail isn't just an expensive toy train for Portland. It's an engine driving growth management for the state's most populated metropolitan area.

Metro, the regional government, has built its planning for the next 50 years around increasingly dense development along light-rail corridors within urban-growth boundaries. Rail is the attractor for that investment.

When was the last time a developer built increased density because his property was served by a bus line?

By contrast, look out the windows of MAX, Portland's eastside light-rail train. Private and public development is growing as fast as zucchini along the line. It's lush. The Oregon Convention Center was sited to be served by light rail. The Rose Garden Arena was expressly located next to light rail. Gresham is planning a high-density residential-commercial-civic-center mix tied to light rail.

Similar density is on the drawing boards for the westside route.

The alternatives: more huge-cost highways chewing up urban lands, housing and tax bases; more sprawl onto farm and forest lands; less money available for rural highways.

Voters of Washington, Clackamas and Multnomah counties authorized $435 million in property taxes last November to match state and federal dollars to hook a south-north line to the region's east-west train.

Yet whom are Oregon legislators listening to? Clark County, Wash., voters, who turned down a tax measure for light rail in March. Seattle-area voters, who turned down a tax

measure for light rail the same month. Neither region has in place the transportation and land-use planning that Oregon and the Portland area have. Oregon needs legislators at the throttle in Salem who hear Oregon voters, not Washington voters.

Republican House leaders, though, are sitting in their caucus on the state's match of the region's $435 million. They refuse to let the full House vote on financing light rail until at least 18 members of the 34-member GOP caucus climb aboard. Only 10 raised their hands for light rail in Friday's count.

House Speaker Bev Clarno, R-Bend, says she supports light rail, and has exercised strong leadership at times during this session. Now's the time to do it again.

Washington County legislators—Republicans among them—made the West Side Light Rail Project happen. It's time for them to see that their track runs all the way to Clackamas County, not just downtown Portland.

If necessary, Republican leaders should quit counting the caucus and start counting the House; Democrats have votes, too.

Managing growth in the state's largest urban area is essential to Oregon's prosperity and livability. Freight doesn't move when traffic is gridlocked. Businesses won't invest and people won't live where jobs and clean air don't matter to legislators.

The 1995 Legislature should ride with local elected officials in the front of the train, not in the caboose, when it comes to managing the growth of the state's primary investment and jobs center.

Oregonian

---

ended with: "The 1965 Legislature should ride with local officials in front of the train, not in the caboose, when it comes to managing the growth of the state's primary investment and jobs center."

FAVORITE SUBJECT

Editorial writers cannot be expected to produce fresh wisdom on every topic, every day. Reiterating a message is one solution to the lack of more inspiring topics. Since most readers don't read the editorial page every day, remaking a point is not likely to seem repetitive. Another, and less defensible, solution is writing on a subject on which the writer has to do little or no research or new thinking. Sometimes the subject is a favorite target. I call this type of editorial "an easy shot."

An example of an easy shot taken every year by some editorial writers is the editorial that appears on the day that average taxpayers have stopped "working for the government" and started earning money to keep for themselves. Every year some tax association notifies newspapers of this date and usually points out that it falls one or two or three days later this year than last year. The first time that editorial appeared it had merit; the idea is clever as a piece of propaganda. Since then, the editorial has become a cliché.

Another perennial piece is the one that criticizes the salaries paid state legislators or members of Congress. This editorial is usually accompanied by

The Assembly Game

Veteran observers dread the return of the General Assembly, which at times seems like a forced march through the Gobi Desert with a garrulous drunk. Those wishing to make the time go by faster might want to play The Assembly Game. The rules are similar to those of The Car Game children play on long trips (one point for a blue car, two for a red, three for a white . . .). Players collect points for following the legislature's progress and spotting the following perennials.

■ A bill is referred to as "leveling the playing field": **1 point**.

■ A bill is referred to as a "slippery slope" or as letting "the camel's nose under the tent": **1 point**.

■ A speaker at a public hearing urges legislators not to "balance the budget on the backs of" his or her favorite special interest: **1 point**.

■ Lawyers get into a contest with another profession—bankers, doctors, real estate agents—over an arcane bill that is of immense interest to the two groups but of approximately zero interest to everyone else: **1 point**.

■ A parental-notification rider is attached to a bill having nothing to do with health care, such as one regarding speed limits on county roads: **2 points**.

■ Lieutenant Governor Don Beyer rules a parental-notification rider non-germane: **2 points**.

■ Something is named an official animal, vegetable, or mineral of the Commonwealth: **2 points**.

■ State colleges and universities complain they are under-funded: **2 points**.

■ Someone gets hurt in the General Assembly's annual basketball game: **3 points**.

■ Roscoe Drummond is spotted on the Capitol grounds: **3 points**.

■ A legislator is photographed (a) asleep, (b) checking his watch, or (c) looking really, really bored: **3 points**.

■ A senior legislator is photographed with his arm around a junior legislator in what looks like camaraderie but what is really a bit of strong-arming: **3 points**.

■ A legislator brings in a ridiculous prop, such as a Civil War–era sword or a large foam "We're No. 1" hand, to buttress a ridiculous argument: **4 points**.

■ Delegate George Grayson trashes Secretary of Natural Resources Becky Norton Dunlop or rakes one of her employees over the coals: **4 points**.

■ Governor Allen is accused of being a "credit-card Governor": **4 points**.

■ Allen blasts Democrats as (a) monarchical elitists, (b) tax-and-spend liberals, (c) pattering nabobs of negativism, or (d) pinheaded cowards who are afraid to come on out and fight like men: **5 points**.

First player to reach 100 points wins.

Richmond Times-Dispatch

A Legislative Goose?

Thank goodness the General Assembly still has time to deal with important matters. Apparently, it will not allow such trivial concerns as budgets and taxes to prevent it from designating an official state reptile. It is moving to bestow that honor on the timber rattlesnake.

Why the legislature favors a poisonous snake over the harmless blacksnake that helps mankind by killing rats and other pests is a mystery. Perhaps there is a subterranean message in the legislators' preference for a reptile that spews venom. When they return next year, will they designate the black widow Virginia's official spider?

The General Assembly seems to designate an official something or other at every session. One of the most interesting examples is the state dog—the foxhound. When that designation was made a number of years ago, two different donors presented the state with portraits of foxhounds to hang on the walls of the Capitol. One portrait was of a champion foxhound named White Ella. The other was of a composite hound. But while the State Art Commission approved both portraits, no Governor has ever had the courage to put up either one.

Because of the Assembly's interest in designating official flora and fauna, many people will wonder why it never has adopted an official mascot. Good idea. May we suggest the goose—as in "silly as a . . . . "?

Richmond Times-Dispatch

an attack on the legislative body for not doing its job and for letting personal interests and pleasures interfere with the public's business. The editorial writer often adds something to this effect: "It is no wonder the voters have lost faith in government." No doubt some legislative bodies deserve criticism for the sneaky ways in which they slip benefits for themselves into legislation and for the seemingly petty politicking that frustrates the legislative process. But an editorial written to condemn a specific misdeed should stick to the particular subject and avoid generalizing about all the wicked ways of government officials. One strange thing about this tendency of editorial writers to pick on legislative bodies is that when it comes time for endorsement of candidates all past sins seem forgotten. Congress is bad, it seems, but our own local member is good enough to merit another term.

The editorial writers on the *Richmond Times-Dispatch* seem to take special delight in needling state legislators. When Virginia lawmakers showed up for the 1997 legislative session, they were greeted with an editorial titled "The Assembly Game" that began: "Veteran observers dread the return of the General Assembly, which at times seems like a forced march through the Gobi Desert with a garrulous drunk." The editorial proposed a game like "The Car Game" children play on long auto trips.

The *Times-Dispatch* poked fun at legislators' naming fad on another occasion ("A Legislative Goose?"), concluding with this paragraph: "Because of the Assembly's interest in designating official flora and fauna, many people will wonder why it never has adopted an official mascot. Good idea. May we suggest the goose—as in 'silly as a . . . .'?"

THE "DUTY" PIECE

"For tomorrow's page we're going to need an editorial on _____. Who's going to write it?" Fill that blank with "Thanksgiving," "the Fourth of July," "the annual United Way campaign," "the state high school basketball championship" or "a highway safety campaign," and you will understand what is meant by a "duty" piece. It is an editorial that you think you ought to run to mark an occasion or boost a good cause, but it is almost impossible to think of anything more to say than you did the last time you wrote on the subject.

A few days before Earth Day 1997 an editorial writer asked other members of the electronic mailing list managed by the National Conference of Editorial Writers (NCEW) whether they had any ideas for an editorial commemorating that day. Barbara Drake of the Peoria, Ill., *Journal Star* suggested calling attention to "extraordinary things" being done by a Scout group, a class or a school. Maury Casey of the *Day* of New London, Conn., also had schools in her sights, but from a different point of view. She said that schools have now so indoctrinated students that they now "lecture their parents [un]mercifully if they try to do anything as innocent as toss out a piece of tinfoil without putting it in the recycling bin first." Even less enthusiastically, Mike Heywood of the *Columbian* of Vancouver, Wash., wrote that Earth Day "ought to be skipped unless you already have a ripping idea so compelling that you cannot type fast enough to get it on the screen or page."[2]

At least two points should be made on behalf of editorials that support worthy causes. The first is that, while an endorsement of an annual fund drive may be repetitious to the veteran editorial writer, whatever is said is usually appreciated by the promoters. If an editorial doesn't actually raise any more money, it at least serves to legitimize the cause. Second, an editorial writer can regard a duty editorial as a challenge to say something creative or imaginative on an old topic.

If a newspaper does publish editorials endorsing causes, it should know what it is backing. Lauren K. Soth of the *Des Moines Register* said that when readers see an editorial supporting a drive for contributions, they ought to be able to assume that the editors have studied the cause and found it to have merit.[3]

Richard B. Childs for the *Flint* (Mich.) *Journal* said his first rule for handling "the drudgery aspects" of "duty" pieces was "to evade." If you are lucky, someone else on the staff will get the job. But if you can't evade, he advised, "relax and enjoy it." Childs said he actually had begun to look forward to Abraham Lincoln's birthday: Each year he tried to find something new to say. He had written about Lincoln's concept of the Constitution, his role as a politician, his faith in people and democracy, his literary abilities, his defense against black writers who sought to picture him a racist and his continuing image as a national hero despite changing national moods.[4]

In a *Masthead* symposium on holiday editorial pages, Jim Wright reported that the *Dallas Morning News* cut back on "well-here-it-is-again editorials, not only for minor holidays like Arbor Day but for annual charity events and the like." Two exceptions were "the opening of Our State Fair (which is a Great State Fair) and the United Way campaign, the sole regular charity event we note." When a need is felt for "inspirational editorials for holidays," the task usually went to new staff writers, "who tend to have less treadwear on their similes, metaphors and quotations dealing with the occasion."[5]

One Christmas the *Fort Worth Star-Telegram* ran a "wish list" discussing what the editorial writers would "ask Santa" for at each level of government: city, county, state and nation.[6] The *Richmond News Leader* has filled its editorial

▬ Toward One Nation, Indivisible

It was 100 years ago—May 18, 1896—that the U.S. Supreme Court in Plessy vs. Ferguson legally established the doctrine of "separate but equal" and made racial segregation, or Jim Crow laws, part of public policy. The end result of the decision was that it led to a strict enforcement of the "separate," with little or no regard for the "equal."

It was the beginning of a sad chapter in American history. And although Plessy was struck down with the Brown vs. Board of Education decision of 1954, the residual effects of the century-old ruling are still evident today in housing, schools and even places of worship. Most Americans would now agree that such a philosophy has no place in today's society.

It would be naive to assert that prejudice and bigotry have disappeared, but there has been a sea change in attitudes and behavior about race relations over the past century. The "color barrier" has been broken in every conceivable area of American life. We are not yet a colorblind society, but we are a lot closer to it than we were 100 years ago.

Many civil rights leaders have claimed that recent Supreme Court decisions in the areas of school desegregation, minority set-asides and black-majority drawn congressional districts are a step back toward Plessy. They are not. The court simply trimmed what it believed to be excessive remedies. Should discrimination occur, legal avenues of redress are available.

AS IT HAS BEEN throughout our history, one faction or another will continue to elevate a separatist agenda. And some of us will continue to associate primarily with those "of our own kind." But today the idea of state-sanctioned segregation is objectionable to most Americans.

Nondiscrimination and equal opportunity are fundamental values of American public policy, well embedded in our collective consciousness. It is unthinkable that "colored only" signs could reappear in public places or that dual school systems could be re-established. That is progress that was unimaginable a century ago, and something we should celebrate today.

Tampa Tribune-Times

---

columns with Christmas poems, carols and stories, the right side of the page with a Christmas sampler of Thomas Nast drawings.[7] For the Fourth of July, the *Hartford Courant*, "the oldest daily newspaper in continuous publication," has dug back in its files of 200 or more years and reprinted contemporaneous accounts of the Revolutionary War.[8] The *Miami Herald* has reprinted the Bill of Rights and the Preamble to the Declaration of Independence.[9]

On the 100th anniversary of *Plessy v. Ferguson*, the Supreme Court case that sanctioned "separate but equal" schools and other facilities for African-Americans, the *Tampa Tribune-Times* concluded that "[w]e are not yet a color-blind society, but we are a lot closer to it than we were 100 years ago." The editorial, "Toward one nation, indivisible," said: "[S]ome of us will continue to associate with those 'of our own kind.' But today the idea of state-sanctioned segregation is objectionable to most Americans."

CONCLUSION

The purpose of this chapter is to suggest that writers, using some imagination and flair, can tackle seemingly dull or clichéd subjects and turn out editorials that are interesting and informative.

Questions and Exercises

1. Find an obituary editorial that is mostly factual and another that goes beyond the facts. What is the difference in the effect of the editorials? What makes the difference?

2. Examine an editorial that expresses pride in the community or some aspect of community life. Is the editorial sheer puffery, or has the writer made an effort to put the event in perspective?

3. Clip some "easy shot" editorials. What makes them fall into this category? What could save them from this category?

4. Find several "duty" editorials. Would you have published them? If not, what could you have written on the same subjects that you would have felt comfortable writing? What angles could the writers have taken that they missed?

CHAPTER 14

Subjects That Are Neglected

Like many journalists with a non-science degree . . . , I previously thought of science as dry and boring. In working with scientists, however, I have learned that science lies at the heart of many of our most important news stories: AIDS, Star Wars, the Challenger disaster, Chernobyl and many others.

—DAVID JARMUL, *NATIONAL ACADEMY SERVICE*[1]

Editorial writers often neglect subjects that are difficult to write about, don't often make the front pages or seem not to involve major public policy issues. As the quotation on the left suggests, however, many difficult subjects can be become pertinent to readers–if writers inform themselves on the subject and write in a way that speaks to those readers. This chapter deals with several kinds of editorials that are frequently neglected: editorials on science, natural resources, other media, lives of people, and humor and satire.

SCIENCE

Science is not a popular or an easy subject for editorials. A survey of five of the nation's largest newspapers found that only 3.7 percent of editorials dealt directly with science or technology.[2] The surveyors found that editorial writers were "most likely to discuss science, technology and health care in the context of some broader issue, such as the economy or a political dispute." They concluded that the science issues are there; "[i]t's the editorials that are lacking." A *New York Times* editor was quoted as saying that "[a]n editorial has to be more than an analysis of something. It has to have some hortatory point."

One reason that science gets little play in editorial columns may be that writers don't feel qualified to comment on science matters. Another may be that, since science supposedly involves facts, what's left to debate in an editorial? The first reason may have a lot of validity, but the second does not. Scientific findings are only the first step toward formulating public policy.

NATURAL RESOURCES

Issues dealing with the environment and natural resources are often skipped over when daily editorial assignments are handed out. These issues don't often capture front page headlines, nor are they easy to frame in simple, clear terms. From time to time, crises arise (partly because of lack of public discussion of these issues). Then an editorial may appear. Even then, and certainly between crises, the editorial writer faces the challenge of enticing readers. The *Missoulian* tried to arouse its readers' interests in a proposal to send more Montana water downstream to the West Coast to save salmon runs ("Water fight continues"). It likened the plan to "cordoning off and reclaiming huge areas of eastern Washington and western Oregon to provide a new habitat for grizzlies." It acknowledged that Montana had some responsibility to help the salmon runs but not at the expense of its own resources.

Timber is another natural resource over which editorial writers in the Northwest disagree. It involves both Canada and the United States. When a

---

Water Fight Continues
Agencies considering reneging on reservoir-tapping agreement

Imagine this scenario: In an effort to protect Montana's threatened population of grizzly bears, federal agencies proposed cordoning off and reclaiming huge areas of eastern Washington and western Oregon to provide new habitat for grizzlies.

Folks on the Coast would go nuts. It would never happen, if for no other reason than there's absolutely no proof that creating huge new bear reserves in those areas of Oregon and Washington would have any good effect on Montana's bears.

Well, of course, no one's asking Montana and Oregon to solve Montana's grizzly problems. But those states are looking to Montana to make extraordinary sacrifices to save runs of salmon imperiled by dams built on the Columbia River.

The federal agencies that manage fish, wildlife and marine fisheries continue to pursue the possibility of virtually draining major western Montana reservoirs in hopes that the water will help young salmon migrate to the Pacific Ocean as it flows down the Columbia River.

Montana's Lake Koocanusa and Hungry Horse Reservoir already are being tapped significantly to aid Columbia River salmon. The reservoirs have managed to fill just twice in the past six years. Those reservoirs have contributed proportionately more water for salmon flushing than those in downriver states have, despite the

fact the only Pacific salmon you'll ever see in Montana will be at the grocery store.

Draining additional water from the reservoirs harms Montana's native fisheries, drastically reduces recreation use of the reservoirs and harms local economies.

This is one of those notions that won't die. Gov. Marc Racicot beat back a plan to increase the drawdown of Montana reservoirs earlier this year. He secured a written agreement from the Bonneville Power Administration, Bureau of Reclamation and Army Corps of Engineers to manage the reservoirs with "minimum outflows" through Labor Day, except for the release of 1.2 million acre feet of water for the benefit of salmon and sturgeon downstream.

But federal officials recently wrote Gov. Racicot to say they are considering a plan to further draft reservoirs, lowering the levels of the Montana reservoirs by an additional 30 feet.

Montanans have a responsibility to participate in efforts to rescue imperiled runs of salmon. They should do their fair share. But just as Montana hasn't asked Washington and Oregon to shoulder the burden of protecting grizzly bears, the coastal states shouldn't expect Montana to sacrifice its water resources for an unproven plan to save their salmon.

Missoulian

━━━ We Lost and We Won Canadian Timber Ruling

A binational appeals panel decision to Canadian timber exports regarding the United States is a defeat . . . sort of.

American officials remain convinced that Canadian timber is being unfairly subsidized. Since about half of its timber ends up in the United States, they contend that's hurting the American logging industry and costing us jobs.

But the appeals committee last week rejected the U.S. International Trade Commission's finding that imports of Canadian lumber injure U.S. industry by suppressing prices. That 3-2 vote was along national lines with the Canadian committee members voting for the Canadian case. The effect is two-fold.

First, the U.S. Commerce Department had imposed a 6.5 percent import duty more than two years ago to level the playing field. Now the federal government will have to return nearly $600 million in duties.

The other effect is that American home-builders should be able to use cheaper lumber from Canada, thus dropping housing costs.

Nearly half of the nation's standing softwood timber is on federal land, and that's increasingly difficult to harvest because of environmental

The issue: An appeals panel recently ruled Canadian timber imports aren't harming the U.S. Industry.

Our opinion: The loss for the timber producers turns out to be a gain for homebuilders who have been strapped with soaring lumber prices in recent years.

lawsuits and the growing public demand that forests be retained for recreation and wildlife habitat.

Thus, U.S. Forest Service logging has decreased dramatically. In 1988, the Forest Service harvested 11.5 billion board feet of timber. By 1992, that figure had dropped to 4.4 billion board feet. Not surprisingly, prices have soared from $206 per thousand board feet in 1990 to $506 last year.

So while America lost its trade dispute with our neighbor to the north, we also have gained a badly needed source of timber to make our housing more affordable.

Great Falls Tribune

---

binational appeals panel ruled in Canada's favor that a U.S. import duty on timber was unfair, the *Great Falls Tribune* ran an editorial, "We lost and we won Canadian timber ruling." Dropping the import duty would increase the competitiveness of Canadian timber, the editorial pointed out, but lower prices would help American home builders—and take pressure off harvesting National Forest lands, which had been declining in production.

Competing interests of Oklahoma and Arkansas were at stake in a series of editorials about the Illinois River run by the *Muskogee* (Okla.) *Daily Phoenix*. Opinion Page Editor Derek R. Melot said the paper "tried to chart a position between the hard lines of 'no use' and 'no protection.'" But that approach produced "grumbling from environmentalists, who say we've saved the float operators and other businesses, and [from] businesses, who claim we want to run them out of business." The editorial noted that neither friends of the river nor state and federal officials seemed to understand that an ecosystem such as the Illinois River doesn't recognize state borders. Consequently, the editorial said, "half-way measures or localized efforts aren't enough."[3] On another occasion, however, the *Phoenix* found Oklahomans at fault for not agreeing on efforts to protect the scenic waterway ("Region needs consensus to protect river"). The editorial asked how Arkansas could be asked to stop dumping waste water into the Illinois basin if Oklahoma couldn't get its act together.

EDITORIALLY SPEAKING Region Needs Consensus to Protect River

The failure of a key bill to give the Oklahoma Scenic River Commission clearer authority to protect the waters of the Illinois River is a setback to conservation efforts. But of even greater concern is the message we are sending to neighboring Arkansas about the Illinois River.

After all, if we can't agree on measures to protect the scenic waterway, how can we ask communities in Arkansas to spend money to stop dumping waste water into the Illinois basin?

Two weeks ago, Rep. Larry Adair, D-Stilwell, removed House Bill 1375 from the House floor and sent it back to the Tourism Committee, effectively ending its legislative life until 1998. But Adair said he did it to avoid an even worse fate for the bill—and the river.

"I made the decision to refer (HB 1375) back to committee rather than see it lose on the House floor," Adair said Thursday. "I didn't want to take a chance on getting the bill killed," he added, for if the House had voted down HB 1375, it could not reconsider the measure until 1999.

"I want to feel comfortable any time I push legislation," Adair explained, "I don't want to force things on people."

That's the key: We, in northeastern Oklahoma, need to get comfortable behind a specific set of goals for protecting the Illinois and convince our fellow Oklahomans of its value.

Some members of the Oklahoma Scenic Rivers Commission express a growing unease that the consensus for protecting the Illinois is unraveling—at just the time Oklahoma needs to be united.

"This will hurt our efforts to work with Arkansas on the waste water issue," said Commission Director Ed Fite.

Fite, who worked closely with Adair on the bill, says HB 1375's failure could affect river visitors this summer. "It will severely limit (the commission's) ability to police areas not under our direct control," Fite said, specifically mentioning fights on private property of the float operators and drunken driving along Oklahoma 10.

But what really made HB 1375 important was it would have laid the foundation for setting numerical standards for the water quality of the Illinois River. Fite and Commission member Ed Brocksmith said that without specific numerical standards it will be more difficult to limit dumping of nitrogen and phosphorous that has clouded both the Illinois and Lake Tenkiller.

Conservation is a tricky political task, for it asks current voters to make commitments and accept limits for benefits that might not be seen for years, or even decades. But, if we fail to act now, we could strip our children and grandchildren of even the chance to enjoy their environment.

Muskogee Daily Phoenix

LEARN MORE
If you are interested in efforts to protect the Illinois River contact:
Oklahoma Scenic Rivers Commission
P.O. Box 292
Tahlequah, OK 74465-0292
Phone: (918) 456-3251 or 3251.

Arguing for one competing interest over the other is not the only way to convince readers of a course of action involving the natural resources. The *Star Tribune* devoted the first half of an editorial ("Dune") to describing the rare sand dunes that were threatened by a proposed golf course. Only a person who was personally knowledgeable and acquainted with the dunes could have described the wrens, the snakes and the grasses and written: "Dried stalks of last year's little bluestem give the land a golden color, but everywhere light green is rising up." After making this description part of the case for the dunes, the writer turned to the more traditional explanation of why the community needed to preserve the natural area.

Dune

Teeing off on a rare prairie

Ten thousand years ago, when the last ice sheets were receding from Minnesota, the Mississippi River was a wide expanse of water, swollen with glacial runoff. Huge deposits of sand accumulated along its route and remained behind as the river cut its way through soil and rock, creating the bluffs that now line its banks. In a few places the sand formed into dunes, sprouting prairie grasses that helped protect the terrain from erosion.

Today those dune prairies are mostly gone. In the Twin Cities area, only one remains, in Cottage Grove. It is for sale. And the question confronting the humans who so recently arrived in the neighborhood is whether to preserve the prairie or turn it into a golf course.

Granted, it would be a very pretty golf course, with a sweeping view of the Mississippi valley. But it would not be the treasure it is today.

Blue and red wildflowers dot the hillsides. Wrens dart from clumps of grass and whiz out of view. A snake moves so suddenly across the path and into the grass that it's hard to identify— maybe a bullsnake, maybe just a garter or little brown snake. Songbirds raise a steady racket. And everywhere stands the evidence of the dune prairie's prime asset—a blend of grasses that would be rare even if prairie land were still plentiful.

Dried stalks of last year's little bluestem give the land a golden color, but everywhere light green is rising up. Soon the dunes will support a lush variety of grasses: big bluestem, Indian grass, sand reed grass, purple lovegrass, sea-beach needle grass, June grass. Here and there, the flowers known as prairie smoke will create little clouds of purplish haze.

The state Department of Natural Resources wants to buy the land, restore it to nearly pristine condition and preserve it. Dr. William Doebler, who already owns one golf course next door, wants to buy the land for another course and a housing development. The owner of the land, Ashland Oil, has agreed to delay sale until the state has had a chance to appraise the property, the first step toward purchase.

Cottage Grove Mayor Jack Denzer, who fears a loss of funds if the land is removed from the tax rolls, has favored the golf-course idea. Counting the prairie, he said, "We're up around 2,800 acres of parks, and I don't think one city needs that many acres of parks."

Bob Djupstrom, who heads the DNR's natural area program, counters that a park is not what the agency has in mind. "We would really like to see this area protected for posterity," he said, adding that the agency plans only an interpretive trail through the dunes and that the state would offer payments in lieu of taxes.

Ashland deserves high praise for waiting to sell the land until the state's appraisal is finished. It will deserve even higher praise if it agrees to sell the land to the DNR at the appraised price. A company spokesman in Kentucky says Ashland would prefer to accommodate the DNR's wish to leave the dunes and grasses undisturbed on the 240-acre site. "But it's really too soon to tell," he added. "The property's still for sale."

Meanwhile, kids with dirt bikes and all-terrain vehicles chew up the prairie sod, exposing sand that washes down the dunes and into gullies. The sand is so fine that a visitor, inspecting his own tracks, can read the trademark of his shoes. If the DNR succeeds in buying the property, it will repair the gullies and stop the joy rides. And a valuable resource that has felt too many footprints will get its chance to heal and survive.

Star Tribune

OTHER MEDIA

Newspapers traditionally have been reluctant to talk about their media competitors, but this reluctance may be changing. When I asked my editorial class to write editorials on a First Amendment issue, more students wrote about the Internet than the traditional mass media. When they were given the chance to write about an entertainment issue, most wrote about television or the movies.

One television issue that editorial writers have not been reluctant to discuss is the effects of violence. A day proclaimed "Turn Off the Violence Day" prompted the *Star Tribune* of Minneapolis to suggest that "parents must do more than take control of the tube. . . . They should express their dismay over violent programming to broadcasters and program sponsors" ("Toxic TV"). On an editorial about stonewalling by the broadcast industry, the *Abilene* (Texas) *Reporter-News* used a teasing headline almost certain to capture readers: "Don't blame violence on Captain Kangaroo." Readers had to read more than half the editorial to figure out what Captain Kangaroo had to do with TV violence.

Toxic TV
A day for turning off violence

The stuff they put on television these days! Adolescents torturing animals; amphibians locked in savage combat with evil; murder and mayhem sauced with salacity. It's hard to raise thoughtful children on a steady diet of such swill, and more than a few Minnesotans would love to call a halt to it all. They might be too genteel, and too hooked, to drop their TVs from an upstairs window. But perhaps they'll consider a tidier alternative: switching off the violence for a single day.

Today presents a fine opportunity for doing just that. Proclaimed "Turn Off the Violence Day" by a throng of anti-violence activists, it's a time to confront the effects of media violence. No one should doubt that youngsters see a lot of it: The typical American kid, it turns out, spends more time watching TV and playing video games than in the classroom. Much of the barbarism children take in isn't even broadcast during prime time: Saturday morning cartoons, for instance, depict 20 to 25 violent acts an hour. The tally-takers thus estimate that, by age 18, the average young viewer will have witnessed more than 200,000 acts of TV violence.

Many parents know in their bones that this can't be healthy, and a torrent of research backs them up: Children who watch a lot of TV, many studies say, are especially prone to violent and aggressive behavior. Of course the surge in youthful cruelty has other antecedents too. But there's little question that TV's ghoulishness adds a lot to the cultural soup that desensitizes children to violence. And it's plainly worth resisting.

Resistance needn't—and shouldn't—mean censorship. As Minneapolis psychologist Dave Walsh argues, all it really entails is following the parental instinct to protect children. Walsh will make that case today in one of many "anti-violence spots" being aired on KTCA-TV to mark Turn Off the Violence Day. Walsh has also teamed up with the Minnesota Medical Association to educate physicians and patients about media violence. The group has distilled its advice in a brochure of TV watching tips—which urges parents to supervise what children watch, keep televisions out of kids' bedrooms, promote high-quality programming and encourage reading and other activities.

But parents must do more than take control of the tube. They must also shake off the notion that consumer power over television stops with the on-off switch. "Imagine if someone were to dump toxins into our water supply," says Walsh, "and we complained about it. Imagine that the response was 'Well, you have a faucet in your kitchen—just turn it off.' We wouldn't tolerate it for a second." Neither should consumers tolerate toxic TV: They should express their dismay over violent programming to broadcasters and program sponsors.

No one should yearn to banish all violence from television. Its portrayal can be essential in documentary and drama—not to mention a good mystery. But only an addled network exec would defend some of the menacing fare now on the airwaves. Everyone else should turn it off, and tell the broadcasters off.

Star Tribune

━━━━━ Don't Blame Violence on Captain Kangaroo

Cause and effect is, sometimes, a difficult relationship to define. For example, if someone wakes up in the morning with a hangover, he might reasonably determine he had too much to drink the night before. His toothache, however, is likely to be a completely unrelated symptom. As the age of violent lawbreakers drops, the public is becoming more and more concerned about the connection between violent television programs and aggressive behavior in children. More than 1,000 studies since 1955 have found a correlation, and the American Academy of Pediatrics has estimated that television violence tripled during the 1980s.

ABC-TV's "Primetime Live" last week clearly demonstrated that even elementary-age youngsters respond immediately to sexual imagery they see on television. Their parents were astounded not only by how fully their children picked up on messages they thought youngsters would ignore, but also by how eager these prepubescent children seemed to be about sexual activity.

Meanwhile, the industry has generally stonewalled attempts to regulate violent programming. Those rebuffs hit a new low point last week when Van Stevenson, a lobbyist for the Motion Picture Association of America, denied any credible scientific evidence proved a relationship between media depictions of sex and violence and real-life behavior like teen-age violence and pregnancy.

In fact, Stevenson argued, the opposite could well be true. The first generation of children TV viewers that grew up watching "Captain Kangaroo" and "Father Knows Best," he said, is the same generation that produced the sexual revolution of the late '60s and early '70s and civil unrest on college campuses. What drivel! While Stevenson was at it, he might as well have pronounced the U.S. Constitution a lousy document because we've ended up with so many criminals in jail!

Such specious reasoning doesn't do anyone any good, least of all concerned parents. More help could be offered by legislation introduced by Sen. Kay Bailey Hutchison to give parents access to a "report card" that rates the violence in television programming. This would at least give parents information to make intelligent decisions to supervise their children's viewing habits.

And as long as television and motion picture industry spokesmen are blaming the problems on Captain Kangaroo, then parents need all the help they can get.

Abilene Reporter-News

LIVES OF PEOPLE

Editorial writers tend to forget that most readers are more interested in their personal lives than they are in public affairs. Except for letters to the editor, they are not likely to find anything on most editorial pages that speaks to them about their daily lives. The editorial that may have received more favorable response than any other I have written was one I hastily typed for use after a Labor Day weekend. My second daughter was to enter kindergarten the following Tuesday. The result was "To a Barefoot Girl," written in the form of a letter to her. At a session of NCEW (the National Conference of Editorial Writers) later that year, other editorial writers questioned whether it was an editorial, since it was written in the first person and did not comment on an issue. But readers of the *Columbian*, especially parents of small children, didn't care whether it met the requirement of an editorial. One woman, several years later, told me she still carried a copy of it in her purse.

Included in this group of editorials could be pieces about the weather, Christmas shopping, summer vacations, new hair styles or clothing trends, the computer game rage and what to do with a stack of old newspapers. These

▬▬▬▬▬ To A Barefoot Girl

Letter to a daughter who went to school for the first time today:

By the time I get home from work tonight, you will have experienced your first day of kindergarten. You'll be bubbling over with stories about the excitement of school—that is, if you aren't already worn out answering questions from your mother, your big sister and the girls next door.

If I know you, you weren't even a little bit scared today. An article in the paper the other evening said parents should expect their five-year-olds to be a little scared the first day, scared of spending two or three hours away from home in a new place. But that's nothing new to you. You've been gone from home longer than that this summer—without telling your mother where you were going. She was the one who was scared.

If your teacher let you paint or color today, I hope she kept a close eye on you. You can do a good job of staying within the lines when you want to. But your mother tells me that every time she turns her back there's a new mark on the living room carpet or your pillow case. How your teacher is going to keep track of you and 29 other children is beyond me. I wish her luck.

I also wish her luck in getting you to stay on your rug when it's rest time. If she has to stand over you the way your mother and I have to when it's nap time at home, 29 other children are going to be up and around and doing whatever they want to.

I hope you came home wearing your shoes, or at least carrying them. You are a big school girl now, and it's time to start learning to keep track of your shoes. It's all right sometimes to take them off, but you've got to stop forgetting where you left them. The tennis shoes you lost this summer didn't cost too much, but those big saddle shoes we bought you for school cost a lot of dollars, a whole lot more than the six cents you charged me yesterday for lemonade. Maybe it would help if you wrote your name on the inside of your shoes.

I hope you're not going to be disappointed with kindergarten. You have been looking forward to school ever since you knew where your big sister went to school. You always thought she was so smart. She could read and write and do numbers. I've heard you tell people that as soon as you went to school you'd be able to read and write and do numbers, too. It will take you quite a while to learn enough so that you can read a book, or the funny papers, or this letter. Kindergartners these days don't get much chance to learn to read. Maybe it's just as well. Maybe kindergarten should be a time only for enjoying your new friends, playing games and painting pictures.

The most important thing about school is being able to enjoy it. A lot of big boys and girls are scared of school—boys and girls who are bigger than your sister. Most of them aren't doing very well in school either. They aren't learning what they should be. Maybe they started out being scared from the first day. But maybe what happened was that somewhere along the line they forgot that school ought to be fun. Maybe they had some cranky teachers. Or maybe their parents put too much pressure on them.

I'm not sure you know what I'm talking about by this time. But I guess what I'm saying is that I hope that, even though you are now a big school girl, you will still be that smiling, laughing little kid who has a mind of her own and who is interested in more important things than keeping track of a pair of shoes. We can always buy another pair of shoes or clean the pillow case. But it's not so easy to repair the damage if you let the big people in the world who have forgotten how to smile and laugh keep you from smiling and laughing.

I hope you have fun in school—even if you come home barefoot.

Columbian

---

editorials may not contribute to the solution of any of the world's problems, but they might help solve some of an editorial writer's problems in getting more people to turn to the editorial page.

Humor and satire

When press critic Ben H. Bagdikian critiqued the pages of editorial writers attending an NCEW convention, he found few examples of humor and the humor that he found was not very good. "Funny" people are hard to find, he said. "Perhaps it isn't a funny world."[4] When columnist Andy Rooney was asked about humor writing in a *Masthead* symposium, he concluded that "[g]enerally speaking . . . editorial pages, like the Bible, are better off without humor." He said he had found that "[a]lmost every time someone sets out, deliberately, to write something funny, the effort falls flat."[5]

Other participants in the symposium were not so pessimistic. "[B]adly executed humor can decapitate an argument faster than a guillotine," but "humor can smooth the way to making [a] point," Nordahl Flakstad of the *Leader-Post* of Regina, Saskatchewan, wrote. "After all, some of the most persuasive writing–running back to Jonathan Swift and earlier–has used a light touch to make a sometimes heavy point." But Flakstad thought it was a wrong use of limited space to "drop a funny piece into editorial pages merely for entertainment and comic relief."[6] Columnist Rick Horowitz saw an "occasional light touch" as the best way to get readers to the page and keep them there. "Being funny doesn't mean you aren't being serious," he said; "it's simply a different way of making points."[7]

Horowitz warned would-be satirical writers that, "[i]f you write satire for a living, you run the risk that somebody just won't get it." He said that one time, when he was attempting to question how Bill Clinton had managed to avoid the Selective Service, he imagined "a news-conference grilling of a certain George Washington" about chopping down a cherry tree. From Portland, Ore., came a letter from a reader who said he "had a hard time believing that a Jew would write this sort of innuendo about America's first president. . . . There is no predicting the level to which you, and your colleagues, will stoop to further the Jewish agenda of division and disloyalty."[8]

Two examples of satire from the *Richmond Times-Dispatch* appear in "The 'Duty' Piece" section in Chapter 13 ("The Assembly Game" and "Legislative

---

Painting Exposed Rocks Dumb

Dumb as a rock.

That is the only way to describe the program created by some pebble brains in the U.S. Forest Service and the Washington State Department of Transportation. Those agencies have been using taxpayers' funds to "colorize" newly exposed rock faces.

Rocks exposed along the highways by construction or landslides sometimes are painted because of concerns it takes too long for them to weather naturally. Apparently, the sight of a newly exposed boulder is disconcerting to passing motorists.

As curious as the program is, however, even more curious was the response by officials to criticism of the practice. They said the project would be put on hold to assess how the rocks were doing on their own in 12 to 18 months.

How's that again? Somebody is going to go out and check the progress of natural color weatherization of rocks?

Next thing you know, somebody will get a federal grant to study the sex life of boulders.

Idaho Statesman

Goose"). An *Idaho Statesman* editorial titled "Painted exposed rocks dumb" ends on a satirical note (about the nature of federal grants).

One risk in writing humorously is that readers might take what you write seriously—and not get the point. That risk is even greater with satire.

In a *Masthead* symposium on satire, Mark L. Genrich of the *Phoenix Gazette* said that, as a person who hates fruitcake, he sometimes writes editorials calling for its abolition. In one editorial he suggested that the state police "establish roadblocks at Christmas time to intercept the transportation of the distasteful stuff." Violators would be "punished by forcing them to eat, on the spot, the fruitcakes they were caught transporting across state lines." Some readers thought he was serious and wrote long letters describing the wonderful taste of fruitcakes. Others accused him of harming the fruitcake industry. On another occasion he wrote an editorial opposing the extension of daylight-saving time, "pointing out that the time change means more hours of sunlight in the afternoon, drying crops and grasslands," leading to the need for farmers and suburbanites to use more water to keep fields and lawns green. Dutifully a number of readers wrote to "explain carefully and patiently that the sun is not controlled by earthly clocks."[9] Satire had gone awry with these readers.

Joseph Plummer of the *Pittsburgh Post-Gazette* said he saw the opportunity for "an occasional alliance between the generally understood mission of the

▬ Nutty Policy
Brits declare war on American squirrels

Two hundred and twenty-one years after "the shot heard 'round the world" at Lexington, Mass., the Redcoats again are taking a licking from the Colonists—but this time, the contenders are rodents and the battlefield is Britain itself.

American gray squirrels, introduced during the last century as a curiosity, have bred so prolifically and foraged so aggressively that they are driving the native British red squirrels toward extinction. The United Kingdom today has an estimated 2.5 million gray squirrels and only 160,000 reds, existing in remote corners of the country.

Displaying an attitude reminiscent of George III at his haughtiest, Britain's red-squirrel fanciers propose to bring the American upstarts under control with a series of distasteful methods: gunfire, poison, sterility drugs and fraud. The [last] involves the installation of trick feeding stations with trapdoors that will eject only the gray squirrels, which outweigh the reds.

Directing the campaign against the detested Yankee rodents is the government's Joint Nature Conservation Committee. Its chairman, appropriately, is an aristocrat, Lord Selborne, who seeks to invoke patriotism among his countrymen.

"Your children and your children's children will be able to watch native British red squirrels in the woods, as well as in the wildlife parks," he says.

"We have nothing against the American gray squirrel," insisted Tom Tew, a committee scientist. "We'd just rather it remain in America."

It must be admitted that the American squirrels' success in the habitat war stems largely from their nature: pushy and competitive. The shy and timid British squirrels, for example, love to eat ripe hazelnuts; the American invaders gobble the nuts before they ripen.

Nevertheless, does such behavior merit a death sentence? Why not let natural competition take its course? As Andrew Butler of the U.K.'s People for the Ethical Treatment of Animals succinctly observes, "Killing one animal to save others is absolute lunacy."

Columbus Dispatch

Welfare: Some Programs

During the National Governors' Association meeting in late January, Michigan
Governor John Engler unrolled a scroll
listing some federal welfare programs. The list is
instructive on several counts. First, it shows
welfare's sheer scope. Second, it indicates the
amount of duplication and waste; does America
really need 46 separate federal child-care
programs for low-income people? And third, it
raises a question: *Given that these programs are
supposed to reduce poverty, and given that poverty
during the past 30 years has become, if anything,
more firmly entrenched, what are the taxpayers
getting for their money?*

Oh, yes, about that money: The amounts
poured into the programs listed below total more
than $108 billion for one year. The average
taxpayer sends about $5,005 to the federal
government yearly—which gives one an idea of
how many taxpayers labor under the yoke of
involuntary servitude to the dubious benefit of
their fellow man.

Herewith, then, a partial list of federal
welfare, housing, employment, and child welfare
programs for low-income people compiled by the
Congressional Budget Office:

Abandoned Infants Assistance; Child Abuse State Grant Program;
Children's Justice Grant Program; Child Abuse Demonstration and
Research Grants; Demonstration Grants for Abuse of Homeless Children;
Community-Based Family Resource Program; Adoption Opportunities
Research Program; Family Violence State Grant Program; Family Support
Centers; Missing and Exploited Children's Program; Temporary Child Care
for Disabilities; Crisis Nurseries; Grants to Improve the Investigation and
Prosecution of Child Abuse Cases; Children's Advocacy Centers; Treatment
for Juvenile Offenders Who Are Victims of Child Abuse or Neglect; Child
Welfare Services.

Child Welfare Training; Child Welfare Research and Demonstration;
Family Preservation and Family Support Program; Independent Living;
Entitlement for Adoption (four programs); Entitlement for Foster Care
(three programs); Criminal Background Checks for Child-Care Providers;
Court-Appointed Special Advocates (CASA) Program; Child Abuse Training
Program for Judicial Personnel and Practitioners; Grants for Televised
Testimony; Victims-of-Crime Program; Grants to Indian Tribes for Child
Abuse Cases; Indian Child and Family Programs; Indian Child Protection
and Family Violence Prevention Programs; Indian Child Welfare Assistance;
Family Unification Program; Food Stamp Program; Student Financial Aid;
Early Intervention Grants for Infants & Families.

Title I (Education for the Disadvantaged); Even Start; Migrant
Education; Native Hawaiian Family Education Centers; School-to-Work
Opportunities; Special Child Care Services for Disadvantaged College
Students; Special Education Pre-School Grants; Vocational Education; Child
and Adult Food Program; Abandoned Infants Assistance Act; Child Care &
Development Block Grant; Child Development Associate Credential
Scholarship; Comprehensive Child Development Centers; Head Start; State
Dependent Care Planning & Development Grants; Temporary Child Care for
Children with Disabilities and Crisis Nurseries; Adult Training Program;
Economic Dislocation & Worker Adjustment Assistance Program; Job Corps;
Migrant & Seasonal Farmworkers Programs; School-to-Work Transition;
Summer Youth Employment & Training Program; Youth Training Program;
At-Risk Child Care; Child Care for Recipients of AFDC; Child Care Licensing
Improvement Grants; Child Welfare Services; Social Services Block Grant;
Transitional Child Care, Child Care and Dependent Care Tax Credit.

Child Care as a Business Expense; Employer Provided Child or
Dependent Care Services; Tax Exemption for Nonprofit Organizations;
National Service Trust Program; Residential Substance Abuse Treatment for
Women; Substance Abuse Prevention and Treatment Block Grant;
Community Development Block Grant; Early Childhood Development
Program; Family Self-Sufficiency Program; Homeless Supportive Housing
Program; Appalachian Childhood Program; Indian Child Welfare Act—Title
II Grants; Guaranteed Student Loans; Pell Grants; Rehabilitation Services
Basic Support; Grants to States; JTPA II-B Training Services for the
Disadvantaged/Summer Youth Employment & Training Program; JTPA Job
Corps; All-Volunteer Force Educational Assistance.

Job Opportunities & Basic Skills Program; State Legalization Impact
Assistance Grants; JTPA II-A Training Services for the Disadvantaged–Adult;
Employment Service/Wagner Peyser State Grants; Vocational
Education–Basic State Programs; JTPA II-C Disadvantaged Youth; Senior
Community Service Employment Program; Community Services Block
Grant; Adult Education–State-Administered Basic Grants Program;
Vocational Rehabilitation for Disabled Veterans; JTPA EDWAA-Dislocated
Workers (Governor's Discretionary); JTPA EDWAA–Dislocated Workers
(Substance Allotment) Trade Adjustment Assistance Workers; Supportive
Housing Demonstration Program; Food Stamp Employment & Training;
Upward Bound; One-Stop Career Centers; Economic Development—Grants
for Public Works and Development; School-to-Work; Federal Supplemental
Education Opportunity Grants; JTPA EDWAA–Dislocated (Secretary's
Discretionary); Student Supportive Services; Survivors & Dependents
Educational Assistance; Vocational Education/TechPrep Education . . .

The list runs on for several more pages, but
space prevents us from continuing. Please bear
in mind that most programs must have their own
bureaucracy. What's more, each has its own
constituency begging for dollars. Yet although
Congress has created a program for seemingly
every interest group under the sun, apparently
no one is looking out for the most beleaguered
Americans of all: the taxpayers.

Richmond Times-Dispatch

---

editorial page as a vehicle for biting criticism and the intent of sarcasm, which
is to deride and taunt," but he wouldn't use it often, "because sarcasm is truly a
blunt instrument." He suggested that sarcasm could be appropriate in "criticizing the egregious misbehavior on the part of a public official" but "unsuitable
when some point of public policy is being weighed in an editorial."[10]

Dave Cummerow of the *Modesto* (Calif.) *Bee* said in a *Masthead* symposium that satire "works best with an overstuffed shirt, a distended balloon, a house of cards" and "the path to successful satire is narrow, with pitfalls on each side."[11] Cummerow occasionally used a character he called Wink van Ripple "who wakes up every once in a while to remark, often sardonically, on the changes in the community and the performances of its leadership."

Editorials don't have to deal with major public issues. A writer on the *Columbus Dispatch* had fun writing an editorial ("Nutty policy") about efforts in Britain to control proliferating American gray squirrels, likening the battle to "the shot heard 'round the world" at Lexington, Mass. The British attitude, the writer said, was "reminiscent of George III at his haughtiest." After poking fun at the British, the editorial ended on a serious note opposing the killing of animals.

One of the most unusual editorials I have seen was one that dealt with a serious subject (welfare programs), but you knew the editors had a lot of fun springing the editorial on their readers. This may be the only editorial that I have seen, in 38 years of dealing with editorials, in which the writer didn't expect his readers to read all the way through. The bulk of the editorial, printed in about six-point type with two points of leading, consisted of "a partial listing of federal welfare, housing, employment and child welfare programs for low-income people." It certainly made a visual impression. The *Times-Dispatch*'s point was that, while Congress responds to every interest group, "no one is looking out for the most beleaguered Americans of all: the taxpayers."

CONCLUSION

Editorial-page readers deserve a break from the traditional topics of government, politics and world-shaking events. Instead of writing only about breaking-news stories, editorial writers can take a broader look at other things their readers are interested in–science and natural resources, for example. Instead of writing only about "serious" subjects, they can try their hand from time to time at writing something personal or humorous.

Questions and Exercises

1. Find an editorial dealing with science. Has the writer been able to achieve a balance between oversimplifying and writing beyond the comprehension of most readers? Has the topic been discussed in terms that are relevant to readers? Does the writer do more than rehash what had appeared in the news columns?
2. Find an editorial dealing with natural resources. Ask the same questions about it.
3. Find a humorous or satirical editorial. Is the humor or satire likely to be misunderstood? Is the use of humor or satire appropriate in this editorial?
4. Find several editorials dealing with everyday life. Do the writers succeed in making the commonplace seem interesting? Might the space have been better used for comment on some public issue?

CHAPTER 15 | Editorials on Elections

Some editorial writers, some scholars and some lay readers think editorial endorsements have little impact on elections. Other writers, other scholars and other readers worry that endorsements carry too much weight with voters, that newspapers control elections. Among the writers who think they have influence, some worry about making mistakes in making endorsements through lack of information about or prejudice toward a candidate.

The endorsement process is a difficult and time-consuming process, if done right. It involves conducting research into backgrounds and political stands of the candidates, conducting interviews, perhaps attending candidates' meetings and then sitting down to figure out whom to endorse. In a local election with several positions on the ballot, or an election that involves statewide and legislative district candidates, scores of candidates may have to be researched and interviewed. Before an election is over, because of this burden, editorial writers may begin to wonder whether newspapers ought to be in the business of endorsing candidates at all. They may wonder even more if they find themselves disagreeing with their editors or publishers about whom to endorse.

The hell that editorial writers feel that they go through during endorsement season may be one reason why some newspapers–although still a minority–forbear from endorsing candidates in some or all races.

WHY ENDORSE?

Most newspapers endorse candidates for public office, but more and more newspaper people, as well as readers, are questioning whether endorsements play a legitimate role in today's changing political world. Some critics contend that endorsements play an unfair role, giving newspapers undeserved power to influence elections. Others contend that endorsements play virtually no role at all in influencing voters.

In any case, the percentage of newspapers that endorse seems to be declining. An editorial in *Editor & Publisher* noted that 30 percent of newspapers polled in the 1996 election cited a "no-endorsement" policy. It said that "[t]his steady trend away from presidential endorsements has been noticeable since 1940 when only 13.4 percent of the newspapers remained neutral."[3] A study made in 1988 found that approximately 90 percent of daily newspapers endorsed candidates in at least some elections.[4] No doubt the percentage is lower now. Some papers make recommendations from president to local judges and school board members. Some endorse in state and local elections; others only in national and state elections. Some newspapers consider it especially important to endorse in local elections. Others avoid endorsing local candidates, either for fear of antagonizing readers or for fear of unduly influencing the vote.[5]

The Case Against Endorsements

Among readers, probably the most frequently heard argument against endorsing is that a paper has no right to use its position of influence to impose its views on the voters. A reader accused the editor-owner of the *Daily News* of Longview, Wash., of inflicting on the community "a slanted and one-sided opinion or recommendation" that "could affect the lives of many people." The letter writer feared that people would "take that recommendation as an easy way out for the solution of their undecided vote." The writer thought that if the editor-owner wanted to express his views, he should take out a political advertisement and label it as such, just like anyone else.[6] A letter writer charged the Eugene, Ore., *Register-Guard* with "meddling into the political affairs of the people of Lane County, dictating to Republicans and Democrats alike." The selection of candidates "belongs to the people. . . . It's their vote," the writer said.[7]

A similar view was expressed by an editor-publisher, Dick Timmons of the *Daily News* of Rhinelander, Wis. "Who are newspapers to tell our readers how to think or how to vote?" he wrote in a letter to *Editor & Publisher*. "[S]top playing God, editors," he wrote. "Readers don't give a hoot whom you vote for."[8]

Another argument against endorsing is that readers will think that, if a paper supports a candidate in its editorial columns, it will be biased in that candidate's favor in the news columns. When the *Los Angeles Times* announced a partial shift away from endorsing, *Times* editors said they hoped to allay suspicions among readers that "editorial page endorsements really affect the news columns," especially in races that arouse the sharpest political passions.[9] A study of newspapers in Chicago and Louisville found some evidence that endorsements do affect how readers perceive the news coverage of a newspaper. Reagan supporters tended to think the papers that endorsed Mondale in 1984 favored Mondale in their news coverage; Mondale supporters tended to think the single paper that endorsed Reagan favored Reagan in its news coverage. (An analysis of the news columns of the major paper in each city found that, indeed, each newspaper gave slightly better coverage to the candidate it endorsed.) A major finding, however, was that less than half the readers surveyed were aware of which candidate their newspapers had endorsed.[10]

The Case for Endorsements

To the charge that newspapers have no right to tell voters what to do, some editors reply that elections are just one aspect of public affairs and should not be treated differently. In answer to the letter writer in Eugene, an editorial in the *Register-Guard* noted the paper's practice of commenting on public matters throughout the year and contended that for the paper "to comment on issues between elections and then to duck the tough choices would be irresponsible."[11] In an NCEW (National Conference of Editorial Writers) online exchange about endorsements, Nancy Q. Keefe, a columnist for Gannett Suburban Newspapers in White Plains, N.Y., said she saw the value of endorsement editorials to be the same as the value of all editorials: "that is, to get people to think[,] [n]ot to think as we do, but simply to butt their heads against a thoughtful opinion and react to it."[12] The extended online exchange on endorsements led Ryan J. Rusak, opinion editor of the *Daily Skiff* of Texas Christian University, to "finally [convince] our editor-in-chief and the rest of the editorial board that we are obligated to endorse candidates in officer elections for our House of Representatives." His reasoning: "We are the only organization on campus with the authority (for lack of a better term, not in a sense of arrogance) to endorse candidates."[13]

Defenders of endorsements contend that the newspaper is unique, not only on college campuses but in most communities, in that no other institution, aside from government and political parties, devotes as much attention to political affairs. "The end result [of not endorsing] leaves the major political campaign largely up to hucksters writing the pitches for print and broadcast political advertising, which isn't known for its fairness, and to the talk show hosts who demonstrate no restraint about their political leanings," said an editorial in *Editor & Publisher*.[14] Aside from professional politicians, political reporters and editorial writers probably know more about the qualifications of candidates and the merits of ballot propositions than anyone else does. They have the added advantage of being less partisan and hence more able to evaluate candidates and issues with some measure of detachment. The editorial columns of a newspaper are among the few places in a community where the pros and cons of issues can be discussed at length and in a logical, factual matter. Why should editorial writers not participate in this forum? According to the writer of the *E&P* editorial, not endorsing "amounts to an abdication of a responsibility that historically has rested on the shoulders of editors—and should remain there."

Of course this argument is good only to the extent that writers of endorsements make certain they are as informed as possible before they share their knowledge and evaluations with readers. Aside from keeping generally informed about government and politics, writers traditionally have invited candidates to the newspaper for in-depth interviews. Interviewing can become a tedious, even horrid, task if an editorial staff faces the necessity to talk to candidates for a long list of positions. In an NCEW online exchange, Kay

Semion reported that writers on the *Tallahassee Democrat* interviewed 100 candidates and wrote 35 editorials during the 1996 election.[15] Phineas Fiske of *Newsday* said his staff conducted 72 interviews in 37 races, but sometimes only two editorial board members were present.

Lynnell Burkett reported that the *San Antonio Express-News* hit on the idea of interviewing all candidates for a particular position at the same time.[16] Robert White said the *Cincinnati Post* helped smooth the interviewing of 50 candidates by sending them questionnaires ahead of time. The newspaper published many of the responses. He anticipated that, in another election, when the Post got its website running, it would "put up the entire text of the questionnaires."[17]

Writing in *The Masthead*, Ed Williams reported that the editorial staff of the *Charlotte Observer* followed a three-point plan to avoid what he called "editorial masochism":

- Do no *pro forma* interviews. Treat candidate endorsements as we do other issues, and interview only the people we need to interview.
- Rather than have all the editorial writers interview a candidate, assign each editorial writer to research specific races and bring the editorial board a recommendation about whom to endorse and whether to interview either or both of the candidates.
- Get out of the office and attend candidate forums around the community. And sponsor some candidate forums ourselves.

Williams reported that in races where interviews were not conducted, when editorial writers showed up at forums, the candidates "knew we were keeping up with their races." He concluded that the *Observer*'s commentary on the election was "better when we're out where the candidates meet the voters—and we learn a lot of things there that we wouldn't learn sitting in the office."[18]

Personal Note

In the years in which I was engaged in writing editorials, the papers on which I worked consistently endorsed candidates and ballot propositions. I was not unsympathetic to the concerns of those who contended that the *Columbian* was trying to impose its candidates on the community. After all, over the years a large majority of the candidates that the paper endorsed were elected. Some critics argued that since the *Columbian* was the sole source of political reporting in the community, the editors should keep their editorial preferences to themselves. But my publishers and I thought that, precisely because we were the only consistent source of political information, we had a responsibility to dig into the backgrounds of candidates, present the arguments for and against propositions and tell our readers what we found and what we had concluded.

WHAT EFFECTS?

Whether endorsement editorials do in fact influence voters has been a matter of speculation and argument for a long time, especially since Democrat

Franklin D. Roosevelt began winning elections in spite of overwhelming opposition from the editorial writers on predominantly Republican newspapers. By 1952, journalism historian Frank Luther Mott, in an article titled "Has the Press Lost Its Punch?" concluded: "There seems to be no correlation, positive or negative, between support of a majority of newspapers during a campaign and victory in a presidential canvass."[19] Following the 1952 election, Professor Nathaniel B. Blumberg noted that "in the 37 presidential campaigns preceding the 1952 election, the winner had the editorial support of a majority of newspapers 18 times and did not have it 19 times."[20] In the 11 elections in the period between 1952 and 1992 the press accumulated a better record, with a majority of newspapers supporting the winning candidate in nine elections, for an improved record of 27 wins and 21 losses. Of course, this tallying proves nothing.

Another way to look at this record: With the exception of the elections of Lyndon Johnson in 1964 and Bill Clinton in 1992, the majority of papers has endorsed a Republican for president at least since the Civil War. This tells you more about the newspapers themselves than it does about their power to influence elections. The presidential race is only one of thousands of contests that take place in the country on a regular basis—and the presidential vote may be the one least influenced by editorials. Voters have many other sources of information in presidential elections. Newspapers may have more impact in state and local races, if only because their editorial endorsements are less predictable. Newspapers are more likely to endorse Democrats in these races.

In spite of the popularity of television news, surveys suggest that the public still tends to look to the print media for guidance in setting the public agenda. Studies show that voters look in particular to newspapers for information about elections at state and local levels.[21] One nationwide study of how much voters knew about the qualifications of candidates for the U.S. Senate found newspapers superior to television "as agents of information to help people identify assets and liabilities of important political contenders." The authors concluded: "If reasoning about political choices depends at all on the features of an area's media system, those characteristics will be found in the newspapers that circulate there, not in television coverage."[22] These studies suggest that voters do, and in fact must, look to newspapers for help in judging candidates.

"Our philosophy is that we don't change many minds endorsing the president," Frank Partsch of the *Omaha World-Herald* said in the NCEW online exchange; "that's more tradition and self-definition. But we can make a difference in a school board race. And that can be important."[23]

Endorsements appear to have more effect on some types of elections and ballot choices than on others. Fred Fedler has concluded that endorsements are most effective when:

- An election is local.
- An election is nonpartisan.
- The candidates are unfamiliar.
- The ballot is long and complicated.
- Voters have received conflicting information or have conflicting loyalties.[24]

Studies that I conducted in California suggested that endorsements have more effect:

- On ballot propositions than candidate races.
- In primary than in general elections.
- On governmental issues (taxes, schools, constitutional amendments) than on emotional issues (death penalty, abortion, gun control, homosexual teachers).[25]

In addition, I found that smaller newspapers seemed to have more influence than larger ones and independent newspapers more than group newspapers.[26] In all of these instances, effects appeared to be modest (from 1 to 5 percent), and hard to measure and prove. Of course, in a close election, a few percentage points can make the difference.

Editorial-writing literature includes several examples of the apparent influence of editorials. During one election, 47 percent of voters leaving the polls in Orlando, Fla., said they had considered the local newspaper's endorsements "very" or "somewhat" helpful; about half of those (23 percent) went a step farther and said the endorsements actually had helped them decide how to vote.[27] A study of the campaigns of congressional candidates found that newspaper endorsement editorials were "the strongest predictor of percent of vote for . . . non-incumbent[s]"–but that incumbents were much more successful in obtaining endorsements.[28] In Cleveland the endorsement of the *Plain Dealer* in a five-way race for mayor was credited with "propell[ing] a longshot . . . into the run-off and to an eventual win."[29] A study concluded that in a series of elections the *Toledo* (Ohio) *Blade* influenced between 4 and 12 percent of the voters in a governor's race but only 2 to 4 percent in a state senate race.[30]

WHOSE VIEWS?

If an editorial should ever represent more than the views of the specific person who wrote it, that time should be during elections. But whether the editorial should be the voice of the owner (publisher), editor or a consensus of staff members is an issue being fought out in newspapers across the country. In most instances the publisher has the power to win in any dispute. But each year an increasing number of newspapers seem to be allowing staff members to influence, if not decide, endorsements.

A 1980 survey of endorsements found some evidence disputing the "critical stereotypes [that] show authoritarian editors and publishers [deciding on endorsements], often on the basis of their own prejudices and in opposition to the wishes of their staffs." Twenty-one editors in the survey volunteered the information that their papers' endorsements were made by the editorial boards.[31] Nevertheless, publishers probably still exercise their final editorial prerogative more strongly and more often on endorsements than on any other type of editorial page decision. One survey found that, while 46 percent of publishers played an active role in determining editorial positions on major political issues, 81 percent exercised a strong voice in endorsements.[32]

John J. Zakarian, then of the *St. Louis Post-Dispatch*, described what he called "the publishers' four-year itch" and the "editorial writers' agony." For 47 months many papers carry moderate-to-liberal editorial policies but "on the 48th month of reckoning turn conservative." He described presidential elections as "sacred cows of the highest order."[33] Byron St. Dizier, professor at the University of Alabama–Birmingham, found evidence of this 48th-month turnaround in a study of newspapers in the 1984 presidential election. Newspapers that supported the Democratic Walter Mondale showed "unswerving loyalty" in support of Democratic positions on issues. Among newspapers that supported the Republican Ronald Reagan, however, more than half opposed his position on six out of nine key issues. "The findings may help to explain why some endorsement editorials fail to mention issues when endorsing a candidate," St. Dizier wrote. "In the case of most of the newspapers supporting Reagan, any discussion of the campaign's issues would make the paper's editorial page appear inconsistent at best."[34]

As might be expected, the 57-to-33 percent ratio of Reagan and Mondale endorsements by the newspapers in the survey (10 percent not endorsing) did not coincide with the opinions of the editors of those papers. The editors supported Mondale over Reagan 55 to 43 percent. Of the Mondale backers, 43 percent said they wrote editorials for newspapers that endorsed Reagan. (They did not say that they themselves wrote the Reagan endorsements.) Only one Reagan supporter worked on a paper that backed Mondale. Although 70 percent of the editors said their publishers were more conservative than they were, and 13 percent said their publishers were more liberal, nine out of 10 editors said they were satisfied with their newspaper's endorsement process. Three out of four said they voted for candidates endorsed by their paper at least three-quarters of the time. These findings suggest that it is principally, if not entirely, in presidential elections that newspapers take stands that run contrary to the preferences of editorial page staffs.

Supposed differences between publisher and editorial page staff became a campaign issue when the *Star-Tribune* of Minneapolis–St. Paul endorsed Democratic Gov. Rudy Perpich for re-election in 1990. A columnist in a rival newspaper had claimed that the editorial staff had preferred write-in candidate Arne Carlson eight to two. Robert J. White, editorial editor of the *Star-Tribune*, reported in a *Masthead* symposium that "we were called undemocratic . . . [a]nd were said to have caved in" to the publisher's wishes. He explained that among all editorial page staff members (including copy editors, artists and the op-ed editor), the preference was for Carlson, but among writers only the split was even, with White and his deputy for Perpich. "But in the end," White said, "the decision was mine, and it was my job to make the recommendation to the publisher. He accepted it."[35] (Carlson won.)

This case, while perhaps not typical, may help make the point that it is not always easy to explain how endorsement decisions get made and who ultimately is responsible for them. Douglas J. Rooks of the *Kennebec Journal* in Augusta, Me., reported that his readers were confused and "felt betrayed by an endorsement they saw as arbitrary and undemocratic." Three years before, the newspaper had created an editorial board that interviewed candidates and made endorsements for the state legislature, city council and school board. The editors felt that their paper and the daily and Sunday papers under the same ownership in Portland, Me., should be responsible for their own endorsements. "But the publisher has decided to continue the previous system," Rooks said, "which—as we were to discover—was poorly understood by many readers." After the *Journal* editorial board had narrowly voted to endorse former Gov. Joseph Brennan, "[w]e were all taken aback when the chairman, acting on previous instructions from the publisher, who did not attend, announced that we would endorse [John] McKernan." Rooks said the board could remember no similar action. "The story of the board's deliberations was quickly out on the street," Rook said, "and was a prominent issue in the waning days of the campaign."[36] (McKernan won by about 2 percent.)

Another variation on disagreement between publisher and editorial page staff was described by Mindy Cameron of the *Seattle Times*. Opponents were seeking to repeal a city ordinance that extended the same sick and bereavement leave benefits to domestic partners that were provided to married persons. "Not surprisingly, the initiative was vigorously opposed by Seattle's sizable gay community," Cameron wrote. "Much of the support for Initiative 35 smacked of gay-bashing, though proponents consistently denied it was an anti-gay measure." Several editorial staff members "were outspoken in our opposition," and "others felt less strongly or had mixed views," but "the publisher had made up his mind [to support the initiative] for practical and symbolic reasons," Cameron said. He thought the policy, if carried out throughout the city, would be too costly and feared that Seattle was becoming too much associated with the image of embracing alternative lifestyles. But in this case, the publisher encouraged staff members who disagreed with him to write signed columns expressing their views. One writer wrote a sharp dissent. Then on the Sunday before the election, below a summary of endorsements, Cameron wrote a column that explained to readers "the endorsement process, the internal disagreement, the publisher's role, my unsuccessful efforts to dissuade him." She concluded: "I'm voting 'no' on the initiative. I hope you will, too."[37] (The initiative was defeated.)

One of the questions raised in recent studies has concerned the role of newspaper groups in making endorsements. Most of the studies have looked only at presidential endorsements and, not surprisingly, found a good deal of homogeneity among endorsements, since most newspapers, group-owned or independent, endorse Republicans for president. But some studies have found differences among groups. Cecilie Gaziano, president of Research Solutions, Inc., of Minneapolis, had divided the groups into three categories: consistently homogeneous in their endorsements, somewhat homogeneous and consistently heterogeneous. The homogeneous groups tended to be regional in nature. Papers in this category tended to be smaller, evening papers with no competition, and Republican. The heterogeneous groups tended to be more national in scope, and to be larger, morning papers with more competition.[38]

Gaziano found that homogeneous newspapers outnumbered heterogeneous papers, but that heterogeneous papers had a larger total circulation. She speculated that in future elections "[t]he growth of the large, heterogeneous groups may reinforce tendencies [of voters] to vote Democratic."

Noting that the largest groups own a wide variety of types of newspapers, John C. Busterna and Kathleen A. Hansen of the University of Minnesota suggested that "[i]t may be that region of the country, circulation size, metro vs. rural, or some other local characteristics have more influence on endorsement decisions than chain ownership per se." They also suggested that group endorsement patterns may result, not from directives from the group, but through other, more subtle, forces: "The socialization of newspapers and newspaper executives, the pressure to conform to professional and industry norms, the need to meet superiors' expectations within the organization, and the desire to please powerful sources outside the organization are recognized as forces that may affect media content." They concluded that "chain ownership may play no role, or only a minor one, in affecting the content performance of daily newspapers. . . . "[39]

One study, concerned with the group homogeneity of Gannett newspapers, examined their stands on three national issues (none of them endorsements). It found a higher uniformity of editorial positions on all three issues among Gannett papers than among other papers included in the study. The authors of the study concluded that "a homogenizing effect on editorial position and policy results from chain ownership" but that "the outstanding question . . . concerns the process through which such uniformity results." The authors expressed the concern that "[a]ny tendency on the part of large newspaper chains to orchestrate editorial opinion on national issues would seem to represent one of the most serious threats posed by chain ownership to freedom of information in a democratic society."[40]

WHAT APPROACH?

Writers generally employ one of two basic approaches to endorsement writing. A form that goes back to the early days of the Republic involves making the strongest possible case for your chosen candidate and either ignoring or criticizing the opposition. The second approach presents the good and bad points of all candidates and then, on the basis of the points made, concludes that one of the candidates is the best. On occasion an editorial will conclude that one candidate is not significantly better than the others.

The endorsement that evaluates all the candidates is similar to the SBA₁A₂DC editorial described in Chapter 10, "Nine Steps to Editorial Writing." We noted that this type of editorial offers a chance to persuade the reader who may have started out disagreeing with the conclusion, in this case the endorsement. It also is appropriate for races in which readers have received little information from other sources. The editorial that basically presents the case for only one candidate, as an SAC editorial might, might be appropriate if the arguments are overwhelming for a candidate, if voters have previously been fully informed on the issues or if the editorial writer is mainly concerned with encouraging readers who already agree with the endorsement position.

To illustrate these types of endorsement, I have selected a sample of editorials written during the 1997 state election in Virginia. Candidates for governor were Democrat Don Beyer, the lieutenant governor, and Republican James Gilmore, who had stepped down as attorney general. Both were well known in state political circles. The candidates seeking to fill the two positions being vacated by Beyer and Gilmore were not previously well known to most voters. All three Republicans won by wide margins.

Our Candidate Only

In its pure form, the one-candidate-only endorsement is not found as often in U.S. newspapers today as it was in the past. Most papers are not so partisan as they once were. Editors recognize that readers who do not agree wholly with an editorial are likely to resent having an endorsement that presents only one side.

Whether there is an editorial decision to talk about only the endorsed candidate may depend on the endorsement policies of the newspaper as well as the nature of a specific race. In 1997 the *Richmond Times-Dispatch* ran editorials that mentioned only the endorsed candidates in the three statewide races. Not even the names of their opponents appeared. In the example published here, "For Mark Earley," starting with the headline, readers had no doubt about the newspaper's preference, but some may have been left with the idea that Earley was the only candidate for attorney general.

Mostly Our Candidate

Other newspapers varied their approaches. The Norfolk *Virginian-Pilot*, the *Roanoke Times* and the Newport News *Daily Press* carried mostly-our-candidate editorials in the attorney general and lieutenant governor races, but published long editorials comparing the candidates and their positions in the governor's race.

The *Virginian-Pilot*'s editorial on the lieutenant governor race was devoted almost exclusively to Democrat L.F. Payne, even to the point of noting where the newspaper differed with Payne over a controversial pipeline. References to his opponent were limited to recognizing that John Hagar was a retired

For Mark Earley

The Attorney General serves as Virginia's lawyer. He not only represents the Commonwealth but also ensures that the Commonwealth plays by the rules. The qualifications for the office include legal skills and philosophy. Mark Earley offers both. Today the *Times-Dispatch* endorses him for Attorney General.

Earley is unique. His entry into politics began not in a campus screaming society but in the Philippines, where the imposition of martial law served as a compelling reminder that democracy is fragile. It cannot be taken for granted. The good work of generations can be undermined in a mischievous moment. He vowed then to defend the principles and institutions defining government of, by, and for the people.

During his decade in the State Senate (he represents Chesapeake), Earley has won the admiration of friends and foes. Those disagreeing with him on specific issues recognize him as an honorable adversary. As Attorney General, he would defend Virginia's interests with tenacious compassion.

Earley's work on behalf of juvenile justice reform suggested his mettle. He supported the abolition of parole not because it was popular but because it was the right thing to do. If compelled to defend policies such as welfare reform, he would do so out of duty and conviction.

The Attorney General counts average Virginians as his clients. In ways large and small, Earley has demonstrated his commitment to his constituents.

On November 4, vote Earley for Virginia's Attorney General.

Richmond Times-Dispatch

tobacco executive, had made "laudable contributions" to the community, had never held office, held a more laudable position on the pipeline and hoped to eliminate much of the property tax on cars and trucks. Seven paragraphs were devoted exclusively to Payne. The editorial lauded Payne for being the "most realistic of the six statewide candidates about Virginia's fiscal condition" and for refusing "to pander to voters by dangling sugar plums that may not be affordable."[41]

More about the Other Candidate

Even though labeled "For governor, Don Beyer," the *Roanoke Times* endorsement editorial devoted more space to Gilmore than to Beyer. The writer said the purpose of the editorial was to cut through "the miasma of campaign bombast to get at the real issues." In spite of what the candidates were saying about each other, neither was "a bumbling incompetent"; "[e]ither could serve capably." More than half of the long editorial was devoted to dispelling "campaign fog" in three areas, all relating to Gilmore: parole reform, Pat Robertson and a proposal to remove the car tax. More important for voters than these matters, the editorial insisted, were "intelligent tax relief" and higher education. On tax relief the editorial found Beyer's ideas more appropriate than Gilmore's. On education the editorial made no mention of Beyer but, instead, concentrated on the weaknesses of Gilmore's proposals. The editorial concluded, rather blandly: "On this—as in the candidates' contrasting views on abortion rights, environmental protection and public schools—Beyer's election would better serve Virginia's future."

One might wonder why an editorial writer would concentrate more on the candidate who was not endorsed. In this instance, the second line of the headline of the editorial suggests an explanation: Beyer had waged "a disappointing campaign." The editorial writer faced the task of trying to change the focus of a campaign dominated by the opposing candidate.

Both Candidates

The gubernatorial endorsement of the *Virginian-Pilot* exemplifies editorials that give both candidates extensive space. Even though the title ("Beyer for governor") and opening paragraphs made it clear that the newspaper favored Beyer, the editorial examined, dispassionately and in depth, the candidates' proposals for tax reform and education as well as their views on "overall vision for Virginia." In each area the editorial found Beyer's ideas more acceptable than Gilmore's. It saw neither candidate, however, holding an advantage in assuring "continued economic prosperity." The editorial concluded by giving credit to both candidates:

Both men also have demonstrated a personal commitment to steady improvement of race relations in the Old Dominion. We have been impressed by Gilmore's willingness to speak out on racial matters.

Despite an ugly and dispirited political campaign, both of these men have the ability and experience to guide the commonwealth. But we believe that Don Beyer will take Virginia in directions that strengthen vital institutions and improve the quality of life for a broader array of citizens. For those reasons, we endorse Beyer for governor.[42]

For Governor, Don Beyer

*Despite a disappointing campaign, Don Beyer comes across as
the gubernatorial candidate with the better grasp of the central
challenge facing Virginia today.*

THE GUBERNATORIAL race of 1997 has left
voters with the tough task of piercing the
miasma of campaign bombast to get at
the real issues that face Virginia and its next
governor.

After attempting to do so, we have arrived at
a couple of conclusions:

■ You wouldn't know it from their
campaigns, but neither Lt. Gov. Don Beyer, the
Democratic candidate, nor former Attorney
General Jim Gilmore, the Republican candidate,
is a bumbling incompetent. Either could serve
capably as governor.

■ The central challenge confronting
Virginia is exploiting the current prosperity to
broaden and make more certain future prosperity. Competitors like the Carolinas, Georgia and
Tennessee are doing so. But in certain key
areas, such as higher education, Virginia is
losing its grip.

Though the need to leverage current prosperity dwarfs all other issues, it has scarcely
been addressed by either campaign. Beyer,
however, appears to grasp the point more fully
than Gilmore. We therefore recommend Beyer's
election.

* * *

Dispelling some of the campaign fog:

Parole reform, which helped propel Republican Gov. George Allen to victory in 1993, is
a dead issue in 1997. It's a done deal that nobody
wants to undo.

As part of the Allen administration, Gilmore
deserves credit for his role in getting the popular deal done. Beyer can take credit, but a
smaller piece of it, for helping get the GOP
initiative through a Democrat-controlled General
Assembly.

Let us further stipulate that Beyer does not
favor releasing child-killers from prison, and
Gilmore does not favor mere slaps on the wrist
for child molesters.

Pat Robertson is a player in this campaign,
and Gilmore cannot pretend otherwise.
Robertson has poured thousands of dollars into
the coffers of statewide GOP candidates;
Robertson's Christian Coalition troops presumably soon will be distributing their GOP-looking
"nonpartisan" voting guides at Robertson-
friendly churches.

Western Virginians might also recall
Gilmore's use of the Robertson connection to
defeat former Republican Del. Steve Agee of
Salem in the 1993 battle for the GOP nomination
for attorney general.

But Gilmore, a product of the more moderate
suburban wing of the Republican coalition, is not
a Robertson toady. The hard questions here have
less to do with Gilmore than with Robertson and
his hypocritical fusion of sanctimony with political hardball.

"Car tax"—known until this year as the
personal-property tax—reduction (and eventual
elimination) is not simply a trivial issue. It is,
strictly speaking, not a state issue at all. The car
tax is a local tax that a county or municipality can

The endorsement editorial in the Newport News *Daily Press* also gave
considerable attention to both candidates, but it was more forceful in indicating its preference for Beyer. The *Daily Press* suggested that, in deciding how to
vote for governor, voters should ask themselves who had the better vision and
better leadership skills. The editorial then devoted a paragraph or more to
education, tobacco, environment, economic development, abortion, taxes and
experience. Positions of both candidates were given attention, but at the beginning of each section the newspaper's preference for Beyer was made clear in
boldface caps. Here is what the *Daily Press* said on the tax issue:

lower or end at any time. Bath County, for one, has all but eliminated it.

The issue arose as a poll-driven ploy by Gilmore to undercut Beyer's base in Northern Virginia, where local government is costlier and the car tax more burdensome. Similarly poll-driven, Beyer responded with his own plan for a state income-tax credit for lower- and middle-income taxpayers to offset personal-property taxes.

Unfortunately, both candidates are too committed to their screwball proposals to drop them after the election. But Beyer's plan is at least honest enough to reduce the state's rather than the localities' revenue streams. Nor would it make localities' fiscal fortunes hostage to Richmond's willingness to keep appropriating offset money long after the next governor leaves office.

* * *

Issues more important than parole reform, Robertson or the car tax? Sure. Here are two, among many:

Intelligent tax relief. Beyer's proposal to remove the state's corporate income tax on small businesses is an example. An earned-income tax credit for the working poor, which Beyer has supported in the past, is another.

You may not know that Virginia has no sales tax on nonprescription medicine, since you're still paying it. The tax has been *repealed*, you see, repeal just hasn't been *implemented*. Before the General Assembly even looks at a Gilmore car-tax bill, it should honor this commitment of several years standing.

Other possibilities: repealing the sales tax on food, raising the personal exemption in the state income tax, broadening state income-tax brackets, dedicating more lottery or sales-tax revenues to the localities.

Keep in mind, though, that Virginia is already a low-tax state by the most valid comparative measure, combined state and local taxes per $1,000 of personal income.

Higher education. Gilmore proposes a blue-ribbon commission on the future of higher education, as if there's some mystery as to where the problem lies. What mystery? It's no secret that Virginia has sunk to near bottom in its per-student higher-ed support.

The result is what former Gov. Gerald Baliles has called "elegant degradation": The machinery still works (Virginia continues to get more value for its higher-ed tax dollar than perhaps any other state), but its useful life is limited without more investment in maintenance and upgrading. That's why a group of leading businessmen from across Virginia has called for nearly $1 billion in additional higher-education spending in just the next biennium.

Continued tuition freezes without sharp increases in state support won't cut it. Neither will Gilmore's plan to squander precious state higher-ed money on scholarships for those who would go to college anyway.

Higher education in Virginia doesn't really need more advice, valuable as that has been and can continue to be. Virginia's colleges and universities need more state dollars, which will require an attitude adjustment in the governor's mansion.

On this—as in the candidates' contrasting views on abortion rights, environmental protection and public schools—Beyer's election would better serve Virginia's future.

Roanoke Times

BEYER WINS ON TAXES. Both candidates want to provide some tax relief. Beyer has a simple plan that would give families with an income below $75,000 a rebate on their state income taxes if they had paid personal property taxes to their local government.

Gilmore's more complicated plan would affect more people, but it would also obligate the state to replace 20 to 25 percent of the local revenue localities collect. That's a considerable burden for a state that has just recovered sufficiently from the recession of the early 1990s to begin restoring funds for such state services as secondary and higher education and transportation.

A brief paragraph concluded the editorial:

Don Beyer deserves your vote on Nov. 4. He deserves to be Virginia's governor, and Virginia deserves to have a man like Don Beyer as its next governor.[43]

Hard to Decide

Sometimes editors have a hard time deciding on an endorsement. The candidates may appear equally attractive or unattractive. Such was the case for the *News-Gazette* of Lexington, Va. After comparing the candidates' proposals on taxation and education and recounting their experiences in government and business, an editorial titled "Beyer For Governor; Re-elect Deeds, Putney" stated:

This race is tough to call. You have two men of similar backgrounds from the Richmond-Washington corridor, who have paid their political dues. Both are pro-education, pro-growth and politically moderate.

Beyer's business experience and his experience in working with the legislature over two terms as lieutenant governor give him the edge in this race and make him the better choice for governor.[44]

To help support this mild endorsement, the editorial then offered additional details about Beyer's ideas on taxation, economic development and education.

Sometimes editorial writers are not especially keen on either candidate. The *Manassas Journal Messenger* began an editorial in this manner: "In lieu of having to choose between candidates Donald S. Beyer Jr. and James A. Gilmore for Virginia governor, many Prince William voters say they wish Gov. George Allen could succeed himself as the state's top official." Many voters "don't find too appealing" the choice between the two candidates. "[W]e are not naive enough to believe all of the campaign promises made by either Gilmore . . . or Beyer," the editorial said, but the newspaper was inclined to go with Gilmore as more likely to carry out the economic measures Allen had started. The editorial unenthusiastically concluded with this sentence: "We see no reason for voters to switch parties in midstream."[45]

Of course, if editorial writers see no real differences in the qualifications of the candidates, they should feel no obligation to endorse one of them. But, in my opinion, whether they endorse or not they have an obligation to use the newspaper's editorial voice to help inform readers about candidates and issues.

Ballot Propositions

In some elections, especially in some states, voters find themselves faced with more ballot propositions than candidate races. Legislatures refer measures to the voters. Citizens use the initiative process to put measures on the ballot. Sometimes propositions receive considerable attention during the campaign period, but more often are buried in a list of little-publicized and little-understood measures. As for propositions that do attract a lot of attention, voters may find themselves more confused than informed as Election Day nears.

In general, newspaper editorials on propositions are likely to have more credibility and greater influence with voters than candidate endorsement editorials do. I found that to be the case in a study of California elections.[46] On lesser issues, aside from official voters' guides, newspapers may be the only source of information. On hot issues, they may be the most reliable source. One reason that endorsements may carry more weight is that voters usually don't approach ballot propositions with their traditional political party biases.

Voters may, however, have other biases or strong feelings concerning some ballot propositions. My own study found that endorsements seemed to carry less weight on emotional and moral issues, where voters could be expected to have strong feelings. A good example was the doctor-assisted suicide referendum that Oregon voters faced in the November 1997 election. Three years before, Oregonians had approved a doctor-assisted suicide initiative by a margin of 1 percent. Implementation had been held up by court suits and legislative concerns about details of the law. Rather than attempt to remedy those concerns, the Legislature referred a proposal to rescind the entire measure to the voters. Not unexpectedly, a highly emotional election campaign resulted. The referendum was rejected (the suicide law sustained) by a surprising 60 percent. Editorials ranged all the way from no stand to extremely strong stands.

No Stand

The *Argus Observer* of Ontario was one of those that took no stand. It noted that it had taken a similar position in 1994. "The issue is too personal for us to tell others how they should vote," said an editorial titled "Whatever your opinion, vote!" Comment on the issue was limited to one paragraph:

There are valid reasons both for and against the issue, and each individual voter must weigh those reasons carefully before making a decision. We urge you, however, not to let propaganda cloud your decision. Check out facts, not statements made by one side or the other.[47]

Responding to Counter-Arguments

When the arguments and claims of the opposing side have received wide publicity during a campaign, one strategy for an editorial writer is to answer, and if possible, refute those arguments and claims. The *Mail Tribune* of Medford, Ore., took this approach in an editorial titled "Measure 51: no" and subtitled "Freedom of choice includes freedom to decide about death." After explaining the background of the ballot measure, the editorial urged voters "to listen to their friends, to their families and to their own hearts" rather than be swayed by "consultants or 30-second spots." More than half the editorial was devoted to citing and attempting to refute five "flawed" arguments made by opponents of the suicide law. The editorial ended with a positive argument: that the suicide law stood in the tradition of Oregonians taking pride in "the power to govern our own lives."

The Fine Print

Sometimes newspapers, like the U.S. Supreme Court, find it appropriate to base an endorsement on something less than the fundamental issue involved. The *East Oregonian* took that approach in an editorial titled "A right to die?"

Measure 51: No

Freedom of choice includes freedom to decide about death

Opponents of the 1994 assisted-suicide law, Measure 16, argue that it is "fatally flawed." They offer many technical arguments for repealing the measure. But the truth is that the real flaw they see is that the law permits physicians to render aid to someone who wants to die—a practice they oppose under all circumstances on moral or religious grounds.

Many of these people believe that God, not the individual, should decide the hour and nature of our deaths.

That's a position we can understand and respect, but still disagree with. We do so without rancor or hostility. Freedom of choice in this world, to be truly free, means freedom for individuals to consult with their doctors about how their lives are concluded. The same freedom gives individuals, doctors or hospitals the freedom to refuse to participate in a practice they feel is wrong.

Measure 51 on the Nov. 4 mail-in ballot would repeal Measure 16, which gave mentally competent, terminally ill Oregonians the right to ask their physician for carefully controlled aid in dying. The *Mail Tribune* editorial board recommends a no vote on Measure 51.

The measure's phrasing is confusing. A yes vote on Measure 51 does away with physician-assisted suicide; a no vote supports the 1994 physician-assisted suicide law.

This inherent confusion is not being eased by the political and ad campaign now under way. Oregon is rightly viewed around the country as a pivotal battleground. The pro–Measure 51 campaign, and to a lesser extent the campaign against it, is being orchestrated or financed by out-of-state interests.

We urge Oregonians to listen to their friends, to their families and to their own hearts. This is a personal matter that should not be decided by consultants or 30-second spots.

Oregon legislators have the power to fix any problem with the law. And opponents had a chance to work with legislators. They decided instead to try to deny everyone a physician's aid in dying.

Now they have the burden of proof. But the case they've made is flawed:

■ **Dying people will flood into Oregon.** Physician-assisted suicide is an option that the weakest, sickest terminally ill will use to die on their own terms, on their home turf. It's hard to believe that armies of terminally ill people will stream across the borders to die alone, far from their homes, families and physicians. The worst

that carried the subhead: "Although crafted in compassion, Measure 16 should be repealed." "Compassion tells us to end the suffering, to let friends and loved ones die with dignity," the editorial said. "But what Measure 16 doesn't do is provide a compelling argument that this will always be the case . . . . [T]aking mass doses of barbiturates orally doesn't always work or have the peaceful effects that are sought in the first place." Recognizing that "basic human rights" must be considered, the editorial asked, but did not answer, the question: "Does a person have the right [to] end his or her life?" For the writer, a more immediate consideration was the flawed nature of the law and the knowledge "that government does a poor job of dealing with issues of such personal consequences." The editorial concluded:

Until a better law is written, and there's no guarantee that will happen, we must protect against possible abuses and the Pandora's box

that such a law could open. That can be achieved only by repealing Measure 16.[48]

of the scare tactics paint a picture of piles of dead people to be buried at public expense.

That's unlikely. But the opposition rhetoric suggests that there is a great need and demand for dignified, individually determined death that is denied people elsewhere.

■ **The law requires no family notification.** Opponents express outrage that grandma might get a doctor's help in dying without consulting her relatives first. Well, of course! Competent adults aren't required to get family approval for anything else in life—and imagine the complications if we were. If we want to encourage family involvement in these final matters, are we going to accomplish that with laws that make suicide shameful, secretive and illegal, and that make criminals out of doctors or relatives who lend aid?

■ **Doctors can be wrong diagnosing terminal illness, or length of life left.** The inspirational stories of people who have survived such diagnoses underscore the most important point: Individuals, not doctors, should decide when life becomes unlivable. People can, and do, battle cancer or other seemingly hopeless ailments, and should get every bit of treatment and hospice care available. But when all those options fail, individuals—not doctors, hospitals or hospice workers—should be able to decide when it's time to die.

■ **Pills don't work, and people who take them can linger on for hours or days.**

Opponents have twisted data from the Netherlands into an argument that a quarter of all attempts "fail." The fact is that most who want to die with oral medicine do so peacefully in their sleep, most in the first few hours, almost all within 10 hours. Researchers in the Netherlands have objected to the way their research has been distorted.

Once assisted suicide becomes legal, doctors and pharmacists can develop prescription pills or elixirs that the law now forbids.

■ **Hospice care makes assisted suicide unnecessary.** Care for the dying is improving, partly as a result of the discussions this issue inspired. Physicians and hospitals (especially those opposed to assisted suicide) have an incentive to make palliative care so good and accessible that assisted suicide is an option few people will ever need.

But that's not the case today. The strongest supporters of assisted suicide are people who have watched a loved one die a long, tortured, powerless death. They know that these last days are not always the brave, noble coming-to-terms glorified by assisted-suicide opponents.

Oregon's proudest history is as a state at the forefront of efforts to give independent citizens the power to govern our own lives. A natural extension of that great tradition is to give individuals—not churches, not doctors, not hospitals—the power to govern our own deaths, too.

Mail Tribune

The Basic Issue

The *Daily Astorian* of Astoria, Ore., in opposing repeal, took a stand on what it saw as the basic issue: "a choice between the sanctity of life and patient autonomy":

Those who seek to repeal Measure 16 (the Death With Dignity Act) believe that the last moments of life are sacred and that there is no ethical justification for allowing people to commit suicide. Those who favor this new law believe that people should be given the means to end their lives in a clinically informed manner, as opposed to pointing a revolver to their head and pulling the trigger.

The editorial accused opponents of the law of being "deceitful and paternalistic." It said that the drive to put the referendum on the ballot "was based on a lie" about supposed new "damaging information" that turned out to be false. It said that putting Measure 51 to a vote was "paternalistic in its inherent notion that people must not be given autonomy in the decision to end their lives. It is doubly paternalistic in its second-guessing of a decision which Oregonians have already made." Furthermore, the editorial said, "We would not be having this vote if it were not for the intense interest of the Vatican. That is not a religious comment; it is an acknowledgment of major league politics, which is based on money."

The final three paragraphs:

Myths abound in the discussion of Measure 51. So does emotion. In approaching this initiative, the challenge is to remove the religious overtones of the debate and strip away the emotional. Underneath that level of vocal argument, there is a serious proposal for your attention.

It comes down to a question of choice that is not unlike that which is presented by abortion. The question is whether people may have the right to end their lives with medical assistance.

We believe that patients should be allowed that freedom. We urge you to vote "no" on Measure 51.[49]

The *Bulletin* of Bend, which supported repeal, also based its editorial on what it saw as the basic issue. Doctor-assisted suicide, it said, represented a "wrenching" shock to "our cultural values." Giving doctors the power to legally take human life "could rip apart the assumed bonds of trust between the health care industry and our society, doctor and patient, family and dying relatives, even rich and poor." The editorial said, "We can only guess at the repercussions of this shattered trust. Certainly our language, our value structure, what we hold to be right or wrong, public or private, legal or illegal, acceptable or commendable, allowed or preferred—all will be affected in some way."[50]

Going All Out

Usually a newspaper will run an editorial or two on a ballot proposition and move on to other issues. But, once in a while, editorial writers feel so strongly that they will launch full campaigns to influence voters. To urge readers to support repeal of doctor-assisted suicide, the *Oregonian* on consecutive days ran five editorials, each 36 inches in length. ("The Vote of Our Lives," October 8–12, 1997, The Oregonian, © 1997 Oregonian Publishing Co. All rights reserved. Reprinted with Permission.) On the first day the editorial argued that studies showed drugs would result in death only about a quarter of the time. "Measure 16 folks say critics are making up potential horrors if the barbiturates and other drugs don't work as planned," the editorial said. "If only this were true." The editorial described what could occur:

In a 1996 report, The American Association of Suicidology's committee on doctor-assisted suicide warned of "the high likelihood of serious accidents" and notes: "Vomiting may occur as the patient slips into a coma, with aspiration of the vomitus."

The report says that barbiturates, morphine and other drugs can at times cause confusion:

"Confused patients in states of intoxification may experience terror, panic, or become assaultive." More proof? A 1971 article—"Acute Barbiturate Poisoning"—warns of these dangers: kidney failure, water on the lung, severe brain damage and blood-clotting in the lungs, causing spasms and severe shortness of breath.[51]

The second editorial dealt with the "cruel" and "undignified" use of a plastic bag over a patient's head in cases in which drugs failed to produce death.

"Somehow we think Oregonians had something other than 'Turkey bags' in mind when contemplating 'death with dignity' in the fall of 1994," the editorial said. "Yet this is just where pills-only Measure 16 would leave terminally ill Oregonians who think they want to end their lives." Oregonians would become "lab rats" in an "experiment" in producing death, the editorial argued.[52]

The third editorial argued that terminal patients who suffered from depression were not likely to make good death-with-dignity decisions.[53]

The fourth editorial contended that advances in the treatment of pain and the greater availability of hospice care made assisted suicide unnecessary.[54]

The final editorial argued that the so-called safeguards in the suicide law would not protect patients but health-care providers. It said:

In short, there are many safeguards for doctors, no matter how fishy their conduct. This in an act that hands doctors awesome new powers and scraps millennia of establishment medical ethics.

The cold truth is that Oregon has more safeguards for death-row murderers than Measure 16 has for the dying.

The editorial concluded:

Here "death with dignity" forms the title of a grotesque law that an American Medical Association News editorial calls "a license to kill."

A license to kill depressed terminally ill Oregonians who will find no refuge in the law's sham safeguards.

A license to kill people who can't advocate for themselves and might be a costly bother to others.

A license to kill vulnerable human beings, who need help—pain relief and hospice—not hemlock.[55]

CONCLUSION

Following an election, editors are likely to find themselves in as untenable a situation as before the election. If most of the candidates they have endorsed win, the editors and their newspapers are accused of controlling the election and influencing the election of the candidates of their choice. If more than a few of the endorsed candidates lose, the newspapers are perceived to have lost credibility.

I have often had voters say to me on election night that the newspaper was, or was not, right in its predictions. Somehow these voters seem to think that a newspaper is calling a horse race—waiting to tie its endorsement to winners.

Election time also can be hazardous for editorial writers. The heightened emotion of a political campaign, plus the black-and-white nature of endorsement decisions, can produce crises and magnify differences of opinion between writers and publishers that might be reconcilable at other times. Perhaps these periodic crises serve a purpose in forcing publishers and writers to re-evaluate whether they still see eye to eye on major issues. Perhaps such crises keep writers from being lulled into writing whatever they know will get by their publishers and not infringe too deeply on their consciences. But in these tense situations both publishers and writers can overreact and later regret that they acted precipitously.

Credibility is the only thing a newspaper has to offer in its editorial endorsements. If a staff thinks it can fairly and knowledgeably endorse one candidate over another, it should be able to do so in a credible manner. If, on the other hand, the staff does not know enough about the candidates, or does not see one candidate as better than another, or lacks the fortitude to risk the wrath of unhappy readers, it should not endorse. A major task of the editorial page is to comment knowledgeably on public issues, whether you prefer to call that urging voters or merely informing them. An editorial page staff that sits out an election loses out on a big part of the political process.

Questions and Exercises

1. What do you think should be the role of the editorial page in an election? Should a newspaper endorse candidates?

2. How do you evaluate the argument that endorsements exert undue and undesirable influence on voters?

3. How do you evaluate the argument that the credibility of the news columns is jeopardized when newspapers endorse candidates?

4. Do you think a presidential nominee has legitimate grounds for complaint when newspaper endorsements are lined up four or five to one against him? Why or why not?

5. Could you work on an editorial page that had "publishers' four-year itch"—a congenial editorial policy for almost four years and then for a month or two a policy with which you did not agree?

6. Ask editors of newspapers in your area or state how editorial endorsements are determined on their papers. Who is involved in the decision-making? Who has the last say if there is disagreement?

7. Ask editors to evaluate the comparative impact they think their editorials have on ballot issues vs. candidate races and on local vs. state and national races.

8. Have any of the papers in your area allowed dissenting editorial staff members to disagree in print with the papers' endorsements? If so, how were the dissents presented? How did the paper explain the presence of more than one opinion? Did publication of the dissent draw comment from readers in the letters column?

9. Find two or more editorials from different newspapers on the same ballot issue or candidate race. Compare their approaches. What type of reader is most likely to be influenced by each approach? For the particular race or issue involved, which editorial do you regard as more appropriate or more likely to influence readers? Why?

10. Write an endorsement editorial that equitably compares two candidates and avoids making a choice between the two until the conclusion. Then rewrite the editorial to make clear from the beginning your choice of candidate. Which was easier to write? Which types of voters are likely to be influenced by each of them?

CHAPTER 16 Other Types of Opinion Writing

Newspaper editorials are not the only type of opinion writing that journalists are likely to have the opportunity to write. In this chapter we will look briefly at:

1. Broadcast editorials
2. Reviews
3. Signed articles

BROADCAST EDITORIALS

Should broadcast station owners feel the same responsibility that newspaper publishers feel to provide for exchanges of opinion on issues of the day?

A strong "yes" was the answer given by Boyd A. Levet of KGW-TV, Portland, and the last president of the National Broadcast Editorial Association, even as his organization was preparing to disband because of a decline in broadcast editorial writing across the country. "Opinion is part of the full venue of journalism," Levet wrote in *The Editorialist.* "I know of no newspaper that earned community respect without opinion. Clearly stations diminish their journalistic influence if they do not air opinion."[3]

Broadcast editorials "show that the station is directly involved in the community—sufficiently involved to be willing to share management's opinions about community issues and events," G. Donald Gale of KSL-TV in Salt Lake City wrote in a *Masthead* article titled "The Need for Broadcast Editorials."[4]

"The editorial is the most mature form of journalism," Daniel W. Toohey wrote, referring specifically to public broadcasting. "Without the right to editorialize, public broadcasting will be relegated to permanent adolescence."[5] He could have said the same about private broadcasting, although public stations are more reluctant to editorialize than private stations are.

In spite of these admonitions, broadcast editorials seem to be in decline. A survey in 1978 found that 61 percent of television stations editorialized. A survey in 1994 found only 33 percent did.[6] In 1981, the National Broadcast Editorial Association (NBEA) had 188 members. The number declined to 65 in 1991, when the NBEA disbanded and surviving members were urged to join the National Conference of Editorial Writers.[7]

One reason for fewer broadcast editorials seems to be financial. Slightly more than half the non-editorializing stations attributed the absence of editorials to "lack of budget for research and writing."[8] A former president of NBEA, Marjorie Arons-Barron, said much of the decline came when mergers and acquisitions of stations across the country resulted in huge new debts for the owners. "It was easiest to cut back in the news department," Arons-Barron said.[9] A former editorial director for WMAG-TV in Chicago, Dillon Smith, said that in his experience the "bottom line was to cut jobs that don't bring in any profits."[10]

Slightly more than a quarter of non-editorializing stations said they did not use editorials because they regarded them as "incompatible" with their news operations. Other reasons included "others in the market do not editorialize" (about 11 percent), "desire not to offend listeners" (almost 9 percent), "desire to avoid controversial programming" (almost 8 percent) and "too many complaints from special interest groups" (almost 8 percent). In short, a substantial number of stations do not editorialize because they lack either the commitment or the courage to speak out.

The networks too have beat a retreat from editorial comment. With the death of Eric Sevareid (CBS), the retirement of John Chancellor (NBC) and the stepping down of Bill Moyers (PBS), network editorials have disappeared.[11] One reason cited was that it is a rare person who has the stature to do the job. "The key to commentary is you have to have a person of just enormous magnitude, and if you don't have that person, don't do it," ABC News *Nightline* producer Tom Bettag was quoted as saying.[12]

At both network and local levels, commentary has been squeezed out because of time limitations. With only 22 minutes available on a nightly news broadcast, news directors resist setting aside a minute or two for a talking head.[13]

The demise of the Fairness Doctrine has been cited as another reason for the decline in broadcast editorializing. In 1941 the Federal Communications Commission (FCC) ruled in the "Mayflower Decision" that a station should not be an advocate (state an opinion). In 1949 the FCC changed its mind but admonished stations to provide a reasonable opportunity for airing all sides of controversial issues. That was the beginning of what became known as the Fairness Doctrine. As part of their public service requirement, stations were expected to provide a balanced presentation of views (including their own) over the course of their broadcast schedule. In 1987 the FCC dropped the Fairness Doctrine. Consequently, "[a]s the regulatory touch grew lighter, and as stations look for ways to cut cost, cutting editorials was a way to save money," Nicholas DeLuca of KCBS-AM of San Francisco told *Quill* magazine.[14] The 1994 survey found that, among the stations that do editorials, only 16 percent said that their primary reason for editorializing was "to satisfy FCC requirements."[15]

One of the strongest statements supporting broadcast editorializing came from Frank Stanton, one-time president of CBS: "Any station manager worth his salt will learn the law, hire the people, sacrifice the time, explore the issues, risk corporate or governmental intervention and welcome adverse public opinion to have said on his station what he thinks needs to—and ought—be said. And if he does not care enough, perhaps because he is afraid of losing sponsors, offending public opinion, or creating problems with stockholders, then he does not deserve the job."[16]

Broadcast vs. Print

Journalists who write in broadcast style are admonished to

- Keep it "short and simple."
- Write in a conversational style.
- Make points quickly and clearly.
- Use short, easily comprehended words.

The result of this type of writing, in the view of a surveyed group of newspaper editorial writers, is likely to be a broadcast editorial that is superficial, oversimplified and lacking in guts. But the broadcast editorial writers who were surveyed expressed a different view. They contended that brief editorials were not necessarily superficial, and that broadcast, especially television, offers a more personal, dynamic approach to offering opinion than the print media do.[17]

Representative of the newspaper writers' views were those of Marcia Sielaff of the *Phoenix Gazette*. She thought that time restrictions and legal restraints push television toward going for "attention grabbers" and aesthetics in lieu of in-depth news and analysis, and that television is not as demanding of its audiences or its writers.[18] One television writer, Phil Johnson of WWL- TV in New Orleans, contended that because television writers face strict time limitations and must make every second count, broadcast editorials are "just the opposite" of superficial. Television writers "must condense the issue and get more meaning in less time," he said.[19] Television, he added, does tend to emphasize personality over content. "Television elevates the [person] with a great personality," Johnson said. Even though "dumb as a piece of wood," if the figure before the camera "smiles at the people, they think it's nice." Lesley Crosson of WCBS-TV in New York noted that television audiences often pay as much attention to inflections, apparel and personality as to the message itself. Another characteristic of broadcast, she said, is that listeners preoccupied with other matters may miss something that was said.[20] With broadcast, they have no second chance to fill in what they missed. They can't reread a paragraph they failed to understand on first reading or return to a vaguely-heard editorial at a more convenient time.

Robert S. McCord, who has written editorials for both television and newspapers, said he was surprised to find that writing 200 words for television was a lot harder than writing 800 words for an op-ed column.[21] "As I have always done, I tried to vary sentence structure and length," he said. "But it doesn't work on television. You have to use simple sentences and be very direct and crystal clear. Elaborate construction, adjectives and similes eat up too much time." He found that he had to try for only one or two main points. He also learned that certain topics don't lend themselves to television commentary: "[T]hey are too minor, too complex or too dull to capture the attention of a man or woman who has put in a hard day's work and is just about to go to bed."

Another surprise was the amount of recognition and reaction he received from the public. "I've never experienced anything like it despite all the years I've been dishing out opinion in Little Rock," he said. "I can't go anywhere without being recognized and stopped by people I have never met. It's not that they agree with what I say or that they are impressed by my brilliance. It's simply that they seem to appreciate being challenged to make a decision about a public issue." He said his experience convinced him that the two-thirds of stations that do not editorialize "are wrong."

Broadcast and print editorials differ most sharply in the manner in which they are presented. A television editorial is likely to include film footage and be delivered by an identifiable person. Even though the opinion expressed may be that of an editorial board, one person (often the station's general manager) makes the presentation. I know of no research that indicates whether such presentations are more or less persuasive with viewers than anonymous print editorials. Probably the range of persuasive effects differs more within each type than between types. As is the case with print editorials, some broadcast editorials are far more effective than others.

Preparing the Broadcast Editorial

Until the time of actual writing, the editorial preparation process for broadcast is basically the same as for a newspaper. As with newspaper editorials, the broadcast editorial presumably represents the views of the management. Similarly, whether the editorial is specifically the opinion of the owner, the general manager, the news director, the editorial director or an individual editorial writer, it must be written by one person, though perhaps edited by others.

The person assigned to write a broadcast editorial should go through the same nine steps of editorial writing described in Chapter 10, "Nine Steps to Editorial Writing": selecting a topic, determining the purpose of the editorial, determining the audience, deciding on the tone of the editorial, researching the topic, determining the general format, writing the beginning of the editorial, writing the body of the editorial and writing the conclusion.

In selecting a topic and determining the audience, broadcast editorial writers probably are more limited than newspaper writers. Newspapers usually publish more than one editorial each day. A reader who is not attracted to one editorial may be attracted to another. Even if none of the editorials appears interesting, the reader can quickly move to other parts of the editorial or another part of the paper without "wasting" more than a few seconds between items of interest. Broadcast viewers and listeners have no such choices, unless they switch channels, which of course no editorial writer wants them to do. Listeners don't enjoy sitting through dull one-minute editorials on topics in which they are not interested. So the first task of the broadcast editorial writer is to pick a topic likely to appeal to the vast majority of listeners.

Broadcast writers also have a more limited range of options for the tone of editorials. Long expository pieces are clearly out. Editorials that require extensive or complex arguments are difficult to present over the air, at least in the framework of a typical news broadcast. Thoughts presented in a subtle or ironic manner may be misinterpreted or missed completely.

Broadcast writers, like print writers, have a choice of starting their editorials by stating their conclusions or reaching conclusions after arguments have been presented. Broadcast writers, like newspaper writers, may sometimes find it more appropriate to present opposing arguments or arguments on only one side. Of course, the time limitations of broadcast preclude the presentation of more than a few arguments, whether on one side or more than one.

Writing the Broadcast Editorial

Here are a few general rules for writing broadcast editorials:

- Writers should remember that they are writing for the ear, not the eye. A broadcast editorial should rate as "easy to read" on the Flesch readability scale mentioned in Chapter 11.

- A broadcast editorial must be brief, clear and interesting. A length of 150 to 250 words is typical.

- Sentences should be short and presented in a straightforward manner. Subjects and verbs should be close together.

- The writing should be free from hard-to-pronounce or easily misunderstood words.

- Strings of modifying words should be avoided. Instead of saying "Virginia Tech Communications Studies Professor Valerie Speer," say: "Valerie Speer, professor of communication studies at Virginia Tech." The latter uses more words but gives listeners a much better chance to comprehend the four separate ideas (name, position, department, university).

- Contractions, such as "The mayor's embarrassed by this," may sound more natural than "The mayor is embarrassed by this."

- Incomplete sentences may be used effectively. Some may start with a conjunction, and even without a subject. Following the statement about the mayor, for instance, may be: "And should be."

- Verbs also may be dropped: "Good news on the economy today."

- "That" and "which" often are dropped if the meaning is clear without them.

Broadcast news writing places a lot of emphasis on "today," to make listeners think they are getting the latest information. Use of the present tense also helps to give listeners the feeling that they are hearing the news as it happens. Editorial writers should keep these listeners in mind, but they should not feel that they have to strain for the "today" angle.

In broadcast writing, it is even more important for writers to outline what they intend to say, to make certain that points are made clearly and in the appropriate order. Broadcast writers may find it helpful to clarify what they mean to say if they apply the designations suggested in Chapter 10: S (statement), A₁ (argument on one side), A₂ (argument on the other side), D (discussion) and C (conclusion).

To provide an example of how broadcast editorial writing differs from newspaper editorial writing, the editorial written in Chapter 10, "The Case of the Dirty Hands," has been rewritten in broadcast style by G. Donald Gale of KSL-TV, Salt Lake City, vice president for news and public affairs for Bonneville International Corp. Gale said that he made four basic changes:

1. Fewer words. Broadcasters have very limited time periods to present their arguments.
2. Fewer secondary ideas. We must focus on a single concept if we hope to communicate.
3. Stronger opening. The first sentence must not only grab the listener but state the case.
4. Shorter sentences. Broadcasters must breathe now and then.

DIRTY HANDS AND JOURNALISM

THE DIRTY HANDS JOURNALISTS EXPOSE SHOULD NOT BE THEIR OWN.

THAT WAS THE CASE IN FOOD LION VERSUS ABC NEWS. A NORTH CAROLINA JURY DECIDED ABC REPORTERS DIRTIED THEIR HANDS WHILE EXPOSING THE DIRTY HANDS OF FOOD LION MEAT HANDLERS.

CLEARLY, FOOD LION AND ITS EMPLOYEES COMPROMISED FOOD HANDLING STANDARDS. VIDEOTAPE FROM THE ABC REPORT PROVES FOOD LION BROKE THE LAW. THE QUESTION FACING THE JURY WAS: DID ABC ALSO BREAK THE LAW WHEN REPORTERS USED DECEPTION TO OBTAIN JOBS AT FOOD LION? THE JURY SAID: "YES."

THE DILEMMA IS AS OLD AS JOURNALISM. IN EVERY NEWSROOM AND EVERY JOURNALISM CURRICULUM, EXPERTS DEBATE HOW FAR REPORTERS SHOULD GO TO GET THE TRUTH. UPTON SINCLAIR WENT UNDERCOVER TO REPORT SHOCKING PRACTICES IN THE MEAT PACKING INDUSTRY. HIS PRINTED WORDS CHANGED THOSE PRACTICES AND DRAMATICALLY IMPROVED THE QUALITY OF MEAT PRODUCTS.

TELEVISION ADDED A NEW DIMENSION. WORDS ARE NO LONGER
ENOUGH; TELEVISION REPORTERS ALSO NEED PICTURES. TODAY'S
TECHNOLOGY MAKES IT POSSIBLE TO HIDE CAMERAS THE WAY UPTON
SINCLAIR HID HIS PENCIL AND NOTEBOOK.

THE JURY HAD NO PROBLEM WITH HIDDEN CAMERAS. THE JURY
OBJECTED TO THE FACT THAT ABC REPORTERS DID NOT TELL THE
TRUTH ON THE JOB APPLICATIONS THEY USED TO GET THEMSELVES
AND THEIR CAMERAS INSIDE FOOD LION STORES.

WE AGREE WITH THE JURY. FRAUD IS NOT AN ACCEPTABLE STRATEGY
FOR NEWS REPORTING. JOURNALISTS LOSE CREDIBILITY WHEN THEY
DIRTY THEIR OWN HANDS IN EFFORTS TO EXPOSE WRONGDOING—NO
MATTER HOW SERIOUS THE WRONGDOING MAY BE.

The original editorial contained 540 words; Gale's editorial 248.
Sentences in the newspaper editorial averaged 23 words; sentences in the
broadcast editorial averaged 12 words. Listeners knew at the beginning of the
broadcast editorial how the writer thought about the Food Lion case. Readers
did not know, for sure, until the end of the newspaper editorial. Those are
some of the differences.

The broadcast editorial writer must remember that television is at least
partly an entertainment medium. Serious subjects don't necessarily have to
be approached in a serious manner. When "Lucy" the sheep was cloned,
Gale's thoughts turned to two-minded Hamlet in an editorial titled "Clone or
Not Clone."

CLONE OR NOT CLONE

TO CLONE OR NOT TO CLONE: THAT IS THE QUESTION.

SHAKESPEARE WOULD TURN OVER IN HIS GRAVE—PERHAPS WITH A
SMILE.

BECAUSE THE POWERFUL SOLILOQUY OF HAMLET ABOUT LIFE AND
DEATH CERTAINLY APPLIES TO TODAY'S DEBATE OVER CLONING.
SCIENTISTS IN ENGLAND MADE AN EXACT PHYSICAL COPY—A CLONE—
OF A SHEEP. IT TOUCHED OFF A WORLDWIDE DEBATE ABOUT THE
ETHICS OF CLONING HUMAN BEINGS.

CAN SCIENTISTS DO IT? PERHAPS. IS IT A GOOD IDEA? PROBABLY
NOT.

AS HAMLET SO ELOQUENTLY ARGUED, THERE ARE TOO MANY UNKNOWNS
TO MAKE THE CHOICE A RATIONAL ONE—EVEN THOUGH THE DECISION
TO CLONE OR NOT TO CLONE HAS MUCH LESS SURFACE FINALITY
THAN THE DECISION TO BE OR NOT TO BE.

IT'S IMPOSSIBLE TO DUPLICATE A HUMAN BEING. MORE THAN ANY
OTHER CREATURE, WE ARE PRODUCTS OF OUR ENVIRONMENT AS WELL
AS OUR HEREDITY. WHO'S TO SAY HOW AN EXACT PHYSICAL COPY OF
YOU MIGHT DEVELOP IN A DIFFERENT ENVIRONMENT? DIFFERENT
PARENTS. DIFFERENT FOOD. DIFFERENT SURROUNDINGS. DIFFERENT
EDUCATION. DIFFERENT EXPERIENCES. DIFFERENT EVERYTHING
EXCEPT BASIC DNA.

SOME YEARS FROM NOW, HE OR SHE MIGHT RESEMBLE YOU,
PHYSICALLY, BUT WOULD ALMOST CERTAINLY NOT BE LIKE YOU,
MENTALLY, EMOTIONALLY, SPIRITUALLY, OR DEVELOPMENTALLY.
"AYE, THERE'S THE RUB," AS HAMLET MIGHT SAY.

EACH OF US IS UNIQUE. EACH OF US IS A MIRACLE. EACH OF US
HAS SINGULAR VALUE.

KSL BELIEVES SCIENCE DESERVES APPLAUSE FOR LEARNING THE
SECRETS OF HEREDITY. BUT SCIENCE, ALONE, CAN NEVER CREATE
ANOTHER SHAKESPEARE—OR ANOTHER YOU.

  KS LAM-TV

Broadcast stations in general have acquired a reputation for being reluctant to speak out on controversial issues—or to speak out at all. But Chuck Stokes of WXYZ/Channel 7 Detroit ("Newspaper Strike Anniversary") admonished both parties in a strike of newspaper workers against the Detroit newspapers. After a year off the job, the editorial said, the workers should have learned that, given today's economic conditions, they would be better off negotiating from inside, and the newspapers should have learned that they had done themselves a disservice with their "self-serving propaganda."

NEWSPAPER STRIKE ANNIVERSARY

THE DETROIT NEWSPAPER STRIKE. ONE YEAR WITH NO SETTLEMENT
IN SIGHT AND NO REAL WINNERS.

BROKEN BONES. BROKEN CAREERS. BROKEN FAMILIES. BROKEN
FRIENDSHIPS. LOST INCOME. LOST PROFITS.

OH SURE, NEWSPAPER MANAGEMENT CAN CLAIM IT NOW HAS A LOT
MORE CONTROL OVER ITS BUSINESS. THAT'S TRUE. THAT'S ALSO A
BIG PLUS TO THEIR CORPORATE HEADQUARTERS AND STOCKHOLDERS.
BUT THEIR CIRCULATION AND REVENUE ARE DOWN CONSIDERABLY.

OVER THE LAST YEAR, THE NEWSPAPERS, THE STRIKERS AND THE
CITY OF DETROIT HAVE SUFFERED A SERIOUS PUBLIC RELATIONS
BLOW. RUNNING A SUCCESSFUL NEWSPAPER IS A LOT DIFFERENT
THAN MOST OTHER BUSINESSES. IT'S A BUSINESS THAT DEPENDS
HEAVILY ON TWO WORDS: "PUBLIC TRUST." TO SOME DEGREE,
THAT'S BEEN LOST. GETTING IT BACK WON'T BE EASY.

AS FOR THE SIX STRIKING UNIONS, THEY HAVE THEIR PRIDE
INTACT, A PRETTY STRIKE NEWSPAPER THEY CAN FLAUNT . . .
BUT NOT MUCH MORE.

A PAINFUL LESSON TO BE LEARNED FROM THIS IS THAT IN THE
1990S UNIONS ARE SAFER—AND PERHAPS WISER—NEGOTIATING FROM
THE INSIDE, EMPLOYED, THAN FROM THE OUTSIDE, UNEMPLOYED.
TIMES HAVE CHANGED. ECONOMICS HAVE CHANGED. AND UNION
LEADERS WHO FAIL TO ADAPT TO THESE CHANGES IN A CREATIVE
WAY PUT THEIR MEMBERS AT GREAT RISK.

THE FREE PRESS AND THE NEWS, ON THE OTHER HAND, HAVE DONE
THEMSELVES A DISSERVICE BY PUBLISHING ADS, NEWS STORIES AND
COLUMNS THAT AT TIMES WERE NOTHING MORE THAN SELF-SERVING
PROPAGANDA.

THIS HAS BEEN A PAINFUL YEAR, NOT JUST FOR THOSE DIRECTLY
INVOLVED BUT FOR THE ENTIRE METRO DETROIT COMMUNITY. IT'S

AN ANNIVERSARY ALL RIGHT . . . BUT IT'S CERTAINLY NOT ONE
WORTH CELEBRATING. WE CAN ONLY HOPE THAT THIS TIME NEXT
YEAR DETROIT'S NEWSPAPER STRIKE WILL BE HISTORY. THERE ARE
NO REAL WINNERS.

I'M CHUCK STOKES AND THAT'S WHERE CHANNEL 7 STANDS.

  WXYZ/Channel 7/Detroit

In broadcast writing, serious subjects don't necessarily have to be treated
in a serious manner. Neil Heinen, editorial director of WISC-TV (Madison,
Wis.), obviously had fun writing about a new commission set up to determine
why Americans are so cynical about public matters ("No, We Don't Want to
Go to Washington to Tell You Why We're Cynical of Washington!").

NO, WE DON'T WANT TO GO TO WASHINGTON TO TELL YOU WHY WE'RE CYNICAL OF WASHINGTON!

THERE'S BEEN A NEW COMMISSION ESTABLISHED TO FIND OUT WHY
AMERICANS ARE "TICKED OFF AT SO MANY THINGS," CYNICAL,
DISTRESSED, ANGRY.

IT'S HEADED BY FORMER EDUCATION SECRETARY WILLIAM BENNET
AND FORMER SENATOR SAM NUNN. IT'S MADE UP PRIMARILY OF
COLLEGE PRESIDENTS, BUSINESS LEADERS AND FOUNDATION HEADS.
IT'S FUNDED BY A MILLION DOLLAR GRANT. HERE'S ITS AGENDA:
THREE PUBLIC HEARINGS IN WASHINGTON. I'M NOT KIDDING.

YOU WANT TO KNOW WHY WE'RE ANGRY, DISTRESSED AND CYNICAL?
BECAUSE NATIONAL CIVICS PROJECTS EXPECT US TO PICK UP AND
GO TO WASHINGTON TO "TESTIFY" IN FRONT OF BUREAUCRATS!

LOOK, WE'RE ALL IN FAVOR OF CIVIC RENEWAL PROJECTS. BUT
LET'S TRY THIS: PUT SOME REGULAR CITIZENS ON THE COMMITTEE,
BREAK INTO SUB-COMMITTEES AND HOLD HEARINGS IN, SAY,
BARNEVELD OR FORT ATKINSON OR TOPEKA OR SPOKANE.

WE'D ACTUALLY BE INTERESTED IN DISCUSSING HOW WE COULD
BETTER CONNECT WITH EACH OTHER AND OUR GOVERNMENT. BUT COME
ON OUT TO OUR PLACE FOR A CHANGE, AND WE'LL TALK.

  WISC-TV

Writing Better Editorials

While the NBEA's magazine, *The Editorialist*, was alive, Professor Richard Elam of the University of North Carolina–Chapel Hill conducted a series of critiques of broadcast editorials. He pointed to faults and good points and suggested how the editorials could be rewritten. One critique was a lesson in "how to sound conversational, but waste words."[22]

"When we 'write as we talk,' that doesn't mean we write as people talk," he wrote. "Heaven forbid. We mean 'create a conversational tone, but not rattle.' Sounding 'folksy' isn't a license to waste words." Eleven "fatty" phrases Elam identified in the following editorial are indicated in bold type. Six uses of the vague word "it" appear in italic. Elam eliminated seven of the "fatty" phrases and five of the six "its" in his rewritten version. The "it" that remains is clear in the rewritten version. The four unchanged "fatty" phrases, or the remaining parts of them, might have been cut out with additional editing, though the same could be said about most editorials.

ORIGINAL EDITORIAL

OUR COUNTY BOARD OF WATER SUPPLY COULD'VE **SAVED ITSELF A LOT OF GRIEF** LAST WEEK. **THOSE PEOPLE FROM** THE OUTLYING AREA WANTED THE BOARD TO DECLARE THE OUTLYING SLAUGHTERHOUSE MATTER A CONTESTED CASE.

NOT AN UNREASONABLE REQUEST, SINCE *IT* IS, **IN FACT**, BEING CONTESTED. BY OFFICIALLY DECLARING *IT* CONTESTED THE BOARD WOULD THEN BE OBLIGATED TO HEAR THE ARGUMENTS OF THOSE PROTESTING THE ISSUING OF WATER PERMITS TO COMPANY PACKERS, AFTER WHICH *IT* COULD RULE **ANY WAY** *IT* PLEASED.

HAD THAT BEEN DONE, EVERYBODY WOULD'VE HAD A CHANCE TO **SPEAK HIS PIECE, AT THE VERY LEAST**. AND WHILE THAT WOULD PROBABLY NOT MOLLIFY THE LOSING SIDE, *IT* CERTAINLY WOULD'VE TAKEN SOME OF THE PASSION **FROM** *ITS* CAUSE.

AS *IT* IS, THE OUTLYING RESIDENTS HAVE MORAL INDIGNATION ON THEIR SIDE. IN EFFECT, THEY HAVE BEEN TOLD **TO SHUT UP AND GO HOME**, WHICH THEY ARE NOT LIKELY TO DO **AT THIS POINT**.

REWRITTEN EDITORIAL

OUR COUNTY BOARD OF WATER SUPPLY COULD'VE SAVED SOME GRIEF LAST WEEK. PEOPLE FROM THE OUTLYING AREA ASKED THE BOARD TO

DECLARE THE OUTLYING SLAUGHTERHOUSE MATTER A "CONTESTED" CASE. CALLING THE CASE "CONTESTED" WOULD HAVE OBLIGATED THE BOARD TO HEAR PROTESTS AGAINST ISSUING WATER PERMITS TO COMPANY PACKERS. AFTER HEARING THE ARGUMENTS, THEN THE BOARD COULD RULE ANY WAY IT PLEASED.

IF THE BOARD HAD RULED THE CASE CONTESTED, THEN EVERYBODY COULD HAVE SPOKEN HIS PIECE. TALKING PROBABLY WOULDN'T MOLLIFY THE LOSING SIDE, BUT DISCUSSION MIGHT HAVE REDUCED SOME OF THE PASSION.

BUT INSTEAD, THE OUTLYING RESIDENTS ARE MORALLY INDIGNANT. THE BOARD, IN EFFECT, TOLD THEM TO SHUT UP AND GO HOME—WHICH THEY ARE NOT LIKELY TO DO.

Other changes:

Passive voice in the original:

. . . THE BOARD WOULD THEN BE OBLIGATED TO HEAR . . . .

Active voice:

CALLING THE CASE 'CONTESTED' WOULD HAVE OBLIGATED THE BOARD . . . .

Wordy in the original:

. . . TO HEAR THE ARGUMENTS OF THOSE PROTESTING THE ISSUING . . . .

More succinct:

. . . TO HEAR PROTESTS AGAINST ISSUING . . . .

Vague and wordy:

HAD THAT BEEN DONE, EVERYBODY WOULD'VE HAD . . . .

Improved:

IF THE BOARD HAD RULED THE CASE CONTESTED, THEN EVERYBODY. . . .

Wordy:

```
. . . . THE OUTLYING RESIDENTS HAVE MORAL INDIGNATION ON
THEIR SIDE . . . .
```

Improved:

```
THE OUTLYING RESIDENTS ARE MORALLY INDIGNANT.
```

A different type of critique, more concerned with content than with wordiness, also was published in *The Editorialist* ("No Liability Insurance").[23] The

■ No Liability Insurance

(ORIGINAL)

No one really knows how many drivers in this state have no liability insurance.

We do know that over one hundred and twenty-five thousand drivers have been caught without insurance the law requires. The State Department of Motor Vehicles suspended the licenses of those drivers following accidents in which they were involved. They also found that these drivers had three times as many traffic violations, committed eight times as many other serious offenses and had 72 percent more accidents than insured drivers.

So why, we might ask, can't there be a crackdown on such people? Why can't we take them off the road?

We were amazed to learn that proof of insurance is not now required to get a driver's license or register a vehicle. Fifteen percent of the state's drivers simply have no insurance.

We find that legislation has often been introduced in recent years to require proof of insurance to get a license. Those laws have all been defeated. It seems that insurance companies have opposed such laws, as they do not want to be forced to cover irresponsible drivers such as we have described.

This major problem, however, is not going to go away until we get tough laws to stop the uninsured motorist.

(CRITIQUE)

Begins with two negatives. Negatives are weak. Turn it around and personalize it to give it more power.

The editorial "we" is okay, but it should not be overused. In this case, it serves only to add to the confusion of the sentence.

Turn this sentence around to build on the strength of the previous sentence.

The reference to "they" is confusing, since the Department is an "it," not a "they."

It would help your general manager to use commas on series, especially lengthy series.

An editorial should answer questions, not ask them.

Why were you amazed? Editorial writers should know such things. This weakens your hard-won credibility.

Again, the editorial "we" distracts in this case.

The laws were not defeated; the proposed laws or bills were.

You let the insurance companies off the hook too easily.

Hardly anyone uses "however" in conversational speech.

This is a weak ending. Call for specific action.

anonymous critic faulted the editorial for a negative opening and advised against overuse of "we" and confusing use of "they." Among other suggestions were that the writer answer questions (not raise them), take a tougher stand on the insurance companies and reach a stronger conclusion. Following these suggestions, the critic revised the editorial.

NO LIABILITY INSURANCE

(REVISED)

THERE'S A GOOD CHANCE THE DRIVER IN THE CAR NEXT TO YOU HAS NO LIABILITY INSURANCE—EVEN THOUGH STATE LAW REQUIRES IT.

LAST YEAR, ONE HUNDRED TWENTY-FIVE THOUSAND DRIVERS WERE CAUGHT WITHOUT INSURANCE. THEY WERE CAUGHT ONLY BECAUSE THEY HAD ACCIDENTS AND THEY COULDN'T COVER THE LOSSES THEY INFLICTED ON THEIR LAW-ABIDING VICTIMS.

VIOLATORS HAD THEIR DRIVER'S LICENSES SUSPENDED.

THAT'S ALL.

IN THE PROCESS, THE DEPARTMENT OF MOTOR VEHICLES LEARNED SOMETHING ELSE. COMPARED TO INSURED DRIVERS, VIOLATORS OF THE STATE INSURANCE LAW HAD THREE TIMES AS MANY TRAFFIC CITATIONS, EIGHT TIMES AS MANY SERIOUS ACCIDENTS AND 72 PERCENT MORE ACCIDENTS. IN OTHER WORDS, THOSE WHO IGNORE THE INSURANCE LAWS ARE LIKELY TO IGNORE OTHER LAWS AS WELL.

BUT THE STATE DOES NOT REQUIRE PROOF OF INSURANCE TO OBTAIN A DRIVERS LICENSE OR TO REGISTER A VEHICLE. AS A RESULT, AT LEAST 15 PERCENT OF THE STATE'S DRIVERS DO NOT HAVE INSURANCE—ONE OF EVERY SEVEN.

THE FAULT LIES PARTLY WITH THE INSURANCE COMPANIES. EVERY TIME THE LEGISLATURE CONSIDERS A BILL TO ENFORCE THE INSURANCE LAW, THE INSURANCE COMPANIES FIGHT AGAINST IT.

COMPANIES ARE AFRAID THEY WILL BE FORCED TO INSURE
IRRESPONSIBLE DRIVERS.

IT'S TIME TO PUT TEETH IN THE LIABILITY INSURANCE LAW.
PROOF OF INSURANCE SHOULD BE PART OF EVERY LICENSE RENEWAL
AND EVERY TRAFFIC CITATION CHECK.

REVIEWS

Reviews can range from A to Z, from art exhibitions to the opening of a new zoo. Most commonly reviewed by newspapers are books, television, films, theater, dance, music and art. Writers associated with the editorial page are most likely to be called upon to write a review of a book.

The task of the reviewer is basically no different from that of the editorial writer. All the advice about opinion writing offered in Chapters 10 and 11 applies to review writing. Reviewers have two responsibilities: briefly describing to their readers the subject of their review and then commenting on the subject. Beyond that, writers basically are free to organize their reviews as they wish.

The purpose of a review is not just to pronounce a production "good" or "bad," but to describe, explain and evaluate. Laura Reina, in an article in *Editor & Publisher*, asked why the "blurbs" for movies in newspaper ads rarely cited newspaper reviewers. Most come from television and other sources. Her explanation was that it is difficult, and unfair, to reduce to a few words "a review that took a lot of time to write" and that broadcast critics seem less critical and more ambitious to get a name.[24]

In writing reviews, a writer should keep in mind both the background and sophistication of the reading audience as well as the level of professionalism of the artists, authors or performers being reviewed. Reviews are likely to be more elaborate and scholarly in the weekly book section of the *New York Times* than on the book page of the *Roanoke Times*. Similarly, amateur performances should not be expected to meet the standards of professional productions.

If the subject matter itself is likely to catch the reader's eye, the reviewer might begin with a description. Otherwise, the reviewer might begin with a provocative comment or evaluation. In most instances, before proceeding more than a sentence or two, reviewers should provide a description of what they are reviewing. Reviewers should not devote too much space to description, however.

Film and Theater

Tim Bywater and Thomas Sobchack have described the reviews that appear in most newspapers as "journalistic reviews."[25] The reviewer generally is writing about a single film (or play or other cultural event) for readers, most of whom have not seen the production. Usually reviewers are "working journalists writing on a deadline, with no special qualifications except [in the case of film] consistent film viewing of weekly releases."[26] The purpose of such reviews is to give general readers some idea of whether they will want to spend their time and money on what is being reviewed. If the performance is past, a review can help readers decide whether to attend future productions of the group or theater.

Readers want to know, first, what the film or play is about. They want to know whether it is a mystery, comedy or musical. They expect a brief description of the plot (without giving away surprises, of course). They want to know who the producers, the directors and the performers are.

Only after they have some idea of whether they are interested in the performance do they concern themselves with the reviewer's opinion (even if that opinion appears early in the review).

The last statement is not intended to suggest all comment should be reserved for the end of the review. As Irving Wardle has noted, "Reviewers soon learn to write to length, knowing that if they overwrite, it is their opinions that will be cut, while all the plottery will be left intact." His advice: "merging the usually segregated categories of fact and comment; a procedure not always appreciated by sub-editors into whose hands the copy . . . falls at dead of night."[27] When the editor begins whacking, for space or other reasons, according to Wardle, the first to go is "colour," then opinion, finally plot. The solution (and a more interesting one, from the reader's point of view) is to include "colour" and comment as the plot is described.[28]

Comment is not just a matter of scoring from one to some other number (although movies commonly are rated with varying numbers of stars). The reviewer should strive to project a personality and write in an interesting, witty manner. One reason, of course, is to attract readers in the first place. It is just as important for the regular reviewer to establish a reputation for liking certain types of productions and disliking others. When readers become accustomed to a reviewer, they have some idea of whether they will like a production based on whether they usually agree or disagree with that reviewer.

A word of advice for journalistic reviewers: Don't pretend to know more than you know. Until you become more knowledgeable and sophisticated, stick primarily to sketching the plot, identifying the principals and making comments that are likely to interest general readers. Even as your expertise grows, don't forget these readers.

Musical Productions

Reviews of musical productions serve a somewhat different purpose. Reviews of single performances are primarily evaluative, not prescriptive. Readers who were present are interested in comparing their impressions with the reviewer's. Those who were not there may be either glad or sad they did something else that evening. Both sets of readers, however, may benefit from a reviewer's comments that will help them decide whether to attend future performances of the same group.

Reviewers may run the greatest risk of getting in over their heads in covering musical events. They need to know about the music and the composer, but also (at least with familiar music) about how passages and instruments should sound. Unfamiliar works may be even harder to interpret, since reviewers have little with which to compare them. Immediately before performances, some conductors provide a brief explanation to audience members (and reviewers) who come early. The Roanoke (Va.) Symphony Orchestra's "Illuminations" include a light dinner as well as pre-concert explanations.

Books

Readers expect book reviewers to comment on the subject matter of the book, the organization, the comparative emphasis given to parts of the book, the quality of the writing, the qualifications of the author, and the adequacy and reliability of the contents. Reviewers should try to explain what the author intended to accomplish with the book and evaluate how well the author accomplished this purpose.

Fairness and Humility

To be persuasive, reviews should appear to be fair and logical. Scathing reviews, like flamboyant editorials, may be fun to read, but emotion is less likely to be convincing than statements of fact and careful evaluations. In the case of reviews, writers should be especially careful not to overreact negatively. In warning reviewers against "heavily negative reviews," William L. Rivers wrote, " . . . whatever the value of a book, be aware that the author has suffered agonies of the creative process that you could not possibly know. Think of the author as an individual who, in the middle of writing, may spend 'endless' periods scratching deep grooves on the table before him or her, waiting for the right words to present themselves."[29]

Reviewers should write with at least some humility, recognizing that the quality of a book, play or musical is likely to be perceived differently by different people. That lesson is often illustrated by the reviews written by my students. For example, four students reviewed a performance by the American Repertory Ballet of Tchaikovsky's "Swan Lake." The four offered sharply contrasting views of the performance.

One reviewer said that, although it was "brilliantly" performed, the production left the largely student audience yawning and snoring, with "several heads . . . on neighbor's shoulders." The reviewer concluded that, "to survive" "Swan Lake" needed a facelift like "Shakespeare's 'Romeo and Juliet' underwent [in] its 'modern day' movie remake."

A second student said the performance might have been enjoyable if there had been fewer distractions and "if the dancers had attended a few more practices." She was the only one who commented specifically about the dancing: ". . . one female dancer stumbled quite ungracefully, and two people dropped their supposed tea cups (which looked like plastic goblets)." She was bothered by children asking pointless questions and a Girl Troop periodically going off to the bathroom. Her view also was blocked by a woman with large hair. She thought the costumes and the music were the best part of the show.

A third reviewer thought the ballet company presented a "masterpiece with youthfulness, athleticism and talent." He wrote that, even though he had not "visit[ed] ballet much," he thought "the American Repertory Ballet's version of 'Swan Lake' will entertain audiences of all levels." He thought the first two acts were too long.

The fourth reviewer, however, found the first act "exciting" and the second act "captivating." ("Loud Applause for Performance of Tchaikovsky's 'Swan Lake.'") She provided the most detailed description of what she called "a pleasant ballet experience." She commented on the performances of the

Loud Applause for Performance of Tchaikovsky's 'Swan Lake'

Finding a professional ballet company in Blacksburg, Va., proves difficult at best. Tuesday night, however, brought a pleasant ballet experience to the stage in Burruss Hall Auditorium.

As part of the Virginia Tech Union's Lively Arts Entertainment Series, the American Repertory Ballet presented Tchaikovsky's "Swan Lake" to a fairly small audience.

"Swan Lake" is a classic tale of Ziegfried, an heir to the fortune of a great New York family, and his struggle to find the fine line between good and evil. This struggle unfolds on stage as Ziegfried, played by Stuart Loungway, fights to keep his dream of the beautiful Odette, played by Mary Barton, alive while his mother, played by Molly Daly, urges him to pair with the dark Odile, also played by Barton.

After the scene with Ziegfried's relationship with his mother was established, the lights dimmed and Loungway gracefully made his way to a chair on the right forestage. The lights proved the most dazzling display of the ballet by signaling the presence of Ziegfried's dream state and the division between good and evil. The lighting was always soft and accented the costumes and movements of each performer.

The first act proved exciting and established the relationship between Loungway and Barton, which set the emotional impact for the rest of the performance. Dancing in front of the huge, stained-glass-like background, both dancers showed exceptional talent and provided emotional performances. Barton's solo performance in the second act was captivating, and when Loungway joined her the two dancers created a beautiful, graceful display intertwined with each other. After the second act, the audience was drawn into the "dream" state by these two dancers.

Once intermission passed, Act Three opened with a grand ballroom scene. This act displayed the most awesome costumes of the show and included a very exciting and fast-paced dance. The satin ball gowns were all boldly colored with lots of grand reds, purples, golds and pinks. This fabulous dance featured lots of bright lighting and grand movements by the performers.

Possibly the greatest moments of Act Three came during a dazzling duet by Loungway and Barton. The couple shined in their dancing. Although at some points Barton's movements as Odile seemed stiff and unemotional, for the most part the dance displayed her graceful and beautiful dancing abilities. At the end of this act the lights again dimmed to signal the entrance of Loungway into the dream state where he loved Odette, the lead swan.

After a confusing pause, which seemed like another intermission, Act Four began with the swans dancing around Barton as Odette. Then Loungway entered again, and another emotional and beautiful performance ensued between Loungway and Barton, but the true star was Loungway.

The obvious talent of Loungway made "Swan Lake" worth seeing. Loungway's grand movements accented by the wonderfully emotional music by Tchaikovsky shined through the rest of the cast and carried the ballet. The fight of Ziegfried to find himself in a world of good and evil was accented by the lighting but was brought to life by Loungway. At the end of the performance, the fighting emotions of Ziegfried consumed the audience, and, when the lights fell signaling the end of the show, a loud display of approval erupted from the audience.

Ballet in Blacksburg may be rare, but with performers like Loungway and Barton, shows like "Swan Lake" should begin to draw larger crowds of ballet lovers.

Abby Legg

two lead dancers, noting that "the greatest moments of Act Three" came during "a dazzling duet performance" by these dancers. At times, however, the movements of the female dancer "seemed stiff and unemotional." She was especially complimentary of the male dancer's talent.

This was the same performance described in such different ways by the other reviewers? Because I did not see the show, it is impossible for me to judge the validity of the students' varied evaluations. But several things can be said.

Although it is appropriate to comment on the environment in which a show is presented (talking children, snoring people, bad acoustics), no review should dwell overwhelmingly on this aspect. If reviewers cannot distance themselves from these distractions, they should pick another line of work.

Unlike the first student, reviewers should attempt to judge a performance on its own merits rather than dismiss it for not being something it does not pretend to be.

Obviously a couple of the students got caught up in the performance. The others seemed not to. Their differing reactions may have reflected the extent of their prior experiences with ballet or classical music, or perhaps only their differences in temperament. It's not at all unusual for experienced reviewers to differ sharply on a performance. Reviewing, after all, is one form of expressing one's opinions, about art, music, dance, books, movies and theater. One student even wrote a "cultural review" of a professional wrestling match.

Not Too Much Detail

Reviews should provide enough information to give readers some idea of whether they are interested in reading a book or going to a movie or concert. If possible, the review should suggest the flavor of the object reviewed. Carl Sessions Stepp, a senior editor of *American Journalism Review* who also teaches at the University of Maryland College of Journalism, did that in "An Inspirational Array of Local Columns." He briefly described the wide range of subject matter (and the wide range of newspapers) of 10 of the 77 columnists represented. Stepp suggested that local columnists can provide a change of pace from the traditional "middle-aged, white male" columnists and explore a wider range of topics.[30]

SIGNED ARTICLES

Editorial writers today probably have more opportunities than ever before to write signed interpretive and opinion pieces. One reason is that more newspapers are providing additional full or partial pages for opinion articles and artwork. This page typically is referred to as the op-ed page (the page opposite the editorial page). Another reason is that publishers seem more willing to allow previously anonymous writers to put their names on articles that are not intended to be the voice of the newspaper. Such articles range from expressions of personal opinion or dissent from the newspaper's editorials, through interpretive and analytical articles, to media criticism.

An Inspirational Array of Local Columns
By Carl Sessions Stepp

The Best of the Rest: Non-Syndicated
Newspaper Columnists Select Their Best Work
Edited by Sam G. Riley
Greenwood Press
341 pages; $49.95

Sam Riley has come up with a wonderful idea for a book, and perhaps for a whole lot more.

Riley, a Virginia Tech communication professor, has collected samples by 77 non-syndicated columnists from papers high and low, dealing with the kinds of outside-the-Beltway themes that America strums to. The range is immense, from okra to the death penalty, a bridge named Bob to sexual harassment. He has tearjerkers, knee slappers, tall tales and, naturally, a few teeth grinders too.

Many columnists share intimate personal meditations. Brian Ojampa (Mankato, Minnesota, *Free Press*) on his son's growing up, Mark Patinkin (*Providence Journal-Bulletin*) on his parents' storybook courtship, Rheta Grimsley Johnson (Memphis *Commercial Appeal*) on her stroke- stricken grandmother.

Others find lessons in local slices-of-life: Lynn Bartels (*Albuquerque Tribune*) on the county fair's sewing competition, Cathy Mauk (Fargo, North Dakota, *Forum*) on the closing of a quaint curiosity shop, Roddy Stinson (*San Antonio Express-News*) on a man driving along an expressway flourishing a baton at an imaginary orchestra.

Several issue public scoldings: Don Bishoff (Eugene, Oregon, *Register-Guard*) to the trains that dump their waste along the tracks, Jim Fitzgerald (*Detroit Free Press*) to fancy restaurants that refuse to provide separate checks. Some detour deep into whimsy: T.J. Gilles (*Great Falls*, Montana, *Tribune*) provides his own entertainingly aggrandized obituary.

Many, many just charm us with lovely writing, like Jack Smith (*Los Angeles Times*) who composes a lyrical parable on hearing Handel's Messiah in a peaceful college chapel:

A girl with a sweet soprano voice and pale gold hair down to her shoulders sang a solo of rejoicing, holding her book high, her elbows out, swaying *slightly with the rhythm of the hymn, and for a moment it was hard not to believe in angels.*

All in all, the book is inspirational and instructive (if stiffly priced). As a bonus, it also plants the idea that more column-type writing could help revive sagging readership.

In a useful introduction on the history and role of columns, Riley praises their humanity, wit and literary freedom.

"All three are qualities that most newspapers could use more of," he adds, especially "at this time, when newspaper publishers, in their dark suits and wing-tip shoes, well dressed but nervous, are employing consultants to tell them how better to compete with television and how to woo a public that, increasingly, seems to regard the act of reading as a form of social punishment to be escaped as soon as one finishes school. . . . "

Unlike the studiedly clinical copy that speaks in a monotone across many front pages, columns have voice and personality. They reflect time and place. They flow from one human being to another. And they prove that short essays can tell power-packed stories. It's no accident that when readers are asked who their favorite newspaper writers are, they tend to name columnists.

Given its virtues, can the column form make a broader contribution? Certainly, columns can add dimension to papers heavy with middle-aged, white male writers and sources. They can expand the monotone to a chorus, incorporating voices of women, young people, members of minority groups and others with special accents.

In addition, columns could increasingly help explain the complexities of business, science, international affairs and other news. This is hardly new; consider the impact of Ernie Pyle's folksy but informative World War II dispatches. Again today in the information age, their agreeableness, accessibility and conversational directness make columns a powerful communication tool.

Riley, a part time columnist himself, doesn't push the matter quite this far. Mostly, he just shows off some fine work, and that is treat enough.

Reprinted by permission of
American Journalism Review

Personal Opinion

An article that expresses a personal opinion may differ little from a signed editorial, aside from being written in the first person singular. But the article is quite likely to be more personal than a regular editorial. (See "An Inspirational Array of Local Columnists," on page 266, for examples of the broad subject matter written about under personal bylines.) For example, a visit by the governor of Florida prompted Philip Gailey, editor of editorials for the *St. Petersburg Times*, to suggest that Gov. Lawton Chiles' legislative priorities were wrong ("A battle worthy of Chiles' efforts").

Interpretive and Analytical

Frequently much longer than editorials, interpretive or analytical articles may reveal the writers' viewpoints, but their primary purpose is to provide readers with information and insights and, perhaps, to raise questions. A suggestion that the Civilian Conservative Corps might be revived, for example, got Blackie Sherrod, columnist for the *Dallas Morning News*, to thinking about his encounter with the CCC in the days before World War II. "For all I know, the CCC might be deemed communistic or, perish forbid, unaffirmative action," Sherrod wrote. "Those are brands I don't care to wear at this late stage. There is also the possibility that anyone who can remember the CCC is beyond recall, with the exception of Mr. [Paul] Harvey [who suggested the idea], Sen. Strom Thurmond, George Burns and a diminishing few of us lesser grumps." To serve in the CCC, "federal supervisors selected more than a half-million young men . . . introducing the frantic unemployed to reforestation, soil erosion prevention, flood control, wildlife protection and roadside parks, which still are seen along our highways." Sherrod recalled that he and his dad had walked to the CCC camp on Thursday evenings.

It looked like an early Army camp hut with wooden floors, half-walls, canvas tops and cots inside. In the center was a wooden tabernacle, with a boxing ring where weekly intra-camp bouts were staged and townspeople welcomed. There was no admission. The CCC guys seemed genuinely glad to see us. The program wasn't perfect. Work was hard, and the desertion rate was 10 percent. Those were the days of segregation, and CCC camps for blacks weren't welcome in the South. Liberals objected to the militarism of the camps. Whatever the drawbacks, by gollies, the guys were *working* and proud of it.[31]

Sherrod suggested a similar program might be one answer to today's "two major problems . . . unemployment and growling stomachs."

Media Criticism

Media criticism is a form of opinion writing in which the microscope is turned around, with the focus placed on the job that the newspaper and other media are doing. My impression is that media criticism reached its high point in the 1970s, in the post-Watergate era. One indication of a more recent decline is the gradual decrease in the number of "ombudsmen" or "reader representatives." When the Organization of News Ombudsmen met in 1995, it had 42 members.[32] A year later, the number of newspaper ombudsmen had dwindled

EDITOR OF EDITORIALS A Battle Worthy of Chiles' Efforts
Philip Gailey

Gov. Lawton Chiles stopped by for a visit last week. He wanted to talk about a recent column I wrote that he said gave him "a case of the reds." That was his folksy way of saying the column had angered and wounded him. I had written that during the 1996 legislative session Chiles seemed obsessed with his war against the tobacco industry and showed— at least publicly—little interest in anything else. I suggested that he should have spent an equal amount of his political energy on other issues important to the state's future.

The governor said the column was terribly unfair. He insisted he had "raised hell" with the Legislature on a number of issues he cares about and was satisfied with the Legislature's overall work. He told me I didn't understand what he was up against in the tobacco war. Big Tobacco, he said, doesn't believe in a fair fight. It spends huge amounts of money to employ an army of lobbyists to sway lawmakers and business groups and mislead the public. He feels he had no choice but to bring the full weight of his political office to bear against the evil empire.

Chiles finally won the fight, heading off an attempt by the tobacco industry and its allies to override his veto of legislation that would have repealed the Medicaid Liability Act, a law that strips the tobacco industry of most of its legal defenses in the lawsuit Chiles filed to recover state Medicaid funds spent on tobacco-related illnesses.

The governor noted that we had known each other for more than two decades and said he had thought he had earned my respect for his generally progressive record in public life. I assured him that he had. I explained that I was not opposed to his taking on the tobacco industry but felt that the issue had become a huge distraction that had consumed too much of his time and energy. I thought he should have fought harder for more money for his Healthy Kids program, human services and education.

Chiles insisted he had won most of what he wanted from the Legislature, although he thinks some parts of the state budget it passed "stink." But the longer we talked, the clearer it became that he had settled for far less than he had asked for.

To increase funding for education, the Legislature shifted money from the Department of Health and Rehabilitative Services, an agency that in recent years has been bled time and time again by lawmakers in a cruel shell game. "Nobody right now is raising a lot of sand," the governor said, "but if we can't run HRS"

to 31.[33] Ombudsmen or reader representatives generally are assigned to critique the content of the newspaper, write op-ed articles responding to readers' complaints and explain newspaper policy. Sometimes they write in-house critiques that are circulated among the news and editorial staffs.

In some instances media criticism has been replaced with articles or columns written by one of the editors. At the *Seattle Times* Editor Michael Fancher replaced the ombudsman column with his own regular column explaining newspaper policies.[34] Simultaneously the *Times* added a syndicated media column. The *Nashville Banner* regularly published an op-ed column titled "20/20" in which "reporters and editors explain various aspects of the *Banner*'s policies and their jobs." One explanation offered for dropping the media critic's position is that "every editor should be an ombudsman."[35]

Readers' most common complaints to media critics concern a liberal bias in the news, factual errors and bad headlines.[36] But a former *Seattle Times* ombudsman, Frank Wetzel, said his experience convinced him that "staff dereliction" was not the principal defect of newspapers. "Rather," he said, "[the with these latest cuts, he will be forced to call a special session of the Legislature to deal with the problem.

Chiles also had sought a $33-million increase to expand the Healthy Kids program, but lawmakers only provided $7 million. Sadly, he added, there is not much of a political constituency for children.

When Chiles' second term as governor expires at the end of 1988, his long career in public service will come to an end. I sense that he is thinking about his legacy and his place in history, especially after his final campaign for office was tarnished by scandal (the phony telephone calls to elderly voters and the yearlong coverup by his top campaign aides). While he is proud of his victory over the tobacco industry, I believe he wants to be remembered for something more lasting, some defining achievement that future generations will look back on with admiration and gratitude.

I suggested there is one issue crying out for leadership. Someone must awaken Floridians to the threat anti-tax politicians pose to the state's future. At some point a governor is going to have to stand up to them. At some point Tallahassee is going to have to come up with new sources of revenue to finance the state's needs in education, human services and economic development.

The governor agreed and suggested that he is ready to throw himself into the fight. He said he is prepared to wage one last campaign to try to educate and arouse the business community and the citizenry to the coming "train wreck" if voters approve the anti-tax amendment that will be on this November's ballot. The proposed constitutional amendment would require a two-thirds vote to write any increase in taxes or fees into the state Constitution.

If that initiative is approved by the voters, it would end any chance for tax reform and permanently cripple Florida's social and economic development. And it certainly would harden the anti-tax mentality of Republicans, making it even more difficult for the Legislature to consider any kind of tax increase.

Chiles said if that amendment can be defeated, he will then devote himself to building public support for tax reform that would include a dedicated funding source for education and the long overdue elimination of certain tax exemptions.

The issue is vital to Florida's future and worthy of Chiles' leadership. It will require an even greater effort than Chiles gave his battle against the tobacco industry. Even if he lost the fight Chiles would be remembered as a governor who had the courage to fight for the state's future. If Chiles makes this his last campaign, he can leave office with his head held high, knowing he rose to Florida's greatest challenge as it moves into a new century.

St. Petersburg Times

---

principal defects] are part of the structure of the American press . . . : 1. Concentration of ownership. 2. Inflated expectations of profitability. 3. Lack of access by the public."[37] He said he thought readers generally get the newspaper they deserve but that was no excuse for editors to "simply dish up what they think the public wants."

CONCLUSION

By no means is the anonymous newspaper editorial the only outlet for opinion. In daily or weekly newspapers, new opportunities are opening in reviewing literary and cultural productions, partly because newspapers are seeking ways to provide more information for consumers. New opportunities also lie on the growing number of op-ed pages, which are open to bylined pieces that range from interpretation to media criticism to personal opinion More and more publishers and editors are relaxing the old rule that editorial writers should remain anonymous.

Until a few years ago, broadcast editorial writing seemed to have a bright future. Then editorial writing jobs began shrinking. Budgets got tight. Broadcast people have always been nervous about having to provide equal time for opinions expressed by themselves and others. But why should broadcast stations allow newspapers to hold a monopoly on opinion in a local community? If owners of broadcast stations were to recommit themselves to offering opinions to their listeners and viewers, radio and television could provide not only jobs for opinion writers but also leadership for their communities.

Questions and Exercises

1. Find a newspaper editorial on a topic that interests you. Rewrite it in broadcast style. Read it aloud to see if any of the wording is awkward or difficult to enunciate clearly. Rewrite to clear up these spots.
2. Keep your ear open for editorials during radio and television news broadcasts. Write to the station manager to ask for a copy. When it arrives, read it aloud. Are there any awkward or difficult spots? How does the editorial approach the subject? Is it analytical or outspoken, one-or two-sided? Is the conclusion at the beginning or the end? Would listeners be convinced?
3. Pick a topic, conduct the necessary research and write an analytical article that would be appropriate for an op-ed page. Then write an editorial based on the article that could run the same day.
4. Write an op-ed piece based on an experience that you have had. Try to make it appeal to as broad an audience as possible.
5. If you can find a media criticism column in one of the newspapers that you read, write the media critic. Ask about the newspaper's policies relating to media criticism and the responsibilities of the media critic.
6. If you spot something that you think merits attention in a newspaper that has a media criticism column, write or call the media critic about it.
7. Select a recent book on a media or current events topic. Write a book review that might be suitable to a book section of a newspaper or an op-ed page. Before writing it, you might read several reviews in newspapers that have strong book departments.
8. Watch for a cultural event that interests you: an art exhibit, a play, a concert, a musical or movie. Write a review for the arts and entertainment section of the paper. Again, it is a good idea to read several reviews before you start writing, and in fact before you attend the event.

Chapter 17 Letters to the Editor

etters to the editor are about the only part of the editorial page that comes free. But in terms of time, effort and headaches, a good letters column is probably the most expensive part. It's quicker and easier for an editorial writer to knock out a couple of paragraphs of prose than to prepare a letter of equal length for print.

"Letters give life to an editorial page," Barry Bingham Sr. of the Louisville *Courier-Journal* said. "They also come near to beating the life out of the fellow who has to handle them. Many are illiterate. Others are long, rambling and inchoate. Still others are so abusive in tone that they recall the Turkish proverb, 'Letters written after dinner are read in Hell.' Some of the ones that come to us must be written in the fine frenzy of after-dinner dyspepsia." Then he added: "Letters are worth every bit of trouble they cause, however."[2]

WHY LETTERS?

Editorial page editors put up with—and encourage—letters for one reason: Letters help give readers a better feeling about the newspaper. Letters give readers, as citizens, one of the few chances they have to speak their mind in public. Letters also help create interest in the editorial page and increase readership.

Surveys consistently show that letters are among the most read parts of the paper. "Some writers put their hearts and souls into one letter of a lifetime, then frame the printed copy and proudly present it as their 'editorial,'" Diane Cole of the *Salt Lake Tribune* wrote in a *Masthead* symposium on letters to the editor. "This process creates a bond between subscriber and newspaper that only a week of late deliveries could break." But the letter column also has its dangers. "Fail to run a writer's masterpiece (or disaster) and you weaken an avid reader loyalty," Cole said. "Get a name wrong or drop a 'key phrase,' and you court alienation."[3]

Letters give readers a chance to talk about what they want to talk about, which is especially important in a one-newspaper town with no built-in voice of opposition. Readers are not stuck with the editor's agenda; they have their own agendas.

Some readers, as well as some legal scholars, think that the public should have a right of access to the letters column and the right to express themselves in any way and at any length they wish. Although the U.S. Supreme Court, in *Miami Herald vs. Tornillo*, held that they have no legal right of access, readers still react vigorously when their letters are shortened, altered or not printed. Editors and publishers, especially in monopoly situations, have a good deal of self-interest, if not legal interest, in helping readers feel that they have access to the printed page.

BUILDING A LETTERS COLUMN

Scholarly studies and reports from editors indicate that readers are increasingly turning to letters columns to express their opinions. A survey by Suraj Kapoor, published in 1995, found that 80 percent of the newspapers reported an increase in letters received over the past 10 years. Seventy-five percent reported an increase in the amount of space devoted to letters.[4] The numbers vary sharply among newspapers. While about one out of 10 reported receiving more than 500 letters a month, almost four out of 10 received 50 or fewer letters. Percentages of letters published varied also, with smaller papers publishing a higher percentage than large papers. Most editors would be delighted to receive more letters, the survey also reported, especially those of good quality.

In the *Masthead* symposium referred to earlier, Keith Carter of the *Desert Sun* in Palm Springs, Calif., offered nine suggestions for building a stronger letters column:[5]

- Localize.
- Print as many letters as possible.
- Encourage debates.
- Set up rules and follow them.
- Identify letter writers.
- Run letters quickly.
- Verify, verify, verify.
- Stay flexible.
- Stimulate interest.

It is clear what Carter had in mind in offering most of these suggestions. The "localize" advice was directed toward urging strong editorials on local topics as a means to stimulate letters. The "stay flexible" advice was intended for editors who seem more concerned with enforcing rigid rules than with printing good (but perhaps excessively long) letters. Probably for as long as there have been letters to newspapers, editors have been concerned with two of Carter's points: stimulating more letters and setting rules for deciding which ones to print. These two areas are discussed at length in the following sections.

STIMULATING INTEREST

In seeking ways to stimulate more and better letters, editors have experimented with ways of displaying letters, methods for speeding the delivery of letters and ideas for encouraging readers to write.

Display of Letters

Displaying letters prominently and attractively is one way editors can indicate to readers that the newspaper takes letters seriously. Letters typically are placed on the right side of the editorial page, beneath the editorial cartoon. When Professor Robert Bohle of Virginia Commonwealth University examined a series of editorial pages, he found no fault with this placement, but said that editors underplayed individual letters. Headlines tended to be small, consisting of one line with few words ("terse and enigmatic," he called them). He preferred two lines to let the reader know what the letter was about.[6]

Bohle applauded papers that worked illustrations or political cartoons into their letter columns. (He might have added photographs.) He urged editors to place the how-to-submit-a-letter box at the top of the column. He suggested that a letter could be made more understandable if a summary of the article or editorial that prompted it could appear at the top of the letter. Bohle also suggested creating a box (perhaps an entire page) that included a news summary of a topic, editorials, letters to the editor and perhaps columns (somewhat on the order of *USA Today*'s theme editorial page).

Transmission of Letters

Editors have been trying for years to improve on the mail for speeding up letters to the editor. Now a whole array of electronic devices is available to them. The newspaper that I have encountered that offers readers the most options for sharing their views is the *Dallas Morning News*. A letters box explains that readers can communicate by mail, fax, modem, America Online, Compuserve, Internet or Prodigy. It is a rare newspaper that has gone to that length to detail how readers can send their comments electronically, but a large, and growing, number receive letters via e-mail and fax. Such transmissions should help enliven the letters column by speeding up the exchange of comments. Newspapers also have experimented with allowing readers to call in letters or brief comments, but the practice remains controversial.

The *Eagle-Tribune* of Lawrence, Mass., runs a "Sound Off" column seven days a week on the editorial page–6,000 items a year, of 18,000 received. The column does not take the place of letters, according to Arthur Hagopian, editorial page editor of the *Eagle-Tribune*, but it "is a point of entry to the opinion pages, and Sound Off, I believe, has bred a whole new younger generation of editorial readers."[7]

Some editors see accepting off-the-cuff phone-in messages as encouraging irresponsible comments that cheapen the editorial page. One editor, Charles Reinken of the *Fayetteville* (N.C.) *Observer-Times*, described phone-in callers as "linguistic infidels" who "hurl verbal Nerf Balls."[8] "I would suggest," he said, "that people who are in the business of writing and editing and peddling the result and allowing ourselves to think that it all might be in some way important would be wise to promote writing and the love of it instead of giving people another cheap out."

Encouraging Writers

To stimulate letters, some editors have staff members call people on the telephone to ask for opinions on topics. Some editors send several letters a day to a sampling of subscribers, asking them to read specific editorials and write their views about them.[9] Some newspapers announce topics and ask readers to submit letters by a certain date. A few editorial pages even carry coupons on which readers can write their opinions. The coupons can be cut out and mailed.[10]

To encourage quality letters, one newspaper puts stars next to the signatures on letters of merit. Some papers pay a few dollars for outstanding letters. Some newspapers hold appreciation banquets for frequent contributors. Some run pictures of regular contributors.[11] The *San Bernardino* (Calif.) *Sun* at one time reproduced one or two letters each day in the original typewritten or handwritten form.

Special efforts may be needed, if a letters column has been neglected, to get readers to start looking at the column. But if editors also offer readers stimulating editorials and other editorial page material, the column should soon begin sustaining itself. James Dix of the *Moline* (Ill.) *Dispatch* said his formula for keeping the letters column fired up was to create "a crossfire of disagreement between us and a column, or between us and a letter."[12] The incoming mail took care of itself.

SETTING UP THE RULES

How readers view a newspaper's letters column and respond to it can depend on how the editors of that newspaper handle the letters they receive. Both the quality of the column and readers' perceptions of it can be affected by the policies of the paper. By no means do editors agree on how best to run the letters column. Policies generally concern seven areas: use of names and addresses, verification of names, subject matter, length and frequency, editing letters, editor's notes and political letters.

Names and Addresses

Whether publication of writers' names and addresses should be required has been debated since the establishment of letters columns. The Kapoor survey found that about 85 percent of newspapers required a name.[13] About 10 percent would withhold a name for good cause and 3.4 percent upon the request of the writer. No major differences were found among newspapers of different sizes. (Editors apparently were not asked about insisting on publishing addresses.) Editors have reported a trend in recent years toward requiring letter writers to include their addresses and telephone numbers but not publishing their addresses (or their phone numbers). Alternatively, some newspapers publish generalized addresses. The *Oregonian*, for example, identifies only the town or the section of town (Southeast Portland, North Portland, etc.). Some newspapers publish street names but not house numbers. The problem with not using addresses of some kind (or some other identification) is that a surprising number of people have similar names.

Some editors have allowed anonymous letters–successfully, in their opinions. The *East Oregonian* in Pendleton reported receiving 240 letters in five weeks, four times the regular volume, in an experiment with permitting anonymous letters.[14]

Verification of Names

Editors these days spend more time verifying the authenticity of letters than in the past. They seem less inclined to presume the good will of letter writers. They also have become more wary of the legal dangers posed by letters. The 1995 survey apparently did not ask editors about verification practices, but an earlier survey found editors about equally divided between those who verified the authors of all letters and those who verified only when their suspicions were aroused. Most relied on the telephone for verification; a third on the mail.[15]

Once in a while an editor will be burned. The *Cleveland Press* once printed a seemingly harmless letter about a streetcar accident. After the first edition appeared on the street, a woman called to say that the professed family name signed to the letter was "an obscene Hungarian word" too nasty to repeat.[16]

James J. Kilpatrick told how a Mr. Stuart Little of New York seduced space from the *Richmond News Leader* with a request for help in finding authentic stories about old crows. His hobby was old crows, he said, the older the better. Many people responded to his requests, including one who sent a package "containing a bottle of an old-time beverage." Another volunteered to send "an elderly female relative by marriage." Kilpatrick reported: "Smiling fondly at the quirks of the amateur ornithologist, we published Mr. Little's letter." Then came a second letter. "But we are not running any more of Mr. Little's crow: We are eating it," Kilpatrick told readers. "For right in the second sentence and in the fourth paragraph was another reference to that 'Kentucky beverage,' and down in the last sentence was still a third mention of this estimable product, and the whole business had about it the faint but unmistakable aroma of the gag, the gimmick, the phonus bolonus." Little turned out to work for a public relations firm that had the account for Old Crow bourbon whiskey. Fifty news-papers had apparently run the first letter.[17]

Subject Matter

Once you decide that a letter is legitimate, you must determine whether the subject matter is appropriate. Most newspapers have rules, published or unpublished, concerning what they will run. Most will not publish a letter unless it pertains to an issue of some public interest.

Letters editors face a dilemma when faced with letters that quote scripture (Christian, Moslem, Jewish or whatever). Most seek to avoid religious pitches and arguments over the meaning of scriptural verses. Some will allow scrip-tural references if they bear on a public issue. With abortion, the death penalty, creationism, prayer in the schools and the rights of gays all matters of public contention, it makes no sense to tell readers they can't draw on, and cite, their religious beliefs in commenting on these issues. Still, as Glenn Sheller of the *York* (Pa.) *Dispatch*, has written: "We don't want to see letters and columns of diverse viewpoint, style and wit driven out by mailbags full of the familiar type in which every sentence ends with a scripture citation and whose 'argument' consists of nothing more than an appeal to supernatural authority."[18]

Many newspapers try to avoid thank-you letters, especially those thanking individuals. Some will weed out publicity seekers who try to get their names in print by praising editorials lavishly. Some are tough on politicians who try to find excuses for getting their names in the letters column.

Many editors will not publish letters from outside their general circulation areas unless they address a local issue or something that appeared in the paper.

Most will not run poetry. "Print a bit of amateur verse and the next day's mail brings a deluge because everyone is a poet at heart if not in pen," M. Carl Andrews of the *Roanoke World-News* warned.[19]

Editors need to be on the lookout for inspired letter-writing campaigns. Sometimes they can tell that several letters have been written on the same typewriter or printer, or have the same wording. Editors can be trapped by letter-writing assignments in the schools, however.

Editors sometimes have to decide to call a halt to the discussion of some issue, when it has gone on so long that nothing new is being said.

Editors are not in agreement on what to do with letters that seemingly don't fall within the range of rationality. Carol Suplee of the Willingboro, N.J., *Burlington County Times* recounted that she had a letter writer who was "blatantly inaccurate and unnecessarily inflammatory when he relate[d] his version of history," especially concerning the Jews. Sometimes she would write to him explaining her reasons for not running a letter. Other times she would run a letter, when she "felt that exposition of his amazing bigotry might serve the community well," but she usually heard objections from local Jewish organizations.[20]

While on the *Columbian*, I was blessed with a persistent letter writer who could start writing on almost any subject but within a couple of handwritten pages would wend her way to talking about sublimating sex as a means of delaying marriage, births and population crisis. She would write several times a week for awhile, then not write for several months. She had been writing to the paper for several years when I took over the editorial page. She was still writing 12 years later when I left. One of her letters consisted of 125 six-by-nine-inch pages. I sometimes could use the first few paragraphs before she headed off into sublimation.

Length and Frequency

Most papers have policies on length and frequency of letters from the same person.

The Kapoor survey found that 35 percent of newspapers limited writers to 250 or few words; 40 percent, 251–500; 2.4 percent, 501–1,000; 15 percent, no limit.[21] Limiting length encourages readers to write succinctly and saves the editor some work, but also may prevent a reader from making as complete an argument as editorial writers allow themselves in the editorial columns. To avoid that problem, editors sometimes will publish a worthy long communication from a reader under a different label, such as "In My Opinion."

Newspapers often limit the frequency with which a letter writer may appear in print. The Kapoor survey found 4.7 percent of the editors would consider publishing a letter writer once a week and 37 percent once a month, but 36 had no prescribed limits.[22] Limiting writers has advantages. When the same names appear again and again, letters become predictable, and other prospective writers are discouraged.

Editing of Letters

Editors disagree on what is desirable or permissible in editing letters. Kapoor found that 96 percent of the papers reserved the right to edit in some form. About 66 percent edited to shorten letters, about 62 percent for grammar, about 26 percent for libel or taste.[23] Not surprisingly, larger newspapers tended to shorten letters more than small papers did. The task facing any editor, of course, is to preserve, or even clarify, the meaning of the original letter. Many letters, after being edited by a skillful editor, will be more effective.

Editor's Notes

Editor's notes following letters used to be more prevalent than they now are. A clever note that sets a letter writer straight may be fun to write, but, as Charles Towne of the *Hartford* (Conn.) *Courant* said, "some editors . . . publish caustic rebuttals out of a feeling of superiority—being so far above such savage assaults as to be immune."[24] Letters columns are meant for exchanges of opinion among readers. If writers have the feeling that the editor is going to have the last word, they are likely to stop writing. If a statement is clearly wrong in its facts, perhaps a note is justified if the letter is judged important enough to run. A note also might be called for when a reader raises a question about something that the newspaper has or has not done. An example: A letter writer asked the Eugene, Ore., *Register-Guard* what had "happened to the photographs that used to accompany the names in the obituary columns." Lack of an editor's note in response must have left other readers wondering as well.

Political Letters

Policies vary widely about what to do with letters relating to elections. Practices run all the way from treating political letters (including candidate endorsements) like other letters to telling writers who want to speak for a candidate to buy an ad.

In a *Masthead* symposium on "The Politics of Letters," Wally Hoffman of the *Salt Lake Tribune* said his paper treated campaign letters like other letters. A signature might be withheld, however, in a "case in which the writer's job might be jeopardized by disclosure of his or her identity."[25]

At the other extreme, Phil Fretz said the *Amarillo* (Texas) *Globe-News* had no trouble with endorsement letters, since it had a policy against running them. "If you run endorsement letters," he said, "you are a masochist. You open yourself to the charge that you didn't run somebody's letter because you endorsed his opponent."[26] On the other hand, if you endorse a candidate and don't give readers a chance to respond, you will almost certainly be accused of being unfair.

To head off last-minute accusations that can't be properly addressed, most newspapers set a deadline for election letters several days before Election Day.

LIBEL IN LETTERS

Marc Franklin, a law professor at Stanford University with expertise in First Amendment issues, has argued that "editors should be protected against libel suits for published letters so long as the letters are authentic and the writers are correctly identified." Letters already serve as a sort of community bulletin board; in Franklin's view, exempting them from the threat of libel suits would make them even more so. Such a bulletin board would "provide access to the media and the community for many who have no other opportunity to get their thoughts before the public," Franklin has written. This access is especially important "as more newspapers become local monopolies." He estimated that about one out of eight letters that are rejected by editors is discarded because of concerns over libel.[27]

For now, however, courts treat letters no differently from the way they treat any other published material in a libel suit. "A long line of case law has held that the author of a libel bears the ultimate responsibility for it, and that everyone who takes part in publication of a libel may be held responsible for it," Professor Steve Pasternack of New Mexico State University warned editors in an article in *The Masthead.* Pasternack noted that a survey had indicated that editors were allowing the use of harsher language in letters columns than elsewhere in their newspapers. He attributed this laxity to the editors' misinformation or lack of knowledge of libel law, and to a reluctance to consult attorneys.[28]

THE LETTERS EDITOR

The job of handling letters is not one for the novice—or for an impatient, careless or uncaring editor. Cliff Carpenter of the *Rochester* (N.Y.) *Democrat and Chronicle* saw some newspapers handling letters lovingly, others handling them ineptly, casually, and with fear or disdain. "Some pages handle letters as if they were ashamed of them," he said. "And by handling them that way, they get only mediocrity to use as letters—and a vicious circle is created."[29] A person who handled letters on the *Kansas City* (Mo.) *Star* was said to have done it "with a certain amount of tender loving care, a bit of prayer and some tearing of hair." Handling letters can take about as much time as an editor can find to work on them, if a paper receives a strong flow of mail.

The letters editor needs a thick skin—literally, at times. Palmer Hoyt of the *Denver Post* told of one letter that began: "Dear Palmer Hoyt: We want you to know that we are going to boil you in oil." A week later Hoyt got a letter that said: "Dear Palmer Hoyt: We want you to know that we are not going to boil you in oil after all. We got bigger turkeys than you to boil."[30] A woman brought to the office of the *Burlington* (Vt.) *Free Press* a three-page letter, typewritten, single-spaced, with a pen name. Franklin Smith tried to explain that the letter was too long for publication and pen names were not permitted. "Finally, after a long, long pause, she looked at me," Smith said, "and said plaintively, 'You don't like me, do you?'"[31]

Letters editors, faceless as they may be to the public, can build special relationships with readers. M. Carl Andrews of Roanoke said that some of his best friends were regular letter writers who had never met him. Three of his most delightful contributors over the years, he said, had been "dear old ladies who always found something good to say about people or things." He reported that two of them had died. One had requested that he be one of her pallbearers.[32]

CONCLUSION

A good letters column can be a lot of work for an editor. Deciding what letters to print and what should be done to get them ready for print requires skill and judgment. Dealing with letter writers requires tact. Editing letters requires sensitivity, a sense of fairness and a heavy editing pencil. But efforts put into the letters column are usually worthwhile in terms of the readability and credibility of the editorial page. Letters bring readers to the page. They also help readers believe they have a voice in their newspaper. Perhaps the clearest sign of a good editorial page is a good letters column, especially one in which readers respond to the editorials, columns and other letters that appear on the page. Such a page is truly a community forum.

Questions and Exercises

1. Examine the letters columns of the newspapers in your area to determine their policies on the use of names and addresses, condensation and frequency of publication. Are these policies spelled out for readers?
2. Compare the letters columns of these papers for quantity and quality of letters published. Which papers seem to have the best letters columns? Is there evidence available to explain the success of these columns?
3. Examine the letters specifically for references to previously published editorials or letters. Such references often indicate that the letters column is providing a lively community forum.
4. Can you find letters that sound as though they were produced by a letters mill that sends the same letter to many newspapers?

5. Can you find political letters that sound as thought they were produced by a letters "sweatshop," letters that support a cause and sound as though they came from the same source?

6. Do the editor's notes seem fully justified in the columns you have examined? Do you think an editor might have been wiser not to have written one or more of the notes? Why?

7. Do any of the papers request letters on specific topics, perhaps in a weekly roundup or in answer to a question? If so, what kind of responses do the papers get?

8. Write a letter to one of the papers. See if any effort is made to verify your name and address. If it is printed, see what changes are made. If you think the changes altered the meaning of the letter, call and inform the editorial page editor. If it was not published, call to ask why.

CHAPTER 18 Columns and Cartoons

Most newspapers devote more space and less attention to syndicated columns and cartoons than to any other element on the editorial page. These features are relatively inexpensive, undemanding of editorial attention and extremely useful for plugging editorial holes of any size and number. Some editors have streamlined their editing to the point that every day they slap a regular liberal columnist in one position on the page, a regular conservative columnist in another spot and maybe an interpretive columnist in a third spot. A cartoon by the same artist sits atop the page every day.

The editorial writer on a one-person staff may be thankful that syndicated features are still available. With these features, the bulk of the editorial page can be filled with a few minutes' work, and the writer can move on to do what most editorial writers prefer to do—write editorials. But even writers who have little time for handling columnists serve readers poorly if they do not give careful attention to which columns and cartoons are selected for print. Deciding which columnists and cartoonists to subscribe to and which to run on any single day can make a difference in how readers regard the page. In this chapter we will talk about the role that columns and cartoons play on the editorial page, how editors decide which ones to use and how they handle the syndicated material. We also will look at efforts to make syndicated writers more credible with editors and readers.

ROLE OF THE COLUMNIST

Signed political columns go back at least to the 1880s. Charles McClatchy, whose father James had worked for Horace Greeley on the *New York Tribune* and founded the

Sacramento Bee, began a political column upon his father's death in 1883. From 1883 to 1897, he called the column "Notes," then, until 1936, "Private Thinks."[3] Heywood Broun began writing a political column in 1911,[4] first for the *New York Tribune*, then the *New York World* and eventually for syndication, until his death in 1931.[5] Arthur Brisbane began writing a signed front-page political column for William Randolph Hearst's newspapers in 1917 and continued writing it until his death in 1936.[6]

Political columnists began to flourish in the early 1920s. David Lawrence, who had accompanied President Wilson to the peace talks in Europe after World War I, began writing a syndicated column in 1919.[7] Walter Lippmann, who had been writing for the *New York World*, on its demise became a syndicated *New York Herald-Tribune* columnist. Lippmann continued writing until 1971, Lawrence until 1973.[8]

Political columnists became popular in the early 1930s. One reason cited for their rise is that, with the coming of the New Deal, editorial page editors were eager to publish interpretive writers who, because of their inside sources, would be able to tell readers what was going on in Washington, D.C. At least some editorial page editors realized that they were unaware of what was going on in the federal government and out of touch with new trends in policy. The syndicated columnists moved in, Robert H. Estabrook of the *Washington Post* said, because newspapers were not doing a "good enough job providing background and interpretation in their news columns . . . and not doing a good enough job of providing informed comment in their editorial columns."[9] Readers wanted to know what was going on, and the columnists fulfilled this function.

Many of the early columnists, more in sympathy with the New Deal than most editors, provided contrasting opinions to the editorials with which they shared pages. Noting that most newspapers were editorially against President Franklin D. Roosevelt, Mark Ethridge of *Newsday* on Long Island wrote: "Rather than rouse the natives, or maybe to silence their protests, publishers thought it the better part of wisdom to let the columnists fight it out on their editorial pages."[10] The columnists who appeared about that time included Raymond Clapper, Tom Stokes, Drew Pearson, the Alsop brothers, Robert Allen, Marquis Childs, Dorothy Thompson and Frank Kent.

Although not among the earliest columnists, David Lawrence followed a career that typified what Ethridge called "both the rise—and . . . fall—of the columnists." Lawrence had been a favorite of Woodrow Wilson and Bernard Baruch, a prominent financier and presidential advisor. "He had the ears and confidence of the mighty, besides the energy to dig," Ethridge recalled. Columnist Walter Lippmann had also been a confidant of Woodrow Wilson and in fact was to pride himself on his close ties with public leaders through more than half a century of editorial and column writing. Robert Allen and Drew Pearson, with their "Washington Merry-Go-Round," provided readers with inside stories. Westbrook Pegler, sometimes published on the editorial page, became known for "reporting" demeaning things about public figures.

Columnist Ed Yoder has recalled that at the end of World War II Lippmann was still "the philosopher-journalist of Jovian perspective," Arthur Krock was "only slightly less Olympian in tenor and tone" and Joseph Alsop, teamed with his brother Stewart, was calling himself a reporter "even when he was most opinionated." "Just below" (Yoder's description) were figures like Pearson, "who specialized in gossip," and Lawrence, "who specialized in indignation."[11]

Eventually the popularity of these columns declined. The David Lawrence columns I edited for the *Des Moines* (Iowa) *Tribune* in the early 1960s were mostly a rehash of the daily news with a little conservative interpretation thrown in. Joseph Alsop was stuck on assuring readers that the war was being won in Vietnam. The news from Washington was reported well in the news columns, and the syndicated columnists had little more inside information than most reporters. The editorial policies of newspapers had also become more moderate. Editorial writers were more informed about and sympathetic toward what was going on in Washington. Readers also were more informed about the federal government and not satisfied with what Ethridge called the "pontificating, . . . griping, . . . off-the-cuff reflections" that came from the traditional columnists.[12]

But columnists have persisted, even though on most newspapers they probably are allotted somewhat less space now than when they first became popular. A new generation of columnists has emerged.

Columnists today serve as more than opinion and information pipelines for public officials and offer more than knee-jerk reactions to the day's news. Looking at changes in column writing, Yoder concluded that busy readers don't particularly care what a columnist thinks about this or that. "My own sense of the columnist's usefulness now is—or some would find it—shockingly esthetic, in the broad sense of that word," Yoder said. "In its new but limited form and function, the column is at best a chance to watch a mind and style at work, through time, on the topics of the day." Columnists, he suggested, should be considering such questions as: "Did the Supreme Court suffer a microbiologist to patent a manmade bug, or discover to the astonishment of many citizens that nude dancing is a form of free speech? . . . Did medical technology raise new questions about the nature of life and death?"[13] Walter Lippmann and Joseph Alsop, mostly concerned with politics and international affairs, would never have raised such questions.

SETTING POLICIES FOR COLUMNS

Editing syndicated columns involves more than placing them in predetermined positions on the editorial page. Editors must decide on the columns that they want to buy and on those that they want to run on any given day. They must make decisions about how extensively they will edit the columns and about how they will identify the columnists that appear on their pages.

Selecting Columnists

How does an editor go about deciding which columnists to subscribe to? Editors must first decide whether to offer readers a variety of viewpoints or a fairly consistent point of view, or whether to select the columnists on another basis. One survey found that 60 percent of the editorial people who responded sought to balance columnists. Only 12 percent said they selected columnists with philosophies similar to the newspaper's, while 27 percent said they picked columnists for their ability to draw readers, regardless of their philosophies.[14]

Since the birth of syndicated column writing generally coincided with the coming of the New Deal, it is not surprising that, during the first years, most columnists wrote from Washington, D.C., and were concerned with—and for the most part supportive of—government initiatives. Even as late as the late 1960s most of the favorite columnists tended to be "liberal": Walter Lippmann, Joseph Kraft, James Reston, Tom Braden, Frank Mankiewicz, Art Buchwald and Art Hoppe. When I was looking for conservative columnists in 1965, editorial page editors generally had a choice of James J. Kilpatrick (who wrote a spritely column), William F. Buckley Jr. (who wrote an erudite column), Arthur Krock (never an easy read) and Richard Wilson (a dull read).

Popular conservatives now include George F. Will, William Safire and Cal Thomas. The most published columnist who might be considered liberal is Ellen Goodman (see below). William Raspberry is the most popular African-American columnist, followed by Carl Rowan and Clarence Page. These three tend to be in the liberal camp. Anthony Lewis and Richard Cohen support liberal causes, as do Mary McGrory and Russell Baker.

The current columnist who has persisted as long as any columnist today is David Broder, whom Kilpatrick described 20 years ago as "the most honest" writer in Washington. He probably is the most respected.

Back in the early days of column writing, Anne O'Hare McCormick of the *New York Times* and Dorothy Thompson of the *New York Herald Tribune* wrote columns on international affairs. Today Georgie Anne Geyer reports and comments on foreign matters. Eleanor Roosevelt wrote a newspaper column, "My Day," during the time her husband was president and later years. Hillary Rodham Clinton resumed the practice.

To what extent do editors rely on syndicated writers today? In looking through a stack of 136 editorial (or editorial and op-ed) pages published between 1990 and 1992, I found 68 writers whom I considered to be syndicated. These writers appeared a total of 180 times. Thus, on the average, each set of pages carried about 1.3 syndicated columns. In 165 set of pages I collected from 1994 to early 1997, 103 writers apparently came from outside the newspaper. They appeared a total of 259 times, or almost 1.6 times for each page. What impressed me most was the number of new names, most of whom only appeared once or twice. Surprising, out of the 73 who showed up fewer than three times, almost half, 35, were listed as officially syndicated in the 1994 *Editor & Publisher's Syndicate Directory*. All but three of the 30 three-time-plus writers were listed. The market may be growing for columnists, but they are being spread thinner. (The *E&P Directory* had 283 entries under "Political Commentary," but these included cartoons, magazine offerings, opinion polls and "This Morning America.")

Being spread thinner, if that perception is accurate, has displeased traditional syndicated columnists who write on a regular basis. They contend that in order to build a following among a newspaper's readers, they need to be carried regularly (one, two or three times a week). It is in a newspaper's interest, they say, for readers to know that a particular columnist will appear on Monday, Wednesday and Friday. Fewer editors apparently buy that argument these days. Editors say they and their readers are more interested in what is said than in who said it. What may be happening is that, through the various media services that get dumped into a newspaper's computer during the day, editors have a wider selection of writers from which to choose.

Still, the two samples suggest editors' preferences for individual columnists have changed little. In both samples only nine columnists appeared more than five times. Six of the nine appeared in both lists, and two in the earlier list ranked not far behind these nine in the later list. The two sets of nine:

1990–92	*1994–early 97*
William Raspberry	Ellen Goodman
James J. Kilpatrick	George F. Will
Mike Royko	Mike Royko
George F. Will	David Broder
Cal Thomas	William Raspberry
David Broder	Cal Thomas
Ellen Goodman	William Safire
Anthony Lewis	Molly Ivins
Richard Cohen	Joan Beck

Among the obvious differences between the two samples is that the more recent list contains three women rather than only one and that Ellen Goodman has jumped from seventh to first place. In the first sample, 10 of the 68, or 15 percent, were women. In the second sample, 28 columnists, or 27 percent, were women.

Among African-Americans, William Raspberry slipped from first to fifth, but columnists that I could identify as African-American increased from five to six.

Columnists with Hispanic surnames increased from two to five.

Perhaps even more encouraging in terms of diversity is the evidence that more columnists are venturing beyond politics. One columnist was identified as dealing with culture and society, another with ethics and religion, several with business, others with the First Amendment.

I found fewer humor columnists in the more recent sample, however. Instead of five, I found only two: Art Buchwald and Art Hoppe.

The impression I get is that editorial page editors, while sticking with some of the familiar faces, are trying to produce fresh editorial and op-ed pages that surprise and challenge their readers.

Another impression is that they are publishing more articles written by (for lack of a better word) lobbyists for causes. Some of these writers express views that are sharply different from the newspapers' editorial policies. Some come from "think tanks," reflecting distinctive political philosophies. I found it not unusual for a newspaper that, say, supported abortion rights to publish a piece from a pro-life spokesperson, or for a newspaper that championed education to run an article taking colleges to task for overspending and protecting lazy tenured professors. I found the contrast refreshing and stimulating, if, from time to time, personally irritating.

Availability of Columnists

One problem facing newspapers, especially smaller papers that are geographically near larger papers, is how to get all the popular columnists (and cartoons). The metropolitan papers like to buy the most popular syndicated features on an exclusive basis, and who can blame them? Many are fighting to preserve their circulation and advertising in the face of competition from suburban newspapers. The suburban (and even fairly far distant) newspapers think it is unfair for the big, rich papers to tie up the best stuff.

A partial victory for the non-metros came in 1975, when, in response to threatened action by the Justice Department, the *Boston Globe* gave up its rights to the exclusive use of syndicated materials in Maine, Vermont, New Hampshire and eastern Massachusetts. But the problem persists. The *Daily Journal-American* in Bellevue, Wash., a paper published across Lake Washington from two Seattle dailies, had trouble obtaining syndicated materials when it went to a daily schedule.[15] The paper I worked for, the *Columbian* in Vancouver, Wash., across the Columbia River from two Portland dailies, had the same problem, particularly when we wanted to add a Sunday edition with a comic section.

The problem remains. In 1996 the U.S. District Court of Appeals held, in a case involving the *Daily Herald*, a suburban Chicago paper, that territorial exclusivity fosters *rather than hampers* competition. The judges' opinion noted that the suburban newspaper "has never tried to outbid the *Tribune* or *Sun-Times*." The response from an attorney for the *Herald* was: "Once the *Tribune* or *Sun-Times* gets it, as long as they continue to pay for it . . . syndicates aren't going to give it to anyone else."[16] My response would have been: How can a small newspaper be expected to outbid a metropolitan daily, or two metropolitan dailies?

Identifying Columnists

It is important for a newspaper to make it clear that syndicated columnists are not staff writers or local people. Naming the columnist's syndicate at the top or the bottom of the column helps. Editors can identify columnists, but it is best to be factual (such as "a *Washington Post* writer") rather than descriptive (such as "liberal"). A good practice, which the *Charlotte Observer* follows, is to provide the postal and e-mail addresses of the columnist at the end of the column.

Conflicts of Interest

Another issue regarding columnists is possible conflict of interest. The issue first arose during the Watergate hearings in 1973 when Jeb Stuart Magruder, former deputy director of the Committee to Re-elect the President (CRP), told an investigating committee that one of the cash distributions he had made was $20,000 to a writer named Victor Lasky. An editor's inquiry to the North American Newspaper Alliance (NANA), for which Lasky wrote, brought the reply that Lasky had received the money for speeches he had written for Martha Mitchell, a neighbor of Lasky's and the wife of the attorney general.[17] The National Conference of Editorial Writers (NCEW) filed charges with the National News Council, alleging that Lasky had engaged in a conflict of interest and that NANA had failed to accept responsibility to inform its clients of the conflict of interest. The council upheld NCEW's complaint.[18]

A 1980 report found that all major syndicates had at least announced that they would hold "their talent to avoidance of undisclosed conflicts of interest in their subject area."[19] Twenty years after the News Council ruling, however, when Gilbert Cranberg of the *Des Moines Register* took another look at the practices of the syndicates, he saw "*deja vu* all over again." The syndicates, at least a good share of them, had slipped back into their old ways of ignoring responses and rebuttals. "Some syndicates need to be reminded that editors are more than just business customers, and the services more than simply go-betweens and conduits," Cranberg wrote in reporting on his findings.[20]

Then, in 1996, when columnist George Will reminded his readers that his wife Mari Maseng was a ranking staff member of presidential candidate Robert Dole, the whole issue of conflict of interest and disclosure was reopened. A month later Maseng left the Dole campaign. Editors who participated in a symposium in *The Masthead* on what was billed as "The George Will/Mari Maseng Affair" generally agreed that Will should give up his column or refrain from commenting on the presidential race. They were still uncomfortable over the continuing potential for conflict. Cranberg said that a one-time disclosure was not sufficient, that Will's syndicate should "append a standing reference to the Will-Maseng connection to every Will column that bears even tangentially on Dole."[21]

ROLE OF THE CARTOONIST

When *Masthead* editors asked *Detroit News* cartoonist Draper Hill to take a look at the development of political cartoons in America, he started with Benjamin Franklin.[22] In 1847 Franklin provided an illustration for the pamphlet *Plain Truth* that, in Hill's view, was "clearly the invention of a wordsmith rather than a draftsman." Both editors and cartoonists are still divided over whether form or content is more important for cartoons, and whether satire or whimsy is more appropriate.

Hill credits Thomas Nast with initiating the "rough-and-tumble era" of the late 19th century, which "petered out with the death of Homer Davenport (1912) and the taming of Art Young." After cartoonists had been exhorted to "bash" the Huns during World War I, the 1920s began an era of "Good Taste." "Information, education and the nurture of consensus" replaced ridicule and satire, Hill wrote. By the end of World War II, and for another decade, cartoonists tended to take a "high-minded, generally predictable, over-labeled, under-caricatured tack . . . more bark than bite."

In 1946 the dominant cartoonists were Daniel Fitzpatrick (*St. Louis Post-Dispatch*), J.M. "Ding" Darling (*Des Moines Register*), Vaughan Shoemaker (*Chicago Daily News*), Herbert L. Block (*Washington Post*) and Bill Mauldin (*St. Louis Post-Dispatch* and, later, *Chicago Sun-Times*). Nearly all cartoons appeared in a vertical format (narrower than they were high).

Then, using the same format, but with more bite and fewer words, came the first wave of younger cartoonists, whom Hill identified as Paul Conrad, Ed Valtman, Hugh Haynie, Jules Fieffer, Bill Mauldin (who had retired and returned) and Bill Sanders.

The second wave was mostly Australian Pat Oliphant, who introduced the horizontal format and a more detailed, more artistic style that did not necessarily rely on humor.

The third wave was led by Jeff MacNelly, who also drew in the horizontal, more artistic style, but used more humor. Hill noted that when MacNelly won his first Pulitzer Prize, in 1972 at the age of 24, Oliphant referred to the cartoonists who had adopted the horizontal style as "those bastards." "Before long the epithet 'clone' achieved a certain popularity," Hill said, and as the MacNelly style became popular, the epithet became "clone of a clone."

In spite of these disparaging labels, Hill concluded that Oliphant's and MacNelly's styles (which he called the phenomenon of "Oliphany" or "MacStyle") "energized committed, aware, talented, college-educated types in unprecedented numbers and propelled them into the profession" of editorial cartooning during the years between the Vietnam War and Watergate. This new generation, Hill said, was younger and more diverse and had "at least as much editorial freedom as they [knew] what to do with."

The author of a book on political cartoons, Professor John Fischer of the University of Minnesota–Duluth, has described 1969 to 1985 as the "golden age" of editorial cartooning. A number of artists did "spectacular" work lampooning Presidents Nixon and Carter, he said, and "futile but heroic" work during the Reagan administration.

According to Fischer, many of today's editorial cartoonists do not enjoy the respect and prominence of their predecessors. One reason, he said, is that newspapers must compete with the Internet, television, radio and other media. Another reason is that newspapers are publishing cartoons in smaller formats than they did in the past.[23]

Cartoonists Today

Newspaper editorial cartoonists have been declining in number. A 1995 study estimated that about 120 cartoonists were working on daily newspapers, compared to 170 in 1980.[24] Signe Wilkinson, then president of the American Association of Editorial Cartoonists, said that cartoonists "are under a lot of pressure" as newspapers fold, make staff cutbacks or encourage "bland, gag-oriented cartoons rather than hardhitting ones."[25] The 1995 study found that, when asked how they rated the status of editorial cartooning, 55 percent of cartoonists made negative remarks and 34 percent mixed remarks. Seventy-one percent said that "political correctness" had made editorial cartooning weaker.[26] Editors who were surveyed were considerably less pessimistic.

More and more, cartoonists are finding themselves without a newspaper as a base (and major source of salary). An article in *Editor & Publisher* told of five cartoonists with no base paper. Pat Oliphant was out of a job when the *Washington Star* went out of business in 1981, but he had a sufficient number of newspaper clients (now about 400) to make it alone. Paul Conrad took a buyout from the *Los Angeles Times*, but he also had a long list of syndicate clients. One of the five was fired from his paper. Neither he nor the other two had, at the time of the article, been able to find newspapers to tie to. One (Ted Rall) had managed to tie into a syndicate and the other two (Ann C. Telnaes and Clay Bennett) had been able to become part of a syndicated package (North American Syndicate's "Best and Wittiest").[27]

Responding to this article, cartoonist Alan Vitiello said more and more cartoonists are having to work their way up through a "farm system." Several weeklies and middle-sized dailies that can't afford their full-time cartoonists have made contracts with him to provide cartoons from time to time. "A few of the newspapers allow me to comment on whatever local subject I see fit," he said, but, "[w]ith the others, I discuss with the editors which ideas would make the best cartoons." He said he didn't make a lot of money, but he gets to see his work in print and the newspapers get localized editorials at relatively low cost.[28]

One cartoonist, Bill Mitchell, formerly of the *Rochester* (N.Y.) *Democrat and Chronicle*, reported finding success on the Internet, where he draws interactive political cartoons. A click on the devil-like tail of a cartoon about House Speaker Newt Gingrich produced a listing of the ethics violations Gingrich faced. A click on his tie brought up a "David Letterman Top 10" list. "There's going to be tons more potential for cartoonists than there ever was in print," Mitchell said. "It's easy to scan the work into a computer."[29]

Ranan Lurie is one of a growing number of cartoonists who provide their work in color. As another innovation, Lurie has started attaching a brief note under each cartoon to describe the background. He said that Americans in particular are not familiar with the international issues in which he specializes.[30]

Today's editorial page editors and cartoonists partly, but only partly, see eye to eye on the role of the editorial cartoonist. Cartoonists, more than editors, tend to think of cartoonists as artists. They also tend to think they should be given more editorial freedom than editors generally would like them to have.

A 1984 survey of cartoonists and editors found that both groups rated "critic" as the first role of the cartoonist.[31] "I believe the fundamental role of an editorial cartoonist is to kick fannies–to convey one's opinion forcefully, graphically and unapologetically," said one cartoonist.

The editor's second most mentioned choice (third among cartoonists) was "opinion leader." One cartoonist who thought "opinion leader" was an inappropriate role wrote: "Editorial cartoons do not persuade. They affirm a reader's perhaps hazy stance on a subject by making concrete and graphic their positions. Readers say 'Aha! That's what I mean.'"

Among cartoonists the second choice (fourth for editors) was "artist." "Too many editors are poor judges of what is good cartoon art," one cartoonist wrote.

Who's in Charge?

Surveys have found that editors and cartoonists have somewhat different ideas about who is best qualified to judge cartoons and who should have the final word on cartoons. In the 1984 survey the largest groups of editors and cartoonists (56 percent in both instances) agreed editors and cartoonists should confer in deciding on cartoons. The remainder had different ideas, with 43 percent of the cartoonists saying cartoonists should make the decision and 35 percent of editors saying the editors should.[32] In the 1995 survey about 38 percent of editors thought they were better than cartoonists at predicting reactions to cartoons. Only about 8 percent of cartoonists agreed. Forty-eight percent of cartoonists thought that editors did not understand the function of editorial cartoons. Only 6 percent of editors agreed.[33]

Cartoonists and editors don't necessarily agree politically. In the 1984 survey cartoonists tended to be more liberal than their newspapers, but most thought cartoonists should conform to the editorial policies of their papers. "Editorial cartoons reflect opinions of the paper and the skill of the cartoonist, and, if not, cartoons don't belong in the paper," one cartoonist wrote. "If he doesn't see things in the same way the publisher does, the cartoonist should look for another publisher," another cartoonist said.[34] But in the 1995 survey only 24 percent of cartoonists and 32 percent of editors said cartoons should reflect the editorial policy of the newspaper. If a cartoon conflicted with the newspaper's policy, 62 percent of cartoonists and 49 percent of editors still would run it on the editorial page. Seventeen percent of cartoonists and 15 percent of editors would run it on the op-ed page. Only 3 percent of cartoonists and 13 percent of editors would not run the cartoon.[35]

So perhaps some cartoonists are being given more opportunities to express views that differ from the newspaper's official editorial policy. The degree of freedom no doubt varies from newspaper to newspaper and from cartoonist to cartoonist. A cartoonist in the 1984 survey pointed out that "[a]n Oliphant, for instance, should never be restricted," but to reach that status, a cartoonist had to be "good, well-versed and responsible enough to tell good slams from cheap shots."

A cartoonist's position can't be allowed to become "too revered," Mindy Cameron of the *Seattle Times* said during an NCEW convention panel on editor-cartoonist relationships. Editors, she said, must make their responsibilities clear to cartoonists, discuss what kinds of cartoons are expected and insist on keeping a dialogue between editor and cartoonist.[36] The cartoonists on the panel said trust was the most important part of their relations with editors. After years of drawing cartoons on the *Austin American-Statesman,* Ben Sargent said his editors "trust me not to do something too *outre,* [and] I trust them to back me up."

In a *Masthead* symposium on "Getting Along With Your Cartoonist," Thomas Gebhardt, associate editor of the *Cincinnati Enquirer,* said that, when Jim Borgman first started as a cartoonist, he drew what was expected of him. But, according to Borgman, as his skill matured and his reputation increased, Borgman began drawing cartoons that reflected his, and not necessarily the paper's, view.[37] "A decade ago it became clear to me that I could only do my best work only if granted that freedom," Borgman wrote for the symposium.[38] Not many cartoonists have this honey of a deal.

Perhaps a more typical relationship exists at the *Lincoln* (Neb.) *Journal.* Editorial Page Editor Dick Herman reported that cartoonist Paul Fell usually offered three or four rough drafts early in the morning. "We confer. We parlay. Sometimes I bounce Satanic counterproposals at him," Herman said. "But increasingly, his own commentary stands. It becomes a finished product by noon or early afternoon."[39]

SETTING POLICIES FOR CARTOONS

Editors face two policy questions when they select cartoons for the editorial page: Should cartoons, especially those at the top of the editorial page, reflect only the editorial policies of the newspaper? In buying syndicated cartoons, should editors seek a broad or a narrow array of opinions?

To Support Editorials?

Some newspapers (the *Seattle Post-Intelligencer*, for example) have a policy that encourages editorial writers and cartoonists to focus on the same subject for a particular day's editorial page. Some studies have indicated that cartoons are more persuasive if they are published in conjunction with editorials expressing the same point of view. On other newspapers that have their own cartoonists, the cartoonists and the editorial writers may have differing agendas, and only by chance hit on the same subject.

On papers that depend on syndicated cartoons, editors must rely on whatever comes in the mail that day. Saving unused–and even used–cartoons can provide a backlog from which to draw when a cartoon is needed to go with an editorial or column. Most cartoons, however, quickly become dated.

A Variety of Opinions?

A more serious question is whether editorials and cartoons on the same page should express the same editorial philosophy. One line of thought among editors is that any cartoon at the top of an editorial page should conform to, or at least not conflict with, the policies of the paper. According to this reasoning, a cartoon at the top of the page will have the most impact if it reflects the paper's position. Some publishers and editors think readers will be confused about the paper's policy if they see a conflict between editorials and the lead cartoon. Other publishers and editors consider cartoons as they do political columns, as intended to present a variety of opinions.

Most editors who subscribe to syndicated cartoons probably take a middle ground. First, they are not likely to subscribe to cartoons that are completely out of sync with their papers' policies. Second, unless editors subscribe to a large number of cartoons, they must take on a daily basis what they are sent by the syndicates. Contemporary layouts of editorial pages have encouraged editors to publish more cartoons. When cartoons are used to illustrate columns or articles, the reader may be less likely to ask, or care, whether they reflect the paper's policies.

In deciding which cartoonists to subscribe to, the editor must decide whether to limit the selection to those that generally agree with the newspaper's policies, to choose from a wide political range, or to seek the best cartoonists. My perusal of editorial pages suggests that a minority of newspapers subscribes strictly to cartoons of one political stripe. Editors may place their favorite cartoonist or cartoonists in the lead spot on the page, but most pages allow for the display of other cartoons. Just as editors are likely to want to provide readers with a variety of columnists, they are likely to want a variety of cartoonists.

In an unscientific search for the cartoonists most popular with editors today, I examined the same stack of editorial and op-ed pages that I used in tallying columnists. I found 308 cartoons by 99 cartoonists. The cartoons appeared on 165 editorial and/or op-ed pages, for an average of 1.86 cartoons per page or set of pages. Of the 99 cartoonists, 55 were listed as syndicated by

Editor & Publisher.[40] These cartoonists appeared 231 times, for an average of 1.4 cartoons per page or set of pages. In a similar survey for an earlier edition I found 47 (apparently syndicated) columnists, who ran a total of 161 times on 136 pages, for an average of 1.2 cartoons per page. These figures would suggest that editors are using slightly more cartoons on their pages than before, but the chances of an individual syndicated cartoonist getting published remain about the same: 2.5 times for every 100 pages. The 55 also are facing more competition from cartoonists such as the 44 who are not syndicated. Of course, a few cartoonists get published a lot more frequently than the rest of them. From year to year the favorites remain about the same.

Here is how the rankings compare for the two surveys (appearing four or more times):

1990–92	*1994–early 97*
Doonesbury	Doonesbury
Jeff MacNelly	Don Wright
Patrick Oliphant	Jim Borgman (tie)
Don Wright	Jeff MacNelly (tie)
Jim Borgman	Mallard Fillmore (tie)
Berry's World	Mike Luckovich
Dunigan's People	Patrick Oliphant (tie)
Dick Wright	Toles (tie)
Henry Payne	Berry's World
Bill Day	Jeff Stahler
Mike Luckovich	Steve Benson
David Horsey	Chip Bok
Steve Benson	Ed Gamble
	Mike Peters
	Margulies

Of the 13 cartoonists on the earlier list, 8 appear among the 15 on the newer list. The most unusual addition is "Mallard Fillmore," which several newspapers now run side-by-side with "Doonesbury," presumably to attain a conservative-liberal balance. "Mallard Fillmore" and "Doonesbury" are the only strip cartoons on the list.

No woman or racial minority cartoonists showed up in the earlier study. The more recent pages contained cartoons by two women (Ann C. Telnaes, mentioned above, and Signe Wilkinson, whose home base is the *Philadelphia Daily News*) and one Hispanic-appearing man (Mike Ramirez). Apparently there are no African-American syndicated cartoonists, since Eric Harrison of the Gary, Ind., *Post-Tribune* has described himself as "the only black [political] cartoonist working for a mainstream paper."[41]

YOUR OWN CARTOONIST?

Surveys show that about 10 percent of daily newspapers have a regular editorial cartoon. Editors who can't afford a full-time cartoonist are sometimes tempted to turn to free-lance artists or artists on their own staffs. Some successes have resulted. Jim Borgman had done only one cartoon a week for his college paper and wasn't particularly interested in public affairs when he went to work for the *Cincinnati Enquirer*.[42] Paul Fell was teaching art in a small college when he started sending an occasional cartoon to the *Lincoln Journal*.[43] (When Fell later was laid off by the *Journal*, he turned to fax and radio. He faxed his daily cartoons to 200 local citizens, then went on the air to take calls from his subscribers.)[44] In looking through a group of Nebraska newspapers, I found a Fell cartoon in the *Kearney Hub*, suggesting he has found additional outlets for his work.

The *Gainesville Sun* found a free-lance cartoonist through a cartoon-drawing contest. Unable to afford a full-time cartoonist, the paper invited readers to draw cartoons on current issues. About 40 responded. The best of the submissions were published in a special Sunday "Issues" section. From the contestants, a *Sun* editor reported, came "the next best thing to an on-staff cartoonist, a talented and prolific free-lancer."[45] The *Arlington* (Mass.) *Advocate* acquired the part-time cartooning talents of a person whose regular job was engraving portraits on tombstones.[46]

One alternative for the newspaper without a cartoonist is to publish a picture on the editorial page. The Big Stone Gap, Va., *Post* ran an old-time picture of a mining camp in Southwest Virginia submitted by a reader. The *Fauquier* (Va.) *Times-Democrat* ran a picture of sign-carrying protestors at a meeting of the county board of supervisors. The *Rappahannock* (Va.) *News* ran a picture of a steel bridge that formed "interesting patterns."

Skilled local artists can bring life and controversy to a page, especially when commenting on local topics. But they must be more than artists or clever gag writers. When asked for ideas on how to get editorial cartoons from a good artist who didn't follow the news, A. Rosen of the Albany, N.Y., *Knickerbocker News*, then president of the National Cartoonist Society, advised: "Give up on that person; you'll never make him or her an editorial cartoonist. Instead, seek out a young person who may not draw well but who is interested in public affairs. Hire that person."[47]

CONCLUSION

Rosen's point was that the message is more important than the medium. Editors should not run syndicated columnists and cartoonists only because it is the standard thing to do, because these features spruce up the page or because they bring wandering eyes to the page.

They should use these syndicated features—and their own local columnists and cartoonists—to present ideas to their readers. They should try to make their readers think—not just entertain them or present them with writers and artists who express opinions and ideas that readers already have. An editorial page should be a place where readers find some familiar faces and names, but also unfamiliar ways of looking at the local community, the state, the nation and the world.

1. Keep track of the syndicated columns in the newspapers of your area to determine whether they tend to run columnists that agree with their own editorial policies, that disagree or that express a variety of opinions.
2. Do these papers run a few columnists consistently or a variety of columnists infrequently? If they run a few, do these columns have something new and different to say each day? If they run a variety, do columns appear often enough to build regular followings among readers?
3. How would you judge the overall quality of the columnists published by the various newspapers you have studied? Do some of the papers seem to spend a lot of money on columnists and others only a little?
4. Do any of the newspapers label the columnists they carry, or attempt to describe the columnists' political positions? If so, are the labels accurate and appropriate?
5. Can you find letters to the editor concerning columns that have been distributed by the syndicates?
6. Which cartoonists seem to be most popular?
7. Do any of the newspapers have their own political cartoonists? Where do they appear on the editorial page? Does the local cartoon always agree with the editorial policies of the paper?
8. Ask editorial page editors in your area whether they have had trouble purchasing a column or cartoon because of territorial exclusivity.
9. While you have the editors' attention, ask them how often they receive letters from syndicates in response to columns and whether they always publish those letters.
10. If you still have the editors' attention, ask about their policies on trimming columns.

CHAPTER 19 Innovations in Design and Content

When editorial page editors sit down to plan the following day's editorial page, and the op-ed page if there is one, they must select editorials, letters, columns, cartoons and other materials. They must also decide on the layout that will best accommodate those features. Some editors, by their own choice or someone else's, are stuck with editorial pages that look the same every day and contain the same mix of features. But the trend among daily newspapers seems clearly to be in the direction of varying the editorial page, from one day to the next, in appearance and content. Varied makeup of a page can help attract readers; varied content can provide pleasant and rewarding surprises for readers. The purpose of this chapter is to trace efforts to transform the editorial page and the op-ed page from among the most stodgy-looking pages into spritely, stimulating pages.

THE "GRAY" TRADITION

For most of the 175 years of the American editorial page's history, editors attempted to gain distinction for their pages through gray respectability. When Professor Robert Bohle of Virginia Commonwealth University was asked to look back over 40 years of newspaper design in 1986, he found that editorial pages had changed the least.[2] The guru of newspaper typography, Edmund C. Arnold, agreed. "The page is still locked into a static page pattern," Arnold said. "It's more interesting than it was 40 years ago, but it's still static."[3]

Except for William Randolph Hearst, who jazzed up his editorial pages 50 years before nearly everyone else, most editors continued through World War II to make up their pages much as their 19th-century predecessors had.

Although the editorial page began to emerge as a separate page, or as a portion of a page, during the first decades of the 19th century, the page was hard to distinguish from other pages. All the type, news and editorial, was set one column in width. News and editorials ran from the bottom of one column to the top of the next column and sometimes from the bottom of one page to the top of the next.

Aside from content, about the only distinguishing mark of an editorial, evident as early as 1835 in the *New York Sun*, was slightly larger type with lines spaced (leaded) a little farther apart. The only headlines were three or four words in italics of the same size and on the same line as the body type. (The *Sun* for Aug. 11, 1835, is displayed in Figure 1, page 299.) This page measured 11 by 15 inches, about the size of the modern-day tabloid, but the type was considerably smaller than the type used in most newspapers today. The size of the *Sun*'s type is hard to measure, but type on the editorial page of the *New York Times* of 1859 was probably 8 points high, compared to $6\frac{1}{2}$ points in the news columns. (Most news columns today are set in $9\frac{1}{2}$ or 10-point type, and editorials are set in 12-point or larger type. The text you are reading now is in $10\frac{3}{4}$-point type.) It takes 72 points to make an inch, so you can see that reading 19th-century newspapers was a strain.

A typical editorial page in Horace Greeley's *New York Tribune* in 1871 contained more than 6,000 words, compared to about 2,600 words (body type) on the editorial page of the *Star Tribune* on page 303 (Figure 4). Part of the difference is accounted for by today's narrower pages, 13 inches compared to 15.5. The printed area of the *Star Tribune* (about 89 percent of Greeley's pages) contains only 43 percent of the words on a Greeley page. Artwork accounts for about 17 percent of the *Star Tribune* page (none for the *Tribune*). The major differences result from artwork, relatively larger body type, substantially larger headline type and more white space. Today's pages certainly are a lot more attractive than those of Greeley's day, but they contain substantially less information and opinion.

Editors were shocked when Hearst and Arthur Brisbane began to set editorials in larger type and wider columns, to run the editorials across several columns (perhaps the original horizontal makeup) and to introduce huge illustrations to the page. Hearst's clouded reputation may even have delayed the brightening of American editorial pages, since "respectable" editors did not want their pages to look like his. An example of the Hearst style, the *New York American* of Oct. 27, 1933 (Figure 2, page 300), uses a banner headline the width of the page for the lead editorial. Above the headline is a scriptural quotation. Columns are separated by white space and wavy lines, unlike most editorial pages of that day, where the columns traditionally were run close together with a thin rule between them. The *American* page is made even more dramatic by a large cartoon.

A textbook copyrighted in 1936 warned editorial page editors:

> In these days, when the average newspaper reader has less time for reading than formerly—when he does more glimpsing than reading, and confines most of that glimpsing to the headlines and leading news stories or entertaining features—he seems to care little or nothing for newspaper editorials. If his attention is to be captured and held by the editorial page,

Figure 1 **New York Sun**

THE NEW YORK SUN.

TUESDAY MORNING, AUGUST 11, 1835.

Distress in Ireland.—Accounts from Ireland, received by the Sheffield, represent many districts of Ireland as suffering great distress from famine. In one parish, consisting of thirty-four families, in the county of Galway, only three possessed provisions for a week. In another, comprising 322 families, only 37 were provisioned till harvest; and, should they extend relief to their famishing neighbors, the whole stock would not hold out a week. "From an authentic source, we have discovered that upwards of 6,000 persons in the barony of Erris, county Mayo, alone, have, on an average, but five days' provision on hand; and in that number there are 106 persons who can command but half a hundred of potatoes amongst them, and 300 without any, whose sole dependence is on chance shell-fish and sea weed, a sample of which we have seen."

Foreigners, and Foreign Influence.—It cannot have escaped the notice of even the most casual observer of what is passing about him in the moral and political world, that within a very short time past, the patriotism of certain of the presses of this city has become most suddenly and most afflictingly sensitive to the appalling dangers which they affect to have discovered overshadowing the liberties and institutions of our republic, by reason of the great influx of emigrants from foreign countries, and the overwhelming influence they are pretended, by these newly fledged patriots, to possess over the judgments and opinions of our native citizens, and the character and destinies of our government. We should do violence to our own imperfect discretion, and to the judgment which our observation of the progress and fruits of the alleged monstrous evil has compelled us to make upon the subject, were we to pretend that we have not ample testimony on every side of us, that the laws of our country, in the premises, do not stand in need of revision and restriction, and that they have entailed upon the country a train of troubles and evils which she could happily dispense with.

But it is not our object now to speak particularly of those evils, or their prospective consequences. Our more immediate purpose, at this time, has been incited by the very recent, and it would seem, almost miraculous discovery, by the presses above referred to, of the stupendous mischiefs against which they are now incessantly harping, and the tremendous and all-devouring force with which this Saul-like conviction has come over them. And, what is most remarkable of all, those very presses which are amongst the loudest in stirring up the bile of native against adopted citizens, are themselves either entirely controlled, or essentially managed by persons coming within the range of their own animadversions, and their most efficient editors are foreigners!

The Courier & Enquirer, for instance, one of the fiercest journals in the city in denunciations of foreigners and foreign influence, numbers among its stipendiary caterers no less than *three* to whom America was a stranger, except by reputation, till within a very few years past; and one of those, the notorious Hoskins, has the supreme control of its course and contents, not excepting even a supervision of the mad ebullitions of Webb himself, who seldom knows, for weeks together, what his paper contains, till it arrives to him at some distant place.

The Evening Star, too, which, under the management of the "King of the Jews"—the demi-American Noah, pretends to a sensibility to foreign encroachment which seems at times half frantic, is indebted for full four-fifths of its editorial matter to the pens of a couple of English scribblers—one of whom sits in the shadow of his principal's huge frame, and bespatters alike the venom of his master's disappointment upon American freemen, and his own spite and petty malice upon his own fellow emigrants, much of which perchance, is engendered by the fact that most of them left home with less sullied reputations than he did himself.

Indeed, almost every large paper in the city which has taken sides with the two above named in this sudden crusade of extermination against foreigners, is in a greater or less degree under the management of men who owe to other hemispheres their birth, breeding, principles, and education; and it is the greatest scandal they can utter against American character, that there is in its composition so great a share of gullibility and sycophancy that *themselves* have obtained the control of so large a portion of the mightiest engine of the land, the public press, hnd wield it with impunity against our purest patriots and most sacred interests and institutions. More hereafter.

Coroner's office, No. 118 Wooster street.—On Saturday evening the Coroner was called on to view the body of Martha Ann Finn, aged 23, born in Massachusetts, who was living as a prostitute at the house of Sallome Blanchard, over Ridgeway's grocery at the corner of Little Water and Anthony streets. It appeared in evidence before the jury, that the deceased was on Friday night in a state of gross intoxication, and that between the hours of 11 and 12 that night, fell out of the second story window of the house upon the side-walk, by which fall her skull was so badly fractured that she died in consequence on Saturday afternoon about half past 5 o'clock. Verdict of the jury: death by falling from the second story window while in a state of intoxication and fracturing her scull.

March of the Drama.—"Who saw the sun to-day?" exclaimed a votary of the sock and buskin, as he passed Park Row a few days since. "Here it is, sir," replied a sprightly little vender of a well-known and interesting penny diurnal, at the same time advancing towards the stage-stricken gentleman. "Begone, fellow—thou troublest me," returned the hero; "do you not readily perceive that I am spouting the immortal!" "Immortal d—l," reiterated the urchin; "you are spouting three-centers!"

Caution.—It has been the practice, for some time, for a great mass of well-grown boys, from 14 to 19 years of age, principally the sons and apprentices of respectable mechanics, to assemble, between 7 and 8 o'clock every night, and to continue, frequently, almost all night, at and about engine house No. 40, in Mulberry street, between Grand and Broome, and to insult and annoy the neighbors and persons passing by, as also to indulge in noise, and riotous and disorderly conduct. The other evening, they broke the windows of Mr. Bogardus, a gentleman residing hard by the place of their assemblage, and enveloped his hired servant girl in a cloud of flour they procured and threw over her. As these boys are known to the police officers, it will be well for them to desist, in future, from their riotous and disorderly assemblages and conduct, unless they wish to be honored with imprisonment, as it is the intention of the officers and some of the neighbors united, to arrest and punish them with the utmost severity, if they continue to indulge in their infamous practices any longer.

Troubles in Baltimore.—Passengers from Baltimore, who arrived here yesterday, state that they were witnesses to a serious riot which took place in that city on Saturday night and Sunday morning.—The mob attacked the houses of Reverdy Johnson and John Glenn, esquires, formerly directors of the bank of Maryland, and caused great destruction in the house of the latter. The citizens flew to arms, and *rumor* says eighteen lives were lost—a great many more were severely wounded;—among the latter Mr. Findlay, Mr. Cheeves, and Mr. Adams. As the passengers left early in the morning, they are not able to state minute partieulars.

The Philadelphia papers of yesterday contain corresponding statements, brought by the Baltimore steamboats, and there is strong and lamentable probability that the above account is not exaggerated.

A Small Deluge.—The immense water tank of the gas works on Eighteenth street, which held 30,000 gallons, burst on Saturday last, when nearly full of water, and deluged the premises. At the time of the occurrence, one of the workmen was on a ladder looking into the tank, and another was standing near it on the floor; they were both swept to a corner of the yard as much as sixty feet distant. A horse and cart, the latter loaded with bricks, were lifted from the ground, and the cart turned bottom side up. Poor Dobbin looked perfectly astonished, and snorted loud his wonderment; but fortunately he was more scared than hurt.

A rumpus at Lynn, Mass.—Thompson, the abolitionist, held forth at Lynn on Thursday evening last. There was a large assembly (mostly females, as usual) in the house, and a still larger one, of men, without. There was a continual hallooing and noise, and about the middle of the lecture the cry of "Fire!" and presently the ringing of the bell at the other end of the Common, created much confusion and affright for a few moments—some persons fainted. After the alarm had subsided in some degree, the cry of fire was again heard, but the audience kept their seats. The crowd and noise outside increasing, Mr. T. closed his harangue. The whole congregation then rose and sung the doxology, and the meeting was closed by prayer. The mob exasperated by the expressions of defiance used by Mr. T. in his discourse, closed round the steps and doors of the house, so as effectually to prevent the egress of the audience. Presently there was a rush at the doors by the mob, who threatened Mr. T., but by the prompt exertions of those within, the doors were closed. Rotten eggs were thrown and a missile came near hitting Mr. T.'s head.

The Wave at Boston.—A few days since we copied from the Boston Transcript a paragraph giving some account of a second race between Capt. Stevens's Wave, and the Sylph of Boston, in which the latter beat the former on rough water. Captain Forbes, of the Sylph has contradicted that assertion, in the Transcript, and states that his boat was fairly beaten both times. He however talks of further experiments.

Mortality among Children.—The deaths among the children in Baltimore have been very distressing. The weekly bills of mortality present more than three children to one adult.

Mrs. Hayes' Syrup.—The numerous instances which have within a few weeks past come to our knowledge, in which afflicting and apparently inveterate cases of dysentary and cholera morbus have been effectually relieved and ultimately cured, by the use of Mrs. Hayes' Syrup, induce us again unsolicitedly to call the attention of our readers to her advertisement on our last last page. A perfect conviction that we are but doing our duty to the community, in this age of quackery and humbug, alone induces us to press this invaluable preparation upon the attention of our readers and the public, to whom we recommend it as being, in our estimation and in the estimation of hundreds of others, who, like ourselves, have experienced its salutary effects, decidedly the most efficient and innocent remedy for complaints incident to the present season, of which we have any knowledge.

A Case of Conscience.—A mate of an East Indiaman, named Dennis Carter, aged 38 years, put an end to his life in London, on the first July, under the following extraordinary circumstances:—Since the return of the deceased from his last voyage, he addicted himself to drinking. Meeting with a Bible, he was struck with his bad conduct, and in it wrote the words as follows: "I promise from this day never to drink grog or blaspheme in the name of the Almighty.—Dennis Carter." In a very short time his passion for liquor overcame his resolution, and he got intoxicated; the next morning he was sadly grieved at having broken his vow, and the circumstances preying on his mind, in the evening he cut his throat.

The London Courier says the talked of marriage of the Queen of Portugal with the Duke de Nemours is now wholly given up on account of the known aversion of England to such a match.

The Office of the Sun has been removed to the corner of Nassau and Spruce streets, opposite the City Hall.

Trieste, June 18.—Shocking Calamity.—We have received the following melancholy intelligence from Malta:—An Austrian merchantman, which had taken in a cargo of cotton and gum at Alexandria, had already arrived off Malta, on its voyage to Leghorn, when three of the crew died of the plague, on which the remainder of the sailors were seized with such alarm that they unanimously declared that they would not continue their voyage in that ship. The captain, therefore, went into Malta, landed his crew, and took another that was not so fearful, with which he proceeded on his voyage to Leghorn. But they had not gone far when some men were seized with the plague and died. The captain adopted the usual precautions, such as fumigation, &c. and already entertained hopes of arresting the disorder, when fire broke out on board, and destroyed the ship and cargo; the captain escaped. It is not stated whether the whole or part of the crew had arrived at Malta.

From Jamaica.—By the arrival of the ship John W. Cater, Capt. Moncrieffe, we are put in possession of Kingston (Jam.) papers to the 17th July.

Previous to the sailing of the Comus, which arrived at Kingston, Jam., on the 15th, from the Caymanas, the island was perfectly quiet. Commander Hamilton brings the intelligence of the wreck of the American ship Atlantic, Balley, belonging to New York.—She went on shore on the east point of the Grand Cayman on the morning of the 23d June—the master, crew, passengers, and the whole of the ship's stores and cargo were saved, and sold with the hull by auction to the inhabitants of the island. She was out fifty-two days from Havre de Grace, bound to New Orleans. The master has freighted a small schooner belonging to the island to convey himself, crew and passengers to New Orleans.

A proclamation has been issued calling on the house of assembly to meet and proceed to business on the 4th of August. [Commercial.

Ship Launch and Dreadful Accident.—On Thursday an immense crowd assembled on the banks of the Dry Dock, Lincoln, to witness the launch of a schooner. Upwards of 100 persons were on board the vessel, which had scarcely entered the water when she turned completely over, and all the persons on board, among whom were several women and children were precipitated into the water and against the banks of the dock. By the praise-worthy exertions of the spectators most of the drowning persons were rescued in a few minutes, and numbers escaped by swimming. The bodies of two children, quite dead have been dragged on shore, and other persons are still missing. [Lincoln Gaz.

More Walloping.—Finnell, of the Lexington Observer, and Vanderslice, of the Georgetown Sentinel, had a battle in Georgetown, on Sunday week. Out of respect to the day, they left their pistols at home and fought with fists; Vanderslice, who was the assailant, is said to have come of second best. We are no friend of Mr. Justice Lynch, but he would certainly do a good thing for these ruffian editors of Kentucky, by rendering them *hors du combat* for a time.

Again.—Charles P. Green, the editor of the Boydstown, Va. Expositor, was attacked a few days since in Warrenton, N. C. by two individuals, named Bragg, one of whom he had assailed in his newspaper. A bloody combat ensued. Green was beaten to the ground with a heavy bludgeon, but rising, he drew a dirk, cut the upper lip of one of his assailants nearly off, stabbed him also in the arm, and buried the weapon in the throat of the other, who is expected to die. A Mr. Somerville, who interfered to keep the peace, was severely wounded by the explosion of a pistol. At the termination of the fight, Green invited two others of the Bragg family to come on, and take a hand, if they felt disposed! Our civilization goes backward like a crab.

Mutiny.—In September last, the crew of the Halcyon, whale ship from New London, mutinied while she was prosecuting her voyage in the Indian Ocean, in consequence of which the captain was obliged to put into Port Louis, in the Isle of France, where he delivered up the mutineers, twenty-one in number, to the custody of the American consul. There they remained in prison sixty three days, during which one of them died, and the American consul sent the remaining twenty to England in the British ship Bencoolen. The American consul at London sent home ten of them, whose names are annexed, by the Toronto which arrived here two or three days back, and on Saturday they were brought to the police office, and temporarily committed to bridewell until they can be handed over to the authorities of the United States. Their names are Isaac Wood, Jason Goodrich, David Kenny, Erastus P. Cartwright, Isaac Delon, Henry Joseph Dower, Patrick M'Keever, and Patrick Cosgrane. [Jour. of Com.

The body of a man, named William Moody, a carpenter by trade, was found dead in the street by the city watch on Wednesday night last. There were no marks of violence on it—and the verdict of the coroner's jury, called by Justice H. T. Cox, was, that the deceased came to his death by intemperance. The deceased was supposed to have been a citizen of Portland, Maine, from his having in his pocket book a letter from his wife, addressed to him from that place. [Mobile Register.

Flood and Loss of Life.—We learn by letter from Mercer, Pa. that on the night of the 12th ult. the rain fell to the depth of fourteen inches in the neighborhood of the country north and west of the Broken Straw Creek, in Warren county, producing an unprecedented rise in the smaller streams, and swelling the Alleghany to a degree heretofore unknown for the season of the year. A number of mill dams were swept away, and the bridges of Broken Straw from its mouth to Sprigh Creek, a distance of thirty or forty miles, were entirely destroyed. Above, the flood was equally destructive. The Mercer Luminary states that at Linzora an accident of a most distressing nature occurred. On Sugar run, in this township, a mill-dam was constructed, part of which ran some distance across the flat; and on this flat, below the dam, the owner had erected his dwelling-house. On the night of the storm he discovered that the water was rising very fast, and opened the flood gate: but finding this did not afford a sufficient outlet, he went a short distance to procure help. On returning, he found, to his utter consternation and distress, that his dam had broken, and swept away his house and its contents with his wife and two children! He arrived in time to hear their screams, but could afford them no relief. The bodies were found on the evening of the ensuing day, some distance below.

Philadelphia Inquirer.

The Cincinnati Whig, of the 30th, states six victims of cholera in Green township, Hamilton county, in that state.

Jackson Mahon, indicted in Baldwin, Superior Court, for the murder of Martin Smith, on the 4th inst., has been found guilty.

[Reported for the Sun.]

Police Office—Yesterday.

MORNING RETURNS.

Lawrence Clark, for intemperance and rioting in the street, was fined $1 and costs and committed.

Archibald Madden, for rioting and assaulting Elizabeth Leacroft; was committed.

Mars Kneas, of No. 9 King street, a young insolent piece of flesh and blood, who because of his name being *Mars*, conceived himself, no doubt, to be the very God of war; was brought up charged with abusing his father Michael Kneas, and the family, he being an inmate of the same house. As his father was not present to prosecute the complaint, he deported himself with the utmost insolence and haughtiness before the magistrate, endeavored to throw the entire blame upon his father, and proved by his own language that if he was not put in prison for abusing his father, he deserved to be for his impudence in the office; but was necessarily discharged.

Susan Sarles, Anthony Dow, a boy from Long Island, and Michael Hogan out of the alms-house, were brought up for lodging in the watch-house habitually; and discharged, the latter to return to the alms house.

Mary Byrnes, a sick vagrant, was sent to the Penitentiary for 3 months.

Frederick Steneck, a German, in a state of inebriate exhilaration, got his ideas raised so high, that he attacked Charlotte Johnson, a well dressed colored woman, of 93 Christie street, in the street, in a most indecent and ruffianly manner; struck her twice in the face, and on her resisting, tore her silk dress almost off her, seized her bonnet and reduced it to a wreck, and was pursuing her with other acts of violence, when he was arrested and brought in. For all of which he was committed to prison.

William Brown was brought in by James Ward, keeper of the Washington Hotel, who found him up stairs in bed in one of the rooms, under suspicious circumstances, and who, when attempting to be ejected, made a stout resistance, for which he received a black eye, was lodged in the watch-house, and in the morning committed.

Hugh McClean and Owen McClean, committed for riotous and disorderly conduct.

Francis Sheridan came in himself, in a state of supposed derangement, but in the morning was deemed sane enough to be discharged.

Juvenile Thieves.—Yesterday, George Burns, who keeps an old iron and junk shop at No. 127 Washington street, discovered three boys named Phillip King, John King, and Peter Coen, enter his premises and steal about 40 pounds of scrap iron, which they placed in a cart, and were conveying away to sell, when he pursued, overtook and arrested one of them, the first named, whom he brought to the police office, the other two escaping. These boys appeared to be not more than from 12 to 13 years old, and Mr. Burns stated, that during the last week, he had had stolen from him, by these and other boys, above 200 pounds of scrap iron, part of which had been taken and sold at the junk shop of his neighbor, Michael Klone, in Carlisle street. The young thief was committed to prison for examination.

Thefts.—The cabin of the brig Cyrus, of Portland, Maine, lying at the foot of Duane street, was entered on Saturday night, and robbed of a frock coat, pantaloons, and three vests. A white merino shawl was stolen from No. 14 Spring street, and a dark green overcoat from No. 4 Forsyth street; and from No. 34 Cedar street, five thick and thin coats, and two pairs of pantaloons.

On Saturday, Mrs. Margaret Navarra, widow, of No. 40 Avenue D, was robbed of a small black silk purse, containing $108 in bills and silver, which was stolen out of a small basket in her possession, and carried away.

Robbing a Sweetheart.—Yesterday about 6 o'clock, a girl of the town named Sarah Rocket, of 57 Orange street, met a young Englishman, named John Johnsoe, in Chatham street, and charged him with robbing her of $7, and a purse worth 50 cents, for which he was committed.

Land Operations.—We learn that a company of gentlemen from this city have recently purchased the principal part of the land at Elizabethtown point, N. J., including the privileges of the ferry, and intend laying it out in streets and lots; and encouraging the speedy settlement of the place as a new city. For manufactures there are great facilities; there is an excellent back country, and by the way of Amboy vessels of large burthen can come up to the dock.—The Sommerville rail road, already chartered, will terminate at this point. [Commercial.

Shocking Affair.—On Friday afternoon a man by the name of Reuben Amadon, Jr. of Sandlake, was in the act of going with his team, on the lands of one of his neighbors, by the name of William Briggs, when he was forbidden by the latter. Some altercation ensued. Amadon threw down his whip, seized a club, and struck Briggs a violent blow on the head, which killed him instantly. Amadon is committed to jail to await his trial. [Troy Whig.

Gen. William Brady, and Henry Bridly, Esq., died of cholera at Murfreesborough on the 23d, after a few hours' illness.

Two criminals escaped form the gaol at Haddam, Middlesex co., by sawing off the grates of their windows. A reward of $60 has been offered for their apprehension.

Cholera.—There has been no case of cholera at Nashville since the 24th.

The Fire Fly locomotive performed a trip from Ballston to Schenectady, N. Y. and back again, last week, in one hour and three minutes. Distance *thirty-one miles!*

Tunnel under our Harbour.—A few days since we gave notice of the commencement of a new entrance to our harbour, we have now to notice that arrangements are being made for the construction of a tunnel under it at the foot of Main street. Such a work when completed will do credit to those engaged in it and be useful to our citizens, there being now a large tract of land in a business part of the city lying almost entirely useless on account of the difficulty of access to it. The work it is thought can be accomplished with a double track, for from $30,000 to $40,000, leaving 12 feet of water on the arch. [Buffalo Trans.

A volume, written and compiled by two of the crew of Captain Ross's late Arctic expedition, has appeared in London; it brings charges of an unparalleled nature against the captain, and gives all the credit to commander Ross; the captain is declared to have monopolized all the trade with the Esquimaux, selling them the presents sent by government, and retaining the proceeds for their own use, &c. They state that the Esquimaux make sledges of salmon sewed in skins, having cross pieces of deer's bones, and in time of scarcity eat their sledges! It is stated in Ross's Narrative that one sledge was seen made of ice.

Practical Knowledge.—A young girl was presented to James I. as an English prodigy, because she was deeply learned. The person who introduced her boasted of her proficiency in ancient languages. "I can assure your Majesty," said he, "that she can both speak and write Latin, Greek and Hebrew."—"These are rare attainments for a damsel," said James, "pray tell me, can she spin?"

Figure 2 **New York American**

TRUTH JUSTICE — FRIDAY—New York American Editorial Page—OCTOBER 27, 1933 — PUBLIC SERVICE

Published Every Day in the Year at 220 South Street, New York City, by the New York American, Inc. President, William R. Hearst, Jr.; Secretary, Austin W. Clark.

Jesus Christ, who hath abolished death, and hath brought life and immortality to light through the gospel.—II Timothy, I, 10.

(The text for today is suggested by Rev. L. D. Woodmancy, D.D., pastor of Grace Methodist Episcopal Church, Manhattan. The next text will be suggested by Rev. Cornelius Greenway, pastor of All Souls Universalist Church, Brooklyn.)

Recognition of Soviet Russia Will Aid World Peace and International Justice

PRESIDENT ROOSEVELT'S effort "to end the present abnormal relations between the 125,000,000 people of the United States and the 160,000,000 people of Russia" ought to commend itself to the thoughtful citizens of both countries. It is a wise act on the President's part and advisable from every point of view.

"It is most regrettable," as Mr. Roosevelt truly says in his cordial message to Mr. Kalinin, president of the All Union Central Executive Committee at Moscow, **"that these great peoples, between whom a happy tradition of friendship existed for more than a century to their mutual advantage, should now be without a practical method of communicating directly with each other."**

To find such a method and to remove the difficulties that have given rise to this anomalous situation are the laudable purpose of the conversations soon to take place in the White House between the President and Mr. Litvinoff, the Russian Commissar for Foreign Affairs.

Mr. Roosevelt does not deny that these difficulties have been serious, but he shares with the American people the hope and the belief that they are no longer "insoluble."

If this free country could continue diplomatic relations with Russia under the government of the old regime, which was opposed to every principle and every ideal on which this nation was founded, we ought to be able to find a way of resuming relations with Russia under the present government, which, although not in accord with our own policies of government, is nevertheless not as diametrically opposed to our ideals as the former despotic autocracy that ruled Russia was.

Nor can we longer question the fact that this form of government is Russia's choice, because it has been firmly established there for fifteen years and there is every indication that it will continue to represent the conceptions of government held by the Russian people.

One of the reasons for this country's refusal to resume diplomatic relations with Russia was the present government's repudiation of pre-war and war-time debts.

This reason seems at present rather ridiculous, as we not only maintain diplomatic relations with France and England, but co-operate in close intimacy with these debt repudiators in regulating the affairs of Europe.

In fact, we have even appeared to be more friendly with these welching nations as they have not paid their just debts and obligations to this country.

• • •

RUSSIA from early days has been the friend of the United States, and a very important friend in past history, and there is every political reason why the two countries should resume this traditional relationship which has proved mutually advantageous in the past and may prove mutually essential in the future.

Japan has of late taken publicly on more than one occasion a very menacing attitude toward the United States.

Some of her less wise but leading statesmen and military commanders have made public utterances which appear to be most menacing in their character.

Furthermore, the moves of Japan, on the diplomatic chessboard, toward absorbing the mandated islands of the Pacific, and her activity in populating the American Territory of Hawaii, and her apparent intention ultimately to take over both the Hawaiian Islands and the Philippine Islands, are developments which would seem to indicate a temptation, if not a disposition, on the part of Japan to disrupt the friendly relations between Japan and this country and to disturb the peace of the Pacific.

Certainly the American people have no desire to see their relations with Japan other than friendly or to be called upon to defend against aggression the peace of the Pacific.

As a great nation and a peace-loving people we cherish nothing but sentiments of friendship for Japan just so long as Japan minds her own business and does not intrude upon American affairs.

But if it be the purpose of Japan, now or later, to dominate the Pacific, violate American rights or menace American territory, insular or continental, America should have an ally or at least a friend in Russia.

Therefore, for the peace of the world and for the establishment of justice among nations of good will, and for the sake of fair dealing and common sense in our international relations, it would seem to be mutually advantageous for the United States and Russia to renew that "happy tradition of friendship" which characterized their relations for more than a century.

We have said little about trade relations because these are, perhaps, the least important consideration. Nevertheless, friendly political relations promote trade relations, and trade relations, when on a basis of fairness, promote friendly political relations, so that the trade aspect of the situation should not be altogether ignored.

• • •

OF THE questions outstanding between Russia and the United States, the most serious is one that can best be removed "by frank, friendly conversations" of the sort that are soon to take place in the White House.

This is the revolutionary activity on American soil against the government and the institutions of the United States, which has been apparently fostered in the past by the government now in power at Moscow.

The American people will share with the President the hope that the Russian Commissar for Foreign Affairs, who is now on his way from Moscow to Washington, will begin his conversations by eliminating, once and for all, this obstacle to the dawn of a new and better day in the relations of these two great nations.

Jobs for Millions

WORK for millions of people would be made possible through a revival of building construction.

It has been estimated that some six million workers are affected by prosperity or lack of prosperity in the building industry. Eighty-five cents out of every building dollar is eventually paid to labor.

Building construction employs thousands of skilled mechanics and laborers. Hundreds of mills and factories employing more thousands of workers must be operated to meet the demand for clay products, woods, metals, cement, paints, textiles, glass, stone and equipment essential to the modern building.

Transportation by rail, air, ship and automobile must be employed to move raw and fabricated materials. Every new building requires new furniture, carpets and rugs, hardware and lighting fixtures. To convert raw material into use for buildings requires tools, machinery and power.

Every building erected means work for architects, engineers, draftsmen and workers in the fields of finance and real estate.

When the amount of direct and indirect employment affected by building is fully realized, the importance of the building industry as an agency for providing jobs for workers is apparent.

• • •

PUTTING men to work is a national and fundamental problem. To quickly accomplish this desirable end it is essential that we concentrate on stimulating those industries which affect the greatest number of workers.

The textile industry excepted, building is responsible for the employment of more persons than any other single industry. Building construction consumes a greater variety of materials produced throughout the United States than any other single industry. Building construction has a greater influence on the trend of general business than any other single industry. The building industry is a barometer that shows the upward and downward movement of all business. Private building construction is the major product of the industry, and therefore is of vast importance in our national economic welfare.

In addition to its Public Works Program the Federal Government should stimulate PRIVATE building construction. The Government should take such steps as may be necessary to remove the obstacles to building, unite forces, and stimulate construction.

To do so will permit employers of labor throughout the United States to put millions of workers back to work.

A Library in Miniature

CRICKETS.

Questions.

1—To what order of insects do crickets belong?
2—Does a cricket leap or walk?
3—What is a katydid?
4—How does a cricket produce its chirp?
5—Why does a cricket chirp?
6—What is a Mormon cricket?
7—Are crickets destructive?

Answers.

1—Orthoptera, a zoological classification which includes cockroaches, mantids, grasshoppers, locusts and their allies.

2—It leaps. Orthoptera are divided into leaping and walking forms, the former being called "saltatory." The saltatory orthoptera include grasshoppers, both long and short horned, true locusts and crickets.

3—A variety of orthoptera closely allied to the grasshopper. Their name was given in reference to the curious strident sound which they emit and which was thought to resemble "Katy did."

4—By rubbing one forewing across the other. The under side of one wing is equipped with a rough saw-like covering which rasps across the projecting edge of the smooth wing.

5—Only the male chirps and his stridulating is a love song intended to attract the female. Succeeding in that, the cricket lowers his tone considerably. An entomologist has discovered that a cricket makes a full-tone slur downward from the fifth "D" above middle "C" in one-fiftieth of a second.

6—The so-called Mormon cricket is not a cricket at all, but a long-horned grasshopper. In 1848, when the Mormons were attempting to settle Great Salt Lake Valley, a horde of these "black crickets" threatened to devour all the crops, but were stopped by myriads of gulls, which appeared suddenly and devoured the insects. In 1913 a monument commemorating the incident was unveiled in Salt Lake City.

7—Yes. They eat clothes, rugs, furniture, meat, bread, and certain kinds do injury to vineyards and gardens.

Copyright, 1933, King Features Syndicate, Inc.

Keep the Air Clean!

Copyright, 1933, by N. Y. American, Inc.

LIBERTY is not LICENSE. Freedom of the press, which the Constitution guarantees, does not mean that irresponsible or malicious persons may defame others by misuse of the public prints.

Libel laws, which all good publications favor and obey, provide redress when such wrongs are committed.

We also have laws to punish slander (which is unwritten libel), but slander is often difficult or impossible to prove. There remains no written record of a conversation, which would be evidential.

Radio is like the press in its access to the public, and should be like the press in responsibility. But such is not the case, because radio is too often merely disseminated conversation. And slanders sometimes occur with little or no redress.

Out in progressive California they have a law to deal with radio slander. Of that law Governor Rolph has said:

"There should be no difference between a newspaper and a radio station as concerns libel. It makes no difference whether a person is slandered in a newspaper or over a radio; he should have recourse by law in either case."

The Governor proposes to amend the law so as to require every radio station in his State to keep a permanent written record of every radio speech.

Not only California but every other State should have such a law.

Thwarting Romance by Law? -:- By Winifred Black

MOVIE FANS, don't go to Germany—not if you want to stay movie fans.

Germany is a nice, green, comfortable country, with plenty of rivers and deep, pleasant valleys and nightingales singing in the moonlight and good beer and the best sausages and pretzels in the world.

There is music in Germany, lots of it, all the time.

Everybody plays something.

The postman, if you please, plays the flute.

The grocer plays the drum and the man behind the counter at the drug store plays the piccolo.

And as for the fiddle—every other boy in high school is a violinist of sorts, and on Saturday nights and all day Sunday there is music in the air in Germany.

Good music, too, if you please. And the German moving pictures—have you seen them? They're very good, don't you think?

But Mr. Hitler is mad at the screen stars. He doesn't want any stars in Germany unless their names begin with H and end with r, it is said.

So he's made a brand new law about picture stars.

• • •

THEY aren't stars any more—not in Germany. They're just numbers.

Their names cannot be printed in big type and the name of the play must come first.

Big salaries for stars are out—in Germany. And woe be to anyone who tries to say that one pretty fraulein or one handsome herr is prettier or handsomer than anyone else.

Down with the movie fans—so says Mr. Hitler.

Now, isn't that just too silly of him?

What would you give for a girl who had never fallen in love with an actor, either on the screen or on the stage?

Not a snap of my finger, for my part.

• • •

KYRLE BELLEW, the handsome Englishman, said something to me once about matinee idols. He was a matinee idol himself, mind you.

Why, the girls used to lie in wait for him at the stage door and fairly tear him to pieces when he came out into the street after an afternoon of "The Romance of a Poor Young Man."

"They aren't crazy about me," said Kyrle Bellew. "They're crazy about romance, that's all.

"I'm always a hero in my plays. I'm poor but honest. I'm young but brave. I am humble but brilliant. I offer my life in defense of the lady of my choice. I defy tyrants. In short, I unfasten the wings of romance—they don't even know me, myself, but, ah! the hero of the play, that's different!

"If I had a daughter she'd bore me to death if she didn't have romance enough in her soul to fall in love with a hero once or twice.

"A faraway hero, of course—but a hero nevertheless."

• • •

NOW, Mr. Hitler, are you going to try to crush romance out of the German heart? You'll have to do a good deal of trying, I'm afraid.

The German fraulein hasn't those blue eyes for nothing, let me tell you.

Copyright, 1933, King Features Syndicate, Inc.

Your November Ballot

PERSONALITIES and bossism are not the only issues on which voters of this city are to pass judgment on November 7th.

The ballot will contain, besides its array of nominees for offices, six referenda, consisting of one State-wide proposition, four proposed amendments to the State Constitution, and a charter revision proposal affecting New York City only.

Little has been said of these referenda amid the wild polemics of an excited local campaign. Nonetheless, all are important.

The proposal that will appear on the ballot as "Proposition No. One" represents the public's inevitable duty to destitute families and other victims of the long depression.

It is a proposal to authorize the issuance of State emergency unemployment relief bonds to the sum total of $60,000,000.

Recommended by Governor Lehman and approved by the Republican leaders in the Legislature, there is no opposition to the measure. It MUST be approved. It should be approved UNANIMOUSLY.

Vote YES on Proposition No. One.

• • •

AMENDMENT NO. ONE to the State Constitution will permit a salutary reform in property condemnation procedure in New York City.

Under the amendment a special court will be established, presided over by competent and experienced judges; trials will be expedited, abuses eliminated and "a harmonious body of law and principles of valuation will be developed."

Vote YES on Amendment No. One.

Amendment No. Two proposes to extend "veterans' preferences" in civil service appointments and promotions, preferences now restricted to veterans who were both American citizens and residents of this State when they entered military service.

Without injustice to deserving veterans and their meritorious claims it is doubtful, indeed, if this proposal would do the public service any good and not do it considerable harm. "Veterans' preferences" are a form of class legislation. The civil service should be based upon ability always, and should not be used as an instrument for any kind of extraneous reward, whether political or otherwise.

In the interests of better civil service instead of worse, vote NO on Amendment No. Two.

Amendment No. Three is to permit a highway to be constructed over State lands in the Adirondacks. Inasmuch as the Association for the Protection of the Adirondacks approves, and the State Conservation Department does not oppose, the amendment may properly be carried.

Vote YES on Amendment No. Three.

Amendment No. Four will allow the State to turn over to New York City the West Fifty-third Street State Barge Canal Terminal.

The State has found the site unsuitable for a canal terminal, and the city needs the land for its West Side waterfront developments.

Vote YES on Amendment No. Four.

• • •

NOW we come to the New York City referendum—proposing a commission of seventeen persons to draft a new charter for the municipality.

The city unquestionably should abandon its present obsolete and detrimental "organic law." A modern and useful charter is a basic essential to good local government—but the pending proposal is no way in which to get a new charter.

In the first place, it is a Tammany scheme, railroaded politically through the Legislature, and as such it presupposes the perpetuation of Tammanyized city government. If the proposal is carried at the polls Mayor O'Brien—irrespective of the results of the mayoral election—will appoint this commission. If Mayor O'Brien is defeated he should not make "lame duck" appointments of such consequence. If he should be re-elected a better method of procuring charter reform should be followed.

In the second place, no special legislation is necessary to institute charter reform. Elected officials, UNDER EXISTING LAW, have the power as well as the obligation to do so.

The Tammany scheme should be defeated overwhelmingly.

VOTE NO ON THE CHARTER REVISION PROPOSAL.

New York American, October 27, 1933

that page must be unusually attractive physically. It must be even more inviting looking than the general-news pages, and even easier to read.[4]

But editors generally ignored this advice. Traditional editorial page makeup in the 1940s, 1950s and 1960s was usually built around a vertical (higher than it was wide) three-column cartoon at the top of the page. The newspaper's own editorials were assigned to one or two columns to the left of the cartoon. Columns and letters filled the remainder of the page. The *Washington Post* of Jan. 20, 1953 (Figure 3, page 302) reflected that makeup arrangement, although the use of white space between the columns represented a step away from tradition. Bohle found at the time of his 40-year look that many newspapers still were using this design.

BOLDER, MORE FLEXIBLE

Partly spurred by editorial page critique sessions at the annual meetings of the National Conference of Editorial Writers (NCEW) and by the needling of designers such as Arnold, editors in the 1960s and 1970s began experimenting with more flexible layouts. Wider columns and "cold type"—which could be pasted anywhere and at any angle on a page—opened new possibilities that not even the most skilled printer could have managed with unwieldy hunks of metal type. Contributing to the flexibility was the introduction of a few cartoons that were wider than they were high.

This combination led to pages that had wider columns, sometimes too wide for easy reading. A rule of thumb suggests that for optimum newspaper reading lines should contain the equivalent of about one and a half-lower case alphabets, or about 39 characters.[5] The Sept. 17, 1995, editorial page (Figure 4, page 303) and op-ed page (Figure 5, page 304) of the Minneapolis–St. Paul *Star Tribune* present a rather bold example of a design with wider columns. In this case the maximum line length in letters and editorial columns is about 40 characters. I will have more comments later about this page as well as a redesign.

Partly because of the flexibility cold type provided, some editors began experimenting with different page arrangements. Professor Bohle, in a critique of editorial pages published in *The Masthead*, said that, in his opinion, the information in an editorial should be the starting point for design. "Newspaper design is functional design, *i.e.*, its primary goal is functional (the reading of the content), not cosmetic," he wrote.[6] He found little evidence of experimenting but offered an example as an inspiration for editors to try something different from time to time. On a model opinion page of his own design (Figure 6, page 306) Bohle placed a five-part editorial across the top: "the facts," arguments "for prayer" at graduation, arguments "against prayer," "local opinions" and "our thoughts." A four-part editorial appears in the lower left corner. A cartoon separates the two editorials. Letters appear in the right two columns beneath the lead editorial.

Note that on this page editorials are set flush left and flush right, the letters flush left. Traditional page designers thought that the formality of the editorial page required that all columns be set flush left and right. Some page designers

Figure 3 Washington Post

The Washington Post

EUGENE MEYER, Chairman of the Board — PHILIP L. GRAHAM, President and Publisher
HERBERT ELLISTON .... Editor — CHARLES C. BOYSEN .... Secretary — DONALD M. BERNARD, Advertising Director
J. R. WIGGINS ...... Managing Editor — JOHN W. SWEETERMAN, Business Manager — JOHN S. HAYES, President WTOP Radio-TV

AN INDEPENDENT NEWSPAPER — TUESDAY, JANUARY 20, 1953 — PAGE 14

Inauguration Day

This is a great day for the American system of government, and a thrilling day for all good citizens of this Republic. Dwight D. Eisenhower will take the oath of office as President of the United States. That means a great change at the White House, not only in occupants, but also in parties. And it is all being done with order and consideration and cooperation, thanks to both the retiring and the incoming Presidents. The transition is something to create pride and awe in the breast of every American.

General Eisenhower will take over the Presidency in the plenitude of the country's power and prosperity. The office is a branch of the American trinity of branches of government. Let us give thanks to our forefathers for the political edifice they outlined. It is refreshing on this day of days to turn back to the *Federalist* to read what the founding fathers had in mind. Madison, Hamilton and Jay were seeking in the *Federalist* to secure ratification of the Constitution. Their basic assumption was that the very definition of tyranny consists of accumulating all powers in the same hands. Whether the hands were hereditary, self-appointed or elected—that made no difference. Thus the founding fathers had already set up a government in three separate and coequal departments in an effort to prevent the rise of tyranny.

The separation of powers upon which our Government rests makes it a tremendously difficult system to operate, because unless there is a considerate relation among the three, the branches could revolve in their respective orbits, and there would be chaos. A balance has somehow to be struck and maintained and be subject, as Dr. Johnson said about friendship, to constant repair in order to irsure the functioning of government.

This constant and continuing need for balance calls for a qualification on the part of a successful President, second only to leadership. The qualification is diplomacy. Leadership is obvious enough as a prerequisite, but diplomacy is not often thought about. A President must do his part in getting along with his partners. Harmony between the White House and the judiciary was difficult till there had been general acceptance of a famous dictum of John Marshall, the country's third Chief Justice. "It is emphatically the province and duty of the judicial department," said the great Marshall, "to say what the law is," and when this statement had become axiomatic, the foundation of our constitutional liberties was well and truly laid.

The prime problem of American government as a day-to-day proposition lies in the relation between the President and Congress. Here there is need for a very high degree of diplomacy—of that kind of diplomacy which recognizes the rights under the organic law of both coordinates, yet seeks consciously to respect what in another connection a great jurist called "the law of the unenforceable." The jurist was talking about the behavior of people in a free society—how 95 percent of their actions are governed not by law but by a feeling of right conduct. The same thought could be applied to relations between a President and Congress under the American system. Ideally, one owes to the other a respect for its individuality and authority—that is to say, power at the other's expense is "an encroaching spirit" that gentlemen must resist. "It is one thing," as Alexander Hamilton said, "to be subordinate to the laws and another to be dependent on the legislative body."

It is said, by way of example, that the men on the Hill feel they are professionals in the business of government and must guide the "amateur in the White House." This kind of arrogance is intolerable to the spirit of the Constitution. The new President could respond to any such outcropping with weapons that would be more than salutary, at least in his initial period—the weapons of his vast public support and of his patronage. It is plain he harbors no idea of using a big stick. He is said to be very conscious of his own responsibilities in creating a smooth-working liaison with Congress. The evidence is the report of his purpose to set up a bipartisan council with which to take counsel on foreign affairs. This will show the President's good intent, and the way that the partnership is worked out will depend upon the conduct of the men involved.

If the new President shows this will to cooperate, then he can legitimately expect Congress to respect his constitutional right to the initiative. For the world of free men will depend upon the wise and swift exercise of the initiative in the conduct of American foreign relations. It was not always so. The framers of the Constitution did not envisage a rank for America of high mightiness. They based the organic law upon the feeling that America would be neutralist in a world of big powers. Even as late as the first edition of *The American Commonwealth* Bryce could write that "four fifths of the President's work is the same in kind as that which devolves on the manager of a railway." Now the President's job is Atlas-like.

With power has come responsibility, and the need to be ready for sure and swift action. Congress must realize that the President's initiative must never be allowed to become palsied, that he must show that "vigor of government" within the "perfect security of freedom" which George Washington said was required of the management of the common interests of Americans. May the new President be aided by Almighty Providence in the discharge of the obligations which he will assume today!

Loyalty And Liberty

The country looks with hope to the great American who assumes the Presidency today for a revitalization of its traditional civil liberties. These liberties have sometimes been curtailed—needlessly curtailed—in the name of national security. They are, of course, a vital source of security. They constitute the real roots of American loyalty.

In the championship of civil liberties which he has promised, President Eisenhower can make no better beginning than to establish a Commission on Internal Security and Individual Rights—made up of distinguished citizens, as was the Nimitz Commission which President Truman vainly tried to set in motion—to advise the country and himself as to the effectiveness of its security precautions and the maintenance of its essential freedoms.

Security and freedom are not in conflict; they are, on the contrary, complementary. The American public needs the reassurance which such a commission could afford that disloyalty is being checked without enthroning demagogy. The President needs the counsel of such a commission in maintaining a wise balance between national needs and individual rights.

Conserving Resources

It was characteristic of President Truman to choose the conservation and development of natural resources as the subject of his final message to Congress. The subject is one respecting which he takes tremendous pride—and justly—in the record of his Administration. It is a subject with a long and highly creditable record of bipartisanship—a fitting subject for the final recommendations of a President about to turn over the reins of authority to his successor. And, finally, these natural resources, as the President observed, "are a foundation upon which rest our national security, our ability to maintain a democratic society, and our leadership in the free world."

The conservation movement got its start under President Theodore Roosevelt in 1902 with the enactment of the reclamation laws. These laws have had the support of every President since then, regardless of party; resource development in a variety of forms was given great impetus during the 20 years of the F. D. Roosevelt and Truman Administrations; and, in particular, the accomplishments since 1945 cited by Mr. Truman indicate how much this kind of conservation and development can mean in terms of living standards and general welfare. Some 1300 new soil conservation districts have been formed during the past eight years; about 2,700,000 irrigated acres have been added to the Nation's farm lands; three million acres have been given flood protection; electricity has been brought to one and one-half million farms that didn't have it prior to 1945, making nearly 9 out of 10 American farms electrified.

This is a proud legacy to leave to one's successor. Mr. Truman leaves it with a dual admonition. "We have learned," he says, "that the mark of a well-managed land lies in the care a Nation gives to its rivers." The Tennessee Valley Authority stands as perhaps the greatest domestic achievement of the last two decades—a symbol of what can be done through Federal-State cooperation, imaginative planning and decentralized, local administration. The rest of his warning to the Eisenhower Administration is that "we must make sure that we safeguard the use of these resources for the benefit of all the people. Where the public moneys are invested, the resulting gains must accrue to the public, and not be diverted to the undue benefit of any private group."

Each generation holds the natural resources of the Nation in trust for its posterity. Mr. Truman can relinquish his trusteeship with a clear conscience. He spoke, in this final message to Congress, in behalf of the most vital interests of the American people.

Symbol Of Tradition

For all the revolutionary spirit which General Eisenhower displayed in spurning a top hat and buying a new homburg for his Inauguration, some devotees of reaction or tradition or just high revelry—whatever you like—have defied the new President and appeared, at least on the pre-Inaugural scene, in tall silk hats. Perhaps they are Democrats! Whoever they are, their defiance of the example of the hero of the day is pardonable, and, indeed, even deserves our salute. After all, the high hat in different colors is the badge for high occasions, and what occasion in the secular calendar of events could be higher than Inauguration? Even if you simply want something to do something with, after your rejoicing over the day's event (such as kicking your hat into the Potomac), what better object than a topper?

Some of the local stores report they have sold out of homburgs since the general announced his decision on their behalf, while the supply of toppers, in view of Ike's decision, is far from exhausted. But other occasions will come around. And the new President may then relent, for it is our surmise that his ukase was a sudden outburst of independence after acquiescence in ritual over many days, and he simply decided that for a change he would be himself.

The Law And Wilson

We reprint below for the benefit of our readers the statute which Senators have raised in connection with the nomination of Charles E. Wilson to be Secretary of Defense:

> Whoever, being an officer, agent or member of, or directly or indirectly interested in the pecuniary profits or contracts of any corporation, joint-stock company, or association, or of any firm or partnership, or other business entity, is employed or acts as an officer or agent of the United States for the transaction of business with such business entity, shall be fined not more than $2000 or imprisoned not more than two years, or both.

This law was enacted in 1948.

Thanks To Neely

As Senator Case takes over the chairmanship of the Senate District Committee, it is important not to overlook the good work done by the retiring Democratic chairman, Senator Neely. The West Virginia legislator has exercised a conscientious stewardship over District affairs for the last two years. His insistence on punctual meetings of the District Committee was an index to his businesslike approach in getting things done. Particularly to his credit was the manner in which, with Senator Case's cooperation, he fought to see the local crime investigation through against considerable odds. He also was a stalwart champion of home rule for Washington. In extending what we feel confident is the thanks of many Washingtonians, we are glad that Senator Neely intends to continue his progressive interest in District affairs in the new Congress.

"The President Of The United States"

Letters To The Editor

Acheson's Record

It is hard for me to imagine just what cerebral steps led the writer of your editorial of January 15 "Four Years of Dean Acheson" to the analysis that ... [illegible]

JAMES ROWE, JR.
Washington.

Arlington Buses

[illegible]

PATRICIA FLEMING.
Arlington.

Communists In Schools

[illegible]

JULIAN F. WILLIAMS.
Mount Rainier, Md.

One-Man Bolt

The strange spectacle of Senator Wayne Morse first bolting the Republican Party and then setting himself up as a one-man Independent, does not surprise people who had occasion to talk with the Senator several years ago—about political matters. [illegible]

FRED REINSTEIN.
Washington.

Missing Fire Boxes

The Washington Post, in glorifying the incident which found a ...-year-old boy pulling a fire alarm box, is a bit off the beam as far as logical reasoning is concerned. [illegible]

W. G. MOORE.
Washington.

"End Of Mob Murder"

[illegible]

ALEXANDER F. MILLER.
Atlanta, Ga.

Eisenhower Maps Middle Road Course

By Marquis Childs

AFTER THE LONG drought, the Republican rejoicing is full of a fine fervor. But when the bunting comes down and the paraders go home, this Capital will see the beginning of one of the most interesting experiments in government in many, many years.

Childs

The outlines of that experiment are already evident. In essence, it is an effort to apply the management techniques of big industry to big government.

The wisecrack about the Eisenhower Cabinet consisting of eight millionaires and a plumber or, more accurately, a steamfitter, misses the real point. These businessmen now in Government have been handsomely rewarded for their ability. But money reward has been secondary to the fact of the power and the skills they have wielded as the managers of industry financed by thousands of investors large and small.

They will now be managers of the far larger enterprises of Government. Often in the past the complaint about the Government administrators has been that they never met a payroll. The men in the Eisenhower Administration have been responsible for meeting some very large payrolls.

But, with two or three exceptions, they have not met the voters at the polling booth. Republicans in Congress, who feel that through the years they put the political capital into this enterprise, look with skepticism on the experiment of managerial government. The Senate hitch over Charles E. Wilson's confirmation as Defense Secretary because of his General Motors stock indicates the relationship between the managers and the politicians may be difficult.

The new Administration is not, however, without its political managers and very skillful ones, indeed. They come out of the hard-boiled organization built up in New York State by Gov. Thomas E. Dewey. They also have roots in California, where Gov. Earl Warren has demonstrated how to build up a political following transcending the two-party system as we have known it in the past 20 years. Significantly, in this connection, it is in California and New York, the two most populous States in the country, that the decay of the Democratic Party is most conspicuous.

THE AIM IS TO go down the middle of the road with a party having few resemblances to the old Republican Party. Thus a minimum of 10 percent, and perhaps nearer to 15 or 20 percent, of the following that has kept the Democrats in power—farmers, labor, minorities—will be permanently won over. This is the pattern evident behind many of the moves made since November 4, and it promises to become increasingly apparent as the new Administration takes over.

One of the able and successful members of the political team which will work toward the long-term goal is Senator Irving Ives of New York. Ives won reelection last fall by the huge plurality of 1,332,198. He carried New York City, which Eisenhower lost, by a plurality of 2743. In a speech in New York last week, Ives said, in effect, that the Republican Congress was Republican because of the personal popularity of General Eisenhower. The people, he said, were still progressive and there could be "no turning back of the clock of progress." Then Ives spoke of what is the biggest hazard faced by the new Administration:

"With a spirit of mutual helpfulness and cooperation the new Administration can and will succeed. Without it, failure is certain and the Republican Party is doomed to defeat in 1956."

A MEMBER OF the Senate Labor Committee, Ives is hoping to head a subcommittee that will study discrimination in industry and business. The political implications of this are obvious. The Republican majority is expected to agree on a compromise civil rights bill providing for a commission to educate and persuade employers that discrimination is not only unfair, but that it does not pay. This would be labeled as a first step and it would be taken by men like Ives as a trial of what can be achieved by a law without power of Federal punishment.

Thus the pattern will be developed if the able political managers working for the Eisenhower Administration can bring it off. They will have many resources, particularly in the honeymoon phase, and they will be working with some shrewd operators.

One of these is Gen. Lucius D. Clay, now retired, an old Eisenhower comrade with a unique influence although he will hold no office. Clay serves as a kind of bridge between the business community and Eisenhower's familiar military associations. A man of outstanding ability, as he demonstrated in his military career which concluded with his appointment as occupying chief in Germany. Clay is now chairman of the board and chief executive officer of the Continental Can Co. He is also on the board of the General Motors Corp., which gives him a link with top Eisenhower Cabinet officers.

The Washington Post
Registered in U. S. Patent Office
Published every day in the year by The Washington Post Company

The Associated Press is entitled exclusively to use for republication of all news dispatches credited to it or not otherwise credited in this paper and local news of spontaneous origin published herein. Rights of republication of all other matter herein are also reserved.

1515 L Street N.W., Washington 5, D. C.
Telephone NAtional 8-4200

Offices of National Advertising Representatives
Sawyer-Ferguson-Walker Co.—
New York .... 60 East 42nd St., Room 822
Chicago .... 333 North Michigan Avenue
Detroit .... 1630 Guardian Building
Atlanta .... 22 Marietta St.
Philadelphia .... 1400 South Penn Square
Los Angeles .... 612 S. Flower St.
San Francisco .... Russ Building
Miami Beach, Fla.—The Hal Winter Co., 9049 Emerson Ave.
London, England—Joshua B. Powers, Ltd., 14 Cockspur St.

CARRIER DELIVERY—WASHINGTON AREA

Daily and Sunday		Sunday Only		Daily Only	
One week	$ .40	One week	$ .10	One week	$ [illegible]
One month	1.75	One month	.45	One month	1.30

Elsewhere

Daily and Sunday		Sunday Only		Daily Only	
One week	$ .40	One week	$ .15	One week	$ .30
One month	1.75	One month	.65	One month	1.30

BY MAIL—PAYABLE IN ADVANCE

[illegible]

Rates outside U. S. A. furnished upon request
Entered at the Postoffice Washington, D. C. as second-class mail matter

20A Sunday/September 17/1995

Star Tribune **Editorial**

Joel Kramer/Publisher

NEWS
Tim McGuire/Editor
Pam Fine/News Leader

EDITORIAL
Susan Albright/Editor, Editorial Pages
Jim Boyd/Deputy Editor, Editorial Pages

OUR PERSPECTIVE

Medicare

The GOP's well-meaning rescue squad

It's hard to be perturbed with the new Republican Medicare plan. After all, it's somewhat ungracious to heckle a lifeguard on the way to a drowning man — even if her sidestroke isn't up to form. Whatever its shortcomings — and there are many — the GOP rescue strategy at least represents an attempt to fish Medicare out of a fix. That's more than can be said about the Democratic response, which so far has amounted to sniping.

> Republicans have taken the bold step of proposing rate hikes for all recipients — including a phase-out of premium subsidies for wealthy seniors. It's the only way to avert the program's bankruptcy.

Much is wrong with the Republican rescue plan. It is overambitious — audacious might be a better word — in aiming to hack $270 billion from Medicare's projected growth in order to fund a whopping tax cut, increase defense spending and still balance the budget within seven years. It is meek and self-deceptive, seeking to reap the savings of the flourishing managed-care system without firmly pushing Medicare recipients into that system.

The proposal is also shortsighted in its reliance on tax-free medical savings accounts, which could spur retirees to leave Medicare in the laps of its sickest and costliest premium-payers. And the plan is half-baked in supposing that Medicare can be saved by hiking premiums and squelching reimbursement rates, when only comprehensive health-care reform can bring lasting stability.

But even with all of its leaks, there's still a lot of buoyancy in this plan. For starters, it comes to grips with Medicare's imminent insolvency. The Republicans have taken the bold step of proposing rate hikes for all recipients — including a phase-out of premium subsidies for wealthy seniors. That proposal is bound to make the Medicare crowd wince, but it's really the only way to avert the program's bankruptcy. Supporting the elderly already swallows up one-third of the federal budget. Unless shifts are made soon, baby boomers will face a grim and threadbare old age.

There's no mystery to all this, of course. President Clinton knows that Medicare is going under, and so do the Democrats in Congress. You'd think the witnesses to such a calamity might be moved to join the rescue team — or at least yell helpful comments. No such luck. Uninclined to get their feet wet, the Democrats seem content to play on the vulnerability of the 37 million Americans holding on to the Medicare lifeline. Their chief contribution to the discussion is the accusation that Republicans are trying to "wreck Medicare."

Surely the Democrats have more to contribute than potshots like that. Just last year, their party was leading the charge for sweeping overhaul of the entire health-care system. The looming dangers for Medicare should revive the reform effort and spur earnest attempts at compromise. Instead of sniping from the safety of the shore, the Democrats should wade in and help with the rescue.

Student loans

Trimming direct loans only helps banks

When congressional Republicans try to put a respectable face on their zeal to scale back or scrap the year-old direct student lending program, a few facts mess up the job.

One fact is this: No decent evidence shows that allowing students to obtain educational loans directly from the government, rather than through private lending institutions, costs taxpayers more. Direct lending's opponents love to cite a Congressional Budget Office comparison of the old system and the new, but the comparison is flawed. It's based on a GOP directive to congressional budgeteers to tally the administrative costs of direct lending, but not of the old guaranteed loan program.

Big blots of partisanship and political pork also mar the Republican crusade against direct lending. It's a program that has become too closely linked to President Clinton for Republican comfort. And its demise would restore money to the pockets of one of the Republican Party's best campaign-contributing friends — the nation's banking industry.

Only two years ago, plenty of Republicans — including former Sen. Dave Durenberger of Minnesota — supported and even sponsored direct lending. Allowing students to obtain loans from the federal government by applying to their colleges, rather than from one of 7,000 government-backed lenders nationwide, was hailed as a breakthrough for simplicity and efficiency.

The colleges that participated in the first year's pilot program reported a positive experience. The application process was simpler for students and loan money came to their schools more quickly than under the bank-dominated guaranteed loan program. The larger second-year pilot program, underway this year, had applications from 800 more colleges than it could accommodate.

And despite the cooked books the Congressional Budget Office served up, the program is still widely expected to benefit taxpayers in the long run. Eliminating the middlefolk and their profits in the loan process should allow a greater share of interest payments to offset the program's administrative costs. By one estimate, taxpayers will save — and banks and private loan guarantors will lose — $12 billion over the next five years if direct lending fully supplants the old lending program on schedule, in 1997-98.

Those facts should trip up Republican efforts to tell the nation there's any real flaw in direct lending. The facts should make clear that banks will be the beneficiaries — and students, colleges and taxpayers the losers — if direct lending is capped or killed.

MUST KEEP AN OPEN MIND.....
UFOs ARRIVE IN L.A. WITH O.J. ALIBI!
COULD HAPPEN....
ELVIS LANDS AT O'HARE IN AMELIA EARHART'S PLANE!!
YOU NEVER KNOW.....
CLONED LOCH NESS MONSTER TO BE LIZ'S 8th HUBBY!!!
I'LL BELIEVE IT WHEN I SEE IT.
REPUBLICANS PROPOSE REDUCING CORPORATE TAX BREAKS
SACK
STAR TRIBUNE

LETTERS FROM READERS

Some standards

So, Gov. Arne Carlson challenges the Star Tribune to publicize its journalistic standards. Mr. Governor, it is amusing to see you hit the Strib where it hurts. Just don't hold your breath.

Remember, the Star Tribune is the newspaper that said we should look at Dan Quayle's service in the National Guard during the Vietnam War as evidence of terribly poor character, but we should forget about Bill Clinton's evasion of the draft because the war was so long ago.

This is the newspaper that refers to upper-echelon gang members as "community leaders," but portrays those with strong religious convictions as dangerous right-wing zealots. And don't forget that this is the newspaper that won't print the names of some professional sports teams for fear they might offend certain political factions of minority groups but deems it appropriate to publish photos of folks in bondage gear who are just out to have some fun.

Perhaps the Strib can create a list of standards that let it take the angles it does, but I'm sure I'd get a headache reading it.

Paul Roberts, Crystal.

Perfect harmony

While attending the outstanding performances of our new orchestra conductor, Eiji Oue and world-famous violinist Itzhak Perlman at the open rehearsal last week, I had a thought about world peace: Would it not be incredibly wonderful if nations would act like the members of the orchestra — tuning up to play in harmony, each one doing their very best to obey the instructions of the composer and the direction of the conductor? May the day dawn when nations act to produce a symphony of peace!

Emily G. White, Minneapolis.

Vouchers' 'danger'

The root of concern over school vouchers appears to the frightening (to the educational establishment) prospect that money will flow from the public system to private schools. The rationalization of the establishment is that this would be a disaster, weakening an already stressed public school system.

Nowhere, however, in its impassioned defense of the status quo, does the public school system even mention the fact that the wealthy already have this choice. All families, not just those with money, should be allowed to choose their educational vendor.

Think about it: If there were only one car manufacturer, would we have the choices, and the consequent quality, that we have in automobiles today? Competition begets quality: If the public schools were forced to improve their product quality in order to stay in existence, you can bet that the quality of the public schools would improve dramatically.

To those who would say otherwise, consider that the proof that competition improves the quality of education already exists in the educational system. Private schools have had to compete since they first came into being — against one another as well as against the public system. They have had to produce a quality product on often a fraction of the money that their public-school counterparts have enjoyed.

Can anyone deny that the quality of a private-school education is far superior, by and large, to that received in public schools? Why, then, is any proposed voucher system so dangerous?

There is danger. The voucher system is dangerous to those who have learned to be comfortable in a second-rate system. Who would not be threatened if they knew they would be forced to improve or slowly cease to exist?

Vouchers would give parents the choice of a school for their children — and if the public schools can provide the same quality as their private counterparts, they will have no worry about their existence.

The well-to-do already enjoy this choice. Why should it be denied to the rest of us?

Tawee Prepodnik, Le Center, Minn.

Flight priorities

Air traffic control computers went down again last week — the sixth time in a year (Sept. 14). We are fortunate there were no collisions resulting in hundreds of deaths. Next time we may not be so lucky.

One of life's enduring mysteries is how the federal government prioritizes its spending. But if money is the holdup in getting state-of-the-art computers to control air traffic, I suggest it be transferred from the billion-dollar space program. Nobody's flying in outer space.

Irene Parsons, Columbia Heights.

Bravo, Betty

Some of us women do care about Betty Crocker (Sept. 12). My 1950 Betty Crocker cookbook is my favorite. I also use and like Betty Crocker products. However, I don't think "she" needs a makeover. I like her present picture just fine.

Bernice Lindskog, Minneapolis.

Primary primer

What if you gave a primary and nobody came?

We are concerned that only 43 citizens (less than 3 percent of our precinct's 1,500 registered voters) came out to vote in Tuesday's Minneapolis primary election for school board members — a turnout that was reflected throughout the city.

The introductory day of Windows 95 was ballyhooed for weeks ahead of time and all that day, but the media has failed to publicize this important contest for the School Board. This, fellow citizens, is where the grass roots are — out here, dealing with kids and their education.

Democracy only works when informed people vote, and part of information availability is the media's responsibility.

Louise Huebner, Judith Duncan and Walter M. Liebenow, Minneapolis.

The Minneapolis school board primary election had a low turnout, but not as low as the "0.05 percent" the Star Tribune reported. Dividing 10,491 voters by 201,580 registered voters gives 5 percent.

There is little solace in either number. My hope for the school board is that we get in return more than we the public deserve.

George R. Anderson, Minneapolis.

Stupid? Not Limbaugh

Jim Heynen, author of the Aug. 30 commentary "Stupidity is taking root in the fears and latent hatreds of America," is identified as a teacher. I would remind him that the first obligation of a teacher is to be clear, which he is not.

In his giant leap to a dubious conclusion, Heynen careens from point to point, and the sum total of his shrillness is that people who do not agree with him are "stupid."

Heynen's hysterical attack is aimed primarily at talk show man Rush Limbaugh. Regardless of how one may feel about Limbaugh, the last thing he is is stupid, and to call also stupid the 20 million listeners he has is childish.

The key issne that completely escapes Heynen is that the reason for Limbaugh's astonishing popularity is that he articulates a point of view very different from 95 percent of the liberal press in America.

There is a reason for Limbaugh, and there will always be a place for someone like he as long as the nation's media keep ladling out their highly convoluted version of what is going on.

Robert B. Pile, Minneapolis.

OTHER POINTS OF VIEW

Women's conference turned out to be not radical at all

By Tom Teepen
Cox News Service

Atlanta, Ga.
The U.N. Conference on Women has come and gone, and there's no detectable change in the Earth's spin. Christendom has not been overthrown. Western culture carries on undeterred. The mystical but dreaded "five genders" have not been established triumphant over the customary two.

Will we ever learn to stop being panicked by the fear-mongering that America's organized reactionaries have taken up as their life's work?

You heard it all before the conference.

This was a plot to bring men low, to reorder the world along the lines of radical feminism, to destroy capitalism and topple God-fearing altars to make room for strange clitoral rites.

Homosexual men and women and bisexuals would be officially declared distinct genders in their own right and every public building would have to set up five restrooms — or, worse, one!

No better proof was needed than the imminent attendance of the horrid Hillary Rodham Clinton — the corporate attorney who is a secret Socialist, the First Lady who sneaks out of state dinners to snack on newborns at wicked covens.

Small wonder President Clinton grew testy ahead of time at press questions driven by the worst-case frights of the busybody right.

The conference turned out to be not at all radical for the simple reason that it was set up not to be radical.

After all, 180-some nations participated, and few are any more left-wing than a Presbyterian elder.

The meeting usefully brought to international view — and in time, one hopes to attention, too — grave gender-based abuses: The forced abortions and sterilizations of Chinese policy. The genital mutilation of girls in some African and Muslim countries, misleadingly labeled "circumcision." The murder of baby girls in societies that place value only on boys.

For the most part, the conference emphasized simple equality for women — in work, education, health care. The World Bank demonstrated in a recent study that the education of women revs up economic growth and cools wildfire birth rates. Doubling female high school enrollment would cut fertility rates by more than a fourth.

There were inevitable differences, of course, and some hair-splitting semantics at the conference. It is difficult, however, to imagine anyone — anyone sensible, that is — finding cause for alarm in the deliberations, though you can be sure our mailing-list hustlers will have heard of one or another oddball episode and soon will be characterizing the conference by fringes it had nothing to do with.

The conference did needed, sober work on behalf of a common-sense agenda.

Hillary Clinton represented Americans adroitly, neatly walking a diplomatic tightrope.

She properly conflated women's rights with human rights generally and firmly held forth for both without either coddling or gratuitously provoking offender nations.

The big losers were China, which in its repressiveness and ineptitude was painfully exposed as a not-ready-for-prime-time nation, and our own ever-panicky right, which in its repressiveness and ineptitude was exposed as not ready for prime time, either, despite all the news time it gets.

Commentary

Sunday/September 17/1995 21A

Childhood looks too dangerous for children

Kristine M. Holmgren

Northfield, Minn.
When 17-year-old Amy left the party and climbed into her daddy's pickup for the 15-minute drive home, she was feeling no pain.

The mortician told me she didn't suffer. "When she flipped the truck and sailed through the windshield," he said, "she didn't know what hit her. She broke her neck as soon as she hit the asphalt. The kid didn't feel a thing."

Lots of other kids were feeling plenty during her funeral. Before we folded her body into the hills of Pierce County, Amy's classmates wept openly. Two cheerleaders distributed roses in her memory and buttons with her picture. Three of her drinking buddies wrote goodbye letters on school poster board, and posted them above pictures of Amy in her prom dress.

"You always had a smile for everyone," one said. "I'll never forget all the good times," said another. "I'll see you again some day." "You were a great kid. Keep smilin'."

Cheap sentiments? Don't be too hard on Amy's heavy drinking friends. Until her death, many of them thought they would live forever. I watched them at the funeral parlor, strutting in front of her casket in last year's tough-guy look. The boys in the class of 1996 can't get their hands on Starter jackets, but they still try for the tough-guy look they see on television. They wear their seed caps backwards.

The young women wear too much Maybelline and not enough blouse. But like Amy, beneath their tough exteriors they are still little girls who desperately need someone to notice the light that shines in their heavily mascara'd eyes.

What adults perceive as risky behavior, these kids see as tickling excitement. They are bored with school, uninspired by the resources of their small towns. For many of them, dangerous sexual experimentation and drunken romps at high speeds on county roads are the only ways they can stem the tide of boredom. No one has ever taught them the subtle benefits of imagination and the life-transforming power of dreams.

To know these roughneck country kids is to love them.

I will think of them this week as I listen to the broadcast of "The Lives of the Children" on 89.3, WCAL-FM. The five one-hour documentaries spotlight the lives of children from many backgrounds, sharing their experiences and perceptions of growing up in America today. I hope that our nation's policymakers will listen and hear the quiet prophecy from the mouths of our babes.

Although the broadcasts originate in Chicago, Portland, San Clemente, New York and St. Paul, the voices could come from Apple Valley, Bloomington or Red Wing. The message they send the nation is a simple one: childhood isn't what it used to be. It certainly isn't what we wish it was.

One of the underwriters for "The Lives of the Children" is the Annie Casey Foundation. Their research indicates that the kids' lives are vastly different today than when their parents were children.

According to their publication, "Kids Count Data Book," in 1950, less than 6 percent of our children were living in mother-only families. Today 24 percent of our children are growing up without a father. The statistics make sense when we learn that more than 30 percent of our nation's men (ages 25-34) earn less than the poverty level for a family of four.

Hiding behind the statistics are the lives and deaths of our nation's children. Amy's automobile accident was the tip of an iceberg of neglect, abuse, boredom and poverty. If she had lived long enough, maybe she would have broken the cycle of early pregnancy and alcohol abuse that penetrates her family and peers.

We will never know. Amy was one of our "throwaway" children, not pretty enough to fuss over and not smart enough to crawl out from under her underclass rural status. Like so many other rural children, her life was a constant flight from monotony and pain.

Undergirding the production of "The Lives of the Children" are Bloomingdale's, the Annie Casey Foundation, the General Mills Foundation, the McKnight Foundation and the members of WCAL.

These corporate and individual sponsors have delivered a genuine service to our nation through their funding of this visionary program. Tune in to 89.3 FM on Monday, Sept. 18, through Friday, Sept. 22, at 3 and 6 p.m.

The innocence in the children's voices will lift your soul. The realities of their lives will break your heart.

Kristine M. Holmgren is a writer and pastor of Laurel Presbyterian Church in Hager City, Wis.

IF YOU RAN THE NEWSPAPER

Readers perceive slant in article on Medicaid

Lou Gelfand

Richard Nelson had a ready answer when I asked him to cite an example of why he believes the Star Tribune slants the news.

"Today's [Sept. 8] article headlined, 'White House goes to bat for Medicaid/ Proposed GOP cuts would end coverage for many, officials say,'" responded Nelson. "In only one of the 13 paragraphs was the Republican point of view [from Rod Grams' office] presented."

The article, by Greg Gordon of the newspaper's Washington bureau, said White House officials "launched a defense for a politically more vulnerable target: the federal health program for the poor."

A principal source was the Urban Institute, which said a preliminary analysis showed 88,000 Minnesotans would lose Medicaid coverage under the GOP plan.

Gordon responded to reader Nelson:

"Grams' office was not the only Republican source. Data on the effects on Hennepin County was originally provided to the paper by Commissioner Randy Johnson, a Republican, who said that he, too, was concerned about the impact of the cuts.

"Second, analyses of the various pending budget proposals in Congress are only beginning to come in. If these analyses include fresh information, we feel an obligation to share them with our readers.

"The story was clearly labeled as a White House analysis and a defense of its program. It included a number of apparently new statistics about Medicaid. Of course, we could have asked other Republicans, besides Grams, to respond.

"But given limited space, we felt that his spokesman's succinct comments were a sufficient rebuttal. After all, Grams seems the perfect person to respond. He is one of the chief backers of the Republican tax-cut proposal that is allegedly being financed in part by $452 billion in Medicare and Medicaid cuts."

Mike Tierney, who also thought the article was slanted to the Democratic side, said it should have told him more about the Urban Institute because, he said, research and so-called think tank groups often are philosophically biased.

He had called the Minneapolis library to inquire about the Urban Institute's directors and was given the names Katherine Graham, publisher of the Washington Post; Eleanor Holmes Norton, a District of Columbia delegate in the U.S. House, and Robert McNamara.

I called the Urban Institute and was told that its directors include Carla Hills, Jack Kemp, Elliot Richardson, William Ruckelshaus and William Scranton, all solid Republicans. The institute calls itself a policy research organization that investigates social and economic problems confronting the nation.

Tierney also called attention to a Sept. 6 article citing a report from the Northeast-Midwest Institute, which said Minnesota would lose money if a proposal by Southern senators for distributing welfare funds is adopted. He asked if I'd heard of the institute.

I found one previous reference to it in the newspaper's electronic library, a June, 1994 story describing the organization as a non profit policy center. The center sent me material showing that its 112 congressional members consist of 66 Democrats, 45 Republicans and one Independent, representing the upper tier of states from Minnesota to Maine.

Comment: Reader Tierney does the newspaper a favor by raising the point of describing organizations not familiar to the average reader.

As for Greg Gordon's Sept. 8 article, on that day the news was the White House initiative to defend Medicaid. On other days, the news has been the Republican effort to slow the growth of Medicaid spending and make it a block grant to the states.

■

Doug de Mille and Stephen Meyer objected to the photograph of Minneapolis City Council Member Brian Herron on the Sept. 5 front page.

Photojournalist Mike Zerby photographed Herron praying in church. Herron was standing, his right arm raised, his mouth open. Meyer said the picture "lampooned Herron, made him look ugly."

Zerby replied: "I thought the picture was the best I had to illustrate the fervor of the man, the power of God in his life."

Herron said the picture probably wasn't the best of him, but he had no objection.

■

"Editorial puffery" was how Charles Hogan stamped the use of "well-regarded" in describing the public relations firm of Mona Meyer McGrath & Gavin in a Sept. 14 story. The article reported that the company had joined the Dorsey & Whitney law firm to form a crisis management service.

Comment: A reporter's opinion of a company does not belong in a news story.

■

Disappointment of the week:

Election Day headline on the Metro/Region cover that appeared in both St. Paul and Minneapolis editions of the "Newspaper of the Twin Cities": "School board primary in Minneapolis is today." The article named the candidates and reviewed the issues.

The only mention of the St. Paul school board primary was a line in a box stating the number to call for results.

■

Richard Franson, whose name continually appears on the election ballot, says he should be identified in news stories as "First Sgt.-retired-Army." He says retired generals are always identified in that manner, why not first sergeants?

Comment: It takes an act of Congress to make a general.

■

The reader representative catches bouquets and brickbats from 8:30 a.m. to 4:30 p.m. Monday through Friday. Call 673-4450. Outside the metro-area call (800) 827-8742.

Federal farm programs have outlived usefulness

From an editorial in the Washington Post:

Do we still need basic federal farm programs? Most are 60 years old, and it isn't clear that they any longer serve agriculture very well. Their critics, both left and right, regard them as costly anachronisms that ought to be cut back or turned into no more than disaster insurance — if they are allowed to live on at all.

These are the kinds of programs that perfectly fit the description of the ones the Republicans want to get rid of, and the chairmen of both the House and Senate Agriculture Committees have proposed extensive reforms.

In the House, the Republican leadership is also behind the changes. But they are meeting stout resistance. Some of it, predictably, is from the president and farm-state Democrats who want the Republicans to be the ones to walk the plank on farm supports a year before the next election. But a number of farm-state Republicans, despite the imaginative stands taken by their two committee chairmen, are also balking. This is a form of welfare they are reluctant to cut; their own strongest constituencies depend on it.

House Agriculture Committee Chairman Pat Roberts would eliminate the existing support system, the cost of which floats from year to year with prices. In its place would be a system of fixed payments — and fixed costs to the government — to farmers who participated in the programs in the past.

For each of the next seven years, the payments would decline. The farmers would meanwhile be free to produce what they pleased; no more acreage or other planting restrictions, and no more producing for the government as distinct from the market.

Roberts still doesn't have the votes to get his bill out of committee; if he gets them, as he likely eventually will, it will be only after a lot more bargaining with the commodity groups, and because he has the House leadership on his side.

Senate Agriculture Committee Chairman Richard Lugar is thought to be in an even weaker position. The leading bills in his committee would pretty well preserve the existing support structure except in reduced form in order to meet the budget requirements, and even those are being challenged.

The president has proposed only marginal changes in the farm programs, which allows him not to offend. But his loose embrace of the continuing system is itself a position that offends those who think the billions spent each year are partly wasted and produce some harmful social as well as environmental results. He has taken a weak stand.

U.S. joins deadbeat countries causing fiscal crisis at U.N.

Robert J. White

When its shining hour arrives next month, the United Nations ought to glow. It will, unless the lights go out. As presidents, kings and prime ministers gather in New York to celebrate the 50th anniversary of the U.N. charter's ratification, officials will probably find a way to pay the organization's electricity bills. But that won't ease the cash crunch.

Critics will point to these financial woes as another example of an extravagant international bureaucracy.

Is there overlap, inefficiency and waste? Certainly. No institution is immune to those ills. But the image of the United Nations as a ravenous money-gobbler is false. The problem is not the size of its budget but the dues unpaid by member nations.

Since the financial problem is unlikely to disappear, the focus of the several high-powered commissions considering the United Nations' future requires a slight shift. The emphasis now is on structure: Security Council membership, weighted votes in the General Assembly, new guidelines for peacekeeping. While none of those considerations should be set aside, the main emphasis needs to be on new ways to raise money to pay the bills.

The United Nations does spend a lot of money — about $1.3 billion a year for basic operations like paying utility bills and meeting the payroll. Dues for peacekeeping, lately a growth industry, are assessed separately to pay costs now at $3.1 billion a year.

That $4.4 billion total is large by any standard. To put the figure in perspective, consider that it's about half the $9 billion spent annually by Minnesota state government.

The comparison is imprecise because the United Nations doesn't really run the world. But neither is Minnesota run entirely from the state Capitol; ask your mayor or county commissioner. Moreover, the state budget is financed almost entirely by Minnesota revenues. U.N. revenue comes from member countries, 25 percent of the total collected from the United States.

Or supposed to be collected. Although the United States is not the only delinquent, its $1.2 billion default is the largest.

The immediate effect of these shortfalls is to cause U.N. budget managers to use money from peacekeeping accounts in order to pay current bills that can't wait. Peacekeeping payments are largely to countries that contribute soldiers and equipment. Deferring U.N. payments to them would seem like a fair penalty on countries whose assessments are past due. But that argument would have merit only if the delinquents and peacekeeping contributors were the same countries. In most cases they are not.

Nor is account juggling the work of amateur bookkeepers. The Bush and Clinton administrations, skeptical of U.N. efficiency, won approval for the appointment of Americans for the job of under secretary general for administration and management.

Former Attorney General Dick Thornburgh served in that post in the early 1990s. His successor is Joseph Connor, former head of the Price Waterhouse accounting firm. Connor warned Congress the other day that increases in peacekeeping costs, past-due assessments and borrowing from peacekeeping accounts are creating a financial crisis. Unfortunately, no solutions are in sight.

The use of dues withholding for political purposes began in the 1960s when the Soviet Union cut back its peacekeeping payments because it objected to U.N. operations in what was then the Congo. Miffed at losing a 1971 vote to keep Taiwan in the United Nations, the United States followed the Soviet precedent by cutting its payment to the regular budget.

Such payments are not optional; member countries are bound by their acceptance of the charter to make them. But no one has figured out a way to enforce payment, and even if the U.N. black helicopters so feared by right-wing militias existed — they don't — they would be unlikely to swoop down on the U.S. treasury.

Inevitably, other countries concluded that if the big guys could break the rules, so could they. At mid-year, only 48 of 185 U.N. members had paid their full assessments. Fiscal foot-dragging has changed from isolated actions in the 1960s and '70s to a global epidemic in the '90s.

While domestic economic pressures account for some of this, in the United States the underlying cause is political. The general complaint is that the United Nations is wasteful and ineffective.

The charge of waste gets weightier when the cost of specialized U.N. functions is added to the regular and peacekeeping budgets. The other functions — for children, for example, or development programs — are separate because they are financed by voluntary contributions rather that mandatory assessments.

Total cost of the U.N. system — $4.4 billion for administration and peacekeeping, together with specialized functions ranging from global AIDS monitoring to the care of 26 million refugees — is somewhat larger than Minnesota's $9 billion annual outlay. To call the $11 billion spent for all U.N.-related functions a waste is ridiculous.

Such criticism gains credence when it comes from the United Nations' putative friends. John Bolton, who managed U.N. affairs at the State Department for President George Bush (elected 1988, defeated 1992), said recently that the United Nations had "almost no role whatever" in the world "until about 1988, and its role lasted until about 1992."

Was the U.N. operation that began in Cambodia in 1992 really insignificant when it oversaw the transition from civil war to elected government? Have U.N. peacekeepers on the Golan Heights played almost no role the past 21 years?

The United Nations has plenty of bureaucratic faults. Insignificance and extravagance are not among them. The large and growing fault lies beyond the U.N. system, in the failure of member countries to pay their obligations. With little prospect for improvement in national dues-paying, talk of alternatives is becoming louder.

James Tobin of Yale once proposed a charge on foreign-exchange transactions to finance the United Nations. Even if that idea is impractical, the principle behind it is not: that the global economic commons, rather than national treasuries, could become the source of U.N. revenue. Among the pieties sure to be forthcoming at next month's anniversary celebration, how refreshing it would be to hear a solid proposal on money-raising.

Robert J. White is a Star Tribune foreign affairs columnist.

today suggest that informality is a desirable attribute of editorials and that ragged right columns can help contribute to that. Bohle's design represents a middle ground.[7]

TODAY'S PAGES

A 1995 survey of editorial page editors found that "virtually all of the nation's larger daily newspapers, and many others, have improved the appearance of their editorial pages in recent decades by using larger body type and wider columns for editorials, adopting easier-to-read type faces and making greater use of white space." According to Ernest C. Hynds, who conducted the survey, the most frequently cited change in the 1990s was "increased use of graphics" (60 percent), followed by "occasionally used cartoons, other elements" (54 percent) and "increased use of drawings" (51 percent). Hynds' survey of editors showed that more than half thought improvements in editorial page design increased readership.[8]

Within about two years, the *Star Tribune* of Minneapolis–St. Paul twice redesigned its opinion pages. The goal in 1993, according to Susan Albright, editorial page editor, was to "create a brighter, cleaner and more dynamic look, as well as to highlight our institutional views as expressed in editorials."[9] Reverse labels—white on black—were designed for headings to divide the page into clearly identifiable sections (Figures 4 and 5, pages 303 and 304). In 1995, as part of a general design of the newspaper, the reverse labels were eliminated as being (in Albright's words) "too harsh within the new design framework, which is more elegant" (Figures 7 and 8, pages 307 and 308). The organizational framework was kept, but fonts and column signatures were changed, again toward a less harsh style. Newsroom design director Anders Ramberg said he thought the previous sans serif bold Helvetica headlines looked dated. He also used the word "elegant" to describe the new combination of san serif Franklin and serif Walbaum, which he thought complemented each other.[10] (The distinctive characteristic of a serif typeface is a smaller line used to finish off a main stroke of a letter. The type you are reading now is serif. The section headlines are sans serif.)

Body type size was increased from 9 points to 10 for the editorials and 9½ for other items on the opinion pages. The first line of a paragraph now is indented, whereas before a blank line set off the paragraphs. Justified letter columns (flush right and left, instead of ragged right) also add to the more formal look of the page, as does centering the editorial headlines. The letters section is simplified with removal of the hairline box. The masthead has been given a more open, modern look.

When I first saw the 1993 design, I thought it was attractive. It had an orderly, bold look. But I like the new version better. It projects a feeling of respectability, dignity and thoughtfulness, and yet has an inviting appearance.

While these pages are attractive, they are not radical departures from the standard opinion page. In fact I found little evidence of a graphics revolution among the 165 editorial pages that I examined in working on this edition. Most editors still place editorials in the upper left corner, with the cartoon in the upper right. The *Chicago Tribune* is one of few newspapers that place the editorial cartoon in the upper left corner with editorials running under the cartoon

Figure 6 **News Regress**

OPINION

". . . and the Truth shall set you free."

PAGE A-4

AUGUST 1, 1992

Prayer at graduation: Issues are complex

THE FACTS

FOR PRAYER

AGAINST PRAYER

LOCAL OPINIONS

OUR THOUGHTS

The Editors

OUR THOUGHTS EXACTLY . . .

CARTOON

Supreme Court in review: Moving to 'Right'

THE FACTS

LOCAL OPINIONS

OUR THOUGHTS

BY THE NUMBERS

The Editors

READERS WRITE

Coverage of softball championship weak

Editor's "an idiot"; publisher agrees

New design looks like a "copycat" winner

Ideas are cheap when learned at U.V.

News-Regress

Universal County's newspaper for 101 years

Thornwell Hugger, *Editor and Publisher*
Y. Elton Hugger, *Vice President and General Manager*
Yvonne MacArthur Hugger, *Business Manager*
Suzanne E. Reid, *Advertising Manager* / Chris Cameron, *News Editor*

Mailing Address: P.O. Box 1570, Universal, VA 23005
Telephone: 804-555-9031 / FAX 804-555-9036

Figure 7 **Star Tribune**

PAGE A18 • STAR TRIBUNE — SUNDAY, FEBRUARY 25 • 1996

Star Tribune Editorial

Joel Kramer: Publisher • *News:* **Tim McGuire** Editor, **Pam Fine** News Leader • *Editorial:* **Susan Albright** Editor, Editorial Pages; **Jim Boyd** Deputy Editor, Editorial Pages

Our perspective

Say more, Bob

Dole must define GOP mainstream

Bob Dole said it plain after Pat Buchanan stung him in New Hampshire last week: The Republican presidential contest has come down to a choice between "mainstream and extreme."

A day later, under fire by Buchanan for name calling, Dole dithered about his phraseology. "Others" have "extreme views," he said he meant to say. "My views are conservative mainstream views."

And those views are . . . ? The candidate never quite said.

So it's been going for the GOP Senate leader for weeks now. A rival ascends. Dole responds with an attack. And the attack becomes the Dole message. Some listeners are turned off; others are reassured. But at the end of the day, nobody knows any more about what Bob Dole would do as president of the United States.

That's a blank the man who would rally anti-Buchanan Republicans had better fill, and fast. This year's primary calendar allows little time for hesitation — and this year's Republican primary voters seem to have little tolerance for equivocation. Now — today — is when Dole should explain what he would do as president to make the American dream come true for a larger share of the nation's citizens.

Former Tennessee Gov. Lamar Alexander isn't being fair when he says repeatedly that Dole is a man with "no ideas." The problem is that Dole's ideas are old-time Republican religion, unrevised to speak to Americans working in a 1990s economy that can soar and leave them strapped at the same time.

Dole extols a balanced federal budget, less government regulation, welfare under state control. It's the Contract with America, warmed up with vague promises to look out for the young and the old, and to provide "strong, steady, faithful, honest leadership."

Does Dole's vision of a smaller federal government leave to others the work of improving worker training, enhancing corporate reinvestment and protecting workers against discrimination and unsafe conditions? The candidate hasn't said.

Dole's post-New Hampshire speech contained an important addendum. He emphasized that his America is a diverse one, and that his Republican tent is big enough to cover people of many classes and colors. That's a point well worth making, especially on the day when Russia's Vladimir Zhirinovsky endorsed Buchanan and suggested that they work together to deport Jews from both nations.

But did Dole mean that he would protect affirmative action from the assaults of his more extreme fellow Republicans? Or that he would extend the federal government's muscular hand to help rebuild America's minority-dominated inner cities? The candidate hasn't said.

These are among the questions Dole must answer. More than the fulfillment of his own long-nursed presidential ambition depends upon it. The direction of his party and, potentially, of the nation are at stake as well. Dole had it right: It has come down to "mainstream vs. extreme" in the Republican Party — and the future of mainstream Republicanism may depend on how clearly and convincingly Dole can defend it in the next month.

Tuning in

Wind-up radio informs South Africans

Among the myriad advances in communications technology shaping this wired age, a particularly ennobling one has been making headlines lately.

It's not a telephone cable that can deliver the Library of Congress in nanoseconds, nor a search engine with links to home pages in Andromeda. It's a simple radio — big as a lunch bucket, ugly as a rutabaga, heavy as a gallon of sherbet, powered by a crank-up motor. And it's bringing the world to villages across South Africa.

Though by averages it is one of the richer nations on its continent, South Africa has a depth of poverty and technological privation that Americans can scarcely imagine.

Half its villages have no electricity. Transistor radios are such coveted rarities that owning one can greatly improve a man's marriage prospects.

The significance of these facts settled on Trevor Baylis, a British inventor, as he listened to a documentary on Africa's AIDS plague and the inability of safe-sex campaigns to get their messages into villages too poor to buy batteries.

Baylis quickly stuck together a seat-belt retractor spring, an electric motor positioned to run backwards, and an AM/FM/shortwave receiver.

After a couple of years of effort, a mix of public and private financing came together. The BayGen Power Co. was established near Cape Town, and the radio known as Freeplay was born.

Most Freeplays are being sold to social-service agencies at wholesale prices around $30; resale prices are often lower. By comparison, operating a battery-powered radio would cost $500 to $1,000 over the three-year period a Freeplay will run before the spring needs replacing.

The Freeplay story is a kind of social and economic miracle in which Baylis' design is just one piece: Lawyers and consultants accepted delayed payment for their startup work. Most BayGen workers are disabled. Agencies that advocate for them own 60 percent of the company stock.

Americans are rightly captivated by the dazzling explosion of computing technology. But it is well to remember, now and then, that half our fellow humans have yet to make a phone call — and that, here and there, a Trevor Baylis is helping them catch up.

A caucus primer

Video explains how to participate

Minnesota citizenship quiz time: Do you know what the purpose of a precinct caucus is? Do you know who can attend one? How would you find out where and when your caucus meets?

Could you explain the difference between "endorsement" and "nomination" of a candidate for elective office in Minnesota? Or how about the difference between a major political party and "registered minor party"? And how many major parties does Minnesota have, anyway?

These and other political mysteries are neatly unraveled in a 15-minute video production of the state League of Women Voters that will air on Metro Cable Network, Channel 6, tonight at 7:30. For anyone a little or a lot confused by the complexities of political participation in Minnesota, it's well worth viewing.

For noncable subscribers, the tape is worth renting or buying from the league's state office, at 224-5445.

The program, produced for the league by KSTP Channel 5 and hosted by its anchors Chris Conangla and Kalley King, offers viewers a clear, concise primer just in time for the state's precinct caucuses on March 5.

The league knows too well that lack of basic political knowledge is a big contributor to low turnout at Minnesota's caucuses, and to declining turnout at the polls. League offices field thousands of calls on caucus and election days from people eager to participate, if they only knew how.

There's ample reason this year for precinct-caucus neophytes to get informed and get involved. A respectable turnout at this year's Republican caucuses could make Minnesota more than the forgotten backwater it has often been in national politics. Minnesotans could make a real difference in the nomination. And, true to its 75-year tradition, the League of Women Voters is there to help.

Letters from readers

Profile of a surgeon

In its Feb. 22 editorial, the Star Tribune indicted and convicted Dr. John Najarian for being "arrogant." Well, if a surgeon is going to cut into my body, take out and successfully replace vital organs, and tend to my healing with a personal sense of commitment and compassion, I'd like a surgeon who thinks highly of himself. In fact, if the surgeon had a proven track record and also thought too highly of himself, I'd feel even better.

Your paper does a disservice to the notion of news when it continues to hound this man with an editorial that rejects his successful development of a drug acknowledged as better than anything else now on the market. ALG saved lives, reduced pain, brought joy to thousands of patients and families, and today I feel deprived by my government of its curative powers should I ever need a transplant. If I may engage in your style of name-calling, I think your paper is arrogant. Pray you don't need ALG to help you recover from a transplant.

— Richard L. Breitman, Minneapolis.

Caring for city students

I was impressed by your Feb. 21 editorial on the Minneapolis schools, particularly the final paragraph calling attention to "the rapidly growing cohort of exceedingly poor and unmotivated children. That group requires massive intervention strategies." You went on to suggest various changes in the operation of the system. I believe that you omitted the most important and effective intervention for that segment of the student population: feed them, beginning at infancy.

The February 1996 Scientific American published a résumé of research showing that undernutrition of infants and young children retards brain development. The résumé concludes: "On balance, it seems clear that prevention of malnutrition among young children remains the best policy — not only on moral grounds but on economic ones as well."

Somehow we must see to it that infants and young children of the poor receive the nourishment they need for normal brain development. By age 7 it's too late; the damage is permanent, and no amount of remedial education will help. Money spent to provide an adequate diet for the most vulnerable members of the community — infants and young children in poverty — will be money returned many times over by a skilled, educated, productive work force.

— Frederick O. Hutchinson, Minneapolis.

Your Feb. 21 editorial gave the Minneapolis schools a "D" for asking parents to live up to their responsibilities. What do you think the school district should do? Start a boarding school for every child whose parents are unable to perform their duties?

— Loren Piller, Minneapolis.

Views on vouchers

Leading citizens of Northern Ireland seek ways to bring Protestant and Roman Catholic children together a few hours a day to reduce "the troubles" there. Our European ancestors, educated in the harm done by aggressive, controlling clerics, blessed us with separation of church and state.

Gov. Arne Carlson and Rep. LeRoy Koppendrayer, R-Princeton, demand vouchers for private schools. Belfast, Mostar, Srebrenica, Sarajevo, Kabul, Beirut and Jerusalem show each day what divisive education can accomplish. Why add St. Paul?

— Daniel P. Norton, Duluth, Minn.

If we didn't have private schools, the taxpayers would be paying for more buildings, teachers and supplies to accommodate the additional students who now attend the private schools.

Does that make school vouchers seem like a better idea? I think it does!

— Rosemary Albrecht, Minneapolis.

Korean memorial

We appreciate your previous articles about Cpl. Harold Motzko, a Minnesotan who was verified missing in action in Korea and never returned. A follow-up letter writer mentioned plans for a Korean War veterans memorial on the Capitol Court of Honor in St. Paul and an address to which contributions may be sent. We would like your readers to know that the Minnesota Korean War Veterans State Memorial now has a new address: P.O. Box 131842, Roseville, Minn., 55113.

— Ed Valle, Stillwater.

All sides of abuse

For years, the media have been siding with feminist groups by implying that the issue of spousal abuse is one-sided; the man is at fault. Thanks to Felicia Moon's testimony, the truth is known: Spousal abuse is not unlike any other issue. It is more than one-sided, and those other sides need to be included in studying the issue.

— Steve Horner, Apple Valley.

Studying annexation law

I agree with the Star Tribune that annexation law changes need to be made, but disagree with several statements in your Feb. 17 editorial.

You state that our current annexation laws are tilted in favor of the townships. Annexation requests in Minnesota over the past few years show the opposite to be true. For example, the 12 most recent contested case annexations reviewed by the Minnesota Municipal Board resulted in 10 approvals and only two denials. In the years from 1982 to 1992, 54 contested case annexations were approved and 18 denied. So, in the most contentious cases annexations are being approved more than 75 percent of the time. Furthermore, 1,064 annexations have occurred since 1992, a 150 percent increase over the previous four years, largely because the Legislature has made it easier for cities to annex surrounding property.

The Legislature also recently took away township residents' right to have a say in the annexation decision. It's odd that we allow city residents to vote when their two cities consider consolidation, but township residents cannot vote when they are being annexed (consolidated) into a city.

Your editorial also urges modeling our annexation process on North Carolina law, but fails to explain that that state doesn't even have townships.

Annexation is one of the most contentious issues I have ever tried to resolve. In my opinion, we first need to encourage joint planning between cities and townships, giving both sides an equal say in the process. Giving more power to cities to take land they want indiscriminately is not the responsible answer to this complex issue.

— Sen. Jim Vickerman, DFL-Tracy; chair, Senate Metropolitan and Local Government Committee.

Next, the G-chip to protect us from ourselves

By Teller

Other points of view

Soon by law all new TVs will carry the V-chip — that cunning little piece of circuitry designed to enable parents (without any attention or effort!) to stop their kids from seeing make-believe violence that an official at the Federal Communications Commission thinks might make them naughty. What a relief.

Later this year Congress will be offering families an even more valuable, worry-saving innovation: the G-chip.

The G-chip will plug into the back of a TV and automatically restrict reception of all depictions of Gluttony.

This is important.

Too many of us are fat.

We waste billions of dollars each year on medical care for victims of Häagen-Dazs.

Furthermore, many criminals became social misfits because they were tubby adolescents.

The G-chip will stop Julia Child and Graham Kerr from leading millions of impressionable moppets down the primrose path to hypercholesterolemia by filling their hungry little heads with visions of zabaglione and chocolate croissants.

With this new technology, parents will no longer have to promote good eating habits by buying wholesome food, preparing balanced meals or teaching the kids about nutrition.

Microchips and legislation will shield the tykes from temptation.

And that is as it should be, for after all, why should a parent bear sole responsibility for the health of a future taxpayer? The government should do its part.

The G-chip will be more practical and cheaper to administer than the V-chip. With the V-chip we'll need to pay expensive experts to decide how many ounces of stage blood are enough to drive a 10-year-old to a life of crime. But with Gluttony, there's no controversy. No one denies that spinach is healthier than spumoni.

TV chips are a great breakthrough in parenting. Once we've gotten the V-chip and the G-chip in place, we'll move on to the P-chip and the S-chip and get rid of Pride and Sloth. Think of the effect that will have on a youngster destined for a career in Congress.

— Teller is the smaller, quieter half of Penn & Teller, the magic duo. He wrote this article for the Washington Post.

WEDNESDAY, JANUARY 10 • 1996

STAR TRIBUNE • PAGE A13

Commentary

A forum for opinions, reactions, dialogue and disagreement

'Diversity training' efforts proceed from false premise

They view others first through prism of race

Katherine Kersten

"Diversity training" has become part of the fabric of American life. Each year, corporations and agencies that accept its premises spend millions trying to bring employees of various races together by stressing how different they are.

Professional groups, too, increasingly instruct members that racial groups think and act in fundamentally different ways. For example, the Minnesota Supreme Court recently ordered that, as of July 1, attorneys must complete periodic diversity training to retain a license here.

The "diversity" mind-set is most firmly entrenched in education circles. In fact, the State Board of Education is about to adopt an "Education Diversity" rule that will make training about racial "differences" an integral part of each Minnesota schoolchild's day.

The Education Diversity rule will require Minnesota school districts to develop curricula that give "special emphasis" to "differing perspectives" of racial/ethnic groups like blacks, Indians and Alaskan natives, Asian/Pacific Americans and Hispanics, plus women and people of "all disability areas."

The rule breaks new ground by mandating that students move beyond instruction to diversity-related "action."

It compels school boards to set "goals and objectives" for students that "reflect movement beyond the level of awareness to a level of making decisions on social issues and taking actions" that demonstrate allegiance to the diversity movement's fundamental premises.

Out of sync with King

Yet there is strong evidence that stressing differences does little to improve race relations, and may even exacerbate them.

For example, the Minneapolis and St. Paul school districts have made costly diversity education a top priority for decades. Nevertheless, the Minneapolis district recently announced that "embedded racism" continues to permeate its schools, while a 1994 study by People for the American Way found that "race relations and tolerance" in St. Paul high schools are "crumbling."

What accounts for diversity programs' failure? They are based on a false premise: That in order to understand our fellow Americans — and learn to treat them decently — we must see them, first and foremost, as representatives of racial and ethnic groups, rather than as unique individuals.

Diversity programs do not teach, with Martin Luther King, that we should judge others by the content of their character, not the color of their skin. On the contrary, these programs suggest that the way a person thinks, what he values, how he behaves, how he sees the world — in short, his "perspective" on life — is to a good extent a function of his color or his grandparents' country of origin. Diversity education claims to seek to banish racial "stereotypes." In fact, they are its stock in trade.

For most Americans, the idea of group identity rings hollow. As a nation of immigrants, our goal has always been not to sanctify old ways, but to create a new way of life — a common culture where each can develop his talents and interests as seems best to him.

Even our children, novelist Mark Helprin has pointed out, shrink instinctively from patronizing exhortations to "celebrate" ethnic differences: "We're so proud to have Melanie in our class, because she's an Eskimo!"

Diversity education's failure to improve race relations in our schools — particularly our elite colleges — is hard to deny. Significantly, however, race relations have generally flourished in another institution charged with acculturating young people: the U.S. Army. In a recent issue of National Review, Chicago writer Steven Sailor explains:

"Through racial quotas, mandatory ethnic studies, minority-only orientation weeks, single-race dormitories, and relentless emphasis on the oppression of minorities, colleges today focus incoming freshmen on what each student is and unalterably will *be*: black or white, Hispanic or Asian."

By contrast, Sailor says, the Army has chosen to ignore "identity politics" and focus exclusively on what each soldier can *become*.

In the early 1970s, the Army discovered firsthand how divisive diversity programs can be. At that time, when relations between black and white soldiers were "viciously hostile," Army brass instituted orthodox "racial sensitivity training" courses, in which outside consultants lectured soldiers about "black victimization and white guilt." Not surprisingly, Sailor notes, this only inflamed racial tensions.

Consequently, the Army developed a radically different approach, replacing outside experts with career soldiers loyal to the institution's best interests.

Instead of lecturing new recruits "on their personal *rights*," instructors now "train sergeants and officers how to carry out their *duty* to the Army of getting full value from each soldier, regardless of race."

Army trainers, Sailor says, see their job as resembling that of college athletic coaches, whose goal is to get black and white players alike to forget what they were — the stars of their high school teams — and "focus on what they can all become together: champions."

Whether used in barracks, corporate boardrooms or elementary schools, programs that encourage people to view others through the prism of race and ethnicity are bound to fail. Mark Helprin — whose ancestors fled czarist Russia's "diversity" policies — has identified the reason: the paradox at the heart of the diversity mind-set.

Programs that pigeonhole people on the basis of race and ethnicity, says Helprin, do not liberate, but imprison them. "Though [people] are forced to dwell on half a dozen categories, told that this is diversity," he observes, "the reduction of 250 million individuals to a handful of racial and ethnic classifications is not the recognition of differences but their brutal suppression." Identity politics, in Helprin's words, is "a triumph of the academic impulse to classify, a triumph of the bureaucratic need to categorize . . . . But it is a defeat for the human spirit."

— Katherine Kersten, an attorney, is vice chair of the Center of the American Experiment in Minneapolis.

Promising new gay candidates for Congress

By Deb Price
Los Angeles Times Syndicate

No matter how eloquently gay-friendly members of Congress champion gay civil rights, there's one vital statement they cannot make about homosexuality: "Hey, that's my life you're talking about!" Massachusetts Democrats Gerry Studds and Barney Frank recently illustrated the importance of having members of Congress who actually can make that statement.

In a debate over rights for domestic partners, several lawmakers accused gay couples of undermining "the family." The openly gay Studds and Frank joined the debate to remind their colleagues of the truth.

"I have a stable, loving family," began Studds, who congenially pointed out that his partner, Dean Hara, is someone "a great many of you consider as a very close friend."

The intelligently combative Frank jumped in, demanding to know how his loving Herb Moses harms anyone else's family. "Herb and I have been together for eight years," he pointed out. "We do not seek your approval . . . . What we do seek is to protect ourselves."

Unfortunately, the half-crazed House, which can ill afford to lose voices of sanity, must kiss two openly gay members goodbye at the end of this year. Studds and Steve Gunderson, R-Wis., are retiring. That leaves only Frank seeking reelection.

But a record number of new House candidates — at least four — are openly gay. They're all hoping to make history by winning election to Congress after coming out — rather than coming out after winning.

"It wouldn't have been honest for me to run as a closeted candidate. It also wouldn't have been possible. Most of my community activism has been with the gay and lesbian community," explains Eric Resnick, a Canton, Ohio, vocational rehabilitation expert. At 32, his long-shot dream is to be the Democrat who throws 12-term Republican Ralph Regula out of work.

Patrick Baikauskas (pronounced bike-cows-kiss), 43, wants to change the House Republican lineup — but by joining it. A former Bush administration appointee, he is legislative liaison for the Illinois Department of Mental Health. Even though he hosts a gay cable TV show, his sexual orientation surprises some party members.

Facing a crowded primary for a shot at Springfield's open seat, he recalls a whispered call from a stranger: "'I want you to know that one of the candidates is going around saying that you're gay.' And I said, 'Well, I am gay.' And he paused for a few seconds and said, 'Well, good; I'm one of those big-tent kind of Republicans.'"

Almost half of U.S. adults don't consider themselves so progressive. In a 1994 Yankelovich poll, 45 percent said they would not vote for "a candidate who is homosexual" while 48 percent would.

But Maine state Sen. Dale McCormick, a Democrat, knows that gay candidates can win once they stop being a faceless abstraction. A 48-year-old carpenter, she'll become the first openly lesbian congresswoman if she defeats freshman Republican James Longley Jr. McCormick has been the lead proponent of a gay civil-rights bill, which she recently withdrew, saying Maine needs "a period of healing and dialogue" after narrowly defeating an antigay referendum.

A continent away in Long Beach, Calif., Rick Zbur, 38, is plotting the ouster of two-term Republican Stephen Horn. A Harvard-educated environmental lawyer who specializes in finding cost-effective, job-saving ways to curb pollution, he's the ideal candidate for everyone outraged by House efforts to Newt-er environmental protections.

The first openly gay partner in the nation's eighth-largest law firm, Zbur's got what he calls "as broad a base of support as you can imagine." Only $10,000 of his impressive first $165,000 in contributions came from gay donors. And already the California League of Conservation Voters and the local Longshoremen's board back this most promising Democrat.

Congress, almost certainly, has always had gay members. We can't be sure. But with the courage of their honesty, today's openly gay members and candidates provide a priceless public service to our nation.

— Deb Price is a columnist for the Detroit News.

Powerful anatomy of disaster that befell Yugoslavia

By Anthony Lewis
New York Times

BOSTON — How did Yugoslavia descend into the savagery that killed 200,000 people and made 2 million refugees? It is a question of signal importance, not just for history but as a key to seeing that it does not happen again, there or elsewhere.

We now have a documented answer, powerfully convincing in its evidence. It is a five-hour television series, "Yugoslavia: Death of a Nation," shown on the BBC and then here, between Christmas and New Year's, on the Discovery Channel.

Western politicians and commentators who wanted to close their eyes to the horror in the former Yugoslavia have often said that it was caused by "ancient hatreds." Americans, they said — or Britons or whoever — should not get involved in such impenetrable ethnic-religious conflicts.

But it was not "ancient hatreds" that produced ethnic cleansing, rape and concentration camps. It was men: ambitious men who stirred up extreme nationalist emotions as a way to power. It was one man above all, Slobodan Milosevic of Serbia. "Death of a Nation" makes that unarguably clear.

We see Milosevic at the beginning of his manipulations: addressing a Serbian crowd in the predominantly Albanian province of Kosovo in 1987. The crowd provokes a police detachment, mostly Albanian. A man shouts, "The police attacked us." Milosevic says, "You will not be beaten again." It was all arranged — and Belgrade television showed the scene with Milosevic as a Serbian hero.

That and many other scenes are amazing examples of contemporaneous footage found by the independent British producers who made the series, Brian Lapping Associates. There is even film taken secretly by Serbian intelligence. And there are gripping interviews.

Radovan Karadzic, the Bosnian Serb leader who has been indicted for war crimes, says that when Bosnia declared its independence in April 1992, Milosevic "couldn't care less if Bosnia was recognized. He said: 'Caligula proclaimed his horse a senator, but the horse never took his seat. Bosnia will get recognition, but . . . .'"

When Milosevic decided to attack Croatia in summer 1991, he used volunteers under the extremist paramilitary leader Vojislav Seselj. The Yugoslav federal army provided weapons, uniforms and transportation. Paramilitaries burned civilians alive and left the bodies as a message.

Again in 1992, when the attack on Bosnia began, Milosevic sought to avoid responsibility. One of his aides says that he "pulled a fast one" — transferred every Serb in the federal army to Bosnian Serb forces while continuing to pay and supply them.

The first major attack was on the town of Zvornik in Bosnia: a terrifying onslaught that left 2,000 Muslim civilians "unaccounted for." Seselj's paramilitaries were there, and he tells an interviewer: "Milosevic was in absolute control. It was all planned in Belgrade."

Milosevic is not the only Yugoslav figure shown in the series as a cold-blooded manipulator, but he is special. The president of Slovenia, Milan Kucan, says: "With Milosevic you never can relax. Show him a finger, and he'll have your arm off."

One of the most arresting aspects of the series is the evidence of how Western weakness encouraged the genocidal aggression. Milosevic sent a secret envoy to Moscow before attacking Croatia, and the Soviet military said its intelligence showed that the West would not respond. It was good intelligence.

Karadzic, speaking to an interviewer, confirms what critics of U.S. and European policy have maintained — that we could have stopped it. "I knew," he says, "that if the West put in 10,000 men to cut off our supply corridor, we Serbs would be finished."

Those who are skeptical of television's potential as a medium for sustained journalism of a high order should see this series and think again. So should those American politicians who tell us that we should be content with the degraded trash that the free market mostly brings to the screen.

There are more remarkable moments in the series than a column can even suggest. For me, the most chilling is the voice of Ratko Mladic, the Bosnian Serb general, telling his men on the hills overlooking Sarajevo: "Shell the presidency and the Parliament. Target Muslim neighborhoods — not many Serbs live there. Shell them till they're on the edge of madness."

Generation X could use a good war to give it some purpose

By Brian Gabriel

LOS ANGELES — It has been said that Generation X — or the MTV Generation, the Slacker Generation, the Baby Busters or whatever it's called — it's been said that this generation of which I, being 27, am part is aimless, apathetic, unmotivated. These twentysomething Americans, it's been said, are spoiled, don't know how good they have it, are nothing but crybabies with degrees. Naturally, all this is said by elders who, no matter the era, always feel it their duty to disparage the younger generation.

But while this younger generation may be apathetic, spoiled, lacking purpose, etc. (just look how many different names it's called and then tell me it doesn't have an identity problem), let me add one more whine and say: It's not our fault.

Throughout this century, the older generation has consistently supplied the younger generation with a cause that conferred an identity: the Lost Generation of World War I, in which the older generation thoughtfully supplied its offspring with a catastrophic war to scar their remaining years; the Depression/World War II Generation, in which the older generation supplied the younger with two catastrophes for the price of one; the Baby Boomer Generation, in which the older generation supplied the young with an unpopular jungle war, causing them to take drugs, protest and drop out.

Which brings us to the present younger generation. Preceding generations' identities were forged mostly in response to war. And therein lies our problem. Our elders have failed to provide us with a suitable war to forge an identity around.

Oh, sure, our noble leaders have done their best to get us one. Ever since the mid-'80s they have tried and tried again with no luck: Panama, Grenada, El Salvador, Somalia, Haiti, the Persian Gulf. Unfortunately, all these efforts failed, either through bungled leadership (Haiti, Somalia) or, worst of all, excessive success — wars that have lasted only a matter of hours or days. How are we supposed to forge an identity around Operation Desert Storm?

That one, by the way, was the great hope. Over the course of a couple of months, while President Bush (God bless him) assembled our military might in the heart of Arabia, I could feel a generation bursting forth: Nirvana played incessantly on the radio, "Slacker" was fast approaching status as an official cult movie and the Clash's "Rock the Casbah" was the first song to be blasted on the armed forces radio in the liberation of Kuwait. I remember being in Santa Cruz in January '91 as students and others took to the park for a protest — a real antiwar protest! — and then, right there on CNN, there it was, a generation forming on the tip of a missile as it pierced the roof of an Iraqi building and blew to pieces everything and everyone inside. What a glorious moment that was.

And then it was over. American troops defeated Iraq in what — six days? Give me a break. World War I lasted about a year and a half after America entered the fray. World War II took almost four. And Vietnam ran somewhere in the neighborhood of 10 years. Six days? What is that?

And so my generation continues to drift here and then there, whining every so often and turning on MTV (but not really watching) and falling asleep and waking up, not knowing really what to do with ourselves, waiting for our fearless leaders to give us a cause, something to care about. The Soviet Union is no more, the Eastern bloc is being swallowed by NATO and Central America is safely capitalist again. Nelson Mandela is president of his country and Manuel Noriega isn't. Sure, there are issues, there always are, but that's not good enough. We need a war.

Where exactly is Bosnia?

— Brian Gabriel, of Los Angeles, wrote this article for the Los Angeles Times.

(Figure 9, page 310). I found no examples of editorials running all the way across the top of the page. The *St. Augustine* (Fla.) *Record* (Figure 10, page 311) ran a two-column editorial approximately two-thirds of the way across the top. (The lines contain a pretty hefty maximum of 60 characters, but some of the lines are a little shorter because of the ragged-right columns.) The *Missoulian* of Missoula, Mont, on a four-column page, ran an editorial (not reproduced here) in columns two, three and four. (The lines, set flush left, varied in length from 43 to 53 characters.) In a design that I found unique, the *Los Angeles Times* (not reproduced here) ran two editorials at the top of the page, side by side, with headlines of the same size. Traditional page designers would describe that as "bumping heads," certain to earn demerits in makeup contests, at least in the old days.

A few editors, following Bohle's advice, have begun to ask whether editorials and cartoons should always get the best play on the page. The *Savannah Morning News* (Figure 11, page 312) provides an example, with a George Will column across the top. The remainder of the page is a standard design, with the editorials in the left columns, beneath the masthead.

INNOVATIVE FEATURES

Editorials, columns, cartoons and letters—plus a Bible verse or short prayer and a "back when" column—have traditionally made up the American editorial page. Most of the religious and reminiscence features have disappeared by now, but I found devotional material on editorial pages of such diverse newspapers as the *Nashville Banner*, the *Abilene* (Texas) *Reporter-News* and the Harrisonburg, Va., *Daily News Record*. In traditional days, except for letters to the editor, those who wrote and drew for the editorial page essentially talked to one another, mostly about politics and government. It was a page that belonged to professionals. But as editors began to search for ways to enliven their pages and keep their readership, they came up with a variety of ideas for attracting more diverse views of more people to the page. The innovations have included guest columns and other contributions from knowledgeable persons, in-depth analyses, a question of the week, pro-con arguments on specific issues, and critiques of and comments on the press. To a large extent these have been made possible through the addition of more editorial space, notably the op-ed (opposite-editorial) page, which will be discussed later.

The innovations generally fall into four broad categories—those that:

- encourage reader participation
- seek a greater diversity of ideas
- simplify the editorial message
- experiment with alternatives to standard editorial pages

ENCOURAGING READER PARTICIPATION

Question of the Week

Some papers have posed a question of the week to help readers feel they can have a say. The *Milwaukee Journal* and the *Philadelphia Evening Bulletin* were among the first to try this feature. One of the newspapers using this feature

Figure 9 **Chicago Tribune**

Chicago Tribune

FOUNDED JUNE 10, 1847

JACK FULLER, *Publisher* HOWARD A. TYNER, *Editor*

N. DON WYCLIFF, *Editorial Page Editor* ANN MARIE LIPINSKI, *Managing Editor*

JAMES O'SHEA, *Deputy Managing Editor/News* GEROULD KERN, *Deputy Managing Editor/Features*

R. BRUCE DOLD, *Deputy Editorial Page Editor* F. RICHARD CICCONE, *Associate Editor*

16 Section 1 Wednesday, January 10, 1996

MacNelly's view

Editorials

The White House deception

Forget, for a moment, the special Senate committee and the Resolution Trust Corp. and the Federal Deposit Insurance Corp. and all the other sleuths who have been investigating the Whitewater affair.

The legal issues will sort themselves out in time. But one thing has now become all too clear: Bill and Hillary Clinton and their aides have made a concerted effort to deceive official investigators and the American public with half-truths and outright lies.

To their detractors, that will come as no surprise. From the start, the foes of this administration have kept up a drumbeat about its supposed failings. That relentless partisanship, in fact, gave reason to wonder whether the Whitewater investigations were a search for truth or for political gain.

But for anyone who attempted to give the Clintons some benefit of the doubt, well, the benefits are expiring. It's not clear what the Clintons want to conceal, but it's clear that they have made extraordinary efforts to do so. They have thereby bought the trouble that now engulfs them.

The latest evidence, perhaps the most damning to date, came last weekend when the White House released copies of billing records that detail the hours of legal work Hillary Clinton did at Little Rock's Rose Law Firm on behalf of Madison Guaranty Savings & Loan, whose failure cost the government $47 million. The records show that Mrs. Clinton had several business discussions with Seth Ward, an Arkansas businessman who was involved in a land deal that led to a $4 million loss for Madison.

These records were subpoenaed by investigators in 1994. They had disappeared from the files of the Rose firm, and the Clintons claimed to have no knowledge of them.

Yet, miracle of miracles, copies showed up in the White House not long after the RTC decided not to bring a civil lawsuit against the Clintons and closed its doors. The records flatly contradict Mrs. Clinton's contention that she had no involvement in the land deal that caused the $4 million loss and little to do at all with Madison Guaranty.

Time and again, the Clintons and their allies have protested their innocence, only to be contradicted by a paper trail or the testimony of others. One more case in point: Hillary Clinton's role in the 1993 decision to fire the White House travel office staff and give the work to an Arkansas firm with Clinton connections.

The Clintons came to the White House with an election victory, but one provided by a skeptical electorate. The president's credibility had been rocked by initial allegations about Whitewater and questions about his character. The first lady's professed faith in her husband had given him a political boost.

Now their credibility is in tatters. Even if the Senate Whitewater committee and the special prosecutor were to close up shop tomorrow, the stain would remain. The Clintons decided that deception and delay were better than forthrightness. They were wrong, deeply wrong.

Caught with a Silver Shovel in hand

In the 1980s, the federal Operation Greylord investigation of the Cook County courts unearthed scores of sleazy lawyers and judges who were sent to jail, disbarred or suspended for their misdeeds. The scope of corruption was incredible.

Yet even more remarkable was that, right when the scoundrels were heading off to jail and everyone knew that the feds were crawling all over the courts, some lawyers and judges kept fixing cases. That produced Operation Gambat, which sent more crooks off to jail.

All that invited the question: If these people were smart enough to get through law school, how come they were so dumb as to keep fixing cases when everyone around them was going off to jail?

There is no bar exam required to join the City Council, no standard of intelligence required. Even so, one has to wonder how investigators are able to pluck off aldermen with as much ease and frequency as Lake Michigan fishermen snag smelt.

Why do they keep taking the bait?

Operation Silver Shovel, the latest sting operation to focus on Chicago politicians, looks like a big haul.

The central accusation is particularly galling: that politicians took bribes to allow the illegal dumping of industrial waste in their own neighborhoods.

The one positive element is that the leaders of the city's Department of Environment apparently have made an honest, dogged and successful legal effort to stop John Christopher, the FBI mole who operated five dump sites in the city.

Those dumps have been closed; the question is who will pay for the cleanup. It will cost an estimated $15 million to clean just one site, a six-square-block expanse on the West Side filled with 600,000 cubic yards of concrete, asphalt, clay and debris that tower over the neighborhood. It must be a depressing sight for the kids who go to classes at Sumner Elementary School, right across the street from the dump.

The city officials who fought Christopher question whether the FBI's embrace of their nemesis in any way hampered their efforts. The question deserves an answer, and the feds ought to provide it.

Time to curb the Harvard curfew

Well-meaning law is not necessarily good law. That about sums up the controversy over Harvard's daytime curfew ordinance, and it is wise that City Council members and Mayor William LeFew now are having second thoughts about keeping it on the books.

The law was adopted last summer as one of a series of steps aimed at heading off a gang problem in Harvard. There's nothing wrong with such preparedness, but this measure is too broad in its reach—the same flaw cited by the Illinois Appellate Court Monday in ruling unconstitutional a Harvard ordinance banning the wearing of gang colors and insignias in public.

The curfew law makes it illegal for anyone aged 7 to 16 to be on the streets of Harvard during school hours, with students and parents subject to fines up to $500. That would have the effect of government intruding on the movements of all young people because of concerns about a few. It would stop such activity as going home or to nearby restaurants for lunch—no small consideration when Harvard High School has a 195-seat cafeteria for 580 students.

It also would put police in the position of being baby-sitters and truant officers when they might have better things to do. Some merchants, for example, have complained of disruptive behavior by some students: cracking down on the problem kids through other ordinances would be more fruitful. As for suspected gang members, it's unlikely that a curfew would deter them if they're bent on trouble.

City officials began having second thoughts after complaints from civil-liberties groups, students and school officials. So-called open campuses—where students are allowed relatively free movement during the day—may or may not be a good idea, depending on the school district and student body. But those policies properly are the province of the schools, working with parents.

In that spirit, students at Harvard High School have proposed a reasonable compromise that would restrict pupils with disciplinary problems from leaving school during school hours, and would require a notice of parental permission on the student identification card for students to eat off campus.

Because of the opposition, Harvard officials have not yet begun enforcing the ordinance. Now they should take the next step and rescind it.

Voice of the people

Protect kids in reforming welfare

EVANSTON—Reforming the nation's welfare system will require a delicate balancing act that will entail far more than just balancing the budget. We must balance the benefits of work against the needs of young children for care and education. If we fail to do so, we will only perpetuate the problems we seek to solve.

We now know that quality early childhood care and education are the bedrock for future success in school and in life. New research shows that most brain development occurs before the age of 4 and that children's ability to learn can increase or decrease by 25 percent or more, depending on whether or not they grow up in a supportive environment.

As a member of the "From Birth to Great" Public Awareness Panel, I am committed to getting this message across to the public and our policymakers, who in their zeal to "fix" a broken budget have lost sight of these fundamental facts.

While most everyone agrees with the goal of breaking the cycle of welfare dependency, the trick is doing it without harming our children and creating bigger, more costly long-term problems in the process. Research shows that children who've been short-changed during the first critical years will operate at a huge disadvantage for the rest of their lives. They are more likely to fail in school, succumb to teen pregnancy or fall into a life of delinquency or crime. Eliminating programs that help kids get a solid start is a sure-fire recipe for sustaining the welfare cycle, not breaking it.

Unfortunately, a welfare-reform bill passed by the U.S. House of Representatives would deny adequate child-care assistance to many welfare recipients who now must go to work, making it more difficult, if not impossible, for parents to place their children in the kind of environments that nurture their development, rather than hinder it.

According to the U.S. Department of Education and a study recently released by the Clinton administration, the impact of the congressional budget plans could mean:

- About 1 million more children could be pushed into poverty.
- Grants would be blocked and funding cut for child care for low-income children. In Illinois, child-care grants would be cut by $112.7 million over seven years, cutting assistance to 15,740 Illinois children.
- Head Start would be denied to 7,417 Illinois children in the year 2002, compared with 1996.
- Goals 2000, the comprehensive reform measure, would be abandoned. As a result, improved teaching and learning will be denied for up to 226,000 Illinois schoolchildren in 1996.
- Some 31,000 of the state's children would be denied basic and advanced skills education in 1996 under plans to cut Illinois Title I funds by $54.3 million.

Slashing the safety net that helps poor families give their kids a decent start is like cutting off our nose to spite our face. Instead, we should devise solutions that offset the negative impact of welfare reform on children. It's one thing to end welfare as we know it for today's generation—but what of tomorrow's? What kind of future are we creating for them if we balance the budget on their backs?

Barbara T. Bowman
President, Erikson Institute

Punish war crimes

CHICAGO—Your Dec. 31 story headlined "War criminals may go free" (Main news) is a sad commentary on U.S. leadership in NATO or this administration's abandonment of its claim to be the world leader in human rights.

War crimes have been charged against Radovan Karadzic, the self-appointed president of the Bosnian Serbs and his military commander Ratko Mladic by the International War Crimes Tribunal. This tribunal was set up after the principle of crimes against humanity was established when the Nazis were tried at Nuremburg. American officers are playing a game of hide-and-seek with these two men, whose charges range from killing unarmed women and children to rape.

If no one is held responsible for such atrocities, then the U.S. has no right to expect any nation, whether it is China, Iraq, Ireland, Israel, Russia, Indonesia, etc., to abide by the concept of protecting human rights. After our government eagerly fought in Europe to defeat the fascists in Germany and Italy, it is a great disappointment to see it betray the principles established in Nuremberg.

These two men must be apprehended and turned over to the international tribunal for a trial. To let them go free will encourage other despots to repeat such horrible crimes there and elsewhere—and why not even here?

Lester Schlosberg

Furlough adversity

OAK PARK—I was beginning to get a little sick and tired of hearing the media tell us about the poor, furloughed federal employees who didn't seem to know how they would cope without being paid during their layoff period. Don't they realize that there are thousands of construction workers laid off during the course of a "slow season" who do not get paid at all, or who get paid through unemployment compensation at not even one-half of their regular salary?

My husband has been a carpenter for 41 years, and I can remember times when he was off for as long as six to eight weeks at a time. At times he had to wait at least three to four weeks for an unemployment check. We learned how to cut corners during these bad times, but our family still flourished, and we adjusted our way of living accordingly, knowing that my husband would never receive "back pay" for the time he lost.

The federal workers should realize that thousands of others have coped under more adverse conditions.

Ruth Schreiber

We invite readers to share their ideas with us in these columns. Write to us at Voice of the People, Chicago Tribune, 435 N. Michigan Ave., Chicago, IL 60611. You also may send e-mail to TribLetter @aol.com. Include your name, address and phone number. The more concise the letter, the less we will have to edit it to fit our space.

On going metric

CHICAGO—Although I agree with Mr. William Holdorf's assertion that "the U.S. has created the greatest financial and industrial nation in the world . . ." ("A foolish U.S. push to go metric," Voice, Jan. 3), I would ask him to contemplate how much more prosperous this nation could be if we offered superior U.S. products and services that utilized the same standards of measurement as used by the other 5.75 billion people on this planet.

Jean-Paul Cushing

Dying with dignity

STURGIS, Mich.—Your Jan. 3 editorial expressing alarm about the way doctors and hospitals treat critically ill patients was a knee-jerk response to a complicated and controversial issue.

The last sentence, suggesting that physicians be prepared for lawyers suing them because of failure to abide by the directives in "living wills," was not only inappropriate but also sadly fanned the flames of litigiousness in our society.

I am a family physician who deals with ethical issues of life, death and illness every day. I am the first to admit that communicating with patients about their mortality is often postponed or neglected by physicians, especially if they are not the primary-care physician. Timing is the essence of the problem and is the reason why "living wills" are mostly useless. These documents are usually mass produced and signed by a person at a time when he or she is healthy and would desire intensive care. The wording is often ambiguous and so couched in subjectivity that neither the patient nor physician clearly knows when it takes effect or exactly what it means.

The simplest way for a patient to assure that he will "die with dignity" is for him to tell both his physician and his family that he does not desire cardio-pulmonary resuscitation (CPR). It would be appropriate to have a legal document that states "no CPR" for use by an appointed guardian if one becomes so ill that he cannot state this himself. These actions should ideally occur at a time before a patient becomes critically ill.

Our society is infused with myths of perpetual youth and fear of death; this carries over into "hospital culture" and complicates appropriate treatment of critically ill patients. It would certainly help if access to a trusted family physician were made available to all Americans during their lives and also at the time of their deaths.

James E. Phillips, M.D.

Coverage 'culprits'

PALATINE—There are just two problems with Mary Beth Lang's letter titled "Insurance dictates medical policy" (Voice, Dec. 31):

First, it is not the insurance companies that dictate the terms of coverage in their policies, as most people seem to think. I can assure you that it is the people who buy the insurance who dictate the terms. Whether it is your employer or you as an individual—believe me, you can buy just about any kind of coverage you want to pay for. The insurance companies are just the messengers of the "bad" news when claimants don't get the coverage they think they should have.

Second, she never did explain how it was that the hospital wanted to discharge her within less than 24 hours of giving birth, when, as she says, "We were entitled to two days' hospital stay, and all suitable pre-arrangements were made with both the hospital and our insurance company." Sounds like the hospital may have goofed, not the insurance company.

No, I don't now nor have I ever worked for an insurance company, but as a certified public accountant, I have worked for and with many large and small employers, and I can speak from experience about who dictates the terms of coverage in health-insurance policies.

Roland G. Ley

Earned or not?

COUNTRYSIDE—Reader George Berliant (Voice, Dec. 30) bemoans the prospect of someone inheriting $10 million not having to pay federal income tax under a flat-tax plan—because it is not "earned" income.

On the contrary: money like that does not magically float down from the sky at nature's behest. A sizable chunk of it would likely have been earned to begin with by an entrepreneur who worked for it, saved it and paid tax on it all his or her working life prior to passing it on. Furthermore, how many Americans does Mr. Berliant think exist who simply loll around day to day with this kind of inheritance in their back pocket?

Harold R. Holm

Gloomy picture

CHICAGO—"The Tribune means the world to Chicago," but I'm not sure I experienced the real world as it was presented in your "Year in Pictures" 1995 special section. The pictures and their stories were important, but I thought the section overemphasized the bad news of 1995. I found it depressing. Beyond the return of Michael Jordan and the success of the Wildcats (an entire page devoted to this team?), it seems there was little good news worthy of an appearance in the section. Am I to believe that the photographers of the Tribune and wire services have not brought any happy news to Chicago?

P. Quinn

Figure 10 **St. Augustine Record**

4A The St. Augustine Record — THE ST. AUGUSTINE RECORD — Sunday, May 12, 1996

OPINION

➤ EDITORIAL

Dole should take tough stance against special-interest money

With Bob Dole down in the polls, some of the best minds in the business are fine-tuning the mix of issues – from taxes to crime to character – to help him get up off the mat during the next six months.

Yet there's a potent issue that he keeps disregarding: the corrupting influence of special-interest money on political campaigns. This money is one of the things that truly sickens millions of Americans about politics.

Not only is reform of the system the right thing to do, it could undo Sen. Dole's image as the ultimate Washington insider – an image that's a millstone at a time when Americans are so bummed out by politics. All that's needed is his willingness to break away from some of his lobbyist pals on K Street.

For maximum impact, his attack on the status quo wouldn't be just another Blue Suit Day on the Hill. Imagine the guy in casual clothes, sitting at a lunch counter like his old one in Russell, Kan., talking to everyday people – clerks and secretaries, teachers and technicians. With the cameras rolling, he glints at the folks and says something like this:

''The big money in politics stinks, and I'm gonna change it. Right now, you don't get heard very well in Congress because special interests can buy so much influence. We're gonna outlaw their PACs. We're gonna give free TV time to candidates who agree to limit their spending. We're gonna clean the pig sty.

''Today, I'm endorsing the best plan to get the job done: the McCain-Feingold bill. Naturally, most special interest PACs are using scare tactics to kill this bipartisan plan. Big Labor, Big Business, the AMA, the tobacco lobby, the Realtors – everybody and his brother are ganging up to beat this bill. But it won't work. I'll push it through the Senate this month.''

By the way, Bill Clinton also supports this bill, but remember – when he had a Democratic Congress in 1993 and 1994, he let his pals Foley and Gephardt and Rosty bury the issue.

''I'm not a summer soldier. When I make the commitment, I get the job done.''

Are you listening, Mr. Dole?

– **Knight-Ridder Newspapers**

Mother's Day: When flowers aren't enough

(Editor's note: This article was first published on Mother's Day, 1993.)

You'd think I'd have it down pat by now. Thirty-something Mother's Days muddled through, and I've yet to give the gift or turn the phrase to show my mother how much I care. How special she's been. How much better my life is today because of the thousands of little things she's done for me (or allowed me the space to do on my own – despite the consequences).

JIM SUTTON
Editor

Born Virginia Louise Dodd on a small dairy farm in Goldenrod, Fla., mom learned early what work was, and how important family becomes when there's little else. Those were Depression years – the bad years – though I've come to understand that the good ones of her childhood were not much better.

Still, she and my two aunts, Mary and Hessie, delivered milk in the pre-dawn hours before school and worked their way off the farm – though in vastly different directions.

Mom married a young man beginning law school, and worked secretarial jobs to help him through Stetson.

At the same time she began the family she'd dreamed about since childhood. Not hesitant about the job (or maybe it was dad), she jumped feet first into motherhood. In five short years she had five long babies – two boys and three girls, though what would have been my younger brother died from a difficult birth.

The early memory of mom that best sums up her motherhood ''style'' revolved around Easter – a big day at the Sutton house. Mom would do the approximately 131 things it took to get four kids from 3 to 6 fed, bathed and in bed – each with a bedtime story or song to snooze on.

But it was then that her real work began. She'd clean the house, then set to work on the Easter clothes. The following morning it looked as if an Easter Fairy had done a little wand work around the place. Three frilly dresses hung outside the girls' room. Three little purses were there along with three Easter Bonnets. At the foot of my bed would be a new Easter suit complete with bow tie, suspenders and a freshly shined pair of saddle oxfords – dapper indeed.

And of course, Easter baskets.

On maybe four hours sleep, mom would get us up, fed, dressed and off to the wooden Windermere Union Church. In our little town, Easter was like a cute kid contest and mothers took it seriously. Those Sundays were an explosion of color. Pastel children were everywhere, set off by the blaze of spring azaleas (where most of the Easter eggs were hidden out on the church grounds).

She was the consummate mother. Buttons were sewn. The house was clean and ready form company. Kids did homework. There was good food, simple food on the table – home cooked. I do remember a time or two mom opened a can of Chef Boyardee spaghetti or slipped some fish sticks into the over if she was going out. But she'd have been horrified if anyone in town had found out her dark secret.

She should have been more ready for the divorce that she was – hardened to being alone. Dad was, at that time, in the Florida Legislature. Gone was the norm for him.

But it shook her to her very being. And, as the years went by, I was troubled by how desperately the hurt held on.

The divorce not only took away a husband, but also fractured the remainder of the family which she had spent so much energy tying together with discipline and love.

My sisters bounced back and forth from my father's new house to my mother's old house, depending on prevailing parental winds and sometimes-selfish whims. It never occurred to me to live with dad. He has so much. Mom so little.

It was in the following years that my love for her turned to sincere

See MOTHER, 8A

➤ YOUR VIEWS

THE ST. AUGUSTINE **RECORD**

A Morris Communications Corp. newspaper

RONNIE J. HUGHES
Publisher

JAMES D. SUTTON
Editor

Phone: 829-6562 • Fax: 829-6664

It's still Nine Mile Road!

Editor:

The Emergency Services Director had said, ''I don't care what they name the road, as long as it's one name.'' But *The Record* misleadingly reported that ''For safety reasons it would be unwise to put the *historic* Nine Mile Road name on even a portion of the nine-mile country lane now designated as International Golf Parkway.''

How and why did it go from ''one name'' to the particular name, IGP?

Would you believe that it was claimed by developer Jim Davidson that he ''had spent hundreds of thousands of dollars to erect signs along the road and along I-95?'' Excuse me – how much was that for the signs, again?

Much more easy to believe are the reports that he had ''... suggested finding another name for Pacetti Road, on which the Ortagus family lives.'' The Florida rapists now dare to openly gloat about their repeated victories over what is left of the real Floridians.

The County Commission had heard Lorna Pacetti Ortagus and other citizens a couple times last fall, and the commission assured them that ''... *history* would be a major consideration'' in ruling on the name change. Equally plausibly did the commission allege that when they had changed the name of Nine Mile, ''... everything was above board.''

In fact, the commission goes through the motions (as required by law) of holding public hearings before they announce the decision which they had already made. (Anyone who votes to re-elect one of these arrogant Brahmins had best have a damn good reason for so doing.)

About all we natives have left is that we will continue to call Nine Mile by its right name – just as we do Bay Street, St. Louis Avenue, Central Avenue and Ripley Road.

R.E. Osteen
St. Augustine

Safety set aside at airport?

Editor:

Points in support of Mr. Furry's recent article in *The Record.*

The crash death of the child pilot (Jessica Dubroff) was a result of poor judgment by the FAA certified flight instructor. As pilot in command it was his decision to allow the child pilot to fly into eternity under the following adverse conditions.

➤ 1. High altitude airport. Less dense airflow over the wings (airfoil) provides less lift than at sea level. Reports say the aircraft was loaded above FAA allowed maximum takeoff weight.

➤ 2. Minimal weather conditions at the airport with hail reported in the vicinity. I have flown miles to the side of my desired track due to reported hail. This in a B 747 jumbo jet with, of course, ATC clearance. As Mr. Furry noted poor little Jessica had a booster seat to see over the cowling plus rudder pedal extensions for her little legs.

Former Vice President Dan Quayle expressed the view of millions of us with the outrage at an aviation system that allowed this child to fly into eternity.

We have a classic case of a FAA ''certified'' flight instructor's poor judgment as pilot in command at our St. Augustine Airport. He crashed an aircraft at St. Augustine while instructing a young student pilot. He then concealed the crash from the FAA and the airport officials. This was in direct violation of numerous federal air regulations. He gave three excuses when found out.

➤ 1. ''The damage was only a dent in the wing tip and not worth reporting.'' A report to our airport authority by Mr. George Erdel, Safety Specialist for the FAA in Jacksonville said ''It was determined significant damage had occurred to the wing and landing gear requiring replacement.''

➤ 2. ''The head of the maintenance department told me not to report this or my insurance premiums would be raised.''

➤ 3. ''I thought the FBO reported the crash.''

All of this tap dancing around the known facts by one of our local FAA ''certified'' flight instructors. He knows as pilot in command it was his responsibility to report his crash.

I and numerous other local pilots are outraged that apparently the FAA is going to continue his ''certification'' as an FAA approved flight instructor for our young pilots. A flight instructor is supposed to not only teach a student how to fly but also to instill in him a respect and necessity to adhere to federal air regulations.

Do you, as I do, question what this devious fellow teaches our fledgling pilots?

Jack Kirkpatrick
St. Augustine

More art, fewer excuses

Editor:

I read and agreed with Mr. Gillilland's letter about *The Record's* unethical treatment of the art galleries in St. Augustine on Sunday, May 5. Ethics aside, The Record's disregard for the local art galleries and many local artists is simply hard to understand.

Your response to Mr. Gillilland does not stand up to scrutiny. You claim that the galleries no longer appear in the Arts and Entertainment section of The Record because ''The Record management made a business decision to discontinue listing of art galleries – and a number of other organizations – last year as part of an effort to conserve space and newsprint'' and because ''space does not permit the publication of several dozen weekly showings at every local art gallery... every week.'' There never were several dozen weekly shows, or even galleries, taking up space in The Record. There was, however, a weekly list of art galleries in the Almanac and you also carried announcements of new monthly shows in the Arts & Entertainment section.

Although there were not several dozen galleries, the list in the Almanac was too long because you made no distinction between true art galleries that made the majority of their revenue on the sale of original works of art and other gift galleries or stores reselling bought merchandise. In fact, any shop that called itself a studio or gallery qualified for your list, or so it seemed. Editorial control and a working definition of art gallery are simple ways of limiting the list so that space would permit its publication.

Neither were there ''dozens'' of ''weekly'' openings to announce. There are very few authentic art galleries in St. Augustine which qualify for the kind of press release Mr. Gillilland described. Such galleries go to the trouble and expense of mounting new shows monthly or less frequently. They host openings to which the public is invited free of charge. Such events involve refreshments, social interaction and cultural benefit to the public and should be announced enthusiastically in the Arts and Entertainment section of any paper. In fact, such press releases are normally welcomed as local newspapers normally help to foster the cultural life of the community. I can think of four such art galleries that would require ''space'' to announce new shows: The Crescent Beach Art Gallery, The St. Augustine Art Center, P.A.St.A. Art Gallery and Art in the Hand. Again, editorial control can and should prevent overuse of such announcements, if space is a problem.

I question your claim that space is the issue. When I read the Arts and Entertainment section these days, the space allotted to generic book revues and movie revues is enormous considering ''space does not permit'' news of the local art galleries.

On the map of the Palm Sunday Arts and Craft Festival (which features few local artists), The Record proclaimed that it supported local artists. Not true. As a gallery owner and local artist I accept your decision to ignore the art gallery community but I do not accept your explanation and still do not understand. And, as an avid reader of your paper, I miss the news about art galleries in St. Augustine.

Manila Clough
St. Augustine

Satanic street entertainers

Editor:

I have worked at a gift shop on St. George Street for the past 10 years. My co-worker for over a year.

We have to be here 40-plus hours a week as we have families to support and care for. Our jobs are based on a commission incentive, and if we cannot concentrate or hear our customers, we cannot make a sale.

In the past three months, our sales have dropped considerably. We have been assaulted by a terrible racket and the gang that accompanies it. Not only is it noisy, but also recently they have become violent, fighting amongst themselves.

We and our customers have witnessed the open use of profanity, violence, drugs and general harassment. But by far the most objectionable practice to us is the recent appearance and use of Satanic or occult items, rites or rituals.

We have become fearful as they come in the shop regularly, we believe, to try and cause a confrontation. Recently, we found it necessary to call the police and report several of them and had ''No Trespassing'' warnings issued to hopefully avoid further confrontations.

We thought we had the right to work in a peaceful and safe environment to support our families!

It appears that we have no rights as it pertains to conduct on a public street. Ever since the ''Street Entertainment'' ordinance was overturned, the corner of St. George and Hypolita has reverted back to the nightmare it was before the ordinance was enacted. We would request that anyone who believes that this type of conduct would be tolerable in his neighborhood simply spend a week or so down here to see what it's like!

It is obvious that not all street performers are disruptive, but if there can be no compromise, and we must vote for ''all or none,'' we vote for none!

Deborah Spengler
Mary Corby
St. Augustine

Can you give a kid a hand?

Editor:

I am eight years old. I am a second grade student at St. Joseph's School in Baytown, Texas. My class is studying the United States. I need your help with a class project. My class is collecting postcards from different states. If you would like to help, please send a postcard showing an interesting feature of Florida. Thank you for helping me.

Matthew Cisneros
1811 Caroline St.
Baytown, TX 77520

Figure 11 **Savannah Morning News**

It's time for Dole to start knocking heads together

Washington

Recollecting in tranquility the delights of politics in 1800, a retired congressman said, "It was a pleasure to live in those good old days, when a Federalist could knock a Republican down in the streets and not be questioned about it." In 1996, Republicans knock Republicans down. Bob Dole, who talks about leadership, should show some by knocking enough heads together to re-store order in his party's ranks.

George Will

Newt Gingrich and Pat Buchanan have been called liabilities by Al D'Amato — talk about being called ugly by a frog — and some conservatives suspect that Govs. Pete Wilson, Christine Todd Whitman, George Pataki and Bill Weld have begun their campaigns for the next Republican nomination by planning to convulse this year's convention with a fight over the platform's pro-life abortion stance. (A stance which did not prevent Reagan and Bush from carrying 133 states in three elections.) The suspicion is that the four would be dry-eyed if a debacle in San Diego — "another Houston" — were followed by defeat in November, allowing them to argue that the party must be "taken back" from . . . ? From some of its most intense and reliable components — religious and pro-life conservatives.

Dole says he is a doer, not a talker, but it is time for him to be more of a talker and less of a doer. He can remain majority leader but must get off the Senate floor and into serious discipline as a talker to the nation, not the other legislators.

By hanging around the Senate he risks convincing the country he should stay there because he thinks the presidency is not important enough to pursue single-mindedly. And when he tells an audience, "Like everyone else in this room, I was born," he calls to mind another Kansan who was a Republican

welfare experiments, embrace of the adoption provision from the Republican Contract, denial of welfare benefits to unwed teen-age mothers who quit school or do not live with responsible adults, and all his other recent political plagiarisms.

They are genuflections to the country's conservatism. So the conservative party should stop complaining and start presenting a coherent conservative rhetoric distinguished from Clinton's by its sincerity.

Dole says he is a doer, not a talker, but it is time for him to be more of a talker and less of a doer. He can remain majority leader but must get off the Senate floor and into serious discipline as a talker to the nation, not the other legislators.

By hanging around the Senate he risks convincing the country he should stay there because he thinks the presidency is not important enough to pursue single-mindedly. And when he tells an audience, "Like everyone else in this room, I was born," he calls to mind another Kansan who was a Republican

can presidential nominee — Alf Landon, who said, "Wherever I have gone in this country I have found Americans."

That was 60 years ago, the last time a Democratic president won a second term. Clinton will win one unless Dole can say, reading carefully crafted speeches, why it is important, even with the world relatively calm and the economy tolerably strong, to change presidents.

Regarding foreign policy, the country is safer than at any time since the 1920s. The stakes of politics were lowered by the end of the Cold War. The electorate's standards have been lowered, too. That is one reason why Clinton is president, and why Dole's strengths of experience, integrity and character may have less salience than he hopes they will in the contrast with Clinton.

However, the country also is more conservative than at any time since the 1920s, so the conservative party's candidate has an advantage Dole has barely begun to exploit. To do so he must do what he is often

uncomfortable doing — voice Americans' anxieties about the coarsening of the culture and the Balkanizing of the citizenry.

He will get help from Hawaii's supreme court if it angers an overwhelming majority of Americans by discovering a right to contract same-sex marriages. He is being helped by the presence on California's ballots this November of the initiative to ban the state government from administering racial preferences.

He must force Clinton to fight for California, lest Clinton linger all autumn where the election will be settled, in the crescent between New Jersey and Wisconsin, where Catholic voters — one-fourth of the population and a bit more of those who vote — will be crucial. Which is why some conservatives, looking for reasons for enthusiasm about Dole, and for a way to stay busy, other than by complaining about Dole, may unite in advocating as his running mate Rep. Chris Cox, an ideologically conservative California Catholic.

Savannah Morning News.
Established 1850

SAVANNAH EVENING PRESS
Established 1891

FRANK T. ANDERSON
Publisher

REXANNA KELLER LESTER
Executive Editor

THOMAS S. BARTON   DAN SUWYN
Editorial Page Editor   Managing Editor

4E   ■ Sunday, May 12, 1996

Use preservation tools

THE CITY of Savannah can demolish an unsafe, dilapidated building regardless of whether the owner can be identified and located.

Yet, when it comes to doing something positive for these structures, such as finding buyers who will renovate them and turn liabilities into community assets, the city has been strangely timid.

Why? The problems are obvious and the solutions are plentiful. What's missing is a concerted effort by city officials and property owners to transfer run-down real estate to those who wish to restore it.

Simply put, most dilapidated properties are held by uncaring, inactive or absentee owners. The Historic Savannah Foundation, which has studied the problem, cites as an example a yellow brick building at the corner of Broughton and Jefferson that was purchased in 1988 by a local attorney and has deteriorated ever since. HSF claims the attorney has refused several reasonable offers to purchase the building and fix it up.

The foundation also is critical of another local property owner who assumed the mortgages held by NationsBank on several hundred properties in a bankruptcy case. The properties are dangerously dilapidated and the city wants to demolish them. Preservationists have found several buyers interested in the buildings, but the owner reportedly won't return phone calls.

The longer these properties and others sit unkempt, the worse the situation becomes. They often accrue significant unpaid city and county tax liens. That tends to scare off potential buyers and leave the city stuck with deteriorating property.

Meanwhile, Savannah's precious historic resource is eroded by these eyesores. Neighborhood revitalization also gets tougher.

But the city doesn't have to sit back passively. It has several options. It just has to take advantage of them.

It could start by getting the courts to enforce its "minimum maintenance ordinance," adopted in 1991. It requires structures be maintained in stable, safe and sanitary condition. Previous attempts to enforce the code were undermined by the judges who gave owners second, third, fourth and more chances to take action. Judges must

start showing more backbone.

Similarly, the courts can utilize "In Rem Foreclosure." That allows local judges to ensure that either property taxes are paid or that the property is sold. That cuts through legal red tape on property foreclosures, which can take up to a decade to clear property titles. Instead, properties are made available to would-be developers within two years.

And what has been the experience of other counties? The Historic Savannah Foundation reports that the Sumter County attorney has found that one-third of property owners faced with In Rem Foreclosure prefer to pay their taxes.

Chatham County has recently approved a resolution to implement the process here. The city is studying it. But with other places in Georgia using it aggressively, Savannah shouldn't wait to be the last in line — especially considering the good it would do in the Historic and Victorian districts.

Finally, the city and Chatham County should take full advantage of "land banks," something the Georgia Legislature created more than five years ago. Land banks can erase liens on properties and give the land to developers, provided they agree in writing to renovate the property by a specific date.

That has worked well in a recent high-profile case involving five dilapidated houses owned by attorney Murray Galin in the Beach Institute neighborhood.

City Council gave City Manager Michael Brown permission to strike a deal with Mr. Galin and developers John Jennings and Jon Larson, who wanted to renovate the houses. If they would pay the $15,000 in taxes owed and half the fees, the city would forgive the other $6,300 in demolition and grass-cutting fees when certificates of occupancy were issued.

So far, the deal has worked to everyone's advantage. The city has its taxes paid. Mr. Galin is rid of property he didn't want. And instead of having crumbling buildings or vacant lots, the developers have been restoring the houses — and significantly improving the neighborhood.

The tools for urban renewal are there. All local officials have to do is open up the tool box and use them.

How to ease the 'Clinton crunch'

Washington

Analysts who believe that economic conditions determine the outcome of presidential elections are on the verge of awarding a second term to President Clinton on the basis of the growth in jobs, profits and overall production in his first 3½ years in office.

David Broder

Republicans, who realize that Sen. Bob Dole, their standard-bearer, cannot concede the pocketbook issue without in effect conceding the election, argue that the record is not as good as it would have been, had their policies been followed.

The reality is that in broad terms, the record looks pretty good, as the Democrats claim, but millions of working families are feeling squeezed by what Republicans like to call "the Clinton crunch" of steep taxes and stagnant or slow-growing take-home pay.

A serious debate about that "crunch" needs to be part of the coming campaign. And it needs to start with an understanding of the sources and dimensions of the problem.

Over time, wages cannot grow faster than productivity gains allow. You boost productivity by investing in machines and equipment and in the education and training of their operators. Investment requires savings, and the surest way to boost savings is to reduce the federal deficits that each year add to the burden of servicing the national debt.

But a point that has been little understood (by me, among others) is that less and less of what employers spend on their workers shows up

The payroll taxes that finance Social Security and Medicare are overdue for re-examination.

in take-home pay. The Bureau of Labor Statistics has reported that real compensation, which includes benefits, has risen about 1 percent a year for the last five years, just about matching the growth in productivity, as it should. But real wages are up only one-fifth as much — a minuscule two-tenths of a percent a year.

The reasons for that are spelled out in two recent reports from the business-sponsored Committee for Economic Development (CED) and the National Association of Manufacturers (NAM), both of which concede that the "crunch" on workers and the problem of growing economic inequality have to be addressed.

The CED report, called "American Workers and Economic Change," is particularly clear about why wages are lagging: "Wages exclude health, pension and other benefits, as well as employer contributions for Social Security and Medicare. These fringe benefit costs and employer social insurance contributions have taken a larger and larger share of compensation."

And then the key points: "Wages fell from 95 percent of compensation in the early 1960s to 81 percent in 1994. A major cause has been the escalating cost of health coverage. . . . The health care issue needs to be on the 1996 campaign agenda. Both Democrats and Republicans have failed so far to restrain the costs and

expand coverage, and the problem has not gone away. It has only grown bigger.

And the payroll taxes that finance Social Security and Medicare are overdue for re-examination. They hit hardest on young workers with modest paychecks who are struggling to pay their bills, because both taxes are imposed on the first dollar of earnings. And the Social Security levy, which is much larger than the Medicare tax, phases out at $61,200, thus reducing the burden on the well-to-do.

The NAM report argues that when it comes to jobs and wages, "the most damaging tax is the payroll tax to fund Social Security and Medicare, which raises the cost of labor by 15.3 percent. . . . Replacing the Social Security tax with a European-style value added tax or another form of taxation that did not directly penalize job creation" could add as many as 2.4 million jobs in five years, the report says.

An influential group of Senate Democrats is thinking along the same lines. A task force headed by Sen. Jeff Bingaman, D-N.M., has recommended a comprehensive package of reforms to Minority Leader Tom Daschle, D-S.D., including a change in the tax system that would allow payroll taxes to be cut in half, exempt small businesses from federal corporation taxes, reduce capital gains taxes on long-term investments and allow workers to deduct the costs of their education and training.

Bingaman would pay for all this with a flat-rate business tax of the type proposed by two conservative senators, Democrat Sam Nunn of Georgia and Republican Pete Domenici of New Mexico.

The time is right for reducing both payroll and capital gains taxes. Dole and Clinton could serve the nation by bringing this discussion into the heart of their campaigns.

Paying the price for negligence

IT HAD to come eventually, and it's about time: Two grossly negligent parents have been convicted of failing to control their criminally active 16-year-old son.

In St. Clair Shores, Mich., Anthony and Susan Provenzino were fined $100 each last week, plus $1,000 in court costs, for failing to keep their son from burglarizing churches — and allowing him to keep a 4-foot marijuana plant in his bedroom.

It can't be said they didn't have time. Their son pleaded no contest in 1995 to charges of burglarizing churches. A month later, he assaulted his father with a golf club. He was arrested again last September on charges of breaking into six

homes. He is serving a one-year sentence in a juvenile jail.

He kept the fruit of his crimes in his bedroom at home, along with the marijuana plant: a gun, a knife and a strong box. He admitted stealing $3,500 from a church collection box.

The Provenzinos, who have four other children, are also paying $155 a day for their son's incarceration. Judges in Georgia should have the authority to take similar action against negligent parents in this state. And if they don't have the authority, then the law needs to be changed to give them that power.

As we welcome the 8th Museum, pray for preparedness

I doubt that the administration's proposed defense budget for 1997, down by nearly a half from what it was in 1994, necessarily reflects the public's esteem for the armed services. I happen to believe the esteem is high.

For example, on a visit to Pensacola, Fla., last year I heard about the new Naval Aviation Museum, and made it my business to pay a visit. Nothing unusual where Yours Truly is concerned because I happen to be a military buff.

Tom Coffey

What I found gratifying, though, was the large number of visitors from elsewhere that day. By sheer numbers it made me aware of the esteem in which the service is held. Many places way off from Pensacola, determined by checking the car tags in the parking

area.

Now, this was not on a weekend, but midweek. It's reasonable to think that the visitors would number far more on weekends.

Smithsonian's Air & Space Museum in Washington, to which I paid my fifth visit two summers ago, was as crowded then as it was on my first visit, the year that it opened. That's another example.

And down at Fort Stewart, whenever there's a change of command, civilians come from all around. Particularly did they flock in for the recent reflagging, when the 3rd Infantry Division's colors supplanted the retired 24th Division's. Same outfit, but by a different designation (and alas, this was one I missed because of sudden and unexpected circumstances). The Fort Stewart-Hunter doings indeed attract the attention of their civilian neighbors, and that's still another example.

Now we have in our very midst the new 8th Air Force Heritage Museum, opening this week in our county, situated in the

shadow of the U.S. 80/I-95 interchange at Pooler. It has been several years in the development, and for the grand opening it will draw veterans of the Mighty Eighth from all the states.

Well and good. Old soldiers and airmen (they were called soldiers before the latter term gained vogue) enjoy reunions, just as old ground troops and sailors do. There's nothing quite like catching up, remembering when, embellishing stories from days of comradeship which are interesting even without the embellishments that the passage of time and the dimming of memory processes induce. Those veterans, and you can bet on it, will enjoy one whale of a time getting together again.

The museum, however, isn't solely for the veterans of that distinguished force of bomber and fighter pilots, bombardiers, navigators, both air and ground crewmen, and all others including those who monitored the weather and radar instruments and those in other varied roles who gave

support to the warriors aloft. It's for all of us, and it establishes in an outward and visible way a depiction, a re-creation if you please, of an important chapter in America's history.

World War II — on land, on sea and in the air — was a bitter and horrifying experience for those who answered the call to bear arms. But its importance to this nation, which is not by nature warlike, overrides the bad aspects by certifying America's unity of purpose when it was challenged and confronted by tyrannous nations which by nature were indeed warlike.

One important legacy of the Eighth, and all the other flying units and the ground and seaborne forces deployed in the far-flung theaters of operations, is that our shores were never invaded by the Axis forces. Instead, our own warriors engaged them where they were while the home front rallied and produced the tools of war, so expeditiously and miraculously that it's still difficult to grasp a half-century later.

Because of a natural curiosity about such

tools of war, I predict that the new museum, after the Eighth's veterans have come and gone, will be drawing thousands of the curious, just as museums commemorating other branches of the service have done. Prompting this prediction is what I have witnessed elsewhere, including the aircraft carrier at Charleston and the battleship in Mobile Bay.

Another important legacy, let's hope and pray, is preparedness. The citizen-soldier warriors of the Eighth flew their missions prepared, representing a nation pulled into that war while initially unprepared though sustained by a national purpose.

Yet, a drastic cutback in defense, even with the Cold War in remission, seems hardly a brilliant tactic of preparedness. No, we don't need what we had while the Cold War flourished. But hope and pray that such a drastic and rapid cutback is not something we soon shall regret. Indeed, hope and pray as we welcome this fine new facility to our neighborhood.

today, the *Gainesville* (Fla.) *Sun* uses several paragraphs to explain an issue and pose "today's question" under the title of "Since we've asked." A week later (on Saturday), under "Last week's responses," the *Sun* notes the number of readers who responded to the question, reports how many readers came down on each side and prints several of the responses. On the page I saw, the *Sun* the previous week had asked whether the government should compensate landowners for losses in property values as a result of environmental laws. (Ten said yes; seven said no.) The new question was whether Congress should dismantle the federal school breakfast and lunch program and turn it over to the states.

Reader Rebuttal

Years ago editors used to relish attaching a stinging editor's note to a letter, setting the letter writer straight. So stung, the writer, and perhaps other potential writers, learned the hard way that the editor has the last word.

The *Roanoke Times* has come up with an ingenious way to remove the sting of the editor's reply. As described by an editor's note, "Talking It Over" is a three-part conversation: "(1) a letter to the editor we've chosen to highlight, (2) a reply by the newspaper, (3) the letter-writer's summing-up response to our reply." The corresponding three labels: "To the Editor," "Our Reply" and "The Last Word." The writers are briefly identified. Issues that have appeared in "Talking It Over" include "deadbeat" dads, teens' access to wheels, the U.S. role in Bosnia and an exchange that was headlined "Are most letter writers naysayers?"

In the naysayers exchange, the reader's letter went to the heart of what editorial pages are about. She noted that on two days the *Times* had printed a total of seven letters opposing a proposed school bond referendum and only two supporting it. She wanted to know whether the paper was promoting its own agenda in the letters column, even to the extent of negative headlines. In its reply, the *Times* explained the letters generally reflected the proportion of responses on the two sides. In this case the newspaper could point out that it had supported the bonds. The reply also said that, "in printing opposing letters, we are, however, promoting another agenda . . . a forum in which wide-ranging viewpoints can find discussion and debate."

Letters to the Editor

To encourage letter writers, several newspapers have devised ways to recognize especially high-quality letters. Each Monday the Spokane, Wash., *Spokesman-Review* puts a "Golden Pen" designation on the letter of the week. At the end of the month one of the winners receives a 10-karat gold Cross pen. The *Richmond Times-Dispatch* from time to time identifies the "Correspondent of the Day." The *Santa Barbara News-Press* honors the "Letter of the Day."

To create a wholly new outlet for letters and other writing, the Newspaper Agency Corporation, which under a joint operating agreement publishes the *Salt Lake Tribune* and the Salt Lake City *Deseret News*, produces a special newspaper supplement titled *Citizens*. Originally mostly ads, *Citizens* eventually became a forum for local residents to express their opinions. To make the letters look more like articles, the names of the writers were given at the tops of their letters. Editors of the *Tribune* reported that the supplement did not affect the volume of regular letters.[11]

The *Roanoke Times* once a week publishes call-in responses to its editorials. An insert run at the bottom of the lead editorial each day states:

> YOUR CALL: What do you think about the issues raised in these editorials? To offer your opinion, please call xxx-xxxx and leave a voice-mail message. We'll publish a selection of responses on Thursday.

Reader Cartoon

The *Spokesman-Review* also encourages readers to submit their own cartoons—"painting, collage, computer art, drawing or artwork in any other style"—especially cartoons concerning Inland Northwest issues. Accepted artists receive no money but are eligible for the paper's "Golden Pen" award. The cartoons are labeled "Your View." (See page 321.)

ENCOURAGING DIVERSITY OF OPINION

Guest Columns and Articles

One of the first successful attempts to bring non-journalists to the editorial page was a column called "In My Opinion," begun by the *Milwaukee Journal* in 1970. An early participant was Milwaukee's mayor, one of the *Journal*'s severest critics.[12] Many newspapers use such columns to specifically invite knowledgeable or opinionated persons to share their views. The *Idaho Statesman* labels a similar feature: "Speaker's Corner." Regarding looking for potential contributors, Rich Bard of the *Miami Herald* had this advice: "As you read your own newspaper or national newspapers and magazines, watch television, hear speeches, or converse with someone at a social gathering, a church event or a school function, take note of particularly knowledgeable, articulate and insightful people."[13]

Boards of Contributors

A board of contributors is a more formal arrangement for obtaining local input. Participants—some knowledgeable in specific areas, some not—are asked to write from time to time on varied subjects. The *Plain Dealer* in Cleveland reported at one time that it had 30 contributors on call.[14]

Community Boards (Advisory Boards)

Another organized effort to bring in outside opinion is the community board (or advisory board). In introducing a *Masthead* symposium on the subject, the magazine's editor, Keith Runyon, noted that busy editorial writers, preoccupied with "officials of government, business and the private sector," tend not to have the time or opportunity to communicate with "average readers." The community board, he said, is an effort to create "mechanisms for readers to participate in the editorial process." Liz Fedor of the *Grand Forks* (N.D.) *Herald* reported that, in her newspaper's experience, "[t]he value of a community board is exposing editorial writers to new perspectives . . . to connect with readers, instead of simply reacting to the readers who contact us."[15]

In an exchange on the Internet mailing list of the NCEW, Richard Hughes of the Salem, Ore., *Statesman Journal* reported that his paper invited three community members to sit in on editorial board meetings (two for six-month periods, the other on an ongoing basis). The community members participated in all editorial board discussions and decisions. "Naturally, most day-to-day editorials don't go to the full board," Hughes said, but on major issues "we have a highly democratic board with the big decisions made by straight vote." He said the board had community members who "got upset when their views didn't prevail" and others "who wanted to argue . . . instead of debating issues." Hughes said he found the community members both "helpful" and "a big pain," but "worth it."[16]

A less formal arrangement has been used at the *Portland* (Maine) *Press Herald* and the *Maine Sunday Telegram.* "We get our community input raw, from the street," George Neavoll said, "as members of the public join us nearly every morning for a free-flowing discussion of events in the news that day." He said "[w]e enjoy ourselves when we look our readers straight in the face, and they look in ours, and we talk directly with one another about things of mutual interest." The sessions are "sometimes rambunctious, often enlightening and always fun as a result."[17]

These boards are not universally seen as an answer to keeping in touch with readers. "Are newspapers now becoming some kind of public utility, subject to review by 'customers,' like citizen utility boards?" asked E.W. Kieckhefer, a retired editorial writer. "Yes, editors and editorial writers should be aware of what their subscribers are thinking and saying, but not necessarily for the purpose of having those thoughts dictate the newspaper's editorial policies."[18]

Pro-Con Arguments

One attempt to give readers the feeling that they were getting a fair debate on issues, and not just the newspaper's viewpoint, is the "pro-con" package developed in 1971 by the editors of the *St. Petersburg* (Fla.) *Times.* They saw the package as a way to "reduce reader resistance to persuasion" without reducing the newspaper's commitment to its own viewpoint. The package contained a question and an explanation of the issue, "yes" and "no" arguments, a brief editorial stating the *Times'* position and a coupon on which readers could write their comments. Readers were urged to cut out the coupon and send it to the newspaper.[19]

USA Today offers "our view" and "opposing view" in the traditional editorial space. In one issue "our view" argued that Congress should give the National Football League and other sports the right to control movement of teams. In the "opposing view," a professor who teaches antitrust and sports law argued that the teams need competition.

The *St. Paul Pioneer-Press* publishes pro/con articles on its op-ed page. In one issue, guest columnists debated whether cameras should be allowed in courtrooms.

The Shreveport, La. newspapers offer readers an unusual alternative of opinions. When the (more liberal) *Shreveport Journal* was sold to the Shreveport *Times*, the arrangement included an agreement that one page each day would be reserved for an editorial page for the *Journal*. The page carries its own editorials, columns, cartoons and letters to the editor.

Media Critics (Reader Advocates, Ombudsmen)

At one time it appeared that a media critic, reader advocate or ombudsman hired by the newspaper might serve both the newspaper and its readers. The person could serve the newspaper by providing a conscience and trying to uphold journalistic standards, and serve readers by listening to and considering their concerns. Once a week or so, the critic/advocate would write a column, generally carried on the editorial page, about good and bad practices or about some journalistic issue. These columns are credible to the extent that the critics/advocates are knowledgeable, fair and free to write what they wish.

Several newspapers that were pioneers in this area no longer provide this service. Apparently, in lean financial times, publishers regard a media critic as a frill, and often an uncomfortable one at that. The newspaper that most consistently has maintained what it continues to call an "ombudsman" is the *Washington Post*. Richard Harwood was appointed to the newly created post in 1970, to be followed by such notable journalistic figures as Ben H. Bagdikian, Robert Maynard and Charles B. Seib.[20] At the time of this writing, the last two had been women, Joann Byrd, who had been editor of the *Post*-owned *Everett* (Wash.) *Herald*, and Geneva Overholser, who had been editor of the *Des Moines Register*. The longest-serving media critic has been David Shaw of the *Los Angeles Times*, who has been reviewing and commenting on the media for a quarter of a century.

Other Newspapers' Opinions

Less popular than in previous days, when newspapers had fewer sources of diverse opinions, are reprints of editorials from other newspapers. The *Denver Post* publishes reprints under the heading "Other Views"; the *Salt Lake Tribune*, "Another view"; the *Daily News* of Newport News, Va., "A Sampling of Editorial Opinion."

MAKING IT EASIER FOR READERS

Summaries

Editors have experimented with a variety of ways to summarize information quickly for readers in a hurry. The *Detroit Free Press* began using a hammer headline for editorials as early as 1978: a large capitalized word or two followed by a summary sentence that continued on to a second line. The *Star Tribune* also uses this device, with a one-line summary. The Cleveland *Plain Dealer* (page 181) uses a two-line headline plus a two-line summary on its first editorial. The *Miami Herald* (page 193) uses a short headline plus a sentence summary but inserts them within the editorial beneath an also-short standard headline.

Several newspapers provide quick summaries. The *Tucson Citizen* (page 182) provides a summary in italic type at the beginning of its lead editorial. The Spokane *Spokesman-Review* (May 29, 1995) runs an italicized summary on top of the headline of the editorial under an "Our View" kicker. *The San Francisco Chronicle* (page 191) inserts a summary partway down the first column.

Some summaries are more elaborate. The *Rocky Mountain News* of Denver briefly summarizes "the issue" and "our view" as an insert at the top of the first column of the editorial (page 177). The *Daily Advertiser* of Lafayette, La., at the beginning of its editorials, capsulizes the issue and offers the newspaper's suggested response. When the state asked local parishes to assess fees on motor vehicle transactions to pay for new motor vehicle offices, this was the *Advertiser*'s summary on May 21, 1996:

THE ISSUE:
Parishes told to
levy fees for
state buildings

WE SUGGEST:
It should be the
responsibility of
the state legislature

The Shreveport, La., *Times*, from time to time, runs a box at the top of the second column of the editorial summarizing its editorial stand. For an editorial urging the local school to seek federal funds under the Goals 2000 program the box said:

> **OUR STAND**
> **Seek federal funding**
> **for local schools**
>
> To contact your school board
> office, write or call:
> **So and so**
> **P.O. Box So and So**
> **Shreveport, La 71130**
> **636-xxxx**

Briefer, Easier-to-Read Editorials

To appeal to readers in a hurry, newspapers have tried a number of ways to present editorial opinions in brief form. Among respondents to a 1994 survey, 70 percent said they were writing shorter editorials than they had in the past, and 65 percent said they were writing easier-to-read editorials.[21]

On Saturday the *Press* of Newport News, Va., under the heading "At week's end," offers half a dozen or so three- or four-paragraph "Capsules of commentary on events in the news." The *Cincinnati Enquirer* publishes bylined moderate-sized comments on Fridays under the heading "Weekend Memos." Several papers offer one-paragraph comments either praising or criticizing. The *Cincinnati Enquirer* calls its feature "Winners and Losers"; the *Gainesville Sun,* "Darts and Laurels"; The *Quad-City* (Iowa) *Times,* "Cheers and Jeers." In the *Times,* thumbs-up and thumbs-down sketches illustrate a partial column of "cheers" and "jeers." The *Dallas Morning News* also uses thumbs, but only singly to illustrate a one-paragraph comment. Sometimes a pink background adds to the impact of a pronouncement.

ALTERNATIVES TO STANDARD EDITORIAL PAGES

Bringing the Community Aboard

To bring their newspapers and communities closer together, some editors have experimented with "civic journalism" or "public journalism." (Sometimes it is called "community journalism," but that term has long been used to refer to weekly newspapers.) Because such journalism is not specifically defined and ranges widely from one newspaper to the next, it inevitably has become the subject of widespread debate and misunderstanding. The sharply different ways in which editors view "civic journalism" are described in Chapter 9, "Relations with the Community." As pointed out in that chapter, this type of journalism raises two questions: How far should editors go to bring the community into the news and editorial processes of the newspaper? How far should editors go in providing leadership in the community?

Here is what four newspapers have done with one form or another of "civic journalism":

In 1994, in the midst of the debate over public journalism, the *Spokesman-Review* of Spokane, Wash., unveiled what it called "reinvented" opinion pages, announcing: "We have turned the majority of the space on these pages over to you—now do something about it."[22] The newspaper did away with the title of editorial page editor, but named two interactive editors who would (as opinion editor John Webster explained in a *Masthead* symposium on "The Future") "go into the community to recruit writers, speak before local civic groups and hold issue forums."[23] Webster reported that, as a result, the number of lengthy guest columns had increased. Twice a week the paper runs a reader-written "Your Turn" column. On the "Opinion" page appearing in Figure 12 (page 320) "an author, educator and consultant" explains how he got duped into making a presentation at an event sponsored by "paramilitary extremists." The paper's "Round Table" page carries a reader-drawn cartoon commentary, "Doonesbury," "Mallard Fillmore" and letters (Figure 13, page 321). "None of this replaces the editorial board, which still takes stands," Webster said. Names of editorial board members are published each day, and a member of the board signs each editorial.

From time to time editorial writers express different points of view on a subject. On Feb. 21, 1997, for example, two writers disagreed over whether the city should "buy the old Salty's restaurant site, or leave it in private hands." The editor of the *Spokesman-Review*, Chris Peck, has said he is convinced that "[p]ublic journalism will save the editorial pages"—at least the type of journalism he sees being practiced in Spokane.[24]

"Convening the community" is the description that the *Charlotte* (N.C.) *Observer* applies to its version of "civic journalism." "Our editorial board forms partnerships for some public events, but only with carefully chosen nonpartisan groups for specific, limited purposes," Ed Williams, the paper's editorial page editor, wrote in the *Masthead* symposium.[25] Williams said the paper sometimes sponsors public debates but more often publishes pro-con pieces. Several times a year the *Observer* devotes a page (or two) to explain an issue in depth, "tell where we stand and (when appropriate) what readers can do."[26]

The *Observer*'s opinion page varies from day to day. On one Friday two standard unsigned editorials were published. On Saturday in that space was a weekly feature titled "Urban Outlook." A photograph showed that the old Carolina Theater was sorely lacking seats and other furnishings. A signed article, written by an associate editor, carried the subtitle: "Does Charlotte have the civic will to save a fabled theater?"

The *St. Paul* (Minn.) *Pioneer-Press* set out to de-emphasize anonymous editorials and bring more community voices onto the page. But its editors also sought to find more imaginative ways to use the talents of its own editorial writers. "Our editorial writers will dig deeper into important subjects that require more illumination, analysis and informed opinion," Ron Clark, editorial page editor, told readers in announcing the changes. He said the paper would carry editorials "when we think the facts or situation warrants, and when we have something we strongly desire to say as a newspaper." The design of the page would be "dictated more often by content rather than by tradition and consistency." As part of the new package, more local writers would be encouraged to submit material. Editorial writers would be encouraged "to work with the community, where appropriate, in the search for solutions to tough public problems."[27]

Figure 12 **Spokesman Review**

Page B6

Friday, February 21, 1997
The Spokesman-Review
Spokane, Wash./Coeur d'Alene, Idaho

OPINION

To submit a letter by phone: (509) 458-8800, code 4853

William Stacey Cowles
Publisher
Christopher Peck
Editor
Shaun Higgins
Director of Marketing and Sales
Douglas Osborn
Director of Operations

From both sides

Should the city of Spokane buy the old Salty's restaurant site, or leave it in private hands?

City purchase best for public

Buy the site

It's best in the long run

If the city of Spokane buys the gorgeous riverbank site of the old Salty's restaurant, the owners of Clinkerdagger restaurant ought to send the city a thank-you note. So should the taxpayers.

A year from now that land will become a construction zone, immersed in the roar of riveters, jackhammers, cement trucks, bulldozers and cranes.

Later, and for decades into the future, the site will bloom again. As a park, perhaps. Or, better yet, as a restaurant, only with better access and parking than is possible with the current building and street configuration.

Meanwhile, as always happens whenever progress threatens to occur in Spokane, a gaggle of naysayers is yelling at City Hall.

It's easy to stand on the sidelines and quibble. It's hard, and always controversial, to build a city.

The Salty's site adjoins the spot where the new Lincoln Street bridge, *replacing* the decrepit Post Street Bridge, will attach to the north bank of the Spokane River. Someday people will look at that new bridge and the new green space around it, and wonder why on earth some local residents opposed it all — just as they opposed the nearby library with its priceless view of the falls, and the World's Fair that became Riverfront Park, and the new arena, and the Ag Trade Center, and on and on.

This fall, after the city hired an engineering firm to design the bridge, it began receiving specific information about how very difficult and expensive it would be to build the bridge while accommodating continued operations at the restaurant site. Meanwhile, Salty's was going under. The building's owner began negotiating with Clinkerdagger, which in spite of the city's warnings wanted to lease the site. Even though it lacked a signed lease, Clinkerdagger gambled that it would get the location and began investing money in its plans.

In December, increasingly alarmed by its engineers' findings, the city began negotiating with the owner to buy the site. Its goal? Eliminate the need to spend a few million in tax dollars shielding the restaurant from construction impacts. As it has an absolute right to do, the owner decided to sell its land to the city.

If the city buys the land both Clinkerdagger and the taxpayers escape an expensive short-term headache. Afterward the land can be resold, the cost can be recovered and the site can be well-used.

John Webster/For the editorial board

Leave business matters to business

Hands off

City should butt out of business decisions

For a city that's too strapped to repair its wretched streets, Spokane is pretty cavalier about paying $2.78 million for the former Salty's property.

It's not just the purchase price. The treasury also will kiss the revenue from private property, business and sales taxes goodbye.

Recognize a pattern? In 1995, the city halted a high-rise condominium project that it had cheered before deciding the building would hide the Spokane River falls from library users' view.

Ironically, the Salty's purchase is tied to the Lincoln Street Bridge project which, critics contend, will ruin a public view of the same falls. Some opponents say the bridge will partly undo what Expo '74 accomplished by removing the railroad trestles that once stretched above the city-center gorge.

Such complaints don't register with city officials who grabbed the Salty's property even as Clinkerdagger restaurant was moving there from the Flour Mill.

Clinkerdagger and the city have conflicting stories of whether the city encouraged or discouraged the restaurant's plans. Still, it's hard to believe a business that has succeeded in Spokane for nearly a quarter century would forge ahead on a project it had cause to think was unattainable.

City officials say the grade of the property and its proximity to the bridge would have made commercial activity untenable during construction and questionable after. They feared lawsuits.

Lawsuits? The city was sued over the library-view property and won. The city was sued over the bridge project and negotiated its way out of it. The city engages year after year in public works projects that disrupt traffic and interfere with commercial activity — and risk lawsuits.

Rather than use speculation about lawsuits as an excuse for displacing desirable downtown business activity, the city should have made its intentions clear, then let Clinkerdagger size up the risks and make its own, informed decision — a weak position to sue.

Now the city says it may lease or sell the property back to a private business when the bridge is built, or convert the site to a public use.

City government ought to leave business decisions to business and concentrate on providing municipal services in a way that is conducive, rather than hostile, to a healthy downtown business climate.

Doug Floyd/Interactive editor

Editorial board

Members of the editorial board are Stacey Cowles, publisher; Chris Peck, editor; Scott Sines, managing editor; John Webster, opinion editor; Rebecca Nappi and Doug Floyd, interactive editors; Anne Windishar, Elana Ashanti Jefferson and D.F. Oliveria, writers; and Milt Priggee, cartoonist.

After 25 years of marriage, life's closest relationship becomes a treasure indeed. **Jennifer Futernick** *describes the evolution of unconditional love.*

Prevailing in chaos of life renewing

By Jennifer Futernick
San Francisco Examiner

SAN FRANCISCO — I was talking on the telephone to my colleague, Harriet Kline, who lives in New York City. I mentioned that my husband and I had just celebrated our 25th anniversary. Her response: "After 25 years, it's roses."

That was the last thing I'd imagined she'd say. Harriet and I have worked at the same company for 16 years. I knew she had two kids in their late 20s but knew nothing about her marriage.

Harriet is a New Yorker, a down-to-earth thinker, not very sentimental. Yet she had just told me something I will remember on my deathbed. She had described my marriage.

Twenty-five years of marriage translates to nearly 10,000 days and billions of moments. Who can give narrative to something so complex?

How do you amply salute something so ripe for dime-store sentiment? In the jumble of marital experiences are delicious moments, passages of despair and, sometimes, not much feeling at all.

Though Valentine cards make it all sound so easy, there are hundreds of reasons why marriages falter. Mine has, numerous times. In fact, after my husband Bob and I had been married for six years, I wanted to leave him.

For three months in 1978, my husband was attracted to another woman. We lived through that painful spring, groping for what had brought us together in the first place.

Patience, tears and even a bit of black humor got us through. By summer, my husband knew he wanted to stay married to me. It was as if our marriage finally had begun.

I think Harriet meant that after a few decades together, you'd found faith in each other.

Then the real work began. We fought every fight in the book, wondered whether this marriage could last (knowing it should), lightened up a lot more, argued less and began really to understand each other. Harmony broke out.

Sometimes, I'll be loading the dishwasher or sitting next to him at a basketball game, or Bob and I will be dancing and I'll look at this man and feel like a teenager in love. Only luckier. We survived the shoals of young love to luxuriate, after 25 years, in mature love.

We never expected to be part of a minority: two people who married young, stayed married to each other, reared our own biological children, lived all of our marriage in the same city (in just two houses) and celebrated our silver anniversary.

Many experiences could have brought us to the brink; chronic pain, back-to-back deaths of parents and a sister, alcoholism in our family, suicide attempts by a nephew, bouts of depression, the harrowing night we thought our son had died, money problems, religious differences and the countless challenges that parents, especially parents of two adolescents, can crash into. The chaos of life.

Yet prevailing is itself renewing.

Now our deepest pleasure is the generosity we feel for each other. The gratitude we share for getting through all those dark moments of the night.

Increasingly, Bob and I delight in each other's successes — and trumpet them shamelessly.

A friend told me, in the bloom of new love, that it was as if she and her boyfriend wanted to proffer the best raspberries on their plate to one another.

Maybe that's what Harriet meant by roses. That feeling of philanthropy toward your partner only deepened by years. Knowing that your children were grown (or nearly so) and you could finally turn to each other — but it was certainly more than that.

I think Harriet meant that after a few decades together, you'd found faith in each other. Understood that troubles would arise, because they always do, but peace in the house would prevail. That maybe, just maybe, you'd fought all your serious arguments. That after 25 years, roses meant unconditional love.

■ Examiner contributor Jennifer Futernick, a San Francisco free-lance writer and poet, is a corporate research librarian.

Why do we deem it modern to put criminals in cages where other criminals can rape them? Peering back into history, **Jeff Jacoby** *suggests that flogging doesn't look so bad.*

For some crimes, whip beats chains

By Jeff Jacoby
Boston Globe

Boston's Puritan forefathers did not indulge miscreants lightly.

For selling arms and gunpowder to Indians in 1632, Richard Hopkins was sentenced to be "whipt, & branded with a hott iron on one of his cheekes." Joseph Gatchell, convicted of blasphemy in 1684, was ordered "to stand in pillory, have his head and hand put in & have his toung drawne forth out of his mouth, & peirct through with a hott iron." When Hannah Newell pleaded guilty to adultery in 1694, the court ordered "fifteen stripes Severally to be laid on upon her naked back at the Common Whipping post." Her consort, the aptly named Lambert Despair, fared worse: He was sentenced to 25 lashes "and that on the next Thursday Immediately after Lecture he stand upon the Pillory for . . . a full hower with Adultery in Capitall letters written upon his brest."

Corporal punishment for criminals did not vanish with the Puritans — Delaware didn't get around to repealing it until 1972 — but for all relevant purposes, it has been out of fashion for at least 150 years. The day is long past when the stocks had an honored place on the Boston Common, or when offenders were publicly flogged. Now we practice a more enlightened, more humane way of disciplining wrongdoers: We lock them up in cages.

Imprisonment has become our penalty of choice for almost every offense in the criminal code. Commit murder; go to prison. Sell cocaine; go to prison. Kite checks; go to prison. It is an all-purpose punishment, suitable — or so it would seem — for crimes violent and nonviolent, motivated by hate or by greed, plotted coldly or committed in a fit of passion. If anything, our preference for incarceration is deepening — behold the slew of mandatory minimum sentences for drug crimes and "three-strikes-you're-out" life terms for recidivists. Some 1.6 million Americans are behind bars today. That represents a 250 percent increase since 1980, and the number is climbing.

We cage criminals at a rate unsurpassed in the free world, yet few of us believe that the criminal-justice system is a success. Crime is out of control, despite the deluded happy-talk by some politicians about how "safe" cities have become. For most wrongdoers, the odds of being arrested, prosecuted, convicted, and incarcerated are reassuringly long. Fifty-eight percent of all murders do *not* result in a prison term. Likewise 98 percent of all burglaries.

Many states have gone on prison building sprees, yet the penal system is choked to bursting. To ease the pressure, nearly all convicted felons are released early — or not locked up at all. "About three of every four convicted criminals," says John DiIulio, a noted Princeton criminologist, "are on the streets without meaningful probation or parole supervision." And while everyone knows that amateur thugs should be deterred before they become career criminals, it is almost unheard-of for judges to send first- or second-time offenders to prison.

Meanwhile, the price of keeping criminals in cages is appalling — a common estimate is $30,000 per inmate per year. (To be sure, the cost to society of turning many inmates loose would be even higher.) For tens of thousands of convicts, prison is a graduate school of criminal studies: They emerge more ruthless and savvy than when they entered. And for many offenders, there is even a certain cachet to doing time — a stint in prison becomes a a sign of manhood, a status symbol.

But there would be no cachet in chaining a criminal to an outdoor post and flogging him. If young punks were horsewhipped in public after their first conviction, fewer of them would harden into lifelong felons. A humiliating and painful paddling can be applied to the rear end of a crook for a lot less than $30,000 — and prove a lot more educational than 10 years' worth of prison meals and lockdowns.

Are we quite certain the Puritans have nothing to teach us about dealing with criminals?

Of course their crimes are not our crimes: We do not arrest blasphemers or adulterers, and only gun-control fanatics would criminalize the sale of weapons to Indians. (They would criminalize the sale of weapons to anybody.) Nor would the ordeal suffered by poor Joseph Gatchell — the tongue "peirct through" with a hot poker — be regarded today as anything less than torture.

But what is the objection to corporal punishment that doesn't maim or mutilate? Instead of a prison term, why not sentence at least some criminals — say, thieves and drunk drivers — to a public whipping?

"Too degrading," some will say. "Too brutal." But where is it written that being whipped is more degrading than being caged? Why is it more brutal to flog a wrongdoer than to throw him in prison — where the risk of being beaten, raped, or murdered is terrifyingly high?

The Boston Globe reported in 1994 that more than 200,000 prison inmates are raped each year, usually to the indifference of the guards. "The horrors experienced by many young inmates, particularly those who . . . are convicted of nonviolent offenses," former Supreme Court Justice Harry Blackmun has written, "border on the unimaginable." Are those horrors preferable to the short, sharp shame of corporal punishment?

Perhaps the Puritans were more enlightened than we think, at least on the subject of punishment. Their sanctions were humiliating and painful, but quick and cheap. Maybe we should re-adopt a few.

■ Jeff Jacoby is a columnist for The Boston Globe.

Figure 13 Spokesman Review

Spokane, Wash. / Coeur d'Alene, Idaho · Friday, February 21, 1997 **Page B7**

Roundtable

Letters

How to write? See "Keep in touch" at the bottom of this page.

Spokane matters

Make GMA serve our future

The key behind the Growth Management Act is planning. Let's be pro-active instead of reactive. Let's take control of our property taxes, traffic congestion, air and water pollution, and maintain the resources we would like to keep.

We need to focus on our future and not on short-term profit. We need to work together on this and think of our children.

Some may feel slighted by not having the opportunity to subdivide land, as they wanted to do to help fund their retirement. Sacrifices will be made for the good of all.

We all share this land and no one owns it. We only rent it for the period we are alive.

As the population expands within our limited space, our biggest challenge will be to change our current way of thinking. It should change from "private property rights" to "rights of everyone."

The Land Use Study Commission concluded that the problem with GMA was not the hearings boards but the fact that some parts of the act are vague. That commission has worked hard to put more specifics into the act. The Legislature should support its recommendations.

We also should support the hearings boards. They are the closest court to the people and for the people. They are the only way to keep government accountable to the people.

Jean Johnson
Mead

Streets lack painted lines

How cheap can we get? Am I the only one in Spokane to notice that we need more paint on our streets?

I was in three lanes of traffic in our city and there were no lane demarcations. I'm glad we know how to follow single file.

I notice this on most of our streets, from downtown to the suburbs. The exceptions are our streets that have been recently renovated.

I know we need to fill our potholes and repair streets as the result of a long, difficult winter, but paint is a given year 'round. As a nurse, I'm concerned for the safety of our citizens.

There are many hazards and obstacles to driving. Please, let's have lane, arrow and crosswalk demarcations on our side. Paint, please.

Nancy Willmek
Spokane

Schools and education

Youths get fine help, opportunity

I was pleased to read the wonderful article (Feb. 14) on the Lionel Hampton Jazz Festival. It's such a great thing that the youths of our community have the opportunity to participate in such a positive manner.

Thousands of young people in numerous choirs, bands and orchestras rehearse all year for the chance to perform with a master. These kids put their hearts and souls into their music.

Hundreds of teachers go beyond the limit in teaching these kids to not only use their talent but also to act like ladies and gentlemen, and to show pride in their community and school.

Special thanks go to Ann Fennessy and Alan Shook of Northwood Junior High. They take these students straight out of elementary schools and nurture and groom them for months to turn these fine young people into musicians and vocalists. They provide these kids with every opportunity to perform and represent their schools at local functions. They give every spare minute of their time and, in the end, it shows.

Last year, our oldest daughter had the privilege of performing at the festival as a member of the Girls Select Choir under Fennessy. They were chosen to perform in the Winners Concert, the highest of honors. This year, she will perform with Jazz'n. Her sister will perform with the Girls Select Group, again under Fennessy's direction. They will carry the memories of these performances forever.

Congratulations, Northwood. Keep up the good work. This is where all the rehearsal and stress pay off. Enjoy yourselves.

Margaret Ellerman
Spokane

Your letter didn't run?

We appreciate all submissions to the Roundtable. However, due to the volume, we cannot answer queries or offer critiques of letters or artwork. Generally, we publish a little over half of the letters we receive.
To increase your submission's chance of being published, please be sure to follow the directions as outlined in the "Keep in touch" box on this page. Also, we prefer commentary on relevant, timely issues.
Artwork lettering must be neat and clear, with correct spelling and grammar; please use ink or other high-contrast medium.

Your view

O.J. SIMPSON SAYS HE WILL NOT REST UNTIL HE HAS TRACKED DOWN THE REAL KILLERS.
SO FAR HIS SEARCH HAS BEEN CONFINED TO THE GOLF COURSE AND HIS TWO SUSPECTS NOW ARE LEE TREVINO AND ARNOLD PALMER!
THE O.J. LEGACY
CHARLES CASTLEMAN

Cartoon commentary by Charles Castleman / Spokane

Cartoon commentary from readers

We encourage you to submit painting, collage, computer art, drawing or artwork in any other style. We are especially interested in art concerning Inland Northwest issues. We do not pay for art, but submissions are eligible for the Golden Pen award. Send your artistic opinions, along with your address and a daytime phone number, to Public art editor, Editorial Art Dept., The Spokesman-Review, 999 W. Riverside Ave., Spokane, WA 99201. Or call 459-5463.

Try surveying ex-college students

With college budgets increasing, conservation of available funds has become paramount.

Members of the class of 1991 have had five years to evaluate the usefulness of the courses they took during their college years. Were they all useful?

If the graduates were sent their college transcripts and asked to rate each course as necessary, helpful or not necessary, the results might prove interesting.

From a survey of this type, could it be an indication of courses not needed which would reduce the cost of a degree?

Archie T. Cernaghan
Coeur d'Alene

Business and labor

Utility's ad sends bad message

We are trying to better the education in this state. Many a high school graduate can only pass an eighth-grade exam.

Along comes a public utilities company, Washington Water Power Co., with a TV campaign selling natural gas. It shows a high school student trying to figure out if $60 is less than $120. What's wrong with these people? Shouldn't we be trying to edify our students instead of making them look dumb?

This ad does nothing for the image of the children of the state of Washington. It makes me angry that WWP uses the profits from my utility bills for its stupid ads. Why doesn't it spend the profits to educate children?

Thank you, WWP, for helping me with the decision to continue home schooling my children.

Kris Whitman
Spokane

Sure, the work is back-breaking, the hours are long, and the pay is lousy—but it beats the heck out of being trapped in a cubicle all day.
PIRARO

Cartoon typifies people's arrogance

The Bizarro cartoon of Feb. 17 is unconscionable. This stereotypical drawing depicts a Mexican farm laborer saying that although the work is back-breaking with long hours and lousy pay, it is still better than working in a cubicle.

Because we pigs of Western civilization demand cheap cucumbers, desperate human beings subject themselves to physically crippling, mind-numbing toil that is guaranteed to dramatically shorten their lives through pesticide contamination. These human beings receive bare subsistence wages, live and work in intolerable conditions and almost none of them receive benefits of any kind.

Little children pick jasmine flowers all night long so we can wear perfumes to smell nice. People slave away in sweatshops, stitching together our designer tennis shoes. Children are chained to looms and forced to weave our kitchen rugs.

What do you suppose goes on in the mind of an exhausted Haitian worker who makes 15 cents an hour as he assembles the 10,000th Hunchback of Notre Dame doll?

Our arrogance is simply astounding.

Margaret Koivula
Spokane

Government and politics

Ms. Smith goes to Washington; Ugh

November 1994 — aided by a groundswell of Republican support, Linda Smith of Vancouver was elected to Congress in a previously strong Democrat-controlled district. This support was enhanced by various local, state and national Republican leaders, most notably Rep. Newt Gingrich and his "Contract With America."

First term, 1995-1996 — bold, intelligent and articulate, Smith speaks out on behalf of the Republican freshmen on many occasions. Nationally, she becomes a rising star.

Somehow, I get on her campaign mailing list. I contribute, even though I live 200 miles outside of her district. I hear her say that she does not accept PAC money (commendable, but tough), or money from outside her district, to which I cringe.

She is re-elected by a narrow margin, coming from behind thanks to absentee ballots. The Washington state Republican Party absentee ballot campaign can be credited with her victory.

January 1997 — Smith refuses to support Gingrich for speaker of the House. He is elected anyway, by a one-vote majority.

February 13 — I get a call from Smith's campaign committee, wanting me to help pay off her campaign debt. I refuse to do so and inform them that I will never contribute to any of her campaigns again.

Smith is probably still electable, but most likely as a Democrat. Under pressure, people tend to show their true colors.

Lord, help me to find the truth but save me from those who have.

Ronald D. Sanders
Spokane

Other topics

Say love and you're saying God

I found the Feb. 13 letter by George Thomas ("Bible is vastly overrated") one of the most ridiculous I've read.

Thomas states that men are good because of the love that dwells in their hearts, not because of some Bible quote. Where does he think love originated?

God is the author of the Bible and the creator of all things, including love. So, whether you believe what the Bible says or not, the fact you love your fellow man means you are abiding by the Bible and doing God's will; whether you're a Jew, Moslem or atheist. And, Jesus does exist. He was God's ultimate gift of love to mankind.

The Bible specifically addresses homosexuality and considers it a sin. However, I do not view the homosexual rights controversy as a war waged against gay people but a spiritual battle between Godly principles and the rulers of this world. Satan continues to deceive people into thinking what they are doing is right. This is another reason God gave us the Bible — so we can discern the works of the enemy.

But, no matter what our personal beliefs, we should have compassion for our fellow man. We are all sinners, none worse or better than the other. However, compromising is not the answer. If we recognize same-sex marriages, it will only support a sinful behavior.

The greatest act of love and the surest way to show our fellow man we care is to pray for them. Then God will do the rest.

Debbie Elduen
Spokane

How foolish, to reject Bible

In response to George Thomas' "Bible is vastly overrated" (Letters, Feb. 13), two sayings come to mind: "When in doubt, it is better to remain silent and be thought dumb than to open mouth and remove all doubt" and "A man with an argument is at the mercy of a man with an experience."

If Thomas could accept Jesus Christ into his life it would revolutionize his life, as it did mine. He called the Bible a collection of scribblings from the imagination of ignorant desert tribesmen. The intelligence of the apostle Paul, who wrote most of the New Testament books, would make Thomas look like an ignorant tribesman by comparison.

The Bible was written over a period of about 1,500 years by God through many prophets, yet they all agree. It's the world's best seller of all time.

All of the Old Testament pointed to the day a savior would come and redeem man from sin. Two thousand years ago, Jesus was born of a virgin. He was God in the flesh. He died for the sins of anyone who will accept him as their savior. He took the cross we deserved and, without sin himself, paid our debt of sin. History records that he rose from the tomb on the third day. So amazed was the world that the calendar was changed to conform to his birth.

Every true scholar who started out determined to prove the Bible a hoax wound up a believer instead.

Then there is prophesy (read II Peter, 1:16-19). All prophesy has been fulfilled except end-time prophesy.

Forrest R. Fichthorn
Spokane

Story brought back memories

Your article about the "Blister rust war" (Feb. 16) brought back memories of my days in the Civilian Conservation Corp in 1938.

We had 200 men in our Maine Woods camp. They were divided into truck groups of about 25 men with four crews per truck. There were seven men to a crew. Six lined up with poles and the end man followed a fence or stone wall. The other end man dropped pieces of paper that provided the guide for the crew's reverse pass.

The crew pulled up the ribes (gooseberries) plants and hung them between tree branches. The leader followed the crew, checking for missed ribes plants.

Thirty years later, I, as a Washington State University geneticist, helped Dick Bingham at the U.S. Forest Intermountain Research Station, Moscow, analyze their selection for rust-resistant Western White Pine. This research has been successful and resistant trees are now being raised.

From one shore of the nation to the other!

Walter A. Becker
Pullman

Quit blaming road for driver errors

Our esteemed news reporters have done it again. They have shown their foolishness and insulted the intelligence of their TV audience and readers of the newspaper.

Last weekend, an unfortunate accident happened near Loon Lake. Our TV news reported, "Another accident on deadly Highway 395." The Feb. 13 Spokesman-Review had a front page report, "Lawmakers told deadly highway must be widened," by staff writer Chris Mulick.

The foolishness referred to is in the inaccuracy of the reporters' phraseology. In reality, there is absolutely nothing deadly about Highway 395. Highway 395 is nothing more than a paved surface that allows inhabitants to travel from one part of this Earth to another.

This highway has not caused any accidents since its construction. I am also sure that a check with law enforcement records would show that drunken driving, improper passing, speeding, primping, talking on the phone, poor vehicle condition, inattention and myriad other reasons are the true causes of these accidents.

In truth, it is the drivers' stupidity that makes the highway deadly.

Put the blame where it belongs — on the drivers.

Jim Barrett
Colbert

Only fair to help ailing soldiers

When our country or its allies need defending, we call on our military. It always responds; that's its job. Why, then, can't our government respond to our military people when they're in need?

Gulf War syndrome is not an imaginary disease of 15,000 people. They need help, physically and mentally. They have a right to this care and all avenues should be explored to find an answer to their illness. If we don't support these people, who will go to our defense next time? Would you?

Kathleen Calohan
Spokane

Keep in touch

We welcome letters of up to 250 words on topics of general interest. All letters are subject to editing. Please include your signature and a daytime telephone number where you can be reached for verification.
Send letters to:
Letters to the Editor
The Spokesman-Review
999 W. Riverside
Spokane, WA 99201
Or fax: (509)459-5482.
Or e-mail: editor@spokesman.com
To dictate a letter by telephone, you must call from a touch-tone telephone. Dial **458-6800** and enter **code 4853**. In Coeur d'Alene, call **765-8811, code 4853.** To contact the managing editor/Opinion, call **459-5405.** To suggest a topic for discussion on the Perspective page, submit it to Perspective at the same address.

Doonesbury By Garry Trudeau

AND IF YOU'LL FORGIVE THE PRESUMPTION, GENTLEMEN, I THINK THE PARALLELS BETWEEN ME AND TEDDY ROOSEVELT ARE ABSOLUTELY STRIKING!
FOR INSTANCE, I INTEND...
EXCUSE ME, SIR, BUT INTENTIONS DON'T CREATE HISTORY— ACTION DOES...
IT'S ONE THING TO TALK ABOUT DRAMATIC CHANGE; IT'S QUITE ANOTHER TO BRING IT ABOUT AS T.R. DID.
WELL, WHO SAYS I WON'T EVENTUALLY ACT?
WELL, YOU DO HAVE A HISTORY, SIR...
I DO? I DO? LIKE WRITTEN DOWN?
YEESS!

Mallard Fillmore By Bruce Tinsley

Mallard interviews James Carville...
GIMME A BREAK, MALLARD! I ONLY MADE FUN OF PEOPLE WHO LIVE IN TRAILER PARKS TO SHOW THAT PAULA JONES IS NO SAINT, OKAY?!
NO, BUT YOU'VE SHOWN AGAIN THAT MARY MATALIN MUST BE ONE...

As an example of the changes, Clark cited an editorial writer's signed analysis examining the movement to reform academic tenure at the University of Minnesota and elsewhere (Figure 14, page 323). It accounted for about 80 percent of the page, with the remainder devoted to letters. "We ran no editorials," Clark said, "but I dare say the tenure analysis had more impact than any editorial we could have run."[28] An in-depth piece that took up about 90 percent of the page took a look at Minnesota's "horribly complex, unfair and inefficient" property tax system. On another occasion, the *Pioneer-Press* invited guest columnists to discuss ("pro-con") the question: "Was the court right to require abortion funding for the poor?" In a change of pace, Clark wrote a full-page article, with full color, on "Glorious Gardens"–"springing up throughout the Twin Cities . . . splashing color everywhere and bringing neighbors closer together."

Most editors no doubt recognize the need to use their editorial staffs more efficiently and to bring more outside opinions onto their pages, but, thus far, few have followed the lead set in Spokane and St. Paul. "I can't conceive of a metropolitan paper with an adequate staff, which I describe the [*Pioneer Press*], turning over its scarce space for editorials–the voice of the paper–to other kinds of opinion material, however useful it might be," wrote Phineas Fiske of *Newsday*.[29]

In responding to the question of "how involved should newspapers be in their community," John H. Taylor Jr. said his experience on the Wilmington, Del., *News Journal* led him to believe there is "no simple answer," but, "with proper care, we can be of real assistance without becoming 'part of the story' in a way that damages credibility." The *News Journal* published a series of articles and editorials called the "Delaware Agenda." One editorial suggested that the governor call an economic summit to discuss where the state ought to be headed economically. When the idea was taken up by a think tank founded by the Delaware State Chamber of Commerce, the newspaper was asked to help convene the meeting. Taylor served as liaison between the paper and the institute, which performed most of the staff work. "While we entered into the cooperative relationship with some trepidation," Taylor said, "in the end we believed we had enhanced the newspaper's image in the community. There was almost no negative reaction."[30]

Some aspects of "civic journalism" are far from new. In the late 1950s, as a beginning reporter, I was assigned to work with local doctors to plan, promote and report an annual series of "Medical Forums." At each forum the public was invited to listen to a panel of four doctors talk about a medical topic and respond to written questions submitted previously by readers. Later I helped promote a series of "Legal Forums." The newspaper regarded these programs as community services and a way to promote the newspaper. (Working with the doctors and the lawyers also gave me ties to the medical and legal communities that paid off later when I was a reporter and an editorial writer.)

Telecommunication

Large, middle-sized and even small newspapers are fast setting up their own Internet websites. Here is another way for newspapers to circulate their editorials and other features to existing and new customers. Most Internet servers

Figure 14 **Pioneer Press**

SAINT PAUL PIONEER PRESS SUNDAY, MARCH 24, 1996

PETER B. RIDDER Publisher/President
WALKER LUNDY Editor/Sr. Vice President
RONALD D. CLARK Editorial Page Editor
KEN DOCTOR Managing Editor
STEVEN DORNFELD Associate Editorial Editor

BERNARD H. RIDDER JR. Chairman Emeritus

OPINION

ST. PAUL PIONEER PRESS
LETTERS TO THE EDITOR 345 Cedar St St. Paul, Minn. 55101
FAX TO: LETTERS TO THE EDITOR Fax Number: 612 228 5564 Internet: letters@pioneerpress.com

We welcome your letters. Make them exclusive to us. Please provide a full signature, city of residence and (for verification) your address and daytime phone. Preference goes to letters under 225 words. All letters are subject to editing. No more than one letter per writer every 60 days. Direct questions to 228 5545.

THE TROUBLE WITH FACULTY TENURE

As higher education dollars become scarce, the U of M may need to foresee a future in which tenured faculty members enjoy fewer protections.

SPOTLIGHT
Faculty Tenure

BY D.J. TICE
EDITORIAL WRITER

The juvenile sea squirt wanders through the sea searching for a suitable rock to cling to and make its home for life. ... When it finds its spot and takes root, it doesn't need its brain anymore, so it eats it! (It's rather like getting tenure.)
— from "Consciousness Explained" by Daniel Dennett

This wry quotation is making the rounds these days on the Internet, which is heavily used by America's academics. Also heating up modems across the land are angry denunciations of efforts in higher education circles to reconsider the venerable institution of academic tenure — the "rock" of a guaranteed job for life to which professors tenaciously aspire and cling.

Nowhere is debate over tenure more intense than at the University of Minnesota. In fact, an ongoing formal review of tenure at the university is the focus of much current Internet fuming.

Tenure has critics these days because the financial realities of higher education are changing, rapidly and harshly. Essentially, the economic and political marketplaces are no longer willing and able to support as large a higher education establishment as academics would like to provide.

After decades of easy expansion, adjusting to this age of limits is proving painful for higher education, and is likely to get worse.

COMING MONDAY:

State Rep. Becky Kelso and University of Minnesota Professor John Adams, leader of a faculty review of tenure, square off in a debate about tenure's value and the need for change.

Criticisms of tenure

The U of M's current tenure trauma began last fall, when the Board of Regents ordered a review of the university's tenure policies, and whether they unacceptably restrict the institution's ability to adjust to a tightening financial pinch.

Tenure definitely limits the university's options. Roughly 74 percent of the 3,500 faculty rank employees are tenured. A professor is typically granted or denied tenure after six years of probationary teaching and research and only after a demanding review.

Once tenured, faculty members are essentially employed for life and immune to pay cuts. Tenured faculty can be fired for extreme misconduct or failure to perform, and some are, but there is no intermediate discipline available. Most observers agree the current procedure for dismissing faculty is so arduous as to discourage action in all but the most outrageous cases.

What's most problematic and controversial is that tenured professors cannot be laid off unless the financial survival of the entire university is at risk. Even if the U chose to cut costs by closing whole programs or departments, the tenured faculty in the shuttered units could not be let go.

Other higher education institutions in Minnesota provide no absolute job security: Substantial job cuts, very much including tenured faculty, have begun within the Minnesota State Colleges and Universities system.

The managerial paralysis that tenure inflicts at the university has become especially critical for its hemorrhaging Academic Health Center. As sweeping change has come to the health care marketplace, revenues at the U hospital and clinics have shrunk disastrously.

The crisis has inspired the university's dramatic decision to merge its hospital with the private Fairview system. Meanwhile, Health Center Provost William Brody has complained that the tenure code prevents his trimming the ranks of tenured clinical faculty or even reducing their U salaries in line with the reduced revenues coming from their practices.

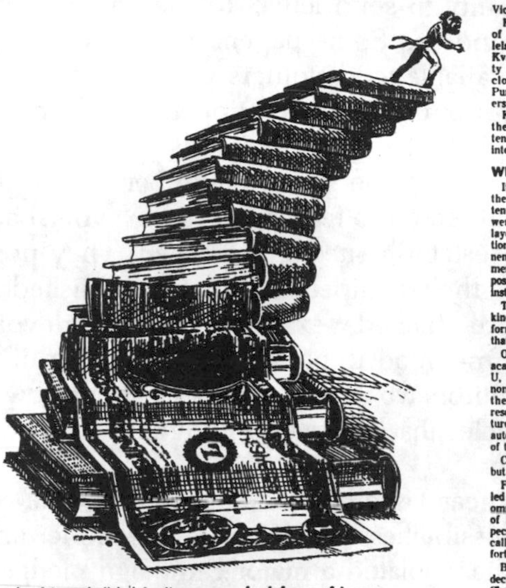

The health center's urgent problems have brought the tenure debate to the state Capitol. Pushing for an emergency infusion of funds for the health center, Rep. Becky Kelso, DFL-Shakopee, has also tied the money to a requirement that tenure rules be changed to give the health center flexibility to make cuts.

But it's not just the health center. The pressure of shrinking resources and rising costs is bearing down upon the university as a whole, as upon virtually all higher education institutions. State and federal funding levels are declining. Tuition has been climbing at punishing rates for years. Many broad budget cuts have already been made. Faculty salaries have sagged well behind those at competitive institutions. Buildings and facilities need major investments.

In short, it's virtually certain that program cuts are in the university's future. But with some 75 percent of its operating budget consumed by personnel costs, the U may not realize the needed savings even from difficult program closures without more flexibility to control faculty costs.

Kelso is troubled — "sickened" she says — by the angry indignation her efforts to encourage minor tenure reform have inspired from many in the university community. She believes the current tenure code makes needed adjustments at the U virtually impossible, and she says lawmakers have little enthusiasm for providing taxpayer support to an institution that is content to remain structurally incapable of adapting to changing times.

In defense of tenure

To many faculty members, all such questioning of tenure undermines the very foundation of the academic enterprise.

The arguments for preserving traditional tenure begin with the powerful case for academic freedom. No one disputes that scholars and researchers must be protected from job-related retribution for expressing unpopular opinions or conducting controversial research. Nor is such intimidation unheard of or difficult to imagine. From research concerning AIDS, to international trade, to the role of genetics in intelligence, a university overflows with projects to offend every constituency.

Many faculty advocates also insist that a guaranteed permanent job is necessary for researchers to feel confident in making long-term commitments to the elaborate studies that typify the best work at a major research university like the U of M — especially because academic pay rarely matches private sector salaries for similar levels of expertise.

That intensive, long-range research has enriched Minnesota is clear. From taconite to pacemakers, whole Minnesota industries owe their existence to U of M research.

Finally, the argument is made that the U stands alone among America's top universities in questioning the role of tenure, and that the U's tenure code is identical to that at competitive institutions. If it ceases to provide competitive tenure protection, goes this argument, the university will be unable to attract or retain top faculty, and will cease to be a top rank school.

These last assertions seem faulty, according to a survey of top American universities recently conducted by University Associate Vice President Robert Kvavik.

Kvavik reports that the "current discussion of tenure ... at Minnesota finds many parallels" at other top universities. What's more, Kvavik found that explicit or assumed authority to lay off tenured faculty when programs close exists at such universities as Duke, Purdue, Washington, Missouri, Kansas and others.

Kvavik also notes, however, that very few of these schools have ever actually laid off tenured faculty, and few express any future interest in doing so.

What can be done

It's hard to imagine, so far as that goes, that the university would ever actually dismiss tenured faculty until all other plausible options were exhausted. But should a small number of layoffs become necessary one day in connection with program changes, would that permanently devastate the confidence and commitment of the entire faculty? Would the mere possibility of layoffs lay waste to the whole institution?

The rest of society functions despite these kinds of uncertainties and pressures to perform. Few Minnesotans seem likely to accept that the U is so utterly different.

One comes back to the impression that the academic world, at least as represented at the U, is simply not yet ready to face hard economic realities. A commission appointed by the Board of Regents to study human resources issues recently reported that "a culture of entitlement and an unusual pursuit of autonomy may be the unintended consequences of tenure ..."

Change won't come easily to such a culture, but it probably will come.

For now, the U's review of tenure is being led by faculty members, who will provide recommendations on tenure revision to the Board of Regents later this spring. This somewhat peculiar procedure seems unlikely to produce calls for dramatic change that might discomfort faculty.

But, in the end, the regents have authority to decide the future of university tenure. Board Chairman Thomas Reagan is clear that the regents will "have to seriously consider whether we want to go further" should the faculty proposals prove timid.

One prudent objective for the regents would be a revised tenure code for the university that parallels the most flexible policies to be found at any comparable top flight research university in America.

On compensation, disciplinary procedures, layoff policies and the authority to gradually reduce the proportion of faculty that is tenured, the university needs every management flexibility it can achieve while remaining competitive with comparable institutions.

Transforming tenure

To be better able to adapt to tightening budgets, the university must pursue key changes to its tenure code. Among them:

- Streamlined disciplinary processes, and creation of levels of discipline less severe than firing for tenured faculty who perform poorly.
- Meaningful post-tenure review of performance for tenured faculty, coupled with flexible salary arrangements under which some merit-based pay can rise or fall with performance.
- Authority to gradually reduce the proportion of faculty that is tenured, through longer probationary periods, more faculty working on contract, etc.
- Greater powers to reassign or lay off tenured faculty when and if needed program changes make it unavoidable.

Readers discuss proposed constitutional 'right' to hunt

LETTERS TO THE EDITOR

Your editorial March 17 missed the major point of the entire issue of the proposed state constitutional right to hunt and fish. The reason sports men and women want this addition to the state constitution is to prevent the animal activist terrorists from interfering with hunting and fishing seasons, and people who enjoy these outdoor activities.

In these days of instant litigation, the same people who burn meat delivery trucks, break windows of butcher shops, endanger hunting dogs with poisoned meat, break into research laboratories and even try to destroy a young boy's final dream of an Alaskan hunting trip could easily find a judge ready and willing to deprive Minnesotans of their outdoor heritage.

It is not a silly game. It is a pre-emptive move to assure a future for Minnesota citizens who hunt and fish.

MICHAEL FISHER
SOUTH ST. PAUL

Thank you for the March 17 editorial regarding a proposed state constitutional amendment to make hunting and fishing a right. There has rarely been as blatant a special interest agenda as far-reaching as this. What may sound rather basic in terms of recreational activity is not a right, no more than skateboarding or water skiing.

What is most insulting is that our elected government officials take their serious occupations so lightly. They waste time on this during the last days of the session, while there are many other pressing matters at hand. The voters of Minnesota should not be bullied by a group that represents approximately 11 percent of the state's population.

COLLEEN MEYER
MINNEAPOLIS

Why not a tunnel?

The March 18 articles about St. Paul Civic Center connections were great to see. This subject deserves careful continued attention. Not mentioned though, and worth public discussion and cost estimates, is a tunnel under Rice Park.

When the Ordway Theater was built, some research looked at putting parking and connecting tunnels under Rice Park with little or no effect on the park's surface. A central hub under Rice Park could provide connections to the St. Paul Hotel, and through the skyway to the Radisson Hotel, as well as the Ordway, Landmark Center, and the central library. A grandiose option would provide coffee, deli, promotion and gift shops along the well-lit and decorated route with a small, public entry on the perimeter of the park.

St. Paul has some of the best conditions in the world for underground construction. .. The hard limestone layer under St. Paul provides a stable roof over a thick layer of fine-grained, light sandstone. Under the limestone, the sandstone can be mined simply with water pressure. The river bluff (and I expect the Civic Center construction) could provide direct access to the sandstone, without having to drill through the limestone. Costs may be much less than would be expected for underground tunneling.

This option deserves exploration before any other choice is made.

JOANNE A. ENGLUND
ST. PAUL

Overlooked facts

In their March 17 opinion piece, Stephen Balch and Rita Zurcher described the results of a study by the National Association of Scholars showing a decline in graduation requirements among the best American colleges. Comparing graduation requirements in 1914, 1939, 1964 and 1993, Balch and Zurcher claimed that typically the best liberal arts colleges no longer require traditional mathematics courses, nor science, English composition, foreign language or history courses.

Balch and Zurcher seemed to long for the days when the sons of well-to-do fathers could study Latin grammar for a few years and then go on to college and get a liberal education. They overlooked two points.

First, the college curriculum has changed. In his book, "Why the Professor Can't Teach," Morris Kline points out that mathematical subjects that were once taught at the college level have been moved down into high school. The courses that are no longer required of college students are studied in high school.

Second, the students who attend the best colleges are much better than they once were. In "The Bell Curve," Richard Herrnstein and Charles Murray point out that in the 1950s, many more of the brightest students began attending college, and the best colleges became much more selective. The best colleges can now fill their freshman class with students who mastered English composition in junior high. For these colleges, English composition is a remedial course.

DICK GREEN
DULUTH

provide access to a bonanza of websites, not just the local newspaper's but those of newspapers across the country and around the world. Computer users can read editorials, save them, download them and print them if they wish. They also have easy access to syndicated columnists and opinion magazines, all for a monthly fee of $20 or so.

As mentioned in Chapter 17, newspapers are also offering their readers an opportunity to send letters to the editor through e-mail, as well as via telephone and fax. Some papers have recorded portions of editorials and made them available to customers who telephone for news and other information. Chat groups on the Internet open up an almost infinite number of possibilities for people to share their opinions.

Faced with the growing number of websites and chat groups, newspapers have real reason to fear losing out to cyberspace competition—hence their mad dash to establish sites of their own. They possess one major advantage over most of their competition: their established news, editorial and advertising staffs are trained, experienced and devoted to the communities they serve. One good thing to look forward to if computers supplant the printed page: Editors won't have to worry about how to cram all the editorials, letters and articles that deserve printing onto one editorial page and one op-ed page each day.

Phineas Fiske of *Newsday*, master of the NCEW's website, has envisioned these possibilities: "Imagine, for example, an editorial pointing out that the mayor has violated a major campaign pledge; now imagine the impact if the mayor can be viewed on the computer monitor actually making that pledge during the campaign—then doing the exact opposite at a city council meeting last night."[31]

OP-ED PAGES

The first op-ed (opposite-editorial) pages may have been produced by the *New York World* in the early 1920s. The executive editor, Herbert Bayard Swope, said he got the idea for an op-ed page when he found that, "in spite of our hard and fast principle," opinion kept creeping into the news columns. "It occurred to me that nothing is more interesting than opinion when opinion is interesting," he recounted later, "so I devised a method of cleaning off the page opposite the editorial page . . . and thereon I decided to print opinions, ignoring facts."[32] The page sparkled with the names of famous writers that Swope recruited: Alexander Woollcott, writing on books and theater; Harry Hansen, on books; Heywood Broun, on whatever he wished. Franklin Pierce Adams (better known as F.P.A.) wrote a witty, acerbic column called "The Conning Tower." The *World*'s op-ed page was heavily oriented toward the arts and culture. (A book on newspaper editing published in 1942 credited the Louisville *Courier-Journal*'s editorial page and "page opposite editorial," or "op-ed" page, with setting one of the outstanding examples in design for editorial pages.[33])

Although the idea and the name of the op-ed page have been around for a long time, the *New York Times* is generally credited with setting the example that has led to a substantial number of such pages in recent years.

Harrison E. Salisbury, the first editor of the *Times'* op-ed page, said the idea emerged when editors were looking for something to attract readers from the *New York Herald Tribune*, which had just folded. A wider diversity of opinion was the immediate aim. The *Times* was also facing the need to raise subscription and advertising rates. The op-ed page was seen as an opportunity "to give the readers something extra for their extra money," Salisbury said. The *Times* moved its own columnists to the op-ed page, leaving room for more letters on the editorial page, and began to publish a variety of articles on the remainder of the page. Salisbury was given only three-quarters of a page; an advertisement occupied the remainder. He said he accepted the ad partly to anchor the page in the real world but also because he feared he would not have enough material to fill a whole page.[34]

When the *Los Angeles Times* joined the movement, according to David Shaw, the paper's media critic, it deliberately planned a less intellectual page than that of the *New York Times*, reasoning that readers got enough reporting on social issues in the opinion columns and from the columnists. "I'd especially like us to give our readers a clear feeling of what it's really like to live in Southern California," the op-ed page editor was quoted as saying. "I want personal experience pieces, stories that tell how it feels to drive the freeway and to suffer a death in the family and to be out of work."[35]

At least one syndicated columnist who appears on op-ed pages thinks such pages no longer present truly diverse views. Norman Solomon sees op-ed pages as presenting "variations of conventional wisdom—spanning only from avowed right-wingers to cautious liberals," expressing "timeworn arguments resembl[ing] billiard balls bouncing between two rails." "No wonder," he added, "so many op-ed pages have a monotonous tone."[36]

A 1994 survey indicated editors themselves were aware of the limitations of their op-ed pages. Although "local, community issues" was rated as the most appealing *theme* for op-ed material (cited by 81 percent of the editors), the most frequently mentioned source of *content* was "syndicated columnists" (used by 87 percent of the editors).[37] Professional journalists, public figures and propagandists were the most frequent contributors. A survey of newspapers reported in 1994 found that fewer than half had op-ed pages. This survey also found that op-ed pages generally were edited by the same person who edited the editorial page. "This greatly reduces the odds favoring an independent public forum disconnected from the agenda of the signature editorial page," the conductors of the survey concluded. While aiming for a balance of opposing points of view, the "op-ed page becomes the flip side of the editorial page, thereby limiting the possibility that an agenda driven primarily by public concerns will emerge."[38]

Checking a stack of 160 or so editorial and op-ed pages, from 1995 to early 1997, tends to confirm what these critics were saying. Most writers on those pages were the standard syndicated columnists discussed and identified in Chapter 18, "Columns and Cartoons."

Here and there, however, local writers appeared. The *Denver Post* carried columns written by local broadcast personalities. The *Roanoke Times* ran a column on Mondays by a woman who writes about everyday (usually rural) life. From time to time newspapers draw on the occasional outside writer. The *Miami Herald* ran a nostalgic piece (with a nostalgic photo) about a Florida retail giant (Burdines) that seemed about to disappear. The *Portland Press Herald* carried an article jointly written by a contractor and a consultant about how Interstate 95 in Maine was "suffering a midlife crisis."

Now and then, I came across a piece that seemed to fall outside the "convention wisdom" decried by syndicated columnist Solomon in commenting on the state of op-ed pages. The *Los Angeles Times* reprinted an article from *Atlantic Monthly* that asked: Since "America and Americans were forged into one Anglo image[,] [w]ho are we to preach to the Bosnias and Chechnyas?" The *Albuquerque Journal* ran an article by a writer identified as an Albuquerque consultant who warned that the "Indian gaming in New Mexico is placing the sovereignty of the Pueblo Indians in jeopardy" by becoming "the tool the [national] gaming industry is now using to pry open New Mexico's doors." The *Tallahassee Democrat* published a piece by a lawyer that opened with a good diss-the-lawyers joke but then undertook the more serious business of arguing against a Supreme Court decision upholding a Florida rule that prohibited lawyers from mail solicitation of accident victims within 30 days of an accident.

The *Chicago Tribune* ran an article by the director of the Harvard University Center of International Affairs that drew conclusions about Americans' weakening community ties from their bowling habits: More were bowling, but fewer were bowling in bowling leagues.

In the Baltimore *Sun*, a person identified as "a writer and farmer" took a look at a deer "hunter as he waits in a tree, arrow nocked, in the cold light of a September morn." The writer described the hunter as dressed in an expensive camouflage outfit with all kinds of high-tech gear—nothing like the old days still recalled by "a few oldtimers" who remember when doe hunting was simpler. The title of the article: "It takes big bucks to bag a doe these days."

The *San Francisco Examiner* printed three locally-written articles under the heading of "The Vocabulary of Hate." One dealt with the use of "'nigger' and other pejoratives." Another cited instances in which "we construct our mental reality with words, which may or may not describe the world with accuracy." An example: In Africa, clashes are "tribal"; in Eastern Europe, they are "ethnic."

Editors have devised a variety of ways to obtain contributions. The *New York Times* and the *Los Angeles Times* generally solicit articles but publish an occasional unrequested piece. The *Nashville Tennessean* first tried for contributions from academic people, but they refused to be rushed, wrote like academics and didn't like to be edited. Community leaders were not much better, so the paper turned to its own reporters and editors for about half of the pieces that were published.[39] The *Tulsa Tribune* set out to establish a base of contributors by contacting between 75 and 100 people. To the half that accepted, the *Tribune* sent out three postcards a week requesting columns (with four-week deadlines).[40]

Some newspapers pay for contributions, notably those they solicit. For some papers, pay depends on who the contributor is. The *Long Beach Press-Telegram* reported paying writers that it solicited and local writers trying to earn a living by their writing, but not politicians or people "who get to champion their favorite cause or point of view."[41]

Editors seem to be running more reprints and more contributions from think tanks, foundations and other interest groups. The contributions generally are offered at no charge; but, if they are responsibly presented, they can provide alternative opinions. Reprints, of course, require prior permission to publish (perhaps at a price). Editorial writers discussed the problem of getting permission in an exchange on the NCEW listserv. One suggestion was to establish a list of the magazines from which articles were most frequently published and arrange some kind of quick way to get approval. Here is the initial list:[42]

American Demographics	*Mother Jones*
American Enterprise	*Nation*
American Spectator	*National Interest*
Atlantic Monthly	*National Review*
Chronicle of Higher Education	*New Republic*
Commentary	*New Yorker*
Commonweal	*Policy Review*
Foreign Affairs	*Progressive*
Foreign Policy	*Public Interest*
Futurist	*Reason*
Governing	*Vanity Fair*
Harper's	*Washington Monthly*

CONCLUSION

The principal purpose of innovation, whether in layout, content or telecommunications, should be to encourage readers to think more deeply about more subjects. The purpose of page design is to get ideas across to readers by attracting them and then holding their attention long enough to stir their thoughts. The makeup of the page itself cannot carry a message to readers, but it can help set the tone of the page. If an editor has a flamboyant editorial style, a flamboyant style of typography will help reinforce the message. Conservative typography will help reinforce a conservative, reserved editorial style.

Whatever style an editor chooses, page design must meet two criteria. The first is to distinguish the opinion pages from the news pages. Readers need constantly to be reminded of this distinction. Editorial columns can be wider than news columns. Body type can be larger. Headlines can use different typefaces. Heads can be centered instead of flush left. Sketches instead of photographs can be used. The page can be run in a distinctive and consistent position in the paper.

The second criterion is to present a page that will attract readers. The makeup should say that this is an important page and that the editors have put a great deal of time, effort and thought into it. Thus the page should be deliberately, carefully and attractively laid out. It should have enough life to it that it is not always the same day by day, yet it also must have enough consistency in page design to suggest that the same editors, with the same editorial philosophy, are producing it each day.

If editors can meet those two criteria, they can design their pages in any manner they wish. In the end, what really counts is what they say on the pages.

The search for new ways to bring more, and more varied, viewpoints to the opinion pages also reflects an effort to keep the pages from becoming routine. Just as readers ought to be surprised from time to time by the appearance of an editorial page, so should they be surprised once in a while by the content. This means that editors must go beyond the traditional staff-written editorials, syndicated columns and cartoons, and letters to the editor. The possibilities are limited only by editors' imaginations and their ability to carry out their ideas, possibilities that may include the features discussed in this chapter—op-ed pages, guest columns, solicited contributions, boards of contributors, questions of the week, pro-con packages, visual illustrations and reprints from other publications as well as criticism of, and comment on, the press itself.

The purpose of all these efforts, of course, is to promote a greater exchange of ideas among readers and to convince readers that their newspaper is doing a thorough and responsible job of serving them. Even more important is actually to do a thorough and responsible job.

Questions and Exercises

1. Examine the makeup of the newspapers in your area. Do you find it easy to distinguish editorial pages from news pages?
2. Does the liberal or conservative nature of the makeup reflect the liberal or conservative editorial policy of the page? Consider the size of headlines, the style of headline type, the use of white space or rules, and the horizontal or vertical nature of the layout.
3. Does the makeup of a specific newspaper change from day to day or remain the same? If it changes, what principles seem to be operating in determining the layout—the relative importance of elements, the readership appeal of the elements or whim? Does the layout change so radically day by day that the page has a disjointed character?
4. What could be done to improve the design of the editorial pages in your area?
5. Which newspaper do you judge to have the best design? Why?
6. Which newspapers in your area have op-ed pages? How often do they appear? Is there a difference between the material that appears on the editorial page and the material on the op-ed page? What seems to be the policy in determining what goes where?
7. Does the editor of the op-ed page seem to be trying hard to bring contrary and different views onto the page? Does the page contain surprises?
8. What devices does the editor use to try to encourage more participation by more people in the opinion pages? A pro-con package? A question of the week? A guest columnist? An in-depth analysis? Articles by experts?
9. Do any of the newspapers have media critics? If so, how free do they appear to be to criticize the newspaper?

CHAPTER 20 The Editorial Page That May, and Must, Be

Truth crushed to earth, shall rise again;
The eternal years of God are hers
But, Error, wounded, writhes in pain,
And dies among his worshippers.
—WILLIAM CULLEN BRYANT[1]

Historians—and newspaper people themselves—have been prophesying the death of the American editorial page since the death of Horace Greeley. Then, they said editorial pages were doomed because of the passing of the great editors. Now, they say editorial pages, and the newspapers they appear in, are doomed because of competition from television, cable and the Internet. If information-seekers can push a button and instantly get the latest news (with sound and motion), the reasoning goes, why would they want to labor through a printed news story or editorial written several hours earlier?

The owner of every newspaper in America is, or should be, trying to find answers to this question. Owners have tried a variety of strategies. They have improved the appearance of their newspapers. They have made their newspapers more accessible, making it easier for readers to locate their favorite features. They have added more photographs and other graphics. They have produced zoned editions to meet the needs of communities within their circulation areas. They have tried to make their newspapers more consumer-friendly, providing useful, everyday information. Some have tried "civic journalism" or "public journalism," using their newspapers to help their communities identify and solve problems.

Few editors, however, have strengthened *news* coverage as a part of their strategy to meet the challenges of the new technology. Even fewer have looked to the *editorial* page as a likely place to start.

I am convinced that the best chance for newspaper owners to stay in business lies in their news and editorial departments. They may not be able to compete with *TV Guide* for information about television and cable, or with consumer and household magazines. Certainly they can't compete with radio and television in providing instantaneous news or the dramatic exposés of the "newsmagazines." And they can't serve the almost infinite variety of special-interest groups as well as the Internet can.

For a time, new, technologically advanced printing presses may help prolong the life of traditional newspapers, especially if they can turn out gorgeous multicolor pages and neighborhood zoned editions—but only so long as the majority of American households are not linked to interactive entertainment and information systems. Once system users reach a critical mass, however, it may be too late for owners of these presses if they have not diversified. Fortunately many newspapers—of all sizes—are trying to prepare for that day. More and more have established their own websites, if for no reason other than to meet or head off the competition.

As of this writing, most websites are money-losers. Readers who are accustomed to paying 25 or 50 cents a day for a newspaper are not yet likely to want to pay more than that for even 10 times or 100 times the information that now is available in a typical newspaper. Eventually, however, the finances will get worked out—between customers and advertisers—and the day will come when most people who are interested in news will get their information electronically, in some form or other.

Among newspapers' competitors will be the telephone companies, the cable companies, Rupert Murdoch, Microsoft, local access firms and national access firms, or a mix of these.

So what does a newspaper offer that these competitors do not? It occurs to me that it offers three things. First, it provides door-to-door distribution of printed products (as well as other products, such as soap samples). Second, it has the largest news-gathering staff in the community. Third, it may have the only staff members in the community whose full-time job it is to look behind the scenes, take a second look and comment on current issues.

For a time newspaper publishers may be able to supplement their incomes by delivering items other than the daily newspaper. But that, at best, is a short-term palliative.

The future of current newspaper companies lies in news and opinion, but not necessarily in a printed format. The computer, in fact, offers news and editorial staffs new opportunities to excel. Instead of being limited to six editorial page columns—with two or three editorials, a cartoon and a half a dozen letters—with the Internet, editors can post an unlimited number of editorials, cartoons and letters. Instead of being limited to four or five pieces on the op-ed page, readers can have access to the opinions of lots of people with a far wider variety of views than normally appear on today's op-ed pages. Posting the columns to a website requires little skill. The expense consists of whatever columns cost these days. Preparing letters to post on a website takes more time, but editing letters is mostly routine.

Provocative, meaty editorials, however, don't come cheap. Sure, it's easy to dash off an editorial on an easy topic. It's easy to fill an editorial column if you rehash what someone else has said or written. It's hard to write an editorial that provides new information and new insights. A few editorial writers can produce two or three editorials a day and even double as publisher. (J.W. "Bud" Forrester, editor and publisher of the *Astorian*, of Astoria, Ore., is the only one I have known who could do this.) For most editorial writers, however, good editorials result when they have an opportunity to discuss issues at an editorial board meeting, when they have time to thoroughly research and write editorials and when they are allowed the intellectual freedom to reach their own conclusions.

Although publishers in general don't seem to be putting much seed money into opinion pages, they do appear to be giving their editorial page staffs a bit more freedom to set editorial policy. One reason may be that publishers are preoccupied with other aspects of the newspaper. That can be good or bad. Many publishers have little or no experience in news or editorials. This is more likely to be bad than good. News and editorial staff members may feel fortunate if a publisher ignores them and goes about other business. But, invariably, there comes a time when publishers suddenly take an interest, usually when something that they don't like appears or happens. By then it's too late to start nurturing and educating the publisher. To prevent such surprises, the strategy for publishers is to hire writers and editors that they trust, take an interest in their work, but give them a lot of freedom to carry out news and editorial policies. The best strategy for writers and editors is to pick companies or newspapers they respect and with whose policies they feel comfortable. Unfortunately for writers and editors, the best is not always, or even often, possible. Job openings are scarce and unpredictable, especially on the newspapers where editors and writers most want to work. Publishers change newspapers. Companies change ownership. In the best relationships, confrontations with bosses, sometimes serious confrontations, happen.

It is no easier for frustrated editors and writers to change jobs or move to new communities than it is for anyone else. Like everyone else, they face weekly grocery bills, mortgages, car payments, child-support payments and tuition for children in college. It may be even more difficult for newspaper people to find new jobs. After all, how many firms within commuting distance employ editorial writers?

Yet, it may be more essential for disenchanted editorial writers than for other workers to move on to more congenial employment. First, there is nothing more miserable for an editorial writer than being at odds with the editorial policies of the newspaper. Second, jobs in journalism are not just jobs. With editorial (and news) jobs comes a commitment to pursuing truth and justice. The freedom of the press prescribed by the First Amendment was not intended to benefit or make life easy for members of the press. This freedom was intended to assure that citizens of this country would have access to all the information they need to make intelligent political and social decisions. The responsibility for assuring that citizens get this information, and that they have ample opportunity to engage in open public dialogue themselves, rests largely with the owners, the writers and the editors of the press. This is a heavy responsibility, but it also can be an exciting and challenging one.

One of the challenges for future writers and editors is to find a new and better way to keep the editorial function of the press alive and healthy. This book is intended to help would-be writers and editors get started down the editorial path. The direction that path takes in the future will be decided by them. Who knows? Down that path may go modern-day equivalents to Horace Greeley, Ralph McGill and David Brinkley.

One final word: If you don't think there are solutions to local, state, national and international problems, don't go into editorial writing. You must believe that efforts of government, private agencies and individuals can make a difference in communities and in the lives of families and individuals. Editorial writing, at heart, is an optimistic business. Each new day, and each new editorial page, offers an opportunity to help make something better.

REFERENCES

Introduction

[1] David Shaw, "The Death of Punditry," *Gannett Center Journal*, 3:1 (Spring 1989).

[2] Rosemary Yardley, "The Editorial Writer (2)," Ibid., p. 43.

[3] Gerald C. Stone and Timothy Boudreau, "1985, 1994: Comparison of reader content preferences," *National Research Journal*, 16:22–23 (Fall 1995).

Chapter 1 The Editorial Page That Used to Be

[1] Rollo Ogden, ed., *The Life and Letters of Edwin Lawrence Godkin* (Westport, Conn., Greenwood Press, 1972), p. 255.

[2] James Parton, "Prestige," *North American Review*, 101:375–76 (April 1866), cited in Frank Luther Mott, *American Journalism* (New York: Macmillan, 1941), p. 385.

[3] Isaiah Thomas, *The History of Printing in America* (New York: Weathervane Press, 1970), p. 508. (First appeared in 1810.)

[4] Wm. David Sloan, Cheryl Watts and Joanne Sloan, *Great Editorials* (Northport, Ala.: Vision Press, 1992), p. 24.

[5] Ogden, *Life and Letters.*

[6] Michael Emery and Edwin Emery, *The Press and America*, 6th ed. (Englewood Cliffs, N.J.: Prentice Hall, 1988), pp. 66–68.

[7] Ishbel Ross, *Ladies of the Press* (New York: Harper, 1936), p. 29.

[8] Ibid., p. 32.

[9] Ibid., p. 37.

[10] Roland E. Wolseley, *The Black Press*, 2nd ed. (Ames: Iowa State University Press, 1990), p. 25.

[11] Ibid., p. 28.

[12] Allen Nevins, *American Press Opinion: Washington to Coolidge* (Boston: Heath, 1928), p. 111.

[13] Parton, "Prestige," p. 385.

[14] Edward P. Mitchell, *Memoirs of an Editor* (New York: Scribner's, 1924), p. 109.

[15] Harold E. Davis, *Henry Grady's New South* (Tuscaloosa: University of Alabama Press, 1990).

[16] Hal Borland, *Country Editor's Boy* (Philadelphia: Lippincott, 1970), pp. 156–69.

[17] Sally Foreman Griffith, *Home Town News: William Allen White and the Emporia Gazette* (New York: Oxford University Press, 1989), pp. 113–38.

[18] Harrison E. Salisbury, *Without Fear or Favor* (New York: Times Books, 1980), p. 26.

[19] Lincoln Steffens, cited in Justin Kaplan, *Lincoln Steffens* (New York: Simon & Schuster, 1974), p. 87.

[20] Upton Sinclair, *The Brass Check* (Pasadena: The Author, 1920), p. 22.

[21] Ibid., p. 14.

[22] Ibid., p. 15.

[23] Griffith, *Home Town News*, p. 138.

[24] Nathaniel B. Blumberg, *One-Party Press?* (Lincoln: University of Nebraska Press, 1954), p. 44.

Chapter 2 The Editorial Page That Should, and Could Be

[1] Alexis de Tocqueville, "A Newspaper's Value," cited in *The Masthead*, 28:29 (Winter 1976).

[2] Robert Reid, "More Hell-Raising Editorials," *The Masthead*, 39:26–27 (Winter 1987).

[3] "A Death Foretold," *Lexington Herald-Leader*, Dec. 2, 1990.

[4] *Bay Guardian*, Jan. 12, 1994.

[5] *Bay Guardian*, May 8, 1996.

[6] Buford Boone, cited in Johanna Cleary, "Lessons in Editorial Leadership," *The Masthead*, 40:46 (Summer 1988).

[7] Hazel Brannon Smith, Ibid., pp. 49–50.

[8] Bernard Kilgore, "A Publisher Looks at Editorial Writing," *The Masthead*, 6:47 (Spring 1954).

[9] Paul Greenberg, "Tyerman Sums Up," *The Masthead*, 17:23 (Winter 1965).

[10] Philip Geyelin, "Who Listens to Your Bugle Calls?" *The Masthead*, 30:9 (Summer–Fall 1978).

[11] Elsa Mohn and Maxwell McCombs, "Who Reads Us and Why," *The Masthead*, 32:24 (Winter 1980–81).

[12] Lenoir Chambers, "Aim for the Mind–and Higher," *The Masthead*, 13:20 (Summer 1961).

[13] James J. Kilpatrick, "Editorials and Editorial Writing," *The Masthead*, 5:7 (Spring 1953).

[14] *Virginia Gazette*, Nov. 8, 1995.

[15] *Southwest Virginia Enterprise*, Oct. 2, 1996.

[16] Ernest Hynds and Erika Archibald, "Improved editorial pages can help papers, communities," *Newspaper Research Journal*, 17:19–20 (Winter/Spring 1996).

[17] Kenneth Rystrom, "The Impact of Newspaper Endorsements," *Newspaper Research Journal*, 7:19–28 (Winter 1986).

[18] Hynds and Archibald, "Improved editorial pages," p. 20.

[19] Jay Rosen, *Community Connectedness Passwords for Public Journalism* (St. Petersburg: Poynter Institute for Media Studies, 1993).

[20] R. S. Baker, "The Editorial Writer: The Man in the Piazza," *Montana Journalism Review*, 15:18–19 (1972).

Chapter 3 Anybody for Editorial Writing?

[1]Robert H. Estabrook, "Why Editorial Applicants Aren't," *The Masthead*, 12:53 (Summer 1962).

[2]G. Cleveland Wilhoit and Dan G. Drew, "Portrait of an Editorial Writer, 1971–88," *The Masthead*, 41:6–7 (Spring 1989).

[3]Wilbur Elston, "The Editor Goes Status Seeking and Image Hunting," *The Masthead*, 15:1–18 (Fall 1963).

[4]William W. Baker, "A Lack of Communication," *The Masthead*, 15:21–22 (Fall 1963).

[5]Elston, "Status Seeking."

[6]Warren H. Pierce, "What Makes a Good Editorial Writer?" *The Masthead*, 10:23–24 (Spring 1958).

[7]David Manning White, "The Editorial Writer and Objectivity," *The Masthead*, 4:31–34 (Fall 1952).

[8]Hoke Norris, "The Inside Dope," *The Masthead*, 8:55–57 (Spring 1956).

[9]Pierce, "What Makes."

[10]Irving Dilliard, "The Editor I Wish I Were," *The Masthead*, 19:51–57 (Summer 1967).

[11]Frederic S. Marquardt, "What Manner of Editor Is This?" *The Masthead*, 19:57–58 (Summer 1967).

[12]G. Cleveland Wilhoit and Dan G. Drew, "Profile of the North American Editorial Writer," *The Masthead*, 31:8–13 (Winter 1979–80).

[13]David E. Klement, "Who we are and what we do," *The Masthead*, 48:54 (Fall 1996).

[14]Ernest C. Hynds, "Improved editorial pages can help papers, communities," *Newspaper Research Journal*, 17:18 (Winter/Spring 1996)

[15]G. Cleveland Wilhoit and Dan G. Drew, "Profile of the North American Editorial Writer," *The Masthead*, 31:8–13 (Winter 1979–80).

[16]Ernest C. Hynds, "Editors at Most U.S. Dailies See Vital Role for Editorial Page," *Journalism Quarterly*, 71:574 (Autumn 1994).

[17]Jean Gaddy Wilson, "Only 68 Years to Go," *Press Women*, 51:1 (January 1988).

[18]Evelyn Trapp Goodrick, "Comparison of Women and Men on Editorial Page Staffs," *The Masthead*, 42:3–7 (Fall 1990).

[19]Klement, "Who we are," p. 54.

[20]Chuck Stokes, "Portrait of NCEW features few minority faces," *The Masthead*, 45:10 (Summer 1993).

[21]Rekha Basu, "Minority voices sound like one hand clapping," *The Masthead*, 45:8–9 (Summer 1993).

[22]Mercedes Lynn de Uriarte, "Inching numbers," *Quill*, 58:16 (May 1966).

[23]Caroline Brewer, "Diverse faces, but not diverse opinions," *The Masthead*, 47:12 (Spring 1995).

[24]James H. Howard, "Feedback From Readers Helps Teach," *The Masthead*, 27:21 (Spring 1975).

[25]Donald L. Breed, "Why Publishers Rarely Write Own Editorials," *The Masthead*, 14:21 (Fall 1962),

[26]John H. Cline, "The Quest for 'Good Editorial Thinking,'" *The Masthead*, 18:17–18 (Fall 1966).

[27]Editor in the West, "Not in That Newsroom," *The Masthead*, 18:7–8 (Fall 1966).

[28]William D. Snider, "Try Law, Politics or Campus," *The Masthead*, 18:10–11 (Fall 1966).

[29]Ben H. Bagdikian, "Editorial Pages Change–But Too Slowly," *The Masthead*, 17:16 (Winter 1965–66).

[30]Jonathan W. Daniels, "The Docility of the Dignified Press," *The Masthead*, 17:8–14 (Winter 1965–66).

Chapter 4 Preparation of an Editorial Writer

[1]LeRoy E. Smith, "The Polls of Journalism Educators," *The Masthead*, 28:25–29 (Spring 1976).

[2]Robert B. Frazier, "What Do You Read, My Lord?" *The Masthead*, 14:10–16 (summer 1962).

[3]Hugh S. Fullerton, cited in Jake Highton, "Perhaps It's Time to Abolish Journalism Schools," *The Masthead*, 40:33 (Winter 1988).

[4]Highton, "Perhaps It's Time," p. 33.

[5]Otis Chandler, cited in LeRoy E. Smith and Curtis D. MacDougall, "What Should Journalism Majors Know?" *The Masthead*, 27:28–32 (Spring 1975).

[6]Smith, "The Poll of Journalism Educators."

[7]Curtis D. MacDougall, "A Modern Journalism Curriculum," *The Masthead*, 28:30–34 (Spring 1976).

[8]Don Carson, "The Goal: Aiming for Perfection," *The Masthead*, 28:34 (Spring 1976).

[9]Kurt Rogahn, NCEW Listserv, Dec. 29, 1997.

[10]Anson H. Smith Jr., "Try an Inspiring Year at Harvard," *The Masthead*, 22:33–5 (Spring 1970).

[11]Sig Gissler, "A Sabbatical: Too Sweet to Be True," *The Masthead*, 29:30–31 (Spring 1977).

[12]Anonymous, "Educational Opportunities," *The Masthead*, 44:28–29 (Spring 1992).

[13]Kenneth Rystrom, "An Editor Returns to Campus," *The Masthead*, 29:12–15 (Winter 1977–78).

[14]Terrence W. Honey, "Our Ivory Tower Syndrome Is Dead," *The Masthead*, 23:26 (Summer 1971).

[15]Maura Casey, "Hosting regionals is easy as 1, 2, 3," *The Masthead*, 45:25–26 (Summer 1993).

[16]Larry Evans, "Regional meetings reach more, cost less," *The Masthead*, 45:24–25 (Summer 1993).

[17]Frazier, "What Do You Read, My Lord?"

[18]Robert B. Frazier, "The Editorial Elbow," *The Masthead*, 15:5–16 (Summer 1963).

[19]James J. Kilpatrick, "Editorials and Editorial Writing," *The Masthead*, 5:1–3 (Spring 1953).

[20]Irving Dilliard, "The Editorial Writer I Wish I Were," *The Masthead*, 19:52 (Summer 1967).

[21]Suraj Kapoor and Janet Blue, "Editorial page editors still call the shots," *The Masthead*, 45:29 (Spring 1997).

[22]Ernest C. Hynds, "Editorial pages become more useful," *The Masthead*, 47:38 (Fall 1995).

[23]Hynds, "Editorial pages."

[24]Kapoor and Blue, "Editorial page editors," p. 29.

[25]Phineas Fiske, "Notes from the Webmaster," *The Masthead*, 48:19–20 (Spring 1996).

[26]Phineas Fiske, "An ongoing electronic conversation," *The Masthead*, 48:21 (Spring 1996).

[27]"Tools of the Trade," *The Masthead*, 49:39 (Spring 1997).

Chapter 5 Who Is This Victorian "We"?

[1]J.G. Saxe, in *The Press*, cited in *The Masthead*, 21:20 (Summer 1969).

[2]Fred C. Hobson Jr., "A We Problem," *The Masthead*, 18:18 (Spring 1966).

[3]Robert E. Kennedy, "(signed) The editorial writer," *The Masthead*, 42:23 (Summer 1990).

[4]Ernest C. Hynds, "Editorial Pages Remain Vital," The *The Masthead*, 27:19 (Fall 1975).

[5]Robert U. Brown, "Shop Talk at Thirty," *The Masthead*, 17:38–39 (Fall 1965).

[6]Floyd A. Bernard, "There Has to Be a Corporate Opinion," *The Masthead*, 23:12 (Spring 1971).

[7]G. Cleveland Wilhoit and Dan G. Drew, "Portrait of an Editorial Writer," *The Masthead*, 41:4–11 (Spring 1989).

[8]Anonymous, "Editors Say More Leeway on Group-Owned Papers," *presstime*, 2:36 (May 1980).

[9]Calvin Mayne, "Gannett Company," in "Symposium: Yeah, What About That Monopoly of Opinion?" *The Masthead*, 26:14 (Fall 1974).

[10]Reese Cleghorn, "Knight Newspapers," "Symposium: Yeah, What," pp. 18–19.

[11]Merrill Lindsay, "Lindsay-Schaub Newspapers," "Symposium:Yeah, What," pp. 22–23.

[12]Daniel B. Wackman, Donald N. Gillmor, Cecille Gaziano and Everett E. Dennis, "Chain Newspaper Autonomy as Reflected in Presidential Campaign Endorsements," *Journalism Quarterly*, 52:411–20 (Autumn 1975).

[13]Brown, "Shop Talk at Thirty."

[14]Kennedy, "(signed) The editorial writer."

[15]George C. McLeod, "The Paper's Masthead Is the Byline," *The Masthead*, 23:13 (Spring 1971).

[16]Ann Lloyd Merriman, "No to Signed Editorials," *The Masthead*, 23:14 (Spring 1971).

[17]Michael J. Birkner, "Behind the Editorial 'We,'" *The Masthead*, 36:20 (Summer 1984).

[18]John J. Zakarian, "The Visiting Board Member," *The Masthead*, 43:19–20 (Summer 1991).

[19]Richard T. Cole, "Pursuing the Elusive Editorial Board," *The Masthead*, 42:24–25 (Summer 1990).

[20]George Neavoll, "We Who Live in Glass Houses," *The Masthead*, 41:11 (Fall 1989).

[21]Sam Reynolds, "Editorial Transubstantiation," *The Masthead*, 27:2 (Fall 1975).

[22]George J. Hebert, "Going Loose and Lively in Norfolk," *The Masthead*, 28:21–22 (Spring 1976).

[23]Warren G. Bovee, "The Mythology of Editorial Anonymity," *The Masthead*, 24:26–35 (Fall 1972) and 24:54–65 (Winter 1972). Copyright 1972 by Warren G. Bovee.

[24]Everett Ray Call, "Yes to Initialed Editorials," *The Masthead*, 23:16–17 (Spring 1971).

[25]Robert Schmuhl, "Accountability Through Initials," *The Masthead*, 39:31 (Winter 1987).

[26]Anonymous, "Report of the 1972 NCEW Continuing Studies Committee," *The Masthead*, 25:37–39 (Spring 1973).

[27]Ernest C. Hynds, "Editorial pages become more useful," *The Masthead*, 47:40 (Fall 1995).

[28]David V. Felts, "Roosevelt's 'I' or Victoria's 'We'?" *The Masthead*, 28:20–21 (Fall 1967).

[29]James Parton, *The Life of Horace Greeley* (New York: Publisher Unknown), 1855), p. 78.

[30]Kenneth Rystrom, "Would You Quit over Editorial Stand?" *The Masthead*, 37:25–26 (Fall 1985).

Chapter 6 Relations with Publishers

[1]Meg Downey, "Editors and Publishers Should Fight," *The Masthead*, 42:18 (Winter 1990).

[2]Hugh B. Patterson Jr., "When Ownership Abdicates Its Responsibilities, Newspaper Suffers," *The Masthead*, 14:16 (Fall 1962).

[3]Bernard Kilgore, "A Publisher Looks at Editorial Writing," *The Masthead*, 6:44 (Spring 1954).

[4]Ibid.

[5]Donald L. Breed, "The Publisher and the Editorial Page," *The Masthead*, 3:34 (Winter 1951).

[6]John Lofton, "Can Editorial Writers Afford to Deal With Their Publishers?" *The Masthead*, 3:1–8 (Winter 1951).

[7]*Group Ownership Survey*, American Society of Newspaper Editors, April 1990, pp. 1–2.

[8]G. Cleveland Wilhoit and Dan G. Drew, "Profile of the North American Editorial Writer, 1971–1979," *The Masthead*, 31:10 (Winter 1979–80).

[9]*Group Ownership Survey*, p. 16.

[10]David Demers, "Corporate Newspaper Structure, Editorial Page Vigor and Social Change," *Journalism and Mass Communication Quarterly*, 73:862 (Winter 1996).

[11]Ibid., pp. 868–70.

[12]Roya Akhavan-Majid and Timothy Boudreau, "Chain Ownership, Organizational Size and Editorial Role Perceptions," *Journalism & Mass Communication Quarterly*, 72:863–73 (Winter 1995).

[13]Edward E. Adams, "A Comparison of Local Editorial Issues in Competitive, Joint Monopoly and Joint Operating Agreement Newspapers," Media Management and Economics Division, annual convention, Association for Education in Journalism and Mass Communication, Montreal, August 1994.

[14]Robert T. Pittman, "How to Free Editorial Writers," *The Masthead*, 22:11 (Spring 1970).

[15] David Halberstam, *The Powers That Be* (New York: Knopf, 1979), p. 573.

[16] Jon G. Udell, *The Economics of the American Newspaper* (New York: Hastings House, 1978), p. 62.

[17] Donald L. Breed, "Why Publishers Rarely Write Own Editorials," *The Masthead*, 14:22 (Fall 1962).

[18] Suraj Kapoor, John Cragan and Irene Cooper, "Publishers' and Opinion-Page Editors' Political Perceptions: A Comparative Analysis," *The Masthead*, 42:7–14 (Winter 1990).

[19] G. Cleveland Wilhoit and Dan G. Drew, "Profile of an Editorial Writer, 1971–88," *The Masthead*, 41:4–11 (Spring 1989).

[20] Robinson Scott, cited in Kilgore, "A Publisher Looks."

[21] Wilhoit and Drew, "Profile of an Editorial Writer."

[22] Downey, "Editors and Publishers Should Fight."

[23] David Holwerk, "Conflicts Are Inevitable–and Even Desirable," *The Masthead*, 42:18 (Winter 1990).

[24] Suraj Kapoor and Janet Blue, "Editorial page editors still call the shots," *The Masthead*, 49:27–29 (Spring 1997).

[25] Kenneth McArdle, "The Real Pressure Is to Make Sense," *The Masthead*, 22:8–9 (Spring 1970).

[26] Kilgore, "A Publisher Looks."

[27] Ibid.

[28] Hoke Norris, "The Inside Dope," *The Masthead*, 8:55 (Spring 1956).

[29] Frank W. Taylor, "Relations with the Publisher," *The Masthead*, 2:21 (Winter 1950).

[30] Houstoun Waring, "Fertilizer for the Grass Roots," *The Masthead*, 4:12 (Spring 1952).

[31] Nathaniel B. Blumberg, "Still Needed: A School for Publishers," *The Masthead*, 22:16 (Spring 1970).

[32] Alan Kern, "Publisher Conflicts Not Often a Problem," *The Masthead*, 42:20–22 (Spring 1990).

[33] Phil Duff, "'Yes, but . . .': Should the Publisher Be Involved in Civic Affairs?" *The Masthead*, 37:3 (Summer 1985).

[34] Breed, "The Publisher," p. 47.

[35] Curtis D. MacDougall, "Our Opportunity to Educate or to Sabotage," *The Masthead*, 22:10 (Spring 1970).

[36] Sam Reynolds, "It's Time We Blew the Whistle," *The Masthead*, 29:45 (Winter 1977).

[37] Steve Parrott and Steve O'Neil, "Wall Between Editorial, News Necessary, Most Editors Agree," *The Masthead*, 41:16–18 (Spring 1989).

[38] Ibid.

[39] Patterson, "When Ownership Abdicates."

[40] Taylor, "Relations."

[41] Sevellon Brown III, "Setting Editorial Policy–Editors vs. Publishers," *The Masthead*, 7:22–24 (Summer 1955).

[42] Kilgore, "A Publisher Looks," p. 46.

[43] William H. Heath, "Editorial Policy," *The Masthead*, 19:66 (Summer 1967).

Chapter 7 Relations with the Newsroom

[1] Clifford E. Carpenter, "When Reporters Speak Up," *The Masthead*, 12:30–32 (Spring 1960).

[2] Steve Parrott and Steve O'Neill, "Wall Between Editorial, News Necessary, Most Editors Agree," *The Masthead*, 41:16–18 (Spring 1989).

[3] Edward M. Miller, "Take a Managing Editor to Lunch," *The Masthead*, 22:31–33 (Spring 1970).

[4] Parrott and O'Neill, "Wall Between," p. 16.

[5] Ellen Belcher, "Election offers insights from other side of the fence," *The Masthead*, 49:8–9 (Spring 1997).

[6] William J. Woods, cited in Anonymous, "Policies and Politics," *The Masthead*, 11:43–44 (Summer 1959).

[7] Parrott and O'Neill, "Wall Between," p. 17.

[8] Desmond Stone, "How Does the News Staff Dissent?" *The Masthead*, 23:24–26 (Spring 1971).

[9] Rufus Terral, "In Conference," *The Masthead*, 3:30 (Summer 1951).

[10] Parrott and O'Neill, "Wall Between," p. 17.

[11] David H. Beetle, "Can a Paper Call on a Reporter for Bylined Opinion?" *The Masthead*, 11:69–71 (Spring 1959).

[12] Fred A. Stickel, "To the People of Oregon," *The Oregonian*, November 1, 1992.

[13] Nathaniel B. Blumberg, "The Case Against Front-Page Editorials," *The Masthead*, 8:17–20 (Summer 1959).

[14] James J. Kilpatrick, "Why Not Throw Outworn Traditions Away?" *The Masthead*, 6:1–5 (Spring 1954).

[15] James C. MacDonald, "'News' and 'Opinion' Get All Mixed Up," *The Masthead*, 6:21 (Summer 1954).

[16] "Symposium: The Role of the Ombudsman/Media Critic," *The Masthead*, 28:3–15 (Spring 1976).

Chapter 8 The Editorial Page Staff

[1] Lawrence J. Paul, "Many Papers Wretchedly Understaffed," *The Masthead*, 24:1 (Spring 1972).

[2] Don Shoemaker, "Mine, by Damn, All Mine," *The Masthead*, 3:10 (Fall 1951).

[3] G. Cleveland Wilhoit and Dan G. Drew, "Profile of the North American Editorial Writer," *The Masthead*, 31:10 (Winter 1979–80).

[4] Wilbur Elston, "Writers Need Topics, Not Orders," *The Masthead*, 28:10 (Spring 1976).

[5] Shoemaker, "All Mine."

[6] Michael Loftin, "Dodging the Daily Boulder," *The Masthead*, 35:6 (Summer 1983).

[7] Karli Jo Hunt, "Read, Read, Read, Clip, Clip, Clip," *The Masthead*, 35:9 (Summer 1983).

[8]Linda Egan, "A Resilient Bunch," *The Masthead*, 38:4 (Winter 1986).

[9]Paul, "Many Papers," pp. 1–3.

[10]John G. McCullough, "Consulting Some Other Oracles," *The Masthead*, 28:5–6 (Spring 1976).

[11]Hugh B. Patterson Jr., "When Ownership Abdicates Its Responsibility, News Suffers," *The Masthead*, 14:18 (Fall 1962).

[12]Pat Murphy, "Fie on Conferences," *The Masthead*, 28:8–9 (Summer 1976).

[13]Gilbert Cranberg, "Skull Sessions Over Lunch," *The Masthead*, 28:10–11 (Summer 1976).

[14]John H. Taylor Jr., "Get back to hands-on control," *The Masthead*, 44:32–33 (Fall 1992).

[15]"How we spend our days," *The Masthead*, 48:22–25 (Winter 1996).

[16]Morgan McGinley, "Get control of your own budget," *The Masthead*, 45:5 (Fall 1993).

Chapter 9 Relations with the Community

[1]Susan Hegger, "Credibility Depends on Being Fair and Appearing Fair," *The Masthead*, 44:9 (Summer 1992).

[2]Norman A. Cherniss, "In Defense of Virtue," *The Masthead*, 18:4 (Summer 1966).

[3]"Symposium: Proposition No. 1: To Be Involved?" *The Masthead*, 18:1–15 (Summer 1996).

[4]G. Cleveland Wilhoit and Dan G. Drew, "Portrait of an Editorial Writer, 1971–88," *The Masthead*, 41:4–11 (Spring 1989).

[5]Paul Greenberg, cited in Sue Ryon, "Editorial Writers Face Classic Dilemma," *The Masthead*, 42:32 (Winter 1990).

[6]David Boeyink, "Anatomy of a Friendship," *The Masthead*, 41:7 (Fall 1989).

[7]James J. Kilpatrick, "How the Question Came Up," *The Masthead*, 18:2 (Spring 1996).

[8]Ibid.

[9]Laird B. Anderson, "A Few Thoughts on the 'Ethics Thing,'" *The Masthead*, 41:8–10 (Fall 1989).

[10]Don Lowery, cited in Ryon, "Editorial Writers Face."

[11]Lewis A. Leader, "Journalism and Joining Just Don't Mix," *The Masthead*, 44:5 (Summer 1992).

[12]Susan Hegger, "Credibility."

[13]Van Cavett, "If Your Paper Supports a Position, Then You Can Too," *The Masthead*, 44:7–8 (Summer 1992).

[14]Charles J. Dunsire, "Stay Away from Causes That Could Become a Topic," *The Masthead*, 44:7 (Summer 1992).

[15]William F. Woo, "Public journalism and the tradition of detachment," *The Masthead*, 47:16 (Fall 1995). (Adapted from a speech delivered in the *Press-Enterprise* Series at the University of California at Riverside.)

[16]Jay Rosen, Community Connectedness Passwords for Public Journalism, (St. Petersburg, FL: Poynter Institute for Media Studies, 1993), frontispiece.

[17]Woo, "Public Journalism," p. 20.

[18]Cited in NCEW mailing list, April 21, 1997.

[19]NCEW mailing list, April 22, 1997.

[20]Ibid.

[21]Ibid.

[22]Ibid.

[23]John Alexander, "Newspapers Took Different Roles as Corporate Citizens," *The Masthead*, 41:6–7 (Fall 1989).

[24]H. Brandt Ayers, "Does a Plane Ticket Buy Your Soul?" *The Masthead*, 28:3–4 (Winter 1976).

[25]John Causten Currey, "Is It Better to Nurture Ignorance?" *The Masthead*, 28: 4–5 (Winter 1976).

[26]Smith Hempstone, "Self-Righteousness Gives Cold Comfort," *The Masthead*, 28:5–6 (Winter 1976).

[27]Richard B. Laney, "Code Gives No Real Guidance," *The Masthead*, 28:6–7 (Winter 1976).

[28]Robert Estabrook, "Those All-Expense Trips," *The Masthead*, 4:39–41 (Fall 1952).

[29]Catherine Ford, "Ethics Are Expensive, But They're Well Worth the Price," *The Masthead*, 41:4 (Fall 1989).

[30]Mark Clutter, "Don't Be Churlish," *The Masthead*, 12:5 (Spring 1960).

[31]Jack Craemer, "One Who Refuses Feels Lonely," *The Masthead*, 12:8 (Spring 1960).

Chapter 10 Nine Steps to Editorial Writing

[1]Vermont Royster, "Parsley and Pot-Boiled Potatoes," *The Masthead*, 8:38 (Fall 1956).

[2]George Comstock, Steven Chafee, Natan Katzman, Maxwell McCombs and Donald Roberts, *Television and Human Behavior* (New York: Columbia University Press, 1978), pp. 318–28.

[3]Werner J. Severin and James K. Tankard Jr., *Communication Theories* (New York: Hastings House, 1979), p. 248.

[4]Wilbur Schramm and William E. Porter, *Men, Women, Messages and Media*, 2nd ed., (New York: Harper & Row, 1982), pp. 110–11.

[5]Elsa Mohn and Maxwell McCombs, "Who Reads Us and Why," *The Masthead*, 32:21 (Winter 1980–81).

[6]W. Phillips Davison, James Boylan and Frederick T. C. Yu, *Mass Media*, 2nd ed. (New York: Holt, Rinehart and Winston, 1982), p. 173.

[7]Alexis S. Tan, *Communication Theories and Research* (Columbus, Ohio: Grid, 1981), p. 103.

[8]Schramm and Porter, *Men, Women,* p. 188.

[9]Tan, *Mass Communication Theories,* p. 149.

[10]Henry M. Keezing, "Who Are Your Brothers?" *The Masthead*, 8:47 (Spring 1956).

[11]James J. Kilpatrick, "Editorials and Editorial Writing," *The Masthead*, 5:5–6 (Spring 1953).

[12]Howard Kurtz and Sue Anne Pressley, "Jury Finds Against ABC for $5.5 Million; Punitive Damages

Awarded to Food Lion Over Hidden-Camera Report," *Washington Post*, Jan 23, 1997.

[13]Barry Meier, "Jury Says ABC Owes Damages of $5.5 Million," *New York Times*, Jan. 23, 1997.

[14]Tan, *Mass Communication*, p. 140.

[15]Schramm and Porter, *Men, Women*, p. 196.

[16]Ibid.

[17]Tan, *Mass Communication*, p. 139.

[18]Davison, Boylan and Yu, *Mass Media*, p. 190.

[19]Paul Starobin, "Why Hidden Cameras Hurt Journalism," *New York Times*, Jan 28, 1997.

[20]Roone Arledge, "Hidden Cameras Find the Truth," *New York Times*, Feb. 1, 1997.

Chapter 11 Nine Steps to Better Writing

[1]James J. Kilpatrick, "Editorials and Editorial Writing," *The Masthead*, 5:5 (Spring 1953).

[2]Vermont Royster, cited in Harry Boyd, "They Write by Ear," *The Masthead*, 8:31 (Fall 1956).

[3]R. Thomas Berner, "Let's Get Rid of Those Pesky Pronouns," *The Masthead*, 31:32 (Summer 1979).

[4]Galen R. Rarick, "The Writing That Writers Write Best," The Masthead, 21:3–5 (Winter 1969–70).

[5]Rudolph Flesch, *The Art of Readable Writing* (New York: Harper, 1949), and *How to Test Readability* (New York: Harper, 1951).

[6]Francis P. Locke, "Too Much Flesch on the Bones?" *The Masthead*, 11:3–6 (Spring 1959).

[7]Wall Street Journal, "On the Other Hand," *The Masthead*, 7:20 (Fall 1955).

[8]Cited in "Words Have Disabling Power," *Roanoke Times & World-News*, Aug. 23, 1992.

[9]Judy E. Pickens, ed., *Without Bias: A Guidebook for Nondiscriminatory Communication* (New York: Wiley, 1992).

[10]Kilpatrick, "Editorials and Editorial Writing," p. 4.

Chapter 12 Subjects That Are Hard to Write About

[1]Creed Black, "Government Is Great, But–," *The Masthead*, 19:23 (Summer 1967).

[2]Lauren K. Soth, "How to Write Understandable Editorials About Economics," *The Masthead*, 6:19 (Winter 1954).

[3]Stein B. Haughlid, "Make international editorials relate to local issues," *The Masthead*, 48:8 (Spring 1996).

[4]Joe Geshwiler, "Find the connection," *The Masthead*, 48:9 (Spring 1996).

[5]Edward Alden, "'Home' is not what it used to be," *The Masthead*, 48:11 (Spring 1996).

[6]Philip Taubman, "Decoding issues across the kitchen table," *The Masthead*, 48:7 (Spring 1996).

[7]Aubrey Bowie, "The Arts Need Same Zeal as Sewers," *The Masthead*, 41:23 (Fall 1989).

[8]D. Michael Heywood, "Health Care Can Be Lethal to Editorial Writing," *The Masthead*, 43:8 (Fall 1991).

[9]Anonymous, "AIDS and the Editorial Page," *The Masthead*, 40:6 (Winter 1988).

[10]Susan Willey, "Journalism and religion," *Quill*, 84:29 (January–February 1996).

[11]*Roanoke Times & World-News*, Feb. 23, 1988.

Chapter 13 Subjects That Are Deceptively Easy

[1]James E. Casto, "Holiday of Headaches," *The Masthead*, 35:15 (Fall 1983).

[2]Barbara Drake, NCEW mailing list, April 16, 1997; Maury Casey, NCEW mailing list, April 17, 1997; Mike Heywood, NCEW mailing list, 1997.

[3]Lauren K. Soth, "From Alpha to Omega," *The Masthead*, 20:3 (Spring 1969).

[4]Richard B. Childs, "When You Can't Pass the Buck," *The Masthead*, 29:3–4 (Summer 1977).

[5]Jim Wright, "It Gets Tough to Give Thanks," *The Masthead*, 35:12 (Fall 1983).

[6]Kyle Thompson, "A Wish List on Christmas Day," *The Masthead*, 35:17 (Fall 1983).

[7]Ann Lloyd Merriman, "It Helps to Be Prepared," *The Masthead*, 35:6 (Fall 1983).

[8]Elissa Papirno, "The Holiday Problem," *The Masthead*, 35:13–14 (Fall 1983).

[9]Joanna Wragg, "Relying on Traditional Material," *The Masthead*, 35:9–11 (Fall 1983).

Chapter 14 Subjects That Are Neglected

[1]David Jarmul, "Ain't Science Articles Fascinating?" *The Masthead*, 39:15 (Summer 1987).

[2]David Jarmul and Leah D. Fine, "Science rare topic of editorial pages," *The Masthead*, 45:10–11 (Winter 1993).

[3]"We can't let artificial lines harm Illinois," *Muskogee Daily Phoenix*, Oct. 12, 1996.

[4]Ben H. Bagdikian, "Editorial Pages Changing–But Too Slowly," *The Masthead*, 17:20 (Winter 1965–66).

[5]Andy Rooney, "Editorial Pages Are Better Off Without Humor," *The Masthead*, 43:9 (Summer 1991).

[6]Nordahl Flakstad, "It's No Laughing Matter, But There's Still Room for Humor," *The Masthead* 43:7–8 (Summer 1991).

[7]Rick Horowitz, "Call Me Irresponsible?" *The Masthead*, 43:8 (Summer 1991). .

[8]Rick Horowitz, "He missed the point–but I'm the target," *The Masthead*, 45:8 (Winter 1993)

[9]Mark L. Genrich, "Down With Fruitcakes," *The Masthead*, 39:5–6 (Spring 1987).

[10]Joseph Plummer, "Use It Selectively," *The Masthead*, 39:10 (Spring 1987).

[11]Dave Cummerow, "Takes a Deft Touch," *The Masthead*, 39:11 (Spring 1987).

Chapter 15 Editorials on Elections

[1]Elizabeth Bird, "Kingmaker or Informer?" *The Masthead*, 40:35–36 (Summer 1988).

[2]Don Robinson, "Newspapers owe it to readers to give editorial endorsements," *The Masthead*, 45:5 (Spring 1993).

[3]"To Endorse, Or Not," *Editor & Publisher*, Oct. 26, 1996, p. 4.

[4]Bird, "Kingmaker or Informer?"

[5]"Electronic report focuses on editorial front," *The Masthead*, 49:13–17 (Spring 1997).

[6]"Paid Ads or Endorsements?" Letter to the Editor, *Daily News*, Longview, Wash., date unknown.

[7]Cited in "Candidate Endorsements–Who, When and Why: A Complaint and a Reply," *The Masthead*, 20:19 (Summer 1968).

[8]Dick Timmons, "Forget endorsements," *Editor & Publisher*, Aug. 10, 1996, p. 9.

[9]"Some Changes in the Editorial Page," *Los Angeles Times*, Sept. 23, 1973, part 6, p. 2.

[10]Hugh B. Culbertson and Guido H. Stempel III, "Public Attitudes About Coverage and Awareness of Editorial Endorsements," in Guido H. Stempel III and John W. Windhauser, eds., *The Media in 1984 and 1988 Elections* (Westport, Conn.: Greenwood Press, 1981), pp. 187–99.

[11]Cited in "Candidate Endorsements–Who, When and Why."

[12]"Electronic report," p. 15.

[13]"Electronic report," p. 17.

[14]"To Endorse, Or Not," p. 4.

[15]Cited in "Electronic report," p. 14.

[16]Cited in "Electronic report," p. 15.

[17]Cited in "Electronic report," p. 14–15.

[18]Ed Williams, "Skip exercises in editorial masochism," *The Masthead*, 45:7 (Spring 1993).

[19]Frank Luther Mott, "Has the Press Lost Its Punch?" *The Rotarian*, Oct. 1952, p. 13.

[20]Nathaniel B. Blumberg, *One-Party Press?* (Lincoln: University of Nebraska Press, 1954), p. 11.

[21]George Comstock, Steven Chafee, Natan Katzman, Maxwell McCombs and Donald Roberts, *Television and Human Behavior* (New York: Columbia University Press, 1978), pp. 136, 319–28.

[22]Peter Clarke and Eric Fredin, "Newspapers, Television and Political Reasoning," *Public Opinion Quarterly*, 42:143–60 (Summer 1978).

[23]"Electronic report," p. 14.

[24]Fred Fedler, "To Endorse or Not to Endorse," *The Masthead*, 36:26 (Summer 1984).

[25]Kenneth Rystrom, "The Impact of Newspaper Endorsements," *Newspaper Research Journal*, 7:19–28 (Winter 1986).

[26]Kenneth Rystrom, "Apparent Impact of Endorsements by Group and Independent Newspapers," *Journalism Quarterly*, 63:449–53, 532.

[27]Fred Fedler, Ron F. Smith and Tim Counts, "Voter Uses and Perceptions of Editorial Endorsements," *Newspaper Research Journal*, 6:20 (Summer 1983).

[28]Ruth Ann Weaver-Lariscy and Spencer F. Tinkham, "News Coverage, Endorsements and Personal Campaigning: The Influence of Non-Paid Activities in Congressional Campaigns," *Journalism Quarterly*, 68:442–43 (Fall 1991).

[29]Mary Ann Sharkey, "Give Each Candidate a Fair Hearing," *The Masthead*, 43:12 (Spring 1991).

[30]Norman Blume and Schley Lyons, "The Monopoly Newspaper in a Local Election: The Toledo Blade," *Journalism Quarterly*, 45:286–92 (Summer 1968).

[31]Fedler, Stephens and Counts, "Endorsement Surprises," pp. 48–49.

[32]Byron St. Dizier, "Republican Endorsements, Democratic Positions: An Editorial Page Contradiction," *Journalism Quarterly*, 63:581–86.

[33]John J. Zakarian, "Speaking of Elections: Sacred Cows of the Highest Order," *The Masthead*, 25:3 (Spring 1973).

[34]St. Dizier, "Republican Endorsements."

[35]Robert J. White, "Endorsement Process Became an Election Issue," *The Masthead*, 43:6 (Spring 1991).

[36]Douglas J. Rooks, "Given a Chance, Candidates Take Issues Seriously," *The Masthead*, 43:14 (Spring 1991).

[37]Mindy Cameron, "Share the Process and Remove Presumptuous Arrogance," *The Masthead*, 43:8–9 (Spring 1991).

[38]Cecilie Gaziano, "Chain Newspaper Homogeneity and President Endorsements, 1972–1988," *Journalism Quarterly*, 66:836–45 (Winter 1989).

[39]John C. Busterna and Kathleen A. Hansen, "Presidential Endorsement Patterns by Chain-Owned Papers, 1976–84," *Journalism Quarterly*, 67:286–94 (Summer 1990).

[40]Roya Akhavan-Majid, Anita Rife and Sheila Gopinath, "Chain Ownership and Editorial Independence: A Case Study of Gannett Newspapers," *Journalism Quarterly*, 68:59–66 (Spring/Summer 1991).

[41]*Virginian-Pilot*, Oct. 25, 1997.

[42]*Virginian-Pilot*, Oct. 26, 1997.

[43]*Daily Press*, Oct. 19, 1997.

[44]*News-Gazette*, Oct. 22, 1997.

[45]*Manassas Journal Messenger*, Nov. 3, 1997.

[46]Rystrom, "The Impact of Newspaper Endorsements."

[47]*Argus Observer*, Oct. 23, 1997.

[48]*East Oregonian*, Oct. 9, 1997.

[49]*Daily Astorian*, Oct. 20, 1997.

[50]*Bulletin*, Sept. 28, 1997.

[51]*Oregonian*, Oct. 8, 1997.

[52]*Oregonian*, Oct. 9, 1997.

[53]*Oregonian*, Oct. 10, 1997.

[54]*Oregonian*, Oct. 11, 1997.

[55]*Oregonian*, Oct. 12, 1997.

Chapter 16 Other Types of Opinion Writing

[1]John Beatty, cited in Anonymous, "Broadcast Editorials: A Dying Breed in a Ripe Market," *Quill*, 80:37 (July/August 1992).

[2]William L. Rivers, *Writing Opinion: Reviews* (Ames: Iowa State University Press, 1988), p. 24.

[3]Boyd A. Levet, "Editorials and the Business of Broadcasting," *The Editorialist*, 17:7 (Spring 1991).

[4]G. Donald Gale, "The Need for Broadcast Editorials," *The Masthead*, 40:37–38 (Spring 1988).

[5]Daniel W. Toohey, cited in Howard W. Kleiman, "Unshackled but Unwilling: Public Broadcast and Editorializing," *Journalism Quarterly*, 64:708 (Winter 1987).

[6]David Spiceland, "Research finds broadcast editorials continue to wane," *The Masthead*, 46:15 (Winter 1994).

[7]Beatty, "Broadcast Editorials," p. 37.

[8]Ibid.

[9]Marjorie Arons-Barron, cited in Elizabeth Aspengren, "Where are the broadcast editorials?" *The Masthead*, 46:10 (Winter 1994).

[10]Dillon Smith, cited in Ibid.

[11]Jill Olmsted, "Whatever happened to network commentary?" *The Masthead*, 44:8 (Winter 1992).

[12]Tom Bettag, cited in Ibid.

[13]Ibid, p. 9.

[14]"Broadcast Editorials," p. 37.

[15]Spiceland, "Research finds," p. 12.

[16]Frank Stanton, cited in Kleiman, "Unshackled but Unwilling," p. 713.

[17]Robert Logan, "TV vs. Print," *The Masthead*, 37:11–25 (Summer 1985).

[18]Martha Sieleff, cited in Ibid., pp 17–18.

[19]Phil Johnson, cited in Ibid., p 19.

[20]Lesley Crosson, cited in Ibid., p. 21

[21]Robert S. McCord, "Move from print to broadcast brings surprises," *The Masthead*, 46:15–6 (Winter 1994).

[22]Richard Elam, "Editorialist Critique," *The Editorialist*, 14:6 (April/May 1988).

[23]Anonymous, "Critics Corner," *The Editorialist*, 10:14 (November–December 1983).

[24]Laura Reina, "Why Movie Blurbs Avoid Newspapers," *Editor & Publisher*, Aug. 31, 1996.

[25]Tim Bywater and Thomas Sobchack, *Introduction to Film Criticism* (New York: Longman, 1989). Other types of reviews include the genre, social science, historical and ideological/theoretical.

[26]Ibid., p. 3.

[27]Irving Wardle, *Theater Criticism* (London: Routledge, 1992), p. 4.

[28]Ibid, p. 14.

[29]Rivers, *Writing Opinion: Reviews*, p. 56.

[30]Carl Sessions Stepp, "An Inspirational Array of Local Columns," *American Journalism Review*, 15:67 (April 1993).

[31]Blackie Sherrod, "Civilian Conservation Corps was good idea then–and now," *Dallas Morning News*, May 18, 1995.

[32]Tony Case, "Ombudsman Overboard?" *Editor & Publisher*, May 25, 1996, p. 8.

[33]Ibid, p. 9.

[34]Bill Kirtz, "The Ombudsman: Cost or Benefit?" *presstime*, 17:43 (June 1995).

[35]Art Nauman, ombudsman, *Sacramento Bee*, cited in Kirtz, "The Ombudsman," p. 43.

[36]Kirtz, "The Ombudsman," p. 43.

[37]Frank Wetzel, "The Ombudsman: Merely a Public-Relations Gimmick?" *Seattle Times*, Sept. 19, 1988.

Chapter 17 Letters to the Editor

[1]Roger O'Dell, "Letters to the editor brighten the day," *Roanoke Times*, March 2, 1996.

[2]Barry Bingham Sr. in "Dear Sir You Cur!" *The Masthead*, 3:38 (Fall 1951).

[3]Diane Cole, "Letters to the Editor: Who Needs 'em? We Do," *The Masthead*, 44:7 (Spring 1992).

[4]Suraj Kapoor, "Most papers receive more letters," The Masthead, 47:18–21 (Spring 1995).

[5]Keith Carter, "Successful Letters Column Requires Ongoing Effort," *The Masthead*, 44:10 (Spring 1992).

[6]Robert Bohle, "Just Running Letters Is Not Enough," *The Masthead*, 43:10–13 (Spring 1991).

[7]Arthur Hagopian, "Sound Off turns readers into participants," *The Masthead*, 45:14–15 (Spring 1993).

[8]Charles Reinken, "Linguistic infidels hurl verbal Nerf Balls," *The Masthead*, 45:16–17 (Spring 1993).

[9]Charles VanDevander, "Building a Readers' Forum," *The Masthead*, 18:16 (Spring 1966).

[10]M. Carl Andrews, "How Letters to the Editor Influence a Community," *The Masthead*, 13:24–26 (Spring 1961).

[11]Anonymous, "Interview Your Letter Writers," *The Masthead*, 17:31 (Spring 1965).

[12]James Dix, "Customers Love Crossfire," *The Masthead*, 20:22 (Fall 1968).

[13]Kapoor, "Most papers receive more letters," p. 19.

[14]Rob Philips, "Anonymous letters turn on readers," *Quill*, 77:8 (December 1989–January 1990)

[15]Suraj Kapoor and Carl Boton, "Studies Compare How Editors Use Letters," *The Masthead*, 44:5–7 (Spring 1992).

[16]John R. Markham, "A Letter Is a Dangerous Thing," *The Masthead*, 5:18– 19 (Fall 1953).

[17]James J. Kilpatrick, cited in Ibid., p. 20.

[18]Glenn Sheller, "Dogma if you do, damned if you don't," *The Masthead*, 46:25 (Summer 1994).

[19]M. Carl Andrews, "Pity the Poor Editor Without Letters," *The Masthead*, 20:12 (Fall 1968).

[20]Carol Suplee, "A Problem," *The Masthead*, 39:32 (Winter 1987).

[21]Kapoor, "Most papers receive more letters," p. 19.

[22]Kapoor, "Most papers receive more letters," p. 19.

[23]Kapoor, "Most papers receive more letters," p. 19.

[24]Charles Towne, "The Trouble with Letters Is Editors," *The Masthead*, 28:9 (Fall 1976).

[25]Wally Hoffman, "Keep a Balance," *The Masthead*, 40:5–6 (Spring 1988).

[26]Phil Fretz, "Don't Run 'em," *The Masthead*, 40:6 (Spring 1988).

[27]Marc Franklin, "Letters and Libel," *The Masthead*, 40:10–13 (Spring 1988).

[28]Steve Pasternack, "Dear Editor–Print This at Your Own Risk," *The Masthead*, 36:5–6 (Spring 1984).

[29]Clifford E. Carpenter, "The Letter Litter, Its Dangers and Potentials," *The Masthead*, 19:80 (Summer 1967).

[30]Palmer Hoyt, "A Publisher Looks at Editorial Writing," *The Masthead*, 6:49 (Spring 1954).

[31]Franklin Smith, "Who Elected the Times?" *The Masthead*, 23:34 (Summer 1971).

[32]Andrews, "Pity the Editor Without Letters," p. 13.

Chapter 18 Columns and Cartoons

[1]Edwin M. Yoder Jr., "In 40 Years, a Sea Change," *The Masthead*, 38:12–13 (Fall 1986).

[2]Donald P. Keith, "Champions of Truth or Claques for Extremists," *The Masthead*, 19:60 (Summer 1967).

[3]Sam G. Riley, *The American Newspaper Columnist* (New York: Praeger, 1998), p. 80.

[4]Riley, *The American Newspaper Columnist*, pp. 82, 83.

[5]Michael Emery and Edwin Emery, *The Press and America*, 6th ed. (Englewood Cliffs, N.J.: Prentice-Hall, 1988), p. 368.

[6]W.A. Swanberg, *Citizen Hearst* (New York: Scribner's, 1961), p. 483.

[7]Riley, *The American Newspaper Columnist*, pp. 80, 81.

[8]Riley, *The American Newspaper Columnist*, pp. 83, 84.

[9]Robert H. Estabrook, "Their Varied Views Are Important," *The Masthead*, 10:22–24 (Fall 1958).

[10]Mark Ethridge, "The Come-Back of Editorial Pages," *The Masthead*, 18:28–32 (Summer 1966).

[11]Yoder, "In 40 Years."

[12]Ethridge, "The Come-Back of Editorial Pages."

[13]Yoder, "In 40 Years."

[14]Ernest C. Hynds, "Editorial Pages Remain Vital," *The Masthead*, 27:19–22 (Fall 1975).

[15]Frank Wetzel, "Territorial Exclusivity Is Attacked," *The Masthead*, 30:3–4 (Winter 1978).

[16]Mark Fitzgerald, "Exclusivity Gets Upheld by Court," *Editor & Publisher*, December 28, 1996.

[17]Lauren Soth, "Conflicts of Interest by Political Writer, Editor," *Des Moines* (Iowa) *Register*, November 29, 1973.

[18]National News Council, "Findings of the National News Council," *The Masthead*, 26:53 (Fall 1974).

[19]Robert Schulman, "The Opinion Merchants," *The Masthead*, 32:21 (Spring 1980).

[20]Gilbert Cranberg, "What syndicates owe to their editors," *The Masthead*, 47:36–37 (Fall 1995).

[21]Gilbert Cranberg, "One-time disclosure misses the point," *The Masthead*, 48:9 (Summer 1996).

[22]Draper Hill, "Cartoonists Are Younger–and Better," *The Masthead*, 38:14–17 (Fall 1986).

[23]Cited in David Astor, "Cartooning Views from Non-Artists," *Editor & Publisher*, July 13, 1996, p. 24.

[24]Chris Lamb and Nancy Brendlinger, "Drawing Conclusions: Are Cartoonists and Editors on the Same Page?" manuscript presented at the Southeast Colloquium, Association for Education in Journalism and Mass Communication, Roanoke, Va., March 15, 1996.

[25]David Astor, "Another Major Newspaper Fires a Political Cartoonist," *Editor & Publisher*, Oct. 29, 1994, p. 33; cited in Lamb and Brendlinger, "Drawing Conclusions."

[26]Lamb and Brendlinger, "Drawing Conclusions," p. 16.

[27]David Astor, "Cartoonists Without a Hometown Newspaper," *Editor & Publisher*, May 18, 1996, pp. 40–41.

[28]Cited in Alan Vitiello, "In defense of editorial cartoonists," *Editor & Publisher*, July 20, 1996.

[29]Cited in Richard Prince, "Black cartoonists missing from pages," *The Masthead*, 48:17 (Spring 1996).

[30]David Astor, "Color Cartoons and Caricatures Coming," Editor & Publisher, July 26, 1997.

[31]Robert Van Ommeren, Daniel Rife and Don Sneed, "What Is the Cartoonist's Role?" *The Masthead*, 36:12–15 (Spring 1984).

[32]Ibid.

[33]Lamb and Brendlinger, "Drawing Conclusions," p. 22.

[34]Ommeren, Rife and Sneed, "What is the Cartoonist's Role?" p. 13.

[35]Lamb and Brendlinger, "Drawing Conclusions," p. 23.

[36]Cited in Signe Wilkinson, "Editors, cartoonists learn to coexist," *The Masthead*, 47:28 (Winter 1995).

[37]Thomas Gebhardt, "A Gamble Paid Off," *The Masthead*, 40:7 (Fall 1988).

[38]Jim Borgman, "No Trench Warfare," *The Masthead*, 40:8 (Fall 1988).

[39]Dick Herman, "Facts Is Facts," *The Masthead*, 40:7–8 (Fall 1988); Paul Fell, "The Self- Imposed Limits of My Cage," *The Masthead*, 40:9 (Fall 1988).

[40]*Editor & Publisher*, "Syndicate Directory Section for 1994," July 30, 1994.

[41]Cited in Prince, "Black cartoonists missing," p. 16.

[42]Gephardt, "A Gamble Paid Off."

[43]Fell, "The Self-Imposed Limits."

[44]Ron Cunningham, "Want Cartoons? Try Asking for Them," *The Masthead*, 45:17–18 (Spring 1993).

[45]Ibid.

[46]Nicole Kirby, "Stability in the midst of change," *Community Newspaper Showcase of Excellence* (1995), p. 21.

[47]A. Rosen, Discussion Session, American Press Institute, Columbia University, New York, May 1972.

Chapter 19 Innovations in Design and Content

[1]Ralph J. Turner, cited in Anonymous, "Professor Gives Tips on Improving Appearances of Editorial Pages," *SNPA Bulletin*, January 3, 1990.

[2]Robert Bohle, "Most Pages Have Resisted Change," *The Masthead*, 38:18–21 (Fall 1986).

[3]Cited in Ibid.

[4]John E. Allen, Newspaper Makeup (New York: Harper, 1936), p. 332.

[5]Miles E. Tinker, *Legibility in Print* (Ames: Iowa State University Press, 1963), pp. 74–107.

[6]Robert Bohle, "Get with the '90s–they're almost over," *The Masthead*, 45 (Winter 1993), 30.

[7]Robert Bohle, "What a good page should look like," *The Masthead*, 44 (Fall 1992), 40–41.

[8]Ernest C. Hynds, "Pages join design revolution," *The Masthead*, 48:19–21 (Winter 1996).

[9]Susan Albright, e-mail letter to the author, April 23, 1997.

[10]Cited in Ibid.

[11]Laura Reina, "Reader-Written Supplement A Success in Utah," *Editor & Publisher*, Oct. 14, 1995, p. 12.

[12]Sig Gissler, "A Forum for Our Readers," *The Masthead*, 23:31–32 (Spring 1971).

[13]Rich Bard, "You can find good opinion writing in unexpected places," *The Masthead*, 45:22–23 (Spring 1993).

[14]Dennis R. Ryerson, "Two Op-ed Pages in Cleveland," *The Masthead*, 36:10 (Fall 1984).

[15]Liz Fedor, "We gained great hindsight from board's demise," *The Masthead*, 47:5–6 (Summer 1995).

[16]Richard Hughes, NCEW mailing list, Feb. 5, 1997.

[17]George Neavoll, "Community input walks in the door every day,"*The Masthead*, 47:7 (Summer 1995).

[18]E.W. Kieckhefer, "Taking orders from customers runs contrary to great tradition," *The Masthead*, 48: 16 (Summer 1996).

[19]Robert T. Pittmann, "Ten Best Bets for Edit Pages," *The Masthead*, 23:33–34 (Spring 1971).

[20]Chalmer Roberts, *The Washington Post: The First 100 Years* (Boston: Houghton Mifflin, 1977), pp. 413–14.

[21]Ernest C. Hynds, "Editorial pages become more useful," *The Masthead*, 47:40 (Fall 1995).

[22]Cited in Judith Sheppard, "Climbing down from the ivory tower," *The Masthead*, 47:7 (Fall 1995).

[23]John Webster, "Spokane experiments with change," *The Masthead*, 48:14–17 (Fall 1996).

[24]Cited in Judith Sheppard, "Climbing down," p. 5.

[25]Ed Williams, "Charlotte takes pride in convening community," *The Masthead*, 48:17 (Fall 1996).

[26]Williams, "Charlotte takes pride," p. 18.

[27]Ron Clark, "Letting go of daily editorials," *The Masthead*, 48: 12–14 (Summer 1996).

[28]Ron Clark, "Reactions to the St. Paul experiment," The Masthead, 48:15 (Summer 1996).

[29]Phineas Fiske, "Reactions to the St. Paul experiment," *The Masthead*, 48:14 (Summer 1996).

[30]John H. Taylor Jr., "Can you be a catalyst without becoming a part of the story?" *The Masthead*, 45:29–30 (Fall 1993).

[31]Phineas Fiske, "Make technology your friend–or else," *The Masthead*, 48:23 (Fall 1996).

[32]E.J. Kahn, Jr., *The World of Swope* (New York: Simon and Schuster, 1965), p. 260.

[33]Norman J. Radder and John E. Stempel, *Newspaper Editing: Makeup and Headlines* (New York: McGraw-Hill, 1942), pp. 332–33.

[34]Harrison E. Salisbury, "An Extra Dimension in This Complicated World," *The Masthead*, 23:29–31 (Spring 1971).

[35]David Shaw, "Newspapers Offer Forum to Outsiders," *Los Angeles Times*, Oct. 13, 1975.

[36]Norman Solomon, "Monotonous Tone of Op-Ed Pages Could Spell Trouble for Newspapers," *Editor & Publisher*, March 29, 1997.

[37]Andrew Ciafalo and Kim Traverso, "Does the op-ed page have a chance to become a community forum?" *Newspaper Research Journal*, 15:51–61 (Fall 1994).

[38]Ibid.

[39]Lloyd R. Armour, "Let the Staff Write Them," *The Masthead*, 36:6–7 (Fall 1984).

[40]John Drummond, "Idea From a Critique Group," *The Masthead*, 36:11 (Fall 1984).

[41]John J. Fried, "From the League and the Campus," *The Masthead*, 36:11 (Fall 1984).

[42]Phineas Fiske, "Magazine Reprints," NCEW listserv, Feb. 24, 1997.

Chapter 20 The Editorial Page That May, and Must, Be

[1]William Cullen Bryant, "The Battle-Field," *Poems* (Philadelphia: Henry Altemus), p. 124.

BIBLIOGRAPHY

Editorial Writing and Editorial Pages

Babb, Laura Longley, ed., *The Editorial Page* [of the *Washington Post*]. Boston: Houghton Mifflin (1977).

Hulteng, John L., *The Opinion Function: Editorial and Interpretive Writing for the News Media*. Hayden Lake, Idaho: Ridge House Press (1973).

Kreighbaum, Hillier, *Facts in Perspective: The Editorial Page and News Interpretation*. Englewood Cliffs, N.J.: Prentice-Hall (1956).

MacDougall, Curtis D., *Principles of Editorial Writing*. Dubuque, Iowa: W.C. Brown (1973).

Rivers, William L., *Writing Opinions: Reviews*. Ames: Iowa State University Press (1988).

Rivers, William L., Bryce McIntyre, and Alison Work, *Writing Opinions: Editorials*. Ames: Iowa State University Press (1988).

Sloan, Wm. David, *Pulitzer Prize Editorials: America's Best Writing, 1917–1979*. Ames: Iowa State University Press (1980).

Sloan, Wm. David, Cheryl Watts and Joanne Sloan, *Great Editorials: Masterpieces of Opinion Writing*. Northport, Ala.: Vision Press (1992).

Stonecipher, Harry W., *Editorial and Persuasive Writing: Opinion Functions of the News Media*. New York: Hastings House (1979).

Waldrop, A. Gayle, *Editor and Editorial Writer*. 3rd ed. Dubuque, Iowa: W.C. Brown (1967).

Press Criticism

Bagdikian, Ben H., *The Effete Conspiracy and Other Crimes of the Press*. New York: Harper & Row (1972).

Blumberg, Nathaniel B., *One-Party Press?* Lincoln: University of Nebraska Press (1954).

Dunsmore, Herman H., *All the News That Fits: A Critical Analysis of the News and Editorial Content of the New York Times*. New Rochelle, N.Y.: Arlington House (1969).

Efron, Edith, *The News Twisters*. Los Angeles: Nash (1971).

Ghiglione, Loren, ed., *The Buying and Selling of America's Newspapers*. Indianapolis: R.J. Berg (1984).

Goldstein, Tom, ed., *Killing the Messenger*. New York: Columbia University Press (1989).

Irwin, Will, *The American Newspaper*. Ames: Iowa State University Press (1969). (First appeared in *Colliers*, January–July 1911.)

Isaacs, Norman A., *Untended Gates*. New York: Columbia University Press (1986).

Lee, Martin A., and Norman Solomon, *Unreliable Sources*. New York: Carol Publishing Group (1990).

Middleton, Neil, ed., *The I.F. Stone's Weekly Reader*. New York: Vintage (1974).

Patner, Andrew, *I.F. Stone: A Portrait*. New York: Pantheon (1988).

Seldes, George, *Lords of the Press*. New York: Julian Messner (1938).

Seldes, George, *The People Don't Know*. New York: Gaer (1949).

Seldes, George, *You Can't Print That*. Garden City, N.Y.: Garden City Publishing (1929).

Sinclair, Upton, *The Brass Check: A Study of American Journalism*. 8th ed. Pasadena: The Author (1920).

Squires, James D., *Read All About It! The Corporate Takeover of America's Newspapers*. New York: Times Books (1994).

Cartoonists

Anonymous, *The Image of America in Caricature and Cartoon*. Fort Worth, Texas: Amon Carter Museum of Western Art (1976).

Block, Herbert, *The Herblock Book*. Boston: Beacon Press (1952).

Block, Herbert, *The Herblock Gallery*. New York: Simon & Schuster (1968).

Block, Herbert, *Herblock's Here and Now*. New York: Simon & Schuster (1955).

Block, Herbert, *Herblock's State of the Union*. New York: Simon & Schuster (1972).

Editors of the Foreign Policy Association, *A Cartoon History of United States Foreign Policy, 1776–1976*. New York: Morrow (1975).

Giglio, James N., and Greg G. Thielen, *Truman in Cartoon and Caricature*. Ames: Iowa State University Press (1984).

Hill, Draper, *Political Asylum*. Winsor, Ontario: Art Gallery of Winsor (1985).

Hill, Draper, *The Young Years, 1982–1985*. Detroit: Detroit News (1986).

Lendt, David L., *Ding: The Life of Jay Norwood Darling* Ames: Iowa State University Press (1979).

Lurie, Ranan R., *Nixon on Rated Cartoons*. New York: New York Times Book Co. (1973).

Mauldin, Bill, *Back Home*. New York: William Sloane (1947).

Mauldin, Bill, *Bill Mauldin's Army*. Novato, Calif.: Presidio Press (1983).

Mauldin, Bill, *The Brass Ring*. New York: Norton (1971).

Mauldin, Bill, *Up Front.* New York: Henry Holt (1945).

Miller, Frank, *Frank Miller Looks at Life.* No publisher, no date.

Nelson, Roy Paul, *Cartooning.* Chicago: Henry Regnery (1975).

Paine, Ralph Bigelow, *Th. Nast: His Period and His Pictures.* Princeton: Pyne Press (1967) (facsimile of 1904 edition).

Pett, Joel, *Rough Sketches.* Lexington, Ky.: Lexington Herald-Leader (1982).

Salzman, Ed, and Ann Leigh Brown, *The Cartoon History of California Politics.* Sacramento: California Journal Press (1978).

Columnists and Opinion Writers

Alsop, Joseph, with Adam Platt, *I've Seen the Best.* New York: Norton (1992).

Baker, Russell, *The Good Times.* New York: Morrow (1989).

Baker, Russell, *Growing Up.* New York: New American Library (1982).

Breslin, Jimmy, *Damon Runyon.* New York: Ticknor & Fields (1991).

Burner, David, and Thomas R. West, *Column Right: Journalists in the Service of Nationalism.* New York: New York University Press (1988).

Childs, Marquis, and James Reston, *Walter Lippmann and His Times.* New York: Harcourt, Brace (1959).

Driscoll, Charles B., *The Life of O.O. McIntyre.* New York: Greystone Press (1938).

Fowler, Will, *The Young Man from Denver: A Candid and Affectionate Biography of Gene Fowler.* Garden City, N.Y.: Doubleday (1962).

Geyer, Georgie Anne, *Buying the Night Flight.* New York: Delacorte Press (1983).

Grayson, David, *American Chronicle: The Autobiography of Ray Stannard Baker.* New York: Scribner's (1945).

Heaton, John L., *Cobb of "The World": A Leader in Liberalism.* New York: Dutton (1924).

Hobson, Fred, *Mencken: A Life.* New York: Random House (1994).

Hopper, Hedda, and James Brough, *The Whole Truth and Nothing But.* Garden City, N.Y.: Doubleday (1963).

Hudson, Robert V., *The Writing Game: A Biography of Will Irwin.* Ames: Iowa State University Press (1982).

Kaplan, Justin, *Lincoln Steffens.* New York: Simon & Schuster (1974).

Klurfled, Herman, *Behind the Lines: The World of Drew Pearson.* Englewood Cliffs, N.J.: Prentice-Hall (1968).

Krock, Arthur, *Memoirs: Sixty Years on the Firing Line.* New York: Funk & Wagnalls (1968).

Krock, Arthur, *Myself When Young.* Boston: Little, Brown (1973).

Kurth, Peter, *American Cassandra: The Life of Dorothy Thompson.* Boston: Little, Brown (1990).

Luskin, John, *Lippmann, Liberty and the Press.* University: University of Alabama Press (1972).

Miller, Lee G., *The Story of Ernie Pyle.* New York: Viking (1950).

Pickett, Calder M., *Ed Howe: Country Town Philosopher.* Lawrence: University Press of Kansas (1968).

Pilat, Oliver, *Drew Pearson: An Unauthorized Biography.* New York: Harper's Magazine Press (1973).

Pilat, Oliver, *Pegler: Angry Man of the Press.* Boston: Beacon Press (1963).

Reston, James, *Deadlines: A Memoir.* New York: Random House (1991).

Reston, James, *Sketches in the Sand.* New York: Knopf (1967).

Ross, Ishbel, *Ladies of the Press.* New York: Harper (1936).

Sanders, Marion K., *Dorothy Thompson.* Boston: Houghton Mifflin (1973).

Sokolov, Raymond, *Wayward Reporter: The Life of A.J. Liebling.* New York: Harper & Row (1980).

Steel, Ronald, *Walter Lippmann and the American Century.* Boston: Little, Brown (1980).

Stone, Melville, *Fifty Years a Journalist.* Garden City, N.Y.: Doubleday (1921).

Weiner, Ed, *The Damon Runyon Story.* New York: Longmans, Green (1948).

Editors and Publishers

Anonymous, *Gardner Cowles.* Des Moines: Des Moines Register and Tribune (1946).

Anonymous, *Life and Labors of Henry W. Grady.* New York: Wm. M. Goldthwaite (1890).

Armstrong, William M., *E.L. Godkin, a Biography.* Albany: State University of New York Press (1978).

Barrett, James Wyman, *Joseph Pulitzer and His World.* New York: Vanguard (1941).

Barrett, James Wyman, *The World, the Flesh and Messrs. Pulitzer.* New York: Vanguard (1931).

Becker, Stephen, *Marshall Field III.* New York: Simon & Schuster (1964).

Bigelow, John, *William Cullen Bryant.* Boston: Houghton Mifflin (1890).

Bond, F. Fraser, *Mr. Miller of "The Times."* New York: Schribner's (1931).

Boswell, Sharon A., and Lorraine McConaghy, *Raise Hell and Sell Newspapers: Alden J. Blethen and the Seattle Times.* Pullman: Washington State University Press (1996).

Bower, Tom, *Maxwell: The Outsider.* New York: Viking (1992).

Bowman, Charles A., *Ottawa Editor*. Sidney, B.C.: Gray's Publishing (1966).

Braddon, Russell, *Roy Thomson of Fleet Street*. London: Collins (1965).

Brenner, Marie, *House of Dreams: The Bingham Family of Louisville*. New York: Random House (1988).

Brown, Francis, *Raymond of the Times*. New York: Norton (1951).

Bruces, Charles, *News and the Southams*. Toronto: Macmillan (1968).

Carlson, Oliver, *Brisbane*. Westwood, Conn.: Greenwood Press (1937).

Carlson, Oliver, *The Man Who Made News: A Biography of James Gordon Bennett*. New York: Duell, Sloane and Pearce (1942).

Carter, Hodding, *Where Main Street Meets the River*. New York: Rinehart and Co. (1952).

Cash, Kevin, *Who the Hell Is William Loeb?* Manchester, N.H.: Amoskeag Press (1975).

Casserly, Jack, *Scripps: The Dynasty Divided*. New York: Donald I. Fine (1993).

Catledge, Turner, *My Life and The Times*. New York: Harper and Row (1971).

Chandler, David Leon, with Mary Voeltz Chandler, *The Binghams of Louisville*. New York: Crown (1987).

Chaney, Lindsay, and Michael Cieply, *The Hearsts: Family and Empire: The Later Years*. New York: Simon & Schuster (1981).

Chisholm, Anne, and Michael Davie, *Lord Beaverbrook: A Life*. New York: Knopf (1993).

Clough, Frank C., *William Allen White of Emporia*. New York: Whittlesey House (1941).

Cochran, Negley D., *E.W. Scripps*. Reprint. Westport, Conn.: Greenwood Press (1972).

Coleridge, Nicholas, *Paper Tigers: The Latest, Greatest Newspaper Tycoons*. New York: Birch Lane (1993).

Cooney, John, *The Annenbergs: The Salvaging of a Tainted Dynasty*. New York: Simon & Schuster (1982).

Cornell, William M., *The Life and Public Career of Hon. Horace Greeley*. Boston: Lee and Shepard (1872).

Cousins, Paul M., *Joel Chandler Harris*. Baton Rouge: Louisiana State University Press (1968).

Cox, James E., *Journey Through My Years*. New York: Simon & Schuster (1946).

Crockett, Albert Stevens, *When James Gordon Bennett Was Caliph of Bagdad*. New York: Funk & Wagnalls (1926).

Crouthamel, James L., *James Watson Webb*. Middletown, Conn.: Wesleyan University Press (1969).

Dabney, Virginius, *Pistols and Pointed Pens: The Dueling Editors of Old Virginia*. Chapel Hill, N.C.: Algonquin (1987).

Daniels, Jonathan, *They Will Be Heard: America's Crusading Editors*. New York: McGraw-Hill (1965).

Daniels, Josephus, *Tar Heel Editor*. Chapel Hill: University of North Carolina Press (1939).

Daniels, Josephus, *Editor in Politics*. Chapel Hill: University of North Carolina Press (1941).

Davies, Marion, *The Times We Had: Life with William Randolph Hearst*. Indianapolis: Bobbs Merrill (1975).

Davies, Nick, *The Death of a Tycoon: An Insider's Account of the Fall of Robert Maxwell*. New York: St. Martin's (1992).

Davis, Deborah, *Katharine the Great: Katharine Graham and Her Washington Post Empire*. New York: Sheridan Square (1991).

Davis, Harold E., *Henry Grady's New South*. Tuscaloosa: University of Alabama Press (1990).

Downing, Sybil, and Robert E. Smith, *Tom Patterson: Colorado Crusader for Change*. Niwot, Colo.: University Press of Colorado (1995).

Duncan, Bingham, *Whitelaw Reid: Journalist, Politician, Diplomat*. Athens: University of Georgia Press (1975).

Eagles, Charles W., *Jonathan Daniels and Race Relations: The Evolution of a Southern Liberal*. Knoxville: University of Tennessee Press (1982).

Ficken, Robert E., *Rufus Woods, the Columbia River and the Building of Modern Washington*. Pullman: Washington State University Press (1995).

Fyfe, Hamilton, *Northcliffe: An Intimate Biography*. New York: Macmillan (1930).

Gies, Joseph, *The Colonel of Chicago* [Robert McCormick]. New York: Dutton (1979).

Graham, Katharine, *Personal History*. New York: Knopf (1997).

Grayson, David, *American Chronicle: The Autobiography of Ray Stannard Baker*. New York: Scribner's (1945).

Griffith, Sally Foreman, *Home Town News: William Allen White and the Emporia Gazette*. New York: Oxford University Press (1989).

Guiles, Fred Laurence, *Marion Davies*. New York: McGraw-Hill (1972).

Haines, Joe, *Maxwell*. Boston: Houghton Mifflin (1988).

Hale, William Harlan, *Horace Greeley: Voice of the People*. New York: Harper (1950).

Harris, William C., *William Woods Holden: Firebrand of North Carolina Politics*. Baton Rouge: Louisiana State University Press (1987).

Hearst, William Randolph, Jr., with Jack Casserly, *The Hearsts: Father and Son*. Niwot, Colo.: Roberts Rinehart Publishers (1991).

Heuterman, Thomas H., *Movable Type: Biography of Legh R. Freeman*. Ames: Iowa State University Press (1979).

Hinshaw, David, *A Man from Kansas: The Story of William Allen White.* New York: Putnam (1945).

Hoge, Alice Albright, *Cissy Patterson.* New York: Random House (1966).

Hough, Henry Beetle, *Country Editor.* New York: Doubleday, Duran (1940).

Jernigan, E. Jay, *William Allen White.* Boston: Twayne (1983).

Johnson, Gerald W., *An Honorable Titan: A Biography of Adolph S. Ochs.* New York: Harper (1946).

Johnson, Gerald W., *William Allen White's America.* New York: Henry Holt (1947).

Kahn, E.J., Jr., *The World of Swope.* [*New York World*]. New York: Simon & Schuster (1965).

Kansas City Star Staff, *William Rockhill Nelson.* Cambridge, Mass.: Riverside Press (1915).

Kneebone, John T., *Southern Liberal Journalists and the Issue of Race, 1920–1944.* Chapel Hill: University of North Carolina Press (1985).

Kroger, Brooke, *Nelly Bly.* New York: Times Books (1994).

Leapman, Michael, *Arrogant Aussie: The Rupert Murdoch Story.* Secaucus, N.J.: Lyle Stuart (1985).

Leidholdt, Alexander S., *Standing Before the Shouting Mob: Lenoir Chambers and Virginia's Massive Resistance to Public School Integration.* Tuscaloosa: University of Alabama Press (1997).

Linn, W.A., *Horace Greeley.* New York: Appleton (1903).

Lundberg, Ferdinand, *Imperial Hearst.* New York: Equinox Cooperative (1936).

Maier, Thomas, *Newhouse.* New York: St. Martin's (1994).

Marberry, M.M., *Vicki* [Victoria C. Woodhull]. New York: Funk & Wagnalls (1967).

Marcosson, Isaac F., *"Marse Henry": Biography of Henry Watterson.* New York: Dodd, Mead (1951).

Martin, Harold H., *Ralph McGill, Reporter.* Boston: Little, Brown (1973).

Martin, Ralph G., *Cissy.* New York: Simon & Schuster (1979).

McFeely, William S., *Frederick Douglass.* New York: Norton (1991).

Meeker, Richard H., *Newspaperman: S.I. Newhouse and the Business of News.* New Haven, Conn.: Ticknor & Fields (1983).

Mills, George, Harvey Ingham and Gardner Cowles, Sr. [*Des Moines Register and Tribune*]. Ames: Iowa State University Press (1977).

Mitchell, Edward, *Memoirs of an Editor.* New York: Scribner's (1924).

Morrison, Joseph L., *W.J. Cash: Southern Prophet.* New York: Knopf (1967).

Moscowitz, Raymond, *Stuffy: The Life of Newspaper Pioneer Basil "Stuffy" Walters.* Ames: Iowa State University Press (1982).

Munster, George, *Rupert Murdoch: A Paper Prince.* New York: Penguin (1985).

Neuharth, Al, *Confessions of an S.O.B.* New York: Doubleday (1989).

Nixon, Raymond B., *Henry W. Grady: Spokesman of the New South.* New York: Knopf (1943).

Noble, Iris, *Joseph Pulitzer: Front Page Pioneer.* New York: Julian Messner (1957).

Nye, Russell B., *William Lloyd Garrison and the Humanitarian Reformers.* Boston: Little, Brown (1955).

Ogden, Rollo, *The Life and Letters of Edwin Lawrence Godkin.* 2 vols. Reprint. Westport, Conn.: Greenwood (1972).

Parton, J., *The Life of Horace Greeley.* New York: Mason Brothers (1855).

Patner, Andrew, *I.F. Stone: A Portrait.* New York: Pantheon (1988).

Pierce, Robert N., *A Sacred Trust: Nelson Poynter and the St. Petersburg Times.* Gainesville: University Press of Florida (1993).

Pfaff, Daniel W., *Joseph Pulitzer II and the Post-Dispatch.* University Park: Pennsylvania State University Press (1991).

Pulliam, Russell, *Publisher: Gene Pulliam, Last of the Newspaper Titans.* Ottawa, Ill.: Jameson Books (1984).

Pusey, Merlo J., *Eugene Meyer.* New York: Knopf (1974).

Raper, Horace W., *William W. Holden: North Carolina's Enigma.* Chapel Hill: University of North Carolina Press (1985).

Reavis, L.U., *A Representative Life of Horace Greeley.* New York: Carleton (1872).

Rosebault, Charles J., *When Dana Was the Sun.* Reprint. Westport, Conn.: Greenwood (1971).

Ross, Ishbel, *Ladies of the Press.* New York: Harper (1936).

Russell, Francis, *The Shadow of Blooming Grove: Warren G. Harding and His Times.* New York: McGraw-Hill (1968).

Russell, Phillips, *Benjamin Franklin: First Civilized American.* New York: Blue Ribbon (1926).

Seitz, Don Carlos, *James Gordon Bennett.* Reprint. New York: Beckman (1974).

Sharpe, Ernest, *G.B. Dealey of the Dallas News.* New York: Henry Holt (1955).

Shawcross, William, *Murdoch.* New York: Simon & Schuster (1992).

Sleeper, Jim, *Turn the Rascals Out: The Life and Times of Orange County's Fighting Editor.* Traabuco Canyon, Calif.: California Classics (1973).

Smith, Rixey, and Norman Beasley, *Carter Glass.* New York: Longmans, Green (1939).

Steele, C. Frank, *Prairie Editor: The Life and Times of Buchanan of Lethbridge.* Toronto: Ryerson Press (1961).

Steele, Janet E., *The Sun Shines for All: Journalism and Ideology in the Life of Charles A. Dana.* Syracuse, N.Y.: Syracuse University Press (1993).

Steffens, Lincoln, *Autobiography of Lincoln Steffens.* New York: Harcourt, Brace (1931).

Stern, J. David, *Memoirs of a Maverick Publisher.* New York: Simon & Schuster (1962).

Stoddard, Henry Luther, *Horace Greeley.* New York: Putnam (1946).

Storke, Thomas L., *California Editor.* Los Angeles: Westernlore (1958).

Streitmatter, Rodger, *Raising Her Voice: African-American Women Journalists Who Changed History.* Lexington: University of Kentucky Press (1994).

Suggs, Henry Lewis, *P.B. Young: Newspaperman: Race, Politics and Journalism in the New South.* Charlotteville: University Press of Virginia (1988).

Swanberg, W.A., *Citizen Hearst.* New York: Scribner's (1961).

Swanberg, W.A., *Luce and His Empire.* New York: Scribner's (1972).

Swanberg, W.A., *Pulitzer.* New York: Scribner's (1967).

Swanson, Walter S.J., *The Thin Gold Watch: A Personal History of the Newspaper Copleys.* New York: Macmillan (1964).

Tagg, James, *Benjamin Franklin Bache and the Philadelphia Aurora.* Philadelphia: University of Pennsylvania Press (1991).

Tebbel, John, *The Life and Good Times of William Randolph Hearst.* New York: Dutton (1952).

Thomson, Lord, of Fleet, *After I Was Sixty.* London: Nelson (1975).

Tifft, Susan E., and Alex S. Jones, *The Patriarch: The Rise and Fall of the Bingham Dynasty.* New York: Summit (1991).

Trible, Vance C., *The Astonishing Mr. Scripps: The Turbulent Life of America's Penny Press Lord.* Ames: Iowa State University Press (1992).

Turnbull, George S., *An Oregon Crusader* [George Putnam]. Portland, Ore.: Binford & Mort (1955).

Villard, Oswald Garrison, *Fighting Years: An Autobiography.* New York: Harcourt, Brace (1939).

Waldron, Ann, *Hodding Carter: The Reconstruction of a Racist.* Chapel Hill, N.C.: Algonquin (1992).

Waldrop, Frank C., *McCormick of Chicago.* Englewood Cliffs, N.J.: Prentice-Hall (1966).

Wall, Joseph Frazier, *Henry Watterson: Reconstructed Rebel.* New York: Oxford University Press (1956).

Wallace, Ernest, *Charles DeMorse: Pioneer Editor and Statesman.* Lubbock: Texas Tech Press (1943).

Watterson, Henry, *"Marse Henry": An Autobiography.* 2 vols. New York: Doran (1919).

Wells, Evelyn, *Fremont Older.* New York: Appleton-Century (1936).

White, William Allen, *Autobiography.* New York: Macmillan (1946).

Whited, Charles, *Knight: A Publisher in the Tumultuous Century.* New York: Dutton (1988).

Wilkinson, J. Harvie III, *Harry Byrd and the Changing Face of Virginia Politics.* Charlottesville: University Press of Virginia (1968).

Williamson, Samuel T., *Frank Gannett.* New York: Duell, Sloan and Pearce (1940).

Wilson, Charles, *First with the News: The History of W.H. Smith 1792–1972.* London: Jonathan Cape (1985).

Wilson, R. Macnair, *Lord Northcliffe: A Study.* Philadelphia: Lippincott (1927).

Winkler, John K., *William Randolph Hearst: A New Appraisal.* New York: Hastings House (1955).

Wright, Elizabeth, *Miller Freeman: Man of Action.* San Francisco: Miller Freeman (1977).

Newspapers

Andrews, J. Cutler, *Pittsburgh's Post-Gazette.* Reprint. Westport, Conn.: Greenwood (1970).

Anonymous, *The History of the Times: "The Thunder" in the Making 1785–1841.* Vol. 1. New York: Macmillan (1935).

Anonymous, *The History of the Times: The Tradition Established 1841–1884.* Vol 2. New York: Macmillan (1939).

Anonymous, *The History of The Times: The Twentieth Century Test 1884–1912.* Vol 3. New York: Macmillan (1947).

Anonymous, *The History of the Times: The 150th Anniversary and Beyond 1912–1948.* Vol. 4. New York: Macmillan (1952).

Anonymous, *The Lee Papers: A Saga of Midwestern Journalism.* Kewanee, Ill.: Star-Courier Press (1947).

Anonymous, *Pictured Encyclopedia of the World's Greatest Newspaper* [*Chicago Tribune*]. Chicago: Chicago Tribune (1928).

Anonymous, *The Virginia Gazette 1775.* Chardon, Ohio: Block (1975).

Ayerst, David, *The Manchester Guardian.* Ithaca, N.Y.: Cornell University Press (1971).

Baehr, Harry W., Jr., *The New York Herald Tribune since the Civil War.* New York: Octagon (1972).

Baker, Thomas Harrison, *The Memphis Commercial Appeal.* Baton Rouge: Louisiana State University Press (1971).

Berger, Meyer, *The Story of the New York Times.* New York: Simon & Schuster (1951).

Berges, Marshall, *The Life and Times of Los Angeles.* New York: Atheneum (1984).

Braley, Russ, *Bad News: The Foreign Policy of the New York Times.* Chicago: Regnery Gateway (1984).

Bruce, Charles, *News and the Southams.* Toronto: Macmillan (1968).

Canham, Erwin D., *Commitment to Freedom: The Story of the Christian Science Monitor.* Boston: Houghton Mifflin (1958).

Catledge, Turner, *My Life and the Times.* New York: Harper (1971).

Chamberlain, Joseph Edgar, *The Boston Transcript: A History of the First Hundred Years.* Boston: Houghton Mifflin (1930).

Chambers, Lenoir, and Joseph E. Shank, *Salt Water and Printer's Ink: Norfolk and Its Newspapers, 1865–1965*. Chapel Hill: University of North Carolina Press (1967).

Chapman, John, *Tell It to Sweeney: An Informal History of the New York Daily News*. Garden City, N.Y.: Doubleday (1961).

Claiborne, Jack, *The Charlotte Observer*. Chapel Hill: University of North Carolina Press (1986).

Coffman, Lloyd W., *5200 Thursdays in the Wallowas* [*Wallowa County Chieftain*]. Enterprise, Ore.: Wallowa County Chieftain (1984).

Cohen, Lester, *The New York Graphic*. Philadelphia: Chilton Books (1964).

Conrad, Will, Kathleen Wilson, and Dale Wilson, *The Milwaukee Journal: The First Eighty Years*. Madison: University of Wisconsin Press (1964).

Copley, *The Copley Press*. Aurora, Ill.: Copley (1953).

Cose, Ellis, *The Press: Inside America's Most Powerful Newspaper Empires*. New York: Morrow (1989).

Cross, Wilbur, *Lee's Legacy of Leadership*. Essex, Conn.: Greenwich Publishing Group (1990).

Crouthamel, James L., *Bennett's New York Herald and the Rise of the Popular Press*. Syracuse, N.Y.: Syracuse University Press (1989).

Dana, Marshall N., *The First Fifty Years of the Oregon Journal*. Portland, Ore.: Binford & Mort (1951).

Diamond, Edwin, *Behind the Times: Inside the New New York Times*. New York: Villard (1994).

Dyar, Ralph E., *News for an Empire: The Story of the Spokesman-Review*. Caldwell, Idaho: Caxton Printers (1952).

Edelman, Maurice, *The Mirror: A Political History*. New York: London House and Maxwell (1966).

Edwards, Jerome E., *The Foreign Policy of Col. McCormick's Tribune*. Reno: University of Nevada Press (1971).

Ferril, Thomas Hornsby, and Helen Ferril, eds., *The Rocky Mountain Herald Reader*. New York: Morrow (1966).

Gottlieb, Robert, and Irene Wolf, *Thinking Big: The Story of the Los Angeles Times: Its Publishers and Their Influence on Southern California*. New York: Putnam (1977).

Goulden, Joseph C., *Fit to Print: A.M. Rosenthal and His Times*. Secaucus, N.J.: Lyle Stuart (1988).

Griffith, Louis Turner, and John Edwin Talmadge, *Georgia Journalism 1763–1950*. Athens: University of Georgia Press (1951).

Grimes, Millard, *The Last Linotype: The Story of Georgia and Its Newspapers since World War II*. Macon, Ga.: Mercer University Press (1985).

Haig, Robert L., *The Gazetteer (1735–1797): A Study of the Eighteenth-Century English Newspaper*. Carbondale: Southern Illinois University Press (1960).

Hooker, Richard, *The Story of an Independent Newspaper: One Hundred Years of the Springfield Republican*. New York: Macmillan (1924).

Hosokawa, Bill, *Thunder in the Rockies: The Incredible Denver Post*. New York: Morrow (1976).

Keeler, Robert F., *Newsday: A Candid History of the Respectable Tabloid*. New York: Arbor (1990).

Kelly, Tom, *The Imperial Post*. New York: Morrow (1983).

King, Charles, *The Ottaway Newspapers: The First 50 Years*. Campbell Hall, N.Y.: Ottaway Newspapers (1986).

Kluger, Richard, *The Paper: The Life and Death of the New York Herald Tribune*. New York: Knopf (1986).

Lyons, Louis, *Newspaper Story: One Hundred Years of the Boston Globe*. Cambridge, Mass.: Belknap Press of Harvard University Press (1971).

MacNab, Gordon, *A Century of News and People in the East Oregonian*. Pendleton, Ore.: East Oregonian (1975).

McClure, Kevin Michael, *The Great American Newspaper: The Rise and Fall of the Village Voice*. New York: Scribner's (1978).

McGivena, Leo E. and others, *The News: The First Fifty Years of New York's Picture Newspaper*. New York: News Syndicate (1969).

McLaws, Monte Burr, *Spokesman for the Kingdom: Early Mormon Journalism and the Deseret News, 1830–1898*. Provo, Utah: Brigham Young Press (1977).

McPhaul, John J., *Deadlines and Monkeyshines: The Fabled World of Chicago Journalism*. Englewood Cliffs, N.J.: Prentice-Hall (1962).

Morison, Bradley L., *Sunlight on Your Doorstep: The Minneapolis Tribune's First Hundred Years*. Minneapolis: Ross & Haines (1966).

Murray, George, *The Madhouse on Madison Street*. Chicago: Follett (1965).

Nevins, Alan, *The Evening Post: A Century of Journalism*. New York: Boni and Liveright (1922).

O'Brien, Frank M., *The Story of the Sun*. Reprint. Westport, Conn.: Greenwood (1968).

Perkin, Robert L., *The First Hundred Years: An Informal History of Denver and the Rocky Mountain News*. Garden City, N.Y.: Doubleday (1959).

Price, Warren C., *The Eugene Register-Guard*. Portland, Ore.: Binford & Mort (1976).

Pritchard, Peter, *The Making of McPaper*. Kansas City: Andrews, McMeel and Parker (1987).

Pugnetti, Frances Taylor, *Tiger by the Tail: Twenty-Five Years with the Stormy Tri-City Herald*. Pasco, Wash.: Tri-City Herald (1975).

Rice, William B., *The Angeles Star: 1851–1864*. Berkeley: University of California Press (1947).

Roberts, Chalmer, *In the Shadow of Power: The Story of the Washington Post.* Cabin John, Md.: Seven Locks (1989)

Roberts, Chalmer, *The Washington Post: The First 100 Years.* Boston: Houghton Mifflin (1977).

Robertson, Charles L., *The International Herald Tribune: The First Hundred Years.* New York: Columbia University Press (1987).

Robertson, Nan, *The Girls in the Balcony: Women, Men and The New York Times.* New York: Random House (1992).

Root, Waverley, *The Paris Edition: 1927–1934.* San Francisco: North Point (1989).

Ross, Margaret, *Arkansas Gazette: The Early Years 1819–1866.* Little Rock: Arkansas Gazette Foundation (1969).

Salisbury, Harrison, *Without Fear or Favor: An Uncompromising Look at the New York Times.* New York: Times Books (1980).

Smith, J. Eugene, *One Hundred Years of Hartford's Courant.* Reprint. Hamden, Conn.: Archon Books (1970).

Talese, Gay, *The Kingdom and the Power* [*The New York Times*]. New York: World (1969).

Tebbel, John, *An American Dynasty: The Story of the McCormicks, Medills and Pattersons.* Garden City, N.Y.: Doubleday (1947).

Toole, John H., *Red Ribbons: A Story of Missoula and Its Newspaper.* Davenport, Iowa: Lee Enterprises (1989).

Turnbull, George S., *History of Oregon Newspapers.* Portland: Binford & Mort (1939).

Veblen, Eric, *The Manchester Union Leader in New Hampshire Elections.* Hanover, N.H.: University Press of New England (1975).

Vigilante, Richard, *Strike: The Daily News War and the Future of American Labor.* New York: Simon & Schuster (1994).

Wendt, Lloyd, *Chicago Tribune.* Chicago: Rand McNally (1979).

Wendt, Lloyd, *The Wall Street Journal.* Chicago: Rand McNally (1982).

Williams, Harold A., *The Baltimore Sun: 1837–1987.* Baltimore, Md.: John Hopkins University Press (1987).

Wolseley, Roland E., *The Black Press, U.S.A.* 2nd ed. Ames: Iowa State University Press (1971).

Wright, Elizabeth, *Independence in All Things, Neutrality in Nothing* [Legh Richmond Freeman]. San Francisco: Miller Freeman Publications (1973).

Works of Opinion Writers

Abell, Tyler, ed., *Drew Pearson Diaries, 1949–1959.* New York: Holt, Rinehart and Winston (1974).

Allen, Robert, and Drew Pearson, *Washington Merry-Go-Round.* New York: Liveright (1931). Published anonymously.

Anderson, Jack, and James Boyd, *Confessions of a Muckraker.* New York: Random House (1979).

Brier, Warren J., and Nathan B. Blumberg, eds., *A Century of Montana Journalism.* Missoula, Mont.: Mountain Press (1971).

Carter, Hodding, *The Angry Scar.* Garden City, N.Y.: Doubleday (1959).

Carter, Hodding, *Southern Legacy.* Baton Rouge: Louisiana State University Press (1950).

Carter, Hodding, *Their Words Were Bullets: The Southern Press in War, Reconstruction and Peace.* Athens: University of Georgia Press (1969).

Chadakoff, Rochelle, ed., *Eleanor Roosevelt's My Day.* New York: Pharos (1989).

Childs, Marquis, *I Write from Washington.* New York: Harper (1942).

Cobb, Irvin S., *Exit Laughing.* Garden City, N.Y.: Garden City Publishing (1942).

Coblentz, Edmund D., ed., *William Randolph Hearst: A Portrait in His Own Words.* New York: Simon & Schuster (1952).

Davis, Richard Harding, *The Notes of a World Correspondent.* New York: Scribner's (1911).

Delaplane, Stanton, *The Little World of Stanton Delaplane.* New York: Coward-McCann (1959).

Frazier, Bob, *Bob Frazier of Oregon.* Eugene: Eugene Register-Guard (1979).

Fuller, Edmund, ed., *The Essential Royster.* Chapel Hill, N.C.: Algonquin (1985).

Golden, Harry, *The Right Time.* New York: Putnam (1969).

Greeley, Horace, *The Reflections of a Busy Life.* 2 vols. Reissued. Port Washington, N.Y.: Kennikat Press (1971).

Harris, Julia Collier, ed., *Joel Chandler Harris: Editor and Essayist.* Chapel Hill: University of North Carolina Press (1931).

Harris, Sydney J., *The Best of Sydney J. Harris.* Boston: Houghton Mifflin (1975).

Harris, Sydney J., *Leaving the Surface.* Boston: Houghton Mifflin (1968).

Hearn, Lacadio, *Editorials.* Boston: Houghton Mifflin Co. (1926).

Hosokawa, Bill, *Thirty-Five Years in the Frying Pan.* New York: McGraw-Hill (1978).

Hutchins, John K., and George Oppenheimer, eds., *The Best in the World.* New York: Viking (1973.)

Kilpatrick, James J., *The Foxes' Union.* McLean, Va.: EPM Publications (1977).

Knight, Oliver, ed., *I Protest: Selected Disquisitions of E.W. Scripps.* Madison: University of Wisconsin Press (1966).

Krock, Arthur, *The Editorials of Henry Watterson.* New York: Doran (1923).

Krock, Arthur, *In the Nation (1932–1966).* New York: McGraw-Hill (1966).

Lampman, Ben Hur, *At the End of the Car Line.* Portland, Ore.: Binford & Mort (1942).

Lampman, Ben Hur, *How Could I Be Forgetting?* Portland, Ore.: Binford & Mort (1926).

Lippmann, Walter, *Early Writings.* New York: Liveright (1970).

McGill, Ralph, *No Place to Hide: The South and Human Rights* (2 vols.) Macon, Ga.: Mercer University Press (1984).

McGill, Ralph, *Southern Encounters: Southerners of Note in Ralph McGill's South.* Macon, Ga: Mercer University Press (1983).

McKabe, Charles R., ed., *Damned Old Crank: A Self-Portrait of E.W. Scripps.* New York: Harper (1951).

Meyer, Karl E., *Pundits, Poets, & Wits: An Omnibus of American Newspaper Columns.* New York: Oxford University Press (1990).

Miller, Joaquin, *Selected Writings of Joaquin Miller.* Eugene, Ore.: Urion Press (1977).

Nichols, David, ed., *Ernie Pyle's America: The Best of Ernie Pyle's 1930s Travel Dispatches.* New York: Random House (1989).

Pyle, Ernie, *Brave Men.* New York: Henry Holt (1944).

Pyle, Ernie, *Ernie Pyle in England.* New York: Robert M. McBride (1941).

Riley, Sam G., *The Best of the Rest: Leading Newspaper Columnists Select Their Best Work.* Westport, Conn.: Greenwood (1993).

Royster, Vermont, *A Pride of Prejudices.* New York: Knopf (1967).

Sulzberger, C.L., *A Long Row of Candles: Memoirs and Diaries, 1934–1954.* New York: Macmillan (1969).

von Hoffman, Nicholas, *Left at the Post.* Chicago: Quadrangle Books (1970).

Watson, Emmett, *Digressions of a Native Son.* Seattle: Pacific Institute (1982).

Winchell, Walter, *Winchell Exclusive.* Englewood Cliffs, N.J.: Prentice-Hall (1975).

Yoder, Edwin M., Jr., *The Night of the Old South Ball.* Oxford, Miss.: Yoknapatawpha Press (1984).

CREDITS AND ACKNOWLEDGMENTS

Grateful acknowledgment is made for permission to use the following:

Permission to reprint sections of articles from *The Masthead* appearing throughout the book: National Conference of Editorial Writers.

The stories entitled "We lost and we won Canadian Timber ruling" and "She was the epitomy of eloquence, grace" are reprinted here with the permission of the Great Falls Tribune, Great Falls, Montana, for whom they were originally written. 1994 Great Falls Tribune.

Chapter 2

"A Death Foretold," *Lexington Herald-Leader*, Dec. 2, 1990.

"The Presidio Precedent," San Francisco *Bay Guardian*, May 8, 1996.

"Toughen up, now," *Virginia Gazette*, March 6, 1996.

"Discipline Dissed," *Virginia Gazette*, March 6, 1996.

"Don't miss the bigger issue," *Southwest Virginia Enterprise*, Oct. 12, 1996.

"CAP's new direction," *Southwest Virginia Enterprise*, April 3, 1996.

R. S. Baker, "The Editorial Writer: The Man in the Piazza," *Montana Journalism Review*, 15:18–19 (1972). Reprinted by permission of *Montana Journalism Review*.

Chapter 5

Warren G. Bovee, "The Mythology of Editorial Anonymity," *The Masthead*, 24:26–35 (Fall 1972) and 24:54–65 (Winter 1972). Copyright 1972 by Warren G. Bovee.

Chapter 9

Basic Statement of Principles, National Conference of Editorial Writers.

Chapter 10

"Don't kill toxics law," *Register-Guard*, June 20, 1967.

"The sanctity of the confessional," *St. Petersburg Times*, May 19, 1996.

"A Word About Libel," W. Wat Hopkins.

Chapter 11

"The Playboy Option," "Sex Objects," "Sex Objects II," by permission of the authors.

Chapter 12

"The birth of Freedom Cabs," *Rocky Mountain News*, Aug. 2, 1995.

"Shirley, you're kidding," *St. Paul Pioneer Press*, Oct. 12, 1995.

"Who needs tax breaks?" *Register-Guard*, July 9, 1995.

"40 years after Brown versus Board," *Plain Dealer*, May 18, 1994.

"Free speech OK'd, not a free-for-all," *Plain Dealer*, Aug. 17, 1996.

"Report shows public records not always public," *Tucson Citizen*, May 18, 1995.

"A Rare, Startling Moment–County Needs More Like It," *Dickinson Star*, Feb. 1, 1995.

"No cause for fear of United Nations," *Shreveport Times*, May 16, 1995.

"Grace, intelligence in evidence as South African nation matures," *Sun-Sentinel*, May 14, 1996. Reprinted with permission from the Sun-Sentinel, Fort Lauderdale, Florida.

"Arts in education: a basic, not a frill," *Roanoke Times*, Feb. 8, 1997.

"So much to do today," *Santa Barbara News-Press*, May 20, 1995.

"The art experience," *Santa Barbara News-Press*, May 25, 1996.

"Marijuana as Medicine," *San Francisco Chronicle*, May 23, 1995. © SAN FRANCISCO CHRONICLE. Reprinted by permission.

"We can see the political ads now," *Roanoke Times*, Feb. 8, 1997.

"The folly of militant creationism," *Chicago Tribune*, Aug. 16, 1996.

"Veto school prayer," *Miami Herald*, May 15, 1996. Reprinted with permission of The Miami Herald.

"Another Evangelist Falls," *Roanoke Times & World-News*, Feb. 23, 1988.

"CSU football team dropped unfairly," *Dayton Daily News*, Aug. 17, 1996.

"Let 'em strike, already," *Des Moines Register*, Aug. 11, 1994.

"Idaho and the Big, Big, Big West? Conference," *Lewiston Morning Tribune*, Aug. 9, 1994.

"Broad plan can control cranes," *Idaho Statesman*, Aug. 14, 1996.

"Repeal state fornication law," *Idaho Statesman*, Aug. 14, 1996.

"No Popularity Contest," *Salt Lake Tribune*, Aug. 14, 1996.

"Needless school upset," *Salt Lake Tribune*, Aug. 14, 1996.

Chapter 13

"Mortimer Charles Lebowitz," *Washington Post*, Feb. 4, 1997.

"Kirsten," *Register-Guard*, June 21, 1997.

"Here's to dynamic downtown," *Idaho Statesman*, Aug. 13, 1996.

"Ferry Farm and its gravel pit," *Free Lance–Star*, Feb. 23, 1996.

"Ferry Farm: Nationally, locally," *Free Lance–Star*, Feb. 24, 1996.

"Push light rail," *Oregonian*, May 24, 1995.

"The Assembly Game," *Richmond Times-Dispatch*, Jan 11, 1997.

"A Legislative Goose," *Richmond Times-Dispatch*, Feb. 3, 1995.

"Toward one nation, indivisible," *Tampa Tribune-Times*, May 19, 1996.

Chapter 14

"Water fight continues," *Missoulian*, May 25, 1994.

"Region needs consensus to protect river," *Muskogee Daily Phoenix*, March 9, 1997.

"Dune," *Star Tribune*, May 26, 1996.

"Toxic TV," *Star Tribune*, Oct. 12, 1995.

INDEX

ABOUT THE AUTHOR

Kenneth Rystrom has spent 20 years in the newspaper business and 20 years teaching journalism. He wrote and edited editorials on the *Register* in Des Moines, Iowa, and the *Columbian* in Vancouver, Wash. He taught at Washington State University, University of Redlands and Virginia Polytechnic Institute and State University. He received a bachelor's degree from the University of Nebraska–Lincoln, a master's degree from the University of California–Berkeley and a Ph.D. from the University of Southern California.

Rystrom has been recognized for his contributions to journalism, journalism education and scholarship. For his contributions to journalism and journalism education, he was awarded a life membership in the National Conference of Editorial Writers, an organization for which he has also served as president. For his scholarly work in journalism, he has four times received the Henry M. Grady Award. Upon his retirement, he was awarded professor-emeritus status at VPI&SU. He is now living in Florence, Ore.